FUNDAMENTALS OF MANAGEMENT

Eighth Canadian Edition

Stephen P. Robbins
San Diego State University

David A. DeCenzo
Coastal Carolina University

Mary Coulter
Missouri State University

Ian Anderson
Algonquin College

PEARSON
Toronto

Editorial Director: Claudine O'Donnell
Acquisitions Editor: Carolin Sweig
Marketing Manager: Lisa Gillis
Program Manager: Karen Townsend
Project Manager: Jessica Hellen
Developmental Editor: Patti Sayle
Media Developer: Kelli Cadet
Production Services: iEnergizer Aptara®, Ltd.
Permissions Project Manager: Joanne Tang
Photo Permissions Research: Melody English, Integra
Text Permissions Research: Renae Horstman, Integra
Interior and Cover Designer: Alex Li
Cover Image: © Taras Kushnir/Shutterstock
Vice-President, Cross Media and Publishing Services: Gary Bennett

Credits and acknowledgments for material borrowed from other sources and reproduced, with permission, in this textbook appear on the appropriate page within the text.

Original edition published by Pearson Education, Inc., Upper Saddle River, New Jersey, USA. Copyright © 2015, 2013 Pearson Education, Inc. This edition is authorized for sale only in Canada.

If you purchased this book outside the United States or Canada, you should be aware that it has been imported without the approval of the publisher or the author.

10 9 8 7 6 5 4 3 2 1 V0RJ

Library and Archives Canada Cataloguing in Publication

Robbins, Stephen P., 1943-, author

Fundamentals of management / Stephen P. Robbins (San Diego State University), David A. DeCenzo (Coastal Carolina University), Mary Coulter (Missouri State University), Ian Anderson (Algonquin College).—Eighth Canadian edition.

Includes bibliographical references and index.
ISBN 978-0-13-385674-3 (paperback)

1. Management—Textbooks.   I. DeCenzo, David A., author   II. Coulter, Mary, author   III. Anderson, Ian (Professor), author   IV. Title.   V. Title: Management.

HD31.R5643 2015   658   C2015-907783-4

ISBN 978-0-13-385674-3

Brief Contents

Contents

Part 4 Leading 185

Part 5 Controlling 259

Preface

Welcome to the eighth Canadian edition of *Fundamentals of Management*, by Stephen P. Robbins, David A. DeCenzo, Mary Coulter, and Ian Anderson. This edition continues the fresh approach to management coverage of the previous editions through the following:

- current and relevant examples
- updated theory
- a new pedagogically sound design

The philosophy behind this revision was to put additional emphasis on the idea that *management is for everyone*. Students who are not managers, or who do not envision themselves as managers, may not always see why studying management is important. We use examples from a variety of settings to help students understand the relevance of studying management to their day-to-day lives.

CHAPTER PEDAGOGICAL FEATURES

We have enhanced the eighth Canadian edition with a rich variety of pedagogical features, including the following:

- Learning outcomes to guide student learning begin each chapter. These questions are repeated at the start of each major chapter section to reinforce the learning outcome.
- An opening case starts the body of the chapter and is threaded throughout to help students apply a story to the concepts they are learning.
- The use of infographics in each chapter presents information graphically to help visual learners with the related concepts. In addition, an increase in photographs enhances business concepts throughout the text.
- *Think About It* questions follow the opening case to give students a chance to put themselves in the shoes of managers in various situations.
- *And the Survey Says . . .* provides relevant Canadian and global data to help students understand business metrics and the Canadian significance of various management topics.
- *Tips for Managers* provide "take-aways" from the chapter—things that managers and would-be managers can start to put into action right now, based on what they have learned in the chapter.

END-OF-CHAPTER APPLICATIONS

The entire end-of-chapter section, *Review and Apply*, provides a wealth of exercises and applications.

- The *Summary of Learning Outcomes* provides responses to the outcome-based questions identified at the beginning of each chapter.
- *Discussion Questions* allow students to review their understanding of the chapter content.
- *Developing Management Skills* lets students apply material to their daily lives as well as to real business situations related to the chapter material, helping them see that planning, leading, organizing, and controlling are useful in one's day-to-day life, too. This feature includes several exercises, such as the ones described below.
- *Dilemma* presents an everyday scenario for students to resolve using management tools.

- *Becoming a Manager* provides suggestions for students on activities and actions they can do right now to help them prepare to become a manager.
- *3BL: The Triple Bottom Line* helps students apply sustainability to business situations.
- *Be the Consultant* emphasizes the importance of interpersonal and organizational skills.
- *Team Exercises* give students a chance to work together in groups to solve a management challenge.
- Two new exercises were added to the eighth Canadian edition: *Hey, You're the Boss Now* and *Diversity Matters*. These exercises increase the diversity component of the text and give students a hands-on perspective of being a supervisor or manager.
- *Your Essential Management Reading List* is new to the eighth edition to give students a glimpse of some of the top management books.
- The *Business Cases* are decision-focused scenarios that ask students to determine what they would do if they were in the situation described.

NEW TO THE EIGHTH CANADIAN EDITION

In addition to the new pedagogical features highlighted above, we have introduced or revised other learning aids and made significant changes to content.

Case Program

This edition offers a variety of cases that can be used in or out of the classroom.

- End of Chapter Cases: At the end of each chapter we offer brief, chapter-specific cases in the *Developing Management Skills* and *Business Cases* sections. These cases include a variety of open-ended questions for classroom discussion or small-group assignment.
- Management Mini-Cases (MyManagementLab): Hosted within MyManagementLab and tied to each chapter are a set of 12 Management Mini-Cases with associated multiple-choice questions. These mini-cases are perfect for assignments, as the students' results feed directly into the MyManagementLab Gradebook.

CHAPTER-BY-CHAPTER HIGHLIGHTS

Below, we highlight the new material that has been added to this edition.

Chapter 1

- New opening case on Calgary mayor Naheed Nenshi
- Expanded section on entrepreneurship

- *And the Survey Says . . .* on female board members in Canada
- New end-of-chapter (EOC) material (*Hey, You're the Boss Now* on mentoring of millennials, *Diversity Matters* on types of diversity, and a new Self-Assessment called *What Skills Do Effective Managers Possess?*)

Chapter 2

- Updated opening case on TransCanada and the Keystone Pipeline Project
- New case on Joe Fresh
- *And the Survey Says . . .* on Canada's trading partners
- Expanded section on Hofstede, including a new exhibit comparing Canada with China and the United States
- New material on the Canadian–EU free trade deal, a new exhibit on styles of three generations, and *Tips for Managers* on how to avoid getting burned by a foreign distributor.
- New EOC material (*Hey, You're the Boss Now* on supervising a diverse workforce, *Diversity Matters* on becoming more culturally aware, and *Your Essential Management Reading List.*)

Chapter 3

- New opening case on Stantec
- *And the Survey Says . . .* on planning
- Four new exhibits on reasons for planning, comparing traditional goal setting with MBO, types of plans, and examples of functional strategies
- New EOC material (*Hey, You're the Boss Now* on setting goals, *Diversity Matters* on diversity and inclusion as a strategic initiative, *Your Essential Management Reading List*, and an updated *Business Case* on the Canadian wine industry)

Supplement 3:

- Brand-new supplement on communication and social media

Chapter 4

- Two new cases on Blue Jays baseball and Coca-Cola and the science of OJ
- *And the Survey Says . . .* on the use of teams
- New EOC material (*Hey, You're the Boss Now* on tips for managing an older employee, *Diversity Matters* on the value of diversity in decision making, *Your Essential Management Reading List.*)

Chapter 5

- New opening case on Sobeys
- New case on Pfizer
- *And the Survey Says . . .* on teleworking
- New material on designing office space, including a new exhibit comparing major office styles

- New EOC material (*Hey, You're the Boss Now* on delegation, *Diversity Matters* on diversity awareness, *Your Essential Management Reading List*, and an updated business case on Levitt)

Chapter 6

- New chapter on operations management
- Two new cases on Apple and the supply chain and the Boeing Dreamliner
- New material on operations management, service versus manufacturing, improving productivity, the role of operations in strategy, supply chain management, value chain management, quality control, project management, and contemporary issues in operations management
- *And the Survey Says* . . . on manufacturing and operations
- Ten new exhibits on the operations system, goods versus services, Deming chain reaction, successful value chain management, Gannt chart, PERT charts, and a PERT network diagram
- New EOC material (*Hey, You're the Boss Now* on being a good project manager, *Diversity Matters* on female representation in the executive ranks, *Be the Consultant*, *3BL, Your Essential Management Reading List.*)

Chapter 7

- New case on love in the workplace
- *And the Survey Says* . . . on sick leave
- New exhibit on the human resource management process, a new table on changes in the labour market, and a new example of a job description for a customer service representative
- Updated exhibits on source of hires by recruitment methods and corporate wellness initiatives
- New information on total rewards
- New EOC material (*Hey, You're the Boss Now* on being an effective interviewer, *Diversity Matters* on the use of immigrant workers, *Your Essential Management Reading List*, and *Tips to be a Successful Volunteer*)

Chapter 8

- New opening case on Sheryl Sandberg of Facebook
- Two new cases on leadership legacy and results only work environments (ROWE)
- *And the Survey Says* . . . on critical leadership capabilities required in Canadian health care
- New mini-supplement *Portraits in Leadership*—profiles of two of Canada's future leaders
- New material on virtual leadership
- New EOC material (*Hey, You're the Boss Now* on tips for a first-time manager, *Diversity Matters* on RBC's Five Core Values, *Your Essential Management Reading List.*)

Chapter 9

- Updated opening case on Yellow House
- Two new cases on DevFacto Technologies and Ubisoft Entertainment SA, and a profile of corporate executive and former NHL player Nevin Markwart
- *And the Survey Says* . . . on investing in corporate social responsibility
- New material on goal-setting theory, open book management, and employee engagement
- New EOC material (*Hey, You're the Boss Now* on motivating employees, *Diversity Matters* on Maslow's equity theory, and *Your Essential Management Reading List*)

Chapter 10

- New opening case on the Virgin Group
- Two new cases on Whole Foods Canada and Toyota Canada
- *And the Survey Says* . . . on teams and motivation
- New exhibits on Belbin's team roles and deciding when to use teams
- Updated exhibit on team development
- New EOC material (*Hey, You're the Boss Now* on team considerations, *Diversity Matters* on managing diverse teams, *Your Essential Reading List.*)

Chapter 11

- Updated opening case on the Canadian Curling Association
- *And the Survey Says* . . . on Canadian debt
- New exhibit on the balanced scorecard
- Material on organizational culture moved to Chapter 12
- Updated exhibit on the service profit chain
- New EOC material (*Hey, You're the Boss Now* on giving feedback, *Diversity Matters* on cultural impact on feedback, *Be the Consultant* on financing a new business venture, *Your Essential Management Reading List.*)

Chapter 12

- New opening case on Men In Kilts
- New material on innovation and creativity, organizational culture's impact on innovation and change
- New *Tips for Managers* on creating a more innovative work environment
- New exhibits on innovation variables and four steps in organizational change
- Updated exhibits on mistakes managers make when leading change and helping employees accept change
- Material on organizational culture (moved from Chapter 11)
- New EOC material (*Hey, You're the Boss Now* on innovation creation, *Diversity Matters* on inherent and acquired diversity, *Your Essential Reading List.*)

SUPPLEMENTS

We have created an outstanding supplements package for instructors, conveniently available online through MyManagementLab in the special instructor area and downloadable from our product catalogue at **www.pearsoncanada.ca.**

Instructor's Resource Manual. This resource includes lecture outlines and chapter overviews, suggested answers to the textbook end-of-chapter exercises, and additional activities.

Computerized Test Bank. Pearson's computerized test banks allow instructors to filter and select questions to create quizzes, tests or homework. Instructors can revise questions or add their own, and may be able to choose print or online options. These questions are also available in Microsoft Word format.

Test Item File. This comprehensive test bank contains more than 1000 multiple choice, true/false, and short essay questions.

PowerPoint® Presentations. PowerPoint slides are available with this edition, with a minimum of 25 slides per chapter.

Image Library. All the figures in the text are provided in electronic format, for use in PowerPoint slides, handouts, or other presentations.

Pearson eText. The Pearson eText gives students access to their textbook anytime, anywhere. In addition to note taking, highlighting, and bookmarking, the Pearson eText offers interactive and sharing features. Rich media options may include videos, animations, interactive figures, and built-in assessments, all embedded in the text. Instructors can share their comments or highlights, and students can add their own, creating a tight community of learners within the class.

The Pearson eText may include a responsive design for easy viewing on smartphones and tablets. Many of our eTexts now have configurable reading settings, including resizable type and night reading mode.

Learning Solutions Managers. Pearson's Learning Solutions Managers work with faculty and campus course designers to ensure that Pearson technology products, assessment tools, and online course materials are tailored to meet your specific needs. This highly qualified team is dedicated to helping schools take full advantage of a wide range of educational resources, by assisting in the integration of a variety of instructional materials and media formats. Your local Pearson Canada sales representative can provide you with more details on this service program.

MyManagementLab

MyManagementLab delivers proven results in helping individual students succeed. It provides engaging experiences that personalize, stimulate, and measure learning for each student. For the eighth Canadian edition, MyManagementLab includes powerful new learning resources, including a new set of online lesson presentations to help students work through and master key management topics, a completely restructured study plan for student self-study, and a wealth of engaging assessment and teaching aids to help students and instructors explore unique learning pathways. MyManagementLab online resources include:

- **NEW Learning Catalytics.** Learning Catalytics is a "bring your own device" student engagement, assessment, and classroom intelligence system. It allows instructors to engage students in class with a variety of questions types designed to gauge student understanding.

- **NEW Personal Inventory Assessment (PIA).** Students learn better when they can connect what they are learning to their personal experience. PIA is a collection of online exercises designed to promote self-reflection and engagement in students, enhancing their ability to connect with concepts taught in principles of management, organizational behaviour, and human resource management classes. Assessments can be assigned by instructors, who can then track students' completions. Student results include a written explanation along with a graphic display that shows how their results compare to the class as a whole. Instructors will also have access to this graphic representation of results to promote classroom discussion.

- **NEW Interactive Lesson Presentations.** Students can now study key chapter topics and work through interactive assessments to test their knowledge and mastery of management concepts. Each presentation allows students to explore through expertly designed steps of reading, practising, and testing to ensure that students not only experience the content, but truly engage with each topic. Instructors also have the ability to assign quizzes, projects, and follow-up discussion questions relating to the online lessons to further develop the valuable learning experiences from the presentations.

- **NEW Study Plan.** MyManagementLab offers students an engaging and focused self-study experience that is driven by a powerful new study plan. Students work through assessments in each chapter to gauge their understanding and target the topics that require additional practice. Along the way, they are recognized for their mastery of each topic and guided toward resources in areas that they might be struggling to understand.

- **NEW Dynamic Study Modules.** These new study modules allow students to work through groups of questions and check their understanding of foundational management topics. As students work through questions, the dynamic study modules assess their knowledge and only show questions that still require practice. Dynamic study modules can be completed online using your computer, tablet, or mobile device.

- **Management Simulations.** Management simulations are real-world scenarios that invite students to apply the concepts they have just learned. Management simulations walk students through key management decision-making scenarios to help them understand how management decisions are made. Students are asked to make important decisions relating to core management concepts. At each point, students receive feedback to help them understand the implications of their choices in the management environment. Both types of simulations can now be assigned by instructors and graded directly through MyManagementLab.

- **NEW Business Today Video Database.** Business Today is a dynamic and expanding database of videos that covers the disciplines of business, marketing, management, and more. In addition to the videos that have been specifically correlated to this text, you will find new videos posted regularly. Check back regularly to see up-to-date video examples that are perfect for classroom use.

ACKNOWLEDGMENTS

A number of people have worked hard to update and enliven this eighth Canadian edition of *Fundamentals of Management*. Patti Sayle was developmental editor on this project. Her understanding, patience, helpfulness, support, and organizational skills made working on this textbook enjoyable and enriching. She also played a key role in handling many aspects of the editorial work needed during the production process. Carolin Sweig, acquisitions editor, was very supportive of finding new directions for the textbook. Karen Townsend, program manager, continues to be easy to work with on various projects and is always in the author's corner.

I'd also like to thank project manager Jessica Hellen, project editor Jogender Taneja, and copy editor Sally Glover, as well as the many others—proofreaders, designers, permissions researchers, marketing and sales representatives—who have contributed to the transformation of my manuscript into this textbook and seen it delivered into your hands. The Pearson Canada sales team is an exceptional group, and I know they will do everything possible to make the book successful.

Finally, I would like to thank the reviewers of this textbook for their detailed and helpful comments:

Kerry Remple, Okanagan College
Tommy Soong, Langara College
Leslie Wilder, Red River College
Geoff Pond, St. Lawrence College
Sharon Hyman, Seneca College
Michael Kelly, Nova Scotia Community College
Kristin Malvar-Oickle, Nova Scotia Community College-
    Lunenburg Campus
Cheryl Dowell, Algonquin College
Wade Hoople, Georgian College
Jai Goolsarran, School of Business, Centennial College
Jorge E. Oceguera, Capilano University
Sharon Archibald, Sir Sandford Fleming College
Carson Rappell, Dawson College
Melanie Simmons MBA, NAIT

I dedicate this book to Tracy, who is my loving support and inspiration; and my two sons, Shaun and Isaac.

Ian Anderson

About the Authors

STEPHEN P. ROBBINS received his Ph.D. from the University of Arizona. He previously worked for the Shell Oil Company and Reynolds Metals Company and has taught at the University of Nebraska at Omaha, Concordia University in Montreal, the University of Baltimore, Southern Illinois University at Edwardsville, and San Diego State University. He is currently professor emeritus in management at San Diego State.

Dr. Robbins's research interests have focused on conflict, power, and politics in organizations, behavioural decision making, and the development of effective interpersonal skills. His articles on these and other topics have appeared in such journals as *Business Horizons*, the *California Management Review, Business and Economic Perspectives, International Management, Management Review, Canadian Personnel, Industrial Relations,* and *The Journal of Management Education.*

Dr. Robbins is the world's best-selling textbook author in the areas of management and organizational behaviour. His books have sold more than 5 million copies and have been translated into 20 languages. His books are currently used at more than 1500 U.S. colleges and universities, as well as hundreds of schools throughout Canada, Latin America, Australia, New Zealand, Asia, and Europe.

Dr. Robbins also participates in masters track competition. Since turning 50 in 1993, he's won 23 national championships and 14 world titles. He was inducted into the U.S. Masters Track & Field Hall of Fame in 2005 and is currently the world record holder at 100m and 200m for men 65 and over.

DAVID A. DECENZO (Ph.D., West Virginia University) is president of Coastal Carolina University in Conway, South Carolina. In his capacity as president, Dr. DeCenzo is responsible for the overall vision and leadership of the university. He has been at Coastal since 2002, when he took over leadership of the E. Craig Wall Sr. College of Business. Since then, the college established an economics major and developed an MBA program. During that period, student enrollment and faculty positions nearly doubled. The college also established significant internship opportunities locally, nationally, and internationally in major *Fortune* 100 companies. As provost, Dr. DeCenzo worked with faculty leadership to pass a revised general education core curriculum as well as institute a minimum salary level for the university's faculty members. Before joining the Coastal faculty in 2002, he served as director of partnership development in the College of Business and Economics at Towson University in Maryland. He is an experienced industry consultant, corporate trainer, and public speaker. Dr. DeCenzo is the author of numerous textbooks that are used widely at colleges and universities throughout the United States and the world.

Dr. DeCenzo and his wife, Terri, have four children and reside in Pawleys Island, South Carolina.

MARY COULTER (Ph.D., University of Arkansas) held different jobs, including high school teacher, legal assistant, and city government program planner, before completing her graduate work. She has taught at Drury University, the University of Arkansas, Trinity University, and Missouri State University. She is currently professor emeritus of management at Missouri State University. Dr. Coulter's research interests were focused on competitive strategies for not-for-profit arts organizations and the use of new media in the educational process. Her research on these and other topics has appeared in such journals as *International Journal of Business Disciplines, Journal of Business Strategies, Journal of Business Research, Journal of Nonprofit and Public Sector Marketing,* and *Case Research Journal.* In additional to *Fundamentals of Management*, Dr. Coulter has published other books with Prentice Hall including *Management* (with Stephen P. Robbins), *Strategic Management in Action*, and *Entrepreneurship in Action.*

When she's not busy writing, Dr. Coulter enjoys puttering around in her flower gardens, trying new recipes, reading all different types of books, and enjoying many different activities with Ron, Sarah and James, Katie and Matt, and especially with her new grandkids, Brooklynn and Blake, who are the delights of her life!

IAN ANDERSON received his Master's of Business Administration in Innovation Leadership from the University of Fredericton. Before commencing his college teaching career, he was the director of human resources for a large Ottawa-based IT company. Ian is also a human resources and management consultant with Association Management, Consulting & Educational Services (AMCES), is a certified Change Management Professional, and has been actively consulting for more than 25 years. At Algonquin College, Ian is a professor in management, leadership, and human resources, and coaches students in business case and college marketing competitions.

In his spare time, Ian enjoys coaching Special Olympics soccer and basketball and volunteering with his favourite charity, the Capital City Condors. He has coached competitive and recreational hockey and soccer for more than 20 years. As a Sommelier, he works regularly with Groovy Grapes to provide tutored tastings and wine and scotch education. You can find Ian's wine reviews via his twitter handle @ #GroovyWineGuy. Ian's parents, Bob and Katharine, are from the Niagara area. Ian recently authored a chapter on knowledge management for CSAE's publication *Canadian Association Management*.

CHAPTER

1

Introduction to Management and Organizations

Jeff McIntosh/Canadian Press Images

LEARNING OUTCOMES

1.1 **Explain** Does studying management make a difference?   2

1.2 **Tell** What makes someone a manager?   3

1.3 **Define** What is management, and what do managers do?   4

1.4 **Describe** What characteristics define an organization?   7

1.5 **Describe** What are the factors that make for successful entrepreneurs?   10

Naheed Nenshi was born in Toronto and completed a master's degree at Harvard in public policy. He worked for the renowned international consulting firm McKinsey, which has been referred to as "special forces training for business leadership."[1] In 2010, at 38 years of age, Nenshi became Calgary's thirty-sixth mayor and the first Muslim mayor of a major North American city.

After leaving McKinsey, Nenshi started a business called Ascend Group to assist public, private, and nonprofit organizations grow their businesses. He developed strategies for the Canadian marketplace for companies like Gap, Banana Republic, and Old Navy. He was Canada's first tenured professor in the field of nonprofit management, at Mount Royal University's Bissett School of Business.

His work as an entrepreneur taught Nenshi the most about business, but designing policy for the Alberta provincial government attracted him to politics. His main focus is to make cities like Calgary run more smoothly. He is the author of *Building Up: Making Canada's Cities Magnets for Talent and Engines of Development*, and his initiatives in Calgary include an ambitious multidecade transit plan.[2]

Naheed Nenshi is a good example of a successful manager today and exemplifies the skills managers must have to deal with the problems and challenges of managing in the twenty-first century. This text is about the important managerial work that Mayor Nenshi and the millions of other managers like him do. It recognizes the reality faced by today's managers: New technologies and new ways of organizing work are altering old approaches. Today's successful managers must be able to blend tried-and-true management styles with new ideas.

Think About It

What kinds of skills do managers need?

In this chapter, we introduce you to managers and management by looking at who managers are, what management is, what managers do, and what an organization is. We will wrap up the chapter by discussing the challenges managers face and why it is important to study management.

1.1 **Explain** Does studying management make a difference?

WHY STUDY MANAGEMENT?

You may be wondering why you need to study management. If you are an accounting major, marketing major, or any major other than management, you may not understand how studying management will help you in your career. We can explain the value of studying management by looking at the universality of management, the reality of work, and how management applies to anyone wanting to be self-employed.

The Universality of Management

Just how universal is the need for management in organizations? We can say with absolute certainty that management is needed in all types and sizes of organizations, at all organizational levels, in all organizational work areas, and in all organizations, no matter what countries they are located in. This reality is known as the **universality of management** (see Exhibit 1-1). Managers in all these settings will plan, organize, lead, and control. However, management is not done the same way in all settings. The differences between what a supervisor in a software applications–testing facility at Microsoft does and what the CEO of Microsoft does are a matter of degree and emphasis, not of function. Because both are managers, they will plan, organize, lead, and control, but how they do so will differ.

Since management is universally needed in all organizations, we have a vested interest in improving the way organizations are managed. Why? We interact with organizations every single day of our lives. Are you irritated when none of the salespeople in a department store seems interested in helping you? Do you get annoyed when you call your computer's technical help desk because your laptop's video player is no longer working, go through seven voice menus, and then get put on hold for 15 minutes? These situations are examples of problems created by poor management. Organizations that are well managed—and we will share many examples of these—develop a loyal customer base, grow, and prosper. Those that are poorly managed find themselves with a declining customer base and reduced revenues. By studying management, you will be able to recognize

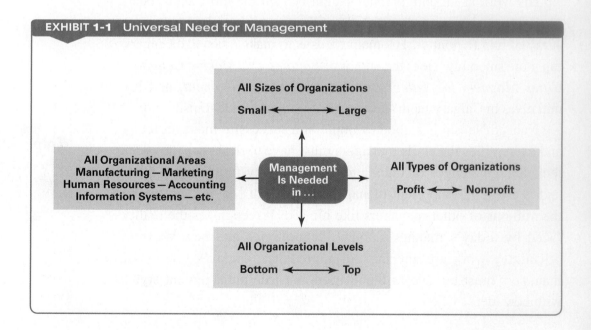

EXHIBIT 1-1 Universal Need for Management

All Sizes of Organizations
Small ←——→ Large

All Organizational Areas
Manufacturing — Marketing
Human Resources — Accounting
Information Systems — etc.

Management Is Needed in …

All Types of Organizations
Profit ←——→ Nonprofit

All Organizational Levels
Bottom ←——→ Top

universality of management
The reality that management is needed in all types and sizes of organizations, at all organizational levels, in all organizational work areas, and in organizations in all countries around the globe.

poor management and work to get it corrected. In addition, you will be able to recognize good management and encourage it, whether it is in an organization with which you are simply interacting or an organization in which you are employed.

The Reality of Work

Most of you, once you graduate and begin your careers, will either manage or be managed. This reality is another reason why you should study management. For those who plan on management careers, an understanding of the management process forms the foundation on which to build management skills. For those of you who do not see yourselves in management positions, this same understanding will help you work more effectively with your future managers. Also, assuming that you will have to work for a living and recognizing that you are very likely to work in an organization, you will probably have some managerial responsibilities, even if you are not managers. Our experience tells us that you can gain a great deal of insight into the way your manager behaves and the internal workings of organizations by studying management. You do not have to aspire to be a manager to gain something valuable from a course in management.

WHO ARE MANAGERS?

As mayor of Calgary, Naheed Nenshi is responsible for more than 13 000 city employees. His focus is on becoming a more effective and disciplined organization. To that end, he has instituted zero-based budget reviews of every business unit at the City. Many initiatives have been citizen-focused, such as a collaborative budgeting process with more than 20 000 Calgarians providing input, or creating video archives of City Council meetings for public review.

Managers may not be who or what you might expect. They could be under age 18 or even over age 80. They run large corporations as well as entrepreneurial startups. They are found in government departments, hospitals, small businesses, nonprofit agencies, museums, schools, and even nontraditional organizations such as political campaign offices and consumer cooperatives. They can be found doing managerial work in every country around the globe and operate at many levels, from top-level managers to first-line managers.

No matter where managers are found or what gender they are, managers have exciting and challenging jobs. And organizations need managers more than ever in these uncertain, complex, and chaotic times. *Managers do matter!* How do we know that? The Gallup Organization, which has polled millions of employees and tens of thousands of managers, has found that the single most important variable in employee productivity and loyalty is neither pay nor benefits nor workplace environment—it is the quality of the relationship between employees and their direct supervisors.[3] A KPMG/Ipsos-Reid study found that many Canadian companies with high scores for effective human resource practices also scored high on financial performance and best long-term investment value.[4] In addition, global consulting firm Watson Wyatt Worldwide found that the way a company manages its people can significantly affect its financial performance.[5] We can conclude from such reports that managers *do* matter!

Defining who managers are used to be fairly simple: Managers were the organizational members who told others what to do and how to do it. It was easy to differentiate *managers* from *nonmanagerial employees*. But life is not quite as simple anymore. In many organizations, the changing nature of work has blurred the distinction between managers and nonmanagerial employees. Many nonmanagerial jobs now include managerial activities.[6] For example, at General Cable Corporation's facility in Moose Jaw, Saskatchewan, managerial responsibilities are shared by managers and team members. Most of the employees at Moose Jaw are cross-trained and multiskilled. Within a single shift, an employee may be a team leader, an equipment operator, a maintenance technician, a quality inspector, and an improvement planner.[7]

1.2 Tell What makes someone a manager?

Think About It
What makes the Calgary mayor a manager?

Ted Hall started Spearhead Timberworks by building a barn for a family friend. Now a multimillion-dollar operation located in Nelson, British Columbia, Hall abandoned conventional tools and embraced digital design and manufacturing. As a manager of 60 employees, Hall must be on top of just-in-time delivery and compressed construction schedules. He has to wear many hats: master carpenter, technology innovator, quality control master, mentor, trainer, and listener. With each role come unique challenges.

How do we define who managers are? A **manager** is someone who works with and through other people by coordinating their work activities in order to accomplish organizational goals. A manager's job is not about *personal* achievement—it is about helping *others* do their work and achieve results.

Types of Managers

Is there some way to classify managers in organizations? In traditionally structured organizations, identifying exactly who the managers are is not difficult, although they may have a variety of titles. **Lower-level managers** are at the lowest level of management and manage the work of nonmanagerial employees who are directly or indirectly involved with the production or creation of the organization's products. They are often called *supervisors*, but may also be called *shift managers*, *district managers*, *department managers*, or *office managers*. **Middle-level managers** include all levels of management between the first-line level and the top level of the organization. These managers manage the work of first-line managers, implement the strategic goals set by top management, and may have titles such as *regional manager*, *project leader*, *plant manager*, or *division manager*. At or near the top of the organization are the **top-level managers**, who are responsible for making organization-wide decisions and establishing the plans and goals that affect the entire organization. These individuals typically have titles such as *executive vice-president*, *president*, *managing director*, *chief operating officer*, *chief executive officer*, or *chair of the board*. In the chapter-opening case, Naheed Nenshi is the popular and successful mayor of Canada's third-largest city. He is involved in creating and implementing broad and comprehensive changes that affect the entire city of Calgary and the province of Alberta.

Not all organizations get work done using a traditional pyramidal form, with the three levels of managers on the top of the pyramid. Some organizations, for example, are more flexible and loosely structured, with work being done by ever-changing teams of employees who move from one project to another as work demands arise. Although it is not as easy to tell who the managers are in these organizations, we do know that someone must fulfill that role—there must be someone who works with and through other people by coordinating their work to accomplish organizational goals.

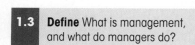

1.3 Define What is management, and what do managers do?

PERSONAL INVENTORY ASSESSMENT

WHAT IS MANAGEMENT, AND WHAT DO MANAGERS DO?

Managers plan, lead, organize, and control, and Naheed Nenshi certainly carries out all of these tasks. He has to coordinate the work activities of over 13 000 city employees efficiently and effectively. Working collaboratively with City Council, he has to make sure that work is carried out consistently to protect his brand. He also has to support his managers. Nenshi likes to joke among his managerial team that the mayor is always right—but only as far as the door of his office. He will defend the decisions of his team even if he didn't agree with them.[8]

---

manager
Someone who works with and through other people by coordinating their work activities in order to accomplish organizational goals.

lower-level managers
Managers at the lowest level of the organization who manage the work of nonmanagerial employees directly or indirectly involved with the production or creation of the organization's products.

middle-level managers
Managers between the first-line level and the top level of the organization who manage the work of first-line managers.

top-level managers
Managers at or near the top level of the organization who are responsible for making organization-wide decisions and establishing the plans and goals that affect the entire organization.

Simply speaking, **management** is what managers do. But that simple statement does not tell us much, does it? Here is a more thorough explanation: Management is coordinating work activities so that they are completed *efficiently* and *effectively* with and through other people. Management researchers have developed three specific categories to describe what managers do: functions, roles, and skills. In this section, we'll consider the challenges of balancing efficiency and effectiveness, and then examine the approaches that look at what managers do. In reviewing these categories, it might be helpful to understand that management is something that is a learned talent, rather than something that comes "naturally." Many people do not know how to be a manager when they first are appointed to that role. See Supplement 1 for the history of management's roots to understand how management theory has developed over time.

Think About It

Naheed Nenshi must balance the needs of efficiency and effectiveness in his role as mayor. What challenges does he face in planning, leading, organizing, and controlling City Hall while running a city of more than 1 million people?

Efficiency and Effectiveness

Efficiency refers to getting the most output from the least amount of inputs or, as management expert Peter Drucker explained, "doing things right."[9] Because managers deal with scarce inputs—including resources such as people, money, and equipment—they are concerned with the efficient use of those resources by getting things done at the least cost.

Just being efficient is not enough, however. Management is also responsible for being effective—completing activities so that organizational goals are achieved. **Effectiveness** is often described as "doing the right things"—that is, those work activities that will help the organization reach its goals. Hospitals might try to be efficient by reducing the number of days that patients stay in hospital. However, they may not be effective if patients get sick at home shortly after being released.

While efficiency is about ways to get things done, effectiveness deals with the ends, or attaining organizational goals (see Exhibit 1-2). Management is concerned, then, not only

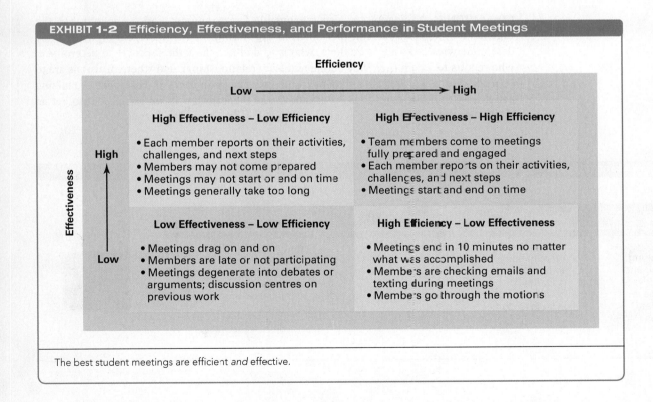

EXHIBIT 1-2   Efficiency, Effectiveness, and Performance in Student Meetings

Efficiency

Low ⟶ High

High Effectiveness – Low Efficiency
- Each member reports on their activities, challenges, and next steps
- Members may not come prepared
- Meetings may not start or end on time
- Meetings generally take too long

High Effectiveness – High Efficiency
- Team members come to meetings fully prepared and engaged
- Each member reports on their activities, challenges, and next steps
- Meetings start and end on time

Low Effectiveness – Low Efficiency
- Meetings drag on and on
- Members are late or not participating
- Meetings degenerate into debates or arguments; discussion centres on previous work

High Efficiency – Low Effectiveness
- Meetings end in 10 minutes no matter what was accomplished
- Members are checking emails and texting during meetings
- Members go through the motions

Effectiveness — High / Low

The best student meetings are efficient *and* effective.

management
Coordinating work activities so that they are completed efficiently and effectively with and through other people.

efficiency
Getting the most output from the least amount of inputs.

effectiveness
Completing activities so that organizational goals are achieved.

with completing activities to meet organizational goals (effectiveness), but also with doing so as efficiently as possible. In successful organizations, high efficiency and high effectiveness typically go hand in hand. Poor management is most often due to both inefficiency and ineffectiveness or to effectiveness achieved through inefficiency.

Management Functions

According to the functions approach, managers perform certain activities or duties as they efficiently and effectively coordinate the work of others. What are these activities or functions? In the early part of the twentieth century, French industrialist Henri Fayol first proposed that all managers perform five functions: planning, organizing, commanding, coordinating, and controlling.[10] Today, most management textbooks (including this one) are organized around four **management functions**: planning, organizing, leading, and controlling (see Exhibit 1-3). But you do not have to be a manager to have a need to plan, organize, lead, and control, so understanding these processes is important for everyone. Let us briefly define what each of these functions encompasses.

PLANNING   If you have no particular destination in mind, then you can take any road. However, if you have someplace in particular you want to go, you have to plan the best way to get there. Because organizations exist to achieve some particular purpose, someone must clearly define that purpose and the means for its achievement. Managers performing the **planning** function define goals, establish an overall strategy for achieving those goals, and develop plans to integrate and coordinate activities. This work can be done by the CEO and senior management team for the overall organization. Middle managers often have a planning role within their units. Planning, by the way, is not just for managers. As a student, for example, you need to plan for exams and for your financial needs.

ORGANIZING   Managers are also responsible for arranging work to accomplish the organization's goals. We call this function **organizing**. When managers organize, they determine what tasks are to be done, who is to do them, how the tasks are to be grouped, who reports to whom (i.e., they define authority relationships), and where decisions are to be made. When you work in a student group, you engage in some of these same organizing activities—deciding on a division of labour and what tasks will be carried out to get an assignment completed.

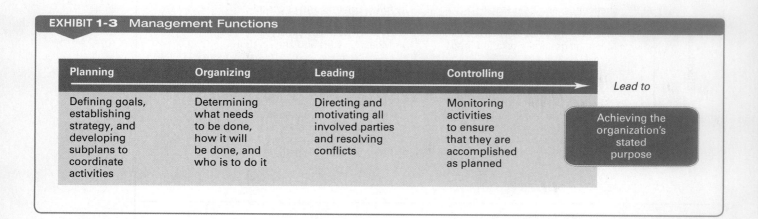

EXHIBIT 1-3 Management Functions

Planning	Organizing	Leading	Controlling	
Defining goals, establishing strategy, and developing subplans to coordinate activities	Determining what needs to be done, how it will be done, and who is to do it	Directing and motivating all involved parties and resolving conflicts	Monitoring activities to ensure that they are accomplished as planned	*Lead to* → Achieving the organization's stated purpose

management functions
Planning, organizing, leading, and controlling.

planning
A management function that involves defining goals, establishing a strategy for achieving those goals, and developing plans to integrate and coordinate activities.

organizing
A management function that involves determining what tasks are to be done, who is to do them, how the tasks are to be grouped, who reports to whom, and where decisions are to be made.

LEADING Every organization contains people. Part of a manager's job is to work with and through people to accomplish organizational goals. This task is the **leading** function. When managers motivate subordinates, direct the work of individuals or teams, select the most effective communication channel, or resolve behaviour issues, they are leading. Knowing how to manage and lead effectively is an important, and sometimes difficult, skill because it requires the ability to successfully communicate. Leading is not just for managers, however. As a student, you might want to practise leadership skills when working in groups or club activities. You might also want to evaluate whether you need to improve your leadership skills in anticipation of the needs of future jobs.

A leader has to be many things.

CONTROLLING The final management function is **controlling**. After the goals are set (planning), the plans formulated (planning), the structural arrangements determined (organizing), and the people hired, trained, and motivated (leading), there has to be some evaluation of whether things are going as planned (controlling). To ensure that work is proceeding as it should, managers need to monitor and evaluate employees' performance. Actual performance must be compared with previously set goals. If the performance of individuals or units does not match the goals set, the manager's job is to get performance back on track. This process of monitoring, comparing, and correcting is what we mean by the controlling function. Individuals, whether working in groups or alone, also face the responsibility of controlling; that is, they must make sure the goals and actions are achieved and take corrective action when necessary. The budget is the most common example of controlling.

The functions approach suggests that managers always plan, organize, lead, and then control, which in practice may not always happen in this logical and sequential order. Regardless of the order in which the functions are carried out, managers do plan, organize, lead, and control as they manage. Some have argued that this approach is not appropriate or relevant.[11] On the next page we will look at another perspective—the management roles perspective, developed by Henry Mintzberg.

As you study management functions in more depth, the exercises in *Team Exercises*, found at the end of each chapter, will give you the opportunity to practise some of the key skills that are part of doing what a manager does. Skill-building exercises cannot make you an instant managerial expert, but they can provide you with a basic understanding of some of the skills you will need to master to become an effective manager.

And the
Survey Says...

Companies with three or more women on their board had

53 percent higher return on equity

42 percent higher return on sales

66 percent higher return on invested capital

Organizations with two or more women on their boards

- demonstrate greater accountability

- conduct more extensive regular reviews of nonfinancial performance indicators

- are far more likely to be revenue and profit leaders over the long term

Fortune 500 companies: 2007 survey[12]

WHAT IS AN ORGANIZATION?

As mayor of Calgary, Naheed Nenshi works closely with City Council, which acts as a de facto board of directors. A municipal government is dramatically different than a federal one. Nenshi says, "If the federal government disappeared while we were talking, it would take a couple of weeks to notice. But if the municipal government disappeared, there go the traffic lights, the water, the electricity, the gas . . . you would, frankly, notice pretty quickly because you might be dead."[13]

1.4 **Describe** What characteristics define an organization?

---

leading
A management function that involves motivating subordinates, directing the work of individuals or teams, selecting the most effective communication channels, and resolving employee behaviour issues.

controlling
A management function that involves monitoring actual performance, comparing actual performance to a standard, and taking corrective action when necessary.

Ways to Look at What Managers Do

Management Roles Approach

- Henry Mintzberg, a prominent management researcher at McGill University, studied actual managers at work and discovered they spent little time in reflection, and most time in reaction.

- **Management roles** refer to specific managerial actions or behaviours. (Think of the different roles you play and the different behaviours you are expected to perform in the roles of student, employee, volunteer, etc.)

- These 10 roles, shown in Exhibit 1-4, are grouped around interpersonal relationships, the transfer of information, and decision making.

EXHIBIT 1-4 Mintzberg's Managerial Roles

Role	Description	Examples of Identifiable Activities
Interpersonal		
Figurehead	Symbolic head; performs routine legal or social duties	Greeting visitors; signing legal documents
Leader	Motivation of subordinates; staffing, training, and associated duties	Performing virtually all activities that involve subordinates
Liaison	Maintains network of contacts who provide favours and information	Acknowledging email; external board work; meeting with stakeholders
Informational		
Monitor	Sifts through a wide variety of internal and external information	Reading periodicals and reports; maintaining business network; LinkedIn
Disseminator	Conveys complex information to members of the organization	Holding informational meetings; phone calls
Spokesperson	Communicates with stakeholders on organizational plans and actions	Holding board meetings and media sessions
Decisional		
Entrepreneur	Identifies opportunities and brings about corrective changes	Organizing strategy to develop new programs
Disturbance handler	Takes corrective action when organization faces major disturbances	Resolving disturbances and crises
Resource allocator	Makes or approves all significant organizational decisions	Scheduling; requesting authorization; budgeting
Negotiator	Represents the organization at major negotiations; sets purchasing and contract terms	Union contract negotiations

Source: Based on H. Mintzberg, *The Nature of Managerial Work*, 1st edition, © 1973. HarperCollins Publishers.

Functions Versus Roles

- Both approaches describe what managers actually do.

- Many of Mintzberg's roles align well with one or more of the functions.

- The functions approach is more useful because of its simplicity and clarity. Managers carry out so many diverse activities and utilize such varying techniques that functions are needed for categorizing ways to achieve organizational goals.[14]

management roles
Specific categories of managerial behaviour.

Managers work in organizations. But what is an **organization**? An organization is a deliberate arrangement of people who act together to accomplish some specific purpose. Your college or university is an organization; so are churches, Amazon.ca, your neighbourhood convenience store, the United Way, the Toronto Raptors basketball team, and the Canadian Tire company. These examples are all organizations because they have three common characteristics:

- *Distinct purpose.* This purpose is typically expressed in terms of a goal or a set of goals that the organization hopes to accomplish.
- *People.* One person working alone is not an organization. An organization requires people to perform the work necessary to achieve its goals.
- *Deliberate structure.* Whether that structure is open and flexible or traditional and clearly defined, the structure defines members' work relationships.

In summary, the term *organization* refers to an entity that has a distinct purpose, includes people or members, and has some type of deliberate structure.

Although these three characteristics are important to our definition of *what* an organization is, the concept of an organization is changing. It is no longer appropriate to assume that all organizations are going to be structured like Air Canada, Petro-Canada, or General Motors, with clearly identifiable divisions, departments, and work units. Just how is the concept of an organization changing? Today's organizations are becoming more open, flexible, and responsive to change.[15]

Why are organizations changing? Because the world around them has changed and continues to change. Societal, economic, political, global, and technological changes have created an environment in which successful organizations (those that consistently attain their goals) must embrace new ways of getting work done. As we stated earlier, even though the concept of an organization may be changing, managers and management continue to be important to organizations.

The Size of Organizations

Managers do not just manage in large organizations, which represent only about 2 percent of all organizations in Canada. Small businesses (those that employ fewer than 100 individuals) represent 98 percent of all Canadian companies. These businesses employ almost half of all Canadian workers. See Supplement 2 for more data on small and medium enterprises and their contribution to the economy.

Managers are also not confined to manufacturing work, as only 10 percent of Canadians work in manufacturing organizations. Most Canadians (around 78 percent) work in the service sector of the economy, with 21 percent working in public sector jobs (those in the local, provincial, or federal government).[16] Industry Canada defines small and medium-sized enterprises (SMEs) as businesses with fewer than 500 employees. SMEs currently make up 48 percent of Canadian businesses.[17] Supplement 1 looks at SMEs in more detail.

The Types of Organizations

Managers work in a variety of situations, and therefore the people to whom they are held accountable vary considerably. Large organizations in the **private sector** are often **publicly held**, which typically means that their shares are available on the stock exchange for public trading. Managers of publicly held companies report to a board of directors that is

organization
A deliberate arrangement of people who act together to accomplish some specific purpose.

private sector
The part of the economy run by organizations that are free from direct government control; enterprises in this sector operate to make a profit.

publicly held organization
A company whose shares are available on the stock exchange for public trading by brokers/dealers.

Canada Post is a Crown corporation that has been in operation for more than 150 years serving more than 15 million Canadian addresses. Its 69 000+ full- and part-time employees run the country's most extensive distribution network, which includes 6500 postal outlets, 20 sorting plants, 500 letter carrier depots, and about 6800 vehicles.[18] How will that change when Canada Post eliminates home mail delivery?

responsible to shareholders (also known as stockholders). There are also numerous **privately held organizations** (whose shares are not available on the stock exchange), both large and small. Privately held organizations can be individually owned, family owned, or owned by some other group of individuals. A number of managers work in the **nonprofit sector**, where the emphasis is on providing charity or services rather than on making a profit. Examples of such organizations include the SPCA (Society for the Prevention of Cruelty to Animals), Toronto's Royal Ontario Museum, and Vancouver's Bard on the Beach Festival. Other organizational forms, such as **nongovernmental organizations (NGOs)**, partnerships, and cooperatives, also require managers. Many of these nonprofit organizations are referred to as SMOs (small and medium-sized organizations). Supplement 2 compares SMOs and SMEs in Canada.

Many managers work in the **public sector** as **civil servants** for the local, provincial, or federal government. The challenges of managing within government departments can be quite different from the challenges of managing in publicly held organizations. Critics argue that working for governments is less demanding because there are few measurable performance objectives, allowing employees to feel less accountable for their actions.

Some managers and employees work for **Crown corporations**, such as Canada Post, the CBC, and the Business Development Bank of Canada. Crown corporations are structured like private sector corporations and have boards of directors, chief executive officers (CEOs), and so on, but are owned by governments rather than shareholders. Employees in Crown corporations are not civil servants, and managers in Crown corporations are more independent than the senior bureaucrats who manage government departments.

Many of Canada's larger organizations are actually subsidiaries of American parent organizations (e.g., Safeway, General Motors, and Ford Motor Company). Their managers often report to American top managers and are not always free to set their own goals and targets. Conflicts can arise when Canadian managers and the American managers to whom they report do not agree on how things should be done.

| 1.5 | **Describe** What are the factors that make for successful entrepreneurs? |

ENTREPRENEURSHIP

You may decide that you want to run your own business rather than work for someone else. This type of employment will require that you manage yourself and may involve managing other people as well. Thus, an understanding of management is equally important whether you are a manager in someone else's business or running your own.

With $25 in allowance savings, Matt Hill started Lawn Troopers at the age of nine. Now an engineering graduate, Matt's lawn care business has 40 employees and has expanded to snow and waste removal. In 2014 he won Youth Entrepreneur of the Year at the Small Business Achievement Awards. One big perk of winning the award—Kevin O'Leary, formerly of CBC's *Dragon's Den*, will serve as his mentor.

There are numerous factors that allow an entrepreneur to be successful. Personal traits such as optimism and dedication are high on the list. For Matt, his path was forged from the outset as a result of determination and hard work. While building his business, he paid for his education out of company profits and completed his degree at Queen's University. Entrepreneurs need access to capital—human, financial, and technological. They need a solid business plan with the right partners. Timing and luck always play a part, but there is no substitute for hard work and "sweat equity."

---

privately held organizations
Companies whose shares are not available on the stock exchange but are privately held.

nonprofit sector
The part of the economy run by organizations that operate for purposes other than making a profit (that is, providing charity or services).

nongovernmental organization (NGO)
A nongovernmental organization that emphasizes humanitarian issues, development, and sustainability.

public sector
The part of the economy directly controlled by government.

civil servants
People who work in a local, provincial, or federal government department.

Crown corporations
Commercial companies owned by the government but independently managed.

Lawn Troopers

Matt Hill, pictured with former star of *Dragon's Den* Kevin O'Leary, accepts the Youth Entrepreneur of the Year Award in 2014

Earlier in the chapter we discussed the four managerial functions. Running a business like Lawn Troopers requires Matt to use each of the functions. Matt has to create a detailed action *plan* aimed at achieving some organizational goal. For example, when Matt wanted to increase sales during the winter months when lawn care business was slow, he added snow removal to his list of services. Matt may have spent time mapping out the necessary steps needed to increase his customer base. Perhaps it involved increasing advertisements in a particular region or contacting prior customers to see if they were interested in purchasing more services. Matt also began a new business, Scooper Troopers, using a revolutionary dog waste collection technology.

Once a plan is in place, Matt has to get busy getting *organized*. He has to allocate resources to any new business venture. He needs to identify different roles and ensure that he assigns the right amount of employees (and perhaps hire more) to carry out the new venture. He then needs to delegate authority, create job descriptions, and provide direction so that his team of sales representatives can work toward higher sales numbers without having barriers in their way. As his two businesses grow, Matt spends more time connecting with his employees on an interpersonal level. He is no longer simply managing the tasks of his employees; he *leads* them. Not all managers can be effective leaders, but Matt is good at communicating, motivating, inspiring, and encouraging his employees to achieve greater productivity. With a plan in place, Matt decided to explore a pilot project of Scooper Troopers prior to launching it fully. This gave him a chance to evaluate his results against his goals. In doing so, Matt exercised *control* over the business. He took corrective actions to work toward his goal of creating another successful business.

Review and Apply

Summary of Learning Outcomes

1.1 Does studying management make a difference? There are many reasons why students end up in management courses. Some of you are already managers and are hoping to learn more about the subject. Some of you hope to be managers someday. Some of you may never have thought about being managers. Career aspirations are only one reason to study management, however. Any organization you encounter will have managers, and it is often useful to understand their responsibilities, challenges, and experiences. Understanding management also helps us improve organizations.

1.2 What makes someone a manager? Managers work with and through other people by coordinating employee work activity in order to accomplish organizational goals. Managers may have personal goals, but management is not about *personal* achievement—it is about helping *others* achieve for the benefit of the organization as a whole.

Naheed Nenshi sees his role as similar to that of an orchestra leader, conducting everyone in the city to do a better job.

1.3 What is management, and what do managers do? Management is coordinating work activities of people so that they are done efficiently and effectively. Efficiency means "doing things right" and getting things done at the least cost. Effectiveness means "doing the right things" and completing activities that will help achieve the organization's goals. To do their jobs, managers plan, organize, lead, and control. In other words, they set goals and plan how to achieve those goals; they figure out what tasks need to be done and who should do them; they motivate individuals to achieve goals and communicate effectively with others; and they put accountability measures into place to make sure that goals are achieved efficiently and effectively.

Naheed Nenshi sets the goals for the overall organization, working closely with City Council and the provincial and federal governments. One of the challenges he faces is determining how rapidly he can change the culture of the municipality to become more client-centric and transparent.

1.4 What characteristics define an organization? There is no single type of organization. Managers work in a variety of organizations, both large and small. They also work in a variety of industries, including manufacturing and the service sector. The organizations they work for can be publicly held (meaning shares are traded on the stock exchange and managers are responsible to shareholders), privately held (meaning shares are not available to the public), public sector (where the government is the employer), or nonprofit (where the emphasis is on providing charity or services rather than on making a profit).

Naheed Nenshi formerly owned a company and thus was ultimately responsible to himself. Now he reports to the 1 million residents of Calgary.

1.5 What are the factors that make for successful entrepreneurs? There is no set formula for what makes a successful entrepreneur, but common traits include optimism, dedication, persistence, and leadership. Most entrepreneurs are innovative, determined, and hardworking. They enjoy the freedom and independence of being their own boss.

Matt Hall started a company at age nine that grew into a successful business employing more than 40 people.

SNAPSHOT SUMMARY

1.1 Why Study Management?
The Universality of Management
The Reality of Work

1.2 Who Are Managers?
Types of Managers

1.3 What Is Management, and What Do Managers Do?
Efficiency and Effectiveness
Management Functions

1.4 What Is an Organization?
The Size of Organizations
The Types of Organizations

1.5 Entrepreneurship

MyManagementLab Study, practise, and explore real management situations with these helpful resources:

- **Interactive Lesson Presentations:** Work through interactive presentations and assessments to test your knowledge of management concepts.
- **PIA (Personal Inventory Assessments):** Enhance your ability to connect with key concepts through these engaging self-reflection assessments.
- **Study Plan:** Check your understanding of chapter concepts with self-study quizzes.
- **Simulations:** Practise decision making in simulated management environments.

Discussion Questions

1. How does a manager's job change with his or her level in the organization?
2. What are the three skills that affect managerial effectiveness?
3. How is management universal?
4. Are effective organizations always efficient? Discuss. If you had to choose between being effective or being efficient, which would you say is more important? Why?
5. Is your instructor a manager? Discuss in terms of planning, organizing, leading, and controlling, and in terms of Mintzberg's managerial roles.
6. What similarities exist with the job activities of the owner of an automotive repair shop that employs two people and the executive director of the Canadian Cancer Society?
7. What are some of the skills that an entrepreneur must possess?

Analysis and Interpretation

Based on the answers above, in which areas are you most effective as a manager? In which areas do you need more development?

Developing Management Skills

Dilemma

Management is about achieving the highest possible return given the investment of money, people, time, and other resources. It is also about achieving results in the most efficient manner. Think about where you hope to be in your life five years from now (that is, your major goal). What is your competitive advantage for achieving your goal? Your education is a way of managing yourself and developing your career, which helps you achieve that goal. Here are some other things you can do to get the most out of yourself.

Becoming a Manager

- What is a better way of completing this task?
- What is my 80/20 rule—what 20 percent of my efforts are resulting in 80 percent of my outputs?
- What is the best use of my time today?
- How can I make better use of the abilities and time of my colleagues, subordinates, and superiors?
- Am I thinking for myself as much as I could?

Your Management Roles

Earlier you learned about Mintzberg's 10 management roles. You can learn to be more effective at managing people by using the following tips to enhance those management roles:

Mintzberg's 10 Roles	How to Enhance Your Managerial Skills
Figurehead	Lead by example, improve your reputation, and be a good role model.
Leader	Improve your emotional intelligence and earn respect from your team.
Liaison	Work on your professional networking skills; use tools such as LinkedIn.
Monitor	Keep up to date with industry news by learning how to gather and process information more effectively.
Disseminator	Develop your communication skills and learn how best to share information through written communication and informal briefings.

(continued)

Mintzberg's 10 Roles	How to Enhance Your Managerial Skills
Spokesperson	Work on your presentation skills; attend conferences and workshops.
Entrepreneur	Develop your creativity and problem-solving skills; learn more about change management.
Disturbance handler	Read about mediation and practise conflict resolution.
Resource allocator	Practise managing budgets and prioritizing your time effectively.
Negotiator	Practise with role playing to learn about win-win negotiations.

Diversity Matters

Innovation is a term that is mentioned frequently as a driver of business growth. More recently diversity among employees and senior leaders has been tied to innovation.[19] The report *Innovation, Diversity and Market Growth* identifies two types of diversity.

Inherent diversity is the gender, racial, and socioeconomic diversity of an organization, which leads to a higher number of innovative ideas. Employees who reflect the diversity of the Canadian and global marketplace are much more able to identify unmet client needs. **Acquired diversity** focuses on how a company's leadership acquires a global mindset and social media skills to enable it to better understand and appreciate diversity.

Studies have demonstrated that organizations with both inherent and acquired diversity were 75 percent more likely to see ideas go to market, 70 percent more likely to have captured a new market in the past 12 months, and 45 percent more likely to have improved market share during that same period than organizations that don't have these traits.[20]

Organizations with strong inherent and acquired diversity are more likely to have a culture with these six key characteristics:

Employees who are

1. listened to frequently
2. encouraged to propose new ideas
3. empowered to make decisions

Leaders who are

1. freely taking advice from their team
2. giving regular and actionable feedback
3. sharing credit for organizational success

Hey, You're the Boss Now!

According to the Canadian Management Centre, millennials (born 1980–2000) make up 29 percent of today's workplace and will constitute roughly 75 percent of the workforce by 2028. This will provide challenges and opportunities for employers. Generation X (born 1965–1979) managers trust themselves and favour action learning, while millennials seek more feedback and value group and team learning.[21] Those styles fundamentally clash, indicating that there is work to be done by the organization to ensure a smooth transition of millennials into the workforce.

As a manager in an organization, mentoring is an excellent way to ease this transition of millennials (including you). Jeanne Meister and Karie Willyerd, cofounders of the executive development firm Future Workplace, identify three kinds of mentoring that can help organizations prepare millennials for success.[22]

With **reverse mentoring**, the purpose of matching you with a senior executive is to provide your insight and expertise on a certain topic of interest to the executive, such as social media, technology, or cloud computing. You will benefit from their experience in other areas, but will bring strengths to the table as well.

In **group mentoring**, millennials have a peer-to-peer connection to deal with common issues of relevance. Use of technology can assist individuals and groups in the sharing of ideas, allowing 24/7 access to virtual members across the globe.

With **anonymous mentoring**, you select a mentor outside your organization. When thrust into a management role without a lot of experience, you may be hesitant to share your shortcomings within your company. An outside mentor provides anonymity and perspective.

Your Essential Management Reading List

Learning from key management experts can help you understand today's management theory and practice. What follows is a list of some influential management books, plus a do-it-yourself guide from a budding entrepreneur:

- *The Essential Drucker* and *The Daily Drucker*—Peter Drucker
- *Competitive Advantage: Creating and Sustaining Superior Performance*—Michael Porter
- *In Search of Excellence: Lessons from America's Best-Run Companies*—Thomas J. Peters and Robert J. Waterman, Jr.
- *The $100 Startup*—Chris Guillebeau

inherent diversity
The gender, racial, and socioeconomic diversity of an organization

acquired diversity
A company's acquisition of a global mindset and social media skills to enable it to better understand and appreciate diversity.

reverse mentoring
A junior employee providing insight and expertise on a certain topic to a senior executive.

group mentoring
Millennials sharing ideas in groups in a peer-to-peer format.

anonymous mentoring
Using a mentor outside an organization who can provide anonymity and perspective.

Team Exercises

3BL: The Triple Bottom Line

WHAT ARE THE BUSINESS CASE BENEFITS OF 3BL?

The components of the triple bottom line are *people*, *profit*, and *planet*. The focus on *people* deals with employee aspects, such as diversity, empowerment, and health and safety. It also expands to charitable contributions and corporate relations. Organizations that focus on more than the financial bottom line typically generate *profit* through ethical behaviour as well as cost savings through sustainable practices. The *planet* element looks beyond environmentalism and finds eco-efficiency in operations, manufacturing, and product development.[23] Over the next 11 chapters, we will examine 3BL in practical circumstances.

THINKING STRATEGICALLY ABOUT 3BL

The business case benefits of 3BL are illustrated in Exhibit 1-5.

Be the Consultant

In teams of four to five people, discuss the following scenario. One person will report back to the class on your recommendations.

Your student association has decided to open a new campus comedy club. They have strong financial backing with a bank loan of $750 000. They have little experience in the hospitality industry or with managing small businesses and have asked your team for advice and support. A student employment program from Human Resources and Skills Development Canada has provided each of you with a six-month contract to help get the club up and running.

How will you split up the key management functions of planning, organizing, leading, and controlling? What are three key decisions that you will have to make in each of the four functions that will help the comedy club become successful? What metrics will you use to evaluate the effectiveness of your managerial roles at the end of six months?

EXHIBIT 1-5   The Business Case Benefits of 3BL

Business Case Benefits	Business Case Components
Reduction in human resources (HR) costs	Recruiting costs are lower due to stronger employer branding; higher employee morale decreases turnover costs.
Reduction in operational costs	Manufacturing expenses are lowered through cost savings and continuous improvement; water, energy, and consumables expenses are reduced.
Decreased risk	Risks of nonsustainable practices are reduced, stakeholder relations are improved, and access to financing is increased.
Business improvements	Productivity is increased due to higher employee morale; sustainability awareness leads to higher innovation.
Financial improvements	Revenue increases due to greater market access and customer loyalty; improved relationships with regulators.

Source: Adapted from B. Willard, *The Next Sustainability Wave* (Canada: New Society Publishers, 2005), p. 130.

Business Cases

Shopify

It may surprise you that two snowboard enthusiasts who simply wanted a better way to sell their snowboards online created an ecommerce platform that now has over 90 000 customers in 80 countries, including Pixar, Angry Birds, and the Foo Fighters.[24] Shopify became Canada's first Internet startup since the dot-com crash to reach a billion-dollar valuation, thanks to $100 million in venture capital raised primarily through the Ontario Municipal Employees Retirement System (OMERS Ventures).[25]

Tobias Lütke, CEO and cofounder, has created a business that allows companies of all sizes to set up online stores, simplifying a task that used to take months and trimming it down to as little as half an hour. Shopify takes care of everything behind the scenes in return for a subscription fee and transaction fees. A typical Shopify customer spends less than $100 per month for the software use, a drop in the bucket compared to the cost to retailers a few years ago to operate an ecommerce site. Retailers using Shopify made more than $1.6 billion in sales in 2013, up from $132 million in 2010.[26]

"I think everyone in the company has a sense Shopify is doing well," said Lütke, noting that the 400+ employees own more than 20 percent of the firm. "Most don't realize *how* well it's going." Joining the "unicorn club" by reaching the $1-billion level is very rare. In the past decade only 40 tech firms, including Facebook and Twitter, have reached this elusive level.

Shopify has been doubling in size every year for the past four years and has emerged as the poster child of a group of online software providers who have substantially reduced the cost of ecommerce, enabling even small companies to build a commanding web presence. The accolades have poured in, with Shopify featured as one of *Fast Company*'s 50 Most Innovative Companies.[27]

Shopify focuses on developing entrepreneurs, both internally and externally. It launched a Build-A-Business contest, inviting online entrepreneurs to dream up something to sell using Shopify and compete to bring in the most revenue within two months for the chance to win more than $500 000 in prizes. "Our first two competitions were extremely successful. In total 4438 new businesses were created, selling over $15 million worth of products," said Lütke.[28] Harley Finkelstein, Shopify's chief platform officer, is a judge for the Future Entrepreneurial Leaders (FuEL) Awards.[29]

Shopify's commitment to its people is evident even in the little details. It has moved its head office for the second time in a year to accommodate its recently doubled workforce. Its new office is in Ottawa's trendy Byward Market area, so staff members have a great variety of fun places to eat and play after work. The office itself is a mix of glass and exposed brick, with open concept workspaces.

Shopify has many benefits and perks, including very popular company video-game tournaments, share options for all employees, daily catered lunches, and even the chance to go to any conference at the company's expense. They believe employees will produce their best work when they can wear their choice of clothing, start work later in the morning, and play video games whenever they need a break.

"Our mission continues to be to make it as easy as possible for retailers of all sizes to start and run a business online," said Lütke.[30] That mission also extends to its employees—hardworking, talented individuals who get things done and always push themselves to improve.

Discussion Questions

1. As a company gets bigger, does it become harder to stay innovative? Why or why not?
2. What are the perks that appeal to you?

Building a Better Boss

Google doesn't do anything halfway. So when it decided to "build a better boss," it did what it does best: Look at data. Using data from performance reviews, feedback surveys, and supporting papers turned in for individuals being nominated for top-manager awards, Google tried to find what a great boss

is and does. The project, dubbed Project Oxygen, examined some 100 variables and ultimately identified seven characteristics or habits of Google's most effective managers. The "big seven" are as follows:

- Provide an unambiguous vision of the future.
- Express interest in employees' well-being. (Make new team members feel welcome and get to know your employees as people.)
- Focus on being productive and on end results. (Focus on helping the team achieve its goals by prioritizing work and getting rid of obstacles.)
- Display good communication skills, especially listening. (Learn to listen and to share information; encourage open dialogue, and pay attention to the team's concerns.)
- Help individuals reach their long-term work goals. (Notice employees' efforts so they can see how their hard work is furthering their careers; appreciate employees' efforts and make that appreciation known.)
- Provide an unambiguous vision of the future. (Lead the team but keep everyone involved in developing and working toward the team's vision.)
- Ensure you have the necessary technical abilities to support employee efforts. (Understand the challenges facing the team and be able to help team members solve problems.)

Now, managers at Google aren't just encouraged to be great managers, they know what being a great manager involves. And the company is doing its part as well. Using the list, Google started training managers, as well as providing individual coaching and performance review sessions.

You can say that Project Oxygen breathed new life into Google's managers. Laszlo Bock, Google's senior vice-president for people operations, says the company's efforts paid off quickly. "We were able to have a statistically significant improvement in manager quality for 75 percent of our worst-performing managers."

Discussion Questions

1. Describe the findings of Project Oxygen using Mintzberg's role approach.
2. Are you surprised at what Google found out about "building a better boss"? Explain your answer.
3. What is the difference between encouraging managers to be great managers and knowing what being a great manager involves?
4. What could other companies learn from Google's experiences?
5. Would you want to work for a company like Google? Why or why not?

2 Environmental Constraints on Managers

ALCE/Fotolia

Social media was a major force in putting pressure on President Barack Obama and the US government in January 2012 to scrap the multibillion-dollar Keystone pipeline project designed to carry oil from Alberta to the Gulf of Mexico. Environmental groups took to Facebook and Twitter to lobby against the deal, despite approval for the project from Canada's National Energy Board and the US Environmental Protection Agency.[1] The pipeline project quickly became a hot topic in the 2014 US midterm election, and Obama decided to delay the pipeline decision.

The United States imports 8.4 million barrels of oil and petroleum products daily, of which Canada provides more than 2.4 million barrels. Canada's oil reserves of over 175 billion barrels rank it third largest in the world. The planned 2736-kilometre Keystone XL pipeline can transport close to a million barrels of oil a day to US refineries, and if approved will create more than 15 000 jobs in Canada.[2]

TransCanada managers were forced to re-evaluate their markets for oil. This reality caused a shift in focus to the Asian market generally and to China specifically. As Obama backtracked, the pace of Asian investment in the Canadian energy sector quickened. Sinopec acquired Daylight Energy for $2.1 billion. Mitsubishi invested $2.9 billion in a joint venture with Encana on its BC gas assets. Both companies are looking at the potential to ship gas to British Columbia for the Asian liquefied natural gas market. PetroChina expanded its oil sands investments by acquiring oil sands assets from Athabasca Oil Sands Corporation and a 20 percent interest in Shell's Groundbirch operations.[3]

As companies like TransCanada and Enbridge diversify away from the United States to Asia, Canada will receive two additional benefits: better oil prices and access to cheap Asian capital. According to a report by oil consultant Wood Mackenzie, Canadian producers will lose $8 billion in revenue a year by 2020 if US bottlenecks are not loosened.

Obama reversed course on the controversial Keystone oil pipeline in March 2012, saying he was fast-tracking approvals on part of

Think About It

Should large corporations have to report the details of all negotiations concerning Canadian natural resources? Put yourself in the shoes of TransCanada's CEO. What responsibilities do organizations have when negotiating international contracts for natural resources?

the project that he had earlier rejected. Obama said the project would create jobs, improve the flow of oil to refineries, and eventually reduce gas prices for Americans.[4] Fast-forward to 2014, and political pressure had Obama delay a decision on Keystone yet again, leaving its future in doubt.

....

Managers at TransCanada are responsible for overseeing the production and sales of oil. But how much actual impact does a manager have on an organization's success or failure? Can managers do anything they want? These questions raise more general questions: Do managers control their environment, or are they controlled by it? Are they affected more by circumstances outside or inside the organization? In this chapter, we consider the impact of an organization's external environment on the ability of managers to act. We begin our exploration by considering the degree of control managers have over an organization's performance.

....

| 2.1 | **Define** What is the external environment for managers? |

THE EXTERNAL ENVIRONMENT

After the United States initially blocked the Keystone XL pipeline project, Canada changed gears, and Prime Minister Stephen Harper visited China to encourage Chinese investment in the oil sector. Harper supports regulatory approval for Northern Gateway and other proposed oil sands pipelines.[5]

Some viewed Canada's overtures to China as leverage in negotiations with the United States. However, David Goldwyn, a former energy official in the Obama administration, does not view China's investment in the Canadian oil sands as a threat. "In the short term it provides additional investment to increase Canadian supply; that's a good thing. Longerterm, if Canadian oil goes to China, that means China's demand is being met by a non-OPEC country, and that's a good thing for global oil supply."[6]

As we discussed in Chapter 1, management is no longer constrained by national borders. Managers in all sizes and types of organizations are faced with the opportunities and challenges of managing in a global environment. For example, global sourcing of ingredients can provide a competitive advantage for food processors, but can also come with risks if the foreign country's food inspection standards are lower than those in North America.

The term **external environment** refers to forces and institutions outside the organization that potentially can affect its performance. The external environment is made up of three components, as shown in Exhibit 2-1: the specific environment, the general environment, and the global environment.

In 2008, the impact of defaults on subprime mortgages in the United States started to have a ripple effect throughout the world. The impact on employment and earnings in Canada was huge, even though Canadian bankers had been far more conservative in their mortgage products. This example illustrates some of the forces in the environment that play a major role in shaping managers' actions. In this section, we identify some of the critical environmental forces that affect managers and show how they constrain managerial discretion.

The Specific Environment

The **specific environment** represents the micro level and includes those external forces that have a direct and immediate impact on managers' decisions and actions and are directly relevant to the achievement of the organization's goals. Each organization's specific environment is unique and changes with conditions. For example, Timex and Rolex both make watches, but their specific environments differ because they operate in

---

external environment
Outside forces and institutions that can potentially affect the organization's performance.

specific environment
The part of the external environment that is directly relevant to the achievement of an organization's goals.

EXHIBIT 2-1 The External Environment

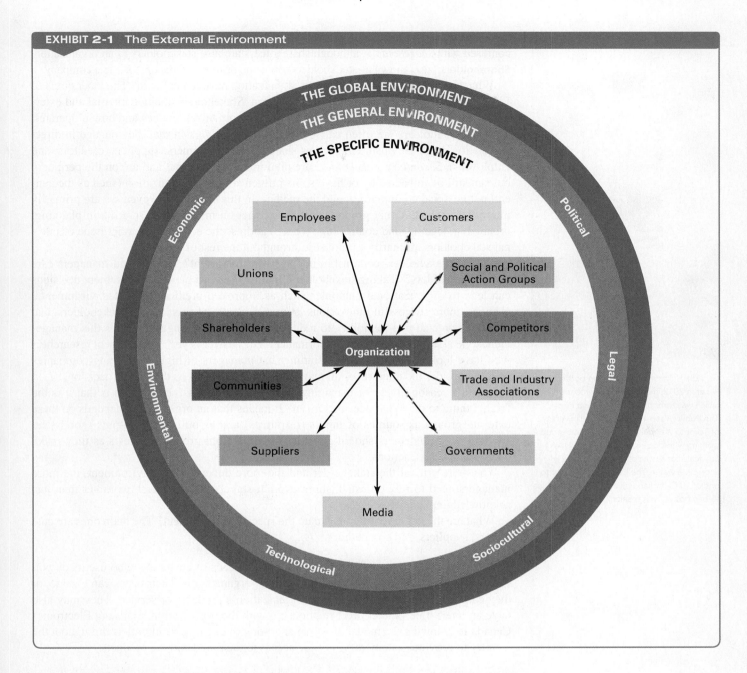

distinctly different market niches. Managers are affected by the nature of the relationships they have with external stakeholders. The more obvious and secure these relationships become, the more influence managers will have over organizational outcomes.

Who are **stakeholders**? We define them as groups in the organization's external environment that are affected by or have an effect on the organization's decisions and actions. These groups have a stake in or are significantly influenced by what the organization does. In turn, these groups can influence the organization. For example, think of the groups that might be affected by the decisions and actions of Starbucks's managers—coffee bean farmers, employees, specialty-coffee competitors, local communities, and so forth. Some of these stakeholders may also affect the decisions and actions of Starbucks's managers. Starbucks recently changed the way it purchased coffee beans after activists pressured the company to

stakeholders
Any constituencies in the organization's external environment that are affected by the organization's decisions and actions.

Canadians spent $2.3 billion on bottled water in 2012, more than 25 percent of which was through Coca-Cola and Pepsi.[7] The Public Water Institute at the University of Toronto is a multipartisan student group working with dozens of organizations to advocate for sustainable, clean, publicly accessible water. The University of Toronto is one of 10 Canadian universities and colleges to ban bottled water sales.

stop buying from plantations that treated their workers poorly. *Stakeholders* should not be confused with *shareholders*, although shareholders are also stakeholders in an organization. **Shareholders** (also known as stockholders) own one or more shares of stock in a company.

What types of stakeholders might an organization have to deal with? The inner circle of Exhibit 2-1 identifies some of the most common. Stakeholders include internal and external groups. Why? Because both can affect what an organization does and how it operates. Internal stakeholders are often called *primary stakeholders* in that they engage in direct transactions with the business (such as shareholders, customers, suppliers, creditors, and employees). *Secondary stakeholders* are predominantly external and are on the periphery but can still be impacted by or have some influence on the organization (such as the general public, local communities, and the media). In this chapter, however, we are primarily interested in the external groups and their impact on managers' discretion in planning, organizing, leading, and controlling. We will address the equally important issue of internal stakeholders, primarily employees, throughout the rest of the text.

Why is stakeholder-relationship management important? Why should managers care about stakeholders?[8] Taking stakeholders' interests into account in management decisions can lead to organizational outcomes such as improved predictability of environmental changes, more successful innovations, a greater degree of trust among stakeholders, and greater organizational flexibility to reduce the impact of change. But does this management style affect organizational performance? The answer is yes! Management researchers who have looked at this issue are finding that managers of high-performing companies tend to consider the interests of all major stakeholder groups as they make decisions.[9]

Another reason given for managing external stakeholder relationships is that it is the "right" thing to do. What does this mean? It means that an organization depends on these external groups as sources of inputs (resources) and as outlets for outputs (goods and services), and managers should consider these external groups' interests as they make decisions and take actions.

The more critical the stakeholder and the more uncertain the environment, the more managers need to rely on establishing explicit stakeholder partnerships rather than just acknowledging their existence.

What are the key forces that make up the specific environment? The main ones are customers, suppliers, and competitors.

CUSTOMERS   An organization exists to meet the needs of customers who use its output. Customers represent potential uncertainty to an organization. Their tastes can change, or they can become dissatisfied with the organization's products or service. They may also have an interest in a more direct relationship with the organization. Samsung Electronics Canada is following the model of Apple and Sony of opening retail outlets throughout the country to provide customers with more access to the brand and the products.

SUPPLIERS   Managers seek to ensure a steady flow of needed inputs (supplies) at the lowest price possible. A limit on an organization's supplies or a delay in delivery can constrain managers' decisions and actions. Walt Disney World, for example, must make sure it has supplies of soft drinks, computers, food, flowers and other nursery stock, concrete, paper products, and so forth. Suppliers also provide financial and labour inputs. A lack of qualified nurses continues to be a serious problem plaguing health care providers, affecting their ability to meet demand and keep service levels high. Virtually all of Alberta's oil and natural gas exports go to the United States, making Alberta a key supplier for the US government.

COMPETITORS   All organizations—profit and nonprofit—have one or more competitors. The major television broadcast networks used to control what you watched on television. Now they face competition from digital cable, satellite, and the Internet, all of which offer

shareholders
Individuals or companies that own stocks in a business.

customers a much broader choice. As US oil production grows, Alberta's role as supplier to the United States will change, and the United States will become a much fiercer competitor to Canadian oil and natural gas exports. In 2011, the United States became a net exporter of petroleum products for the first time since 1949.[10] As production increases, dependence on Alberta petroleum will decrease.

The General Environment

The **general environment** represents the macro level and includes the broad political, economic, sociocultural, technological, environmental, and legal conditions that *may* affect the organization. Changes in any of these areas usually do not have as large an impact as changes in the specific environment, but managers must consider them as they plan, organize, lead, and control. PESTEL is an acronym for the six macro environmental factors and will be discussed in more detail in Chapter 3.

POLITICAL CONDITIONS Political conditions include the political climate, the general stability of a country in which an organization operates, and the attitudes that elected government officials hold toward business. The political environment influences businesses and also has a major impact on consumer confidence and spending.

In Canada, organizations have generally operated in a stable political environment. The stability of the Canadian political landscape allows businesses to invest in and enter new markets. One challenging aspect of the Canadian marketplace is the government policies concerning taxation and regulation, which may vary from province to province.

Organizations spend a great deal of time and money meeting government regulations, but the effects of these regulations go beyond time and money.[11] They can also reduce managerial discretion by limiting the choices available to managers. In a 2004 COMPAS survey of business leaders, most respondents cited interprovincial trade barriers as a significant hurdle to doing business in this country, calling the barriers "bad economics." One respondent to the survey noted that the federal government fails "to realize that in today's global economy, our real 'competitors' are no longer in the next province (or the next city), not even in the United States or Mexico but are the emerging economies of Asia and Europe."[12]

The *Competition Act of 1985* created the Bureau of Competition Policy (now called the Competition Bureau) to oversee and encourage competition in Canada. For example, if two major competing companies consider merging, they will come under scrutiny from the Bureau. Heather Reisman and Gerry Schwartz's purchase of Chapters in 2001 needed approval before they could merge Chapters with their Indigo bookstores. Before approving the merger, the bureau imposed a number of conditions, including the sale or closing of 20 stores and a code of conduct for dealing with publishers. The code of conduct was the result of publishers' complaints about the way Chapters had treated them in the past. These rules affected the way Chapters Indigo could do business until 2006. Beyond that time, the bookseller was allowed to operate without restraint by the Competition Bureau.[13]

To protect farmers, the Canadian government has created marketing boards that regulate the pricing and production of such items as milk and eggs. Those who decide they want to manufacture small amounts of cheese would have great difficulty doing so, because the Canadian government does not open production quotas to new producers very often. Marketing boards restrict imports of some products, but the unintended result is that foreign governments oppose exports from Canada.

ECONOMIC CONDITIONS Interest rates, inflation, changes in disposable income, stock market fluctuations, and the stage of the general business cycle are some of the economic factors that can affect management practices in Canada. For example, many specialty

general environment
Broad external conditions that may affect the organization.

retailers such as IKEA, Roots, Birks, and Williams-Sonoma are acutely aware of the impact consumer disposable income has on their sales. When consumers' incomes fall or confidence about job security declines, such as happened in 2009, consumers will postpone purchasing anything that is not a necessity. Even charitable organizations such as the United Way and the Heart and Stroke Foundation feel the impact of economic factors. During economic downturns, not only does the demand for their services increase, but their contributions also typically decrease.

Economic indicators such as gross domestic product, price indices, and unemployment are used to reflect the health of the economy. The gross domestic product (GDP) is the broadest indicator of a country's economic activity, expressed in the market value of goods and services produced in a country. The consumer price index (CPI) measures purchasing power and rises and falls with inflation and deflation. It has an impact on wages paid and the prices of products and services. The Bank of Canada's commodity price index (BCPI) measures the price of 24 Canadian commodities on the world market, while the MLS® Home Price Index (HPI) compares home prices across the country. The unemployment rate is calculated by the number of workers above age 16 who are not working. There are several complicating factors, such as seasonal and cyclical changes, but the unemployment rate is used by government and businesses for planning purposes.

SOCIOCULTURAL CONDITIONS Responding to societal dietary concerns, Frito-Lay Canada announced that it was eliminating trans fatty acids (TFAs) from Doritos, Tostitos, and SunChips (it had already done so for its Lay's, Ruffles, and Miss Vickie's chips). Marc Guay, president of Frito-Lay Canada, explained his decision at the time: "Eliminating trans fat is a major step in Frito-Lay Canada's on-going commitment to offer consumers a wide variety of great-tasting snacks made with more healthful oils."[14]

Burlington, Ontario–based Voortman Cookies was the first Canadian cookie maker to drop TFAs from its products. President and cofounder Harry Voortman said he dropped the TFAs after his daughter, Lynn, a naturopathic doctor, became concerned enough that she stopped eating her father's cookies altogether.[16]

Why did Frito-Lay Canada and Voortman Cookies change their products? Because health officials and consumers became increasingly anxious about the link between TFAs and heart disease.[15] Managers must adapt their practices to the changing expectations of the societies in which they operate. As societal values, customs, and tastes change, managers also must change. For example, as employees have begun seeking more balance in their lives, organizations have had to adjust by offering family leave policies, more flexible work hours, and even on-site childcare facilities. These trends may pose a constraint on managers' decisions and actions. If an organization does business in other countries, managers need to be familiar with those countries' values and cultures and manage in ways that recognize and embrace those specific sociocultural aspects.

Demographics are part of socialcultural conditions and encompass trends in the physical characteristics of a population such as gender, age, level of education, geographic location, income, family composition, and so forth. Changes in these characteristics may constrain how managers plan, organize, lead, and control.

The three largest demographic groups are demonstrated in Exhibit 2-2. The aging of the Baby Boomers will leave Canada's workforce with major skill shortages. Alberta alone faces a shortage of more than 75 000 workers within the next 10 years.[17]

TECHNOLOGICAL CONDITIONS In terms of the general environment, the most rapid changes have occurred in technology. We live in a time of continuous technological change. Information gadgets are getting smaller and more powerful. We have automated offices, electronic meetings, robotic manufacturing, lasers, integrated circuits, faster and more powerful microprocessors, synthetic fuels, and entirely new models of doing business in an electronic age. Companies that capitalize on technology, such as Apple, eBay, and Google, prosper. In addition, many successful retailers such as Walmart use

EXHIBIT 2-2 The Styles of Three Generations[18]	
Baby Boomers (born 1946–1964)	Competitive, idealistic, team players
	Enjoy being in leadership roles
	Like recognition for their actions
Generation X (born 1965–1979)	Trust themselves more than institutions
	Avoid rules and bureaucracy
	Favour learning in an action-oriented way
Millennials (Born 1980–2000)	Technologically advanced, connected globally
	Appreciate feedback more than recognition
	Value learning in a group or team setting

Sources: Adapted from Pew Research Center, "Millennials—A Portrait of Generation Next," 2010; D. Piktialis and K. A. Greenes, *Bridging the Gaps*, The Conference Board, 2008.

sophisticated information systems to keep on top of current sales trends. Similarly, hospitals, universities, airports, police departments, and even military organizations that adapt to major technological advances have a competitive edge over those that do not. The whole area of technology is radically changing the fundamental ways that organizations are structured and the way that managers manage.

ENVIRONMENTAL CONDITIONS The environment has become a bigger issue in terms of sustainability of raw materials. The triple bottom line approach discussed throughout the text indicates the importance of the environmental bottom line for companies. Reducing the carbon footprint has become a focus for many organizations as they attempt to reduce waste; protect air, water, and land quality; and increase biodegradable and recyclable packaging. The Canadian Association of Petroleum Producers developed a Responsible Canadian Energy program to track greenhouse gas emissions, fresh water usage, and land cleared and reclaimed for mining operations.[19] For the oil industry, becoming more environmentally responsible is as much about financial and marketing conditions as it is about the environment. Cleaner extraction methods make oil more marketable in markets with low carbon-fuel standards such as California.[20]

LEGAL CONDITIONS The legal environment is often closely related to the political environment, because laws and regulations are enacted by politicians. Laws related to employment, health and safety, and product safety can have a major impact on how businesses operate.

Federal, provincial, and local governments influence what organizations can and cannot do. Some federal legislation has significant implications. The *Canadian Human Rights Act* makes it illegal for any employer or service provider falling within federal jurisdiction to discriminate on the following grounds: race, national or ethnic origin, colour, religion, age, sex (including pregnancy and childbirth), marital status, family status, mental or physical disability (including previous or current drug or alcohol dependence), pardoned conviction, or sexual orientation. The Act covers federal departments and agencies, Crown corporations, chartered banks, national airlines, interprovincial communications and telephone companies, interprovincial transportation companies, and other federally regulated industries, including certain mining operations.

Canada's *Employment Equity Act* of 1995 protects several categories of employees from employment barriers: Aboriginal peoples (whether First Nation, Inuit, or Métis); persons with disabilities; members of visible minorities (non-Caucasian in race or nonwhite in colour); and women. This legislation aims to ensure that members of these four groups are treated equitably. Employers covered by the *Canadian Human Rights Act* are also covered by the *Employment Equity Act*.

2.2 Describe What challenges do managers face in a global environment?

UNDERSTANDING THE GLOBAL ENVIRONMENT

Menu Foods was founded in 1971 and bought its first US factory in New Jersey in 1977, hoping to use that factory to launch an expansion into the US market.[21] Today the global company has four pet food processing plants: one in Canada (Mississauga, Ontario) and three in the United States (Emporia, Kansas; Pennsauken, New Jersey; and North Sioux City, South Dakota). The company's Canadian and American plants operate close to the areas they serve, which reduces shipping expenses.

Menu Foods buys the ingredients for its pet food products from a variety of companies, and those companies in turn may buy ingredients for their products from other companies around the world. As the tainted pet food investigation found, an ingredient that originated in China was responsible for the deaths caused by Menu Foods' various pet foods. Menu Foods gets some of its ingredients from suppliers, who may themselves rely on external suppliers. As a result, Menu Foods may not always be aware of the original source of every ingredient it uses.

Historically, Canada has been slow to face the global challenge, although the relatively small size of many Canadian firms may be a contributing factor in this pattern.[22] The *Fortune* list of the Top 100 Global Companies of 2013 does not include any Canadian firms (although there are 9 in the Top 500).[23] The majority of firms listed are American, but the number of Chinese firms on the list has grown from only 11 in 2001 to over 60 companies.[24]

The global environment presents both opportunities and challenges for managers. With the entire world as a market and national borders becoming increasingly irrelevant, the potential for organizations to grow is expanding dramatically.

However, even large successful organizations with talented managers face challenges in managing in the global environment. Managers must deal with cultural, economic, and political differences. Meanwhile, new competitors can suddenly appear at any time from any place on the globe. Managers who make no attempt to learn and adapt to changes in the global environment end up reacting rather than innovating. As a result, their organizations often become uncompetitive and fail.[25] Below, we discuss the issues managers have to face in managing in a global environment.

Global Trade

What is the global environment like? An important feature is global trade. Global trade is not new. Countries and organizations have been trading with each other for centuries. According to the World Trade Organization (WTO), "Trade is central to human health, prosperity, and social welfare."[26] When trade is allowed to flow freely, countries benefit from economic growth and productivity gains because they produce the goods they are best at producing and import goods that are more efficiently produced elsewhere. Global trade is being shaped by two forces: regional trading alliances and agreements negotiated through the WTO.

REGIONAL TRADING ALLIANCES   The major regional trading alliances are as follows:

- The **European Union (EU)**: The signing of the Maastricht Treaty (named for the Dutch town where the treaty was signed) in February 1992 created the European Union (EU), a unified economic and trade entity with 12 member countries—Belgium, Denmark, France, Greece, Ireland, Italy, Luxembourg, the Netherlands, Portugal, Spain, the United Kingdom, and Germany. By 2007, the EU comprised 27 countries. Three other countries (Croatia, the former Yugoslav Republic of Macedonia, and Turkey) have

European Union (EU)
A union of 27 European countries that forms an economic and political entity.

submitted applications to join the EU. The EU's economic power has diminished somewhat with the European economic crisis, but the current EU membership encompasses more than 490 million people.[27]

- The **North American Free Trade Agreement (NAFTA)**: When agreements in key issues covered by the North American Free Trade Agreement (NAFTA) were reached by the Canadian, US, and Mexican governments in August 1992, a vast economic bloc was created in which barriers to free trade were reduced. In 2011, Canadian exports to the United States were $331 billion, which accounted for 72 percent of our total exports.[28] Canada's exports to Mexico have quadrupled since the NAFTA agreement was signed, and its foreign investments in Mexico increased by a factor of five.[29] Westcoast Energy, Scotiabank, and BCE are just a few Canadian companies that have expanded their operations to Mexico. Many economists argue that reducing the barriers to trade (tariffs, import licensing requirements, customs user fees) has resulted in a strengthening of the economic power of all three countries. Free trade did not eliminate all trade problems between Canada and the United States, however, as the ongoing softwood lumber negotiations show. Canada and the United States first started negotiations in 1986, and they have continued to the present, with the latest agreement signed in 1994, with no expiration date.

- The **Association of Southeast Asian Nations (ASEAN)**: A trading alliance of 10 Southeast Asian countries, including Brunei Darussalam, Cambodia, Indonesia, Laos, Malaysia, Myanmar, Philippines, Singapore, Thailand, and Vietnam, ASEAN encompasses a region with a population of about 500 million and a combined gross domestic product of $1496 billion.[30] During the years ahead, the Southeast Asian region promises to be one of the fastest-growing economic regions of the world. It will be an increasingly important regional economic and political alliance whose impact eventually could rival that of both NAFTA and the EU.

- **Trans-Pacific Partnership (TPP)**: The TPP is a group of nine countries comprising the United States, Australia, New Zealand, Singapore, Peru, Vietnam, Malaysia, Brunei, and Chile, which is intending to revolutionize Asian trade relations. Canada joined the TPP in October 2015.[31]

- **Brazil, Russia, India, China, and South Africa (BRICS)**: BRICS is not a political alliance or a trading association, but it is a unique grouping with shared opportunities and common challenges. South Africa joined in 2011, and the group currently meets to create mechanisms for consultation and cooperation.[32]

- **Caricom Single Market and Economy (CSME)**: The CSME is intended to provide better opportunities to produce and sell local goods and services and to attract investment. It will create one large market among the participating member states, which include 15 Caribbean countries such as Bahamas, Barbados, Guyana, Grenada, Saint Lucia, and Jamaica.

THE WORLD TRADE ORGANIZATION The **World Trade Organization (WTO)** is a global organization that sets rules for international trade and helps countries negotiate trade problems and settle trade disputes.[33]

The WTO was formed in 1995 and evolved from the General Agreement on Tariffs and Trade (GATT), an agreement in effect since the end of World War II. Today, the WTO is the only *global* organization dealing with the rules of trade among nations. Its membership

---

North American Free Trade Agreement (NAFTA)
An agreement among the Canadian, American, and Mexican governments in which barriers to free trade are reduced.

Association of Southeast Asian Nations (ASEAN)
A trading alliance of 10 Southeast Asian countries.

Trans-Pacific Partnership (TFP)
A group of nine countries that is intending to revolutionize Asian trade relations.

Brazil, Russia, India, China, and South Africa (BRICS)
An association of leading emerging economies aiming to create mechanisms for consultation and cooperation.

Caricom Single Market and Economy (CSME)
An association of Caribbean countries aiming to create one large market.

World Trade Organization (WTO)
A global organization of 153 member countries that deals with the rules of trade among nations.

And the Survey Says...

Canada's trade has always focused on the United States and to a lesser extent China. The other countries with which Canada is conducting tariff-free trade are

- $86.2 billion with the **EU**
- $24.4 billion with **Japan**
- $11.4 billion with the **European Free Trade Association**
- $10.8 billion with **South Korea**
- $9.9 billion with the **Trans-Pacific Partnership**
- $5.8 billion with **India**
- $3.7 billion with **Peru**

Source: Leading Indicator—Trading Nations, *Canadian Business*, May 2014, pp. 10–11.

consists of 153 member countries and 31 observer governments (which have a specific time frame within which they must apply to become members). At its core are various trade agreements negotiated and ratified by the vast majority of the world's trading nations. The goal of the WTO is to help businesses conduct trade between countries (importing and exporting) without undesired side effects. Although a number of vocal critics have staged highly visible protests and criticized the WTO, claiming that it destroys jobs and the natural environment, the WTO appears to play an important role in monitoring and promoting global trade.

Canada spent four years negotiating a new free trade agreement with the EU, which will be Canada's largest trade initiative since NAFTA. The agreement should boost bilateral trade by 20 percent, growing the Canadian economy by $12 billion a year and creating 80 000 new jobs.[34] The agreement covers goods and services as well as procurement and provisions on labour and the environment. Canada has also completed eight rounds of negotiation with India, a massive market that currently represents less than 1 percent of Canadian exports.

PESTEL—Global Environment

Canadian managers are accustomed to stable legal and political systems. Changes are slow, and legal and political procedures are well established. The stability of laws governing the actions of individuals and institutions allows for accurate predictions. The same cannot be said for all countries. Managers in a global organization must stay informed of the specific laws in countries where they do business.

Some countries have a history of unstable governments. Managers of businesses in these countries face dramatically greater uncertainty as a result of political instability or interference. The Chinese government controls what organizations do and how they do it within China's borders. Google has struggled with determining how to manage its website in China. "Figuring out how to deal with China has been a difficult exercise for Google," said Elliot Schrage, former vice-president of global communications and public affairs at Google. "The requirements of doing business in China include self-censorship—something that runs counter to Google's most basic values and commitments as a company."[35]

The legal and political environments do not have to be unstable or revolutionary to be a concern to managers. Just the fact that a country's laws and political system differ from those of Canada is important. Managers must recognize these differences to understand the constraints under which they operate and the opportunities that exist.

The global manager must also be aware of economic issues when doing business in other countries. Understanding the type of economic system under which the country operates is crucial. The two major types are a market economy and a planned economy. A **market economy** is one in which resources are primarily owned and controlled by the private sector. A **planned economy** is one in which all economic decisions are planned by a central government. In actuality, no economy is purely market or planned. Canada and the United States are two countries at the market end of the spectrum, but they do have some governmental control. The economies of Vietnam and North Korea, however, are more plan based. Then there is China, a country that has utilized a planned economy for decades but is moving toward becoming more market based. Why would managers need to know about a country's economic system? Because it has the potential to constrain decisions and actions. Other economic issues a manager would need to understand include currency exchange rates, inflation rates, and diverse tax policies.

market economy
An economic system in which resources are primarily owned and controlled by the private sector.

planned economy
An economic system in which all economic decisions are planned by a central government.

What is National Culture?

Which is more important to a manager: national culture or organizational culture?

- Geert Hofstede, a professor at Maastricht University in the Netherlands, developed one of the most widely referenced approaches to understanding six key dimensions of **national cultures** (see Exhibit 2-3).

- Hofstede indicates that national culture has a greater effect on employees than does their organization's culture.[36]

- Imagine Swedish employees at IKEA in Vancouver. The organizational culture will certainly shape the employees, but not nearly as influentially as the Canadian culture.

EXHIBIT 2-3   Hofstede's Six Dimensions

Power Distance	Hofstede used the term *power distance* as a measure of the extent to which a society accepts the fact that power in institutions and organizations is distributed unequally.
	High power distance—Accepts wide differences in power; great deal of respect for those in authority; titles, rank, and status carry a lot of weight.
	Low power distance—Plays down inequalities; employees are not afraid to approach, nor are they in awe of the boss.
Individualism vs. Collectivism	Individualism is the degree to which people in a country prefer to act as individuals rather than as members of groups. Collectivism is characterized by a social framework in which people prefer to act as members of groups.
	Individualistic—People look after their own and family interests because of the freedom afforded by society.
	Collectivistic—People expect the group to look after and protect them.
Masculinity vs. Femininity	The masculinity side of this dimension represents a preference in society for achievement, while the femininity side is more nurturing.
	Achievement—Values such as assertiveness, acquiring money and goods, and heroism prevail. Society is competitive.
	Nurturing—Values such as relationships, concern for others, cooperation, and the quality of life prevail. Society is consensus-oriented.
Uncertainty Avoidance	Uncertainty avoidance describes the degree to which people tolerate risk and prefer structured over unstructured situations. Since the future is uncertain, should we try to control the future, or just let it happen?
	High uncertainty avoidance—Threatened by ambiguity and experience high levels of anxiety and stress; intolerant of unorthodox ideas.
	Low uncertainty avoidance—Comfortable with risk; tolerant of different behaviours and opinions.
Pragmatic vs. Normative	This dimension describes how people relate to the fact that so much that happens around us cannot be explained.
	Normative—In societies with a normative orientation, most people have a strong desire to explain as much as possible. People in such societies have a strong concern with establishing the absolute truth and a need for personal stability. They exhibit great respect for social conventions and traditions, a relatively small propensity to save for the future, and a focus on achieving quick results

(Continued)

national culture
The values and attitudes shared by individuals from a specific country that shape their behaviour and beliefs about what is important.

EXHIBIT 2-3 Hofstede's Six Dimensions (*Continued*)

Pragmatic—In societies with a pragmatic orientation, most people do not have a need to explain everything, as they believe that it is impossible to understand fully the complexity of life. The challenge is not to know the truth but to live a virtuous life. In societies with a pragmatic orientation, people believe that truth depends very much on situation, context, and time. They show an ability to accept contradictions, adapt according to the circumstances, show a strong propensity to save and invest, and demonstrate thriftiness and perseverance in achieving results.

Indulgence vs. Restraint — Indulgence in society refers to willingness to have fun and enjoy life, while restraint refers to suppression of the gratification of needs through social norms.

Indulgent—People look to the future and value gratification and freedom of expression.

Restrained—People value tradition and the past and are comfortable suppressing their needs.

The ratings in each of the six dimensions for Canada, the United States, and China are illustrated in Exhibit 2-4.

Hofstede's findings may help your future interactions. As you appreciate different cultural perspectives, your interactions will improve and you will face less conflict. *Diversity Matters— Becoming More Culturally Aware* on pages 38–39 encourages you to think about how to become more comfortable when interacting with people from different cultures.

EXHIBIT 2-4 Hofstede's 6-D Model

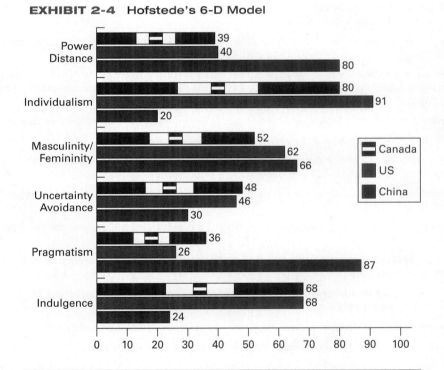

Source: Based on Intercultural Management Courses, Retrieved from http://geert-hofstede.com/intercultural-management-courses.html

DOING BUSINESS GLOBALLY

Menu Foods was forced to remove 60 million packages of its wet pet foods off grocery and pet food store shelves in March 2007.[37] The pet food had been contaminated with melamine, a nonfood product. Investigators found that the melamine had been mixed with wheat gluten (an ingredient in pet food) at Xuzhou Anying factory in China. Employees apparently deliberately mixed the melamine into the wheat gluten because melamine mimics protein when mixed with gluten. The resulting product would then appear to have a higher nutrient value than it actually did.

China's animal feed producer had been supplementing the feed with melamine for a number of years. "Many companies buy melamine scrap to make animal feed, such as fish feed," said Ji Denghui, general manager of the Fujian Sanming Dinghui Chemical Company, which sells melamine. The additive is inexpensive, thus it reduces product costs. Ji also explained, "I don't know if there's a regulation on it. Probably not. No law or regulation says 'don't do it,' so everyone's doing it. The laws in China are like that, aren't they? If there's no accident, there won't be any regulation."[38] How should companies that import from China deal with the lack of product quality legislation? What about patent and copyright infringement, which is rampant in China?

Organizations in different industries and from different countries are pursuing global opportunities. In this section, we look at different types of global organizations and how they do business in the global marketplace.

Different Types of International Organizations

Although doing business internationally is widespread, the terms used to describe the different types of international companies are not standardized—different authors use different terminology. In this text, we use the terms *multinational*, *multidomestic*, *global*, and *transnational* to describe the various types of international organizations.[39]

MULTINATIONAL CORPORATIONS Organizations doing business globally are not anything new. DuPont started doing business in China in 1863. H. J. Heinz Company was manufacturing food products in the United Kingdom in 1905. Ford Motor Company set up its first overseas sales branch in France in 1908. But it was not until the mid-1960s that international companies became commonplace. A **multinational corporation (MNC)** is a broad term normally used to refer to any and all types of companies that maintain operations in multiple countries but manage them from a base in the home country. Today, most companies have some type of international dealings.

MULTIDOMESTIC CORPORATIONS A **multidomestic corporation** is an MNC that maintains significant operations in more than one country but decentralizes management to the local country. This type of organization does not attempt to manage foreign operations from its home country apart from the common practice of centralizing cash management. Instead, local employees typically are hired to manage the business, and marketing strategies are tailored to that country's unique characteristics. Switzerland-based Nestlé can be described as a multidomestic corporation. With operations in almost every country on the globe, its managers match the company's products to its consumers. In parts of Europe, Nestlé sells products that are not available in North America or Latin America. Another example of a multidomestic corporation is Frito-Lay, a division of PepsiCo, which markets a Doritos chip in the UK market that differs in both taste and texture from the Canadian and US versions. Many consumer companies manage their global businesses using this approach because they must adapt their products and services to meet the needs of the local markets.

GLOBAL COMPANIES A **global company** is international in scope but centralizes its management and other decisions in the home country. These companies treat the world

2.3 Explain How do organizations do business globally?

---

multinational corporation (MNC)
A broad term referring to any and all types of international companies that maintain operations in multiple countries.

multidomestic corporation
An international company that decentralizes management and other decisions to the local country.

global company
An international company that centralizes management and other decisions in the home country.

market as an integrated whole and focus on the need for global efficiency. Although these companies may have considerable global holdings, management decisions with company-wide implications are made from headquarters in the home country. Some examples of companies that can be considered global companies include Montreal-based transport manufacturer Bombardier, Montreal-based aluminum producer Rio Tinto Alcan, Tokyo-based consumer electronics firm Sony, Frankfurt-based Deutsche Bank AG, and New York City–based financial services provider Merrill Lynch.

TRANSNATIONAL OR BORDERLESS ORGANIZATIONS Many companies are going global by eliminating structural divisions that impose artificial geographical barriers. This type of global organization is called a **transnational corporation (TNC) or borderless organization**. For example, IBM dropped its organizational structure based on country and reorganized into industry groups such as business solutions, software, IT services, and financing. Borderless management is an attempt by organizations to increase efficiency and effectiveness in a competitive global marketplace.[40]

BORN GLOBALS Our classification of different types of international organizations tends to describe large international businesses. However, an increasing number of businesses, called **born globals**, choose to go global from inception.[41] These companies (also known as *international new ventures* or *INVs*) commit resources up-front (material, people, financing) to doing business in more than one country and are likely to continue to play an increasingly important role in international business.

How Organizations Go Global

When organizations do go global, they often use different approaches depending on whether they are just starting or whether they have been doing business internationally for a while (see Exhibit 2-5). During the initial stages of going global, managers look at ways to get into a global market without having to invest a lot of capital. At this stage, companies may start with **global sourcing** (also called *global outsourcing*), which refers to the purchasing of materials or labour from around the world, wherever it is cheapest. The goal is to take advantage of lower costs in order to be more competitive. In 2006, for example, Montreal-based Bell Canada contracted with Sitel India and two other Indian companies to provide technical

EXHIBIT 2-5 How Organizations Go Global

Minimal Global Investment ←→ Significant Global Investment

- Global Sourcing
- Exporting and Importing
- Licensing
- Franchising
- Strategic Alliance/ Joint Venture
- Foreign Subsidiary

---

transnational corporation (TNC) or borderless organization
A type of international company in which artificial geographical barriers are eliminated.

born globals
International companies that choose to go global from inception.

global sourcing
Purchasing materials or labour from around the world, wherever they are cheapest.

support and customer care to Canadian customers. Some of that business was pulled back in 2009 due to Canadian customer complaints, but outsourcing call centres globally continues to rise. Recently, the Philippines overtook India as the hub of call centres.[42] Although global sourcing is often the first step in going global, many organizations continue to use this approach, even as they become more international, because of the competitive advantages it offers. Beyond global sourcing, however, each successive stage of becoming more international requires more investment and thus entails more risk for the organization.

IMPORTING AND EXPORTING   An organization can go global by **exporting** its products to other countries—that is, by making products at home and selling them overseas. In addition, an organization can go global by **importing** products—that is, by selling products at home that are made abroad. Both exporting and importing are small steps toward becoming a global business and usually involve minimal investment and minimal risk. Many organizations start doing business globally this way. Many, especially small businesses, continue with exporting or importing as the way they do business globally. For example, Haribhai's Spice Emporium, a small business in Durban, South Africa, exports spices and rice to customers all over Africa, Europe, and the United States. Montreal-based Mega Brands (now owned by Mattel), with sales in over 100 countries, focuses on exporting. The company holds the number-one position in Canada and Spain, and has a 43 percent share of the UK market.[43] The company operates in eight countries, with more than 1000 employees. Mega Brands is only one example of Canada's increasing reliance on export business. The value of merchandise exported from Canada totalled $471 billion in 2013, growing each year since a loss in 2009.[44,45] Of that amount, over 75 percent was exports to the United States. China was the second largest destination for exports, at 4 percent.[46] Transportation equipment manufacturing, primary metal manufacturing, and paper manufacturing account for the largest volume of Canadian exports.

LICENSING AND FRANCHISING   Some managers use licensing or franchising in the early stages of doing business internationally. Licensing and franchising are similar in that they both involve one organization giving another the right to use its brand name, technology, or product specifications in return for a lump-sum payment or a fee that is usually based on sales. The only difference is that **licensing** is primarily used by manufacturing organizations that make or sell another company's products, and **franchising** is commonly used by service organizations that want to use another company's name and operating methods. For example, Russian consumers can enjoy McDonald's hamburgers because McDonald's Canada opened the first Russian franchise in Moscow. Franchises have also made it possible for Mexicans to dine on Richmond, BC–based Boston Pizza food and Koreans to consume frozen yogurt from Markham, Ontario–based Coolbrands' Yogen Früz. Currently, US franchisors are making Canada a priority for growth. Puroclean, a US property disaster restoration firm, is aggressively expanding into the Canadian market, and franchises have been performing twice as well as those in the United States.[47] Licensing and franchising involve more investment and risk than exporting and importing because the company's brand is more at stake.

Fast-food giant McDonald's, like many big franchise firms, is opening more new outlets overseas. Along the way, the company is making appropriate changes in its menu offerings, such as providing vegetarian burgers for India's Hindus, who believe that killing cows and eating beef are against religious rules. In Spain, McDonald's sells gazpacho, while in Australia you can order vegemite.

exporting
An approach to going global that involves making products at home and selling them abroad.

importing
An approach to going global that involves acquiring products made abroad and selling them at home.

licensing
An approach to going global in which a manufacturer gives another organization the right to use its brand name, technology, or product specifications.

franchising
An approach to going global in which a service organization gives a person or group the right to sell a product, using specific business methods and practices that are standardized.

STRATEGIC ALLIANCE Typically, once an organization has been doing business internationally for some time and has gained experience in international markets, managers may decide to make a more direct investment. One way they can do this is through a **strategic alliance**—a partnership between two companies in which both share resources and knowledge in developing new products or building production facilities. The partners also share the risks and rewards of this alliance. Finding a partner, however, is not always easy. When Starbucks decided to open coffee shops in France, four major French food companies it approached as possible joint venture partners turned the proposal down. Jean-Paul Brayer, former head of one of the food companies Starbucks approached, commented, "Their contract was way too expensive. It was a win-win situation—but only for Starbucks."[48] Starbucks ended up partnering with a Spanish firm, Grupo VIPS, and together they opened the first Parisian Starbucks in January 2004.

A specific type of strategic alliance in which the partners agree to form a separate, independent organization for some business purpose is called a **joint venture**. Hewlett-Packard (HP) has had numerous joint ventures with various suppliers around the globe to develop different components for its computer equipment, such as Tokyo-based Hitachi, which supplies hard drives for HP. These partnerships provide a faster and more inexpensive way for companies to a compete globally than doing it on their own.

TIPS (FOR) GLOBAL MANAGERS

FXR Racing, a Canadian manufacturer of snowmobile and motorcross racing gear, learned a difficult lesson when working with European suppliers. Founder Milt Reimer shares his strategies to avoid getting burned by a foreign distributor:[49]

✳ Get references.

✳ Consider all tax implications.

✳ Do not use the same model in all countries.

✳ Create safeguards.

FOREIGN SUBSIDIARY Managers can make a direct investment in a foreign country by setting up a **foreign subsidiary**, a separate and independent production facility or office. This subsidiary can be managed as an MNC (domestic control) or a TNC or borderless organization (foreign or global control). As you can probably guess, this arrangement involves the greatest commitment of resources and poses the greatest amount of risk. Many of the larger companies operating in Canada are actually subsidiaries of US corporations, including GM Canada, Procter & Gamble Canada, and McDonald's Canada. Canadian subsidiaries manage their operations and set their own targets and goals, but they also report to a head office in the United States.

| 2.4 | **Explain** How does the environment affect managers? |

HOW THE ENVIRONMENT AFFECTS MANAGERS

Knowing *what* the various components of the environment are is important to managers. However, understanding *how* the environment affects managers is equally important. The environment affects managers through the degree of environmental uncertainty that is present, through the various stakeholder relationships that exist between the organization and its external constituencies, and through the challenges of managing in a global environment.

strategic alliance
An approach to going global that involves a partnership between a domestic and a foreign company in which both share resources and knowledge in developing new products or building production facilities.

joint venture
An approach to going global in which the partners agree to form a separate, independent organization for some business purpose; it is a type of strategic alliance.

foreign subsidiary
An approach to going global that involves a direct investment in a foreign country by setting up a separate and independent production facility or office.

Assessing Environmental Uncertainty

Not all environments are the same. They differ by what we call their degree of **environmental uncertainty**, which can be defined as the degree of change and complexity in an organization's environment (see Exhibit 2-6).

The first dimension is the degree of change. If components in an organization's environment change frequently, we call it a *dynamic* environment. If change is minimal, we call it a *stable* one. A stable environment might be one in which there are no new competitors, few technological breakthroughs by current competitors, little activity by pressure groups to influence the organization, and so forth. Zippo Canada, best known for its Zippo lighters, enjoys a relatively stable environment, with few competitors and little technological change. The main environmental concern for the company is the declining trend in tobacco smokers, although the company's lighters have other uses and global markets remain attractive.

In contrast, the recorded music industry faces a highly uncertain and unpredictable environment. Digital formats such as MP3, music-streaming Internet services like VEVO, online piracy, and the ability to buy individual songs from companies such as iTunes have turned the industry upside down. The global music market declined a staggering 30 percent from 2004 to 2009, despite a total increase in digital sales of 940 percent. The trend slowed to an 8 percent decline in 2010 and to 4 percent in 2011.[50] Although music companies traditionally earned revenues by selling physical products such as LP records, cassettes, and CDs, the digital future represents chaos and uncertainty. Companies are trying to harness the mobile music environment and to stem the illegal downloading of music.[51] This environment can definitely be described as dynamic.

What about predictable rapid change? Is this type of change considered a dynamic environment? Bricks-and-mortar retail department stores provide a good example. They typically make one-quarter to one-third of their sales in December. The drop-off from December to January is significant. However, because the change is predictable, we do not consider the environment to be dynamic. When we talk about degree of change, we mean unpredictable change. If change can be accurately anticipated, it does not represent uncertainty that managers must confront.

EXHIBIT 2-6 Environmental Uncertainty Matrix

	Degree of Change	
	Stable	**Dynamic**
Simple	**Stable and predictable environment** Few components in environment Components are somewhat similar and remain basically the same Minimal need for sophisticated knowledge of components	**Dynamic and unpredictable environment** Few components in environment Components are somewhat similar but are in continual process of change Minimal need for sophisticated knowledge of components
Complex	**Stable and predictable environment** Many components in environment Components are not similar to one another and remain basically the same High need for sophisticated knowledge of components	**Dynamic and unpredictable environment** Many components in environment Components are not similar to one another and are in continual process of change High need for sophisticated knowledge of components

(Degree of Complexity — vertical axis label)

---

environmental uncertainty
The degree of change and the degree of complexity in an organization's environment

The second dimension of uncertainty describes the degree of **environmental complexity**. Degree of complexity refers to the number of components in an organization's environment and the extent of the knowledge the organization has about those components. For example, Hasbro, the world's second-largest toy manufacturer (behind Mattel), has simplified its environment by acquiring many of its competitors, such as Tiger Electronics, Wizards of the Coast, Kenner Toys, Parker Brothers, and Tonka Toys. The fewer competitors, customers, suppliers, government agencies, and so forth that an organization must deal with, the less complexity and, therefore, the less uncertainty there is in its environment.

Complexity is also measured in terms of the knowledge an organization needs to have about its environment. For example, managers at the online brokerage E*TRADE must know a great deal about their Internet service provider's operations if they want to ensure that their website is available, reliable, and secure for their stock-trading customers. On the other hand, managers of grocery stores have a minimal need for sophisticated knowledge about their suppliers.

How does the concept of environmental uncertainty influence managers? Looking again at Exhibit 2-6, each of the four cells represents different combinations of degree of complexity and degree of change. Cell 1 (an environment that is stable and simple) represents the lowest level of environmental uncertainty. Cell 4 (an environment that is dynamic and complex) represents the highest. Not surprisingly, managers' influence on organizational outcomes is greatest in cell 1 and least in cell 4.

Because uncertainty is a threat to an organization's effectiveness, managers try to minimize it. Given a choice, managers would prefer to operate in environments such as those in cell 1. However, they rarely have full control over that choice. Most industries today are facing greater dynamic change, making their environments more uncertain. Thus, managers, as planners, need to consider the environment they currently face, as well as thinking ahead about possible changes in the environment, and act accordingly. In a simple, stable environment, a manager may decide to continue doing things in the usual way. In a dynamic, complex environment, a manager may want to establish plans to keep the organization ahead of competitors or develop new niches in which to operate.

THE PROS AND CONS OF GLOBALIZATION

Doing business globally today isn't easy! Advocates praise the economic and social benefits that come from globalization. Yet that very globalization has created challenges and controversy because of the potential negative impact it can have on the world's poor. Instances of the use of child labour to produce North American goods have come to light. Also, globalization has led to the economic interdependence of trading countries. If one country's economy falters, it could potentially have a domino effect on other countries with which it does business.

Some have predicted that globalization is dead, including Canadian philosopher John Ralston Saul. However, Joel Bakan, a University of British Columbia law professor who wrote *The Corporation* and coproduced the documentary of the same name, claims, "It's overly optimistic to say globalization is dead."[52]

Although supporters of globalization praise it for its economic benefits, others think globalization is simply a euphemism for "Americanization"—that is, the spread of US cultural values and business philosophy throughout the world.[53] Critics claim that this attitude of the "almighty American dollar wanting to spread the American way to every single country" has created many problems.[54] Exhibit 2-7 examines some of the pros and cons of globalization. Some of the dominant opponents of globalization include the

environmental complexity
The number of components in an organization's environment and the extent of the organization's knowledge about those components.

EXHIBIT 2-7 Pros and Cons of Globalization	
Pros	**Cons**
• Globalization has led to free trade, which provides consumers with a greater choice of goods and services and lower overall prices of goods.	• Globalization may lead to a labour drain, meaning countries with more limited job opportunities may find it difficult to encourage skilled workers to stay in their countries.
• Free trade allows exporters to sell their goods to wholesalers and consumers in a large variety of countries, which allows nations to specialize and produce higher quality goods at better prices.	• There are environmental, social, and economic costs to globalization.
• Globalization encourages the efficient use of natural resources and raises environmental awareness and, thus, helps protect the environment.	• Large-scale immigration can weaken domestic cultures.
• Globalization minimizes government intervention, which can hinder development in business and in people's lives.	• Globalization can lead to the exploitation of workers' rights and human rights.
	• Globalization can harm economies that are at an early stage of development.
• Globalization has allowed the free movement of labour, which benefits workers and also countries that can fill "gaps" that exist in their labour market.	• Globalization can have a major negative impact on taxation, as countries move operations abroad to tax havens to avoid paying taxes.

International Institute for Sustainable Development; the International Forum on Globalization; Greenpeace; the Canadian-based Centre for Research on Globalization; and Canadian author, journalist, and activist Naomi Klein, who is well known for her book *No Logo: Taking Aim at the Brand Bullies*. Some of the main supporters of globalization include the London-based International Policy Network, the Washington-based Competitive Enterprise Institute, and the Cato Institute.

Because Canada is not seen as a country that wants to spread Canadian values and culture, Canadian managers may have some advantages over their American counterparts in doing business internationally. Managers will need to be aware of how their decisions and actions will be viewed, not only by those who may agree, but, more importantly, by those who may disagree. They will need to adjust their leadership styles and management approaches to accommodate these diverse views. Yet, as always, they will need to do this while still being as efficient and effective as possible in reaching the organization's goals. There can be some great added benefits to diversity, such as organizations that can operate 7/24/365 because of a workforce in which some employees work on Christmas Day because of their religious beliefs.

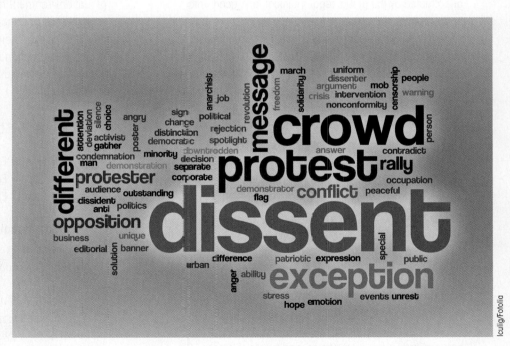

loulig/Fotolia

The Occupy movement, which started in New York in 2011, aims to redress economic and social disparity, including the impact of globalization on costs, worker safety, and local employment. Currently the movement is focused on massive public education and targets issues such as low-wage worker reform. In the United States, 13 states increased their minimum wage in 2014.[55]

2 Review and Apply

Summary of Learning Outcomes

2.1 What is the external environment for managers? The external environment plays a major role in shaping managers' actions. In the specific environment, managers have to be responsive to customers and suppliers while being aware of competitors and public pressure groups. As well, political, economic, sociocultural, technological, environmental, and legal conditions in the general environment affect the issues managers face in doing their job.

TransCanada and other Canadian energy exporters provided more than 80 percent of their exports to the US market. When political decision making was pressured by environmental interest groups, the Canadian companies needed to look at other markets such as China for their exports.

2.2 What challenges do managers face in a global environment? When managers do business in other countries, they are affected by the global legal, political, and economic environments of those countries. Differing laws and political systems can create constraints as well as opportunities for managers. The type of economic system in some countries can place restrictions on how foreign companies are able to conduct business there. In addition, managers must be aware of the culture of the countries in which they do business to understand *how* business is done and what customers expect.

Conducting business in China is different than in the United States. Canada and the United States impose far stricter rules on the environmental impact of the oil sands than does China. Social media pressure by Chinese citizens is almost a non-issue, whereas in North America it was the major factor in Obama's stance to delay the decision on the Keystone project.

2.3 How do organizations do business globally? Organizations can take on a variety of structures when they go global, including multinational corporations, multidomestic corporations, global companies, and transnational or borderless organizations. An organization can opt for lower-risk and lower-investment strategies for going global through importing or exporting, hiring foreign representation, or contracting with foreign manufacturers. It can also increase its presence in another country by joining with another business to form a strategic alliance or joint venture. Or it can

set up a foreign subsidiary in order to have a full presence in the foreign country.

TransCanada is a global energy company that focuses on pipelines, power generation, and oil and gas storage. Its headquarters are in Canada, and it has customers around the world. It uses pipelines such as Keystone XL to safely and efficiently transport crude oil and natural gas.

2.4 How does the environment affect managers? Because environments can change, sometimes even unexpectedly, managers have to be aware of the degree of environmental uncertainty they face. They also have to be aware of the complexity of their environment. Managers need to manage relationships with their stakeholders—individuals who are influenced by and have an influence on the organization's decisions and actions. Successfully managing in today's global environment requires incredible sensitivity and understanding. Canadian managers may have some advantages over their American counterparts in doing business internationally, because American companies are sometimes viewed as trying to impose American culture on foreign countries.

SNAPSHOT SUMMARY

2.1 The External Environment
The Specific Environment
The General Environment

2.2 Understanding the Global Environment
Global Trade
PESTEL—Global Environment

2.3 Doing Business Globally
Different Types of International Organizations
How Organizations Go Global
Tips for Global Managers

2.4 How the Environment Affects Managers
Assessing Environmental Uncertainty

The Pros and Cons of Globalization

MyManagementLab Study, practise, and explore real management situations with these helpful resources:

- **Interactive Lesson Presentations:** Work through interactive presentations and assessments to test your knowledge of management concepts
- **PIA (Personal Inventory Assessments):** Enhance your ability to connect with key concepts through these engaging self-reflection assessments.
- **Study Plan:** Check your understanding of chapter concepts with self-study quizzes.
- **Simulations:** Practise decision making in simulated management environments.

Discussion Questions

1. Describe the components of the specific and general environments.

2. Contrast multinational corporations, multidomestic corporations, global companies, and transnational or borderless organizations.

3. Why is it important for managers to understand the external forces that act on them and their organizations?

4. Compare the advantages and disadvantages of the various approaches to going global.

5. What challenges might confront a Mexican manager transferred to Canada to manage a manufacturing plant in Winnipeg? Will these be the same for a Canadian manager transferred to Guadalajara, Mexico? Explain.

Developing Management Skills

Dilemma

You are considering organizing an event to raise funds for a special cause (children living in poverty, breast cancer research, illiteracy, or another cause of your choice). Think about who you might invite to this event (that is, your "customers"—those who will buy tickets to the event). What type of event might appeal to them? What suppliers might you approach for help in organizing the event? What legal issues might you face in setting up this event? After considering all these specific environmental forces, describe the challenges you could face in holding this event.

Becoming a Manager

- Familiarize yourself with current global political, economic, and cultural issues.
- If given the opportunity, try to have your class projects or reports (in this class and other classes) cover global issues or global companies.
- Talk to instructors or students who are from other countries and ask them what the business world is like in their countries.
- When you evaluate companies for class assignments (for this class and others you may be enrolled in), make a habit of looking at the stakeholders that might be affected by these companies' decisions and actions.

Hey, You're the Boss Now!

Being a successful supervisor of a diverse workforce is not easy, especially when it comes to dealing with cultural differences. If you think of another culture as an iceberg, the top

15 percent is easy to see, such as food, appearance, language, and so on. Although these elements themselves can be complicated, it is the other 85 percent of the iceberg, which is not initially apparent, that managers need to be especially concerned about. What does that include? Workplace issues such as communication styles, prioritizing, role expectations, work tempo, negotiation styles, nonverbal communication, attitudes toward planning, and so forth. Understanding these issues requires developing a global mindset and skill set. Many organizations are relying on cultural awareness training to help them do just that.

Having outsourced some engineering jobs to India, Axcelis Technologies had its North American–based employees go through a training program in which they role-played scenarios with one person pretending to be Indian and the other his or her North American coworker. One of the company's human resources directors said, "At first I was skeptical and wondered what I'd get out of the class, but it was enlightening for me. Not everyone operates like we do in North America." In our global world, successful managers must learn to recognize and appreciate cultural differences and to understand how to work effectively and efficiently with employees, no matter what their nationality.

Questions

1. UK-based company Kwintessential has several cultural awareness "quizzes" on its website (www.kwintessential. co.uk/resources/culture-tests.html). Go to the company's website and try two or three of these quizzes. Were you

surprised at your score? What does your score tell you about your cultural awareness?

2. What advice might you give to a supervisor who has little experience working with people from other countries?

Diversity Matters

BECOMING MORE CULTURALLY AWARE

Workplaces around the world are becoming increasingly diverse. Thus, managers need to recognize that not all employees want the same thing, act in the same manner, and can be managed in the same way. What is a diverse workforce? It is one that is heterogeneous in terms of gender, race, ethnicity, age, and other characteristics that reflect differences. Valuing diversity and helping a diverse workforce achieve its maximum potential are becoming indispensable skills for more and more managers.

STEPS IN DEVELOPING THE SKILL

The diversity issues an individual manager might face are many. They could include communicating with employees whose familiarity with the language might be limited; creating career development programs that fit the skills, needs, and values of a variety of employees; helping a diverse team cope with a conflict over goals or work assignments; or learning which rewards are valued by different groups of employees. You can improve your handling of diversity issues by following these eight behaviours:[56]

1. **Fully accept diversity.** Successfully valuing diversity starts with each individual accepting the principle of multiculturalism. Accept the value of diversity for its own sake—not simply because you have to. Accepting and valuing diversity is important because it is the right thing to do. And it is important that you reflect your acceptance in all you say and do.

2. **Recruit broadly.** When you have job openings, work to get a diverse applicant pool. Although referrals from current employees can be a good source of applicants, they tend to produce candidates similar to the current workforce.

3. **Select fairly.** Make sure that the selection process does not discriminate. One suggestion is to use job-specific tests rather than general aptitude or knowledge tests. Such tests measure specific skills, not subjective characteristics.

4. **Provide orientation and training for minorities.** Making the transition from outsider to insider can be particularly difficult for an employee who belongs to a minority group. Provide support either through a group or through a mentoring arrangement.

5. **Sensitize nonminorities.** Not only do you personally need to accept and value diversity, but as a manager you need to encourage all your employees to do so. Many organizations do this through diversity training programs, in which employees examine the cultural norms of different groups. The most important thing a manager can do is show by his or her actions that diversity is valued.

6. **Strive to be flexible.** Part of valuing diversity is recognizing that different groups have different needs and values. Be flexible in accommodating employees' requests.

7. **Seek to motivate individually.** Motivating employees is an important skill for any manager; motivating a diverse workforce has its own special challenges. Managers must be more in tune with the background, cultures, and values of employees. What motivates a single mother with two young children who is working full-time to support her family is likely to be different from the needs of a young, single, part-time employee or an older employee who is working to supplement his or her retirement income.

8. **Reinforce employee differences.** Encourage individuals to embrace and value diverse views. Create traditions and ceremonies that promote diversity. Celebrate diversity by accentuating its positive aspects. However, be prepared to deal with the challenges of diversity, such as mistrust, miscommunication, lack of cohesiveness, attitudinal differences, and stress. Be aware of differences in the Hofstede's six dimensions of national cultures.

PRACTISING THE SKILL

Read the descriptions of the following employees who work for the same organization. After reading each description, write a short paragraph describing what you think the goals and priorities of each employee might be. With what types of employee issues might the manager of each employee have to deal? How could these managers exhibit the value of diversity? How can they manage issues of communicating with heavy accents or the significance of cultural garments?

Vincenzo is 57 years old, a college graduate, and a vice-president of the firm. His family was all born in Canada, but he is from Italy and still has a very strong accent. He is busy with volunteer work and is active in his church. Vincenzo is healthy and likes to stay active, both physically and mentally.

Sanjyot is a 40-year-old clerical worker who came to Canada from Indonesia last year. She has begun to attend evening classes at a local college to improve her English. Sanjyot likes to wear cultural garments at the office.

Yuri is a recent immigrant from one of the former Soviet republics. He is 42 years old and his English communication skills are quite limited. He has an engineering degree from his country, but since he is not licensed to practise in Canada, he works as a parts clerk.

Bobby is a 21-year-old from a farm in the Ottawa Valley, an area without a lot of ethnic diversity. He has just finished an advanced diploma at the local college. This is his first job, and he loves to play hockey and go hunting.

Your Essential Management Reading List

Learning from key management experts can help you understand today's management theory and practice. What follows is a list of some of the more influential management books:

- *Why Nations Fail*—Daron Acemoglu and James Robinson
- *China Shakes the World*—James Kynge
- *Breakout Nations*—Ruchir Sharma

3BL: The Triple Bottom Line

WHAT SHOULD KINDER MORGAN CANADA DO WHEN IT ANTICIPATES OPPOSITION TO EXPANSION OF ITS OIL PIPELINE IN BC?

Kinder Morgan Canada has been running the Trans Mountain pipeline for more than 60 years. In 2008, with little fanfare, the company spent $750 million and added 13 new pump stations to increase capacity by 75 000 barrels for the Edmonton-to-Vancouver pipeline. With oil and gas pipeline projects very much under the public eye in 2014, company president Ian Anderson expects significant opposition to a $5-billion pipeline expansion. The issue is no longer a simple matter of profit—people are concerned about oil sands growth and its impact on communities and workers.

The profit bottom line is straightforward—expanding pipeline capacity is good business for oil sands producers, refiners, and overseas customers. The expansion will provide a building block for the development of the Asian market.

People are concerned because Kinder Morgan Energy Partners is a Houston-based infrastructure giant, so Kinder Morgan Canada may have to increase its presence in Vancouver. A Vancouver presence would mean more jobs for local workers and higher tax revenues for governments and First Nations groups.

The main concern stems from the potential environmental impact of the oil sands generally, and the Trans Mountain pipeline specifically. Increasing capacity means more tankers in the Vancouver harbour, which increases the chance of an oil spill. An oil spill would hurt both Vancouver's tourism industry and its image as a "green" city. In fact, Kinder Morgan has been using tankers for more than 60 years without any incidents, but the perception of that reality is distorted by incidents such as the BP oil spill in the Gulf of Mexico.

Opposition is expected from Vancouver and Burnaby municipal politicians, First Nations peoples, including the Tsleil-Waututh Nation near Burrard Inlet, and the broader environmental movement. Kinder Morgan has split the environmental stakeholders into three groups. The first group includes organizations like the Pembina Institute, a Canadian think-tank concerned about sustainable energy solutions. Anderson feels that meaningful dialogue about environmental impact is possible with this group. The second group encompasses environmental activists who use lobbying, campaigns, and protest to make their viewpoint heard. Anderson acknowledges that discussions and progress will be harder to make with these stakeholders. The third group is what Kinder Morgan calls the larger group in the middle, who are interested in the specifics of why the pipeline should be expanded and how to minimize the environmental risks of the project.

THINKING STRATEGICALLY ABOUT 3BL

Anderson's game plan involves building alliances among business groups like the BC Chamber of Commerce, with First Nations and environmental organizations across BC, and with municipal politicians. He plans to meet with various stakeholders for a full two years before entering the regulatory process. How should he approach each of the three environmental factions? What are the differing environmental stakeholder perspectives on the pipeline expansion?

Source: C. Cattaneo, "Trans Mountain: Same Pipeline, New Realities," *Financial Post*, April 27, 2012.

Team Exercises

Be the Consultant: Ethical Decision Making

In teams of five or six people, discuss each of the following scenarios and come to an agreement on the most ethical courses of action in each situation.

Scenario 1: You work for a large Canadian nonprofit organization that holds a big annual conference. The conference rotates throughout Canada on a yearly basis. A resort and conference company in Hawaii invites you and one other person down for a one-week paid vacation so that you can check out their conference facilities. Should you:

(a) Accept the vacation?
(b) Turn down the vacation?
(c) Accept the vacation if your boss poses no objection?
(d) Accept the vacation if the majority of the conference attendees are in favour of holding the conference in Hawaii?

Scenario 2: You work for a large manufacturer of farm equipment in Saskatchewan. You are anticipating that a bid you submitted for a big project is going to be successful. The final decision is being delayed by bureaucracy with the international combine manufacturer. It is likely that you are to be awarded the contract, and the tight timelines mean that you need to get started right away. You begin negotiations with a supplier and decide to tell them:

(a) "Approval is done. We can skip the technical details and start production immediately."
(b) "Start producing the product and we'll cover your costs when we sign the contract."
(c) "We are anticipating that the proposal will be approved. We can sign an interim contract to cover the first phase of the project, which we will initiate on a tentative basis."
(d) "The deal is almost done. It is going to be a big deal for both of us, but we need you to shoulder the startup costs until the contract is signed. Then we can work out a contract between the two of us."

Scenario 3: You work for a medium-sized IT consulting firm in Quebec. You submit the lowest bid for a government contract. You do not have the staffing in place to meet the contract at the moment and you anticipate that it will take you three months longer than your main competitor to build the IT infrastructure awarded in the contract. Your government client asks for details on your schedule before awarding the contract to you or your main competitor. What do you do?

(a) Indicate that your schedule is "basically the same" as what you believe your competitor's is to build the infrastructure.

(b) Commit to completing the job in the same time frame as your competitor and tell your internal team that they must shorten their time frame by three months or else.

(c) Ignore the scheduling question and focus on the quality of your firm's work and the lowest cost component of your bid.

(d) Admit that your schedule is longer than your competitor's, but reconfirm the quality of your work and hope that you do not lose too many points in the evaluation process.

Scenario 4: Your newest hire is a friend of yours. Her performance is lacking and her relationships with her coworkers are poor. What do you do?

(a) Call her in to discuss her poor performance.

(b) Meet with her coworkers and tell them to give her some slack.

(c) Ask HR to meet with her and develop a performance management plan.

(d) Do nothing because she is new on the job and will perform better.

Assessing Employees' Global Aptitudes

Moving to a foreign country is not easy, no matter how many times you have done it or how receptive you are to new experiences. Successful global organizations are able to identify the best candidates for global assignments, and one of the ways they do this is through individual assessments prior to assigning people to global facilities. Form groups of three to five individuals. Your newly formed team, the Global Assignment Task Force, has been given the responsibility for developing a global aptitude assessment form for Zara, the successful European clothing retailer.[57] Although the company is not well known in North America, Zara's managers have positioned the company for continued global success. Their success is based on a simple principle—in fashion, nothing is as important as time to market.

Zara's store managers (more than 600 worldwide) offer suggestions every day on cuts, fabrics, and even new lines. After reviewing the ideas, a team at headquarters in La Coruna, Spain, decides what to make. Designers draw up the ideas and send them over the company's intranet to nearby factories. Within days, the cutting, dyeing, sewing, and assembling start. In three weeks, the clothes will be in stores from Barcelona to Berlin to Buenos Aires. That is 12 times faster than its competitors. Zara has a twice-a-week delivery schedule that restocks old styles and brings in new designs. Competitors tend to get new designs once or twice a season.

Because Zara is expanding its global operations significantly, management wants to make sure they are sending the best possible people to the various global locations. Your team's assignment is to come up with a rough draft of a form to assess people's global aptitudes. Think about the characteristics, skills, attitudes, and so on that you think a successful global employee would need. Your team's draft should be at least a half page but not longer than one page. Be prepared to present your ideas to your classmates and instructor.

Business Cases

Earth Rated

Fashionable. Affordable. Earth-friendly. Poop bags. Abby Gnanendran, president and cofounder of Montreal-based Earth Rated, started his business when grocery stores began charging for plastic bags. Pet owners now had to pay for bags, and Gnanendran realized that an affordable and eco-friendly bag would be a big hit in the marketplace.[58]

The pet supply market is very strong, with more than 12.5 million pets in Canada alone.[59] Research conducted by the Pet Industry Joint Advisory Council of Canada revealed that half of Canadian households own some kind of pet, and Canadians spent $6.5 billion on them in 2012.[60] Market growth continues to be strong, and as the economy improves, consumers are more likely to increase spending on pets. From the outset, Gnanendran sold his product exclusively online through his company's website, http://www.earthrated.com/home. The company relied on Google AdWords and Facebook to generate interest and sales. Increasing fan numbers have opened up avenues to share stories and keep fans up to date on environmental issues as well as animal care, rescue, and shelter programs.

Going retail was not part of the original plan, but repeated calls from pet supply stores convinced Earth Rated to move from online to retail. The company used a long-term strategy that sacrificed short-term profits as it distributed more than 5 million free bags to retail stores, dog walkers, and bloggers. The move paid off: The conversion rate was higher than 70 percent, with retailers placing orders within a month of receiving the samples. The poop bags are now carried in more than 4900 stores in North America and parts of Europe. Company sales were 10 times higher in Earth Rated's second year of operation, and sales tripled in 2012. The company moved away from online sales and instead uses its web presence to communicate via social media with customers, retailers, and the charities it supports. It has built high awareness and now needs to turn that into higher sales and engagement.

Discussion Questions

1. What strategies can Gnanendran use to maintain social media momentum?
2. How can Earth Rated continue to expand into the US and European markets?
3. What world market should Earth Rated target next?

Joe Fresh

Joe Fresh was founded in 2006 as one of Canada's premiere sources for modern style and accessible design collections for men, women, and children. Joe Fresh products are available in over 340 Loblaw Companies Ltd. stores in Canada, as well in 650 JCPenney stores in the United States. Pioneered by one of Canada's leading fashion moguls, Joe Mimran, Joe Fresh signed three partnership agreements in 2014 that brought the brand into 23 new countries. The agreements represented the first expansion beyond North America into key growth markets in the Middle East, North Africa, Europe, and South Korea.[61]

With the backing of grocery giant Loblaw, the discount clothing line will roll out up to 141 Joe Fresh stores in 23 countries over the next four years. "This is representative of what has been a long-standing belief on our part that there is an international level of opportunity for the Joe Fresh brand," said Galen G. Weston, Loblaw's executive chairman.[62]

Going global for Joe Fresh meant partnering with companies that had integral knowledge and expertise of the local retail dynamics and consumer preferences.[63] When Joe Fresh entered the United States, it chose to stay away from the large capital cost of opening stand-alone stores and entered into a supply arrangement with JCPenney. Weston said the deal hasn't gone according to plan due to restructuring and leadership changes at the struggling US retailer.[64] So instead of putting clothing in existing stores, the global strategy is a partnership to build new stores and leverage local expertise from companies such as Fawaz A. Alhokair & Co. and Retail Arabia International.

Joe Fresh's "extreme pricing" is one of its selling points, but in 2013 that approach was brought into question with the collapse of a factory in Dhaka, Bangladesh, killing 1100 people.[65] Called the worst disaster in the history of the garment industry, the tragedy spurred Loblaw to join fellow retailers Sears Canada and Walmart Canada at an emergency meeting of the Retail Council of Canada to make plans to improve working conditions in sweatshops.[66] These types of tragedies typically bring enormous pressure on retailers to investigate the rights of Third World factory workers. In these countries, rampant corruption exists at every level, where garment factories are policed by thugs who threaten workers who do not want to enter unsafe premises or who try to leave before working 13- or 14-hour shifts, typically seven days a week.[67]

Loblaw provided compensation for the families of victims, as well as aid and resources to the neighbourhood of Savar, where the collapse took place. Senior Loblaw executives met with local officials to discuss "finding an approach that ensures safe working conditions, drives lasting change in the industry and [helps prevent] other tragedies," the company said in a press release.[68]

Queen's University marketing professor Tandy Thomas said Loblaw has the power to ensure working conditions are up to a certain standard by saying, "You're not gonna get our business unless you do things correctly."[69] This type of economic pressure is effective in eliciting a faster response than waiting for local governments to make changes. The typical consumer reaction to this sort of incident, Thomas said, is usually boycotting, but she felt Loblaw was doing the things it should be doing to make it right. Rather than using a PR firm to boost its image, Loblaw is working at a local level to prevent these tragedies from happening in the future. Thomas said consumers will take notice of the mistake and the response of Joe Fresh. Thomas believes consumers will forgive, "and, in many cases, they come back with a stronger level of loyalty because they know they can trust the company to do the right thing again in the future."[70]

Who is to judge what is morally correct for companies operating in the global marketplace? Joe Fresh continues to manufacture clothing in Bangladesh. Do you believe this is ethical behaviour?

CHAPTER
3
Planning and Strategic Management

Stefan Riches/Stantec

LEARNING OUTCOMES

Think About It

Stantec follows a long-range, five-year strategy process that includes review of current strategies, plans made, and challenges in its business environment. As you learn more about this company, its business, and the challenges it has faced in recent years, think about all the different aspects of the business that the company's managers and board of directors have to consider when making their plans for the future.

Planning provides companies an opportunity to align their resources with their key priorities. Stantec is a professional consulting firm focusing on planning, engineering, architecture, interior design, surveying, environmental sciences, and project economics. With 8400 Canadian employees and 15 000 in total in more than 200 locations, Stantec is striving to become a top-10 global design firm. In 2014, the company aligned its internal structure to mesh more closely with that of its clients, and began to focus on three business operating units: buildings, energy and resources, and infrastructure. This realignment provides enhanced client support and greater leadership accountability, and better positions Stantec for future growth and success while maintaining the core strategic elements.

This change in strategic focus was all about creating vibrant communities and designing with community in mind, Stantec's new mantra. The philosophy was linked with company values, and then initiatives were developed relating to employees, clients, business processes, and overall firm performance. In 2013, Stantec focused on organization-wide communication of the values that provide the foundation of its strategic plan.

....

Managers everywhere need to plan. In this chapter, we present the basics of planning: what it is, why managers plan, and how they plan. We also discuss the importance of strategic management and choosing effective strategies to develop a competitive advantage. The success of any strategy depends partly on how effectively it is communicated to employees, clients, and investors. In the Communications supplement at the end of the chapter, we will examine how Stantec connects its brand and communications with its strategy.

....

WHAT IS PLANNING?

As we stated in Chapter 1, **planning** involves defining goals, establishing an overall strategy for achieving those goals, and developing a comprehensive set of plans to integrate and coordinate the work needed to achieve the goals. It is concerned both with ends (what is to be done) and means (how it is to be done). For example, you and your classmates may want to organize a large graduation dinner dance. To do so, you would set goals, establish a strategy, develop plans, and assign committees to get the work done.

Planning can either be formal or informal. In informal planning, nothing is written down, and there is little or no sharing of goals with others. Informal planning is general and lacks continuity. Although more common in smaller organizations where the owner-manager has a vision of where he or she wants the business to go and how to get there, informal planning does exist in some large organizations. At the same time, some small businesses may have very sophisticated planning processes and formal plans.

When we use the term *planning* in this book, we mean *formal* planning. In formal planning, specific goals covering a period of years are defined. These goals are written and shared with organization members. Then a specific action program for the achievement of these goals is developed: Managers clearly define the path they want to take to get the organization and the various work units from where they are to where they want them to be.

Setting goals, establishing a strategy to achieve those goals, and developing a set of plans to integrate and coordinate activities seem pretty complicated. So why would managers want to plan? Does planning affect performance? We address these issues next.

Effective plans need to be ongoing, accurate, and flexible.

3.1 **Tell** What does planning involve?

HOW DO MANAGERS PLAN?

Planning is often called the primary management function because it establishes the basis for all the other functions that managers perform. Without planning, managers would not know what to organize, lead, or control. In fact, without plans, there would not be anything to organize, lead, or control! So how do managers plan?

Planning involves two important elements: goals and plans. **Goals (objectives)** are the desired outcomes for individuals, groups, or entire organizations.[1] Goals and objectives are very similar and are often confused with each other. The main differences between goals and objectives are in scope, specificity, and time frame. Goals tend to be broader, more general, and have a longer time frame. Objectives are narrow and more specific, with a shorter time frame (think of precise short-term targets). Goals provide the direction for all management decisions and form the criteria against which actual work accomplishments can be measured. That is why they are often called the foundation of planning. You have to know the desired target or outcome before you can establish plans for reaching it. **Plans** are documents that outline how goals are going to be met and that typically describe resource allocations, schedules, and other necessary actions to accomplish the goals. As managers plan, they are developing both goals and plans.

3.2 **Define** How do managers set goals and develop plans?

planning
A management function that involves defining goals, establishing a strategy for achieving those goals, and developing plans to integrate and coordinate activities.

goals (objectives)
Desired outcomes for individuals, groups, or entire organizations.

plans
Documents that outline how goals are going to be met and describe resource allocations, schedules, and other necessary actions to accomplish the goals.

Planning for Success

1 Reasons for Planning

Managers plan for at least four key reasons (see Exhibit 3-1).

- **Planning provides *direction* to both managers and employees.** When everyone in the organization or work unit understands what they must contribute to reach goals, they can coordinate their activities, cooperate with each other, and do what it takes to accomplish those goals. Without planning, departments and individuals might work at cross purposes, preventing the organization from moving efficiently toward its goals.

- **Second, planning *reduces uncertainty*** by forcing managers to look ahead, anticipate change, consider the impact of change, and develop appropriate responses. This increased preparation for change helps develop managers' skills and provides flexibility to the organization.

- **Third, planning *reduces overlapping and wasteful activities.*** Coordinating work activities in advance is likely to uncover redundancy and enhance time management. Furthermore, when means and ends are made clear through planning, inefficiencies become obvious and can be corrected or eliminated.

- **Finally, planning *establishes the goals or standards* that facilitate control.** If employees are unsure of what they are trying to accomplish, how can they determine whether they have actually achieved it? When managers plan, they develop the goals and the plans. When managers control, they compare actual performance against the goals, identify any significant deviations, and take any necessary corrective action. Without planning, there are no goals against which to measure or evaluate work efforts.

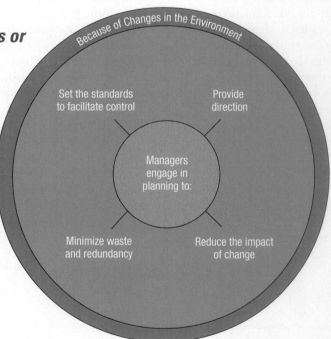

EXHIBIT 3-1 Reasons for Planning

2 Planning and Performance

Is planning worthwhile? Do managers and organizations that plan outperform those that do not? Intuitively, you would expect the answer to be a resounding yes. While results from studies examining performance in organizations that plan are generally positive, we cannot say organizations that formally plan *always* outperform those that do not plan.

Studies show that **formal planning** is associated with **higher profits** and **higher return on assets**.[2]

Golden Pixels LLC/Shutterstock

Planning is like a blueprint for growing a business. What actions must be taken and expenditures must be made to accelerate the company's revenue growth?

3 Criticisms of Planning

It makes sense for an organization to establish its direction. But critics have challenged some of the basic assumptions underlying planning.

- **Planning may create rigidity.**[3] Formal planning efforts can lock an organization into specific goals to be achieved within specific timetables. Such goals may have been set under the assumption that the environment would not change. Forcing a course of action when the environment is fluid can be a recipe for disaster.

  What to do about it? Managers need to remain flexible and not be tied to a course of action simply because it is the plan.

- **Formal plans cannot replace intuition and creativity.**[4] Successful organizations are typically the result of someone's innovative vision, which have a tendency to become formalized as they evolve. If formal planning efforts turn that vision into a programmed routine, disaster may be awaiting the firm.

  What to do about it? Planning is meant to enhance and support intuition and creativity instead of replacing it.

- **Planning focuses managers' attention on today's competition, not on tomorrow's survival.**[5] Formal planning has a tendency to focus on how to capitalize on existing business opportunities within an industry. It often does not allow managers to consider creating or reinventing an industry.

  What to do about it? Managers need to be open to untapped opportunities and new directions.

- **Formal planning reinforces success, which may lead to failure.**[6] A familiar adage is, "If it ain't broke, don't fix it." However, successful plans may provide a false sense of security, generating more confidence in the formal plans than is warranted. Many managers will not face the unknown until they are forced to do so by environmental changes. By then, it may be too late!

  What to do about it? Managers need to face the unknown and be prepared to adapt before environmental changes make it too late to do so.

Approaches to Establishing Goals

Goals provide the direction for all management decisions and actions, and form the criteria against which actual accomplishments are measured. Everything organizational members do should be oriented toward helping both their work units and the organization achieve the goals that have been set. **Traditional goal setting** features goals set at the top of the organization and then broken into subgoals for each organizational level. This process works reasonably well when an organization is hierarchically structured. This traditional perspective assumes that top managers know what is best because they see "the big picture." Thus, the goals that are established and passed down to each succeeding level serve to direct and guide, and in some ways constrain, individual employees' work behaviours. Employees work to meet the goals that have been assigned in their areas of responsibility.

As an alternative to traditional goal setting, many organizations use **management by objectives (MBO)**, a process of setting mutually agreed-upon goals and using those goals to evaluate employee performance. Managers would jointly determine performance goals with employees, periodically review progress toward accomplishing these goals, and allocate rewards based on this progress. Rather than using goals only as controls, MBO uses them to motivate employees as well. Employees will be more committed to goals that they help set. These goals must align with the overall organizational goals set by top management.

Management by objectives consists of four elements: goal specificity, participative decision making, an explicit time period, and performance feedback.[7] Its appeal lies in its focus on the accomplishment of participatively set objectives as the reason for and motivation behind individuals' work efforts. Exhibit 3-2 lists the steps in a typical MBO program. Studies of actual MBO programs confirm that they can increase employee performance and organizational productivity, provided top management involvement and commitment was present.[8]

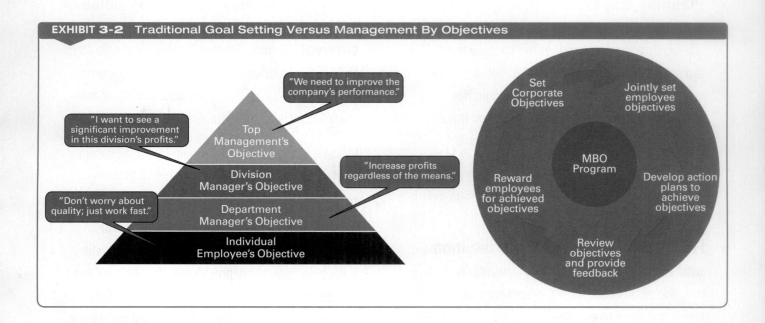

EXHIBIT 3-2 Traditional Goal Setting Versus Management By Objectives

traditional goal setting
An approach to setting goals in which goals are set at the top of the organization and then broken into subgoals for each organizational level.

management by objectives (MBO)
An approach to goal setting in which specific measurable goals are jointly set by employees and their managers, progress toward accomplishing those goals is periodically reviewed, and rewards are allocated on the basis of this progress.

CHARACTERISTICS OF WELL-DESIGNED GOALS Goals are not all created equal. Some goals are better than others. How can you tell the difference? "Well-designed" goals should have the following characteristics:[9]

- written in terms of outcomes rather than actions
- measurable and quantifiable
- clearly specify a time frame
- challenging yet attainable
- flexible
- feature participation and feedback from all necessary organizational members

Steps in Goal Setting

What steps should managers follow in setting goals? The goal-setting process consists of six steps:

1. *Review the organization's vision and mission.* The **vision and mission** reflect the purpose of an organization as statements of what the organization hopes to accomplish. Reviewing these statements before writing goals is important, because the goals need to reflect what is contained in the vision and mission statements.

2. *Evaluate available resources.* Avoid setting goals that are impossible to achieve given your available resources. Goals that are challenging and realistic considering the resources for employees to work with have a greater chance of being met.

3. *Determine the goals individually or with input from others.* The goals reflect desired outcomes and should be consistent with the organization's mission and goals in other organizational areas. These goals should be measurable, specific, and include a time frame for accomplishment.

4. *Ensure the goals are well-written and communicated to all who need to know.* Writing down and communicating goals forces people to think them through.

5. *Review results and assess whether goals are being met.* If goals aren't being met, change them as needed.

6. *Link rewards to goal attainment.* Linking rewards to goals answers the question "What's in it for me?" for the employees.

TYPES OF PLANS The most popular ways to describe an organization's plans are by their breadth (strategic vs. operational), time frame (short term vs. long term), specificity (directional vs. specific), and frequency of use (single use vs. standing). These planning classifications are not independent. As Exhibit 3-3 illustrates, plans change depending on the level of management. Strategic plans are long term, directional, and single use, while operational plans are short term, specific, and standing. Let us examine some examples of plans at each level of management.

Breadth **Strategic plans** are plans that apply to the entire organization, establish the organization's overall goals, and seek to position the organization in terms of its environment. Plans that specify the details of how the overall goals are to be achieved are called **operational plans**. How do the two types of plans differ? Strategic plans tend to cover a longer time frame and a broader view of the organization. Strategic plans also include the formulation of goals, whereas operational plans define ways to achieve the goals. Also, operational plans tend to cover short time periods—monthly, weekly, and day-to-day.

vision and mission
The purpose of the organization.

strategic plans
Plans that apply to the entire organization, establish the organization's overall goals, and seek to position the organization in terms of its environment.

operational plans
Plans that specify the details of how the overall goals are to be achieved.

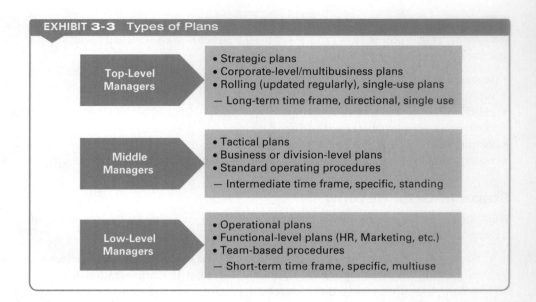

EXHIBIT 3-3 Types of Plans

Top-Level Managers
- Strategic plans
- Corporate-level/multibusiness plans
- Rolling (updated regularly), single-use plans
— Long-term time frame, directional, single use

Middle Managers
- Tactical plans
- Business or division-level plans
- Standard operating procedures
— Intermediate time frame, specific, standing

Low-Level Managers
- Operational plans
- Functional-level plans (HR, Marketing, etc.)
- Team-based procedures
— Short-term time frame, specific, multiuse

Time Frame The number of years used to define short-term and long-term plans has shortened significantly due to environmental uncertainty. Thus **long-term plans** are defined as those with a time frame beyond one year.[10] **Short-term plans** cover one year or less. For example, a company may decide that it will increase sales by 10 percent over the next year.

Specificity Intuitively, it would seem that specific plans would be preferable to directional, or loosely guided, plans. **Specific plans** are plans that are clearly defined and leave no room for interpretation. They have clearly defined objectives. There is no ambiguity and no problem with misunderstanding. For example, a manager who seeks to increase his or her unit's work output by 8 percent over a given 12-month period might establish specific procedures, budget allocations, and schedules of activities to reach that goal. The drawbacks of specific plans are that they require clarity and a sense of predictability that often do not exist.

When uncertainty is high and managers must be flexible in order to respond to unexpected changes, directional plans are preferable. **Directional plans** are flexible plans that set out general guidelines. They provide focus but don't lock managers into specific goals or courses of action. Instead of detailing a specific plan to cut costs by 4 percent and increase revenues by 6 percent in the next six months, managers might formulate a directional plan for improving profits by 5 to 10 percent over the next six months. The flexibility inherent in directional plans must be weighed against the loss of clarity provided by specific plans.

Some plans that managers develop are ongoing, while others are used only once. A **single-use plan** is a one-time plan specifically designed to meet the needs of a unique situation. Budgets and projects are examples of single-use plans. For example, when Charles Schwab introduced its online discount stock-brokerage service, top-level executives used a single-use plan to guide the creation and implementation of the new service. In contrast, standing plans are ongoing and provide guidance for activities performed repeatedly. **Standing plans** include policies, rules, and procedures, which we define in Chapter 4.

long-term plans
Plans with a time frame beyond one year.

short-term plans
Plans with a time frame of one year or less.

specific plans
Plans that are clearly defined and leave no room for interpretation.

directional plans
Plans that are flexible and that set out general guidelines.

single-use plans
A one-time plan specifically designed to meet the needs of a unique situation.

standing plans
Ongoing plans that provide guidance for activities performed repeatedly.

An example of a standing plan would be the discrimination and harassment policy developed by the University of British Columbia. The policy provides guidance to university administrators, faculty, and staff as they perform their job duties.

PLANNING TOOLS AND TECHNIQUES Managers use various tools and techniques to maximize the benefits of planning.[11]

Forecasting	Attempting to predict the future and developing plans accordingly
Contingency planning	Identifying alternative plans for outcomes that are different than expected
Scenario planning	Predicting various future outcomes and making plans for each
Benchmarking	Developing plans based on the practices of competitors
Process planning	Creating a framework for the general process necessary to reach an ultimate goal, such as a marketing campaign

FORECASTING Forecasting is the attempt to predict future trends based on past events and management insight. Expert opinions and statistical analysis are two types of forecasting techniques.[12] Canadian financial analysts regularly predict what will happen with the Canadian and world economies, and businesses use that information to help plan their strategy.

CONTINGENCY PLANNING Contingency planning features an alternative course of action to be followed if a preferred plan fails. The process of developing these plans is influenced by changing circumstances in the environment.[13] When environmental uncertainty is high, plans should be specific, but flexible. Managers must be prepared to amend plans as they are implemented. At times, managers may even have to abandon their plans.[14]

SCENARIO PLANNING Scenario planning is a type of contingency planning that involves a longer time frame. Royal Dutch Shell has used scenarios since the early 1970s as part of a process for generating and evaluating its strategic options. Shell used these scenarios to develop better oil forecasts than its competitors and to predict the overcapacity issue in the tanker business earlier.[15]

BENCHMARKING Benchmarking involves the search for the best practices among competitors or noncompetitors that lead to their superior performance.[16] The basic idea underlying benchmarking is that management can improve quality by analyzing and then copying the methods of leaders in various fields. A local charity organization can benefit from the experience and successful practices of other Canadian charities.

PROCESS PLANNING Process planning is used in project management to help select resources for use in the execution and completion of a project. Organizations use project planning when structuring a new project or strategic direction.

ORGANIZATIONAL STRATEGY: CHOOSING A NICHE

Maple Leaf Foods combines strategy and innovation to stay abreast of the trends in consumer purchasing. Each year, it introduces up to 100 new products. In 2009, Maple Leaf opened the ThinkFOOD! Centre, created to provide customers with an opportunity to collaborate with the product development team and culinary experts. By involving

And the Survey Says...

51% of managers said they are using more business scenarios and data-driven approaches in their planning.

47% of managers surveyed say their organization's projects always or often meet their goals.

46% of executives at smaller companies are likely to take a collaborative approach to developing strategy.

29% of executives at larger companies are likely to take a collaborative approach to developing strategy.

60% of companies believe that their employees are not prepared for future company growth.

75% of managers surveyed said their company's planning approach wasn't working.

51% of executives said that planning was an important skill.

3.3 Describe What are the steps in strategic management?

Think About It

Think about the different aspects of the business that Maple Leaf Foods's managers and board of directors have to consider when they are making their plans for the future. For example, Maple Leaf Foods previously used acquisitions to diversify its product mix. How would some acquisitions be more effective than others?

customers in the design of food products, Maple Leaf hopes to increase sales for its global baker and protein businesses.[17]

To begin to understand why organizational strategy matters, you need look no further than at what has happened in the discount retail industry in Canada. The industry's largest current competitor—Walmart—battled with Zellers for market dominance since Walmart entered Canada in 1992. Walmart's performance (financial and otherwise) took market share from Zellers every single year until U.S. retailer Target purchased 220 of the Zellers store to compete head to head in Canada with Walmart. The two chains have some striking similarities: store atmosphere, markets served, and organizational purpose. Organizations vary in how well they perform because of differences in their strategies and differences in competitive abilities.[18] Walmart excels at strategic management, while Target's struggle to understand Canadian customers and supply chain management led to its exit from Canada in 2015.

Strategic management is what managers do to develop the organization's strategies. What are an organization's **strategies**? They are the plans for how the organization will do whatever it is in business to do, how it will compete successfully, and how it will attract and satisfy its customers in order to achieve its goals.[19]

One term that is often used in conjunction with strategic management and strategies is **business model**, which is a strategic design for how a company intends to profit from its strategies, work processes, and work activities. A company's business model focuses on two things: (1) whether customers will value what the company is providing and (2) whether the company can make any money doing that.[20] Stantec has a focused business model that allows for managing risk while pursuing continued growth. The model is organized around geographic diversification and business operating units—to provide better support for clients, to create stronger accountability for the leadership team, and to better position the company for future growth and success while maintaining the core elements of its strategy.

The **strategic management process**, as illustrated in Exhibit 3-4, is a six-step process that encompasses strategic planning, implementation, and evaluation. Although the first four steps describe the planning that must take place, implementation and evaluation are just as important! Even the best strategies can fail if management does not implement or evaluate them properly.

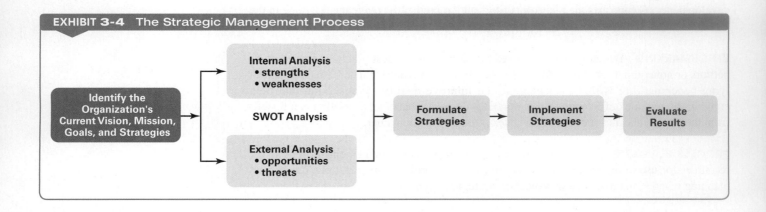

EXHIBIT 3-4   The Strategic Management Process

strategic management
What managers do to develop the organization's strategies.

strategies
The decisions and actions that determine the long-run performance of an organization.

business model
A strategic design for how a company intends to profit from its strategies, work processes, and work activities.

strategic management process
A six-step process that encompasses strategic planning, implementation, and evaluation.

Step 1: Identify the Organization's Current Vision, Mission, Goals, and Strategies

Together the vision and mission provide an organization's statement of purpose. The vision answers the question: What will this business be in the future?[21] The mission answers the question: What is our reason for being in business? Think of yourself. A personal vision might be who you want to be in five years, and a personal mission might be the specifics of how you will get there. Defining the organization's mission forces managers to identify what it is in business to do. Exhibit 3-5 describes the components of Stantec's mission statement and some examples of each element.

It is important for managers to identify goals and strategies consistent with the vision and mission being pursued. Stantec's vision and mission is what it calls its promise: design with community in mind. In one instance where a pipeline crossing was required for a project in the Atlantic Ocean, Stantec created a fish ladder to preserve the environment (see Exhibit 3-6 on page 52).

EXHIBIT 3-5 Components of Stantec's Mission Statement

Customers:	**Who are the organization's customers?**
	Public and private clients needing engineering, consulting, and design services.
Markets:	**Where does the organization compete geographically?**
	We are focused on designing for the world around us. We operate in three main geographic regions: Canada, the United States, and International. Our aim is to leverage global expertise while focusing on our strong local presence.
Concern for survival, growth, and profitability:	**Is the organization committed to growth and financial stability?**
	We are committed to being a top-10 global design firm, and plan on achieving an average compound growth rate of 15 percent.
Philosophy:	**What are the organization's basic beliefs, values, and ethical priorities?**
	We make a difference in the world by creating communities. Achievement at every level begins and ends with a firm commitment to being the best that we can be.
Concern for public image:	**How responsive is the organization to societal and environmental concerns?**
	Our high standard of business practices is articulated in our project management frameworks, code of ethics, and policies and practices. Working with integrity is a promise we make to our clients, colleagues, and shareholders.
Products or services:	**What are the organization's major products or services?**
	We provide services in three business operating units: Buildings, Energy and Resources, and Infrastructure.
Technology:	**Is the organization's technology current?**
	We design flexible facilities and processes that respond easily to changing requirements, maximize the number of innovations produced, and minimize the time and costs to develop them.
Self-concept:	**What are the organization's major competitive advantage and core competencies?**
	Stantec is recognized as a leader in our industry because we perform consistently for our clients and staff. Because of the diversity of our model, we can adapt to changes in market conditions and manage risk while continuing to increase our revenue and earnings.
Concern for employees:	**Are employees a valuable asset of the organization?**
	We put people first. We will evolve by attracting talent and developing our people. We will engage and develop leadership and focus on a diverse and inclusive work environment.

Source: From 2013 Annual Report, Stantec. Copyright © 2013 by Stantec. Reprinted by permission.

EXHIBIT 3-6 Stantec's Vision and Mission Statements

Vision	How do we make a difference in the world? Design with community in mind. Community is who we are and how we design.
Mission	At Stantec we look at every challenge as an opportunity to bring communities together. We make lasting connections with the people and places we serve. Our work—professional consulting in planning, engineering, architecture, interior design, landscape architecture, surveying, project management, environmental sciences, and project economics—begins at the intersection of community, creativity and client relationships.
Values	We put people first. We are better together. We do what is right. We are driven to achieve.

Sources: "Design with Community in Mind," http://www.stantec.com/content/dam/stantec/files/PDFAssets/2015/Company%20Profile.pdf; "Our Values," Stantec, http://www.stantec.com/about-us/our-values.html. Copyright © 2015 by Stantec. Reprinted by Permission.

Step 2: Do an Internal Analysis

Now we move from looking outside the organization to looking inside. The internal analysis provides important information about an organization's specific resources and capabilities. An organization's **resources** are its assets—financial, physical, human, intangible—that are used by the organization to develop, manufacture, and deliver products or services to its customers. Its **capabilities** are its skills and abilities in doing the work activities needed in its business. The major value-creating capabilities and skills of the organization are known as its **core competencies**.[22] Both resources and core competencies can determine the organization's competitive weapons. Procter & Gamble's (P&G) core competencies were historically based on innovation and brand-building.[23] Supply chain management has become a core competency through increasing forecasting accuracy, and the company has earned very high rankings annually, including the fifth spot in the Gartner 2014 Supply Chain Top 25.[24] Companies like P&G or Stantec that are committed to continually improving the quality of their products and services are attempting to use **quality management**.

After doing the internal analysis, managers should be able to identify organizational strengths and weaknesses. **Strengths** are any activities the organization does well or any unique resources that it has. **Weaknesses** are activities the organization does not do well or resources it needs but does not possess. This step forces managers to recognize that their organizations, no matter how large or successful, are constrained by the resources and capabilities they have.

Doing an internal analysis of an organization's financial and physical assets is fairly easy because information on those areas is readily available. However, evaluating an organization's intangible assets—things such as employees' skills, talents, and knowledge; databases and other IT assets; organizational culture; and so forth—is a bit more challenging. Organizational culture, specifically, is one crucial part of the internal analysis that is often overlooked.[25] Assessing the company's culture is critical because strong and weak cultures have different effects on strategy, and the content of a culture has a major effect on strategies pursued. What is a strategically appropriate culture? It is one that supports the firm's chosen strategy. Stantec's objective is to be a top-10 global design firm. In the communications supplement at the end of the chapter, we will discuss how Stantec strengthened its brand and launched a new identity.

Another intangible asset that is important but difficult to assess during an internal analysis is corporate reputation. Does the fact that Montreal-based aluminum producer Rio Tinto

resources
An organization's assets—financial, physical, human, intangible—that are used to develop, manufacture, and deliver products or services to customers.

capabilities
An organization's skills and abilities that enable it to do the work activities needed in its business.

core competencies
An organization's major value-creating skills, capabilities, and resources that determine its competitive weapons.

quality management
A philosophy of management driven by continual improvement and responding to customer needs and expectations.

strengths
Any activities the organization does well or any unique resources it has.

weaknesses
Activities the organization does not do well or resources it needs but does not possess.

Alcan is ranked as one of Canada's "most admired corporations" make a difference? Does the fact that Calgary-based WestJet Airlines often makes the list of "Canada's 10 Most Admired Corporate Cultures™" mean anything? Does the fact that Coca-Cola has the world's most powerful global brand give it any edge? Studies of reputation on corporate performance show that it can have a positive impact.[26] As one researcher stated, "[A] strong, well-managed reputation can and should be an asset for any organization."[27]

Step 3: Do an External Analysis

In Chapter 2 we described the external environment as an important constraint on a manager's actions. Analyzing that environment is a critical step in the strategic management process. Managers in every organization need to do an external analysis. They need to know, for example, what the competition is doing, what pending legislation might affect the organization, or what the labour supply is like in locations where it operates. In analyzing the external environment, managers should examine both the specific and general environments to see what trends and changes are occurring.

After analyzing the environment, managers need to assess what they have learned in terms of opportunities the organization can exploit and threats it must counteract. **Opportunities** are positive trends in external environmental factors; **threats** are negative trends. Amazon has thrived on the opportunity of online book sales. Threats to Amazon include a decreasing number of people who read books and greater competition from alternative sources of entertainment, including movies, radio, and streaming video. As a result, Amazon's book sales are being replaced by electronics, home decor, and gifts.

One last thing to understand about external analysis is that the same environment can present opportunities to one organization and pose threats to another in the same industry because of their different resources and capabilities. For example, WestJet Airlines has prospered in a turbulent industry, while Air Canada has struggled.

The combined external and internal analyses are called the **SWOT analysis**—an analysis of the organization's *s*trengths, *w*eaknesses, *o*pportunities, and *t*hreats. After completing the SWOT analysis, managers are ready to formulate strategies that take advantage of strengths and opportunities, protect the organization from threats, and correct critical weaknesses. For example, owner Leonard Lee started Ottawa-based Lee Valley Tools in 1982 to help individual woodworkers, and later gardeners, find just the right tools for their tasks. This niche strategy enabled Lee to grow Lee Valley into one of North America's leading garden and woodworking catalogue companies.

SWOT analysis is effective when the analysis helps companies make specific observations and draw conclusions, and allows them to develop plans to act upon this information. Exhibit 3-7 shows some common areas to investigate when performing SWOT analysis.

PESTEL ANALYSIS PESTEL is an acronym for six contextual factors that shape a company's external environment: *p*olitical, *e*conomic, *s*ociocultural, *t*echnological, *e*nvironmental, and *l*egal. The questions in Exhibit 3-8 help determine the nature of opportunities and threats facing a company in the future. **PESTEL analysis** is a way for a company to align its strategy with the external environment.[28]

Paul Holland, CEO of Vancouver-based A&W, celebrates with employee Fatemeh Divsaler Mohajer. A&W's sales have increased due to Holland's strategy of focusing on Baby Boomers' taste for nostalgia.

Mark Van Manen/The Vancouver Sun

---

opportunities
Positive trends in external environmental factors.

threats
Negative trends in external environmental factors.

SWOT analysis
An analysis of the organization's strengths, weaknesses, opportunities, and threats.

PESTEL analysis
A way for a company to align its strategy with the external environment by analyzing six contextual factors that shape the external environment: political, economic, sociocultural, technological, environmental, and legal.

EXHIBIT 3-7 SWOT Analysis

Strengths

- Financial condition: adequate resources, returns, revenues, profit
- Operations: cost advantages, economies of scale, location/geographic coverage, good supply chain management
- Product: product innovation, price/value/quality, product line breadth
- Management: proven management team, history of success, succession planning
- Competition: insulated from competitive pressures, market leader
- Technology: proprietary technology, patents
- Marketing: brand awareness and recognition, brand equity, distribution, strong advertising
- Customers: attractive customer base, well thought of by buyers
- Strategies: powerful strategy, key functional area strategies
- Organization: strong culture, climate
- History: track record of success, experience, knowledge, data
- People: accreditations, qualifications, training, low turnover, high customer service, intellectual capital
- Competencies/capabilities suited to industry
- IT: strong processes, systems, infrastructure, communications
- Alliances/joint ventures with key industry partners
- Innovation: proven and unique

Weaknesses

- Financial condition: inadequate resources, debt, declining revenues, subpar profitability
- Operations: obsolete facilities, weak R&D, internal operating problems, underutilized capacity, weak dealer network
- Product: too narrow a product line, cannibalization, saturation, limited features
- Management: lack of depth and talent, key executive departures
- Competition: losing market share, inferior intellectual capital
- Technology: lack of presence in ecommerce
- Marketing: weak brand image or reputation, no unique sales proposition, lack of reach
- Customers: declining customer base, poorly regarded by buyers
- Strategies: lacking clear strategic direction, poor track record in strategy implementation
- Organization: weak culture, climate
- History: still overcoming negative trends, poor triple bottom line reputation
- People: high turnover, poor training, low morale, poor customer service, missing key skills or competencies
- Lack of developed or proven competencies
- IT: weak processes, systems, infrastructure, communications
- Lack of alliances/joint ventures with key industry partners
- Innovation: weak or unproven

Opportunities

- Markets: new markets or segments, vertical/horizontal integration, niche markets
- Customers: serve additional customer groups, lifestyle or demand trends
- Product: PL expansion (broader range of customer needs), add complementary products, diversification
- Competition: complacency among rivals, rival vulnerabilities, winning market share
- Market developments: faster market or industry growth
- Technology: development/adaptation innovation, online sales/ecommerce
- Operational: using existing skills/know-how to enter new product lines or new businesses, production economies, supply chain integration
- Integration: forward/backward
- Global: new influences, export/import, lowering trade barriers
- Tactics: surprise element, major contracts, alliances/joint ventures/partnerships, acquisition of rivals
- Seasonal: weather, fashion influences, trends
- Marketing: research, product development

Threats

- Competition: likely entry of new competitors, existing competition, substitute products
- Buyers: changing needs and preferences, growing purchasing power
- Demographics: adverse changes, skills shortages
- Supply: limited supply, growing bargaining power of suppliers
- Economy: home and abroad, vulnerability to recession and business cycle
- Political/legislative: effects from changes, restrictive trade policies, costly new regulatory requirements
- Market: slower growth, decreasing demand
- Environmental: seasonality, weather effects
- Technology: new services, technologies, ideas
- Organization: loss of key staff, insurmountable weaknesses, vital contracts and partners

---

EXHIBIT 3-8 PESTEL Analysis

Political

- How stable is the political environment?
- What are local taxation policies, and how do these affect your business?
- Is the government involved in trading agreements such as EU, NAFTA, ASEAN, or others?
- What are the foreign-trade regulations?
- What are the social-welfare policies?

Economic

- What are current and projected interest rates?
- What is the level of inflation, what is it projected to be, and how does this projection reflect the growth of your market?
- What are local employment levels per capita, and how are they changing?
- What are the long-term prospects for gross domestic product (GDP) per capita and so on?
- What are exchange rates between critical markets and how will they affect production and distribution of your goods?

Sociocultural

- What are local lifestyle trends?
- What are the current demographics, and how are they changing?
- What is the level and distribution of education and income?
- What are the dominant local religions, and what influence do they have on consumer attitudes and opinions?
- What is the level of consumerism, and what are popular attitudes toward it?
- What pending legislation affects corporate social policies (e.g., maternity/paternity leave)?
- What are the attitudes toward work and leisure?

Technological

- What is the level of research funding in government and industry, and are those levels changing?
- What is the government's and industry's level of interest and focus on technology?
- How mature is the technology?
- What is the status of intellectual-property issues in the local environment?
- Are potentially disruptive technologies in adjacent industries creeping in at the edges of the focal industry?

Environmental

- What are local environmental issues?
- Are there any pending ecological or environmental issues relevant to your industry?
- How do the activities of international pressure groups (e.g., Greenpeace, Earth First, PETA) affect your business?
- Are there environmental protection laws?
- What are the regulations regarding waste disposal and energy consumption?

Legal

- What are the regulations regarding monopolies and private property?
- Does intellectual property have legal protections?
- Are there relevant consumer laws?
- What is the status of employment, health and safety, and product safety laws?

Source: Carpenter, Mason; Sanders, Gerry, Strategic Management: Concepts and Cases, 2nd Ed., ©2009, pp.110, 118. Reprinted and Electronically reproduced by permission of Pearson Education, Inc., New York, NY.

Step 4: Formulate Strategies

Once the SWOT analysis is complete, managers need to develop and evaluate strategic alternatives and then select strategies that either capitalize on the organization's strengths and exploit environmental opportunities or correct the organization's weaknesses and buffer it against threats. Strategies need to be established for the corporate, business, and functional levels of the organization, which we will describe shortly. This step is complete when managers have developed a set of strategies that gives the organization a relative advantage over its rivals. Professor Henry Mintzberg of McGill Business School notes that strategies often emerge from actions that organizations take rather than simply reflect the original strategic intent of the organization.[29]

Step 5: Implement Strategies

After strategies are formulated they must be implemented. No matter how effectively an organization has planned its strategies, it cannot succeed if the strategies are not implemented properly. Involving all members of the organization in strategic planning is also important.

Ecotrust Canada successfully implemented a turnaround strategy to improve the triple-bottom-line (3BL) performance of Iisaak Forest Resources, a 100-percent First Nations forest operator on the BC coast. Iisaak has outperformed its competitors while receiving the Forest Stewardship Council certification for meeting strict environmental standards.

What Strategies Do Managers Use?

EXHIBIT 3-9   Types of Organizational Strategy

Corporate
Multibusiness Corporation

Competitive
Strategic Business Unit 1 | Strategic Business Unit 2 | Strategic Business Unit 3

Functional
Research and Development | Manufacturing | Marketing | Human Resources | Finance

3.4 Explain What kinds of strategies can managers use?

1 Corporate Strategy

Multibusiness Corporation

Specifies *what businesses* to be in and *what to do with those businesses*.

⟫⟫ **3 main corporate strategies**

① **Growth Strategy:** Organization expands the number of markets served or products offered, either through its current business(es) or through new business(es).

WAYS to grow:

- **Concentration:** Growing by focusing on a primary line of business and increasing the number of products offered or markets served in this primary business.

- **Vertical integration:** Growing by gaining control of inputs or outputs or both.
  - Backward vertical integration—organization gains control of inputs by becoming its own supplier
  - Forward vertical integration—organization gains control of outputs by becoming its own distributor

- **Horizontal integration:** Growing by combining competitors.

- **Diversification:** Growing by moving into a different industry.
  - Related diversification—different but related industries. "Strategic fit."
  - Unrelated diversification—different and unrelated industries. "No strategic fit."

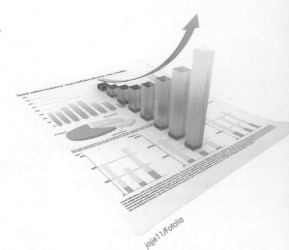

jolje11/Fotolia

② **Stability Strategy:** Organization continues—often during periods of uncertainty—to do what it is currently doing; to maintain things as they are.

- **Examples:** Continuing to serve the same clients by offering the same product or service, maintaining market share, and sustaining current business operations.

The organization **does not grow**, but it **does not fall** behind, either.

③ Renewal Strategy: Organization is in trouble and needs to address declining performance.

- **Retrenchment strategy:** Minor performance problems—need to stabilize operations, revitalize organizational resources and capabilities, and prepare organization to compete once again.

- **Turnaround strategy:** More serious performance problems requiring more drastic action.

  In both renewal strategies, managers can **(1) cut costs** and **(2) restructure organizational operations**, but actions are more extensive in a turnaround strategy.

2 Competitive Strategy

| Strategic Business Unit 1 | Strategic Business Unit 2 | Strategic Business Unit 3 |

How an organization will compete in its business(es).

- A small organization is only one line of business *or* a large organization that has not diversified: Competitive strategy describes *how it will compete in its primary or main market.*

- Organizations in multiple businesses:

Each business will have its own competitive strategy.

  - Those single businesses that are independent and formulate their own competitive strategies are often called **strategic business units (SBUs)**.

▶ **Important Role of Competitive Advantage:**

Developing an effective competitive strategy requires understanding **competitive advantage**, which is what sets an organization apart; that is, its distinctive edge, which comes from:

- The organization's core competencies—doing something that others cannot do or doing it better than others can do it.
- The company's resources—having something that its competitors do not.

▼ **Types of Competitive Strategies:**

Porter's **competitive strategies** framework:

1 Cost leadership strategy	2 Differentiation strategy	3 Focus strategy	4 Stuck in the middle
Having the lowest costs in its industry and aimed at a broad market	Offering unique products that are widely valued by customers and aimed at a broad market	A cost advantage (cost focus) or a differentiation advantage (differentiation focus) in a narrow segment or niche (which can be based on product variety, customer type, distribution channel, or geographical location)	What happens if an organization can't develop a cost or differentiation advantage—a bad place to be

- **Cost leadership:**
  - Highly efficient
  - Overhead kept to a minimum
  - Does everything it can to cut costs
  - Product must be perceived as comparable in quality to that offered by rivals or at least acceptable to buyers

- **Differentiation:**
  - Product differences: exceptionally high quality, extraordinary service, innovative design, technological capability, or an unusually positive brand image

arturs2o/Fotolia

Use **strategic management** to get a **sustainable competitive advantage**.

3 Functional Strategy

| Research and Development | Manufacturing | Marketing | Human Resources | Finance |

Those **strategies used by an organization's various functional departments** (marketing, operations, finance/accounting, human resources, and so forth) to support the competitive strategy.

Step 6: Evaluate Results

The final step in the strategic management process is evaluating results. How effective have the strategies been? A winning strategy is one that provides competitive advantage, leads to improved performance, and fits the industry and competitive situation.[30] What adjustments, if any, are necessary? Revisions become necessary for several reasons: specific company performance, changing environmental conditions, and new opportunities.[31] We discuss this step in our coverage of the control process in Chapter 11.

In any industry, Michael Porter's five competitive forces dictate the rules of competition. Together, these forces plus the element of complementors (see Exhibit 3-10) determine industry attractiveness and profitability. Managers assess an industry's attractiveness using these forces:

- *Threat of new entrants.* Factors such as economies of scale, brand loyalty, and capital requirements determine how easy or hard it is for new competitors to enter an industry.

EXHIBIT 3-10 Forces in an Industry Analysis

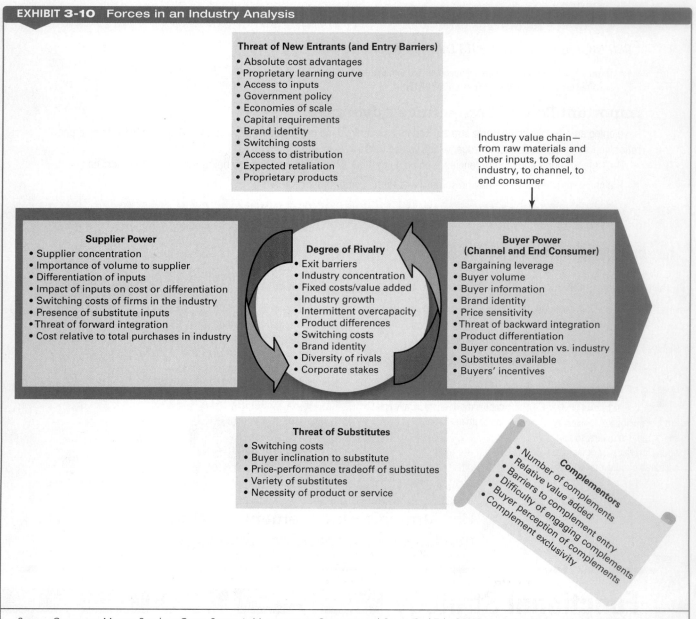

Source: Carpenter, Mason; Sanders, Gerry. Strategic Management: Concepts and Cases, 2nd Ed., ©2009, pp.110, 118. Reprinted and Electronically reproduced by permission of Pearson Education, Inc., New York, NY.

EXHIBIT 3-11 Critical Success Factors for Pursuing Porter's Competitive Strategies

Generic Strategy	Target	Examples	Critical Success Factors
Cost leadership	Broad (mass market)	Walmart Ikea	Large customer base, low prices Economies of scale Supply chain management expertise
Differentiation	Broad (mass market)	Nordstrom Holt Renfrew	Top quality merchandise Exceptional service Brand recognition, high advertising
Focus (differentiation)	Narrow (niche market)	Whole Foods Cinnabon	Unique, innovative Special features for smaller segments Customized products
Focus (cost)	Narrow (niche market)	Dollar store Claire's	Low costs Inexpensive products Moderate quality

Source: Based on M.E. Porter, *Competitive Strategy: Techniques for Analyzing Industries and Competitors* (New York: Free Press, 1980).

- *Threat of substitutes.* Factors such as switching costs and buyer loyalty determine the degree to which customers are likely to buy a substitute product.
- *Bargaining power of buyers.* Factors such as number of customers in the market, customer information, and the availability of substitutes determine the amount of influence that buyers have in an industry.
- *Bargaining power of suppliers.* Factors such as the degree of supplier concentration and availability of substitute inputs determine the amount of power that suppliers have over firms in the industry.
- *Current-competitor rivalry.* Factors such as industry growth rate, increasing or falling demand, and product differences determine how intense the competitive rivalry will be among firms currently in the industry.
- *Power of complementors.* A complementor is another industry whose product tends to increase the sales of a product in another industry.[32] Companies in the computer and electronics industries sell products that must be used together.[33]

Other stakeholders such as special interest groups, trade associations, and local communities can also wield powerful influence and therefore impact the competitive landscape of an industry. Browse YouTube for many examples of Porter's analysis as applied to various industries such as airlines and automobiles.

Once managers have assessed the six forces and determined what threats and opportunities exist, they are ready to select an appropriate competitive strategy. According to Porter, no firm can be successful by trying to be all things to all people. He proposes that managers select a strategy that will give the organization a competitive advantage, which he says arises out of either having lower costs than all other industry competitors or by being significantly different from competitors. On that basis, managers can choose one of three strategies: cost leadership, differentiation, or focus. Which strategy managers select depends on the organization's strengths and core competencies and its competitors' weaknesses (see Exhibit 3-11).

Functional strategies are the strategies used by an organization's various functional departments to support the business strategy. For organizations with traditional functional departments such as manufacturing, marketing, human resources, research and development, and finance, these strategies must support the business strategy. Exhibit 3-12 shows some functional strategies that support the business strategies of cost leadership and differentiation.

EXHIBIT 3-12 Examples of Functional Strategies		
Functional Area	**Cost Leadership**	**Differentiation**
Marketing	• Finding new customers • Reducing advertising or sales budget with lower-cost alternatives	• Adapt products to meet the needs of customers • Spend money on building brand awareness and loyalty
Operations	• Just-in-time, continuous improvement; computerization • Improve efficiency of processes, equipment, and machinery	• Provide flexible shipping options, reduce shipping time • Increase quality of suppliers • Enhance existing products
Human Resources	• Lower cost of recruitment and training • Reduce turnover, increase employee productivity	• Invest in specialty training to meet customer needs • Hire more skilled employees

3 Review and Apply

Summary of Learning Outcomes

3.1 What does planning involve? Planning is the process of defining goals and assessing how those goals can best be achieved. The goals are written and shared with organizational members. Once the goals are agreed on, specific action plans are created to achieve the goals. The purpose of planning is to provide direction, reduce uncertainty, reduce overlapping and wasteful activities, and establish the goals or standards used in controlling. Without planning, managers would not know what to organize, lead, or control.

Stantec is a professional consulting firm that focuses on planning, engineering, architecture, interior design, surveying, environmental sciences, and project economics. It uses a rigorous and creative planning process that balances culture, data, and financial realities.

3.2 How do managers set goals and develop plans? Planning involves two important elements: goals and plans. Goals are the desired outcomes for individuals, groups, or entire organizations. They provide the direction for all management decisions and form the criteria against which actual work accomplishments can be measured. Goals can be set at the top of the organization or through management by objectives (MBO), in which employees and managers jointly develop goals. Once goals have been established, managers develop plans to achieve them, either on their own or with the help of employees. Plans outline how goals are going to be met. They typically describe resource allocations, schedules, and other necessary actions to accomplish the goals. Planning can lock people into a particular way of behaving, which might not be appropriate at a later point. Therefore, plans need to be somewhat flexible so that managers can respond to environmental changes.

Stantec developed a new strategic focus on creating communities and designing with community in mind—Stantec's new mantra. The philosophy was linked with company values, then initiatives were developed relating to employees, clients, business processes, and overall firm performance. Stantec focused on organization-wide communication of the values that provide the foundation of its strategic plan.

3.3 What are the steps in strategic management? The strategic management process is a six-step process that encompasses strategic planning, implementation, and evaluation. The first four steps involve planning: identifying the organization's current mission, goals, and strategies; analyzing the internal environment;

analyzing the external environment; and formulating strategies. The fifth step is implementing strategies, and the sixth step is evaluating the results. Even the best strategies can fail if management does not implement or evaluate them properly.

Stantec follows a long-range, five-year strategy process that includes reviewing current strategies, plans made, and challenges in its business environment.

3.4 What kinds of strategies can managers use? There are three levels of organizational strategies: corporate, business, and functional. They relate to the particular level of the organization that introduces the strategy. At the corporate level, organizations can engage in growth, stability, and renewal strategies. At the business level, strategies look at how an organization should compete in each of its businesses: through cost leadership, differentiation, or focus. At the functional level, strategies of the various functional departments support the business strategy.

Stantec aligned its internal structure to mesh more closely with that of its clients and began to focus on three business operating units: buildings, energy and resources, and infrastructure. This realignment provides enhanced client support and greater leadership accountability and better positions Stantec for future growth and success while maintaining the core strategic elements.

SNAPSHOT SUMMARY

3.1 What Is Planning?

3.2 How Do Managers Plan?
Approaches to Establishing Goals
Steps in Goal Setting

3.3 Organizational Strategy: Choosing a Niche
Step 1: Identify the Organization's Current Vision, Mission, Goals, and Strategies
Step 2: Do an Internal Analysis
Step 3: Do an External Analysis
Step 4: Formulate Strategies
Step 5: Implement Strategies
Step 6: Evaluate Results

3.4 What Strategies to Managers Use

Discussion Questions

1. Contrast formal and informal planning.
2. Describe the differences and explain the relationships between (a) strategic and operational plans, (b) short- and long-term plans, and (c) specific and directional plans.
3. Describe the six-step strategic management process.
4. What is the difference between SWOT and PESTEL analysis?
5. "Organizations that fail to plan are planning to fail." Do you agree or disagree with this statement? Explain your position.
6. Using Michael Porter's generic strategies (cost leadership, differentiation, and focus), describe the strategy used by each of the following companies in the automotive industry: Kia, Toyota, and Ferrari.
7. "The primary means of sustaining a competitive advantage is to adjust faster to the environment than your competitors do." Do you agree or disagree with this statement? Explain your position.

Analysis and Interpretation

Successful people have goals and establish plans to help them achieve those goals. The following exercise is designed to get you to think about goal setting as it relates to your school and personal life.

Developing Management Skills

Dilemma

Think ahead to five years from now, to consider what it is that you might like to be doing with your life. Develop your own vision and mission statements. Conduct a personal SWOT analysis. Establish a set of goals that will help you achieve your vision and mission. Develop a five-year plan that maps out the steps you need to take to get to where you want to be with your life at that time. Use this plan as a basis for prioritizing tasks with your time management techniques.

Becoming a Manager

- Write a personal mission statement in under 200 words
- What are your strengths and weaknesses as a student? What opportunities and threats exist in your college or university environment?

- Develop some specific and challenging goals for various aspects of your life, such as academic studies, career preparation, family, and so forth.
- Set some deadlines and milestones for your goals. Monitor and evaluate your performance every six to twelve months.
- For goals that you have developed, write out plans for achieving those goals.
- Think of a job that you would like to have five years from now. See if your goals and plans will help you to obtain this job.

Developing Your Interpersonal Skills: Goal Setting for Your Professor

ABOUT THE SKILL

Management by objectives was described earlier in the chapter. Setting objectives jointly provides for greater commitment and motivation.

PRACTISING THE SKILL

Have a discussion with your professor. Provide responses to the following three questions as they relate to your classroom:

1. What should the professor stop doing?
2. What should the professor start doing?
3. What should the professor continue doing?

Now develop a list of three goals that would be critical to your professor's performance, and ensure that they meet the characteristics of well-designed goals. Now develop an action plan for your professor to achieve the goals.

Your Essential Management Reading List

Learning from key management experts can help you understand today's management theory and practice. What follows is a list of some of the more influential management books:

- *The Lords of Strategy*—Walter Kiechel
- *The End of Competitive Advantage*—Rita Gunther McGrath
- *Good Strategy Bad Strategy*—Richard Rumelt

Team Exercises

3BL: The Triple Bottom Line

ETHICAL COMPETITIVE INTELLIGENCE

Some companies use competitive intelligence to get a sense of a competitor's possible strategic options, to find out information on their cost structure, or even to get an early read on a new product. If a firm does so unethically, the profit bottom line may create a negative tradeoff on the people bottom line in the organization. Acting unethically, even if it generates more profit, can lead employees to believe that their interests and those of the broader community are no longer being served.

In 2004, Air Canada filed a $5 million lawsuit against rival WestJet, alleging that WestJet executives used a former Air Canada employee's password to gain access to confidential information on flight load schedules. WestJet used this information to increase service out of Toronto and adjust US routes to the detriment of Air Canada. The case was settled in 2006, when WestJet paid $5.5 million to Air Canada in damages and agreed to donate $10 million to children's charities in the names of both airlines.

THINKING CRITICALLY ABOUT ETHICAL COMPETITIVE INTELLIGENCE

Which of the following situations would be examples of ethical competitive intelligence? Why or why not?

- Attending a trade show with a name badge and gathering information at the competitor's booth
- Accessing annual reports and industry market surveys
- Obtaining information from the competitor's public website
- Interviewing competitors' employees to access confidential information
- Hiring professional investigators to get some specific details about the competitor
- Secretly monitoring statements made by competitors' employees

Your College or University's Vision, Mission, and Strategies

You might not pay much attention to the goals and objectives of your college or university because you are focusing on your studies. But your college or university had to carve out its niche in an effort to provide something of value to its students, and it must continue to monitor its performance.

For this exercise, break up into small groups. The task of each group is to prepare responses to the following questions and present your findings to the class:

1. What is your college or university's vision and mission? What resources does your college or university have that support its vision and mission?
2. How would you describe your college or university's environment in terms of PESTEL?
3. What do you believe are the strengths and weaknesses of your college or university? What are its opportunities and threats?
4. Obtain the strategic plan for your college or university. Which corporate strategy is your college or university following? How does this relate to its strengths, weaknesses, opportunities, and threats?
5. Which of Porter's generic strategies is evident at your college or university?
6. What do you believe is your college or university's competitive advantage? What do you think your college or university should do to sustain its competitive advantage?
7. Is strategic planning as important in education as it is in business?

Be the Consultant: Making Meetings More Effective

Try these tips at your next group meeting, and discuss the impact they made on your meeting.

Objectify Yourself	The meeting needs to have a clear outcome: "At the end of the meeting, we will . . . "	Make a decision? Generate ideas? Update status?
The Basket Case	Collect everyone's PDA, tablet, or cell phone at the start of the meeting and return them at the end of the meeting.	Collecting electronic devices will reduce distractions and keep people on task.
Share and Share Again	Distribute the agenda in advance. Get the minutes out quickly.	Attendees can prepare more effectively in advance. Having an agenda allows you to keep the meeting on track and on time. Momentum will not be lost if you can get the action items in the hands of the participants.
Take a Stand	Motivational speaker and author Jon Petz suggests having the meeting in a space with no chairs, tables, or laptops—only a whiteboard.	People will work more quickly and will not extend the time of the meeting unnecessarily.
Two-minute Warning	Petz suggests that each participant gets two minutes uninterrupted to state his or her case or provide information.	Participants must stay focused. Cut people off if they go over and reward them if they finish sooner.

Pressmaster/Shutterstock

A two-hour meeting with four people leads to a potential productivity loss of eight hours.

Hey, You're the Boss Now!

In addition to your own focus on goals, employees should also have a clear understanding of what they're attempting to accomplish. Managers have the responsibility to help employees with this understanding as they set work goals.

You can be more effective at setting goals if you use the following eight suggestions:

- *Identify an employee's key job tasks.* Goal setting begins by defining what it is that you want your employees to accomplish. The best source for this information is each employee's job description.
- *Establish measurable, specific, and challenging goals for each key task.* Identify the level of performance expected of each employee. Specify the target toward which the employee is working.
- *Specify the deadlines for each goal.* Putting deadlines on each goal reduces ambiguity. Deadlines, however, should not be set arbitrarily. Rather, they need to be realistic given the tasks to be completed.

- *Allow the employee to participate actively.* When employees participate in goal setting, they're more likely to accept the goals. However, it must be sincere participation. That is, employees must perceive that you are truly seeking their input, not just going through the motions.
- *Prioritize goals.* When you give someone more than one goal, it's important to rank the goals in order of importance. The purpose of prioritizing is to encourage the employee to take action and expend effort on each goal in proportion to its importance.
- *Rate goals for difficulty and importance.* Goal setting should not encourage people to choose easy goals. Instead, goals should be rated for their difficulty and importance. When goals are rated, individuals can be given credit for trying difficult goals, even if they don't fully achieve them.
- *Build in feedback mechanisms to assess goal progress.* Feedback lets employees know whether their level of effort is sufficient to attain the goal. Feedback should be

both self-generated and supervisor-generated. Feedback should also be frequent and recurring.

- *Link rewards to goal attainment.* It's natural for employees to ask, "What's in it for me?" Linking rewards to the achievement of goals will help answer that question.[34]

Diversity Matters

The Canadian Institute of Diversity and Inclusion (CIDI) surveyed Canadian employers and found that 80 percent of them considered diversity a key strategic initiative; yet only 20 percent measured it in terms of return on investment (ROI). The first step toward diversity is for an organization to conduct an employee census or ask employees to self-identify based on demographic categories. Understanding demographics allows organizations to identify gaps in representation and determine inclusion issues and barriers to advancement, helping them set goals, establish appropriate programs and initiatives, and measure results, and ensuring that they are building a pipeline of the leaders of tomorrow.

CIDI found that the following standard metrics were commonly used:[35]

- Representation of diverse/underrepresented groups by job level
- Recruitment, promotion, and turnover statistics by demographic group
- Employee engagement scores by demographic group
- Diversity-related or inclusiveness questions on employee surveys
- Human rights, harassment, or discrimination complaints
- Participation in training and diversity, inclusiveness, equity, and human rights
- Participation in employee resources/networking groups

Business Cases

SilverBirch Hotels & Resorts

The name SilverBirch Hotels & Resorts may be unfamiliar, but you have likely heard of brands such as Radisson, Hilton, Best Western, and Ramada. Vancouver-based SilverBirch is one of Canada's leading hotel management companies, managing over 20 hotels and resorts across Canada—both independent hotels and hotels operating under the major franchise brands listed previously.

Over the past decade, SilverBirch Hotels & Resorts has experienced success due in large part to a strong regional infrastructure, sales growth, marketing programs and support, excellent franchise relations, and an unusual approach to branding. For consumer marketing purposes, the name GreatCanadianHotels is used instead of SilverBirch to address the lack of a franchise brand.

SilverBirch entered into a partnership with Marriott International Inc. to open the first branded extended-stay hotel in the summer of 2012. The partnership gives Marriott a partner who is familiar with the Canadian market, while aligning with a strong international brand is helping SilverBirch with its strategy of acquiring and building new branded properties across the country.

SilverBirch has also shown a strong environmental ethic since it was established in 1997. Its vision, mission, and values include "safety and respect for the environment." The Hotel Association of Canada (HAC) administers a Green Key Eco-Rating Program, and SilverBirch was the first hotel management company in Canada to have all of its properties certified by HAC.[36]

Determine whether the following SilverBirch decisions are strategic (S) or operational (O):

_____ Partnering with Marriott International
_____ Planting 1800 trees at one of its hotels to offset the greenhouse gas emissions produced by meetings and events at its property
_____ Creating educational internship programs for students at culinary and hospitality training schools
_____ Installing a computerized reservation system
_____ Developing a new vision statement: "We excite our markets with the liveliest hotels in Canada, each with its own rich, Canadian sense of place."
_____ Holding a wine-and-food pairing fall promotion in its Saskatoon hotel

Canadian Wine Industry

The Canada-US free trade agreement was expected to destroy the Canadian wine industry. Initially, market share and vineyard hectarage were both reduced. The increase of competition forced the remaining Canadian wineries to increase product quality and find new markets. The Canadian wine industry overcame a very sluggish period in the 1990s with growth of more than 7 percent annually thanks to a shift in higher quality grape species (*vitis vinifera*), the establishment of the Vintners Quality Alliance (VQA), and new markets for cool climate wines. The industry is fragmented, with only two major players: Vincor and Andrés Wines. This fragmentation provides major challenges through the lack of economies of scale and brand recognition. The industry is concentrated in Ontario and British Columbia, with small operations in Quebec and other provinces. Canadian provincial distribution monopolies (except in Alberta and Quebec) lead to heavy mark-ups and high sales taxes, which hurt domestic wine sales.

Imports once made up only 25 percent of domestic consumption, but now total two-thirds of domestic market share. Canadian wine consumption is growing at a faster rate than that of beer and spirits, but import growth has been spurred by the reduction of nontariff barriers, the strength of the Canadian dollar, and geographic limitations on red wine production in Canada. Climate conditions hamper Canadian wine production both in scale and competitiveness. Poor weather leads to a short season and major fluctuations in quality from year to year for all wines except ice wine, in which Canada has become a world leader. Canada has successfully exploited the cool climate wine niche, and exports in this area reached $15.6 billion in 2012, over 50 percent of that to China alone.

Other domestic challenges include the absence of external credibility due to poor export market penetration and persisting perceptions of low-quality wines, which date back to the lower-quality grape species used in the 70s and 80s. Exporting challenges for Canadian wines include lack of capacity, lack of marketing expertise, and insufficient financial resources.

Ontario, which accounts for 80 percent of domestic production, developed a strategic plan in the early 2000s to optimize land use planning, increase wine quality through VQA, and increase wine tourism. A recent study by the Canadian Vintners Association had the following key findings:

- Canadian wine industry production has an annual national economic impact of $6.8 billion. For every bottle of wine produced in Canada, it generates $31 of domestic economic impact in the country.
- The wine and grape industry is responsible for more than 31 000 jobs in Canada from manufacturing, agriculture, tourism, transportation, research, restaurants, and retail.

- Wine-related tourism welcomes more than 3 million visitors each year, generating more than $1.2 billion annually in tourism revenue and employment.
- The wine industry generates $1.2 billion in federal and provincial tax revenue and liquor board mark-up.
- Canadians enjoy over 1 billion glasses or 220 million bottles of wine produced by the Canadian wine industry each year.

The strategic dilemma facing Canadian winemakers is whether to focus on domestic or international markets. While exports are likely to remain small in the short term, it is possible to target smaller, fast-growth markets.[37]

Questions

1. How is the planning process in the wine industry similar to that in other manufacturing industries?
2. What kinds of contingency plans are required in the Canadian wine industry?
3. What elements would be required in a Canadian national or provincial exporting strategy?
4. What growth strategies are most suitable for the Canadian wine industry?

Communication and Social Media

EXHIBIT S3-1   What are Canadians doing online?

Desktop
1 Playing games
2 Social media
3 General browsing
4 Banking
5 Hobbies/interests and news

Laptop
1 Social media
2 General browsing
3 Playing games
4 Banking
5 Hobbies/interests

Tablet
1 Social media
2 Playing games
3 General browsing
4 Entertainment
5 News and hobbies/interests

Mobile
1 Social media
2 Messaging
3 Taking/editing photos
4 Playing games
5 General browsing

Source: From CIRA: Canadian Internet Registration Authority 2014 Factbook. Copyright © 2014 by Canadian Internet Registration Authority (CIRA). Reprinted by permission.

EXHIBIT S3-2   Top social networking sites in Canada by unique visits

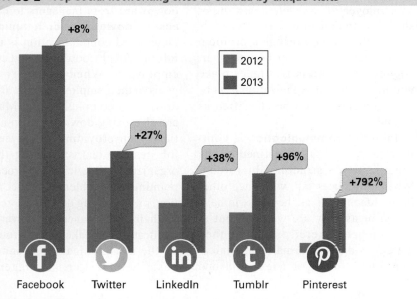

Source: CIRA: Canadian Internet Registration Authority Factbook, 2014. Copyright © 2014 by Canadian Internet Registration Authority (CIRA). Reprinted by permission.

And the Survey says...

Canadians have the highest social media network penetration in the world. Eighty-two percent of Canadians use a social network versus 75 percent of Americans.

Canadians spend an average of 2 hours 19 minutes on social networks each day.

91% of Canadian Internet users have social media accounts, and 66 percent have used social media in the past month.

85% have a Facebook account, and 57 percent have used Facebook in the past month.

46% have a Twitter account, and 22 percent have used Twitter in the past month.

45% have a Google+ account, and 13 percent have used Google+ in the past month.

30% have a LinkedIn account, and 11 percent have used LinkedIn in the past month.

26% have a Pinterest account, and 10 percent have used Pinterest in the past month.[1]

ORGANIZATIONAL COMMUNICATION

The business community recognizes social media as a multifaceted tool. Some employers prescreen job applicants by searching their Facebook and LinkedIn profiles or reading their Twitter feeds. "While the majority of Canadian companies are engaging in social media, most of them aren't combining the two fundamental pillars—posting information and monitoring what people are saying—with enough frequency to build lasting relationships with their customers," said Katie Delahaye Paine, CEO of KDPaine & Partners.[2] Some employers, such as the City of Toronto, have blocked the use of social media at work, while others are creating their own company networks on Facebook to allow employees to use social media as one of their communication tools.

Communication between managers and employees provides the information necessary to get work done effectively and efficiently in organizations. As such, communication is fundamentally linked to managerial performance.[3]

Stantec went through a major strategic planning renewal process, followed by a coordinated brand repositioning based on the community theme. The overall strategic platform featured five main aspects. The first was the company's purpose statement, which is essentially a mission statement. Next was the listing of core values, followed by the promise—another version of a vision statement. The fourth aspect was the company's voice, or its communications plan. This is where communications strategy must be aligned with Stantec's overall strategy. The last aspect was implementation, or living with the new brand and strategy. Prior to the public launch, it was crucial to collect feedback from employees and ensure they were on board.

Stantec's brand strategy launched in September 2013, but prior to that much work took place. A 2011 strategic planning session in Boston featured the company's leaders talking about a need to unite the company under a common purpose: community. In 2012, Stantec partnered with a large global brand consultant and conducted research with its 13 000 employees. This ensures that each employee is able to be a brand ambassador and can communicate the strategic plan and platform to their clients and the general public. This massive communication strategy featured formal communication channels such as office meetings and email and informal channels such as the company's social networking site, StanNet.

Formal Versus Informal Communication

Communication within an organization is often described as either formal or informal. **Formal communication** refers to communication that follows the official chain of command or is part of the communication required to do one's job. When a manager asks an employee to complete a task, he or she is communicating formally. So is the employee who brings a problem to the attention of his or her manager. Any communication that takes place within prescribed organizational work arrangements would be classified as formal.

Informal communication is communication that is not defined by the organization's structural hierarchy. When employees talk with each other in the lunchroom, as they pass in hallways, or as they are working out at the company exercise facility, they are engaging in informal communication. Employees form friendships and communicate with each other. The informal communication system fulfills two purposes in organizations: (1) it permits employees to satisfy their need for social interaction; and (2) it can improve an organization's performance by creating alternative, and frequently faster and more efficient, channels of communication.

Direction of Communication Flow

Organizational communication can flow downward, upward, laterally, or diagonally. Let us look at each of these types of communication.

Downward Communication Every morning and often several times a day, managers at UPS package delivery facilities gather employees for mandatory meetings that last precisely three minutes. During those 180 seconds, managers relay company announcements and go over local information such as traffic conditions or customer complaints. Each meeting ends with a safety tip. The three-minute meetings have proved so successful that many of the company's office employees are using the idea.[4]

Any communication that flows downward from managers to employees is **downward communication**. Downward communication is used to inform, direct, coordinate, and evaluate employees. When managers assign goals to their employees, they are using downward communication. Managers are also using downward communication when providing employees with job descriptions, informing them of organizational policies and procedures, pointing out problems that need attention, or evaluating and giving feedback on their performance. Downward communication can take place through any of the communication channels we described earlier. Managers can

---

formal communication
Communication that follows the official chain of command or is part of the communication required to do one's job.

informal communication
Communication that is not defined by the organization's structural hierarchy.

downward communication
Communication that flows downward from managers to employees.

improve the quality of the feedback they give to employees if they follow the advice given in *Tips for Managers—Suggestions for Giving Feedback*.

Upward Communication Any communication that flows upward from employees to managers is **upward communication**. Managers rely on their employees for information. Reports are given to managers to inform them of progress toward goals and any current problems. Upward communication keeps managers aware of how employees feel about their jobs, their coworkers, and the organization in general. Managers also rely on it for ideas on how things can be improved. Some examples of upward communication include performance reports prepared by employees, suggestion boxes, employee attitude surveys, grievance procedures, manager–employee discussions, and informal group sessions in which employees have the opportunity to identify and discuss problems with their manager or even representatives of top management.

The extent of upward communication depends on the organizational culture. If managers have created a climate of trust and respect and use participative decision making or empowerment, there will be considerable upward communication as employees provide input to decisions. Ernst & Young encourages employees to evaluate the principals, partners, and directors on how well they create a positive work climate. A partner in the Montreal office was surprised to learn that people in her office found her a poor role model, and she took care to more carefully explain her actions as a result.[5] In a highly structured and authoritarian environment, upward communication still takes place, but is limited in both style and content.

Lateral Communication Communication that takes place among employees on the same organizational level is called **lateral communication**. In today's often chaotic and rapidly changing environment, lateral communication is frequently needed to save time and facilitate coordination. Cross-functional teams, for example, rely heavily on this form of communication. However, it can create conflicts if employees do not keep their managers informed about decisions they have made or actions they have taken.

Diagonal Communication Communication that cuts across both work areas *and* organizational levels is **diagonal communication**. When an analyst in the credit department communicates directly with a regional marketing manager—note the different department and different organizational level—about a customer problem, they are engaging in diagonal communication. In the interest of efficiency and speed, diagonal communication can be beneficial. Email facilitates diagonal communication. In many organizations, any employee can communicate by email with any other employee, regardless of organizational work area or level. However, just as with lateral communication, diagonal communication

has the potential to create problems if employees do not keep their managers informed.

TIPS FOR MANAGERS

Suggestions for Receiving Feedback

Managers can use the following tips to receive feedback more effectively:

* Seek clarification and **specific examples**.
* Share your feelings about the message.
* Observe the **nonverbal cues** from the sender.
* Be open and avoid being **defensive**.
* Verify assumptions and **summarize**.

Suggestions for Giving Feedback

Managers can use the following tips to give more effective feedback:

* Relate feedback to existing performance goals and clear expectations.
* Give **specific feedback** tied to observable behaviour or measurable results.
* Channel feedback toward **key result areas** and things the person can do something about.
* Give feedback **as soon as possible**.
* Give positive **feedback for improvement**, not just final results.
* Focus feedback on performance, not personalities.
* Speak directly and without judgment.
* Base feedback on accurate and credible information.[6]

---

upward communication
Communication that flows upward from employees to managers.

lateral communication
Communication that takes place among employees or the same organizational level.

diagonal communication
Communication that cuts across both work areas and organizational levels.

EXHIBIT S3-3 Barriers to effective interpersonal communication

Barrier	Definition	Example
Filtering	Manipulation of information to make it more favourable to the receiver	An employee telling his or her manager what the manager wants to hear
Emotions	How a receiver feels when a message is received influences how he or she interprets it	Reacting negatively to a message when you are upset
Information Overload	Information exceeds a person's processing capacity	Texts, emails, phone calls, and meetings can create an onslaught of data that leads to ignoring or even forgetting
Selective Perception	Interpreting reality based on personal needs, motivations, experience, background, and personality	Employers believing that Millennials spend too much time on social media and that they won't work long hours
Defensiveness	People feeling threatened, which leads to reactions that reduce effective communication	Verbal attacks, sarcastic remarks, questioning motives
Mental Models	How we perceive the world through a frame of reference or assigning certain meanings to communication	A manager who feels an employee is always complaining may use negative nonverbal signals
Language	Words have different meanings for different people	Jargon may be used to communicate among a group, limiting understanding for some members
Culture	Cultural differences can lead to differences in communication patterns, body language, and the way a person communicates	Canadian communication patterns are detail oriented and focus on the individual; Japanese communications focus more on face-to-face and consensus-based open communication

EXHIBIT S3-4 Overcoming the barriers to effective communication

Use Feedback	You can ask the receiver if they understood what you said, or you could ask the receiver to restate the message in their own words.
Simplify Language	Ensure the message is received and understood by using language that is appropriate for the audience.
Listen Actively	More than hearing but actively listening for full meaning without making judgments or interpretations; place yourself in the sender's position and empathize with them
Constrain Emotions	If you are emotionally upset over an issue, you could refrain from communicating until you regain your composure.
Watch Nonverbal Cues	If actions speak louder than words, ensure your actions and nonverbal cues align with the message.

EXHIBIT S3-5 Active listening behaviours

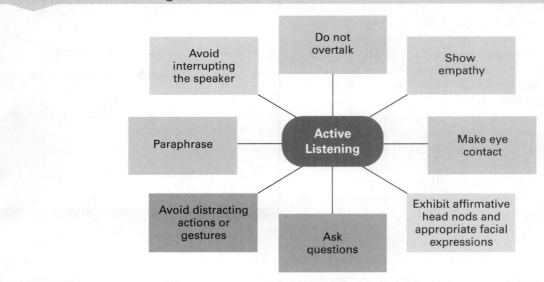

Source: P. L. Hunsaker, *Training in Management Skills*, 1st Ed., 2001. Reprinted and electronically reproduced by permission of Pearson Education, Inc., New York, NY.

HOW INFORMATION TECHNOLOGY AFFECTS ORGANIZATIONAL COMMUNICATION

Information technology has radically changed the way organizational members communicate. For example, it has

- significantly improved a manager's ability to monitor individual or team performance
- allowed employees to have more complete information to make faster decisions
- provided employees with more opportunities to collaborate and share information
- made it possible for employees to be fully accessible, any time, regardless of where they are

Several developments in information technology appear to have the most significant impact on current managerial communication: email, instant messaging, wikis and blogs, and social networking websites such as Facebook and LinkedIn.

Email   Email is a quick and convenient way for organization members to share information and communicate. However, many people complain about email overload, and it is not always used effectively. A recent study found that opening nasty messages from your boss can harm your health over time.[7] While negative email messages from anyone had health consequences, those from superiors resulted in the most significant increase in a person's blood pressure.

Individuals should remember that email tends to be permanent, which means that a message sent in anger could come back to hurt the sender later on. Christina Cavanagh of the University of Western Ontario's Richard Ivey School of Business[8] suggests sleeping on angry emails before sending to be sure you are sending the right message. Email is also not necessarily private communication, and organizations often take the position that they have the right

to read your email. To learn more about email communications protocols, see *Writing Better Emails* at the end of the supplement.

Instant Messaging   Instant messaging (IM) first became popular among teens and preteens who wanted to communicate online immediately with their friends. Now it has moved to the workplace. IM provides immediate and collaborative communication and may replace the desk phone and email in the future.[9] However, IM has drawbacks. Unlike email, it requires users to be logged on to the organization's computer network in order to communicate with one another, which leaves the network open to security breaches. As a result, some organizations have limited which employees can use IM in the workplace.

Wikis and Blogs   Wikis and blogs are sites for open discussion and collaborative information sharing that have quickly replaced the company newsletter. Both can be used effectively internally and externally, allowing employees and customers to distribute and document information quickly.

Social Networking Websites   Social networking websites such as Facebook, Twitter, and LinkedIn have drawn millions of subscribers who voluntarily post information about themselves that can be viewed by any other subscriber, unless the user deliberately sets privacy restrictions.

Some employers post job offerings on sites such as Facebook and LinkedIn; others post recruitment videos on sites such as YouTube. In a recent twist, some employers have conducted virtual interviews through *Second Life*, an online virtual community.[10] Job seekers create an avatar—a computer-generated image that represents themselves—and then communicate with prospective employers through IM. A recent virtual job fair on *Second Life* included employers Hewlett-Packard, Microsoft, Verizon, and Sodexho Alliance SA, a food and facilities-management services company.

Individuals who use websites such as Facebook may want to consider the lack of privacy such sites afford when it comes to employers and evaluations. Individuals may forget that once something has been posted to the Web, it is difficult to erase. Although sharing photos of drunken partying may seem like a good idea, the portrait created might not leave a good impression on potential employers. Many employers regularly use social media sites when recruiting potential employees. Though people may feel they have separate private lives and work lives, the internet makes that line blurry. Every job seeker would be wise to Google themselves and see what cyber footprint they have left, since employers can and may be doing the same thing.

HOW INFORMATION TECHNOLOGY AFFECTS ORGANIZATIONS

Employees—working in teams or as individuals—need information to make decisions and do their work. After describing the communication capabilities managers have at their disposal, it is clear that technology *can* significantly affect the way that organization members communicate, share information, and do their work. Information technology also creates opportunities for organizations. For example, colleges and universities now have the capability to offer online courses and degrees. Over time, these courses could decrease the number of students taught in face-to-face settings, while increasing the overall number of students who can be reached because of online methods of teaching.

Communication and the exchange of information among organization members are no longer constrained by geography or time. Collaborative work efforts among widely dispersed individuals and teams, information sharing, and the integration of decisions and work throughout an entire organization have the potential to increase organizational efficiency and effectiveness. While the economic benefits of information technology are obvious, managers must not forget to address the psychological drawbacks.[11] For example, what is the psychological cost of an employee being always accessible? Will there be increased pressure for employees to "check in" even during their off hours? How important is it for employees to separate their work lives and their personal lives? While these questions have no easy answers, they are issues that managers will have to face.

The widespread use of voice mail and email at work has led to some ethical concerns as well. These forms of communication are not necessarily private, because employers have access to them. The federal *Privacy Act* (which protects the privacy of individuals and provides individuals with the right to access personal information about themselves) and the *Access to Information Act* (which allows individuals to access government information) apply to all federal government departments, most federal agencies, and some federal Crown corporations. However, many private-sector employees are not covered by privacy legislation. Only Quebec's *Privacy Act* applies to the entire private sector. Managers need to clearly convey to employees policies on such things as personal Internet and email use, and the extent to which their communications will be monitored.

SOCIAL MEDIA

Social networking websites such as Facebook and LinkedIn have become resources for employers seeking job candidates.[12] Companies large and small are using these resources to do research, form relationships, and fill positions. More than 350 companies broadcast their job listings to more than 10 million registered users of LinkedIn. A manager looking to fill a key position can use LinkedIn to view posted résumés and read an individual's postings, and can even check out a competitor's site for potential candidates.

Brian Drum, president of executive search firm Drum Associates, uses social

Big data can be an effective counterpart to the information exchange gathered through social media. When Walmart began looking at its enormous database, it noticed that when a hurricane was forecasted sales of batteries, flashlights and Pop-Tarts increased. Now when hurricanes threaten, Walmart stocks additional Pop-Tarts along with emergency storm supplies at the front door.[13]

networking sites such as MySpace to see if there is any information about a job candidate's character that might suggest an inability to perform reliably. "Sometimes all we find is meaningless chit-chat," says Drum, "but once in a while we'll turn up something useful, like an unflattering picture or a piece of information that really shows what the person is made of."

Some businesses are not just using social networking sites for recruiting, however. They have also placed their own company profiles on such sites, allowing employees to interact with each other. They realize that a number of younger employees are using social networking sites, so they might as well encourage productive use of the medium.

The world of communication is not what it used to be. Managers are challenged to keep their organizations functioning smoothly while continually improving work operations *and* staying competitive, even though both the organization and the environment are changing rapidly. Although changing technology has been a significant source of the environmental uncertainty facing organizations, these same technological advances have enabled managers to coordinate the work efforts of employees in ways that can lead to increased efficiency and effectiveness. Information

technology now touches every aspect of almost every company's business. The implications for the ways individuals communicate are profound.

HOW BUSINESSES CAN USE SOCIAL MEDIA

Social media is a peer-to-peer network based on some type of user profile, which allows people to connect with others who may share their interests, activities, or even contacts. Because of this link, social networks can be created that allow companies to communicate with audiences in a much more personal way. Social media can play an integral role in engaging employees, consumers, suppliers, partners, and even investors. Building relationships and brand loyalty through social media can be faster and lower in cost than through traditional marketing.[14]

Organizations that use social media for employees to interact with management can make internal communication more stimulating, strengthening the culture of the organization and loyalty to the brand.[15]

Stantec had an intranet portal called StanNet. With the brand repositioning strategy came an opportunity to harness social media in a coordinated fashion. StanNet 2.0 was introduced to give

Rawpixel.com/Shutterstock

Employers have now begun to use social media in the collective bargaining process to keep employees updated and to quash any false rumours. Unions use social media to gain support and to keep their members aware of what is happening on their side. "In collective bargaining . . . a lot of employers are using social media or controlled websites about the status of collective bargaining," says Len Polsky, a Calgary-based employment lawyer with MacPherson Leslie and Tyerman LLP. Polsky recalls one case where the union leadership negotiated agreements that the membership took issue with. "Had they taken advantage of social media in a greater way . . . maybe the leadership could have aligned itself better with the members' thinking."[16]

employees features from the social networking sites they were using elsewhere, such as Facebook, Blogger, YouTube, LinkedIn, and others. The StanNet 2.0 community sites were launched with the internal brand launch and have been tremendously successful at engaging employees in communications strategies. Social media proved to be a powerful ally in helping employees understand, digest, and articulate the new strategic platform.

A sound social media strategy should be based on clear metrics benchmarks in terms of sales, brand awareness, and customer service.[17] Organizations need to plan in advance for criticisms and complaints so that responses are quick and show that the company takes its customers' concerns seriously. A little pre-planning can help turn a negative experience around when necessary.[18] See *Tips for Managers—Getting Started with Social Media* on how a business can get social media up and running.

DIVERSITY MATTERS: THE COMMUNICATION STYLES OF MEN AND WOMEN

"You don't understand what I'm saying, and you never listen!" "You're making a big deal out of nothing." Have you said (or heard) these statements or ones like them when communicating with friends of the opposite sex? Most of us probably have. Research shows that men and women tend to have different communication styles.[20] Let us look more closely at these differing styles and the problems that can arise and try to suggest ways to minimize the barriers.

Deborah Tannen, professor of linguistics at Georgetown University, has studied the ways that men and women communicate and reports some interesting differences. According to her research, men use talk to emphasize status, while women use it to create connection. Tannen states that communication between the sexes can be a continual juggling act to balance our conflicting needs for intimacy, which emphasizes closeness and commonality, and independence, which emphasizes separateness

TIPS FOR MANAGERS

Getting Started with Social Media

* Explore. What platforms are your customers and employees using?

* Listen. Use Google, Twitter, and Facebook to see what people are saying about your industry, your company, and your products.

* Create a strategy. What business goals can social media support?

* Choose the right platform. B2B customers are more likely to be reached via blogs, LinkedIn, and Twitter, while YouTube and Facebook are better for contact with consumers.

* Offer unique content. Provide insight on hot topics, VIP offers, or special deals.

* Manage the conversation. Nurture your brand ambassadors and follow up on all feedback.

* Coordinate channels. Ensure your social media platforms are linked with your website and other communication channels.

* Think mobile. Everything needs to be accessible on a mobile device.

* Build relationships. Stay connected in real time and build gradually.

Source: Based on *Connecting With Social Media* by Debbie. Dimoff, Vice-President, Consulting, PricewaterhouseCoopers (PwC).[19]

and differences. No wonder communication problems arise! Women hear and speak a language of connection and intimacy. Men hear and speak a language of status and independence. For many men, conversations are merely a way to preserve independence and maintain status in a hierarchical social order. For many women, however, conversations are a way to negotiate closeness and seek out support and confirmation. Let us look at a few examples of what Tannen has described.

Men frequently complain that women talk on and on about their problems. Women, however, criticize men for not listening. What is happening? When a man hears a woman talking about a problem, he frequently asserts his desire for independence and control by offering solutions. Many women, in contrast, view conversing about a problem as a way to promote closeness. The woman talks about a problem to gain support and connection, not to get the man's advice.

Here is another example: Men are often more direct than women in conversation. A man might say, "I think you're wrong on that point." A woman might say, "Have you looked at the marketing department's research report on that issue?" The implication in the woman's comment is that the report will point out the error. Men frequently misread

women's indirectness as "covert" or "sneaky," but women are not as concerned as men with the status and one-upmanship that directness often creates.

Finally, men often criticize women for seeming to apologize all the time. Men tend to see the phrase "I'm sorry" as a sign of weakness because they interpret the phrase to mean the woman is accepting blame, when he may know she is not to blame. The woman also knows she is not at fault. She is typically using "I'm sorry" to express regret: "I know you must feel bad about this and I do too." Women learn to listen with empathy, which helps them maintain collaborative relationships.

Here are some guidelines to help facilitate communications when gender diversity is present:

- *Assume differences more than similarity.* Avoid stereotypes, and do not assume the other person will react in the same way as you do.
- *Focus on description rather than evaluation.* Delay your judgment until you have interpreted the situation from the other person's perspective.
- *Be empathetic.* Viewing behaviours from your perspective might lead you to misinterpret; try instead to simply understand the other person's actions and behaviours.

WRITING BETTER EMAILS

The purpose of the table at the bottom of this page is to learn when to use the active or passive voice, when to be direct or indirect, and how to avoid jargon in emails.

Procedure

Form groups of five or six individuals. Prepare emails that are active, direct, and clear for each of the following four scenarios:

1. The company has been approached by a large competitor who wishes to acquire the company. Staff are worried the takeover might result in some employee layoffs within the next three months.
2. A customer has complained about an employee via email. You have investigated and found the complaint justified. How do you convey this to the employee?
3. Bonus decisions have been made. Not all individuals will receive a bonus.
4. An employee has gone above and beyond in meeting a customer's request. You want to acknowledge the employee's efforts.

Active	Passive
• "The committee determined that the report was inconclusive." • "I am writing the report." • "Please contact Brian to discuss his concerns about your meeting."	• "It was determined by the committee that the report was inconclusive." • "The report is being written by me." • "It is suggested that your meeting with Brian was less than effective and that it would be appropriate that the matter had further discussions."
Direct	Indirect
• "I plan to reassign you to one of two different projects. Please let me know if you have any preferences on which application you would like to develop." • "We have selected another candidate for the promotion. Thank you for your consideration."	• "We hope to develop two new applications this year. To best use your skills, I plan to reassign all team members to one of two different projects. Please let me know if you have any preferences." • "Thank you for your hard work this quarter. Our selection of a candidate for promotion was taken very seriously. We considered your application very carefully, but another candidate was selected."
Clear	Jargon
• "When is the proposal expected?" • "Be creative in meeting the target and make sure we're well organized." • "Regarding" • "To be clear"	• "What is the ETD of the RFP?" • "Push the envelope; get our ducks in a row." • "With reference to" • "To tell the truth"

NAVIGATING THE WORKPLACE COMMUNICATION PROTOCOLS IN A TECHNOLOGY AGE

In 2000, faxing and letters were commonplace forms of communication in the office setting. Technology has advanced rapidly and changed the rules, but maintaining social protocols remains important. Poor etiquette and the excessive use of smartphones and cellphones have led to the term "cell-fishness." Here are some tips on how to be professional in the age of thumb typing and finger swiping.[21]

Social Media

- Do not gripe about or jab at your company, even as a joke—the digital record is permanent.
- Accept Facebook requests from your superiors but not your subordinates.
- Keep your LinkedIn network primarily for business purposes.

Email

- Be discriminating with the urgent flag.
- Stay away from u, ttyl, 2nite, and other email slang.
- Avoid the one-word responses "okay" and "thanks."
- Reply-all is not your friend.

Texting/IM

- Forget the emoticons.
- Do not text or use IM for business purposes unless these forms of communication are a big part of your client's or company's culture—they are too informal.
- Keep in mind that throwing a "jk" after a jab does not make it less of a jab.

Voice Mail

- Use office voice mail mainly to let people know how they can find you.
- Leave messages longer than the five-second "Hey it's me, call me back" and shorter than 30 seconds.
- Be aware that caller ID is reducing the need for messages—more and more people do not retrieve their messages.

Telephone

- Consider the telephone when you need to deal with personal, complex, or multiple issues—voice can help you detect tone.
- Ensure that the background noise does not overwhelm the conversation.
- Never, never, ever call in the bathroom.

Face to Face

- Set your phone on vibrate unless you must receive a very important call, in which case ask the person if it is all right to leave the phone on.
- Do not check your phone every two minutes when you are with someone face to face.
- Do not be "cell-fish"—have an uninterrupted, focused conversation.

Business Cards

- Hand out your card only on request—it is not candy.
- Keep your hashtag, blog, and url off the card—just give basic contact information.

Maridav/Fotolia

CHAPTER

4 Decision Making

LEARNING OUTCOMES

Think About It

Put yourself in Lucie Shaw's shoes. What steps would you have taken to determine whether you should leave a corporate job and purchase a Nurse Next Door franchise? How could you evaluate the risk and return parameters of the decision to purchase the franchise? What decision criteria might you use?

Lucie Shaw saw firsthand a market niche not being well served as she struggled to find home health care services for her in-laws. Because North Americans are living longer, elder care is putting a stress on Baby Boomers, who try to keep their parents living on their own as long as possible, and on the already squeezed health care system. Shaw left her job as an operations manager at Air Canada and purchased a Nurse Next Door franchise.

More and more women are making the decision to become entrepreneurs. At Nurse Next Door, 68 percent of franchisees are women. According to TD economists Beata Caranci and Leslie Preston, "[P]rospects are looking brighter for women entrepreneurs."[1] Female franchise owners have a higher percentage of post secondary education than their male counterparts and are more likely to expand their businesses, but face slightly lower revenue growth.[2] The Canadian franchise industry is the second largest in the world, with more than $100 billion in sales annually. At present, the highest franchise growth is in home-based businesses such as Nurse Next Door.[3]

Nurse Next Door founders John DeHart and Ken Sim acknowledge that running a home-care business can be very challenging due to all the administrative demands such as employee and client scheduling, which happens on a 24/7 basis. So they decided to offer 24/7 scheduling for their franchise partners, allowing the franchise managers to focus on the more important decisions regarding how to develop the business.[4]

Making good decisions is something that every manager strives to do, since the overall quality of managerial decisions has a major influence on organizational success or failure. In this chapter, we examine the concept of decision making and how managers can make ethical decisions.

THE DECISION-MAKING PROCESS

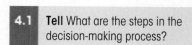
4.1 **Tell** What are the steps in the decision-making process?

While watching a sports competition, have you ever felt that you could make better decisions than the coaches on the field or court?

In the Helsinki, Finland, suburb of Pukinmaki, the fans of PK-35, an amateur soccer team, get that chance![5] The coach does not make decisions about what to do on the field by himself, but instead relies on 300 fans who text message their instructions via their cellphones. Each week the coach posts between three and ten questions about training, team selection, and game tactics to the fans. They have three minutes to respond via cellphone text messaging, and they receive immediate feedback on what others think.

Does shared decision making work? During the first season of the experiment, the team won first place in its division and was promoted to the next higher division. Although we are unlikely to see this type of wireless interactive decision making in organizations any time soon, it does illustrate that decisions, and maybe even how they are made, play a role in performance.

Individuals must continually make **decisions**. Although decision making is typically described as "choosing among alternatives," that view is simplistic. Why? Because decision making is a comprehensive process, not just a simple act of choosing among alternatives.[6] Even for something as straightforward as deciding where to go for lunch, you do more than just choose burgers or pizza. You may consider various restaurants, how you will get there, who might go with you. Granted, you may not spend a lot of time contemplating a lunch decision, but you still go through a process when making that decision. What *does* the decision-making process involve?

Exhibit 4-1 illustrates the **decision-making process**, a set of eight steps that begins with identifying a problem, the decision criteria, and the weights for those criteria; moves to developing, analyzing, and selecting an alternative that can resolve the problem; then moves to implementing the alternative; and concludes with evaluating the decision's effectiveness. Many individuals use most or all of the steps implicitly, if not explicitly. Often, when a poor decision is made, it is because one of the steps was not carefully considered.

This process is as relevant to your personal decision about what movie to see on a Friday night as it is to a corporate action such as a decision to use technology in managing client relationships. The process can also be used to describe both individual and group decisions. Let us take a closer look at the process in order to understand what each step involves. We will use an example—a manager deciding what tablet is best to purchase—to illustrate these steps.

Step 1: Identify a Problem

The decision-making process begins with the existence of a **problem** or, more specifically, a discrepancy between an existing and a desired state of affairs.[7] Take Amanda, a sales manager whose sales representatives need new tablets because their old laptops are inadequate to do their jobs efficiently and effectively. For simplicity's sake, assume that Amanda has determined that it is not economical to simply add memory to the old computers and that the organization's policy prefers managers to purchase new computers rather than lease them. Now we have a problem. There is a disparity between the capabilities of the sales reps' current computers and the capabilities that the sales reps require of their new tablets in order to do their jobs properly. Amanda has a decision to make.

PERSONAL INVENTORY ASSESSMENT

Step 2: Identify Decision Criteria

Once a manager has identified a problem, the **decision criteria** important to resolving the problem must be identified. Managers must determine what is relevant in making a

decision
A choice from two or more alternatives.

decision-making process
A set of eight steps that includes identifying a problem, selecting an alternative, and evaluating the decision's effectiveness.

problem
A discrepancy between an existing and a desired state of affairs.

decision criteria
Criteria that define what is relevant in making a decision.

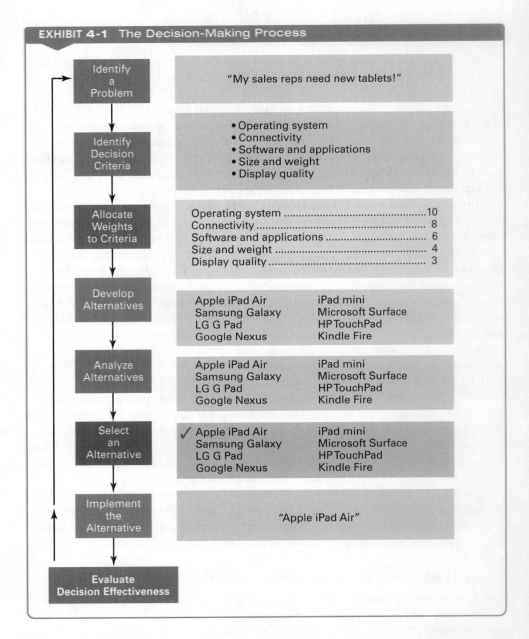

EXHIBIT 4-1 The Decision-Making Process

Identify a Problem
"My sales reps need new tablets!"

Identify Decision Criteria
- Operating system
- Connectivity
- Software and applications
- Size and weight
- Display quality

Allocate Weights to Criteria
Operating system 10
Connectivity 8
Software and applications 6
Size and weight 4
Display quality 3

Develop Alternatives
Apple iPad Air   iPad mini
Samsung Galaxy   Microsoft Surface
LG G Pad   HP TouchPad
Google Nexus   Kindle Fire

Analyze Alternatives
Apple iPad Air   iPad mini
Samsung Galaxy   Microsoft Surface
LG G Pad   HP TouchPad
Google Nexus   Kindle Fire

Select an Alternative
✓ Apple iPad Air   iPad mini
Samsung Galaxy   Microsoft Surface
LG G Pad   HP TouchPad
Google Nexus   Kindle Fire

Implement the Alternative
"Apple iPad Air"

Evaluate Decision Effectiveness

decision. Whether explicitly stated or not, every decision maker has criteria that guide his or her decisions. These criteria are generally determined by one's objectives. For example, when you buy a car, your objective might be to have a car that shouts "status symbol." Or you might want a car that is low maintenance. With your objective in mind, you might consider speed, fuel efficiency, colour, manufacturer, size, and so on as criteria on which to evaluate which car to buy. In our tablet purchase example, Amanda has to assess what factors are relevant to her decision. These factors might include criteria such as price, connectivity, software and applications, operating system, memory and storage capabilities, display quality, battery life, expansion capability, warranty, and carrying weight. After careful consideration, she decides that operating system, connectivity, software and applications, size and weight, and display quality are the relevant criteria in her decision.

Step 3: Allocate Weights to Criteria

If the criteria identified in Step 2 are not equally important, the decision maker must weight the items in order to give them the correct priority in the decision. How do you weight criteria? A simple approach is to give

The choice of a new tablet relies on specific decision criteria such as price, connectivity, operating system, software and applications, display quality, battery life, and size and weight.

Natalia Merzlyakova/Fotolia

EXHIBIT 4-2 Criteria and Weights for Tablet Replacement Decision

Criterion	Weight
Operating System	10
Connectivity	8
Software and Applications	6
Size and Weight	4
Display Quality	3

the most important criterion a weight of 10 and then assign weights to the rest against that standard. Thus, a criterion with a weight of 10 would be twice as important as one given a 5. Of course, you could use 100 or 1000 or any number you select as the highest weight. The idea is to prioritize the criteria you identified in Step 2 by assigning a weight to each.

Exhibit 4-2 lists the criteria and weights that Amanda developed for her computer replacement decision. As you can see, operating system is the most important criterion in her decision, and display quality is the least important. Amanda chose operating system because it was a major aspect in evaluating other factors. She had to choose between the Android system (Google), iOS (Apple), webOS (HP), and Windows (Microsoft).

Step 4: Develop Alternatives

The fourth step requires the decision maker to list viable alternatives that could resolve the problem. No attempt is made to evaluate the alternatives, only to list them. Our sales manager, Amanda, identified eight tablets as possible choices, including Apple iPad Air, Samsung Galaxy, Microsoft Surface, LG G Pad, Google Nexus, Apple iPad mini, HP TouchPad, and Amazon Kindle Fire.

Step 5: Analyze Alternatives

Once the alternatives have been identified, a decision maker must analyze each one. How? By appraising each against the criteria established in steps 2 and 3. From this comparison, the strengths and weaknesses of each alternative become evident. Exhibit 4-3 shows the assessed values that Amanda gave each of her eight alternatives after she had talked to some tablet experts and read the latest information from computer magazines, blogs, and user reviews.

Keep in mind that size and weight is easy to determine by looking at descriptions online or in computer magazines. However, the assessment of display quality is more of a personal judgment. The point is that most decisions by managers involve judgments—the criteria chosen in Step 2, the weights given to the criteria in Step 3, and the analysis of alternatives in Step 5. This fact explains why two tablet buyers with the same amount of money may look at two totally different sets of alternatives or even rate the same alternatives differently.

EXHIBIT 4-3 Assessed Values of Tablets Using Decision Criteria

	Operating System	Connectivity	Software and Applications	Size and Weight	Display Quality
Apple iPad Air	10	9	9	7	10
Samsung Galaxy	9	10	8	9	7
LG G Pad	6	6	7	7	8
Google Nexus	7	7	8	6	8
iPad mini	8	8	6	8	7
Microsoft Surface	7	7	8	5	8
HP TouchPad	7	7	8	5	7
Kindle Fire	9	10	6	8	6

EXHIBIT 4-4 Evaluation of Tablet Alternatives Against Weighted Criteria

	Operating System	Connectivity	Software and Applications	Size and Weight	Display Quality	Total
Weight	**10**	**8**	**6**	**4**	**3**	
Apple iPad Air	100 (10*10)	72 (9*8)	54 (9*6)	28 (7*4)	30 (10*3)	**284**
Samsung Galaxy	90 (9*10)	80 (10*8)	48 (8*6)	36 (9*4)	21 (7*3)	275
LG G Pad	70 (7*10)	56 (7*8)	48 (8*6)	24 (6*4)	24 (8*3)	222
Google Nexus	80 (8*10)	64 (8*8)	36 (6*6)	32 (8*4)	21 (7*3)	233
iPad mini	70 (7*10)	56 (7*8)	48 (8*6)	20 (5*4)	24 (8*3)	218
Microsoft Surface	90 (9*10)	56 (7*8)	54 (9*6)	24 (6*4)	24 (8*3)	248
HP TouchPad	70 (7*10)	56 (7*8)	48 (8*6)	20 (5*4)	21 (7*3)	215
Kindle Fire	60 (6*10)	48 (6*8)	42 (7*6)	28 (7*4)	24 (8*3)	202

Exhibit 4-3 represents only an assessment of the eight alternatives against the decision criteria. It does not reflect the weighting done in Step 3. If you multiply each alternative's assessed value (Exhibit 4-3) by its weight (Exhibit 4-2), you get the scores presented in Exhibit 4-4. The sum of these scores represents an evaluation of each alternative against both the established criteria and weights. At times a decision maker might not have to take this step. If one choice had scored 10 on every criterion, you would not need to consider the weights. Similarly, if the weights were all equal, you could evaluate each alternative merely by summing up the appropriate lines in Exhibit 4-3.

Step 6: Select an Alternative

Step 6 is choosing the best alternative from among those considered. Once all the pertinent criteria in the decision have been weighted and viable alternatives analyzed, we simply choose the alternative that generated the highest total in Step 5. In our example (Exhibit 4-4), Amanda would choose the Apple iPad Air because it scored highest (284 total) on the basis of the criteria identified, the weights given to the criteria, and her assessment of each tablet's ranking on the criteria.

That said, occasionally when one gets to this step the alternative that looks best according to the numbers may not feel like the best solution (e.g., your intuition might suggest some other alternative). Often the reason is that the individual did not give the correct weight to one or more criteria (perhaps because one criterion was actually much more important than the individual realized initially, when assigning weights). Thus, if the individual finds that the "best alternative" does not seem like the right alternative, the decision maker needs to decide before implementing the alternative if a review of the criteria is necessary.

Step 7: Implement the Alternative

Step 7 is concerned with putting the decision into action. This step involves conveying the decision to those affected by it and getting their commitment to it. Managers often fail to get buy-in from those around them before making a decision, even though successful implementation requires participation. One study found that managers used participation in only 20 percent of decisions, even though broad participation in decisions led to successful implementation 80 percent of the time. The same study found that managers most commonly tried to implement decisions through power or persuasion (used in 60 percent of decisions). These tactics were successful in only one of three decisions, however.[8] If the people who must carry out a decision participate in the process, they are more likely to enthusiastically support the outcome than if they are just told what to do. Parts 3, 4, and 5 of this text discuss how decisions are implemented by effective organizing, leading, and controlling.

Step 8: Evaluate Decision Effectiveness

The last step in the decision-making process involves evaluating the outcome of the decision to see if the problem has been resolved. Did the alternative chosen in Step 6 and

What Are the Three Approaches Managers Use to Make Decisions?

Decision making is the **essence of management**.[9]

- Everyone in an organization makes decisions, but it is particularly important to managers.

- Managers make decisions—mostly routine ones like which employee will work what shift, what information to include in a report, how to resolve a customer's complaint, and so on—as they **plan, organize, lead,** and **control**.

EXHIBIT 4-5 Decisions in the Management Functions

Planning	Leading
• What are the organization's long-term objectives?	• How do I handle employees who appear to be low in motivation?
• What strategies will best achieve those objectives?	• What is the most effective leadership style in a given situation?
• What should the organization's short-term objectives be?	• How will a specific change affect worker productivity?
• How difficult should individual goals be?	• When is the right time to stimulate conflict?
Organizing	**Controlling**
• How many employees should I have report directly to me?	• What activities in the organization need to be controlled?
• How much centralization should there be in the organization?	• How should those activities be controlled?
• How should jobs be designed?	• When is a performance deviation significant?
• When should the organization implement a different structure?	• What type of management information system should the organization have?

- Managers want to be good decision makers and exhibit good decision-making behaviours so they appear competent and intelligent to their boss, employees, and coworkers.

1 Rational Model

- This approach assumes that decision makers must act rationally.[10] How? Use **rational decision making**—that is, make logical and consistent choices to maximize value.[11]

rational decision making
Making decisions that are consistent and value-maximizing within specified constraints.

2 Bounded Rationality

- **Bounded rationality** means managers make rational decisions but are limited (bounded) by their ability to process information.[12]

- Most decisions managers make do not fit the assumption of perfect rationality.

- No one can possibly analyze *all* information on *all* alternatives, so they **satisfice**—that is, they accept solutions that are "good enough," rather than spend time and resources trying to maximize.

- Most managerial decisions do not fit the assumptions of perfect rationality, but can still be influenced by (1) the organization's culture, (2) internal politics, (3) political considerations, and (4) a phenomenon called escalation of commitment—an increased commitment to a previous decision despite evidence that it may have been wrong.[13]

- Why would anyone—especially managers—escalate commitment to a bad decision? Two reasons: (1) They hate to admit that their initial decision may have been flawed; and (2) they do not want to search for new alternatives.

Example: As a newly graduated finance major, you look for a job as a financial planner—minimum salary of $47k and within 100 kilometres of your hometown. After searching several different options, you accept a job as a business credit analyst at a bank 50 kilometres away at a starting salary of $42k. Hooray! If, however, you had *maximized*—that is, continued to search all possible alternatives—you would have found this financial planning job at a trust company 25 kilometres away with a starting salary of $43k. However, the first job offer was *satisfactory*—"good enough." Your decision making was still rational . . . but within the bounds of your ability to process information!

iQoncept/Fotolia

EXHIBIT 4-6 Bounded Decision Making

	Definition	Example
Bounded Awareness	People overlooking important information during the decision-making process	The music industry's failure to see the threat of Napster and file sharing
Bounded Ethicality	Personal ethical preferences may not be in sync with our actual behaviour	A hiring manager who views himself/herself as egalitarian but has different eye contact and body language with one group of people versus another
Bounded Rationality	We employ shortcuts (heuristics) to help make sense of things	Limited time to perform or a lack of understanding of financial ratios might lead to decisions made with improper financial support
Bounded Willpower	We give too much focus to the present and not enough to the future	A person not saving enough for retirement early in their career
Bounded Self-Interest	Attaching a priority to the outcomes of others rather than simply trying to maximize our own payoffs	Employing principles of fairness rather than trying to crush your competitors

Source: Based on *Rotman Magazine*, Winter 2009, Q&A with Dolly Chugh—The NYU professor discusses the foibles of bounded willpower, bounded awareness and bounded self interest and what can be done to combat them, interview by Karen Christensen, pp. 91–95.

bounded rationality
Limitations on a person's ability to interpret, process, and act on information.

satisfice
To accept solutions that are "good enough."

Intuition and Managerial Decision Making

When deciding yay or nay on new shoe styles, Diego Della Valle, chairman of Tod's luxury shoe empire, does not use common decision-making tools like focus groups or poll testing. Nope . . . he wears the shoes for a few days. If they are not to his liking, his verdict: No! **His intuitive decision approach has helped make Tod's a successful multinational company.**[14]

Smalik/Fotolia

- **Intuitive decision making**—also described as "unconscious reasoning"—is making decisions on the basis of experience, feelings, and accumulated judgment.

- Exhibit 4-7 illustrates five different aspects of intuition.

EXHIBIT 4-7 What Is Intuition?

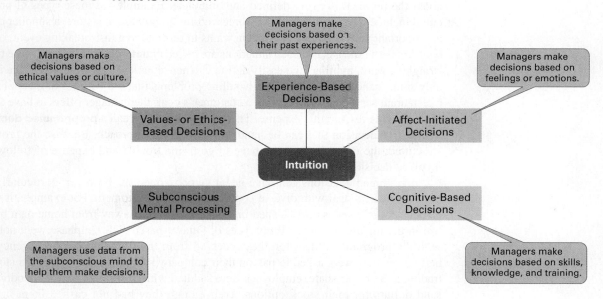

Source: Based on "Exploring Intuition and Its Role in Managerial Decision Making," *Academy of Management Review,* January 2007, pp. 33–54; M. H. Bazerman and D. Chugh, "Decisions Without Blinders," *Harvard Business Review,* January 2006, pp. 88–97; C. C. Miller and R. D. Ireland, "Intuition in Strategic Decision Making: Friend or Foe in the Fast-Paced 21st Century," *Academy of Management Executive,* February 2005, pp. 19–30; E. Sadler-Smith and E. Shefy, "The Intuitive Executive: Understanding and Applying 'Gut Feel' in Decision-Making," *Academy of Management Executive,* November 2004, pp. 76–91; L. A. Burke, and J. K. Miller, "Taking the Mystery Out of Intuitive Decision Making," *Academy of Management.*

intuitive decision making
Making decisions on the basis of experience, feelings, and accumulated judgment.

implemented in Step 7 accomplish the desired result? In Part 5 of this text, in which we look at the controlling function, we will see how to evaluate the results of decisions.

What if the evaluation shows the problem still exists? The manager would need to assess what went wrong. Was the problem incorrectly defined? Were errors made in the evaluation of the various alternatives? Was the right alternative selected but poorly implemented? Answers to questions such as these might send the manager back to one of the earlier steps. It might even require re-doing the whole decision process. To learn more about creativity and decision making, see *Be the Consultant—Solving Problems Creatively* on page 99 at the end of the chapter.

Types of Problems and Decisions

Managers at eating establishments in Whitehorse, Yukon, make decisions weekly about purchasing food supplies and scheduling employee work shifts. It is something they have done countless times. But in 2007 they faced a decision they had never encountered—how to adapt to a newly enacted no-smoking bylaw in public places, which included restaurants and bars. This situation is not all that unusual. Managers in all kinds of organizations will face different types of problems and decisions as they do their jobs. Depending on the nature of the problem, a manager can use different types of decisions.

STRUCTURED PROBLEMS AND PROGRAMMED DECISIONS   Some problems are straightforward. The goal of the decision maker is clear, the problem is familiar, and information about the problem is easily defined and complete. Examples of these types of problems could include what to do when a customer returns a purchase to a store, a supplier delivers an important product late, a news team wants to respond to a fast-breaking event, or a student wants to drop a class. Such situations are called **structured problems** because they are straightforward, familiar, and easily defined. When situations are structured, there is probably some standardized routine for handling problems that may arise. For example, when a restaurant server spills a drink on a customer's coat, the manager offers to have the coat cleaned at the restaurant's expense. This action is what we call a **programmed decision**—a repetitive decision that can be handled by a routine approach. Because the problem is structured, the manager does not have to go to the trouble and expense of following an involved decision process.

Programmed decisions can have negative consequences, however, particularly when decision makers deal with diverse populations/clients/customers. For example, it may be difficult to have one's coat cleaned immediately if one is away from home on a business trip in the middle of winter. Employees of Ottawa-based JDS Uniphase were not happy with the programmed decision they received from the Canada Revenue Agency about hefty taxes they were asked to pay on their company stock options. When JDS stock was trading at $300 per share, employees were saddled with tax bills of several hundred thousand dollars for their stock options, even though they had not cashed them in. When employees asked the Canada Revenue Agency how they could be expected to pay such big tax bills when they earned only $50 000 per year, the agency responded unsympathetically that they had to pay up.[15]

Managers make programmed decisions by falling back on procedures, rules, and policies.

A **procedure** is a series of interrelated, sequential steps that a decision maker can use to respond to a structured problem. The only real difficulty is in identifying the problem. Once it is clear, so is the procedure. When bad weather grounds airplanes, airlines have procedures for helping customers who miss their flights. Customers may request that they be put up in a hotel for the night. The customer service agent knows how to make this decision—follow the established airline procedure for dealing with customers when flights are grounded.

---

structured problems
Problems that are straightforward, familiar, and easily defined.

programmed decision
A repetitive decision that can be handled by a routine approach.

procedure
A series of interrelated sequential steps that a decision maker can use to respond to a structured problem.

A **rule** is an explicit statement that tells a decision maker what he or she can or cannot do. Rules are frequently used because they are simple to follow and ensure consistency. For example, rules about lateness and absenteeism permit supervisors to make disciplinary decisions rapidly and fairly.

A **policy** is a guideline for making a decision. In contrast to a rule, a policy establishes general parameters for the decision maker rather than specifically stating what should or should not be done. Policies typically contain an ambiguous term that leaves interpretation up to the decision maker. "The customer always comes first and should always be *satisfied*" is an example of a policy statement. While ambiguity of policies is often intended to allow more flexibility in action, not all employees and customers are comfortable with flexibly determined policies.

UNSTRUCTURED PROBLEMS AND NONPROGRAMMED DECISIONS Many organizational situations involve **unstructured problems**, or new or unusual problems for which information is ambiguous or incomplete. Whether to build a new manufacturing facility in Beijing is an example of an unstructured problem.

Nonprogrammed decisions are unique and nonrecurring and require custom-made solutions. For example, if an office building were to be flooded because sprinklers went off accidentally, CEOs with businesses in the buildings would have to decide when and how to start operating again and what to do for employees whose offices were completely ruined. When a manager confronts an unstructured problem, there is no cut-and-dried solution. The problem requires a custom-made response through nonprogrammed decision making.

Few managerial decisions in the real world are either fully programmed or nonprogrammed. These are extremes, and most decisions fall somewhere in between. Few programmed decisions are designed to eliminate individual judgment completely. At the other extreme, even a unique situation requiring a nonprogrammed decision can be helped by programmed routines. It is best to think of decisions as *mainly* programmed or *mainly* nonprogrammed, rather than as completely one or the other.

The problems confronting managers usually become more unstructured as they move up the organizational hierarchy. Why? Because lower-level managers handle the routine decisions themselves and let upper-level managers deal with the decisions they find unusual or difficult. Similarly, higher-level managers delegate routine decisions to their subordinates so they, the managers, can deal with more difficult issues.[16]

One of the more challenging tasks facing managers as they make decisions is analyzing decision alternatives (Step 5 in the decision-making process). In the next section, we look at analyzing alternatives under different conditions.

Decision-Making Conditions

When managers make decisions, they face three conditions: certainty, risk, and uncertainty. What are the characteristics of each?

CERTAINTY The ideal condition for making decisions is one of **certainty**—that is, a condition in which a decision maker can make accurate decisions because the outcome of every alternative is known. For example, when Alberta's finance minister Joe Ceci is deciding in which bank to deposit provincial funds, he knows the exact interest rate being offered by each bank and the amount that will be earned on the funds. He is certain about the outcomes of each alternative. As you might expect, most managerial decisions are not like this.

One of the easiest ways to practise decision making is to list all the pros and cons of an alternative.

rule
An explicit statement that tells a decision maker what he or she can or cannot do.

policy
A guideline for making a decision.

unstructured problems
Problems that are new or unusual and for which information is ambiguous or incomplete.

nonprogrammed decisions
Decisions that are unique and nonrecurring, and require custom-made solutions.

certainty
A condition in which a decision maker can make accurate decisions because the outcome of every alternative is known.

Estimating the outcomes of risk is like navigating with a compass.

RISK A far more common condition is one of **risk**, a condition in which a decision maker is able to estimate the likelihood of certain outcomes. The ability to assign probabilities to outcomes may be the result of personal experiences or secondary information. With risk, managers have historical data that let them assign probabilities to different alternatives. Let us work through an example.

Suppose that you manage a ski resort in Whistler, British Columbia. You are thinking about adding another lift to your current facility. Obviously your decision will be influenced by the additional revenue that the new lift would generate, and additional revenue will depend on snowfall. The decision is made somewhat clearer because you have fairly reliable weather data from the past ten years on snowfall levels in your area—three years of heavy snowfall, five years of normal snowfall, and two years of light snowfall. Can you use this information to help you make your decision about adding the new lift? If you have good information on the amount of revenues generated during each level of snowfall, the answer is yes.

You can calculate expected value—the expected return from each possible outcome—by multiplying expected revenues by snowfall probabilities. The result is the average revenue you can expect over time if the given probabilities hold. As Exhibit 4-8 shows, the expected revenue from adding a new ski lift is $687 500. Of course, whether that justifies a decision to build or not depends on the costs involved in generating the revenue, such as the cost to build the lift, the additional annual operating expenses for the lift, the interest rate for borrowing money, and so forth.

PERSONAL INVENTORY ASSESSMENT

UNCERTAINTY What happens if you have a decision where you are not certain about the outcomes and cannot even make reasonable probability estimates? We call such a condition **uncertainty**. Managers do face decision-making situations of uncertainty. Under these conditions, the choice of alternative is influenced by the limited amount of information available to the decision maker and by the psychological orientation of the decision maker. The optimistic manager will follow a *maximax* choice (maximizing the maximum possible payoff) in order to get the largest possible gain. The pessimist will follow a *maximin* choice (maximizing the minimum possible payoff) to make the best of a situation should the worst possible outcome occur. The manager who desires to minimize his or her maximum "regret" will opt for a *minimax* choice, to avoid having big regrets after decisions play out.

Decision-Making Styles

Suppose that you are a new manager at Sony or at the local YMCA. How would you make decisions? Decision-making styles differ along two dimensions.[17] The first dimension is an individual's *way of thinking*. Some of us are more rational and logical in the

EXHIBIT 4-8	Expected Value for Revenues from the Addition of One Ski Lift				
Event	Expected Revenues	×	Probability	=	Expected Value of Each Alternative
Heavy Snowfall	$850 000		0.3		$255 000
Normal Snowfall	725 000		0.5		362 500
Light Snowfall	350 000		0.2		70 000
					$687 500

risk
A condition in which a decision maker is able to estimate the likelihood of certain outcomes.

uncertainty
A condition in which a decision maker is not certain about the outcomes and cannot even make reasonable probability estimates.

way we process information. A rational type processes information in order and makes sure that it is logical and consistent before making a decision. Others tend to be creative and intuitive. An intuitive type does not have to process information in a certain order and is comfortable looking at it as a whole.

The other dimension is an individual's *tolerance for ambiguity*. Some of us have a low tolerance for ambiguity. These types need consistency and order in the way they structure information so that ambiguity is minimized. On the other hand, some of us can tolerate high levels of ambiguity and are able to process many thoughts at the same time. When we diagram these two dimensions, four decision-making styles are evident: directive, analytic, conceptual, and behavioural (see Exhibit 4-9). Let us look more closely at each style.

- *Directive style.* Individuals with a **directive style** have low tolerance for ambiguity and are rational in their way of thinking. They are efficient and logical. Directive types make fast decisions and focus on the short run. Their efficiency and speed in making decisions often result in decisions that are made with minimal information and assessment of few alternatives.
- *Analytic style.* Individuals with an **analytic style** have much greater tolerance for ambiguity than do directive types. They want more information before making a decision and consider more alternatives than directive-style decision makers do. Analytic-style decision makers are characterized as careful decision makers with the ability to adapt to or cope with unique situations.
- *Conceptual style.* Individuals with a **conceptual style** tend to be very broad in their outlook and consider many alternatives. They are intuitive, focus on the long run, and are very good at finding creative solutions to problems. They are also adaptive and flexible.
- *Behavioural style.* Individuals with a **behavioural style** have a low tolerance for ambiguity and an intuitive way of thinking. They are sociable, friendly, and supportive.

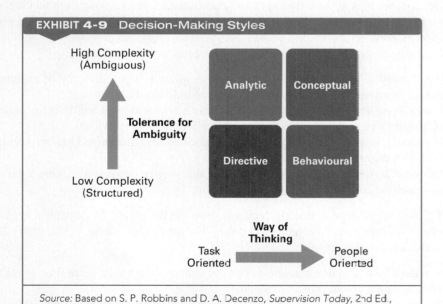

EXHIBIT 4-9 Decision-Making Styles

Source: Based on S. P. Robbins and D. A. Decenzo, *Supervision Today,* 2nd Ed., 1998. Reprinted and electronically reproduced by permission of Pearson Education, Inc., Upper Saddle River, New Jersey.

directive style
A decision-making style characterized by a low tolerance for ambiguity and a rational way of thinking.

conceptual style
A decision-making style characterized by a high tolerance for ambiguity and an intuitive way of thinking.

analytic style
A decision-making style characterized by a high tolerance for ambiguity and a rational way of thinking.

behavioural style
A decision-making style characterized by a low tolerance for ambiguity and an intuitive way of thinking.

They work well with others, are concerned about the achievements of those around them, and are receptive to suggestions from others. They often use meetings to communicate, although they try to avoid conflict. Acceptance by others is important in this decision-making style.

Although these four decision-making styles are distinct, most managers have characteristics of more than one style. It is probably more realistic to think of a manager's dominant style and his or her alternative styles. Although some managers will rely almost exclusively on their dominant style, others are more flexible and can shift their style depending on the situation.

Managers should also recognize that their employees may use different decision-making styles. Some employees may take their time, carefully weighing alternatives and considering riskier options (analytic style), while other employees may be more concerned about getting suggestions from others before making decisions (behavioural style). These differences do not make one approach better than the other. The decision-making styles are just different. For a look at the issues associated with diversity and making decisions, see *Diversity Matters—The Value of Diversity in Decision Making* on page 101 at the end of the chapter.

Group Decision Making

Many organizational decisions are made by groups. It is a rare organization that does not at some time use committees, task forces, review panels, study teams, or similar groups to make decisions. Studies show that managers may spend up to 30 hours a week in group meetings.[18] Undoubtedly, a large portion of that time is spent identifying problems, developing solutions, and determining how to implement the solutions. It is possible, in fact, for groups to be assigned any of the eight steps in the decision-making process. In this section, we look at the advantages and disadvantages of group decision making, discuss when groups would be preferred, and review some techniques for improving group decision making.

What advantages do group decisions have over individual decisions?

Do you think individuals or groups make better decisions?

- *More complete information and knowledge.* A group brings a diversity of experience and perspectives to the decision process that an individual cannot.
- *More diverse alternatives.* Because groups have a greater amount and diversity of information, they can identify more diverse alternatives than an individual.
- *Increased acceptance of a solution.* Group members are reluctant to fight or undermine a decision they have helped develop.
- *Increased legitimacy.* Decisions made by groups may be perceived as more legitimate than decisions made unilaterally by one person.

If groups are so good at making decisions, how did the phrase "A camel is a horse put together by a committee" become so popular? The answer, of course, is that group decisions also have disadvantages:

- *Increased time to reach a solution.* Groups almost always take more time to reach a solution than it would take an individual.
- *Opportunity for minority domination.* The inequality of group members creates the opportunity for one or more members to dominate others. A dominant and vocal minority frequently can have an excessive influence on the final decision.
- *Ambiguous responsibility.* Group members share responsibility, but the responsibility of any single member is diluted.
- *Pressures to conform.* There can be pressures to conform in groups. This pressure undermines critical thinking in the group and eventually harms the quality of the final decision.[19]

GROUPTHINK   The pressure to conform is what social psychologist Irving Janis called the "groupthink" phenomenon. Have you ever been in a situation in which several people were sitting around discussing a particular item and you had something to say that ran contrary to the consensus views of the group, but you remained silent? Were you surprised to learn later that others shared your views and had also remained silent? What you experienced is what Janis termed **groupthink**.[20]

Groupthink applies to a situation in which a group's ability to appraise alternatives objectively and arrive at a quality decision is jeopardized. Because of pressures for conformity, groups often deter individuals from critically appraising unusual, minority, or unpopular views. Consequently, an individual's mental efficiency, reality testing, and moral judgment deteriorate.

How does groupthink occur? The following are examples of situations in which groupthink is evident:

- Group members rationalize any resistance to the assumptions they have made.
- Members apply direct pressure on those who momentarily express doubts about any of the group's shared views or who question the validity of arguments favoured by the majority.
- Those members who have doubts or hold differing points of view seek to avoid going against what appears to be group consensus.
- There is an illusion of unanimity. If someone does not speak, it is assumed that he or she is in full agreement.

Does groupthink really hinder decision making? Yes. Several research studies have found that groupthink symptoms were associated with poorer-quality decision outcomes. But groupthink can be minimized if the group is cohesive, fosters open discussion, and has an impartial leader who seeks input from all members.[22]

This behaviour is a form of conformity in which group members withhold deviant, minority, or unpopular views in order to give the appearance of agreement. As a result, groupthink undermines critical thinking in the group and eventually harms the quality of the final decision.

Individual Versus Group Decision Making

Determining whether a group or an individual will be more effective in making a particular decision depends on the criteria you use to assess effectiveness.[23] Group decisions are preferable when accuracy, creativity, and degree of acceptance are required, while individual decision making offers greater speed and efficiency.

Keep in mind, however, that the effectiveness of group decision making is also influenced by the size of the group. Although a larger group provides greater opportunity for diverse representation, it also requires more coordination and more time for members to contribute their ideas. So groups should not be too large. Evidence indicates, in fact, that groups of five, and to a lesser extent, seven, are the most effective.[24] Having an odd number in the group helps avoid decision deadlocks. These groups are large enough for members to shift roles and withdraw from unfavourable positions, but still small enough for quieter members to participate actively in discussions.

Employee involvement, present in every organization to some extent, leads to higher commitment from the employees for the decisions. A recent study found that employee involvement also increases skill variety and feelings of autonomy, which results in higher job enrichment and motivation.[25] What is the right amount of employee involvement? Exhibit 4-10 looks at the situational factors that have an impact on the effectiveness of employee involvement outcomes.[26] The four contingencies are:

- *Decision structure.* Programmed decisions require less employee involvement.
- *Source of decision knowledge.* Employees may have more relevant and timely information than managers, increasing the need for involvement.

In 2003, Richard Branson, founder of the Virgin Group of companies, wanted to compete with Apple's entry in the MP3 music player industry—the iPod. Virgin's management team was strongly opposed to Virgin producing its own MP3 player. Branson insisted they launch the Virgin Pulse, at a design cost of $20 million. However, it bombed and they had to write off the investment. Had Branson listened more to his management employees, the huge investment failure could have been avoided.[21]

groupthink
The withholding by group members of different views in order to appear to be in agreement.

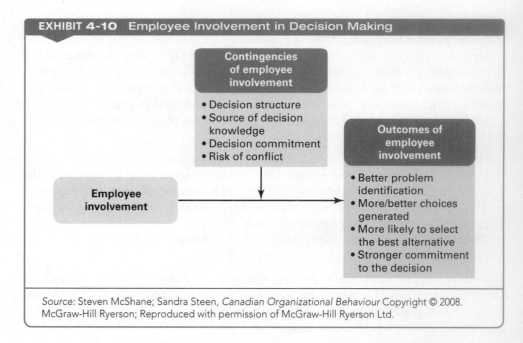

EXHIBIT 4-10 Employee Involvement in Decision Making

Contingencies of employee involvement

- Decision structure
- Source of decision knowledge
- Decision commitment
- Risk of conflict

Employee involvement

Outcomes of employee involvement

- Better problem identification
- More/better choices generated
- More likely to select the best alternative
- Stronger commitment to the decision

Source: Steven McShane; Sandra Steen, *Canadian Organizational Behaviour* Copyright © 2008. McGraw-Hill Ryerson; Reproduced with permission of McGraw-Hill Ryerson Ltd.

- *Decision commitment.* If participants might be against a decision without their input, then involvement is more necessary.
- *Risk of conflict.* If there are conflicting employee and organizational goals, involvement is useful in minimizing conflict.

Decision-Making Biases and Errors

When managers make decisions, not only do they use their own particular style, but many use "rules of thumb," or **heuristics**, to simplify their decision making. Rules of thumb can be useful to decision makers because they help make sense of complex, uncertain, and ambiguous information.[27] Even though managers may use rules of thumb, that does not mean those rules are reliable. Why? Because they may lead to errors and biases in processing and evaluating information. Exhibit 4-11 identifies seven common decision-making biases and errors. Let us take a quick look at each of them.[28]

- *Overconfidence bias.* Decision makers tend to think they know more than they do or hold unrealistically positive views of themselves and their performance. For

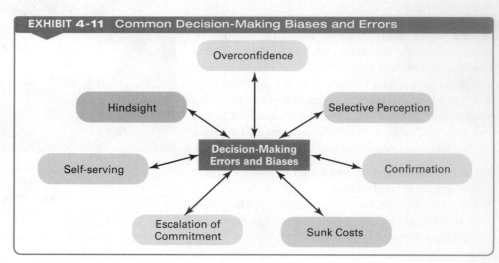

EXHIBIT 4-11 Common Decision-Making Biases and Errors

- Overconfidence
- Hindsight
- Selective Perception
- Self-serving
- **Decision-Making Errors and Biases**
- Confirmation
- Escalation of Commitment
- Sunk Costs

heuristics
Rules of thumb that managers use to simplify decision making.

example, a sales manager brags that his presentation was so good that there is no doubt the sale will be his. Later he learns that he lost the sale because the client found him obnoxious.

- *Sunk-costs error.* Decision makers forget that current choices cannot correct the past. They incorrectly fixate on past expenditures of time, money, or effort in assessing choices rather than on future consequences. For example, Hakan has spent thousands of dollars and several months introducing new procedures for handling customer complaints. Both customers and employees are complaining about the new procedures. Hakan does not want to consider the possibility that the procedures are needlessly complicated because of the investment in time and money he has already made.

Rob Byron/Fotolia

- *Selective perception bias.* Decision makers selectively organize and interpret events based on their biased perceptions. This bias influences the information they pay attention to, the problems they identify, and the alternatives they develop. For example, before John meets with two job candidates, he learns that one went to his alma mater. He does not seriously consider the other job candidate because he believes that graduating from the same university as he did makes the first candidate superior.

- *Confirmation bias.* Decision makers seek out information that reaffirms their past choices and discount information that contradicts past judgments. These people tend to accept at face value information that confirms their preconceived views and are critical and skeptical of information that challenges these views. For example, Pierre continues to give business to the same supplier, even though the supplier has been late on several deliveries. Pierre thinks the supplier is a nice person, and the supplier keeps promising to deliver on time.

- *Escalation-of-commitment error.* Decisions can also be influenced by a phenomenon called **escalation of commitment**, which is an increased commitment to a previous decision despite evidence that it might have been wrong.[29] For example, studies of the events leading up to the space shuttle *Columbia* disaster in 2003 point to an escalation of commitment by decision makers to ignore the possible damage that foam striking the shuttle at takeoff might have had, even though the decision was questioned by some individuals. Why would decision makers want to escalate commitment to a bad decision? Because they don't want to admit that their initial decision might have been flawed. Rather than search for new alternatives, they simply increase their commitment to the original solution.

7 percentage points higher financial results is what organizers gained from reducing bias in their decision-making processes.

20+ options and people's decision making is more likely to be paralyzed or frustrated.

84% of companies use teams to solve special projects.[31]

40% more ideas are generated with electronic brainstorming than with individuals brainstorming alone.

- *Self-serving bias.* Decision makers take credit for their successes and blame failure on outside factors. For example, Jesse dismisses his team's efforts when he wins a contract, although he blames them for the small error that was in the final report.

- *Hindsight bias.* Decision makers falsely believe that they would have accurately predicted the outcome of an event once that outcome is actually known. For example, after a client cancelled a contract that had been drawn up, Cindy tells her manager she knew ahead of time that was going to happen, even though she'd had no such thoughts before the contract was cancelled. After the fact, some outcomes seem more obvious than they did beforehand.

59% of employees say a key obstacle to their job is more attention is paid to placing blame than to solving problems.

77% of managers said the number of decisions they make during a typical workday has increased.

How can managers avoid the negative effects of these decision errors and biases? The main strategy is to be aware of them and then try not to exhibit them. Beyond that, managers should also pay attention to "how" they make decisions: They should try to identify the heuristics they typically use and critically evaluate how appropriate those are. Finally, managers might want to ask people around them to help identify weaknesses in their decision-making style and try to improve.

43% of managers said the amount of time given to each decision has decreased.

escalation of commitment
An increased commitment to a previous decision despite evidence that the decision might have been wrong.

4.3 **Describe** How do ethics and social responsibility relate to decision making?

ETHICS, CORPORATE SOCIAL RESPONSIBILITY, AND DECISION MAKING

When you see top managers such as those formerly at Merrill-Lynch, AIG, and some of the other major financial institutions acting with greed and using financial manipulations, lying, and group pressure to deceive others, you might conclude that corporations have no ethics. Although that is by no means true, what *is* true is that managers—at all levels, in all areas, and in all kinds of organizations—will face ethical issues and dilemmas. As managers plan, organize, lead, and control, they must consider ethical dimensions.

What do we mean by ethics? The term **ethics** refers to rules and principles that define right and wrong behaviour.[32] Unfortunately, the ethics of a situation are not always black and white. For some decisions, you can make choices exercising complete freedom of choice, with no regard for others. For other decisions, your behaviour will be guided by a set of laws. In between are situations where you might want to consider the impact of your decision on others, even though there are no laws regarding your behaviour. This middle zone is the grey area of behaviour. Laws often develop because people did not act responsibly when they had a choice. For example, not too long ago drinking and driving did not have the penalties that are in place now. Many people have talked about laws banning cellphones in various situations for much the same reason: Individuals may not think about the impact of cellphone use on others.

In this section, we examine the ethical dimensions of managerial decisions. Many decisions that managers make require them to consider who may be affected—in terms of the result as well as the process.[33] To better understand the complicated issues involved in managerial ethics, we will look at four different views of ethics and the factors that influence a person's ethics, and offer some suggestions for what organizations can do to improve the ethical behaviour of employees.

Four Views of Ethics

There are four views of ethics: the utilitarian view, the rights view, the theory of justice view, and the integrative social contracts theory.[34]

The **utilitarian view of ethics** maintains that ethical decisions are made solely on the basis of their outcomes or consequences. Utilitarian theory uses a quantitative method for making ethical decisions by looking at how to provide the greatest good for the greatest number. Following the utilitarian view, a manager might conclude that laying off 20 percent of the workforce in the plant is justified because it will increase the plant's profitability, improve job security for the remaining 80 percent, and be in the best interest of shareholders. Utilitarianism encourages efficiency and productivity and is consistent with the goal of profit maximization. However, it can result in biased allocations of resources, especially when some of those affected by the decision lack representation or a voice in the decision. Utilitarianism can also result in the rights of some stakeholders being ignored.

The **rights view of ethics** is concerned with respecting and protecting individual liberties and privileges such as the rights to privacy, freedom of conscience, free speech, life and safety, and due process. This view would include, for example, protecting the free speech rights of employees who report legal violations by their employers. The positive side of the rights perspective is that it protects individuals' basic rights. The drawback, however, is that it can hinder productivity and efficiency by creating a work climate more concerned with protecting individuals' rights than with getting the job done. For example, an individual's right to privacy might make it difficult to make special arrangements for an employee whose illness is preventing her or him from carrying out job responsibilities.

---

ethics
Rules and principles that define right and wrong behaviour.

utilitarian view of ethics
A view of ethics maintaining that ethical decisions are made solely on the basis of their outcomes or consequences.

rights view of ethics
A view of ethics concerned with respecting and protecting individual liberties and privileges.

According to the **theory of justice view of ethics**, managers impose and enforce rules fairly and impartially, and do so by following all legal rules and regulations. A manager following this view would decide to provide the same rate of pay to individuals who are similar in their levels of skills, performance, or responsibility, and not base that decision on arbitrary differences such as gender, personality, race, or personal favourites. Using standards of justice also has pluses and minuses. It protects the interests of those stakeholders who may be underrepresented or lack power, but it can encourage a sense of entitlement that might make employees reduce risk-taking, innovation, and productivity.

The **integrative social contracts theory** proposes that ethical decisions be based on existing ethical norms in industries and communities in order to determine what constitutes right and wrong. This view of ethics is based on the integration of two "contracts": the general social contract that allows businesses to operate and defines the acceptable ground rules, and a more specific contract among members of a community that addresses acceptable ways of behaving. In deciding what wage to pay employees in a new factory in Ciudad Juarez, Mexico, Canadian managers following the integrative social contracts theory would base the decision on existing wage levels in the community, rather than paying what Canadians might consider a "fair wage" in that context. Although this theory focuses on looking at existing practices, the problem is that some of these practices may be unethical.[35]

Which approach to ethics do most businesspeople follow? Not surprisingly, most follow the utilitarian approach. Why? It's consistent with such business goals as efficiency, productivity, and profits. However, that perspective needs to change because of the changing world facing managers. Trends toward individual rights, social justice, and community standards mean that managers need ethical standards based on nonutilitarian criteria. This new demand is an obvious challenge for managers, because making decisions based on such criteria involves far more ambiguities than using utilitarian criteria such as efficiency and profits. The result, of course, is that managers increasingly find themselves struggling with the question of the right thing to do.

Improving Ethical Behaviour

Managers can do a number of things if they are serious about reducing unethical behaviour in their organizations. They can seek to hire individuals with high ethical standards, establish codes of ethics and decision rules, lead by example, delineate job goals and performance appraisal mechanisms, provide ethics training, conduct independent social audits, and provide support to individuals facing ethical dilemmas. Taken individually, these actions will probably not have much impact. But when all or most of them are implemented as part of a comprehensive ethics program, they have the potential to significantly improve an organization's ethical climate. The key term here, however, is *potential*. There are no guarantees that a well-designed ethics program will lead to the desired outcome.

The complexity of ethical dilemmas requires organizations to balance transparency with confidentiality. A focus on ethics is a constant part of day to day actions and not just something to consider when facing a crisis. As an employee you can learn to recognize ethical warning flags associated with comments such as "no one will ever know", "well maybe just this once", or "everyone does it".

Ethical decision making is based on the same principles as discussed earlier in the chapter. Start by getting the facts and identifying whether the problem is an ethical one. Are there societal or organizational rules or values that apply? Identify alternative solutions from multiple stakeholder perspectives and implement the decision that is not only the "best" but also the "most ethical". Some firms implement codes of ethics to help encourage regular discussion of ethical issues both within organizations and across the industry.

---

theory of justice view of ethics
A view of ethics in which managers impose and enforce rules fairly and impartially, and do so by following all legal rules and regulations.

integrative social contracts theory
A view of ethics proposing that ethical decisions be based on existing ethical norms in industries and communities in order to determine what constitutes right and wrong.

CODES OF ETHICS AND DECISION RULES   Toronto-based Royal Bank of Canada has had a corporate code of conduct for more than 25 years. Christina Donely, the bank's senior adviser on employee relations and policy governance, says that the code "focuses on outlining behaviours that support honesty and integrity . . . and covers environmental [and] social issues."[36] However, that is not the way it is in all organizations. The US government passed the *Sarbanes–Oxley Act* in 2002 to crack down on business wrongdoing in publicly traded companies. Following the American example, the Canadian Securities Administrators put best corporate governance practices into effect in March 2004, although these are not as tough as the American rules.[37] As well, the securities regulators in all ten provinces and three territories have proposed that all public companies adopt written codes of ethics and conduct, or explain why they do not have them.[38] But these proposals carry no enforcement requirements or mechanisms.

Ambiguity about what is and is not ethical can be a problem for employees. A **code of ethics**—a formal statement of an organization's primary values and the ethical rules it expects its employees to follow—is a popular choice for reducing that ambiguity. About 60 percent of Canada's 650 largest corporations have some sort of ethics code.[39] Codes of ethics are also becoming more popular globally. A survey of business organizations in 80 countries found that 80 percent have formally stated ethics standards and codes of ethics.[40]

What should a code of ethics look like? It has been suggested that codes should be specific enough to show employees the spirit in which they are supposed to do things yet loose enough to allow for freedom of judgment.[41] A survey of companies' codes of ethics found their content tended to fall into three categories: (1) be a dependable organizational citizen; (2) don't do anything unlawful or improper that will harm the organization; and (3) be good to customers.[42]

How well do codes of ethics work? In reality, they are not always effective in encouraging ethical behaviour in organizations. While no comparable Canadian data are available, a survey of employees in US businesses with ethics codes found that 75 percent of those surveyed had observed ethical or legal violations in the previous 12 months, including such things as deceptive sales practices, unsafe working conditions, sexual harassment, conflicts of interest, and environmental violations.[43] Companies with codes of ethics may not do enough monitoring. For example, David Nitkin, president of Toronto-based EthicScan Canada, an ethics consultancy, notes that "only about 15 percent of [larger Canadian corporations with codes of ethics] have designated an ethics officer or ombudsman" or provide an ethics hotline, and less than 10 percent offer whistle-blower protection.[44] Vancouver public employees were concerned enough about whistle-blower protection that the issue was one of the major stumbling blocks in reaching an agreement for a new collective agreement in summer 2007, leading to a 12-week strike.

Does this mean that codes of ethics should not be developed? No. But there are some suggestions managers can follow. First, an organization's code of ethics should be developed and then communicated clearly to employees. Second, all levels of management should continually reaffirm the importance of the ethics code and the organization's commitment to it, and consistently discipline those who break it. When managers consider the code of ethics important, regularly affirm its content, and publicly reprimand rule breakers, ethics codes can supply a strong foundation for an effective corporate ethics

Aleksandar Mijatovic/Fotolia

One of Canada's infamous cases of political corruption occurred under Jean Chrétien's leadership, when three contracts worth $1.6 million were awarded to Montreal-based Groupaction Marketing Inc. to write three reports on ways to improve the federal government's profile in Quebec. An audit was called for after it was discovered that two of the three reports were virtually identical, even containing the same spelling errors. The third report was never found.

code of ethics
A formal statement of an organization's primary values and the ethical rules it expects its employees to follow.

EXHIBIT 4-12 10 Questions for Examining the Ethics of a Business Decision

1. Have you defined the problem or issue correctly?

2. How much harm or benefit will occur to others as a result of this action?

3. Will your decision be valid in a month or year from now?

4. Would you view the situation differently from another party's perspective?

5. How does this activity fit with your own beliefs, values and conscience?

6. How long after the action will the consequences occur and what is the likelihood of the consequences being bad?

7. How did this situation occur in the first place?

8. Can you discuss the problem with the affected parties before you make the decision?

9. How many people are affected by this action?

10. How would you feel if your actions were published in the newspaper for your mother to read?

Source: Based on Ethics Without the Sermon" by Laura L. Nash. Harvard Business Review, Nov. 1981. Harvard Business Publishing.

---

program.[45] Finally, an organization's code of ethics might be designed around the 12 questions listed in Exhibit 4-12, which can be used as decision rules to guide managers when they handle ethical dilemmas in decision making.[46]

Corporate Social Responsibility

We define **corporate social responsibility** as a business's obligation, beyond that required by law and economics, to do the right things and act in ways that are good for society.[47] Note that this definition assumes that a business obeys laws and pursues economic interests. But also note that this definition views business as a moral agent—that is, in its effort to do good for society, a business must differentiate between right and wrong. A great deal of attention has been focused on the extent to which organizations and management should act in socially responsible ways. On one side, there is the classical—or purely economic—view, and on the other side is the socioeconomic view.

THE CLASSICAL VIEW The **classical view** holds that management's only social responsibility is to maximize profits. The most outspoken advocate of this approach is the late economist and Nobel laureate Milton Friedman.[48] He argues that managers' primary responsibility is to operate the business in the best interests of the shareholders (the owners of a corporation). What are those interests? Friedman contends that shareholders have a single concern: financial return. He also argues that any time managers decide to spend the organization's resources for "social good," they are adding to the costs of doing business. These costs have to be passed on to consumers either through higher prices or absorbed by shareholders through a smaller profit returned as dividends. We must be clear that Friedman is not saying that organizations should *not* be socially responsible; he thinks they should. But the extent of that responsibility is to maximize organizational profits for shareholders.

Joel Bakan, professor of law at the University of British Columbia, author of *The Corporation,* and co-director of the documentary of the same name, is more critical of organizations than Friedman, although he finds that current laws support corporate behaviour

---

corporate social responsibility
A business's obligation, beyond that required by law and economics, to do the right things and act in ways that are good for society.

classical view
The view that management's only social responsibility is to maximize profits.

some might find troubling. Bakan suggests that today's corporations have many of the same characteristics as a psychopathic personality (that is, self-interested, lacking empathy, manipulative, and reckless in one's disregard of others). Bakan notes that even though companies have a tendency to act psychopathically, this behaviour is not why they are fixated on profits. Rather, though they may have social responsibilities, the only *legal* responsibility corporations have is to maximize organizational profits for shareholders.[49] He suggests that more laws and more restraints need to be put in place if corporations are to behave more socially responsibly, because current laws direct corporations to be responsible to their shareholders and make little mention of responsibility toward other stakeholders.

THE SOCIOECONOMIC VIEW   The **socioeconomic view** maintains that management's social responsibility goes beyond making profits to include protecting and improving society's welfare. This position is based on the belief that corporations are *not* independent entities responsible only to shareholders. They also have a responsibility to the larger society that endorses their creation through various laws and regulations and that supports them by purchasing their products and services. In addition, proponents of this view believe that business organizations are not mere economic institutions. Society expects and even encourages businesses to become involved in social, political, and legal issues. Proponents of the socioeconomic view would say that Avon Products was being socially responsible when it initiated its Breast Cancer Crusade to provide women with breast cancer education and early detection screening services, which, after 14 years, has raised more than $815 million worldwide.[50]

Educational programs implemented by Brazilian cosmetics manufacturer Natura Cosméticos SA in public primary schools in São Paulo to improve children's literacy and decision-making skills are also viewed as socially responsible.[51] Why? Through these programs, the managers are protecting and improving society's welfare. More and more organizations around the world are taking their social responsibilities seriously, especially in Europe, where the view that businesses need to focus on more than just profits has a stronger tradition than in North America.[52] Some even try to measure their "triple bottom line," which takes into account not only financial responsibilities but social and environmental ones as well.[53] Examples of triple bottom line (3BL) issues are presented at the end of each chapter throughout the text.

COMPARING THE TWO VIEWS   The key differences between the two views of corporate social responsibility are easier to understand if we think in terms of the people to whom organizations are responsible. Classicists would say that shareholders, or owners, are the only legitimate concern. Those supporting the socioeconomic view would respond that managers should be responsible to any group affected by the organization's decisions and actions—that is, the stakeholders (such as employees and community members).[54] Exhibit 4-13 shows four different approaches an organization can take toward corporate social responsibility.[55] The defensive approach is consistent with the classical view, while the accommodative and proactive approaches are consistent with the socioeconomic view.

A proactive approach requires strong leadership to guide employees to become socially responsible.

CORPORATE SOCIAL RESPONSIBILITY AND ECONOMIC PERFORMANCE   How do socially responsible activities affect a company's economic performance? Findings from a number of research studies can help us answer this question.[56] The majority of these studies show a

---

socioeconomic view
The view that management's social responsibility goes beyond making profits to include protecting and improving society's welfare.

EXHIBIT 4-13 Approaches to Corporate Social Responsibility

Obstructionist Approach	**Defensive Approach**	**Accommodative Approach**	**Proactive Approach**
Disregard for social responsibility	Minimal commitment to social responsibility	Moderate commitment to social responsibility	Strong commitment to social responsibility

← No Social Responsibility ————————————————— High Social Responsibility →

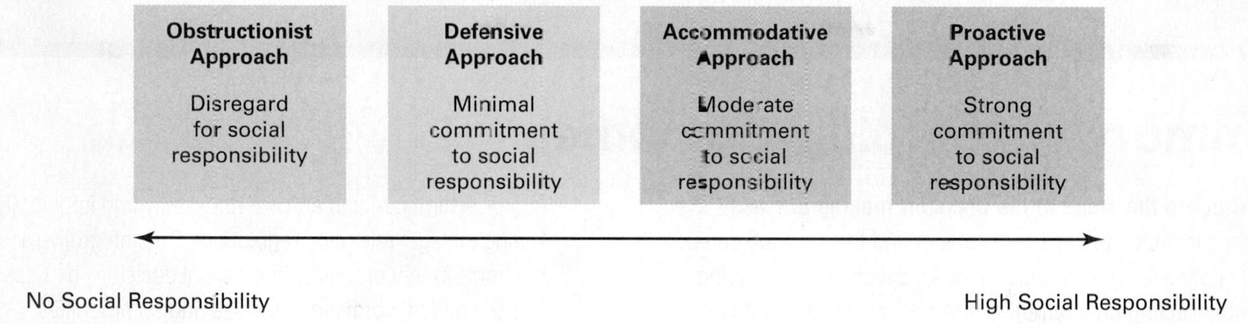

positive relationship between social involvement and economic performance. One study found that firms' corporate social performance was positively associated with both *prior* and *future* financial performance.[57] But we should be cautious about making any compelling assumptions from these findings because of methodological questions associated with trying to measure "corporate social responsibility" and "economic performance."[58] Most of these studies determined a company's social performance by analyzing the content of annual reports, citations of social actions in news articles on the company, or "reputation" indexes based on public perception. Such criteria certainly have drawbacks as reliable measures of corporate social responsibility.

We can also look at what consumers say about corporate social responsibility. A recent survey conducted by GlobeScan, which specializes in corporate issues, found that "83 percent of Canadians believe that corporations should go beyond their traditional economic role; 51 percent say they have punished a socially irresponsible company in the past year."[59] As for naming a socially responsible company, 43 percent of Canadians said they could not do so.

What conclusion can we draw from all of this? Corporate social responsibility is generally good for the bottom line. It matters to consumers, and there is little evidence to say that a company's social actions hurt its long-term economic performance. Given political and societal pressures on business to be socially involved, managers would be wise to take social goals into consideration as they plan, organize, lead, and control.

Summary of Learning Outcomes

4.1 **What are the steps in the decision-making process?** The steps include identifying a problem and the decision criteria; allocating weights to those criteria; developing, analyzing, and selecting an alternative that can resolve the problem; implementing the alternative; and evaluating the decision's effectiveness.

Lucie Shaw realized there was a strong market for providing health care to seniors and recognized that a Nurse Next Door franchise was a good way to exploit that opportunity and quench her thirst for entrepreneurship. However, Shaw had a well-paying operations manager job at Air Canada, and starting a franchise was risky. Which was the best alternative?

4.2 **What factors affect how decisions are made?** It is often assumed that managers make decisions that follow the steps of the rational decision-making process. However, not all decisions follow that process for a variety of reasons. Often managers work with bounded rationality, because they are not able to collect and process all the information on all possible alternatives. Or they might make a satisficing decision—one that is "good enough" rather than the "best." Managers sometimes use intuition to enhance their decision-making process. Managers also need to decide whether they should make decisions themselves or encourage a team to help make the decision. Teams can make better decisions in many cases, but the time to make the decision generally increases. Managers are affected by a variety of biases and errors: overconfidence bias, selective perception bias, confirmation bias, sunk-costs error, escalation-of-commitment error, self-serving bias, and hindsight bias.

Lucie Shaw was aware of a variety of positives and negatives in the decision to start her own Nurse Next Door franchise. It was important for her to recognize that her preference for work that inspired her passion and the desire to see her in-laws and other seniors taken care of might affect how she made her decision.

4.3 **How do ethics and social responsibility relate to decision making?** Ethics refers to rules and principles that define right and wrong conduct. There are four views of ethics: the utilitarian view, the rights view, the theory of justice view, and the integrative social contracts theory. The utilitarian view of ethics maintains that ethical decisions are made solely on the basis of their outcomes or consequences. The rights view of ethics is concerned with respecting and protecting individual liberties and privileges. According to the theory of justice view of ethics,

managers impose and enforce rules fairly and impartially, following all legal rules and regulations. The integrative social contracts theory proposes that ethical decisions be based on existing ethical norms in industries and communities.

To improve ethical behaviour, managers can hire individuals with high ethical standards, design and implement a code of ethics, lead by example, undertake performance appraisals, provide ethics training, conduct independent social audits, and provide formal protective mechanisms for employees who face ethical dilemmas.

Beyond ethics, managers are increasingly asked to be more socially responsible in the decisions they make. In doing so, some organizations are likely to simply give lip service to social responsibility, while others are much more committed to actually being socially responsible.

SNAPSHOT SUMMARY

4.1 **The Decision-Making Process**
Step 1: Identify a Problem
Step 2: Identify Decision Criteria
Step 3: Allocate Weights to Criteria
Step 4: Develop Alternatives
Step 5: Analyze Alternatives
Step 6: Select an Alternative
Step 7: Implement the Alternative
Step 8: Evaluate Decision Effectiveness

4.2 **What Are the Three Approaches Managers Use to Make Decisions?**
Types of Problems and Decisions
Decision-Making Conditions
Decision-Making Styles
Group Decision Making
Individual Versus Group Decision Making
Decision-Making Biases and Errors

4.3 **Ethics, Corporate Social Responsibility, and Decision Making**
Four Views of Ethics
Improving Ethical Behaviour
Corporate Social Responsibility

MyManagementLab Study, practise, and explore real management situations with these helpful resources:

- **Interactive Lesson Presentations:** Work through interactive presentations and assessments to test your knowledge of management concepts.
- **PIA (Personal Inventory Assessments):** Enhance your ability to connect with key concepts through these engaging self-reflection assessments.
- **Study Plan:** Check your understanding of chapter concepts with self-study quizzes.
- **Simulations:** Practise decision making in simulated management environments.

Discussion Questions

1. Describe a decision you have made that closely aligns with the assumptions of perfect rationality. Compare this with the process you used to select your major. Did you depart from the rational model in your choice of major? Explain.

2. Is the order in which alternatives are considered more critical under assumptions of perfect rationality or bounded rationality? Why?

3. Explain how a manager might deal with making decisions under conditions of uncertainty.

4. Give an example drawn from your personal decision making that illustrates satisficing. What steps would be necessary to make a better decision in that situation?

5. How does escalation of commitment affect decision making? Have you had an example of this in your decision making?

6. Discuss the role that stakeholders play in the four approaches to corporate social responsibility.

Developing Management Skills

Dilemma

Suppose you are sitting at your desk examining a request a customer has just emailed to you. The customer is proposing a project that would be very lucrative for your company but has an extremely demanding time schedule over the next two weeks. Yesterday, one of your long-time employees gave two weeks' notice of his desire to leave the company and spend more time with his ailing mother.

Your employee is well qualified to meet the requirements of the request but it would force his last two weeks to be tremendously busy. How would you decide whether you should take the customer up on her request?

Becoming a Manager

- Pay close attention to decisions you make and how you make them.
- When you feel you have not made a good decision, assess how you could have made a better one. Which step of the decision-making process could you have improved?
- Work at developing good decision-making skills.
- Read books about decision making.
- Ask people you admire for advice on how they make good decisions.

Be the Consultant: Solving Problems Creatively

Creativity is a frame of mind. You need to expand your mind's capabilities—that is, open up your mind to new ideas. Every individual has the ability to improve his or her creativity, but many people simply don't try to develop that ability. In a global business environment, where changes are fast and furious, organizations desperately need creative people. The uniqueness and variety of problems that managers face demand that they be able to solve problems creatively.

STEPS IN DEVELOPING THE SKILL

You can be more effective at solving problems creatively if you use the following 10 suggestions:[60]

1. **Think of yourself as creative.** Although this may be a simple suggestion, research shows that if you think you cannot be creative, you won't be. Believing in your ability to be creative is the first step in becoming more creative.

2. **Pay attention to your intuition.** Every individual has a subconscious mind that works well. Sometimes answers will come to you when you least expect them. Listen to that "inner voice." In fact, most creative people keep

notepads near their beds and write down ideas when the thoughts come to them. That way they don't forget them.

3. **Move away from your comfort zone.** Every individual has a comfort zone in which certainty exists. But creativity and the known often do not mix. To be creative, you need to move away from the status quo and focus your mind on something new.

4. **Determine what you want to do.** Make sure you include taking time to understand a problem before attempting to try to resolve it, getting all the facts in mind, and trying to identify the most important ones.

5. **Look for ways to tackle the problem.** This process can be accomplished by setting aside a block of time to focus on it; working out a plan for attacking it; establishing subgoals; imagining or actually using analogies wherever possible (e.g., could you approach your problem like a fish out of water and look at what the fish does to cope? Or can you use the things you have to do to find your way when it's foggy to help you solve your problem?); using different problem-solving strategies such as verbal, visual, mathematical, theatrical (e.g., you might draw a diagram of the decision or problem to help you visualize it better or you might talk to yourself out loud about the problem, telling it as you would tell a story to someone); trusting your intuition; and playing with possible ideas and approaches (e.g., look at your problem from a different perspective or ask yourself what someone else, such as your grandmother, might do if faced with the same situation).

6. **Look for ways to do things better.** Find new approaches by trying consciously to be original, not worrying about looking foolish, eliminating cultural taboos (such as gender stereotypes) that might influence your possible solutions, keeping an open mind, being alert to odd or puzzling facts, thinking of unconventional ways to use objects and the environment (e.g., thinking about how you could use newspaper or magazine headlines to help you be a better problem solver), discarding usual or habitual ways of doing things, and striving for objectivity by being as critical of your own ideas as you would be of those coming from someone else.

7. **Find several right answers.** Being creative means continuing to look for other solutions even when you think you have solved the problem. A better, more creative solution might be just around the corner.

8. **Believe in finding a workable solution.** Like believing in yourself, you also need to believe in your ideas. If you don't think you can find a solution, you probably won't.

9. **Brainstorm with others.** Creativity is not an isolated activity. Bouncing ideas off others creates synergy.

10. **Turn creative ideas into action.** Coming up with creative ideas is only part of the process. Once the ideas are generated, they must be implemented. Keeping great ideas in your mind, or on papers that no one will read, does little to expand your creative abilities.

PRACTISING THE SKILL
How many words can you make using the letters in the word *brainstorm*? (There are at least 95.)

Hey, You're the Boss Now! Tips for Managing a Diverse Workforce

As millennials take on increasing responsibilities at work among a diverse population, managing and leading employees of different ages, genders, races, and religions becomes the reality. By utilizing the right combination of tact, consideration, and strategy, you can successfully navigate the potential career minefield. Use the following tips to deal with your older and more experienced employees:

1. **Be confident.** You are in the position for a reason, so have conviction in what you know and do not second guess yourself. People tend to believe you when you sound like you know what you are talking about!

2. **Ask for input, not guidance.** Your employees' life or cultural experiences may give you added perspective, and learning from them makes you a stronger manager. Solicit feedback regularly. When you are open to feedback, you will get it.

3. **Be open-minded.** Avoid making assumptions, and try to understand your employees' challenges. Older workers are more accustomed to face-time than using technology. They are familiar with meeting regularly to discuss goals and projects, and they may have different perspectives on loyalty and work-life balance. Men may be more interested in conveying facts, while women may pay attention to emotions.

4. **You do not have to "be the boss."** Give your employees time to get used to you instead of appearing to be the heavy. Your lack of experience can be complemented by their individual skills.

5. **Communicate.** Constantly keep your employees informed. Understand that communication styles may be different. An older employee might prefer a two-minute conversation instead of, "Shoot me an email," while other cultures have different communication needs.

6. **Show respect and motivate your team.** Treat older employees like everyone else on your team, but recognize that they may have different hot buttons. Educate the team on respecting individual differences, whether based on age, gender, religion, or culture.

7. **Start a mentorship program.** A diverse workforce has so much knowledge to pass on. Validate your employees' experience by demonstrating that their opinion and experience count.

8. **Train them.** There may be things your older employees need to learn. Remember that they can learn from you, too.

Diversity Matters: The Value of Diversity in Decision Making

Have you decided what your major is going to be? How did you decide? Do you feel your decision is a good one? Is there anything you could have done differently to make sure that your decision was the best one?[61]

Making good decisions is tough! Managers are continuously making decisions—for example, developing new products, establishing weekly or monthly goals, implementing advertising campaigns, reassigning employees to different work groups, resolving customers' complaints, or purchasing new tablets for sales representatives. One important suggestion for making better decisions is to tap into the diversity of the work group. Drawing upon the ideas of diverse employees can prove valuable to a manager's decision making. Why? Diverse employees can provide fresh perspectives on issues. They can offer differing interpretations on how a problem is defined and may be more open to trying new ways of doing things. Diverse employees usually are more creative in generating alternatives and more flexible in resolving issues. Getting input from diverse sources increases the likelihood of finding creative and unique solutions.

Even though diversity in decision making can be valuable, it has drawbacks. The lack of a common perspective usually means that more time is spent discussing the issues. Communication may be a problem, particularly if language barriers are present. Seeking out diverse opinions can make the decision-making process more complex, confusing, and ambiguous. With multiple perspectives on the decision, it may also be difficult to reach a single agreement or to agree on specific actions. Although these drawbacks are valid concerns, the value of diversity in decision making outweighs the potential disadvantages.

When you have worked in teams, what advantages and disadvantages arose because of the diversity (or lack of diversity) in the group? What measures could be taken to make sure that diversity is an asset for a team, rather than something that causes problems?

Your Essential Management Reading List

Learning from key management experts can help you understand today's management theory and practice. What follows is a list of some of the more influential management books:

- *Creativity, Inc.: Understanding the Unseen Forces That Stand in the Way of True Inspiration*—Ed Catmull and Amy Wallace
- *The Art of Choosing*—Sheena Iyengar
- *Behind Every Good Decision: How Anyone Can Use Business Analytics to Turn Data into Profitable Insight*—Piyanka Jain and Puneet Sharma
- *Thinking Fast and Slow*—Daniel Kahneman

Team Exercises

3BL: The Triple Bottom Line

A Canadian clothing company was losing market share to some of its US competitors and began to outsource manufacturing of most of its products to Sri Lanka. This practice resulted in a negligible increase in product defects, but the cost savings were driving increased profitability by upward of 15 percent per month. Management was thrilled, and the company shareholders were buoyed by the results.

An investigative journalism report uncovered some illegal practices at the Sri Lankan factory. Toxic effluent was being disposed of without proper handling and safeguard protections, and much of the waste was being dumped in back alleys and open spaces. Wages were paid on productivity targets, and basic pay was cut if management targets were not achieved. Intimidation and abuse were common when workers failed to reach production targets—in one example, 50 workers were locked in an unventilated room without access to toilet facilities, water, and food for over four hours as a punishment.

The report found that excessive overtime was an accepted practice, and workers were forced to work up to 130 hours per month in overtime, with a quarter of the employees not receiving any additional pay for their overtime. Three-quarters of the workers at this factory in Sri Lanka were young women from rural areas. They were told when recruited that the factories prefer them not to marry and were given pregnancy tests to weed out pregnant women. Sexual intimidation and abuse were common.

A decision that was having a positive impact on profit was turning out to be negative for people and the planet. What could the company do to deal with this situation?

THINKING STRATEGICALLY ABOUT 3BL

There are eight steps that can be used to help navigate confusing ethical issues such as the Sri Lankan factory problems.

1. Recognize the ethical issue.	Although labour practices may be more lax in Sri Lanka, the treatment of the workers is an ethical dilemma.
2. Who will be affected?	Company employees and shareholders might be concerned, but the buck stops with the management team of the Canadian company.
3. Get the facts.	The investigative report may have its own agenda. Get information from workers at the factory as well as the company running it on behalf of the Canadian company.
4. Is it a case of right versus wrong?	Could you defend your choice to the broader public? To your friends and family?
5. Is it a choice between two "goods" or between two "bads"?	Are there core values that are pitted against each other? Is it business needs (like staying in business) versus the needs of the broader community? Is it a truth versus loyalty situation (that exists for whistle-blowers)?
6. Apply ethical standards and principles to evaluate alternative courses of action.	Which option will produce the most good and do the least harm? Which option best serves the community as a whole?
7. Make a decision.	You can bury yourself in facts and opinions, but at some point you just have to make the ethical decision.
8. Act and reflect on the outcome.	How can you apply this learning to future decisions? What ethical dilemmas can we anticipate?

Individual Versus Group Decisions

Objective: To contrast individual and group decision making.

Time: 15 minutes.

Step 1: You have five minutes to read the following story and individually respond to each of the 11 statements as either true, false, or unknown.

THE STORY

A salesclerk had just turned off the lights in the store when a man appeared and demanded money. The owner opened a cash register. The contents of the cash register were scooped up, and the man sped away. A member of the police force was notified promptly.

STATEMENTS ABOUT THE STORY

1. A man appeared after the owner had turned off his store lights. True, false, or unknown?
2. The robber was a man. True, false, or unknown?
3. The man did not demand money. True, false, or unknown?
4. The man who opened the cash register was the owner. True, false, or unknown?
5. The store owner scooped up the contents of the cash register and ran away. True, false, or unknown?
6. Someone opened a cash register. True, false, or unknown?
7. After the man who demanded the money scooped up the contents of the cash register, he ran away. True, false, or unknown?
8. The cash register contained money, but the story does not state how much. True, false, or unknown?

9. The robber demanded money of the owner. True, false, or unknown?
10. The story concerns a series of events in which only three persons are referred to: the owner of the store, a man who demanded money, and a member of the police force. True, false, or unknown?
11. The following events in the story are true: Someone demanded money; a cash register was opened; its contents were scooped up; a man dashed out of the store. True, false, or unknown?

Step 2: After you have answered the 11 questions individually, form groups of four or five members each. The groups have 10 minutes to discuss their answers and agree on the correct answers to each of the 11 statements.

Step 3: Your instructor will give you the correct answers. How many correct answers did you get at the conclusion of Step 1? How many did your group achieve at the conclusion of Step 2? Did the group outperform the average individual? Who was the best individual? Discuss the implications of these results.

Step 4: Analyze your team's decision making by answering the following questions:

- Did you clearly identify the desired outcome?
- Were all members prepared to discuss the statements?
- Did you encourage open and active discussion of the story?
- Did you make and communicate guidelines for the decisions?
- Did you direct and manage the discussion?
- Did you get a commitment from all members of the team on the correct answers?

Business Cases

The Business of Blue Jays Baseball

Baseball has long been called "America's national pastime" with a long history of traditions such as large groups of scouts watching thousands of games to find players for their ball club. Commonly used statistics such as stolen bases, runs batted in, and batting averages that were typically used to evaluate players' abilities and performances were becoming inadequate and poor gauges of potential.

The game changed with Sabermetrics, the use of advanced statistics to predict a player's future performance. As the film *Moneyball* (based on an earlier book by the same name) emphasized, statistics—the "right" statistics—are crucial aspects of effective decision making in the sport of baseball. The central premise of *Moneyball* was that the collected wisdom of baseball insiders (players, managers, coaches, scouts, the front office) had pretty much been flawed almost from the onset of the game. Rigorous statistical analysis showed that on-base percentages and slugging percentages were better indicators of a player's offensive potential.

It has turned the game of baseball into a game of number crunching. Take, for instance, Alex Anthopolous, the general manager of the Toronto Blue Jays. In 2013, he hired a baseball operations analyst to capitalize on Sabermetrics. He took a bold move in sending talented prospects to acquire R. A. Dickey, Mark Buehrle, Jose Reyes, and Melky Cabrera. Las Vegas odds had the Blue Jays as favourites to win the 2013 World Series. The Jays used an advanced metric called fWAR (Wins Above Replacement), a complete measure of a player's contributions to his team. The WAR value indicates how many more wins the player contributed for his team than a replacement player would produce. The following table illustrates the projected fWAR in 2013 for the acquired star players and the actual 2013 data. It is not hard to see why the Jays did not make the playoffs.[62]

Player	Projected fWAR	Actual fWAR	Difference
R. A. Dickey	4.0	2.0	−2.0
Mark Buehrle	2.5	2.5	0.0
Jose Reyes	4.3	2.2	−1.9
Melky Cabrera	2.5	−0.9	−3.6

Source: "Toronto Blue Jays: Built to Win Yesterday," Batting Leader, http://battingleadoff.com/2014/01/09/toronto-blue-jays-builtto-win-yesterday/

The goal of all this number crunching? To make better decisions. Team managers want to allocate their limited payroll in the best way possible to help the team be a winner. The move to more systematic data usage can also be seen in college baseball. At this level, coaches have long used their faces (touching their ears, noses, and chins continually and constantly) to communicate pitch selection to the catcher. Now, however, hundreds of college teams at all levels have abandoned these body signals

and are using a system in which the coach yells out a series of numbers. "The catcher decodes the sequence by looking at a chart tucked into a wristband—the kind football quarterbacks have worn since 1965—and then relays the information to the pitcher the way he always has." Coaches say this approach is not only faster and more efficient, but it is not decipherable by opponents wanting to steal the signs. Since the method allows for many combinations that can mean many different pitches, the same number sequence will not be used for the rest of the game—and maybe not even for the rest of the season. The use of this kind of data analysis helps balance qualitative and quantitative decision making. It is not just the Blue Jays. The Edmonton Oilers and Toronto Maple Leafs have also begun working with advanced data analysis to make hockey decisions.

Questions

1. Is it appropriate for baseball managers to use only quantitative, objective criteria in evaluating their players? Why?
2. Describe how baseball front-office executives and college coaches could use each of the following to make better decisions: (a) rationality; (b) bounded rationality; and (c) intuition.
3. Can there be too much information in managing the business of baseball? Discuss.

Coca-Cola and the Science of OJ

The Coca-Cola Company (Coke) is in a league by itself.[63] As the world's largest and number one nonalcoholic beverage company, Coke makes or licenses more than 3500 drinks in more than 200 countries. Coke has built $15-billion brands and also claims four of the top five soft-drink brands (Coke, Diet Coke, Fanta, and Sprite). Each year since 2001, global brand consulting firm Interbrand, in conjunction with *Bloomberg BusinessWeek*, has identified Coke as the number one best global brand. Coke's executives and managers are focusing on ambitious, long-term growth for the company—doubling Coke's business by 2020.

A big part of achieving this goal is building up its Simply Orange juice business into a powerful global juice brand. Decision making is playing a crucial role as managers try to beat rival PepsiCo, which has a 40 percent market share in the not-from-concentrate juice category compared to Coke's 28 percent share. And those managers are not leaving anything to chance in this hot—umm, cold—pursuit!

You would think that making orange juice (OJ) would be relatively simple—pick, squeeze, pour. While that would probably be the case in your own kitchen, in Coke's case, that glass of 100 percent OJ is possible only through "satellite imagery, complicated data algorithms, and even a juice pipeline." The purchasing director for Coke's massive Florida juice packaging facility says, "Mother Nature doesn't like to be standardized." Yet standardization is what it takes for Coke to make this work profitably. And producing a juice beverage is far more complicated than bottling soda.

Using what it calls its "Black Book model," Coke wants to ensure that customers have consistently fresh, tasty OJ 12 months a year despite a peak growing season that is only three months long. To help in this, Coke is relying on a "revenue analytic consultant." He says, "Orange juice is definitely one of the most complex applications of business analytics." To consistently deliver an optimal blend given the challenges of nature requires some 1 quintillion (that is 1 followed by 18 zeroes) decisions.

There is no secret formula to Black Book; it is simply an algorithm. It includes detailed data about the more than 600 different flavours that make up an orange and about customer preferences. This data is correlated to a profile of each batch of raw juice. The algorithm then determines how to blend batches to match a certain taste and consistency. At the juice bottling plant, "blend technicians carry out Black Book instructions prior to bottling." The weekly OJ recipe they use is "tweaked" constantly. Black Book also includes data on external factors such as weather patterns, crop yields, and other cost pressures. This is useful for Coke's decision makers as they ensure they will have enough supplies for at least 15 months. One Coke executive says, "If we have a hurricane or freeze, we can quickly replan the business in five or ten minutes just because we've mathematically modeled it."

Questions

1. Which decisions in this story could be considered unstructured problems? Structured problems?
2. How does the Black Book help Coke's managers and other employees in decision making?
3. What does Coke's big data have to do with its goals?

CHAPTER 5

Organizational Structure and Design

Felix Choo/Alamy

You might not have heard of Empire Company Limited, but you've probably shopped at one of their Sobeys, Safeway, or IGA grocery stores. Empire is a Canadian food-retailing and real estate company based in Stellarton, Nova Scotia, with more than $17 billion in annual sales and more than 124 000 employees. Sobeys has been serving Canadians for over 100 years, and one of the secrets to its competitive success is the synergy that comes from owning its own retail real estate. With a lofty goal of being recognized as the best food retailer and workplace environment in Canada, Empire has moved away from a regional management structure in order to reduce complexity and eliminate duplication.

The company streamlined its organizational structure to reflect its transition to an operationally focused grocery retailer with related real estate interests on the heels of an October 2013 announcement appointing Marc Poulin as CEO of both Empire Company Ltd. and Sobeys Inc.[1]

For Empire to be successful, the management structure requires simplicity and clarity. What kind of organizational structure can support the operations of retail stores and real estate assets? The CEO has a great deal of flexibility in determining some parts of the structure and less flexibility in determining others. As a business with significant family ownership, Empire has been able to pursue a long-term growth strategy rather than focusing on short-term financial results. Empire continues to expand, adding gas stations from Shell Canada in 2014.

In this chapter, we present information about designing appropriate organizational structures. We look at the various elements of organizational structure and the factors that influence their design. We also look at some traditional and contemporary organizational designs, as well as organizational design challenges that today's managers face.

Think About It

How do you run retail stores and invest in real estate ventures? Put yourself in CEO Marc Poulin's shoes. How can you continue to make Empire successful? What organizational structure will best ensure Empire's goals?

5.1 **Tell** What are the major elements of organizational structure?

PERSONAL INVENTORY ASSESSMENT

miskolin/Fotolia

Work specialization is the division of individual tasks into separate jobs.

DEFINING ORGANIZATIONAL STRUCTURE

No other topic in management has undergone as much change in the past few years as that of organizing and organizational structure. Managers are questioning and re-evaluating traditional approaches to organizing work in their search for organizational structures that can achieve efficiency but also have the flexibility necessary for success in today's dynamic environment. Recall from Chapter 1 that **organizing** is defined as the process of creating an organization's structure. That process is important and serves many purposes (see Exhibit 5-1). The challenge for managers is to design an organizational structure that allows employees to work effectively and efficiently.

Just what is **organizational structure**? It is how job tasks are formally divided, grouped, and coordinated within an organization. When managers develop or change the structure, they are engaged in **organizational design**, a process that involves decisions about six key elements: work specialization, departmentalization, chain of command, span of control, centralization and decentralization, and formalization.[2]

Work Specialization

Adam Smith first identified division of labour and concluded that it contributed to increased employee productivity. Early in the twentieth century, Henry Ford applied this concept in an assembly line, where every Ford employee was assigned a specific, repetitive task.

Today we use the term **work specialization** to describe the degree to which tasks in an organization are subdivided into separate jobs. The essence of work specialization is that an entire job is not done by one individual but instead is broken down into steps, and each step is completed by a different person. Individual employees specialize in doing part of an activity rather than the entire activity. When work specialization was implemented in the early twentieth century, employee productivity rose initially, but when used to extreme, human diseconomies from work specialization—boredom, fatigue, stress, poor quality, increased absenteeism, and higher turnover—more than offset the economic advantages. Most managers today see work specialization as an important organizing mechanism but not as a source of ever-increasing productivity. McDonald's uses high work specialization to efficiently make and sell its products, and employees have precisely defined roles and standardized work processes. However, other organizations, such as Bolton, Ontario–based Husky Injection Molding Systems and Ford Australia, have successfully increased job breadth and reduced work specialization. Still, specialization has its place in some organizations. No hockey team has anyone play both goalie and centre positions. Rather, players tend to specialize in their positions.

EXHIBIT 5-1 Purposes of Organizing

- Divides work to be done into specific jobs and departments
- Assigns tasks and responsibilities associated with individual jobs
- Coordinates diverse organizational tasks
- Clusters jobs into units
- Establishes relationships among individuals, groups, and departments
- Establishes formal lines of authority
- Allocates and deploys organizational resources

---

organizing
A management function that involves determining what tasks are to be done, who is to do them, how the tasks are to be grouped, who reports to whom, and where decisions are to be made.

organizational structure
How job tasks are formally divided, grouped, and coordinated within an organization.

organizational design
The process of developing or changing an organization's structure.

work specialization
The degree to which tasks in an organization are subdivided into separate jobs; also known as division of labour.

Departmentalization

Does your college or university have an office of student affairs? A financial aid or student housing department? Once jobs have been divided up through work specialization, they have to be grouped back together so that common tasks can be coordinated. The basis on which jobs are grouped together is called **departmentalization**. Every organization will have its own specific way of classifying and grouping work activities. Exhibit 5-2 shows the five common forms of departmentalization.

Functional departmentalization groups jobs by functions performed. This approach can be used in all types of organizations, although the functions change to reflect the organization's purpose and work. **Product departmentalization** groups jobs by product line. In this approach, each major product area is placed under the authority of a manager who is responsible for everything having to do with that product line. For example, Estée Lauder sells lipstick, eyeshadow, blush, and a variety of other cosmetics represented by different product lines. The company's lines include Clinique and Origins, in addition to Canadian-created MAC Cosmetics and its own original line of Estée Lauder products, each of which operates as a distinct company.

Geographical departmentalization groups jobs on the basis of territory or geography, such as the East Coast, Western Canada, or Central Ontario, or maybe by US, European, Latin American, and Asia–Pacific regions. **Process departmentalization** groups jobs on the basis of product or customer flow. In this approach, work activities follow a natural processing flow of products or even of customers. For example, many beauty salons have separate employees for shampooing, colouring, and cutting hair, all different processes for having one's hair styled. Finally, **customer departmentalization** groups jobs on the basis of customers who have common needs or problems that can best be met by having specialists for each. There are advantages to matching departmentalization to customer needs.

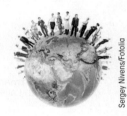

Large organizations often combine forms of departmentalization. For example, a major Canadian photonics firm organizes each of its divisions along functional lines: its manufacturing units around processes, its sales units around seven geographic regions, and its sales regions into four customer groupings. Two popular trends in departmentalization are the use of customer departmentalization and the use of cross-functional teams. Toronto-based Dell Canada is organized around four customer-oriented business units: home and home office; small business; medium and large business; and government, education, and health care. Customer-oriented structures enable companies to better understand their customers and to respond faster to their needs.

Managers use **cross-functional teams**—teams made up of groups of individuals who are experts in various specialties and who work together—to increase knowledge and understanding for some organizational tasks. Scarborough, Ontario–based Aviva Canada, a leading property and casualty insurance group, puts together cross-functional catastrophe teams, with trained representatives from all relevant departments, to more quickly help policyholders when a crisis occurs. During the BC wildfires of summer 2003, the catastrophe team worked on both local and corporate issues, including managing information technology, internal and external communication, tracking, resourcing, and vendors. This type of organization made it easier to meet the needs of policyholders as quickly as possible.[3] We discuss the use of cross-functional teams more fully in Chapter 10.

Burnaby, British Columbia–based TELUS is structured around four customer-oriented business units to improve customer response times: consumer solutions (focused on services to homes and individuals); business solutions (focused on services to small and medium-sized businesses and entrepreneurs); TELUS Québec (a TELUS company focused on services for the Quebec marketplace); and partner solutions (focused on services to wholesale customers, such as telecommunications carriers and wireless communications companies).

---

departmentalization
The basis on which jobs are grouped together.

functional departmentalization
Grouping jobs by functions performed.

product departmentalization
Grouping jobs by product line.

geographical departmentalization
Grouping jobs on the basis of territory or geography.

process departmentalization
Grouping jobs on the basis of product or customer flow.

customer departmentalization
Grouping jobs on the basis of customers who have common needs or problems.

cross-functional teams
Work teams made up of individuals who are experts in various functional specialties.

EXHIBIT 5-2 The Five Common Forms of Departmentalization

Functional Departmentalization

```
                        Plant Manager
   ┌──────────┬──────────┬──────────┬──────────┬──────────┐
 Manager,   Manager,   Manager,    Manager,    Manager,
 Engineering Accounting Manufacturing Human Resources Purchasing
```

+ Efficiencies from putting together similar specialties and people with common skills, knowledge, and orientations
+ Coordination within functional area
+ In-depth specialization
– Poor communication across functional areas
– Limited view of organizational goals

Geographical Departmentalization

```
                  Vice-President
                    for Sales
   ┌──────────────┬──────────────┬──────────────┐
 Sales Director, Sales Director, Sales Director, Sales Director,
 Western Region  Prairies Region Central Region  Eastern Region
```

+ More effective and efficient handling of specific regional issues that arise
+ Better service of needs of unique geographic markets
– Duplication of functions
– Feelings of isolation from other organizational areas possible

Product Departmentalization
Source: Bombardier Annual Report

```
                        Bombardier
            ┌──────────────────┴──────────────────┐
      Bombardier                            Bombardier
      Aerospace                             Transportation

   Commercial Aircraft                      Rail Vehicles
   Regional Aircraft                        Total Transit Systems
   Business Aircraft                        Propulsion and Controls
   Amphibious Aircraft                      Services
   Military Aviation Training               Retail Control Solutions
   Flexjet                                  Bogies
   Skyjet
```

+ Specialization in particular products and services possible
+ Managers able to become experts in their industry
+ Closer to customers
– Duplication of functions
– Limited view of organizational goals

Process Departmentalization

```
                        Plant
                     Superintendent
   ┌──────────┬──────────┬──────────┬──────────┬──────────┐
 Sawing    Planing    Assembling  Lacquering  Finishing   Inspection
 Department and Milling Department  and Sanding Department  and Shipping
 Manager   Department Manager      Department  Manager     Department
           Manager                 Manager                 Manager
```

+ More efficient flow of work activities
– Use possible only with certain types of products

Customer Departmentalization

```
                    Director
                    of Sales
   ┌──────────────┬──────────────┐
 Manager,      Manager,        Manager,
 Retail Accounts Wholesale Accounts Government Accounts
```

+ Specialists able to meet customers' needs and problems
– Duplication of functions
– Limited view of organizational goals

Chain of Command

The **chain of command** is the continuous line of authority that extends from upper organizational levels to the lowest levels and clarifies who reports to whom. It helps employees answer questions such as "Who do I go to if I have a problem?" or "To whom am I responsible?"

You cannot discuss the chain of command without discussing these other concepts: authority, responsibility, accountability, unity of command, and delegation. **Authority** refers to the rights inherent in a managerial position to tell people what to do and to expect them to do it.[4] To facilitate decision making and coordination, an organization's managers are part of the chain of command and are granted a certain degree of authority to meet their responsibilities.

As managers coordinate and integrate the work of employees, those employees assume an obligation to perform any assigned duties. This obligation or expectation to perform is known as **responsibility**. Responsibility brings with it **accountability**, which is the need to report and justify work to a manager's superiors. Sobeys maintains an environmental scorecard where it tracks its performance on environmental pledges such as reducing greenhouse gas emissions by 15 percent, reducing landfill waste by 30 percent, and selling only sustainable seafood products.

The **unity of command** principle helps preserve the concept of a continuous line of authority. It states that every employee should receive orders from only one superior. Without unity of command, conflicting demands and priorities from multiple managers can create problems.

Because managers have limited time and knowledge, they may delegate some of their responsibilities to other employees. **Delegation** is the assignment of authority to another person to carry out specific duties, allowing the employee to make some of the decisions. Delegation is an important part of a manager's job, as it can ensure that the right people are part of the decision-making process. *Hey, You're the Boss Now—Delegating 101* gives more tips on how to do a better job of delegating. These concepts are far less important today. For example, at the Michelin plant in Tours, France, managers have replaced the top-down chain of command with "birdhouse" meetings, in which employees meet for five minutes at regular intervals throughout the day at a column on the shop floor to study simple tables and charts to identify production bottlenecks. Instead of being bosses, shop managers are enablers.[5] In addition, information technology has provided employees with immediate access to information instead of waiting to hear from someone higher up in the chain of command.

PERSONAL INVENTORY ASSESSMENT

LINE AND STAFF AUTHORITY In many organizations, a distinction can be made between line and staff authority. **Line managers** are responsible for the essential activities of the organization, including production and sales. Line managers have the authority to issue orders to those in the chain of command. The president, the production manager, and the sales manager are examples of line managers. **Staff managers** work in the supporting activities of the organizations, such as human resources or accounting. Staff managers have advisory authority and cannot issue orders to those in the chain of command (except those in their own department). The vice-president of

---

chain of command
The continuous line of authority that extends from the top of the organization to the lowest level and clarifies who reports to whom.

authority
The rights inherent in a managerial position to tell people what to do and to expect them to do it.

responsibility
The obligation or expectation to perform any assigned duties.

accountability
The need to report and justify work to a manager's superiors.

unity of command
The management principle that states every employee should receive orders from only one superior.

delegation
The assignment of authority to another person to carry out specific duties, allowing the employee to make some of the decisions.

line managers
Managers responsible for the essential activities of the organization, including production and sales.

staff managers
Managers who work in the supporting activities of the organizations (such as human resources or accounting).

accounting, the human resources manager, and the marketing research manager are examples of staff managers. Matthew Malek, Manager of Talent Management and Organizational Development at Empire Company Limited, may have recommendations about potential real estate opportunities, but CEO Marc Poulin is likely more interested in Malek's advice about managing employees.

Span of Control

How many employees can a manager efficiently and effectively manage? This question of **span of control** is important because, to a large degree, it determines the number of levels and managers an organization needs. All things being equal, the wider or larger the span, the more efficient the organization. An example can show why.

Assume that we have two organizations, both of which have 64 employees. As Exhibit 5-3 shows, if one organization has a uniform span of four and the other a span of eight, the wider span will have one fewer level and approximately 12 fewer managers. If the average manager made $50 000 a year, the organization with the wider span would save more than $600 000 a year in management salaries alone. Obviously, wider spans are more efficient in terms of cost. However, at some point, wider spans reduce *effectiveness*. When the span becomes too large, employee performance can suffer because managers may no longer have the time to provide the necessary leadership and support. The top performing manufacturing plants have up to 40 production workers per supervisor.[6] In a large call centre, that number can be as high as 50 customer service representatives per supervisor.

TODAY'S VIEW The contemporary view of span of control recognizes that many factors influence the appropriate number of employees a manager can efficiently *and* effectively manage. These factors include the skills and abilities of the manager and the employees, and the characteristics of the work being done. For example, the more training and experience employees have, the less direct supervision they need. Therefore, managers with well-trained and experienced employees can function quite well with a wider span. Other contingency variables that determine the appropriate span include similarity of employee tasks, the complexity of those tasks, the physical proximity of subordinates, the degree to which standardized procedures are in place, the sophistication of the organization's information system,

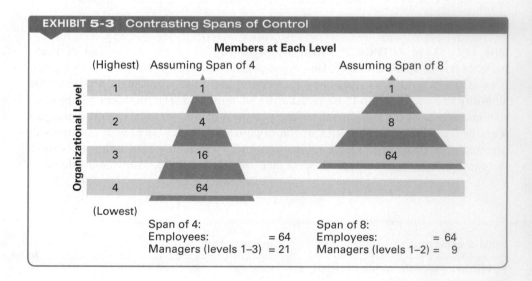

EXHIBIT 5-3 Contrasting Spans of Control

Members at Each Level

	(Highest) Assuming Span of 4	Assuming Span of 8
1	1	1
2	4	8
3	16	64
4	64	

Organizational Level (Highest to Lowest)

Span of 4:
Employees: = 64
Managers (levels 1–3) = 21

Span of 8:
Employees: = 64
Managers (levels 1–2) =   9

span of control
The number of employees a manager can efficiently and effectively manage.

the strength of the organization's culture, and the preferred style of the manager.[7] Wider spans of control are also possible due to technology—it is easier for managers and their subordinates to communicate with each other, and there is often more information readily available to help employees perform their jobs.

The trend in recent years has been toward larger spans of control, which are consistent with managers' efforts to reduce costs, speed up decision making, increase flexibility, get closer to customers, and empower employees. However, to ensure that performance does not suffer because of these wider spans, organizations are investing heavily in employee training. Managers recognize that they can handle a wider span when employees know their jobs well or can turn to coworkers if they have questions.

Centralization and Decentralization

In some organizations, top managers make all the decisions and lower-level managers and employees simply carry out their orders. At the other extreme are organizations in which decision making is pushed down to the managers who are closest to the action. The former organizations are centralized, and the latter are decentralized.

Centralization describes the degree to which decision making is concentrated at a single point in the organization. If top managers make the organization's key decisions with little or no input from below, then the organization is centralized. In contrast, the more that lower-level employees provide input or actually make decisions, the more **decentralization** there is. Keep in mind that the concept of centralization/decentralization is relative, not absolute—an organization is never completely centralized or decentralized. Few organizations could function effectively if all decisions were made by only a select group of top managers; nor could they function if all decisions were delegated to employees at the lowest levels. Nestlé uses decentralized marketing with centralized production, logistics, and supply chain management.[8]

TODAY'S VIEW Most organizations start with a centralized model, where a founder makes all the decisions. As the businesses grow and diversify their environments become complex. These businesses need to become more flexible and responsive, resulting in decentralized decision making. In large companies especially, lower-level managers are "closer to the action" and typically have more detailed knowledge about problems and how best to solve them than do top managers. For example, the Bank of Montreal's some 1000 branches are organized into "communities"—a group of branches within a limited geographical area. Each community is led by a community area manager, who typically works within a 20-minute drive of the other branches. This area manager can respond faster and more intelligently to problems in his or her community than could a senior executive in Toronto.

Another term for increased decentralization is **employee empowerment**, which means giving more decision-making authority to employees.

Kingsey Falls, Quebec–based Cascades, a leading manufacturer of packaging products and tissue paper, uses decentralization effectively with more than 100 operating units located in Canada, the United States, and Europe.[9] Companies are treated as separate entities, based on product, and operate like a federation of small and medium-sized businesses. Each mill is accountable for its own bottom line, and employees are motivated through profit sharing in the profits generated by their own mill. The emphasis on decentralized, entrepreneurial management has been copied by other Canadian forest products companies, such as Domtar.

picsfive/Fotolia

---

centralization
The degree to which decision making is concentrated at a single point in the organization.

decentralization
The degree to which lower-level employees provide input or actually make decisions.

employee empowerment
Giving more authority to employees to make decisions.

What determines whether an organization will move toward more centralization or decentralization? Companies facing dynamic environments are more likely to need to adapt quickly to change, and thus decentralize decision making. Stable environments allow for more rules and procedures, so decision making can be centralized more easily. A community college with one location is more likely to be centralized, while a college in a major metropolitan area with five campuses might treat each of the campuses as a separate unit and decentralize decision making to support a more complex environment.

Formalization

Formalization refers to the degree to which jobs within the organization are standardized and the extent to which employee behaviour is guided by rules and procedures. If a job is highly formalized, the person doing that job has little freedom to choose what is to be done, when it is to be done, and how he or she does it. Employees can be expected to handle the same input in exactly the same way, resulting in consistent and uniform output. Organizations with high formalization have explicit job descriptions, numerous organizational rules, and clearly defined procedures covering work processes. On the other hand, where formalization is low, job behaviours are relatively unstructured, and employees have a great deal of freedom in how they do their work.

The degree of formalization varies widely among organizations and even within organizations. For example, at a newspaper, news reporters often have a great deal of discretion in their jobs. They may pick their news topics, find their own stories, research them the way they want to, and write them up, usually within minimal guidelines. In contrast, employees who lay out the newspaper pages do not have that type of freedom. They have constraints—both time and space—that standardize how they do their work.

TODAY'S VIEW Although some formalization is important and necessary for consistency and control, many of today's organizations seem to be less reliant on strict rules and standardization to guide and regulate employee behaviour. Consider the following situation:

It is 2:37 p.m. and a customer at a watch repair store is trying to drop off a watch for same-day repair. Store policy states that items must be dropped off by 2:00 p.m. for this service. The clerk knows that rules like this are supposed to be followed. At the same time, he wants to accommodate the customer, and he knows that the watch could, in fact, be repaired that day. He decides to accept the watch and, by so doing, to violate the policy. He just hopes that his manager does not find out.[10]

Has this employee done something wrong? He did "break" the rule. But by breaking the rule, he actually brought in revenue and provided the customer good service—so good, in fact, that the customer may be satisfied enough to come back in the future.

Because such situations where rules may be too restrictive frequently arise, many organizations allow employees some freedom to make decisions they feel are best under the circumstances. However, this freedom does not mean that all organizational rules are thrown out the window. There *will* be rules that are important for employees to follow, and these rules should be explained so employees understand the importance of adhering to them. But for other rules, employees may be given some leeway in application.[11]

---

formalization
The degree to which jobs within the organization are standardized and the extent to which employee behaviour is guided by rules and procedures.

What Contingency Variables Affect Structural Choice?

John Cogill/AP Images

Identify the contingency factors that favour either the mechanistic model or the organic model of organizational design.

IF these are the contingency factors,
THEN this is the most appropriate structure.

MECHANISTIC

ORGANIC

EXHIBIT 5-4
Mechanistic Versus
Organic Organizations

MECHANISTIC	ORGANIC
☐ Rigid hierarchical relationships	☐ Collaboration (both vertical and horizontal)
☐ Fixed duties	☐ Adaptable duties
☐ Many rules	☐ Few rules
☐ Formalized communication channels	☐ Informal communication
☐ Centralized decision authority	☐ Decentralized decision authority
☐ Taller structures	☐ Flatter structures

113

Mechanistic or Organic[12]

Mechanistic organization (or bureaucracy)

- Rigid and tightly controlled structure
- Combines traditional aspects of all six elements or organizational structure:
  - High specialization
  - Rigid departmentalization
  - Clear chain of command
  - Narrow spans of control leading to taller structure
  - Centralization
  - High formalization

MECHANISTIC

Organic organization

ORGANIC

- Highly adaptive and flexible structure
  - Collaboration (both vertical and horizontal)
  - Adaptable duties
  - Few rules
  - Informal communication
  - Decentralized decision authority
  - Wider spans of control leading to flatter structures
- Loose structure allows for rapid adjustment to change[13]

The "If": Contingency Variables

1 Strategy—Structure

- Based on work of Alfred Chandler[14]
- Goals are important part of organization's strategies; structure should facilitate goal achievement
- Simple strategy → simple structure
- Elaborate strategy → more complex structure
- Certain structural designs work best with different organizational strategies[15]
  - Passionate pursuit of innovation → organic
  - Passionate pursuit of cost control → mechanistic

Coloures-pic/Fotolia

mechanistic organization
An organization that is rigid and tightly controlled.

organic organization
An organization that is highly adaptive and flexible.

❷ Size—Structure

- Considerable evidence that size (number of employees) affects structure[16]

- Magic number seems to be 2000 employees

- **LARGE** organizations (>2000 employees)—mechanistic

- When an organization reaches this number, size is *less influential;* adding more employees has little impact as structure is already fairly mechanistic

Adding a significant number of new employees to **a smaller organization that has a more organic structure** will force it to become more mechanistic

ORGANIC

MECHANISTIC

❸ Technology—Structure

- Technology is used—by every organization—to convert inputs into outputs (see Exhibit 5-5)

EXHIBIT 5-5   Woodward's Findings on Technology and Structure

	UNIT PRODUCTION	MASS PRODUCTION	PROCESS PRODUCTION
Structural characteristics:	Low vertical differentiation	Moderate vertical differentiation	High vertical differentiation
	Low horizontal differentiation	High horizontal differentiation	Low horizontal differentiation
	Low formalization	High formalization	Low formalization
Most effective structure:	Organic	Mechanistic	Organic

Talex/Fotolia

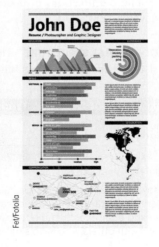

Fet/Fotolia

Rvlsoft/Fotolia

❹ Environment—Structure

- Environment is a constraint on managerial discretion

- Environment also has a major effect on an organization's structure

  - Stable environment: mechanistic structure
  - Dynamic/uncertain environment: organic structure
  - Helps explain why so many managers today have restructured their organizations to be lean, fast, and flexible[17]

5.3 **Describe** Beyond traditional organizational designs, how else can organizations be structured?

COMMON ORGANIZATIONAL DESIGNS

What types of organizational designs exist in small businesses or in big companies such as Ford Canada, Corel, McCain Foods, Procter & Gamble, and eBay? When making organizational design decisions, managers can choose from traditional organizational designs and contemporary organizational designs.

Traditional Organizational Designs

In designing a structure to support the efficient and effective accomplishment of organizational goals, managers may choose to follow more traditional organizational designs. These designs—the simple structure, functional structure, and divisional structure—tend to be more mechanistic. Exhibit 5-6 summarizes the strengths and weaknesses of each design.

SIMPLE STRUCTURE Most organizations start as entrepreneurial ventures with a simple structure consisting of owners and employees. A **simple structure** is an organizational structure with low departmentalization, wide spans of control, authority centralized in a single person, and little formalization.[18] This structure is most commonly used by small businesses in which the owner and manager are one and the same.

Most organizations do not remain simple structures. As an organization grows, it generally reaches a point where it has to add employees. As the number of employees rises, the structure tends to become more specialized and formalized. Rules and regulations are introduced, work becomes specialized, departments are created, levels of management are added, and the organization becomes increasingly bureaucratic. At this point, a manager might choose to organize around a functional structure or a divisional structure.

FUNCTIONAL STRUCTURE A **functional structure** is an organizational structure that groups similar or related occupational specialties together. It is the functional approach to departmentalization applied to the entire organization. Revlon, for example, is organized around the functions of operations, finance, human resources, and product research and development.

DIVISIONAL STRUCTURE The **divisional structure** is an organizational structure that consists of separate business units or divisions.[19] In this structure, each unit or division has

EXHIBIT 5-6 Strengths and Weaknesses of Common Traditional Organizational Designs

Structure	Strengths	Weaknesses
Simple Structure	Fast; flexible; inexpensive to maintain; clear accountability	Not appropriate as organization grows; reliance on one person is risky
Functional Structure	Cost-saving advantages from specialization (economies of scale, minimal duplication of people and equipment), and employees are grouped with others who have similar tasks	Pursuit of functional goals can cause managers to lose sight of what is best for the overall organization; functional specialists become insulated and have little understanding of what other units are doing
Divisional Structure	Focuses on results—division managers are responsible for what happens to their products and services	Duplication of activities and resources increases costs and reduces efficiency

simple structure
An organizational structure with low departmentalization, wide spans of control, authority centralized in a single person, and little formalization.

functional structure
An organizational structure that groups similar or related occupational specialties together.

divisional structure
An organizational structure that consists of separate business units or divisions.

relatively limited autonomy, with a division manager responsible for performance who has strategic and operational authority over his or her unit. In divisional structures, however, the parent corporation typically acts as an external overseer to coordinate and control the various divisions, and often provides support services such as financial and legal. For example, Maple Leaf Sports & Entertainment has three divisions, including two sports teams, the Raptors and the Maple Leafs.

Contemporary Organizational Designs

Managers in contemporary organizations often find that traditional hierarchical designs are not appropriate for the increasingly dynamic and complex environments they face. In response to marketplace demands to be lean, flexible, and innovative, managers are developing creative ways to structure and organize work and to make their organizations more responsive to the needs of customers, employees, and other organizational constituents.[20] At the Canada Revenue Agency, the workforce is spread out, and employees rely on shared workspaces, mobile computing, and virtual private networks to get work done. Nevertheless, work gets done effectively and efficiently.[21] Exhibit 5-7 summarizes some of the newest concepts in organizational designs.

TEAM STRUCTURE   Larry Page and Sergey Brin, cofounders of Google, have created a corporate structure that "tackles most big projects in small, tightly focused teams."[22] In a **team structure**, the entire organization is made up of work groups or teams that perform the organization's work.[23] Employee empowerment is crucial in a team structure, because there is no line of managerial authority from top to bottom. Rather, employee teams are free to design work in the way they think is best. However, the teams are also held responsible for all work and performance results in their respective areas. Let us look at some examples of organizations that are organized around teams.

EXHIBIT 5-7   Contemporary Organizational Designs

Structure	Description	Advantages	Disadvantages
Team	A structure in which the entire organization is made up of work groups or teams.	Employees are more involved and empowered. Reduced barriers among functional areas.	No clear chain of command. Pressure on teams to perform.
Matrix–Project	Matrix is a structure that assigns specialists from different functional areas to work on projects but who return to their areas when the project is completed. Project is a structure in which employees continuously work on projects. As one project is completed, employees move on to the next project.	Fluid and flexible design that can respond to environmental changes. Faster decision making.	Complexity of assigning people to projects. Task and personality conflicts.
Boundaryless	A structure that is not defined by or limited to artificial horizontal, vertical, or external boundaries; includes *virtual* and *networked* types of organizations.	Highly flexible and responsive. Draws on talent wherever it is found.	Lack of control. Communication difficulties.

team structure
An organizational structure in which the entire organization is made up of work groups or teams.

Whole Foods Market, the largest natural-foods grocer in the United States, now has nine stores in Ontario and British Columbia. Each Whole Foods store is an autonomous profit centre composed of an average of 10 self-managed teams, each with a designated team leader. The team leaders in each store are a team; store leaders in each region are a team; and the company's six regional presidents are a team.[24] At the Sun Life Assurance Company of Canada (US) office in Wellesley Hills, Massachusetts, customer representatives work in eight-person teams trained to expedite all customer requests. When customers call in, they are not switched from one specialist to another, but to one of the teams, who takes care of every aspect of the customer's request. Together, team members work to make resolving insurance difficulties go much smoother.

In large organizations, the team structure complements what is typically a functional or divisional structure. This structural addition enables the organization to have the efficiency of a bureaucracy while providing the flexibility that teams provide. To improve productivity at the operating level, for example, Toyota's CAPTIN plant (based in Delta, British Columbia), Motorola, and Xerox use self-managed teams extensively.[25]

MATRIX AND PROJECT STRUCTURES Other popular contemporary designs are the matrix and project structures. The **matrix structure** is an organizational structure that assigns specialists from different functional departments to work on one or more projects led by project managers. Once a project is completed, the specialists return to their functional departments. Exhibit 5-8 shows an example of the matrix structure used in an aerospace firm. Along the top are the familiar organizational functions. The specific projects the firm is currently working on are listed along the left-hand side: aircraft, mission systems and avionics, engines and parts, and space technologies. Each project is managed by an individual who staffs his or her project with people from each of the functional departments. Adding this vertical dimension to the traditional horizontal functional departments in effect "weaves together" elements of functional and product departmentalization, creating a matrix arrangement. Another unique aspect of this design is that it creates a *dual chain of command*, which explicitly violates the classical organizing principle of unity of command.

How does a matrix structure work in reality? Employees in a matrix organization have two managers: their functional department manager and their product or project

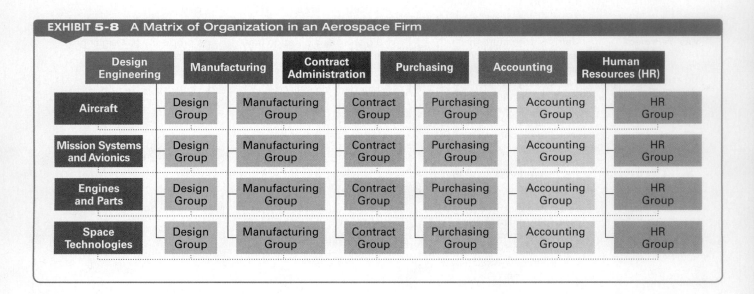

EXHIBIT 5-8 A Matrix of Organization in an Aerospace Firm

matrix structure
An organizational structure that assigns specialists from different functional departments to work on one or more projects.

manager, who share authority. The project managers have authority over the functional members who are part of their project team in areas relative to the project's goals. However, decisions such as promotions, salary recommendations, and annual reviews remain the functional manager's responsibility. To work effectively, project and functional managers have to communicate regularly, coordinate work demands on employees, and resolve conflicts together.

Although the matrix structure continues to be an effective organizational structure choice for some organizations, many are using a **project structure**, in which employees continuously work on projects. Unlike the matrix structure, a project structure has no formal departments that employees return to at the completion of a project. Instead, employees take their specific skills, abilities, and experiences to other projects. All work in project-structured organizations is performed by teams of employees who become part of a project team because they have the appropriate work skills and abilities.

Oticon A/S, a Danish hearing-aid manufacturer, has no departments or employee job titles. All work is project based, and project teams form, disband, and form again as the work requires. Employees "join" project teams because they bring needed skills and abilities to that project. Once the project is completed, they move on to the next one.[26]

Project structures tend to be fluid and flexible organizational designs. This type of structure has no departmentalization or rigid organizational hierarchy to slow down decision making or taking action. Managers act as facilitators, mentors, and coaches. They "serve" the project teams by eliminating or minimizing organizational obstacles and by ensuring that the teams have the resources they need to effectively and efficiently complete their work.

BOUNDARYLESS ORGANIZATIONS Another approach to contemporary organizational design is the **boundaryless organization**, an organization whose design is not determined by a predefined structure. Instead the organization seeks to eliminate the chain of command, places no limits on spans of control, and replaces departments with empowered teams.[27] The term *boundaryless organization* was coined by Jack Welch, former chair of General Electric (GE), who wanted to eliminate vertical and horizontal boundaries within GE and break down external barriers between the company and its customers and suppliers. This idea may sound odd, but many successful organizations are finding they can operate more effectively in today's environment by remaining flexible and *un*structured: The ideal structure for them is *not* having a rigid, predefined structure.

What do we mean by "boundaries"? A typical organization has internal boundaries—horizontal boundaries imposed by work specialization and departmentalization, and vertical boundaries created by separating employees into organizational levels and hierarchies. The organization also has external boundaries, which separate the organization from its customers, suppliers, and other stakeholders. To minimize or eliminate these boundaries, managers might use virtual or network organizational structures.

How does a boundaryless organization operate in practice? General Electric is made up of a number of companies, including GE Money, which provides financial services to consumers and retailers; GE Water & Process Technologies, which produces water treatment, wastewater treatment, and process systems products; GE Energy, which supplies technology to the energy industry; and NBC Universal Studios, a leading media and entertainment company. Anyone working in any division of GE can learn about opportunities available in the other business units and how to move into those units, if so desired. Mobility is one way a boundaryless organization functions for its employees. Outside the company, the boundaryless structure allows GE customers to ask factories to increase inventory when the customer needs more product. Thus, the customer makes a decision about inventory that was once made inside the organization. GE also encourages customers and suppliers to evaluate its service levels, giving direct and immediate feedback to employees.

---

project structure
An organizational structure in which employees continuously work on projects.

boundaryless organization
An organization that is not defined by a chain of command, places no limits on spans of control,

and replaces departments with empowered teams.

New Westminster, British Columbia–based iGEN Knowledge Solutions uses its virtual form to bring technical solutions to its business clients. iGEN associates work from home offices connected by wireless technologies to solve client problems collaboratively. This structure allows faster idea implementation, product development, and service delivery. The company finds it easy to set up operations in different regions of the country without large overhead costs because of its virtual structure.

Companies such as Cisco Systems, Nike, Ericsson, Reebok, and Mitel have found that they can do business worth hundreds of millions of dollars without owning manufacturing facilities. San Jose, California–based Cisco Systems is essentially a research and development company that uses outside suppliers and independent manufacturers to assemble the Internet routers its engineers design. Similarly, Beaverton, Oregon–based Nike is a product development and marketing company that contracts with outside organizations to manufacture its athletic footwear. Ottawa-based Mitel Networks designs computer equipment but outsources manufacturing and repair to BreconRidge, another Ottawa high tech firm.[33]

VIRTUAL ORGANIZATIONS A **virtual organization** has elements of a traditional organization, but also relies on recent developments in information technology to get work done.[28] Thus, the organization could consist of a small core of full-time employees plus outside specialists hired on a temporary basis to work on opportunities that arise.[29] The virtual organization could also be composed of employees who work from their own home offices—connected by technology but perhaps occasionally getting together face to face. An example of a virtual organization is Strawberry Frog, an international advertising agency based in Amsterdam. The small administrative staff accesses a network of more than 100 people around the globe to complete advertising projects. By relying on this global web of freelancers, the company enjoys a network of talent without the overhead and structural complexity of a more traditional organization.

The inspiration for virtual organizations comes from the film industry. If you look at the film industry, people are essentially "free agents" who move from project to project applying their skills—directing, talent search, costuming, makeup, set design—as needed.

Some organizations are now testing out a new form of virtuality, using the virtual online world *Second Life* to create a different type of organization. Vancouver-based Davis LLP is the first Canadian law firm to have a presence in *Second Life*.[30] Lawyer Dani Lemon, whose online avatar (the digital version of a real person) is Lemon Darcy, said that "the online world gives [Davis LLP] an opportunity to interact with clients and meet new ones who are comfortable in that setting."

Lemon believes that being part of *Second Life* will bring new clients to Davis and give the company an opportunity to communicate in new ways. Several of her colleagues have joined her in this virtual office, including Sarah Dale-Harris (BarristerSolicitor Underwood), Pablo Guzman (PabloGuzman Little), Chris Bennett (IPand Teichmann), David Spratley (DaveS Blackadder), and Chris Metcalfe (IP Maximus).

Davis LLP's *Second City* office has a boardroom off the lobby that can be used for online conferences, a room containing recruiting information from Davis, and a library that will house online legal information. "I think it will be an evolving process," Lemon said of the online office. "We will use it as a networking tool and as a way to meet clients."[31] The law firm plans to hold online events in *Second Life*, conduct seminars, and give talks that might be of value to potential clients.

NETWORK ORGANIZATIONS Another structural option for managers wanting to minimize or eliminate organizational boundaries is the **network organization**, which is a small core organization that outsources major business functions.[32] This approach allows organizations to concentrate on what they do best and to contract out other activities to companies that specialize in those activities. Many large organizations use the network structure to outsource manufacturing.

While many companies use outsourcing, not all are successful at it. Managers should be aware of some of the problems involved in outsourcing, such as the following:

- choosing the wrong activities to outsource
- choosing the wrong vendor
- writing a poor contract
- failing to consider personnel issues
- losing control over the activity

virtual organization
An organization that has elements of a traditional organization, but also relies on recent developments in information technology to get work done.

network organization
A small core organization that outsources major business functions.

- ignoring the hidden costs
- failing to develop an exit strategy (for either moving to another vendor or deciding to bring the activity back in-house)

A review of 91 outsourcing activities found that the two most likely reasons for an outsourcing venture failure were writing a poor contract and losing control of the activity.[34] Canadian managers say they are reluctant to outsource.[35] The PricewaterhouseCoopers (PwC) 2011 Business Insights survey[36] showed outsourcing as the lowest priority in terms of improving the competitiveness of Canadian businesses, while innovation and reducing costs were perceived as more important than outsourcing for dealing with volatility. In some cases, companies formerly used as outsourcers are now direct competitors due to globalization.

Organizational Design Challenges

As managers look for organizational designs that will best support and facilitate employees doing their work efficiently and effectively in today's dynamic environment, certain challenges arise with which they must contend. These challenges include designing office space, keeping employees connected, building a learning organization, and managing global structural issues.

DESIGNING OFFICE SPACE Office space has always been a battle between freeing employees to work and maximizing space to minimize costs (see Exhibit 5-9). In the early 1900s, Frederick Taylor suggested that properly organized offices would boost productivity. In 1964, Herman Miller designed the Action Office, with clusters of barrier-free offices. Openness and proximity were meant to break down barriers and encourage "meaningful traffic". When the furniture was reduced in size and interlocked a few years later, the Action Office really took off.[37] The Cube Farm was the next phase as furniture firms were imitating Miller's design and using cheaper materials to make mass cubicles. Today's office spaces are collaborative, accommodating virtual workers with group spaces to engineer interaction and foster creativity. International design firm Gensler conducted a study

EXHIBIT 5-9 Comparison of the Major Office Styles

Office Style	Space/Cost	What They Got Right	What They Got Wrong
The Action Office (1960s–70s)	Average space per employee 500 sq ft $22/sq ft (Toronto)	• Flexibility for employers to choose elements • Well-designed desk spaces gave better access to tools and resources	• High-quality components were very expensive • Open environment was noisy and distracting
The Cube Farm (1980s–90s)	Average space per employee 144 sq ft $40/sq ft (Toronto)	• Cubes offered some privacy and the ability to personalize • Businesses found cubicles flexible and affordable	• Quarters became cramped • Bad air and artificial light left workers unmotivated and anxious to leave • "Prairie-dogging," or the tendency of workers to pop their heads up to communicate with others
The Collaborative Office (present)	Average space per employee 176 sq ft $68/sq ft (Toronto)	• Open designs encourage interaction • Workers can adapt to the environment that is best for them • Smaller footprint equals lower costs	• Open-concept offices distract from the ability to be deep in focus • Less efficiency in shared spaces

Source: Adapted from Steve Brearton, "Circles and Squares," *Canadian Business*, November 2014, pp. 57–63.

in 2013 that found workers spent about one-quarter of their workday collaborating and more than half in deep focus. That means employers need to provide office environments that facilitate interaction while allowing freedom from interruption.[38]

KEEPING EMPLOYEES CONNECTED Many organizational design concepts were developed during the twentieth century, when work tasks were fairly predictable and constant, most jobs were full-time and continued indefinitely, and work was done at an employer's place of business under a manager's supervision.[40] However, many organizations today are not like that, as you saw in our preceding discussion of virtual and network organizations. A major structural design challenge for managers is finding a way to keep widely dispersed and mobile employees connected to the organization. We cover information on motivating these employees in Chapter 9.

BUILDING A LEARNING ORGANIZATION Doing business in an intensely competitive global environment, managers at British retailer Tesco realize how important it is for stores to operate smoothly behind the scenes. At Tesco, they do so through the use of a proven tool—a set of software applications called Tesco in a Box, which promotes consistency in operations and acts as a way to share innovations. Tesco is an example of a learning organization, an organization that has developed the capacity to constantly learn, adapt, and change.[41] In a learning organization, employees continually acquire and share new knowledge and apply that knowledge in making decisions or doing their work. Some organizational theorists even go so far as to say that an organization's ability to learn and to apply that learning may be the only sustainable source of competitive advantage.[42]

What structural characteristics does a learning organization need? First, members of a learning organization must be able to share information and collaborate on work activities throughout the entire organization—across different functional specialties and even at different organizational levels. This sharing and collaboration requires that structural and physical barriers be minimal. In such a boundaryless environment, employees can work together and collaborate in doing the organization's work the best way they can and learn from each other. Second, because of the need to collaborate, teams tend to be an important feature of a learning organization's structural design. Employees work in teams empowered to make decisions about doing whatever work needs to be done and to resolve issues. With empowered employees and teams, the organization has little need for "bosses" to direct and control. Instead, managers serve as facilitators, supporters, and advocates.

MANAGING GLOBAL STRUCTURAL ISSUES Are there global differences in organizational structures? Are Australian organizations structured like those in Canada? Are German organizations structured like those in France or Mexico? Given the global nature of today's business environment, managers need to be familiar with the issues surrounding structural differences. Researchers have concluded that the structures and strategies of organizations worldwide are similar, "while the behavior within them is maintaining its cultural uniqueness."[43] What does this mean for designing effective and efficient structures? When designing or changing structure, managers may need to think about the cultural implications of certain design elements. One study showed that formalization—rules and bureaucratic mechanisms—may be more important in less economically developed countries and less important in more economically developed countries, where employees may have higher levels of professional education and skills.[44] Other structural design elements may be affected by cultural differences as well, such as chain of command and span of control.

A Final Thought

No matter what structural design managers choose for their organization, the structure should help employees work in the most efficient and effective way possible to meet the organization's goals. After all, structure is simply a means to an end. To understand your reaction to organizational structure, see at the end of the chapter.

5 Review and Apply

Summary of Learning Outcomes

5.1 **What are the major elements of organizational structure?** Organizational structure is the formal arrangement of jobs within an organization. Organizational structures are determined by six key elements: work specialization, departmentalization, chain of command, span of control, centralization and decentralization, and formalization. Decisions made about these elements define how work is organized; how many employees managers supervise, where in the organization decisions are made; and whether employees follow standardized operating procedures or have greater flexibility in how they do their work.

For Empire Company Limited, separating the operation of the grocery retail and related real estate because of the work specialization involved makes sense. For example, Sobeys executives would not necessarily make good decisions about which Shell stations to acquire.

5.2 **What factors affect organizational structure?** No one organizational structure is best. The appropriate structure depends on the organization's strategy (innovation, cost minimization, imitation), its size, the technology it uses (unit production, mass production, or process production), and the degree of environmental uncertainty the organization faces.

For Empire, organizing its grocery businesses by brand makes sense—Sobeys, Safeway, and IGA are different "brands" with different types of customers. Each brand has a similar organizational structure, as size, technology, and environmental uncertainty would not differ in any meaningful way among the brands.

5.3 **Beyond traditional organizational designs, how else can organizations be structured?** The traditional structures of organizations are simple, functional, and divisional. Contemporary organizational designs include team structure, matrix and project structures, and boundaryless organizations.

Empire moved from a regional management structure to one that resembles a traditional divisional structure for its two businesses. Other structures might be considered to operate its grocery business, such as a project structure or a boundaryless organization, because retail stores can be managed in a variety of ways.

SNAPSHOT SUMMARY

5.1 **Defining Organizational Structure**
Work Specialization
Departmentalization
Chain of Command
Span of Control
Centralization and Decentralization
Formalization

5.2 **What Contingency Variables Affect Structural Choice?**

5.3 **Common Organizational Designs**
Traditional Organizational Designs
Contemporary Organizational Designs
Organizational Design Challenges
A Final Thought

MyManagementLab Study, practise, and explore real management situations with these helpful resources:

- **Interactive Lesson Presentations:** Work through interactive presentations and assessments to test your knowledge of management concepts.
- **PIA (Personal Inventory Assessments):** Enhance your ability to connect with key concepts through these engaging self-reflection assessments.
- **Study Plan:** Check your understanding of chapter concepts with self-study quizzes.
- **Simulations:** Practise decision making in simulated management environments.

Discussion Questions

1. Describe what is meant by the term *organizational design*.
2. What is the difference between a mechanistic and an organic organization?
3. Describe the characteristics of a learning organization. What are its advantages?
4. Which do you think is more efficient: a wide or a narrow span of control? What is an example of a company that would benefit from a narrow span of control? A wide span of control?
5. Do you think the concept of organizational structure, as described in this chapter, is appropriate for charitable organizations? If yes, which organizational design do you believe to be most appropriate? If no, why not? Explain your position.
6. Why should structure follow strategy instead of the reverse?
7. What functions could your college or university outsource? Why?

Developing Management Skills

Dilemma

Choose an organization for which you have worked. How did the structure of your job and the organization affect your job satisfaction? Did the tasks within your job make sense? In what ways could they be better organized? What structural changes would you make to this organization? Would you consider making this a taller or flatter organization (that is, would you increase or decrease the span of control)? How would the changes you have proposed improve response to customers and your job satisfaction?

Becoming a Manager

- If you belong to a student organization or are employed, notice how various activities and events are organized through the use of work specialization, chain of command, authority, responsibility, and so forth.
- As you read current business periodicals, note what types of organizational structures businesses use and whether or not they are effective.
- Talk to managers about how they organize work and what they have found to be effective.
- Look for examples of organizational charts (visual representations of organizations' structures) and use them to try to determine what structural design the organization is using.

Diversity Matters

Most companies recognize the benefits of employing a diverse workforce. Along with its many advantages, diversity also presents challenges for managers. Managers must dedicate focus to creating a cohesive work environment. Organizational leaders can ensure that workplace diversity is successful by enacting effective policies, communicating the organization's diversity vision, and providing employees with diversity training.

Many organizations are moving toward a full-time diversity champion role. Often that role is housed within HR, which can lead to misalignment with the organization's structure and operations. Diversity planning should align with an organization's vision and strategy. To do so, the diversity role should reside outside a functional area like marketing or HR.

The goal of diversity awareness is to create a workplace where employees appreciate differences in race, gender, religion, cultural values, and thinking styles. As an example, diversity can help teams in the workplace develop a wider variety of problem-solving strategies and approaches. Diversity training is often necessary to reduce employee conflict.

Companies can use evaluations to measure the effectiveness of its diversity workforce through employee turnover, and employee satisfaction with their job and the work environment. Using formal evaluation allows companies to reward individuals and teams that follow company diversity policies and guidelines.

Hey, You're the Boss Now! Delegating 101

ABOUT THE SKILL

Managers get things done through other people. Because any manager's time and knowledge is limited, effective managers need to understand how to delegate. Delegation is the assignment of authority to another person to carry out specific duties. It allows an employee to make some of the decisions. Delegation should not be confused with participation. In participative decision making, authority is shared. In delegation, employees make their own decisions.

STEPS IN DEVELOPING THE SKILL

A number of actions differentiate the effective delegator from the ineffective delegator. You can be more effective at delegating if you use the following five suggestions:[45]

1. **Clarify the assignment.** Determine what is to be delegated and to whom. You need to identify the person

who is most capable of doing the task and then determine whether he or she has the time and motivation to do the task. If you have a willing and able employee, your responsibility is to provide clear information on what is being delegated, the results you expect, and any time or performance expectations you may have. Unless there is an overriding need to adhere to specific methods, you should specify only the results expected. Get agreement on what is to be done and the results expected, but let the employee decide the best way to complete the task.

2. **Specify the employee's range of discretion.** Every situation of delegation comes with constraints. Although you are delegating to an employee the authority to perform some task or tasks, you are not delegating unlimited authority. You are delegating authority to act on certain issues within certain parameters. You need to specify what those parameters are so that employees know, without any doubt, the range of their discretion.

3. **Allow the employee to participate.** One of the best ways to decide how much authority will be necessary to accomplish a task is to allow the employee who will be held accountable for the task to participate in that decision. Be aware, however, that allowing employees to participate can present its own set of potential problems as a result of employees' self-interests and biases in evaluating their own abilities.

4. **Inform others about the delegation.** Delegation should not take place behind the scenes. Not only do the manager and employee need to know specifically what has been delegated and how much authority has been given, so does anyone else, both inside and outside the organization, who is likely to be affected by the employee's decisions and actions. Essentially, you need to communicate what has been delegated (the task and amount of authority) and to whom.

5. **Establish feedback channels.** To delegate without establishing feedback controls is to invite problems. The establishment of controls to monitor the employee's performance increases the likelihood that important problems will be identified and the task will be completed on time

and to the desired specifications. Ideally, these controls should be determined at the time of the initial assignment. Agree on a specific time for the completion of the task and then set progress dates on which the employee will report back on how well he or she is doing and on any major problems that may have arisen. These controls can be supplemented with periodic checks to ensure that authority guidelines are not being abused, organizational policies are being followed, proper procedures are being met, and so forth.

PRACTISING THE SKILL

Ricky Lee is the manager of the contracts group of a large regional office-supply distributor. His manager, Anne Zumwalt, has asked him to prepare, by the end of the month, the department's new procedures manual, which will outline the steps followed in negotiating contracts with office products manufacturers who supply the organization's products. Because Ricky has another major project he is working on, he went to Anne and asked her if it would be possible to assign the rewriting of the procedures manual to Bill Harmon, one of his employees, who has worked in the contracts group for about three years. Anne said she had no problems with Ricky reassigning the project as long as Bill knew the parameters and the expectations for the completion of the project. Ricky is preparing for his meeting in the morning with Bill regarding this assignment. Prepare an outline of what Ricky should discuss with Bill to ensure the new procedures manual meets expectations.

Your Essential Management Reading List

Learning from key management experts can help you understand today's management theory and practice. What follows is a list of some of the more influential management books:

- *Change by Design*—Tim Brown
- *Building the Awesome Organization*—Katherine Catlin and Jana Matthews
- *The Culture Game*—Dan Mezick

Team Exercises

3BL: The Triple Bottom Line

INTEGRATING SUSTAINABILITY INTO THE ORGANIZATIONAL STRUCTURE

Sustainability. Social responsibility. The environment. These concepts are buzzwords for regulators and stakeholders who put pressure on organizations to deal with 3BL issues, urging companies to determine how best to incorporate 3BL as part of their organizational structure.[46]

Organizations are concerned both with structure—where will 3BL decision-making authority reside?—and with the processes and flow of information across the organization. What kind of internal structure and support would magnify their 3BL efforts?

Organizations typically feature one of three 3BL structures.[47] The first is the traditional model, in which 3BL is an initiative or a few activities. Minimal resources are allocated to 3BL, and they may be spread across many departments or business units. The second is the federated model, where the organization has likely created a 3BL business unit and engaged an executive such as a Chief Sustainability Officer or a Chief Responsibility Officer. This unit is able to liaise with other business units and starts to align 3BL priorities with business strategy. The last model is an embedded structure, where 3BL is no longer a separate initiative but integrated into the company's business model, structure, and culture. Companies at this point view 3BL as a major source of competitive advantage.

THINKING STRATEGICALLY ABOUT 3BL

Some best practices for ensuring 3BL success in an organization include the following:

- *Tie responsibility with senior executives.* You need more than "support" from the CEO—the CEO needs to drive the bus and set up a cross-functional 3BL committee with employee participation.
- *Establish regular target setting and reporting.* The focus on accountability builds traction within an organization.
- *Use employees, partners, and collaborators to leverage 3BL capabilities.* Achieve greater outcomes by working collaboratively with everyone in your sphere of influence.
- *Recruit 3BL change agents.* These champions of change will help embed a culture of concern for people, profit, and the planet.

How Is Your School Organized?

Every university or college displays a specific type of organizational structure. For example, if you are a business major, your classes are often housed in a department, school, or faculty of business. But have you ever asked why? Or is it something you just take for granted?

In Chapter 3 you had an opportunity to assess your college or university's strengths, weaknesses, and competitive advantage and see how these fit into its strategy. In this chapter, we argued that structure follows strategy. Given your assessment in Chapter 3 (if you have not done so, you may want to refer to page 63 for the strategy part of this exercise), analyze your college or university's overall structure in terms of its degree of formalization, centralization/decentralization, and complexity. Look at the departmentalization that exists. Is your college or university more organic or mechanistic? How well does your college or university's structure fit with its strategy? Do the same thing for your college or university's size, technology, and environment. Assess its size, degree of technological routineness, and environmental uncertainty. Based on these assessments, what kind of structure would you predict that your college or university has?

Does it have this structure now? Compare your findings with those of other classmates. Are there similarities in how each viewed the college or university? Differences? To what do you attribute these findings?

Be the Consultant: The Nova Scotia Association of Social Workers

The Nova Scotia Association of Social Workers (NSASW) contracted your management consulting firm to conduct an operational structure review.[48] The size of social worker governance councils varies across Canada, with larger associations like NSASW having professional staff to carry out association activities. The NSASW has a governance council of 30, as well as a Board of Examiners to provide oversight for the association. The Council is the governance body for the association and is responsible to follow the association bylaws and the *Social Workers Act of Nova Scotia*. The Board is responsible for registration and renewal of provincial social workers, regulation of the members' practice to protect the public, and dealing with discipline and complaints. The Council and the Board have a difficult relationship, and staff roles, responsibilities, and reporting relationships are not clearly defined. The executive director complains about being stressed and overworked and is not conducting performance evaluations. The membership has increased dramatically, putting a burden on the association's financial resources, staff, and volunteers.

Your analysis leads you to discover that Council meetings regularly run late and not all of the agenda items are accomplished. Consensus is almost impossible to reach, and decision making is ineffective at times. The Board plays a valuable role in assuring the public and professional interests are safeguarded, but no formal communication mechanism between the Board and the Council has been established.

You provided an interim report with many recommendations. Specifically, the Board has brought you in to discuss three of your recommendations:

1. reduction of the governance council size to 15 members
2. creation of a liaison committee to work with both the Council and the Board to develop a stronger working and reporting relationship
3. formal approval of staff position descriptions by Council, with the executive director responsible for their implementation, to facilitate the association's performance management system

What information will you provide to the Council to support your recommendations?

Business Cases

Pfizer: A New Kind of Structure

Admit it.[49] Sometimes the projects you are working on (school, work, or both) can get pretty boring and monotonous. Do you ever dream about having a magic button you could push to get someone else to do the boring, time-consuming stuff for you? At Pfizer, such a button is a reality for a large number of employees.

As a global pharmaceutical company, Pfizer is continually looking for ways to be more efficient and effective. The company's head of pfizerWorks (aka Office of the Future), Jordan Cohen, found that the "Harvard MBA staff we hired to develop strategies and innovate were instead Googling and making PowerPoints." Indeed, internal studies conducted to find out just how much time its valuable talent was spending on menial tasks was startling. The average Pfizer employee was spending 20 to 40 percent of his or her time on support work (creating documents, typing notes, doing research, manipulating data, scheduling meetings) and only 60 to 80 percent on knowledge work (strategy, innovation, networking, collaborating, critical thinking). The problem was not just at lower levels. Even the highest-level employees were affected. So Cohen began looking for solutions. The solution he chose turned out to be the numerous knowledge-process outsourcing companies based in India.

Initial tests of outsourcing support tasks did not go well. However, Cohen continued to tweak the process until everything worked. Now Pfizer employees can click the OOF (Office of the Future) button in Microsoft Outlook, and they are connected to an outsourcing company where a single worker in India receives the request and assigns it to a team. The team leader calls the employee to clarify the request. The team leader then emails back a cost estimate for the requested work. At this point, the Pfizer employee can say yes or no. Cohen says that the benefits of OOF have been unexpected. Time spent on data analysis has been cut—sometimes in half. The financial benefits are also impressive. Pfizer employees love it. "It's kind of amazing," Cohen says, "I wonder what they used to do."

Questions

1. Describe and evaluate what Pfizer is doing.
2. What structural implications—good and bad—does this approach have? (Think in terms of the six organizational design elements.)

3. Do you think this arrangement would work for other types of organizations? Why or why not?
4. What role do you think organizational structure plays in an organization's efficiency and effectiveness? Explain.

Levitt-Safety Limited

Levitt-Safety Limited is Canada's largest specialist supplier of safety equipment and services.[50] Like many Canadian companies, it looked to emerging foreign markets for growth opportunities. However, globalization and outsourcing are no longer a one-way street. Foreign competitors are eyeing the Canadian market, because barriers to entry, such as the North American regulatory and approval bodies, are easier to navigate in Canada. To be successful in the Canadian marketplace, foreign companies need to spend a lot of time and money to build up their brands. Or they could form an alliance with a company like Levitt-Safety to piggyback on a brand that is already established and well known after 36 years of business.

Increased competition has led to downward pressure on profit margins. To counter this, CEO Bruce Levitt created an intermediary company to import product and resell it to Levitt-Safety's distribution business. The company sales teams now have a much better understanding of inventory carrying costs, stock-outs, dead stock, and other often hidden costs. Levitt-Safety also has a separate manufacturing business, NL Technologies, run by Heidi Levitt, which has become a world leader in the manufacturing and design of mining technology.

Levitt-Safety has created an effective organizational structure, with an intermediary and a separately managed company. Levitt-Safety is looking at adding another brand that it can sell to others in the industry.

Questions

1. Should Bruce Levitt set up another company or, instead, set up an alliance with a foreign company that would sell its products under the Levitt-Safety name?
2. How has Levitt-Safety remained a family business for over 75 years?

dantien/Fotolia

CHAPTER

6 Operations Management

Think About It

What uncertainties does Starbucks face in its value chain? Can Starbucks manage those uncertainties? If so, how? If not, why not?

That coffee you love so much at your local Starbucks location starts as coffee beans (berries) plucked from fields of coffee plants.[1] From harvest to storage to roasting to retail to cup, Starbucks understands the important role each value chain participant plays. Starbucks offers a selection of coffees from around the world, and its coffee buyers personally travel to the coffee-growing regions of Latin America, Africa/Arabia, and Asia/Pacific to select and purchase the highest-quality *arabica* beans. There are many potential challenges in "transforming" the raw material into the quality product and experience that customers expect at Starbucks—weather, shipping and logistics, technology, political instability, and so forth.

Although these operations management challenges are significant, the most challenging issue facing Starbucks today may be balancing its vision of the uniquely Starbucks coffee experience with the realities of selling a $5 latte in today's world. Starbucks products have become an unaffordable luxury for many. As revenues and profits declined during the economic downturn, CEO Howard Schultz realized that "the company needed to change almost everything about how it operates." Recessionary and competitive pressures forced Starbucks away from its "anti-fast-food" focus to become more streamlined. Stores implemented "lean" initiatives such as keeping items in the same place, moving drink toppings closer to where drinks are handed to customers, and altering the order of assembly. Stores witnessed increases of up to 20 percent in transactions.

Lean techniques have to be balanced with quality objectives. Starbucks sped up drink preparation using a model in which baristas produced as many drinks as possible, but later chose to reduce the speed of service to ensure the highest customer value experiences.

Every organization produces something, whether it's a good or a service. Some, like Starbucks, produce both a good and a service. Technology has changed how production is done. This chapter focuses on organizations' processes of operations management.

We also look at the important role that managers play in managing those operations.

WHY IS OPERATIONS MANAGEMENT IMPORTANT TO ORGANIZATIONS?

6.1 **Tell** What is operations management, and what is its role?

You've probably never given much thought to how organizations "produce" the goods and services that you buy or use. But it's an important process. Without it, you wouldn't have a car to drive or McDonald's fries to snack on, or even a hiking trail in a local park to enjoy. *Organizations need to have well-thought-out and well-designed operating systems, organizational control systems, and quality programs to survive in today's increasingly competitive global environment.* And it's the manager's job to manage those things.

What Is Operations Management?

The term **operations management** refers to the design, operation, and control of the **transformation process** that converts such resources as labour and raw materials into goods and services that are sold to customers. Exhibit 6-1 portrays a simplified overview of the transformation process of creating value by converting inputs into outputs. The system takes inputs—people, technology, capital, equipment, materials, and information—and transforms them through various processes, procedures, and work activities into finished goods and services. These processes, procedures, and work activities are found throughout the organization. For example, department members in marketing, finance, research and development, human resources, and accounting convert inputs into outputs such as sales, increased market share, high rates of return on investments, new and innovative products, motivated and committed employees, and accounting reports.

As a manager, you'll need to be familiar with operations management concepts, regardless of the area in which you're managing, in order to achieve your goals more effectively and efficiently. Operations management focuses on several key competitive priorities: cost, quality, delivery, flexibility, and service.

Why is operations management so important to organizations and managers?

---

1. It encompasses processes in services and manufacturing organizations.
2. It is important in effectively and efficiently managing productivity.
3. It plays a strategic role in an organization's competitive success.

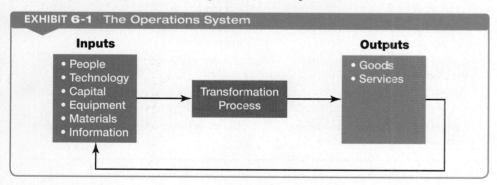

EXHIBIT 6-1 The Operations System

Inputs
- People
- Technology
- Capital
- Equipment
- Materials
- Information

Transformation Process

Outputs
- Goods
- Services

---

operations management
The study and application of the transformation process.

transformation process
The process that converts resources into finished goods and services.

Some economists think the shipping container has done more for global trade than every trade agreement signed over the past 50 years. One proposal sees containers made from carbon-fibre composites to lower cost, increase security, and enhance tracking.[6]

How Do Service and Manufacturing Firms Differ?

With a menu that offers more than 200 items made fresh each day, The Cheesecake Factory restaurants rely on a finely tuned production system. One food-service consultant says, "They've evolved with this highly complex menu combined with a highly efficient kitchen."[2]

All organizations produce goods or services through the transformation process. Simply stated, every organization has an operations system that creates value by transforming inputs into finished goods and services outputs. For manufacturers, the products are obvious: cars, cellphones, or food products. After all, **manufacturing organizations** produce physical goods. It's easy to see the operations management (transformation) process at work in these types of organizations because raw materials are turned into recognizable physical products. But that transformation process isn't as readily evident in **service organizations** because they produce nonphysical outputs in the form of services. For instance, hospitals provide medical and health care services that help people manage their personal health; taxi companies provide transportation services that move people from one location to another; cruise lines provide vacation and entertainment services; and residential plumbers and electricians ensure that we have running water and electricity where we live. All of these service organizations transform inputs into outputs. For example, look at your college. College administrators bring together inputs—instructors, books, academic journals, multimedia classrooms, and similar resources—to transform "unenlightened" students into educated and skilled individuals. Exhibit 6-2 illustrates the difference between goods and services.

The reason we're making this point is that the Canadian economy, and to a large extent the global economy, is dominated by the creation and sale of services. Most of the world's developed countries are predominantly service economies. In Canada, for instance, almost 78 percent of all economic activity is services, and in the United States it is nearly 77 percent.[3] In lesser developed countries, the services sector is less important. For instance, in Nigeria it accounts for only 33 percent of economic activity; in Laos, only 37 percent; and in Vietnam, 38 percent.[4,5]

EXHIBIT 6-2 Goods Versus Services	
Goods	**Services**
Tangible—have a physical form	Intangible—are experienced
Can be stored in inventory	Production and consumption happen at the same time
Ownership is transferred	Ownership of service is not transferred to the customer
Can be produced independently of the customer	Customers are much more involved
Delays can be tolerated	Time is more important and delays are more challenging
Quality can be measured by defects or deviations in manufacturing	Quality is based on customer perceptions

manufacturing organizations
Organizations that produce physical goods.

service organizations
Organizations that produce nonphysical products in the form of services.

How Do Businesses Improve Productivity?

One jetliner has some 4 million parts. Efficiently assembling such a finely engineered product requires intense focus. Boeing and Airbus, the two major global manufacturers, have copied techniques from Toyota. However, not every technique can be copied because airlines demand more customization than do car buyers, and there are significantly more rigid safety regulations for jetliners than for cars.[7] Amazon purchased robotics company Kiva Systems as part of its push to speed delivery and reduce order costs. Amazon is using 1400 Kiva robots in three of its warehouses, which could save the company almost $900 million per year due to higher operating efficiency across its massive order fulfillment–centre network. Another interesting potential is for Amazon to begin selling robots to other companies. Prior to its purchase, Kiva was charging about $2 million for a kit of robots and another $20 million for large installations.[8]

Although most organizations do not make products that have 4 million parts, and most organizations are unable to function without people, *improving productivity has become a major goal in virtually every organization.* For countries, high productivity can lead to economic growth and development. Employees can receive higher wages and company profits can increase without causing inflation. For individual organizations, increased productivity gives them a more competitive cost structure and the ability to offer more competitive prices.

Over the past decade, Canadian businesses have made dramatic improvements to increase their efficiency. However, it is important to balance those improvements with effectiveness. For example, H.J. Heinz Company's frozen-food plant in Pocatello, Idaho, was the highest ranked factory for safety, cleanliness, and efficiency in 2011. In 2014, the plant was closed because of ineffective logistics, such as shipping frozen enchiladas more than 1000 miles away from San Diego to Idaho, and from there to distribution centres on the East Coast.[10] These changes impacted Canadian operations as well, with the century-old Leamington, Ontario, plant closed amid much acrimony in November 2013.

Organizations that hope to succeed globally are looking for ways to improve productivity. For example, Tim Hortons began offering double lanes in many of its drive-throughs to improve speed and accuracy. The two-lane system would likely be more effective if one lane was dedicated for coffee-only customers. McDonald's generates 70 percent of its revenues from drive-through customers and recently added a third high-speed window in many stores to counter the fact that the company's drive-through time of 189 seconds is longer than Wendy's (158 seconds) or Taco Bell (134 seconds).[11] According to a study from Gad Allon, a professor at Northwestern University in Chicago, "Every seven seconds of improvement amounts to an average gain of one percent of market share."[12] The Canadian Imperial Bank of Commerce, based in Toronto, automated its purchasing function, saving several million dollars annually.[13] And Skoda, the Czech car company owned by Germany's Volkswagen AG, improved its productivity through an intensive restructuring of its manufacturing process.[14]

The advent of robots that are cheap and safe enough to be used outside big factories is one factor in the rise of the robots. Amazon is imagining a world where drones will deliver products to customers. Companies have used robots as grips on film sets and panel installers at solar-power plants. Aerial robots—drones—are used by farmers to tend crops, by broadcasters to monitor traffic, and by architects to look for infrastructure in need of repair.[9]

Productivity = People + Operations Variables

Productivity is a composite of people and operations variables. To improve productivity, managers must focus on both. William Edwards Deming was an American statistician, professor, author, lecturer, and consultant.[15] He is widely credited with improving production in the United States during World War II, although he's probably best known for his work in Japan. From 1950 onward, he taught Japanese top managers how to improve product design and product quality, testing, and sales, primarily through applying statistical methods. Deming believed that managers, not workers, were the primary source of increased productivity. He outlined 14 points for improving management's productivity (see Exhibit 6-3 for a visual representation of Deming's work). A close look at these suggestions reveals Deming's understanding of the interplay between people and

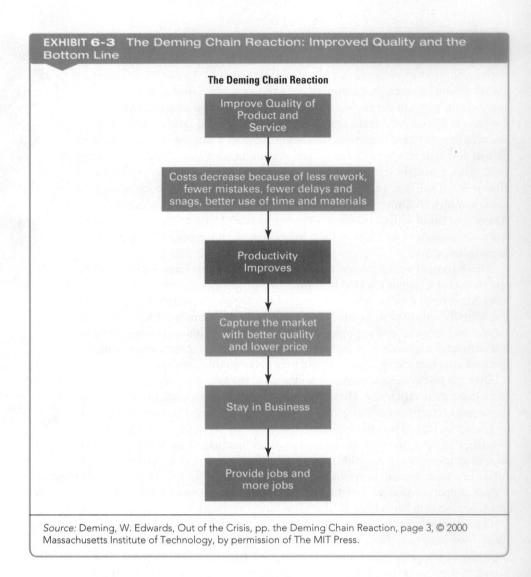

EXHIBIT 6-3 The Deming Chain Reaction: Improved Quality and the Bottom Line

The Deming Chain Reaction

Improve Quality of Product and Service

↓

Costs decrease because of less rework, fewer mistakes, fewer delays and snags, better use of time and materials

↓

Productivity Improves

↓

Capture the market with better quality and lower price

↓

Stay in Business

↓

Provide jobs and more jobs

Source: Deming, W. Edwards, Out of the Crisis, pp. the Deming Chain Reaction, page 3, © 2000 Massachusetts Institute of Technology, by permission of The MIT Press.

operations. High productivity can't come solely from good "people management." The truly effective organization will maximize productivity by successfully integrating people into the overall operations system. For instance, customer lines snaking out the door have been an issue for the burrito chain Chipotle. The fast-food chain, with six locations in Canada, recently sped up service by six transactions per hour by implementing a system to leverage the strengths of its employees.[16] Exhibit 6-4 illustrates the four pillars of its operations system.

Chiptole is a company that understands the important interplay between people and the operations system.

EXHIBIT 6-4 The Four Pillars of Chipotle's Operations System

Pillar	Purpose
Expediters	An extra person between cooks and cashiers
Linebackers	The people who patrol the countertops, serving-ware, and bins of food so that the people servicing customers never turn their backs on them
Mise en place	A zero tolerance policy for not having everything ready and in place for peak periods
Aces in their places	Having each branch's top servers in the most important positions at peak times

What Is Value Chain Management and Why Is It Important?

6.2 **Define** What is the nature and purpose of value chain management?

1

What Is Value Chain Management?

Let's start from the beginning . . .

- Every organization needs customers to survive and prosper.

- Customers want value from the goods and services they purchase or use, and *they decide what has value*.

- Organizations must provide that value to attract and keep customers.

- **Value** is defined as the performance characteristics, features and attributes, and any other aspects of goods and services for which customers are willing to give up resources (usually money).

vege/Fotolia

The following examples of **closely integrated work activities among many different players are brought to you by . . . VALUE CHAIN MANAGEMENT!**

- **Big management assignment due in one week and your computer crashes! NO!** Your custom-designed dream computer is built to your exact specifications and delivered three days later. Management assignment **DONE!**

- **Zero inventory warehousing**. Order processing that involves only one change of hands. It's happening at Siemens AG's Computed Tomography manufacturing plant in Forchheim, Germany, because its 30 supplier partners share responsibility with the plant for overall process performance.

- Black & Decker's handheld glue gun—**totally outsourced to the leading glue gun manufacturer**.[17]

Marek Kosmal/Fotolia

value
The performance characteristics, features, attributes, and other aspects of goods and services, for which customers are willing to give up resources.

- Value is provided to customers through transforming raw materials and other resources into some product or service that end users need or desire when, where, and how they want it.

That seemingly simple act of turning varied resources into something that customers value and are willing to pay for involves a vast array of interrelated work activities performed by different participants (*suppliers, manufacturers, and even customers*)—that is, it involves the **value chain**.[17]

- **Value chain management (VCM)** is *externally* oriented and focuses on both incoming materials and outgoing products and services. VCM is effectiveness oriented and aims to create the highest value for customers.[18]

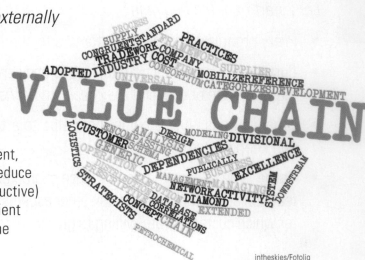

intheskies/Fotolia

  - Contrast VCM with supply chain management, which is efficiency oriented (its goal is to reduce costs and make the organization more productive) and *internally* oriented by focusing on efficient flow of incoming materials (resources) to the organization.

- **Who has the power in the value chain?**

  - Is it the supplier providing needed resources and materials? After all, suppliers have the ability to dictate prices and quality.

  - Is it the manufacturer that assembles those resources into a valuable product or service? A manufacturer's contribution in creating a product or service is critical.

  - Is it the distributor that makes sure the product or service is available where and when the customer needs it?

 Actually, it's none of these!

In value chain management, **customers** are the ones with the power.[19]

---

value chain
The entire series of work activities that add value at each step from raw materials to finished product.

value chain management (VCM)
The process of managing the sequence of activities and information along the entire value chain.

- They define what value is and how it is created and provided.

- Using VCM, managers seek to find that unique combination in which customers are offered solutions that truly meet their needs and at a price that cannot be matched by competitors.[20]

Goals of Value Chain Management

- Sequence of participants work together as a team, each adding some component of value—*such as faster assembly, more accurate information, or better customer response and service*—to the overall process.[21]

- The better the collaboration among the various chain participants, the better the customer solutions.

- When value is created for customers and their needs and desires satisfied, everyone along the chain benefits.[22]

Durand Florence/Newcom

2 How Does Value Chain Management Benefit Businesses?

- improved procurement (acquiring needed resources)

- improved logistics (managing materials, service, and information)

- improved product development (close relationships with customers leads to developing products they value)

- enhanced customer order management (managing every step to make sure customers are satisfied)[23]

nickylarson974/Fotolia

beawolf/Fotolia

Ford's operations management allows it to produce cars that are greener and cleaner. A typical car is made with 100 kinds of plastic, and Ford has begun to replace many of these with plant-based materials. Seats are filled with foam made from soybeans; coconut husks are being used in sound-absorbing carpet underlay; and latex extracted from dandelion roots is producing natural rubber instead of synthetic rubber made from petroleum.

What Role Does Operations Management Play in a Company's Strategy?

Modern manufacturing originated more than 100 years ago in the United States, primarily in Detroit's automobile factories. The success that U.S. manufacturers experienced during World War II led manufacturing executives to believe that troublesome production problems had been conquered. These executives focused, instead, on improving other functional areas, such as finance and marketing, and paid little attention to manufacturing. However, as Canadian and U.S. executives neglected production, managers in Japan, Germany, and other countries took the opportunity to develop modern, technologically advanced facilities that fully integrated manufacturing operations into strategic planning decisions. The competition's success realigned world manufacturing leadership. North American manufacturers soon discovered that foreign goods were being made not only less expensively but also with better quality. To counter this, they invested heavily in improving manufacturing technology, increased the corporate authority and visibility of manufacturing executives, and began incorporating existing and future production requirements into the organization's overall strategic plan.

Today, successful organizations recognize the crucial role that operations management plays as part of the overall organizational strategy to establish and maintain global leadership.[24] Organizations face many operational strategy issues: location, capacity, supply chain integration, choice of production process, quality management, control process, workforce composition, and organizational structure. Each of these operational variables must align with overall organizational strategy.

The strategic role that operations management plays in successful organizational performance can be seen clearly as more organizations move toward managing their operations from a value chain perspective, which we're going to discuss next.

6.3 **Describe** How is value chain management done?

HOW IS VALUE CHAIN MANAGEMENT DONE?

Supply Chain Management

A supply chain is the organizations that are involved in the production and delivery of a product or service. These include facilities such as factories, warehouses, distribution outlets, retail stores, and offices. Supply chains also include functions and activities, such as forecasting, purchasing, inventory management, information management, quality control, scheduling, procurement, distribution, delivery, and customer service. Supply chains are often referred to as value chains, indicating that value is added as goods and services progress through the chain.

Supply chain management is the coordination of activities across the supply chain. Exhibit 6-5 lists the key elements of supply chain management and some of the typical issues faced in each element.

EXHIBIT 6-5 Elements of Supply Chain Management	
Customers	Forecasting the quantity and timing of customer demand
Facilities	Location, capacity, operational design
Inventory	Meeting demand while managing inventory and safety stock
Production	Product/service design, controlling quality, scheduling work
Transportation	Method of transportation, route, logistics
Information	Information sharing, technology
Suppliers	Monitoring supplier quality, flexibility, maintaining relationships, evaluating suppliers

Supply chains and value chains are susceptible to changes in environmental circumstances. The Japanese earthquake and tsunami in 2011 was one of the biggest supply chain disruptions in modern history. A study by AON Risk Solutions found that the percentage of companies reporting income loss due to supply chain disruption increased from 28 percent in 2011 to 42 percent in 2013. One startling statistic revealed that 60 percent of surveyed managers do not utilize supply chain risk management or do not consider their risk management practices to be effective. Operations executives at Cisco have learned to integrate supply chain design and risk management with proactive capabilities to keep the supply chain resilient, effective, and as profitable as possible.[25] Protecting a supply chain from disruption involves increasing inventory, adding capacity at various locations, and using a mix of different suppliers. These tactics to increase supply chain resilience may undermine efforts to improve supply chain efficiency. Recurrent risks cause companies to focus on efficiency while managing demand fluctuations; disruptive risks require companies to increase costs to reduce risk. To balance both types of risk requires segmenting or regionalizing the supply chain.[26]

The dynamic, competitive environment facing contemporary global organizations demands new solutions.[27] Understanding how and why value is determined by the marketplace has led some organizations to experiment with a new **business model**—that is, a strategic design for how a company intends to profit from its broad array of strategies, processes, and activities. For example, IKEA, the home furnishings manufacturer, transformed itself from a small, Swedish mail-order furniture operation into the world's largest retailer of home furnishings by reinventing the value chain in the home furnishings industry. The company offers customers well-designed products at substantially lower prices in return for the customers' willingness to take on certain key tasks traditionally done by manufacturers and retailers—such as getting the furniture home and assembling it.[28] The company's adoption of a unique business model and willingness to abandon old methods and processes have worked well. It also helped that IKEA recognized the importance of managing its value chain.

Like the diagram, the value chain contains hundreds of linked activities that ultimately provide value to the customer

What Are the Requirements for Successful Value Chain Management?

So what does successful value chain management require? Exhibit 6-6 summarizes the six main requirements. Let's look at each of these elements more closely.

1. **Coordination and collaboration.** For the value chain to achieve its goal of meeting and exceeding customers' needs and desires, comprehensive and seamless integration among all members of the chain is absolutely necessary. All partners in the value chain must identify things that they may not value but that customers do. Sharing information and being flexible as far as who in the value chain does what are important steps in building coordination and collaboration. This sharing of information and analysis requires open communication among the various value chain partners. BMW's South Carolina plant faced a shortage of workers knowledgeable about diesel engines. In Germany, industry commonly partners with schools to create an advanced industrial capacity and lower unemployment levels. In North America, these collaborative partnerships are less frequent. BMW's apprenticeship program allowed South Carolina to attract France's Michelin and Germany's Continental Tire to expand in the state.[29]

business model
A strategic design for how a company intends to profit from its broad array of strategies, processes, and activities.

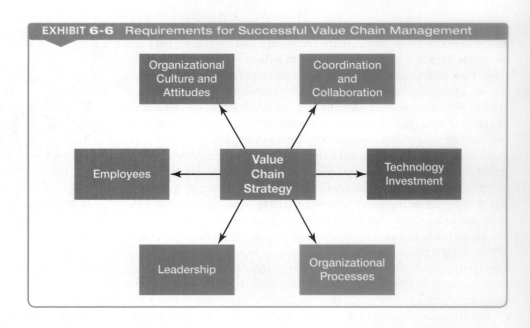

EXHIBIT 6-6 Requirements for Successful Value Chain Management

And the
Survey Says...[35]

22% of manufacturers introduced product innovations during a recent three-year time span.

58% of companies are looking to connect better with their suppliers.

56% of those companies hope to reduce procurement costs.

16% of employers prefer using employee referrals to locate quality employees.

12% of companies say that sustainability is among their top three supply chain priorities.

63% of those companies see sustainability as an opportunity for revenue growth.

64% of manufacturers say that they currently have wireless networks or intend to have them.

2. **Technology investment.** Successful value chain management isn't possible without a significant investment in information technology. The payoff from this investment is that information technology can be used to restructure the value chain to better serve end users.[30] For example, Rollerblade invested heavily in developing a website and used it to educate customers about its products. Although the company has chosen not to sell its products over the Web for fear of antagonizing its dealer network, managers remain flexible about the issue and would reconsider if they felt that value could be better delivered to customers by doing so.[31]

What types of technology are important? According to experts, the key tools include a supporting enterprise resource planning software (ERP) system that links all of an organization's activities, sophisticated work planning and scheduling software, customer relationship management systems, business intelligence capabilities, and e-business connections with trading network partners.[32] For instance, Dell manages its supplier relationships almost exclusively online. The company has one website for customers and one for suppliers. The supplier website is the primary mode of communication between Dell and 33 of its largest suppliers. The company's investment in this type of information technology allows it to meet customers' needs in a way that competitors haven't been able to match.[33] Mercy Hospital in St. Louis has used medication-tracking to save US$600 000 per year in time lost from pharmacists, technicians, and nurses locating medications. Other hospitals are using RFID tags and mobile robots for delivery of meds to reduce the instances of drugs being misplaced or stolen.[34]

3. **Organizational processes.** Value chain management radically changes **organizational processes**—that is, the way organizational work is done.[36] Managers must critically evaluate all organizational processes from beginning to end by looking at core competencies—the organization's unique skills, capabilities, and resources—to determine where value is being added. Non-value-adding activities are eliminated. Questions such as "Where can internal knowledge be leveraged to improve the flow of material and information?" "How can we better configure our product to satisfy both customers and suppliers?" "How can the flow of material and information be improved?" and "How can we improve customer service?" should be asked for each process. For example, when managers at Deere & Company implemented value

organizational processes
The way organizational work is done.

chain management in its Worldwide Commercial and Consumer Equipment Division, a thorough process evaluation revealed that work activities needed to be better synchronized and interrelationships between multiple links in the value chain better managed. They changed numerous work processes division-wide to improve these relationships.[37] Airlines have struggled with speeding up the boarding process, as delays are estimated to cost airlines more than $30 billion in the United States alone. Researchers at Clarkson University have proposed assigning seats to airline passengers based on the number of bags they carry. Each row of seats would balance customers with two bags, one bag, and no bags to shave off boarding time and distribute luggage more evenly throughout the plane.[38] United Air has boarded passengers by location, using what they call the "WilMA" (Window, Middle, Aisle) system, which is saving the airline four to five minutes per flight and almost $1 million annually.[39]

Three important conclusions can be made about how organizational processes must change:

- First, better demand forecasting is necessary and possible because of closer ties with customers and suppliers. For example, in an effort to make sure that Listerine was on the store shelves when customers wanted it, Walmart collaborated with product manufacturer Pfizer Consumer Healthcare on improving product demand forecast information. Through their mutual efforts, the partners boosted Walmart's sales of Listerine by $6.5 million. Customers also benefited because they were able to purchase the product when and where they wanted it.

- Second, selected functions may need to be done collaboratively with other partners in the value chain. This collaboration may even extend to sharing employees. For instance, CAE Aviation in Edmonton was facing a shrinking Canadian defence budget and needed to become more productive to compete internationally. The company changed from single-trade work groups to cross-functional teams, which required a cultural change to a participatory style of management.[40]

- Finally, new measures are needed for evaluating the performance of various activities along the value chain. Because the goal in value chain management is meeting and exceeding customers' needs and desires, managers need a better picture of how well value is being created and delivered to customers. For instance, the Canadian lamb chain was established in an effort to secure an increased supply of Canadian lamb to meet rising domestic demand. Processors, who slaughter, process, and package meat, encouraged farmers to diversify operations and increase lamb production.

4. **Leadership.** The importance of leadership to value chain management is plain and simple—successful value chain management is not possible without strong and committed leadership.[41] From top organizational levels to lower levels, managers must support, facilitate, and promote the implementation and ongoing practice of value chain management. Managers must make a serious commitment to identifying what value is, how that value can best be provided, and how successful those efforts have been. That type of organizational atmosphere or culture in which all efforts are focused on delivering superb customer value is not possible without a serious commitment on the part of the organization's leaders. Also, it is important that leaders outline expectations for what is involved in the organization's pursuit of value chain management. Ideally, articulating expectations should start with a vision or mission statement that expresses the organization's commitment to identifying, capturing, and providing the highest possible value to customers. For example, the Alberta Barley Commission was looking for a way to make people aware that barley was used for more than beer and animal feed, but is also a very healthy grain that could be used in baking due to its low glycemic index. They worked with the Good Earth Café, a coffee house and restaurant that differentiates itself by serving healthy alternatives to mainstream baked goods.[42] Throughout the organization, then, managers should clarify expectations regarding each employee's role in the value chain. Being clear about

michaeljung/Fotolia

Canadian consumers purchased more than 12 million roses for Valentine's Day in 2010. Getting fresh roses to Canadian lovers takes speed, the right temperature, and skill. As with other perishable products, flowers require specific temperatures to maintain freshness and stay in bloom. Eighty percent of all flowers sold for Valentine's Day are shipped from Latin America, with 12 percent coming from U.S. production and 8 percent arriving from other locations.

expectations also extends to partners. The Barley commission created promotional materials for the Good Earth Café and barley producer Hamilton's Milling helped out with recipe development and how bakers could best make use of barley for healthy baked goods. The barley commission worked with barley producers and food retailers to deliver better value to customers.

5. **Employees/human resources.** We know from our discussions of management theories and approaches throughout this text that employees are the organization's most important resource. So, not surprisingly, employees play an important part in value chain management. Three main human resources requirements for value chain management are flexible approaches to job design, an effective hiring process, and ongoing training. Flexibility is the key description of job design in a value chain management organization. Traditional functional job roles—such as marketing, sales, accounts payable, customer service, and so forth—are inadequate in a value chain management environment.

   Instead, jobs need to be designed around work processes that link all functions involved in creating and providing value to customers. This type of flexible job design supports the company's commitment to providing superb customer value.[43] In designing jobs for a value chain approach, the focus needs to be on how each activity performed by an employee can best contribute to the creation and delivery of customer value, which requires flexibility in what employees do and how they do it.

   The fact that jobs in a value chain management organization must be flexible contributes to the second requirement: Flexible jobs require flexible employees. In a value chain organization, employees may be assigned to work teams that tackle a given process and are often asked to do different things on different days, depending on need. In an environment focusing on collaborative relationships that may change as customer needs change, employees' ability to be flexible is critical. Accordingly, the organization's hiring process must be designed to identify those employees who have the ability to quickly learn and adapt.

   Finally, the need for flexibility also requires a significant investment in ongoing employee training. Whether the training involves learning how to use information technology software, how to improve the flow of materials throughout the chain, how to identify activities that add value, how to make better decisions faster, or how to improve any number of other potential work activities, managers must see to it that employees have the knowledge and tools they need to do their jobs. For example, Carswell, a division of Thomson Reuters Canada, uses training to grow leaders from within. The Toronto company developed an in-house leadership intern program for its 850 staff, as well as courses that teach new recruits about the business and their role in it, that included 90-minute sessions that help staff navigate the myriad resources available, especially online. As one of Canada's Top 100 employers, Carswell also uses internal training, cross-functional assignments, mentoring, and coaching directed at staff already in management or on their way there. An impressive 80 percent of those in the two-year internship program are promoted when finished.[44]

6. **Organizational culture and attitudes.** The last requirement for value chain management is having a supportive organizational culture and attitudes. Those cultural attitudes include sharing, collaborating, openness, flexibility, mutual respect, and trust. And these attitudes encompass not only the internal partners in the value chain but external partners as well. For instance, American Standard has chosen to practise these attitudes the old-fashioned way—with lots of face time and telephone calls. However, as we mentioned earlier, Dell has taken a completely different approach, as it works with its value chain partners almost exclusively through cyberspace.[45] Both approaches, however, reflect each company's commitment to developing long-lasting, mutually beneficial, and trusting relationships that best meet customers' needs.

What Are the Obstacles to Value Chain Management?

As desirable as value chain management may be, managers must tackle several obstacles in managing the value chain—organizational barriers, cultural attitudes, required capabilities, and people (see Exhibit 6-7).

EXHIBIT 6-7 Obstacles to Successful Value Chain Management

```
Organizational          Cultural
  Barriers              Attitudes

           Obstacles to
           Value Chain
           Management

   People               Required
                       Capabilities
```

ORGANIZATIONAL BARRIERS Organizational barriers are among the most difficult obstacles to handle. These barriers include refusal or reluctance to share information, reluctance to shake up the status quo, and security issues. Without shared information, close coordination and collaboration is impossible. And the reluctance or refusal of employees to shake up the status quo can impede efforts toward value chain management and prevent its successful implementation. Finally, because value chain management relies heavily on a substantial information technology infrastructure, system security and Internet security breaches are issues that need to be addressed.

CULTURAL ATTITUDES Unsupportive cultural attitudes—especially trust and control—also can be obstacles to value chain management. The trust issue is a critical one—both lack of trust and too much trust. To be effective, partners in a value chain must trust each other.

There must be a mutual respect for, and honesty about, each partner's activities all along the chain. When that trust doesn't exist, the partners will be reluctant to share information, capabilities, and processes. But too much trust also can be a problem. Just about any organization is vulnerable to theft of intellectual property—that is, proprietary information that is critical to an organization's efficient and effective functioning and competitiveness. You need to be able to trust your value chain partners so your organization's valuable assets are not compromised.[46] Another cultural attitude that can be an obstacle is the belief that when an organization collaborates with external and internal partners, it no longer controls its own destiny. However, this just isn't the case. Even with the intense collaboration that is important to value chain management, organizations still control critical decisions such as what customers value, how much value they desire, and what distribution channels are important.[47]

REQUIRED CAPABILITIES We know from our earlier discussion of requirements for the successful implementation of value chain management that value chain partners need numerous capabilities. Several of these—coordination and collaboration, the ability to configure products to satisfy customers and suppliers, and the ability to educate internal and external partners—are not easy. But they are essential to capturing and exploiting the value chain. Many of the companies we have described throughout this section endured critical and oftentimes difficult self-evaluations of their capabilities and processes in order to become more effective and efficient at managing their value chains.

PEOPLE The final obstacles to successful value chain management can be an organization's people. Without their unwavering commitment to do whatever it takes, value chain management will not be successful. If employees refuse to be flexible in their work—how and with whom they work—collaboration and cooperation throughout the value chain will be hard to achieve. In addition, value chain management takes an incredible amount of time and energy on the part of

Starbucks CEO Howard Schultz visits with coffee bean growers around the globe to discuss the importance of producing high-quality beans and establishing responsible growing practices. Schultz's personal visits with external partners illustrate his support of Starbucks's cultural attitudes of sharing, openness, collaborating, and mutual respect.

elena.rudyk/Fotolia

an organization's employees. Managers must motivate those high levels of effort from employees, which is not an easy thing to do.

6.4 **Discuss** What are some contemporary issues in managing operations?

WHAT CONTEMPORARY ISSUES DO MANAGERS FACE IN MANAGING OPERATIONS?

Redesigned milk jugs that have been adopted by Walmart and Costco are cheaper to ship, better for the environment, cost less, and keep the milk fresher. Experts say this type of redesign is "an example of the changes likely to play out in the Canadian economy over the next two decades. In an era of soaring global demand and higher costs for energy and materials, virtually every aspect of the economy needs to be re-examined and many products must be redesigned for greater efficiency."[48]

If you somehow thought that managing operations did not really matter in today's online 24/7 global economy, think again. It does matter . . . a lot. We're going to look at five contemporary issues that managers face in managing operations.

What Role Does Technology Play in Operations Management?

As we know from our previous discussion of value chain management, today's competitive marketplace has put tremendous pressure on organizations to deliver products and services that customers value in a timely manner. Smart companies are looking at ways to harness technology to improve operations management. Many fast-food companies are competing to see who can provide faster and better service to drive-through customers. With drive-through now representing a huge portion of sales, faster and better delivery can be a significant competitive edge. For instance, Wendy's added awnings to some of its menu boards and replaced some of the text with pictures. Others use confirmation screens, a technology that helped McDonald's boost accuracy by more than 11 percent. And technology used by two national chains tells managers how much food they need to prepare by counting vehicles in the drive-through line and factoring in demand for current promotional and popular staple items.[49]

Although an organization's production activities are driven by the recognition that the customer is king, managers still need to be more responsive. For instance, operations managers need systems that can reveal available capacity, status of orders, and product quality while products are in the process of being manufactured, not just after the fact. To connect more closely with customers, production must be synchronized across the enterprise. To avoid bottlenecks and slowdowns, the production function must be a full partner in the entire business system. Walmart is trying to compete with major online rivals like Amazon by offering speedy, same-day grocery delivery. To do so, Walmart is using "dark stores"—spaces that are used only for online order fulfillment. Its inaugural store in Mexico handles the same volume of orders as five regular Walmart stores.[50]

What makes such extensive collaboration possible is technology. Technology also allows organizations to control costs, particularly in the areas of predictive maintenance, remote diagnostics, and utility cost savings. For instance, Internet-compatible equipment contains embedded Web servers that can communicate proactively—that is, if a piece of equipment breaks or reaches certain preset parameters indicating that it is about to break, it asks for help. But technology can do more than sound an alarm or light up an indicator button. For instance, some devices have the ability to initiate email or signal a pager to a supplier, the maintenance department, or contractor describing the specific problem and requesting parts and service. How much is such e-enabled maintenance control worth? It can be worth quite a lot if it prevents equipment breakdowns and subsequent production downtime.

blueringmedia/Fotolia

Lowe's is battling with Home Depot for hardware superstore supremacy and has turned to technology to improve customer service. Lowe's is using satellites to gauge traffic at its 1900 stores, scanning images of parking lots to determine how many shoppers it can expect on an hourly basis. It can then analyze how many transactions are occurring at various traffic levels and adjust scheduling in accordance.

TIPS (FOR) MANAGERS

Technology and the Manager's Job

What would the ideal factory of the future look like?[51] Experts at Georgia Tech's Manufacturing Research Center say that three important trends are driving what tomorrow's factories will look like. One trend is *globalization of the supply chain*. In the factories of the future, design and business processes will be performed where it is most efficient and effective to do so. For example, parts for Boeing's 787 Dreamliner are produced around the world and then come together in Boeing's US facilities. The second trend is *technology that simultaneously dematerializes the product while vastly increasing complexity*. The challenge for managing operations is that despite simplicity in products, the production process is becoming more complex. The third trend is *demographics and the impact on demand patterns*. Products will have shorter life cycles and more variety and choices. The key characteristic of the factory of the future will be its ability to change to accommodate whatever product is being produced in the needed time frame. And it will be particularly important that these factories be efficient and effective.

Given these trends, it is clear that technology will continue to play a key role in transformation processes that need to be collaborative, adaptive, flexible, and responsive. But keep in mind that technology is simply a tool. Future factories will also require a talented and skilled workforce and a clear understanding of managing operations processes. Those are the challenges facing managers who want their organizations to survive and thrive.

Technology allows the production of far more output with far fewer people. Consider the shift that has taken place in agriculture. The number of North American workers employed in agriculture was more than 35 percent a century ago, and currently sits at less than 2 percent.[52] Agriculture is adapting quickly to technology. Farmers use global positioning systems to plant straighter rows and use "prescriptive planting" technology to collect data on crops and soil and adjust planting depth and distance between crop rows. Data-driven planting is expected to increase worldwide crop production by about $20 billion per year.[53]

Managers who understand the power of technology to contribute to more effective and efficient performance know that managing operations is more than the traditional view of simply producing the product. Instead, the emphasis is on working together with all the organization's business functions to find solutions to customers' business problems.

How Do Managers Control Quality?

Quality problems are expensive. For example, even though Apple has had phenomenal success with its iPod, the batteries in the first three versions died after four hours instead of lasting up to 12 hours, as buyers expected. Apple's settlement with consumers cost close to $100 million. At Schering-Plough, problems with inhalers and other pharmaceuticals were traced to chronic quality control shortcomings, for which the company eventually paid a $500 million fine. And the auto industry paid $14.5 billion to cover the cost of warranty and repair work in one year.[54]

Many experts believe that organizations unable to produce high-quality products will not be able to compete successfully in the global marketplace. What is quality? When you consider a product or service to have quality, what does that mean? Does it mean that the product doesn't break or quit working—that is, it is reliable? Does it mean that the service is delivered in the way that you intended? Does it mean that the product does what it is supposed to do? Or does quality mean something else? Exhibit 6-8 provides a description of several quality dimensions. We are going to define quality as the ability of a product or service to reliably do what it is supposed to do and to satisfy customer expectations.

HOW IS QUALITY ACHIEVED? How quality is achieved is an issue managers must address. A good way to look at quality initiatives is with the management functions—planning, organizing, leading, and controlling—that need to take place.

When *planning for quality*, managers must have quality improvement goals and strategies and plans to achieve those goals. Goals can help focus everyone's attention toward

---

EXHIBIT 6-8 What Is Quality?

Product Quality Dimensions

1. Performance—Operating characteristics

2. Features—Important special characteristics

3. Flexibility—Meeting operating specifications over some period of time

4. Durability—Amount of use before performance deteriorates

5. Conformance—Match with pre-established standards

6. Serviceability—Ease and speed of repair or normal service

7. Aesthetics—How a product looks and feels

8. Perceived quality—Subjective assessment of characteristics (product image)

Service Quality Dimensions

1. Timeliness—Performed in the promised period of time

2. Courtesy—Performed cheerfully

3. Consistency—Giving all customers similar experiences each time

4. Convenience—Accessibility to customers

5. Completeness—Full service, as required

6. Accuracy—Performed correctly each time

Sources: Based on J. W. Dean and J. R. Evans, *Total Quality: Management, Organization, and Society* (St. Paul, MN: West Publishing Company, 1994); H. V. Roberts and B. F. Sergesketter, *Quality Is Personal* (New York: The Free Press, 1993); D. Garvin, *Managed Quality: The Strategic and Competitive Edge* (New York: The Free Press, 1988); and M. A. Hitt, R. D. Ireland, and R. E. Hoskisson, *Strategic Management*, 4th ed. (Cincinnati: South-Western Publishing, 2001), p. 121.

---

some objective quality standard. For instance, Caterpillar's goal is to apply quality improvement techniques to help cut costs.[55] Although this goal is specific and challenging, managers and employees are partnering together to pursue well-designed strategies to achieve the goals, and are confident they can do so.

When *organizing and leading for quality,* it is important for managers to look to their employees. For instance, at the Moose Jaw, Saskatchewan, plant of General Cable Corporation, every employee participates in continual quality assurance training. In addition, the plant manager believes wholeheartedly in giving employees the information they need to do their jobs better. He says, "Giving people who are running the machines the information is just paramount. You can set up your cellular structure, you can cross-train your people, you can use lean tools, but if you don't give people information to drive improvement, there's no enthusiasm." Needless to say, this company shares production data and financial performance measures with all employees.[56]

Organizations with extensive and successful quality improvement programs tend to rely on two important people approaches: cross-functional work teams and self-directed or empowered work teams. Because achieving product quality is something that all employees from upper to lower levels must participate in, it is not surprising that quality-driven organizations rely on well-trained, flexible, and empowered employees.

Finally, managers must recognize when *controlling for quality* that quality improvement initiatives are not possible without having some way to monitor and evaluate their progress. Whether it involves standards for inventory control, defect rate, raw materials procurement, or other operations management areas, controlling for quality is important.

Delcan is one of Canada's 50 Best Managed Companies[57] and is a leader in quality management and control. Delcan provides

Italian carmaker Ferrari competes successfully in the global marketplace by developing and producing high-quality cars in terms of design, performance, and reliability.

quality management of some of the world's most impressive infrastructure programs and has won numerous industry quality awards.

Quality improvement success stories can be found globally. For example, at a Delphi assembly plant in Matamoros, Mexico, employees worked hard to improve quality and made significant strides. For instance, the customer reject rate on shipped products is now 10 ppm (parts per million), down from 3000 ppm—an improvement of almost 300 percent.[58] Quality initiatives at several Australian companies, including Alcoa of Australia, Wormald Security, and Carlton and United Breweries, have led to significant quality improvements.[59] At Valeo Klimasystemme GmbH of Bad Rodach, Germany, assembly teams build different climate-control systems for high-end German cars, including Mercedes and BMW. Quality initiatives by those teams have led to significant improvements.[60]

WHAT QUALITY GOALS MIGHT ORGANIZATIONS PURSUE? To publicly demonstrate their commitment to quality, many organizations worldwide have pursued challenging quality goals. The two best-known are the following:

1. ISO 9000/9001 is a series of international quality management standards established by the International Organization for Standardization (www.iso.org), which set uniform guidelines for processes to ensure that products conform to customer requirements. These standards cover everything from contract review to product design to product delivery. The **ISO 9000** standards have become the internationally recognized standard for evaluating and comparing companies in the global marketplace. In fact, this type of certification can be a prerequisite for doing business globally. Achieving ISO 9000 certification provides proof that a quality operations system is in place. As of 2013, more than 1 million certifications had been awarded to organizations in 175 countries. Almost 9000 Canadian businesses are ISO 9000 certified,[61] and the town of Ajax, Ontario, was the first fully registered municipality in North America to have ISO 9000 certification.[62] Ajax strives to achieve excellence in the delivery of services to its residents and business owners.

2. More than 30 years ago, Motorola popularized the use of stringent quality standards through a trademarked quality improvement program called Six Sigma.[63] Very simply, **Six Sigma** is a quality standard that establishes a goal of no more than 3.4 defects per million units or procedures. What does the name mean? Sigma is the Greek letter that statisticians use to define a standard deviation from a bell curve. The higher the sigma, the fewer the deviations from the norm—that is, the fewer the defects. At one sigma, two-thirds of whatever is being measured falls within the curve. Two sigma covers about 95 percent. At six sigma, you're about as close to defect-free as you can get.[64] It is an ambitious quality goal! Although it is an extremely high standard to achieve, many quality-driven businesses are using and benefitting from it. Other companies pursuing Six Sigma include BMW, Dow Chemical, 3M Company, American Express, Kraft, Sony Corporation, Nokia Corporation, and Johnson & Johnson.[65] Although manufacturers seem to make up the bulk of Six Sigma users, service companies such as financial institutions, retailers, and health care organizations are beginning to apply it. What impact can Six Sigma have? Let us look at an example.

Staples's Lean Six Sigma program has been the impetus for dozens of improvements that have generated tens of millions of dollars in benefit for

tashatuvango/Fotolia

The National Quality Institute (NQI) has certification and training programs and annually recognizes organizations with the Canada Awards for Excellence. While the NQI has made significant advances in promoting Canadian quality improvements, other developed countries are moving faster in this area, giving them a competitive advantage over Canada.

ISO 9000

A series of international quality standards that set uniform guidelines for processes to ensure that products conform to customer requirements.

Six Sigma

A quality standard that establishes a goal of no more than 3.4 defects per million units or procedures.

Staples and produced a tenfold return on the company's investment in the process improvement program:

- improved lease negotiations and enhanced architecture and construction processes that have shaved four weeks off the time needed to open a new store
- streamlined the item-order cycle that freed space and generated inventory savings of $3.3 million
- reconfigured the loading dock layout to eliminate extra handling of merchandise, efforts that improved on-time to due-date performance by 21 percent
- achieved a 50 percent reduction in budget for freight distribution and fulfillment centres[66]

Although it is important for managers to recognize that many positive benefits come from obtaining ISO 9000 certification or Six Sigma, *the key benefit comes from the quality improvement journey itself.* In other words, the goal of quality certification should be having work processes and an operations system in place that enable organizations to meet customers' needs and employees to perform their jobs in a consistently high-quality way.

How Are Projects Managed?

A **project** is a one-time-only set of activities with definite beginning and ending points.[67] Projects vary in size and scope, from a NASA space shuttle launch to a wedding. **Project management** is the task of getting the activities done on time, within budget, and according to specifications. Project management has actually been around for a long time in industries such as construction and movie making, but now it has expanded into almost every type of business. What explains the growing popularity of project management? It fits well with a dynamic environment and the need for flexibility and rapid response. Organizations are increasingly undertaking projects that are somewhat unusual or unique, have specific deadlines, contain complex interrelated tasks requiring specialized skills, and are temporary in nature. These types of projects do not lend themselves well to the standardized operating procedures that guide routine and continuous organizational activities.[68] Managing projects tends to happen in one of four key areas: people, communications, change, and risk. Often a project charter is used, which outlines the project scope, objectives, constraints, and assumptions. In project management, one key aspect is the need to make tradeoffs in the areas of cost, time, and scope—known as the *triple constraint.*

In the typical project, team members are temporarily assigned to and report to a project manager, who coordinates the project's activities with other departments and reports directly to a senior executive. The project is temporary: It exists only long enough to complete its specific objectives. Then it is wound down and closed up; members move on to other projects, return to their permanent departments, or leave the organization. If you were to observe a group of supervisors or department managers for a few days, you would see them regularly detailing what activities have to be done, the order in which they are to be done, who is to do each, and when they are to be completed. What the managers are doing is called scheduling. The following discussion reviews some useful scheduling devices.

HOW DO YOU USE A GANTT CHART? The **Gantt chart** is a planning tool developed around the turn of the century by Henry Gantt. The idea behind the Gantt chart is relatively simple. It is essentially a bar graph, with time

mybaitshop/Fotolia

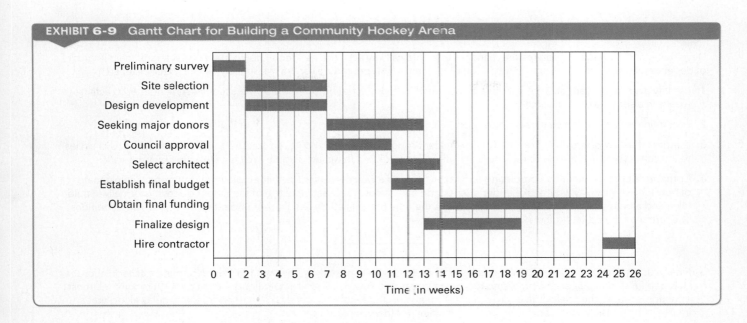

EXHIBIT 6-9 Gantt Chart for Building a Community Hockey Arena

Time (in weeks)

on the horizontal axis and activities to be scheduled on the vertical axis. The bars show output, both planned and actual, over a period of time. The Gantt chart visually shows when tasks are supposed to be done and compares the assigned date with the actual progress on each. This simple but important device allows managers to detail easily what has yet to be done to complete a job or project and to assess whether it is ahead of, behind, or on schedule. Exhibit 6-9 shows a Gantt chart that was developed for building a community hockey arena. Time is expressed in months across the bottom of the chart. Major activities are listed down the left side (see Exhibit 6-9 for more details). The planning comes in deciding what activities need to be done to get the arena built, the order in which those activities need to be done, and the time that should be allocated to each activity. The blue shading represents actual progress made in completing each activity.

A Gantt chart, then, actually becomes a managerial control device as the manager looks for deviations from the plan. In this case, most activities were completed on time. If, for example, the "seeking major donors" activity was two weeks behind, the manager might want to take some corrective action to make up the lost time and to ensure that no further delays will occur. At this point, the manager can expect that the arena will be built at least two weeks late if no corrective action is taken.

WHAT IS A PERT NETWORK ANALYSIS? Gantt and load charts are helpful as long as the activities or projects being scheduled are few and independent of each other. But what if a manager had to plan a large project—such as a complex reorganization, the launching of a major cost-reduction campaign, or the development of a new product—that required coordinating inputs from marketing, production, and product design personnel? Such projects require coordinating hundreds or thousands of activities, some of which must be done simultaneously and some of which cannot begin until earlier activities have been completed. If you are constructing a shopping mall, you obviously cannot start erecting walls until the foundation has been laid. How, then, to schedule such a complex project? Use PERT.

A PERT network is a flowchart-like diagram that depicts the sequence of activities needed to complete a project and the time or costs associated with each activity. With a PERT network, a project manager must think through what has to be done, determine which events depend on one another, and identify potential trouble spots (see Exhibit 6-10). PERT also makes it easy to compare the effects alternative actions will have on scheduling and costs. PERT allows managers to monitor a project's progress, identify possible bottlenecks, and shift resources as necessary to keep the project on schedule.

EXHIBIT 6-10   Developing PERT Charts

Developing a PERT network requires the manager to identify all key activities needed to complete a project, rank them in order of dependence, and estimate each activity's completion time. This procedure can be translated into five specific steps:

1. Identify every significant activity that must be achieved for a project to be completed. The accomplishment of each activity results in a set of events or outcomes.

2. Ascertain the order in which these events must be completed.

3. Diagram the flow of activities from start to finish, identifying each activity and its relationship to all other activities. Use circles to indicate events and arrows to represent activities. The result is a flowchart diagram that is called the PERT network.

4. Compute a time estimate for completing each activity, using a weighted average that employs an optimistic time estimate (t_o) of how long the activity would take under ideal conditions, a most-likely estimate (t_m) of the time the activity normally should take, and a pessimistic estimate (t_p) that represents the time that an activity should take under the worst possible conditions. The formula for calculating the expected time (t_e) is then

$$t_e = \frac{t_o + 4t_m + t_p}{6}$$

5. Finally, using a network diagram that contains time estimates for each activity, the manager can determine a schedule for the start and finish dates of each activity and for the entire project. Any delays that occur along the critical path require the most attention because they delay the entire project. That is, the critical path has no slack in it; therefore, any delay along that path immediately translates into a delay in the final deadline for the completed project.

To understand how to construct a PERT network, you need to know three terms: *events*, *activities*, and *critical path*. Let us define these terms, outline the steps in the PERT process, and then develop an example.

- **Events** are end points that represent the completion of major activities. Sometimes called milestones, events indicate that something significant has happened (such as receipt of purchased items) or an important component is finished. In PERT, events represent a point in time.
- **Activities**, on the other hand, are the actions that take place. Each activity consumes time, as determined on the basis of the time or resources required to progress from one event to another.
- The **critical path** is the longest or most time-consuming sequence of events and activities required to complete the project in the shortest amount of time.[69]

Let us apply PERT to a construction manager's task of building a hockey arena. As a construction manager, you recognize that time really is money in your business. Delays can turn a profitable job into a money loser. Accordingly, you must determine how long it will take to complete the arena. You have carefully dissected the entire project into activities and events. Exhibit 6-11 outlines the major events in the arena construction project and your estimate of the expected time required to complete each activity. Exhibit 6-12 depicts the PERT network based on the data in Exhibit 6-11.

HOW DOES PERT OPERATE?   Your PERT network tells you that if everything goes as planned, it will take just over 32 weeks to build the arena. This time is calculated by tracing the network's critical path: A C D E F H J. Any delay in completing the events along this path will delay the completion of the entire project. For example, if it took six weeks instead of four to get city council approval for the arena (event E), the entire project would be delayed by two weeks (or the time beyond that expected). But a one-week delay for establishing the final budget (event G) would have little

---

events
End points that represent the completion of major activities.

activities
Actions that take place.

critical path
The longest or most time-consuming sequence of events and activities required to complete a project in the shortest amount of time.

EXHIBIT 6-11 Major Activities in Building a Community Hockey Arena

Activity	Immediate Predecessor(s)	Time (weeks)
A. Needs analysis/survey	None	2
B. Determine location for hockey arena	A	5
C. Develop preliminary design	A	5
D. Source donations to support funding base	C	6
E. Obtain council approval	B, D	4
F. Select architect	E	3
G. Establish final budget	E	2
H. Secure outstanding funding	F, G	10
I. Finalize arena design	G	6
J. Hire contractor	H, I	2

EXHIBIT 6-12 A PERT Network for Building a Community Arena

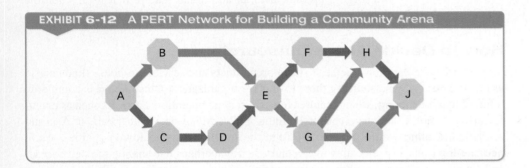

effect because that event is not on the critical path. By using PERT, the construction manager would know that no corrective action would be needed. Further delays in installing the brick, however, could present problems—for such delays may, in actuality, result in a new critical path. Now back to our original critical path dilemma.

Slack time is the time difference between the critical path and all other paths. What use is there for slack? If the project manager notices some slippage on a critical activity, perhaps slack time from a noncritical activity can be borrowed and temporarily assigned to work on the critical one. As you can see, PERT is both a planning and a control tool. Not only does PERT help estimate the times associated with scheduling a project, but it also gives clues about where controls should be placed. Because any event on the critical path that is delayed will delay the overall project (making it not only late but also probably over budget), attention needs to be focused on the critical activities at all times.

As stated at the beginning of this chapter, it is the manager's job to manage the organization's operating systems, organizational control systems, and quality programs. That is the only way organizations will survive in today's increasingly competitive global economy.

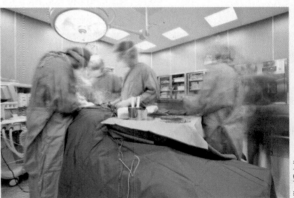

St. John's regional health centre in Missouri was running operating rooms at 100 percent capacity. Emergency cases—about 20 percent of the full load—were causing the hospital to bump long-scheduled surgeries. Doctors often waited several hours to perform routine surgeries, and staff members regularly worked unplanned overtime. The solution was to leave an operating room empty. Crazy idea? The empty room added much needed slack to the system. After implementing the idea, the hospital was able to reduce the number of surgeries performed at night by 45 percent and increase overall surgical volume by 11 percent.[70]

slack time
The time difference between the critical path and all other paths.

A mining alliance in Australia is applying lean principles to coal mining. It is using modular building design to save time and money in construction of processing plants. Engines in the alliance's $5-million trucks are being replaced just-in-time rather than as prescribed by manufacturers, which has increased productivity by 13 percent. Some mines are even using Formula One–style pit stops to improve refuelling of trucks and other vehicles.[71]

How Does Lean Manufacturing Work?

Lean manufacturing and just-in-time (JIT) production are concerned with the timing and flow of parts through the operations system and ensuring it is using very little "fat" (e.g., excess inventory, employees, or space). The JIT approach was developed at Toyota to schedule production with low levels of inventory. But JIT and lean are philosophies that have principles to eliminate disruptions and waste and make the system as flexible as possible.

If lean principles are implemented poorly, it may negatively affect product quality. However, the lean philosophy will alter a company's fundamental definition of quality to focus on those things that are defined by the customer as adding value. If a particular process or feature does not add value for the customer, it should be eliminated. The end user defines "quality" as it relates to the product or service. If the customer receives a product that includes all those features (s)he defines as valuable, it must also be available when (s)he wants it. A customer would forgo a product with an additional feature if it means that the product is not produced quickly enough.

How to Decide About Outsourcing

Managers have a decision whether to develop products and services in-house (known also as **insourcing**) or by outsourcing them to another organization. **Outsourcing** is commonly referred to as **offshoring**, which features relocation of an operational process such as manufacturing to another country, typically in India, China, Malaysia, or other parts of Asia and Africa. **Onshoring** would relocating within the same country to low-cost cities, while **nearshoring** is usually relocating to a country nearby, perhaps one sharing the same border and a market with many geographic, economic, and political similarities. This is becoming more common for Canadian and American companies.

Otis Elevator relocated its plant from Mexico to South Carolina to save money and help fill orders faster by putting the manufacturing of elevators closer to the engineers who design them and their customers. The reshoring initiative has not gone easily, with production delays, a backlog of orders, and customer cancellations.[73]

Outsourcing offers many advantages, including cost savings, external expertise, and an ability to grow more rapidly. Globalization and the Internet have allowed companies to focus on their core competencies and farm out the rest of their operational processes or functional activities, such as IT, accounting, and technical support. This may provide companies with better access to technology, faster speed to market, increased operational flexibility, and lower risk exposure.

Recently there has been a backlash against companies using outsourcing, leading companies to bring back production of goods to the home country, or **reshoring**. Rising energy prices, wage inflation, and customer demand are some of the factors leading Canadian and U.S. companies to bring back the production of goods bound for domestic markets. Firms that reshore successfully take the time to understand the domestic market in terms of labour, utility services and rates, taxation, government support, transportation costs, and product demand.[72] In Ontario, plant closures and an aging workforce have depleted the pool of skilled manufacturing workers.

---

reshoring
Companies that bring back production of goods to the home country.

insourcing
Developing products and services in-house.

outsourcing
Relocation of an operational process such as manufacturing to another country.

offshoring
Relocation of an operational process to a country not connected by land.

onshoring
Relocating to lower-cost cities within the same country.

nearshoring
Relocating to a nearby country, perhaps one sharing the same border and a market with many geographic, economic, and political similarities.

6 Review and Apply

Summary of Learning Outcomes

6.1 **What is operations management, and what is its role?**
Operations management is the transformation process that converts resources into finished goods and services. Manufacturing organizations produce physical goods. Service organizations produce nonphysical outputs in the form of services. Productivity is a composite of people and operations variables. A manager should look for ways to successfully integrate people into the overall operations systems. Organizations must recognize the crucial role that operations management plays as part of their overall strategy in achieving successful performance.

For Starbucks, recessionary and competitive pressures forced Starbucks away from its "anti-fast-food" focus to become more streamlined. Stores implemented "lean" initiatives such as keeping items in the same place, moving drink toppings closer to where drinks are handed to customers, and altering the order of assembly. Stores witnessed increases of up to 20 percent in transactions.

6.2 **What is the nature and purpose of value chain management?** The value chain is the sequence of organizational work activities that add value at each step from raw materials to finished product. Value chain management is the process of managing the sequence of activities and information along the entire product chain.

The goal of value chain management is to create a value chain strategy that meets and exceeds customers' needs and desires and allows for full and seamless integration among all members of the chain.

Four benefits from value chain management include improved procurement, improved logistics, improved product development, and enhanced customer order management.

Lean techniques have to be balanced with quality objectives. Starbucks has sped drink preparation using a model in which baristas produced as many drinks as possible, but later chose to reduce the speed of service to ensure the highest customer value experiences.

6.3 **How is value chain management done?** The six main requirements for successful value chain management include coordination and collaboration, investment in technology, organizational processes, leadership, employees or human resources, and organizational culture and attitudes. The obstacles to value chain management include organizational barriers (refusal to share information, reluctance to shake up the status quo, or security issues), unsupportive cultural attitudes, lack of required capabilities, and employees unwilling or unable to do it.

6.4 **What are some contemporary issues in managing operations?** Companies are looking at ways to harness technology to improve their operations management by extensive collaboration and cost control. ISO 9000 is a series of international quality management standards that set uniform guidelines for processes to ensure that products conform to customer requirements. Six Sigma is a quality standard that establishes a goal of no more than 3.4 defects per million units or procedures. Project management involves getting a project's activities done on time, within budget, and accomplished to specifications. A project is a one-time-only set of activities that has a definite beginning and ending point in time. Popular project scheduling tools include Gantt charts, load charts, and PERT network analysis. Lean manufacturing and just-in-time are philosophies about minimizing waste. Organizations need to decide if outsourcing is right for them and consider the various options, such as offshoring, onshoring, and nearshoring.

SNAPSHOT SUMMARY

6.1 Why Is Operations Management Important to Organizations?

What Is Operations Management?

How Do Service and Manufacturing Firms Differ?

How Do Businesses Improve Productivity?

What Role Does Operations Management Play in a Company's Strategy?

6.2 What Is Value Chain Management and Why Is It Important?

6.3 How Is Value Chain Management Done?

Supply Chain Management

What Are the Requirements for Successful Value Chain Management?

What Are the Obstacles to Value Chain Management?

6.4 What Contemporary Issues Do Managers Face in Managing Operations?

What Role Does Technology Play in Operations Management?

How Do Managers Control Quality?

How Are Projects Managed?

How Does Lean Manufacturing Work?

How to Decide About Outsourcing

MyManagementLab Study, practise, and explore real management situations with these helpful resources:

- **Interactive Lesson Presentations:** Work through interactive presentations and assessments to test your knowledge of management concepts.
- **PIA (Personal Inventory Assessments):** Enhance your ability to connect with key concepts through these engaging self-reflection assessments.
- **Study Plan:** Check your understanding of chapter concepts with self-study quizzes.
- **Simulations:** Practise decision making in simulated management environments.

Discussion Questions

1. What is operations management, and what strategic role does it play?

2. Do you think manufacturing or service organizations have greater need of operations management? Explain.

3. What are supply and value chains? What is value chain management? What is the goal of value chain management?

4. What types of organizational benefits does value chain management provide? What obstacles stand in the way of successful value chain management?

5. Explain why managing productivity is important in operations management.

6. Select a company you are familiar with. Describe its value chain. Be as specific as possible in your description. Evaluate how it "uses" the value chain to create value.

WHAT IS MY NEGOTIATION STYLE?

Listed in Exhibit 6-13 are seven characteristics related to a person's negotiating style. Each characteristic demonstrates a range of variation. Indicate your own preference by selecting a point along the 1-to-5 continnuum for each characteristic.

EXHIBIT 6-13	What Is My Negotiation Style?		
Approach	Confrontational	1 2 3 4 5	Collaborative
Personality	Emotional	1 2 3 4 5	Rational
Formality	High	1 2 3 4 5	Low
Communication	Indirect	1 2 3 4 5	Direct
Candidness	Closed	1 2 3 4 5	Open
Limited	Limited	1 2 3 4 5	Many
Willingness to use power	Low	1 2 3 4 5	High

Source: Based on R. Fisher and W. Ury, *Getting to Yes* (New York: Penguin, 1981); and J. W. Salacuse, "Ten Ways That Culture Affects Negotiating Style: Some Survey Results," *Negotiation Journal* (July 1998), pp. 221–239.

Analysis and Interpretation

People differ in the way they handle negotiations. Exhibit 6-13 attempts to tap the key dimensions that differentiate preferences in negotiation style. Add up the scores for the seven items. Your score will range between 7 and 35. Research indicates that negotiation style is influenced by a number of factors—including the situation, your cultural background, and your work occupation. Nevertheless, experts in negotiation generally recommend individuals use a style that will result in a high score on this test. That is, they favour collaboration, rationality, a direct communication style, and so on. We think it best to consider your total score in a situational context. For instance, while a high total score may generally be favourable, the use of an informal style may be a handicap for North Americans or Europeans when negotiating with Nigerians, who favour high formality. Similarly, Latin Americans tend to show their emotions in negotiation. So if you're negotiating with Brazilians or Costa Ricans, a more emotional approach on your part may be appropriate or even expected.

Practising the Skill

1. Negotiate with a course instructor to raise the grade on an exam or paper on which you think you should have received a higher grade.
2. The next time you purchase a relatively expensive item (e.g., automobile, apartment lease, appliance, jewellery), negotiate a better price and gain some concessions such as an extended warranty, smaller down payment, maintenance services, or the like.

Developing Management Skills

Diversity Matters

One of the key challenges in organizations today is the lack of female representation in the executive ranks. Lack of diversity can be approached as an operations management challenge to be overcome. The operational measure of *control* can be utilized if the company was to implement key performance indicators for gender diversity and then move toward making the necessary changes to meet the metrics. Monitoring such metrics serves as a tool for defining and directing priorities for action.

Indicators could be developed for the following:

- the proportion of women in the company's levels of management and among new recruits
- pay levels and attrition rates between men and women working in similar functions
- the ratio of women promoted to women eligible for promotion

Operations management uses policies, procedures, and processes to ensure gender diversity change occurs. Employers could enact policies that would encourage women to grow into management careers, such as flexible working hours and career breaks like maternity leave. During the breaks the company could maintain contact to enable easy reintegration into the workforce. Human resources processes may need to be adapted to ensure women are not held back in their professional development. Operations managers are adept at reengineering processes as needed, and could implement coaching, network-building, or mentoring programs to raise awareness of the limitations that are imposed on women.[74]

Hey, You're the Boss Now!

BEING A GOOD PROJECT MANAGER

Managing any project requires good negotiation skills. You will typically have to work across vertical and horizontal levels in an organization, deal with people over whom you have no formal authority, and negotiate schedules, deadlines, work assignments, and the like with people possibly both inside and outside the organization.

You can be more effective at negotiating if you use the following five recommended behaviours:

- *Begin with a positive overture.* Studies on negotiation show that concessions tend to be reciprocated and lead to agreements. As a result, begin bargaining with a positive overture—perhaps a small concession—and then reciprocate the other party's concessions.

- *Address problems, not personalities.* Concentrate on the negotiation issues, not on the personal characteristics of the individual with whom you're negotiating. When negotiations get tough, avoid the tendency to attack this person. Remember, it is that person's ideas or position you disagree with, not him or her personally. Separate the people from the problem, and do not personalize differences.

- *Pay little attention to initial offers.* Treat an initial offer as merely a point of departure. Everyone must have an initial position. These initial offers tend to be extreme and idealistic. Treat them as such.

- *Emphasize win–win solutions.* Inexperienced negotiators often assume that their gain must come at the expense of the other party. That does not need to be the case. Assuming a zero-sum game means missed opportunities for trade-offs that could benefit both sides. So if conditions are supportive, look for an integrative solution. Frame options in terms of the other party's interests and look for solutions that can allow this person, as well as yourself, to declare a victory.

- *Create an open and trusting climate.* Skilled negotiators are better listeners, ask more questions, focus their arguments more directly, are less defensive, and have learned to avoid words or phrases that can irritate the person with whom they are negotiating (such as "generous offer," "fair price," or "reasonable arrangement"). In other words, they are better at creating the open and trusting climate that is necessary for reaching a win–win settlement.[75]

3BL: The Triple Bottom Line

Lean production is geared toward eliminating waste to increase efficiency. Waste is something that uses resources without creating value. Imagine a company that sold highlighters and dry erase markers that used hundreds of different types of blister packs for packaging. If the company reduced the number of packages by half, it would eliminate not only the waste in extra packaging, but would reduce setup time for packaging, cut tooling costs, and reduce warehouse costs. That is the power of lean.

THINKING STRATEGICALLY ABOUT 3BL

Lean thinking applies also to companies in the service sector, even though customers are often involved in the provision of the service. Canadian Tire is a company that has successfully applied lean techniques in its distribution centres and wondered if it could do the same with the company's recruitment.

Liza Provenzano, Associate Vice-President of Human Resource Operations, looked at every aspect of their heavy recruitment workload, from the time a manager indicated the need for a new hire to the time that new recruit walked in the door, and found a lot of variations in workload, delays, duplication, and unnecessary steps.[76] The Canadian Tire team met weekly, using a large whiteboard to brainstorm ideas that could change the company's HR processes.

Ontario's Institute for Competitiveness and Prosperity has called lean retailing a best practice that "achieves highly efficient operations through a relentless drive to reduce waste of time and resources."[77] The results for Canadian Tire were impressive: Recruitment time fell by 25 percent, the number of steps in the hiring process was cut in half, turnover rates fell, and the cost per hire dropped 34 percent.

Your Essential Management Reading List

Learning from key management experts can help you understand today's management theory and practice. What follows is a list of some influential operations management books and two useful Twitter hashtags to watch:

- *The Goal*—Eliyahu Goldratt
- #pmot—Project Managers on Twitter is a useful hashtag used by professionals willing to share their experiences and insight
- #ftpm—The First Time Project Managers hashtag is useful for those just getting started or who are project managers "by accident"

Team Exercises

Be the Consultant

As marketing director for Done Right, a regional home-repair chain, you've come up with a plan you believe has significant potential for future sales. Your plan involves a customer information service designed to help people make their homes more environmentally sensitive. Then, based on homeowners' assessments of their homes' environmental impact, your firm will be prepared to help them deal with problems or concerns they may uncover. You are really excited about the competitive potential of this new service. You envision pamphlets, in-store appearances by environmental experts, and contests for consumers and school kids.

After several weeks of preparations, you make your pitch to your boss, Nick Castro. You point out how the market for environmentally sensitive products is growing and how this growing demand represents the perfect opportunity for Done Right. Nick seems impressed by your presentation, but he's expressed one major concern. He thinks your workload is already too heavy. He does not see how you are going to have enough time to start this new service *and* still be able to look after all of your other assigned marketing duties.

People in the class should form pairs. One will play the marketing director; the other will play the role of Nick Castro. Nick seems convinced you cannot handle your present responsibilities and start the new service. Negotiate a solution.

Business Cases

Apple and the Supply Chain

When the iPhone 5 was launched in 2012, it was labelled as Apple's most aggressive production-and-launch schedule given its scale, speed, and complexity. In just over a month it was selling in 100 countries at a rate of 3.7 million per week in the model's first three months.[78] One of Apple's largest suppliers is Flextronics International, a contract manufacturer based in Singapore with about 28 million square feet of factory space spread across four continents, including a plant in an industrial area south of Kuala Lumpur. Flextronics is one of Apple's top 10 suppliers, employing about 150 000 workers in 30 countries.[79]

To meet Apple's supply chain requirements, Flextronics had to put its own supply chain into overdrive, seeking 1500 men to make cameras. Companies use an informal, unregulated network of thousands of recruiters and subagents who fan out into the farm fields and impoverished cities of Indonesia, Cambodia, Myanmar, and Vietnam. Because jobs are difficult to find, the 1500 positions were basically sold as brokers took fees from families, representing as much as a year or more of wages. Often the workers had to take loans that would take years to pay off. Since the workers owed money to recruiters, the companies would keep their passports to guarantee they paid up. This practice led many migrant workers to be trapped abroad for months or even years because of seized passports, debts, and interest.[80]

On the assembly lines the number of failures was growing. Apple was rejecting 7 out of every 10 cameras. Because of the high failure rate at Flextronics's Bukit Raja facility, Apple removed it from its supply chain. Production was shut down and the workers were terminated on "grounds of redundancy." The workers were instructed not to leave the hostel and were told nothing for weeks on end. Many of the workers' visas had expired, and they were vulnerable to arrest if they left the hostel. Some Flextronics recruits who left the hostel were shaken down for cash by local police. Soon the workers ran out of cash and food, and eventually they smashed windows and threw things out of the building. Police arrived, but rather than arresting the men, they ordered Flextronics to send food and expedite the process of returning the workers to their villages.[81]

Apple has been aggressively investigating claims of "bonded labour" such as the case in Kuala Lumpur. To do so requires a substantial auditing of its supply chain to uncover the abuse of migrant workers. Apple initiated a program to mandate reimbursement to employees who were charged excessive recruitment fees, which has funnelled $16.4 million back to contract workers since 2008.[82]

Ernst and Young released a report in 2014 titled *Human Right and Professional Wrongs*, along with the following five recommendations for companies such as Apple:[83]

1. Use third-party certifiers and auditors more strategically to source out unethical practices.
2. Tighten procurement systems to prevent working with factories that have not had their social compliance status assessed.
3. Establish stronger social compliance expectations with agents.
4. Maintain longer relationships with a smaller number of suppliers.
5. Incorporate human rights agreements prior to commencing manufacturing operations or offshoring agreements.

Discussion Questions

1. Discuss the Flextronics case from a value chain management perspective. How did it happen? Why did it happen?

2. What can managers learn about managing operations from this situation?
3. Although enforcement of worker safety in Kuala Lumpur is clearly lax, government officials clearly do not want global businesses withdrawing from the country and driving it deeper into poverty. Discuss.

Dreamliner Nightmare

The 787 Dreamliner was born out of desperation.[84] The year was 2003 and Boeing had just lost its title as the world's largest plane manufacturer to European rival Airbus. Boeing's then CEO had just resigned in a defense-contract scandal. And the company's stock price had plunged to its lowest price in a decade. Remember, this was two years after the 9/11 terrorist attacks, and financially troubled airlines were reluctant to invest in new equipment. Boeing needed something revolutionary to win back customers. The Boeing 787 program descended from Boeing's lean philosophy. Boeing initially consulted with 20 international systems suppliers, leading to the selection of carbon-fibre materials for the Dreamliner. Composites provided many benefits: reduced weight leading to 20 percent fuel reduction; enhanced modularity of the plane reducing assembly time by 75 percent; ability to withstand higher pressure and suffer less corrosion; and higher cabin humidity leading to a more comfortable interior cabin.[85] During the Dreamliner's development, Boeing's board was primarily focused on keeping costs down. It was this priority focus that allowed Boeing to devise a unique approach in which suppliers would become partners and would finance and produce entire sections of the 787, taking on greater risk and also benefitting from a larger share of revenue from each jet sold. Boeing would manufacture 30 percent of each 787 and outsource the remainder. Main suppliers would build large sections of the plane that would be flown to Boeing's factory to be assembled in three days and delivered to customers.

The result was a technologically advanced aircraft that would be built by a global network of suppliers in three days, compared with a month the traditional way. And it was Boeing's first aircraft built with lightweight composite materials (graphite, titanium, carbon fibre) rather than traditional metals, making the 787 a lighter and more efficient aircraft than previous models. Why was this so revolutionary? The 787 could fly farther, burn less fuel, and offer more passenger comforts than what was currently available. The 787 had built-in sensors designed to help counter the effects of turbulence, making for a smoother flight. And it was designed to have more humid air, quieter engines, improved lighting, and the largest windows in the industry. Of course, airlines were eager to save money and entice customers, and ordered a record number of the planes.

Despite its innovative features (or, as some critics said, maybe because of), the 787 faced many production setbacks and delays (the plane was originally scheduled to be delivered in May 2008). These delays were due to several issues, including design and manufacturing challenges—coordinating that many global suppliers, using new materials in the plane, and

---

EXHIBIT 6-14 e-Enabled Supply Chain Process

Design	Source	Procurement
eCollaboration	**eSourcing**	**eProcurement**
• Build teams across functional enterprise boundaries in secure, virtual workplaces • Manage complex projects and project documentation electronically • Share data with secure, format-neutral tools	• Trading partner directory • Integrated suite of sourcing tools • Develop and manage requests for information and requests for quotes • Conduct real-time online negotiations • Integrated to enterprise requirements and procurement systems	• Host procurement onramp and electronic catalogues • Suppliers manage customer purchase orders and other transaction documents via the Web • Establish integrated "machine-to-machine" connections with the Boeing supply chain

Source: Adapted from L. M. Applegate, J. S. Valacich, M. E. Vatz, and C. Schneider (2006), "Boeing's e-Enabled Advantage," *Harvard Business Publishing*, retrieved from each case collection.

---

assembling the sophisticated components. However, three years after its first expected delivery date, Boeing handed over the first 787 on a rainy and blustery day in Everett, Washington, to Japan's All Nippon Airways Co. on September 26, 2011. The chief executive of Boeing's commercial airplanes division said, "Today . . . will always be remembered as the dawn of a new day in commercial aviation."

Boeing utilized what was called a Global Collaborative Environment (GCE), a virtual environment for constant collaboration. This new e-enabled environment (see Exhibit 6-14) would integrate every aspect of Boeing's and the suppliers' operations through information technology. Each partner was provided with the same tools, technologies, and processes to collaborate electronically.[86]

In the 787's first year of service, at least four aircraft suffered some type of electrical problem. Although such problems are not unusual, especially in the first year of a newly designed aircraft, a number of incidents, including an electrical fire aboard an All Nippon Dreamliner plane and a similar fire aboard a landed 787 at Boston's Logan International Airport, led the U.S. Federal Aviation Administration (FAA) to order a review of the design and manufacture of the Dreamliner. There obviously was concern over what the FAA found, because it proceeded to ground the entire Boeing 787 fleet. Aviation safety investigators focused their attention on the 787's lithium-ion batteries, manufactured by a Japanese company GS Yuasa of Kyoto. Boeing's team

immediately set to work to solve the issue because a grounded fleet is a *big* problem! In mid-March 2013, Boeing announced that it had come up with solutions for the Dreamliner problems. The 787's chief engineer said, "We may never get to a single root cause." But the engineers had looked at some 80 potential problems that could lead to a battery fire, categorized them into four groups, and come up with solutions for each group. A major part of the "fix" was a battery enclosure made of stainless steel, not designed to contain a fire, but to prevent the battery from ever having a fire to begin with by quickly starving any flame of oxygen. With the fix in place and approved by the FAA, a team of Dreamliner technicians fanned out around the globe modifying the 787's batteries. By the end of April 2013, the Dreamliner fleet went back into service.

Discussion Questions

1. What role does innovation play in managing an organization's operations?

2. Describe the operations management issues that the Dreamliner team faced. Could these issues have been avoided? Why or why not?

3. Is a global network of suppliers the future of operations management? Discuss.

4. What other lessons about operations management can you see in this story?

CHAPTER

7 Human Resource Management

FotolEdhar/Fotolia

The Calgary Chamber of Voluntary Organizations (CCVO) is the largest and strongest voluntary sector chamber in Canada and recently developed *A Guidebook for Building an Immigrant Workforce in the Nonprofit Sector* to help employers develop an inclusive strategy for attracting, recruiting, and retaining the most qualified candidates.[1] A future labour supply shortage looms in the nonprofit sector due to demographic shifts. Targeting immigrants can provide many benefits, including higher levels of skills and education, increased community responsiveness and representation, and lower recruitment and turnover costs.[2]

Alberta's nonprofit sector employs more than 100 000 staff[3] but will face dramatic competition from the private and public sectors as Baby Boomers retire. Organizations need to make changes to their systems to overcome the challenges of attracting immigrants. A diversity strategy may require nonprofit employers to change aspects of their organizations as varied as their values, communication, branding, and recruitment advertising.

THE HUMAN RESOURCE MANAGEMENT PROCESS

"Our people are our most important asset." Many organizations use this phrase, or something close to it, to acknowledge the important role that employees play in organizational success. These organizations also recognize that *all* managers must engage in some human resource management (HRM) activities—even in large ones that have a separate HRM department. Managers interview job candidates, orient new employees, and evaluate their employees' work performance. Because human resources (HR) also involves appropriate ways of treating coworkers, even nonmanagers must be aware of basic HR principles and practices.

Can HRM be an important strategic tool? *Can* it help establish an organization's sustainable competitive advantage? The answer to these questions seems to be yes. Various studies have concluded that an organization's human resources can be a significant source of competitive advantage.[4] That conclusion is true for organizations around the world, not just for Canadian firms. The Human Capital Index, a

LEARNING OUTCOMES

Think About It

What are the barriers to hiring immigrants? What do employers need to do to build a more diverse workforce?

7.1 Tell What factors affect human resource planning?

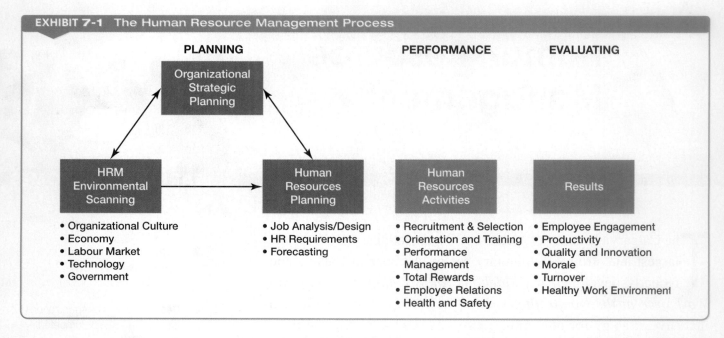

EXHIBIT 7-1 The Human Resource Management Process

comprehensive global study of more than 2000 firms conducted by consulting firm Watson Wyatt Worldwide, concluded that people-oriented HR gives an organization an edge by creating superior shareholder value.[5]

Human resource professionals are actively involved in strategy formulation and implementation. Thus, human resource practices must support the organization's distinctive competencies, its competitive advantage (e.g., superior customer service, innovation, efficient production), and the long-term objectives of the organization (such as growth or market share).

Exhibit 7-1 introduces the key components of an organization's **human resource management process**, which consists of three key areas: *environmental factors* that impact HRM, such as organizational culture, economic conditions, labour market issues, government legislation, and technology; *human resource requirements and performance and reward factors*, such as planning, recruitment, training, and total rewards;[6] and *employee relations factors*, including employee engagement and occupational health and safety.

Environmental Factors Affecting HRM

Notice in Exhibit 7-1 that the entire HRM process is influenced by the internal and external environments as well as the organization's strategy. Whatever effect the external environment has on the organization ultimately affects the organization's employees. We elaborated on the constraints that the environment puts on managers in Chapter 2. The external environmental factors that most directly influence the HRM process are economic conditions, labour market issues, government legislation, and technology. The key internal factor shaping an organization's ability to meet its strategic objectives is the organizational culture.

ORGANIZATIONAL CULTURE Culture consists of the organization's set of beliefs, values, and norms.[7] A positive **organizational culture** provides many benefits to an organization, including loyalty, commitment, direction, productivity, and retention. The Calgary Chamber of Voluntary Organizations suggests an inclusive workplace culture can be created through cross-cultural awareness and communication training, as well as through sessions where employees learn about different cultural practices.[8] StarTech of London, Ontario,

human resource management process
Activities necessary for staffing the organization and sustaining high employee performance.

organizational culture
A system of shared values, norms, and beliefs held by organizational members that determines, in large degree, how employees act.

EXHIBIT **7-2** Changes in the Labour Market, 2008–2013

	2008	2013	Change	
	000s	000s	000s	%
Total employed	17 087	17 731	644	3.8
Full-time	13 923	14 380	457	3.3
Part-time	3165	3351	187	5.9
Underemployed part-time	710	914	203	28.6
Going to school	1009	959	−50	−5.0
Other voluntary	1445	1478	33	2.3
Unemployed	1117	1348	232	20.8
Not in the labour force	8703	9594	890	10.2
Wanted work	391	469	78	19.9
Did not want work	8313	9125	813	9.8

Source: Canadian Labour Congress, "Underemployment Is Canada's Real Labour Market Challenge," March 2014. Reprinted by permission.

has created an entrepreneurial culture by involving employees and ensuring that they enjoy what they do. "We bring in all employees to get their final input before finalizing our strategic plan," says cofounder Paul Seed.[9]

ECONOMIC CONDITIONS Canada's labour market features 19 million people, of which 14 million are employed full-time and 3.3 million part-time, and 1.3 million are unemployed.[10] Another 9.5 million are not in the labour force. In 2012, about 76 percent of Canadian men aged 15 to 74 participated in the labour force, ranking Canada sixth highest in the OECD (the OECD average was 73 percent). Women continue to have lower participation rates than men, as in other OECD countries. However, at 68 percent, Canada's labour force participation rate for women aged 15 to 74 ranked fourth in the OECD and was 9 percentage points higher than the OECD average (59 percent).[11] See Exhibit 7-2 for further details.

The ability of employers to recruit is dependent on local (and national) unemployment rates, competition in regional and local labour markets, and industry-specific labour market conditions. For example, hospitals across the country are facing a shortage of nurses, so provinces compete with each other, and recruitment, training, and retention strategies in this sector become more important. When the unemployment rate is high, employers have more potential employees to choose from.

LABOUR MARKET ISSUES According to the Canadian Chamber of Commerce, the number one concern of its members is "finding the right people to do the job," which has led to a skills shortage "crisis."[12] The Government of Canada is revamping its Skilled Worker Program to help fill vacancies in skilled trades.[13]

The Canadian population is aging. In 2013, the median age in Canada was 40 years, up from 26 years in 1971. Seniors make up the fastest-growing age group with close to 5 million Canadians aged 65 and older, a number expected to double by 2036. Over the next 10 years, one in four Canadian workers will be above 55 years old. The percentage of the population in this age group is growing rapidly due to the aging of the Baby Boom generation, high life expectancy, and a decreased fertility rate.[14] Canada also admits more immigrants per capita than any other country. According to the last census, the proportion of the population born outside the country was 20 percent in 2011.[15] These factors combine to provide challenges and opportunities for HR managers.

A unique labour market issue is unionization. In North America, many of the privileges that workers can count on are a result of the labour union movement. Government programs such as employment insurance, workers compensation, and pensions are a direct result of the union movement. Minimum wage, eight-hour workdays, 40-hour workweeks, and even weekends off are also due to unions.[16]

A **labour union** is an organization that represents employees and seeks to protect their interests through collective bargaining. Labour unions try to improve pay and benefits and working conditions for members. They also try to have greater control over the rules and procedures covering issues such as promotions, layoffs, transfers, and outsourcing.

In unionized organizations, many HRM decisions are regulated by the terms of collective agreements, and management has much less flexibility in terms of HR policies, procedures, and practices. Collective agreements usually define such things as recruitment sources; criteria for hiring, promotions, and layoffs; training eligibility; and disciplinary practices. About 30 percent of Canadian employees belong to labour unions, a figure that has been consistent for the past 25 years.[17] Wages, working conditions, lack of respect by managers, unfair working hours, job security, and the desire for safer workplaces all contribute to unionization.

GOVERNMENT LEGISLATION The federal government has greatly expanded its influence over HRM by enacting a number of laws and regulations, including Employment Standards legislation, the *Charter of Rights and Freedoms*, and the *Canadian Human Rights Act*. The provincial governments also have their own labour legislation that governs the workplace, meaning that employment law in Canada involves 14 different jurisdictions.[18]

The Canada Labour Code establishes the right of employees to join labour unions if they desire. Part II of this legislation outlines the health and safety obligations of federal employers to prevent accidents and injury to their employees.

Each province and territory has health and safety regulations that cover most nonfederal workplaces in its region. Separate legislation covers workplace hazards. The Workplace Hazardous Materials Information System (WHMIS) is a comprehensive plan for providing information on the safe use of potentially hazardous materials in the workplace.

Employment standards legislation sets minimum employment standards in the private sector in Canada. It covers such things as the minimum age of employees, hours of work and overtime pay, minimum wages, equal pay, general holidays and annual vacations with pay, parental leave, and termination of employment.

The *Charter of Rights and Freedoms* and the *Canadian Human Rights Act* require employers to ensure that equal employment opportunities exist for job applicants and current employees. Decisions regarding who will be hired, for example, or which employees will be chosen for a management training program must be made without regard to race, sex, religion, age, colour, national origin, or disability.

Trying to balance the "shoulds and should-nots" of these laws often falls within the realm of employment equity. The *Employment Equity Act* creates four "protected categories"—women, Aboriginal peoples, people with disabilities, and visible minorities. These groups must not be discriminated against by federally regulated employers or any employers who receive federal contracts worth more than $200 000. Employment equity is intended to ensure that all citizens have an equal opportunity to obtain employment regardless of gender, race or ethnicity, or disabilities.

The intent of the Canada Labour Code, *Occupational Health and Safety Act*, employment standards legislation, *Charter of Rights and Freedoms*, and *Canadian Human Rights Act* is to ensure that all employees have a safe work environment, that they are not asked to work too many hours, that they have reasonable opportunities to be considered for jobs, and that pay for jobs is not discriminatory. Because an increasing number of workplace lawsuits are targeting supervisors, as well as their organizations, managers need to be aware of what they can and cannot do by law.[19]

TECHNOLOGY Companies use technology in many areas of their operations, including HRM. Some companies use a Human Resources Information System (HRIS) to capture and manage employee data. An HRIS can help reduce administrative costs, provide information more quickly, ensure legal compliance, provide for better talent management and enhanced decision making, and streamline the entire people management function. By decreasing transactional activities, technology allows HR practitioners to increase their client and

labour union
An organization that represents employees and seeks to protect their interests through collective bargaining.

customer focus, solving problems and meeting their needs faster than was ever dreamed of previously. Technology can be a catalyst for innovation and productivity, providing organizations with new ways to create value.[20] Technology also allows HR to strategically manage human capital proactively and has been shown to positively impact the organizational bottom line.[21]

Other technology applications for HRM include applicant tracking, performance management, elearning, online selection testing, computer monitoring, software-as-a-service (SaaS), and cloud computing.[22]

Oracle and SAP are examples of major companies that provide SaaS technologies, applications hosted by the vendor and made available via a network or the cloud.[23] Companies have to decide whether to rely on software and an internal HRIS or to use external vendors such as Oracle and SAP. HR practitioners work with these vendors to determine a system that aligns best with their needs, budget, and management requirements.

Small firms can benefit from outsourcing or vendor applications as well, especially in payroll, talent management, and learning management solutions.

Mobile and self-service applications will lead to a consumer-driven user experience[24] that emphasizes efficiency and ease of use. Watson Wyatt consultants have identified other trends in technology, including the following:[25]

- optimization of existing HR technology and systems
- enhanced focus on workforce analytics
- increased focus on reducing costs
- heightened data privacy issues

HUMAN RESOURCE REQUIREMENTS

Canada will experience a shortage of 1 million skilled workers over the next 20 years, according to the Conference Board of Canada.[26] The Canadian Restaurant and Foodservices Association states that 36 percent of Canadian restaurants report that a shortage of skilled labour is having a negative effect on their business, while the Forest Products Association of Canada calls the 60 000 employees at all skill levels needed in the forest products sector by the end of the decade an ongoing challenge. The predicted shortage in the IT sector is more than 100 000 workers by 2016.[27] Aware of these predictions, managers in all industries and sectors are developing plans to ensure that they will have enough qualified people to fulfill their human resource needs.

HR requirement planning involves job analysis and design, HR planning and recruitment, and selection. Managers begin human resource planning by reviewing the organization's current human resource status, usually through a *human resource inventory*. This information is taken from forms filled out by employees, and includes things such as name, education, training, prior employment, languages spoken, special capabilities, and specialized skills. Many firms have introduced HRIS to track employee information for policy and strategic needs. For example, these systems can be used for salary and benefits administration. They can also be used to track absenteeism, turnover, and health and safety data. More strategically, HRIS can be used to keep track of employee skills and education and match these to ongoing needs of the organization.

Job Analysis and Design

The initial part of HR requirement planning is **job analysis**, an assessment that defines jobs and the behaviours necessary to perform them. Information for a job analysis can be gathered by directly observing or videotaping individuals on the job, interviewing employees individually or in a group, having employees complete a structured questionnaire, having job "experts" (usually managers) identify a job's specific characteristics, or having employees record their daily activities in a diary or notebook.

7.2 Define How do organizations assess their human resource needs?

And the Survey Says...

$5 billion: Ottawa's sick leave liability

$27 million: liability faced by Winnipeg over banked sick days for its firefighters

$20 million: cost incurred by the Vancouver School Board for absenteeism in 2012

$9 million: Calgary Transit's overtime costs in 2011 when drivers took an average of 15 days off

18.2 Sick days per year taken by the average federal civil servant

90 Sick days per year that can be taken by Calgary schoolteachers[28]

---

job analysis
An assessment that defines jobs and the behaviours necessary to perform them.

With information from the job analysis, managers develop or revise job descriptions and job specifications. A **job description** is a written statement of what a jobholder does, how the job is done, and why the job is done. It typically describes job content, environment, and conditions of employment. A **job specification** states the minimum qualifications that a person must possess to perform a given job successfully. It identifies the human traits, knowledge, skills, and attitudes needed to do the job effectively. The job description and the job specification are both important documents that aid managers in recruiting and selecting employees. Here is an example of a job description used by many employers on Monster for their online recruitment of customer service representatives:

Description: Customer Service Representative

Customer Service Representative Job Purpose: Serves customers by providing product and service information; resolving product and service problems; upselling products to customers.

Customer Service Representative Job Duties:

- Manages large amounts of incoming calls.
- Generates sales leads by answering product and service questions; suggesting information about other products and services.
- Provides accurate, valid and complete information by using the right methods and tools.
- Handles complaints, provides appropriate solutions and alternatives within the time limits and follows up to ensure resolution.
- Maintains financial accounts by processing customer adjustments.
- Recommends potential products or services to management by collecting customer information and analyzing customer needs.
- Keeps records of customer interactions, processes customer accounts and files documents.
- Meets personal/team sales targets and call handling quotas.

Skills/Qualifications:

- Proven customer support experience.
- Product knowledge.
- Familiarity with CRM systems and practices.
- Problem solving.
- Excellent communication, presentation and documentation skills.
- Resolving conflict.
- Ability to multi-task, prioritize, and manage time effectively.

The second part of HR requirement planning is **job design**, which refers to specifics of how a job is organized. Various activities and duties are typically grouped together to allow for enhanced employee performance.[29] Grouping allows organizations to enrich, enlarge, or even rotate jobs. Job design can help an organization address problems such as work overload/underload, repetition, isolation, work design, and other risks related to breaks and excessive hours of work.

Having a better idea of the various tasks required in a position provides the employee with more control and a better understanding of the job process, and it allows the organization to reduce delays in filling vacant positions.

Human Resource Planning

Through **human resource planning**, managers ensure that they have the right number and kinds of people in the right places at the right times, who are capable of effectively

---

job description
A written statement of what a jobholder does, how the job is done, and why the job is done.

job specification
A statement of the minimum qualifications that a person must possess to perform a given job successfully.

job design
The process of looking at a job to determine what set of tasks is required, how they are done, and in what order.

human resource planning
The process by which managers ensure that they have the right number and kinds of people in the right places at the right times, who are capable of effectively and efficiently performing assigned tasks.

and efficiently performing assigned tasks. Through planning, organizations can avoid sudden talent shortages and surpluses.[30] Human resource planning can be condensed into two steps: (1) assessing current human resources; and (2) assessing future human resource needs and developing a program to meet those future needs.

Meeting Future Needs

Future human resource needs are determined by the organization's mission, goals, and strategies. Demand for employees is a result of demand for the organization's products or services. On the basis of its estimate of total revenue, managers can attempt to establish the number and mix of employees needed to reach that revenue. In some cases, however, that situation may be reversed. When particular skills are necessary but in short supply, the availability of appropriate human resources determines revenues.

HTML500 was an event hosted by 50 employers in Vancouver, including TELUS and Hootsuite. These employers took the unusual approach to remedying the skill gap by providing a free one-day learn-to-code event.

After they have assessed both current capabilities and future needs, managers are able to estimate human resource shortages—both in number and in type—and to highlight areas in which the organization will be overstaffed. Managers can then develop replacement charts for managerial positions to outline which employees are available to fill future managerial needs and to indicate who might be ready for promotion and who might need more training to move into upper-level positions. Succession planning has taken on a greater importance for employers.

With all of this information, managers are ready to proceed to the next step in the HRM process.

STAFFING THE ORGANIZATION

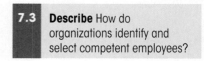

7.3 Describe How do organizations identify and select competent employees?

Decisions made about staffing a business are very important for a manager or even a business owner. Those decisions impact the quality of the workforce and the level of customer service provided. The purpose of staffing an organization is to find the right people and put them in the best role to help achieve your organizational goals. Careful planning ensures that the appropriate staff are in place as needed.

To deal with recruiting issues, Scotiabank has developed a Careers webpage to target young graduates and encourage them to think about working for the bank.[31] Scotiabank recognized that its target audience would best be reached through the Internet and mobile devices. The site gives corporate information, and users can do job searches and read about what makes Scotiabank a good employer.

Scotiabank supplements e-recruiting with more traditional staffing vehicles such as print advertising and recruitment fairs. Arlene Russell, Scotiabank's Vice-President of Human Resources, recognizes the importance of understanding job seekers, especially when and how to communicate with them. As much as Scotiabank must be an expert in mobile banking, it must also be adept at mobile recruitment and ensuring that it has a mobile interface that appeals to job seekers.

Once managers know their current human resource status and their future needs, they can begin to do something about any shortages or excesses. If one or more vacancies exist, they can use the information gathered through job analysis to guide them in **recruitment**—that is, the process of locating, identifying, and attracting capable applicants.[32]

How can using social media for recruitment bias decision making in the selection process? What steps can companies like Scotiabank take to avoid this bias?

recruitment
The process of locating, identifying, and attracting capable applicants.

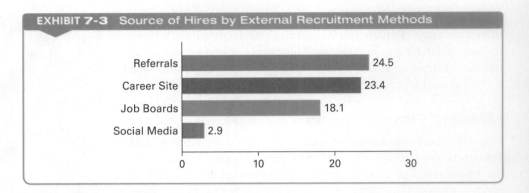

EXHIBIT 7-3 Source of Hires by External Recruitment Methods

Source	Value
Referrals	24.5
Career Site	23.4
Job Boards	18.1
Social Media	2.9

Recruitment

At a career fair and expo at Edmonton City Centre mall, the Edmonton Police Service tried to convince high school students to consider a career with the police force. To show that there are many different opportunities in police service, they brought their vehicles, including police motorcycles and dirt bikes. Potential job candidates can be found through several sources, as Exhibit 7-3 shows.[33]

Social networking offers organizations a chance to attract young, tech-savvy candidates through virtual recruitment booths, company Facebook pages, and even job postings through Twitter.

Web-based recruiting, or e-recruiting, has remained a popular choice for organizations and applicants. After the Vancouver Police Department (VPD) examined what kinds of recruits would be needed over the next several years, the department decided to launch a recruitment seminar inside *Second Life*, the online alternative universe. The police recruiters

The Vancouver Police Department has started recruiting through an online presence on *Second Life*. They created special avatars (shown here) to interview prospective candidates.

Vancouver Police Department

created their own avatars (*Second Life* persona) dressed "in a specially designed VPD uniform, badge, belt, and radio." Inspector Kevin McQuiggen, head of the department's tech crimes division, explains why recruiting on *Second Life* makes sense: "If people are on *Second Life*, they're likely to be web-savvy, a quality the police department is looking for in new recruits." The department has seen an increasing number of Internet and technology-related crimes in recent years, and hiring people who can help detect those crimes would be an advantage to the Vancouver police.[34]

Although e-recruiting has been gaining in popularity (Scotiabank, for example, allows applicants to fill out information forms online and upload their résumés with the forms), employers use other recruitment sources as well. Burnaby, British Columbia–based Electronic Arts Canada, following the lead of some other Canadian companies, decided to recruit at universities and colleges in recent years to win "the best and the brightest" from computer science programs.[35] Pat York, Director of Human Resources, is pleased with the results, because the interviews have led to hires more than one-third of the time. Many companies continue to use print advertising and employment agencies.

Despite the popularity of new recruiting techniques, the majority of studies have found that employee referrals generally produce the best candidates.[36]

Strezhnev Pavel/Fotolia

Selection

Once the recruiting effort has developed a pool of candidates, the next step in the HRM process is to determine who is best qualified for the job. This step, called the **selection process**, is the process of screening job applicants to ensure that the most appropriate candidates are hired. Errors in hiring can have far-reaching implications, as the average cost of turnover can be as high as 150 percent of the employee's salary![37] Some selection practices may screen out applicants who have transferable skills. CCVO suggests that employers need to have a broader understanding of foreign credentials to avoid missing out on immigrants with valuable knowledge, skills, and abilities. Turning down candidates for a lack of Canadian experience might be overlooking the skills and competencies required for the position. If human resource planning shows a surplus of employees, management may want to take steps to reduce the organization's workforce, as Exhibit 7-4 demonstrates.

EXHIBIT 7-4 Workforce Reduction Options	
Option	**Description**
Firing	Permanent involuntary termination
Layoffs	Temporary involuntary termination; may last only a few days or extend to years
Attrition	Not filling openings created by voluntary resignations or normal retirements
Transfers	Moving employees either laterally or downward; usually does not reduce costs but can reduce supply–demand imbalances within organizations
Reduced workweeks	Having employees work fewer hours per week, share jobs, or perform their jobs on a part-time basis
Early retirements	Providing incentives to older and more senior employees for retiring before their normal retirement dates
Job sharing	Having employees share one full-time position

selection process
The process of screening job applicants to ensure
that the most appropriate candidates are hired.

EXHIBIT 7-5 Selection Decision Outcomes

		Selection Decision	
		Accept	Reject
Later Job Performance	Successful	Correct Decision	Reject Error
	Unsuccessful	Accept Error	Correct Decision

bluebay2014/Fotolia

Choosing the right person for the organization can be very difficult when there are many suitable candidates

WHAT IS SELECTION? Selection is an exercise in prediction. It seeks to predict which applicants will be successful if hired. *Successful* in this case means performing well on the criteria the organization uses to evaluate employees. In filling a sales position, for example, the selection process should be able to predict which applicants will generate a high volume of sales; for a position as a network administrator, it should predict which applicants will be able to effectively oversee and manage the organization's computer network.

Consider, for a moment, that any selection decision can result in four possible outcomes. As shown in Exhibit 7-5, two of these outcomes would be correct, and two would indicate errors.

A decision is correct when the applicant was predicted to be successful and proved to be successful on the job, or when the applicant was predicted to be unsuccessful and would have been so if hired. In the first case, we have successfully accepted; in the second case, we have successfully rejected.

Problems arise when errors are made by rejecting candidates who would have performed successfully on the job (reject errors) or by accepting those who ultimately perform poorly (accept errors). These problems can be significant. Given today's human resource laws and regulations, reject errors can cost more than the additional screening needed to find acceptable candidates. They can expose the organization to charges of discrimination, especially if applicants from protected groups are disproportionately rejected. The costs of accept errors include the cost of training the employee, the profits lost because of the employee's incompetence, the cost of severance, and the subsequent costs of further recruiting and screening. The major thrust of any selection activity should be to reduce the probability of making reject errors or accept errors while increasing the probability of making correct decisions. How do managers do this? By using selection procedures that are both valid and reliable.

VALIDITY AND RELIABILITY Any selection device that a manager uses should demonstrate **validity**, a proven relationship between the selection device and some relevant job criterion. For example, the law prohibits managers from using a test score as a selection device unless there is clear evidence that, once on the job, individuals with high scores on the test outperform individuals with low test scores. The burden is on managers to show that any selection device they use to differentiate between applicants is related to job performance.

In addition to being valid, a selection device must also demonstrate **reliability**, which indicates whether the device measures the same thing consistently. For example, if a test is reliable, any single individual's score should remain fairly consistent over time, assuming that the characteristics being measured are also stable. No selection device can be effective if it is low in reliability. Using such a device would be like weighing yourself every day on an erratic scale. If the scale is unreliable—randomly fluctuating, say, four to seven kilos every time you step on it—the results will not mean much. To be effective predictors, selection devices must possess an acceptable level of consistency.

TYPES OF SELECTION DEVICES Managers can use a number of selection devices to reduce accept and reject errors. The best-known devices include application forms, written tests, performance-simulation tests, interviews, background investigations, and, in some cases, physical examinations. Exhibit 7-6 lists the strengths and weaknesses of each of these devices.[39]

EXHIBIT 7-6 Selection Devices

Selection Device	Strengths	Weaknesses
Application forms	Relevant biographical data and facts that can be verified have been shown to be valid performance measures for some jobs. When items on the form have been weighted to reflect job relatedness, this device has proved to be a valid predictor for diverse groups.	Usually only a couple of items on the form prove to be valid predictors of job performance and then only for a specific job. Weighted-item applications are difficult and expensive to create and maintain.
Written tests	Tests of intellectual ability, spatial and mechanical ability, perceptual accuracy, and motor ability are moderately valid predictors for many semi-skilled and unskilled lower-level jobs in manufacturing. Intelligence tests are reasonably good predictors for supervisory positions.	Intelligence and other tested characteristics can be somewhat removed from actual job performance, thus reducing their validity.
Performance-simulation tests	Tests are based on job analysis data and easily meet the requirement of job relatedness. Tests have proven to be valid predictors of job performance.	They are expensive to create and administer.
Interviews	Interviews must be structured and well organized to be effective predictors. Interviewers must use common questions to be effective predictors.	Interviewers must be aware of the legality of certain questions. Interviews are subject to potential biases, especially if they are not well structured and standardized.
Background investigations	Verifications of background data are valuable sources of information.	Reference checks are essentially worthless as a selection tool.
Physical examinations	Physical exams have some validity for jobs with certain physical requirements.	Managers must be sure that physical requirements are job related and do not discriminate.

HR PERFORMANCE To increase job satisfaction among employees and reduce turnover, organizations can provide a **realistic job preview (RJP)**. An RJP includes both positive and negative information about the job and the company. For example, in addition to the positive comments typically expressed during an interview, the job applicant might be told that there are limited opportunities to talk to coworkers during work hours, that promotional advancement is rare, or that work hours fluctuate so erratically that employees may be required to work during what are usually off hours (nights and weekends). Research indicates that applicants who have been given a realistic job preview hold lower

validity
The proven relationship that exists between the selection device and some relevant job criterion.

reliability
The ability of a selection device to measure the same thing consistently.

realistic job preview (RJP)
A preview of a job that includes both positive and negative information about the job and the company.

and more realistic job expectations for the jobs they will be performing and are better able to cope with the frustrating elements of the job than are applicants who have been given only positive information.

7.4 **Explain** How do organizations help employees adapt and stay up-to-date?

ORIENTATION AND TRAINING

Thirty-year-old Roxann Linton is enthusiastic about her career at Scotiabank.[40] "Working with an international and diverse organization like Scotiabank, there are so many opportunities," says Linton. The young woman was chosen for Leading Edge, Scotiabank's fast-track leadership program. In the application process, she had to prepare a challenging business case analysis, go through psychometric testing, and be interviewed twice by a total of eight executives. The Leading Edge program prepares employees for senior management positions by rotating them through a series of assignments.

Linton worked for the bank for about five years in the bank's internal audit department in Kingston, Jamaica. She then transferred to Halifax and worked in commercial banking. During the first 15 months of the Leading Edge program, Linton managed more than 100 people in the electronic banking contact centre. Her next assignment was as director of special projects at Scotia Cassels Investment Counsel, part of the bank's wealth management division. She launched a new corporate bond fund during her first three months in that assignment. She will have one more 12- to 18-month assignment in another part of the bank, and then she can start applying for vice-president positions.

Organizations have to introduce new members to the work they will do and to the organization. They do this through their orientation programs. As time goes by, employees may need to increase their skills. This need is handled through training. We review the strategies that organizations use for orientation and training below.

Think About It

What kinds of orientation and training methods do organizations that you have worked for use to help employees develop their skills and learn about the businesses?

Orientation

Did you participate in some type of organized introduction to campus life when you started college or university? If so, you might have been told about your school's rules and regulations or about the procedures for activities such as applying for financial aid, cashing a cheque, or registering for classes, and you were probably introduced to some of the campus administrators. A person starting a new job needs the same type of introduction to his or her job and to the organization. This introduction is called **orientation**.

There are two types of orientation. *Work unit orientation* familiarizes the employee with the goals of the work unit, clarifies how his or her job contributes to the unit's goals, and includes an introduction to his or her new coworkers. *Organization orientation* informs the new employee about the organization's objectives, history, philosophy, procedures, and rules. This information should include relevant human resource policies and benefits such as work hours, pay procedures, overtime requirements, and fringe benefits. In addition, a tour of the organization's work facilities is often part of the organization orientation.

Managers have an obligation to make the integration of the new employee into the organization as smooth and as free of anxiety as possible. They need to openly discuss employee beliefs regarding mutual obligations of the organization and the employee.[41] It is in the best interests of the organization and the new employee to get the person up and running in the job as soon as possible. Successful orientation, whether formal or informal, results in an outsider–insider transition that makes the new member feel comfortable and fairly well adjusted, lowers the likelihood of poor work performance, and reduces the probability of a surprise resignation by the new employee only a week or two into the job.

orientation
The introduction of a new employee to his or her job and to the organization.

Training

Employee training is an important HRM activity. As job demands change, employee skills have to be altered and updated. In 2011, U.S. business firms budgeted over $59 billion on workforce formal training.[42] Canadian companies spend far less than American firms on training and development—about $852 per employee compared with $1273 by the Americans in 2006.[43] Managers, of course, are responsible for deciding what type of training employees need, when they need it, and what form that training should take.

TYPES OF TRAINING When organizations invest in employee training, what are they offering? Some of the most popular types of training that organizations provide include information on sexual harassment, safety, management skills and development, and supervisory skills.[44] For many organizations, employee interpersonal skills training—communication, conflict resolution, team building, customer service, and so forth—is a high priority. Shannon Washbrook, Director of Training and Development for Vancouver-based Boston Pizza International, says, "Our people know the Boston Pizza concept; they have all the hard skills. It's the soft skills they lack." To address that gap, Washbrook launched Boston Pizza College, a training initiative that uses hands-on, scenario-based learning about many interpersonal skills topics.[45] Technology-based training is becoming more popular. Exhibit 7-7 describes the major training methods that organizations use.

EXHIBIT 7-7 Employee Training Methods

bluebay2014/Fotolia

Traditional Training Methods

- *On-the-job*—Employees learn how to do tasks simply by performing them, usually after an initial introduction to the task.

- *Job rotation*—Employees work at different jobs in a particular area, getting exposure to a variety of tasks.

- *Mentoring and coaching*—Employees work with an experienced worker who provides information, support, and encouragement; also called *apprenticing* in certain industries.

- *Experiential exercises*—Employees participate in role playing, simulations, or other face-to-face types of training.

- *Workbooks/manuals*—Employees refer to training workbooks and manuals for information.

- *Classroom lectures*—Employees attend lectures designed to convey specific information.

Technology-Based Training Methods

- *CD-ROM/DVD/videotapes/audiotapes*—Employees use selected media to listen to information or watch demonstrations of certain techniques.

- *Videoconferencing/teleconferencing/satellite TV*—Employees listen or participate as information is conveyed or techniques demonstrated.

- *E-learning*—Internet-based learning in which employees participate in multimedia simulations or other interactive modules.

7.5 **Explain** What can organizations do to help employees achieve high performance throughout their careers?

PERSONAL INVENTORY ASSESSMENT

PERFORMANCE MANAGEMENT

Managers need to know whether their employees are performing their jobs efficiently and effectively or whether improvement is needed. Employees are often compensated based on those evaluations.

Performance Management System

Evaluating employee performance is part of a **performance management system**, which is a process of establishing performance standards and appraising employee performance in order to arrive at objective human resource decisions and to provide documentation in support of those decisions. Performance appraisal is a critical part of a performance management system. Some companies invest far more effort in it than others.

Performance appraisal is not easy to do, and many managers do it poorly. Both managers and employees often dread the appraisal process. A survey found that 41 percent of employees report having had a least one incident of being demotivated after feedback from their managers.[46] Performance appraisal can also be subject to politics, not unlike the 2002 Olympic Winter Games ice skating controversy in which the French judge was accused of manipulating her scores to enable the Russian skaters to win the gold over Canadians Jamie Salé and David Pelletier. Let us look at some different methods of doing performance appraisal.

PERFORMANCE APPRAISAL METHODS   Managers can choose from six major performance appraisal methods. The advantages and disadvantages of each of these methods are shown in Exhibit 7-8.

EXHIBIT 7-8 Advantages and Disadvantages of Performance Appraisal Methods		
Method	**Advantage**	**Disadvantage**
Critical incidents	Rich examples; behaviourally based	Time-consuming; lack quantification
Graphic rating scales	Provide quantitative data; less time-consuming than others	Do not provide depth of job behaviour assessed
Behaviourally anchored rating scales (BARS)	Focus on specific and measurable behaviours	Time-consuming; difficult to develop job behaviours
Multiperson comparisons	Compare employees with one another	Unwieldy with a large number of employees; legal concerns
Management by objectives (MBO)	Focuses on end goals; results oriented	Time-consuming
360-degree feedback	Thorough	Time-consuming

CRITICAL INCIDENTS   The use of **critical incidents** focuses the evaluator's attention on critical or key behaviours that separate effective from ineffective job performance. The evaluator writes down anecdotes describing what an employee did that was especially effective or ineffective. The key here is that only specific behaviours, not vaguely defined personality traits, are cited.

GRAPHIC RATING SCALES   One of the most popular performance appraisal methods is **graphic rating scales**. This method lists a set of performance factors such as quantity and quality of work, job knowledge, cooperation, loyalty, attendance, honesty, and initiative. The evaluator then goes down the list and rates the employee on each factor using an incremental scale, which usually specifies five points. A factor such as job knowledge, for example, might be rated from 1 ("poorly informed about work duties") to 5 ("has complete mastery of all phases of the job").

performance management system
A process of establishing performance standards and evaluating performance in order to arrive at objective human resource decisions and to provide documentation in support of those decisions.

critical incidents
A performance appraisal method in which the evaluator focuses on the critical or key behaviours that separate effective from ineffective job performance.

graphic rating scales
A performance appraisal method in which the evaluator rates an employee on a set of performance factors.

BEHAVIOURALLY ANCHORED RATING SCALES Another popular performance appraisal method is **behaviourally anchored rating scales (BARS)**. These scales combine major elements from the critical incident and graphic rating scale approaches. The evaluator rates an employee according to items along a numeric scale, but the items are examples of actual job behaviours rather than general descriptions or traits.

MULTIPERSON COMPARISONS **Multiperson comparisons** compare one individual's performance with that of others.[47] Made popular by former General Electric (GE) CEO Jack Welch, this system rates employees as top performers (20 percent), middle performers (70 percent), or bottom performers (10 percent). Advocates of the system believe that by using this type of "rank and yank" appraisal, a company can rid itself of slackers and thus be more productive. However, critics say that the rankings unfairly penalize groups made up of star performers and hinder risk-taking and collaboration.[48] For example, Sprint used forced rankings for a year and discontinued the program because it found more effective ways to differentiate performance.[49] Are forced rankings a good idea or a bad idea? According to research, companies that used forced rankings and fired the bottom 5 percent to 10 percent of employees saw productivity increase by an impressive 16 percent over the first couple of years. However, in subsequent years, productivity gains dropped off considerably.[50] Companies are therefore questioning the wisdom of strict forced ranking. Even GE has been looking at ways to make its system more flexible and has encouraged its managers to use more common sense in assigning rankings.[51]

MANAGEMENT BY OBJECTIVES We previously introduced management by objectives (MBO) when we discussed planning in Chapter 3. If you have discussed planning in your management studies, you may have already been introduced to **management by objectives (MBO)**—an approach in which specific performance goals are jointly determined by employees and their managers, progress toward accomplishing these goals is periodically reviewed, and rewards are allocated on the basis of this progress. MBO is also a mechanism for appraising performance. In fact, it is often used for assessing managers and professional employees.[52] With MBO, employees are evaluated according to how well they accomplish specific goals that have been established by them and their managers.

360-DEGREE FEEDBACK **360-degree feedback** uses feedback from multiple sources, including supervisors, employees, coworkers, and customers. In conjunction with another appraisal method, this appraisal uses information from the full circle of people with whom the employee interacts. Of the 101 large Canadian organizations surveyed by professors Mehrdad Debrayen and Stephane Brutus of the John Molson School of Business at Concordia University, 43 percent used 360-degree feedback.[53] Toronto-based Hill & Knowlton Canada, a public relations firm, uses 360-degree feedback to help employees learn what they need to do to get to the next level of the organization. The feedback has had the added benefit of reducing turnover to 18 percent.[54]

Users caution that although this method of appraisal is effective for career coaching and helping a manager recognize his or her strengths and weaknesses, it is not appropriate for determining pay, promotions, or terminations. Managers using 360-degree feedback also have to carefully consider the pros and cons of using anonymous evaluations.[55]

Not all organizations conduct performance evaluations; in particular, smaller organizations often do not. Consequently, it can be useful as an employee to ask your manager for an annual appraisal, if you do not routinely receive one. The feedback will allow you to determine your goals for the following year and identify anything for which you need improvement or training.

---

behaviourally anchored rating scales (BARS)
A performance appraisal method in which the evaluator rates an employee on examples of actual job behaviours.

multiperson comparisons
A performance appraisal method in which one individual's performance is compared with that of others.

management by objectives (MBO)
An approach to goal setting in which specific measurable goals are jointly set by employees and their managers, progress toward accomplishing those goals is periodically reviewed, and rewards are allocated on the basis of this progress.

360-degree feedback
A performance appraisal method that uses feedback from supervisors, employees, coworkers, and customers in conjunction with another appraisal method.

Total Rewards: Five Key Components

Total Rewards

- strategic compensation
- benefits
- work–life balance
- performance management
- career development

7.6 **Tell** How do total rewards motivate employees?

The five components combine into one reward strategy that is integrated and results in happy, committed, and productive employees.[56] The total rewards model does not exist in a vacuum—rewards must be linked very closely with the organization's strategy.

1 Strategic Compensation

Most of us expect to receive appropriate compensation from our employers. Therefore, developing an effective and appropriate compensation system is an important part of the HRM process.[57] Why? Because it helps attract and retain competent and talented individuals who help the organization accomplish its mission and goals. Compensation is typically the largest expense for an employer, so it becomes critical for compensation strategy to be directly linked with organizational strategy. An organization's compensation system has been shown to have an impact on its strategic performance and value creation.[58]

Managers must develop a compensation system that reflects the changing nature of work and the workplace to keep people motivated. Organizational compensation can include many different types of rewards and benefits such as base wages and salaries, wage and salary add-ons, incentive payments, as well as other benefits and services such as vacation time, extended health care, training allowances, and pensions. Benefits often amount to one-third or more of an individual's base salary and should be viewed by the employee as part of the total compensation package.

How do managers determine who gets paid $9 an hour and who gets $350 000 a year? Several factors influence the differences in compensation and benefit packages for different employees. Exhibit 7-9 summarizes these factors, which are both job-based and business- or industry-based.

Many organizations use an alternative approach to determining compensation called **skill-based pay**. In a skill-based pay system, an employee's job title does not define his or her pay category; skills do.[59] Research shows that these types of pay systems seem to be more successful in manufacturing organizations than in service organizations or organizations pursuing technical innovations.[60] Skill-based pay systems seem to mesh nicely with the changing nature of jobs and today's work environment. On the other hand, many organizations are using **variable pay** systems, in which an individual's compensation is contingent on performance—81 percent of Canadian and Taiwanese organizations use variable pay plans, and 78 percent of U.S. organizations do.[61]

skill-based pay
A pay system that rewards employees for the job skills and competencies they can demonstrate.

variable pay
A pay system in which an individual's compensation is contingent on performance.

EXHIBIT 7-9 Factors That Influence Compensation and Benefits

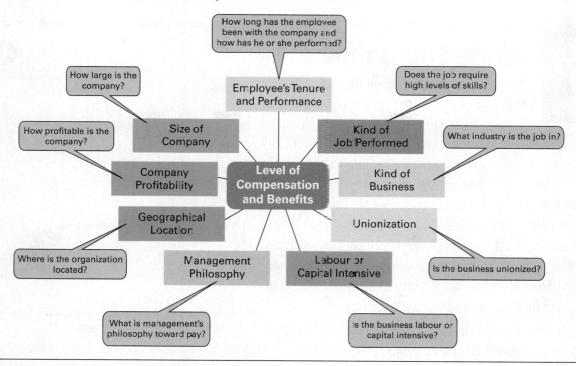

How long has the employee been with the company and how has he or she performed?

Employee's Tenure and Performance

How large is the company?

Size of Company

How profitable is the company?

Company Profitability

Does the job require high levels of skills?

Kind of Job Performed

What industry is the job in?

Kind of Business

Level of Compensation and Benefits

Geographical Location

Where is the organization located?

Management Philosophy

What is management's philosophy toward pay?

Unionization

Is the business unionized?

Labour or Capital Intensive

Is the business labour or capital intensive?

Sources: A. Murray "Mom, Apple Pie, and Small Business," Wall Street Journal, August 15, 1994, p. A1.

Although many factors influence the design of an organization's compensation system, flexibility is a key consideration. The traditional approach to paying people reflected a time of job stability when an employee's pay was largely determined by seniority and job level. Given the dynamic environments that many organizations face in which the skills that are absolutely critical to organizational success can change in a matter of months, the trend is to make pay systems more flexible and to reduce the number of pay levels. However, whatever approach managers take, they must establish a fair, equitable, and motivating compensation system that allows the organization to recruit and keep a productive workforce.

John Lund/Getty Images

Canada's top 100 highest-paid CEOs make 171 times the earnings of an average Canadian wage—a jump from 105 times in 1998. That works out to $7.96 million for the CEOs and $46 634 for the average Canadian. Did greed and executive compensation cause the 2009 financial crisis?

2 Benefits

Benefits are programs and services meant to supplement the cash component of compensation. Some benefits, such as employment insurance, workers' compensation, and the Canada Pension Plan, are mandatory. Other benefits a company may offer include time off with pay, savings and retirement programs, and supplementary health and life insurance. Employee services are divided between personal services such as counselling and employee assistance programs (EAPs), and job-related services such as child care, food services, and family-friendly benefits, which are discussed in more detail as part of work–life balance.[62]

alexmillos/Fotolia

Employee services were traditionally a small part of total rewards but have increased with the aging workforce and lower job security.

3 Work–Life Balance

Professors Linda Duxbury of the Sprott School of Business at Carleton University and Chris Higgins of the University of Western Ontario are the leading Canadian researchers on the issue of work–life balance. Their research shows that employees are working long hours and are also increasingly being asked to work a number of unpaid hours a week. This workload affects employees' abilities to manage their family lives. In response, most major organizations have taken actions to make their workplaces more family-friendly by offering **family-friendly benefits**, which include a wide range of work and family programs to help employees.[63]

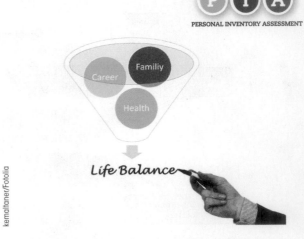

kemalttaner/Fotolia

Companies have introduced programs such as on-site child care, summer day camps, flextime, job sharing, leaves for school functions, telecommuting, and part-time employment.

Work–life conflicts are as relevant to male employees with children and female employees without children as they are to female employees with children. Heavy workloads and increased travel demands, for example, are making it increasingly hard for many employees, male and female, to meet both work and personal responsibilities. A *Fortune* survey found that 84 percent of male executives surveyed said that "they'd like job options that let them realize their professional aspirations while having more time for things outside work." Also, 87 percent of these executives believed that any company that restructured top-level management jobs in ways that would both increase productivity and make more time available for life outside the office would have a competitive advantage in attracting talented employees.[64] Younger employees, particularly, put a higher priority on family and a lower priority on jobs and are looking for organizations that give them more work flexibility.[65]

Today's progressive workplace is becoming more accommodating of the varied needs of a diverse workforce. It provides a wide range of scheduling options and benefits that give employees more flexibility at work and allow employees to better balance or integrate their work and personal lives. Large groups of women and minority employees remain unemployed or underemployed because of family responsibilities and bias in the workplace.[66] What can managers do?

DOC RABE Media/Fotolia

Despite these organizational efforts, work–life programs have room for improvement. Workplace surveys still show high levels of employee stress stemming from work–life conflicts.

Total rewards necessitate looking at the whole picture, and work–life balance must fit within the compensation and benefit strategy. Research has shown a significant, positive relationship between work–family initiatives and an organization's stock price.[67] Managers need to understand that people do differ in their preferences for work–family life scheduling options and benefits.[68] Some people prefer organizational initiatives that better *segment* work from their personal lives. Others prefer programs that facilitate *integration*. Flextime schedules segment because they allow employees to schedule work hours that are less likely to conflict with personal responsibilities. On the other hand, on-site child care integrates by blurring the boundaries between work and family responsibilities. People who prefer segmentation are more likely to be satisfied and committed to their jobs when offered options such as flextime, job sharing, and part-time hours. People who prefer integration are more likely to respond positively to options such as on-site child care, gym facilities, and company-sponsored family picnics.

4 Performance and Recognition

Performance can be addressed through performance management, as described earlier in the chapter, through pay-for-performance strategies, and through recognition. The goal of recognition is to reinforce positive behaviours either formally or informally. It can reinforce performance improvement and meet intrinsic needs for appreciation, positive communication, and feedback.[69]

5 Career Development

The term *career* has several meanings. In popular usage, it can mean advancement ("she is on a management career track"), a profession ("he has chosen a career in accounting"), or a lifelong sequence of jobs ("his career has included 12 jobs in 6 organizations"). For our purposes, we define a **career** as the sequence of positions held by a person during his or her lifetime.[70] Using this definition, we all have, or will have, a career. Moreover, the concept is as relevant to unskilled labourers as it is to software designers or physicians.

A key concept in total rewards is that you are responsible for your own career! Organizations can assist with coaching, mentoring, networking opportunities, and training and development, but you have to take charge and find your dream job.

One of the first career decisions you have to make is career choice. The optimum career choice is one that offers the best match between what you want out of life and your interests, abilities, and market opportunities. Good career choice outcomes should result in a series of positions that give you an opportunity to be a good performer, make you want to maintain your commitment to your career, lead to highly satisfying work, and give you the proper balance between work and personal life. A good career match, then, is one in which you are able to develop a positive self-concept, to do work that you think is important, and to lead the kind of life you desire.[71] Exhibit 7-10 describes the factors Canadian, American, and UK college and university students look for in a job. How would you rank these items?

EXHIBIT 7-10 What Do College and University Grads Want from Their Jobs?

Top Factors for Canadian Students	Top Factors for U.S. Students	Top Factors for UK Students
• Opportunities for advancement in position	• Work–life balance	• International career opportunities
• Good people to work with	• Annual base salary	• Flexible working hours
• Good people to report to	• Job stability and security	• Variety of assignments
• Work–life balance	• Recognition for a job done well	• Paid overtime
• Initial salary	• Increasingly challenging tasks	
	• Rotational programs	

family-friendly benefits
Benefits that accommodate employees' needs for work–life balance.

career
The sequence of positions held by a person during his or her lifetime.

What Happens When Performance Falls Short

So far, our discussion has focused on the performance management system. But what if an employee is not performing in a satisfactory manner? What can you do?

If, for some reason, an employee is not meeting his or her performance goals, a manager needs to find out why. If it is because the employee is mismatched for the job (a hiring error) or because he or she does not have adequate training, something relatively simple can be done: The manager can either reassign the individual to a job that better matches his or her skills or train the employee to do the job more effectively. If the problem is associated not with the employee's abilities but with his or her desire to do the job, it becomes a **discipline** problem. In that case, a manager can try counselling and, if necessary, can take disciplinary action such as oral and written warnings, suspensions, and even termination.

Employee counselling is a process designed to help employees overcome performance-related problems. Rather than viewing the performance problem as something that needs to be punished (discipline), employee counselling attempts to uncover why employees have lost their desire or ability to work productively. More important, counselling is designed to find ways to fix the problem. In many cases, employees do not go from being productive one day to being unproductive the next. Rather, the change happens gradually and may be a function of what is occurring in their personal lives. Employee counselling attempts to assist employees in getting help to resolve whatever is bothering them.

TIPS (FOR) LAID-OFF EMPLOYEES

* Looking for work is a full-time job.
* Be prepared for rejection—stay positive.
* Networking is more important than job advertisements.
* Continue upgrading your skills.

7.7 Define What can organizations do to maximize employee relations?

EMPLOYEE RELATIONS

Once an organization has attracted and motivated employees, retention becomes the next crucial component. Employee relations is the final part of the HRM process identified earlier in the chapter and completes the toolkit that is an effective and integrated model for the successful management of an organization's human resources.

Occupational Health and Safety

Every province and territory has occupational health and safety legislation, which is based on joint responsibility of workers and employers.[72] Both sides are meant to take reasonable care and precaution. Employers can prevent workplace accidents by reducing unsafe conditions in the workplace and unsafe acts by employees. Employee wellness is an area that falls under the overall healthy workplace desired by employers and employees. Exhibit 7-11 lists some of the more common corporate wellness initiatives.

Organizational performance can be reduced by several issues that can exist in the workplace, including alcohol and substance abuse, stress, repetitive strain injuries, workplace violence, and harassment.[73]

Sexual harassment is a serious issue in both public- and private-sector organizations. A survey by York University found that 48 percent of working women in Canada reported they had experienced some form of "gender harassment" in the year before they were surveyed.[74] Barbara Orser, a research affiliate with the Conference Board of Canada, notes

Andreas Mueller/Fotolia

Aldo HQ is a footwear giant in Montreal with 1200 employees. The company has an atrium in the lobby along with an art gallery, wood-clad employee lounges on every floor, VIP parking spots for carpoolers, and open concept workspaces with abundant natural light.

---

discipline
Actions taken by a manager to enforce an organization's standards and regulations.

employee counselling
A process designed to help employees overcome performance-related problems.

EXHIBIT 7-11 Corporate Wellness Initiatives

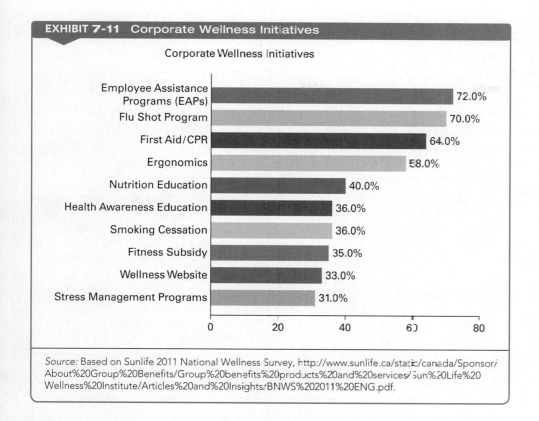

Corporate Wellness Initiatives

Initiative	Percentage
Employee Assistance Programs (EAPs)	72.0%
Flu Shot Program	70.0%
First Aid/CPR	64.0%
Ergonomics	58.0%
Nutrition Education	40.0%
Health Awareness Education	36.0%
Smoking Cessation	36.0%
Fitness Subsidy	35.0%
Wellness Website	33.0%
Stress Management Programs	31.0%

Source: Based on Sunlife 2011 National Wellness Survey, http://www.sunlife.ca/static/canada/Sponsor/About%20Group%20Benefits/Group%20benefits%20products%20and%20services/Sun%20Life%20Wellness%20Institute/Articles%20and%20Insights/BNWS%202011%20ENG.pdf.

that "sexual harassment is more likely to occur in workplace environments that tolerate bullying, intimidation, yelling, innuendo, and other forms of discourteous behaviour."[75]

Employee Engagement

Employees in 2011 and beyond have experienced a severe economic downturn, have witnessed issues with governmental and personal debt, and have likely faced wage freezes, downsizing, and increased job demands. All of these factors combine to provide a new challenge for employers—keeping employees engaged.

The Conference Board of Canada published a report entitled *Employee Engagement: A Review of Current Research and Its Implications*, in which it defined employee engagement as "a heightened emotional connection that an employee feels for his or her organization that influences him or her to exert greater discretionary effort to his or her work."[76] Organizations with high employee engagement likely have a high level of employee involvement, commitment to the organization, and job satisfaction.

Studies have proven that employee engagement leads to higher organizational performance.[77] Engaged employees are happier and have more pride in their work. They are more likely to collaborate with coworkers, invest more effort and take additional responsibility, and remain with the organization than employees who are less engaged.[78]

The Conference Board summarized more than 12 major studies on employee engagement and discovered key drivers that were consistent in many of the reports. Exhibit 7-12 lists the eight most common drivers of employee engagement.

PERSONAL INVENTORY ASSESSMENT

Engagement and work–life balance go hand in hand.

EXHIBIT 7-12 Key Drivers of Employee Engagement

Key Driver	Checkpoint
Trust and integrity	How well do managers communicate and "walk the talk"?
Nature of the job	Is the job mentally stimulating day-to-day?
Line of sight between employee performance and company performance	Does the employee understand how his or her work contributes to the company's performance?
Career growth opportunities	Are there future opportunities for growth?
Pride about the company	How much self-esteem does the employee feel by being associated with the company?
Coworkers/team members	How well does the employee get along with his or her coworkers/team members? (These relationships significantly influence one's level of engagement.)
Employee development	Is the company making an effort to develop the employee's skills?
Relationship with one's manager	Does the employee value the relationship with his or her manager?

Source: The Conference Board Inc.'s publication "Employee Engagement: A Review of Current Research and Its Implications," November 2006, John Gibbons. www.conference-board.org

7 Review and Apply

Summary of Learning Outcomes

7.1 What factors affect human resource planning? The human resource management (HRM) process consists of three key areas: *environmental factors* that impact HRM, such as organizational culture, economic conditions, labour market issues, and technology; *human resource requirements and performance and reward factors*, such as planning, recruitment, training, and total rewards;[79] and *employee relations factors*, including health and safety and employee engagement.

Canada's workforce is aging and its demographics are changing, leading to projected employee skill shortages. CCVO recommends that nonprofit organizations need to include diversity initiatives as part of their HRM strategy.

7.2 How do organizations assess their human resource needs? Human resource managers do a human resource inventory to discover what skills and capabilities current employees have. They map that inventory against what might be needed in the future, based on the organization's mission, goals, and strategies.

Organizations need to identify and assess the strengths and limitations of their employees. CCVO suggests using targeted training to overcome skill gaps in language, writing, presentation skills, communication, numeracy, and thinking skills.

7.3 How do organizations identify and select competent employees? Organizations first need to assess their current and future needs for employees to make sure they have enough of the right people to accomplish the organization's goals. When selecting new employees, organizations need to determine whether potential employees will be successful once they are on the job. To do this, managers use application forms, written tests, performance-simulation tests, interviews, background investigations, and, in some cases, physical examinations to screen employees. Managers also need to make sure that they do not engage in discrimination in the hiring process.

Organizations can develop more inclusive recruitment practices by advertising in various ethnic media sources and providing job descriptions without jargon or technical language.

7.4 How do organizations help employees adapt and stay up-to-date? Organizations, particularly larger ones, have orientation programs for new employees. The orientation introduces the new employee to his or her job, and also to the organization. As job demands change, employees may need to have their skills updated through training programs. Companies use a variety of training methods, from on-the-job training to classroom work to technology-based training.

CCVO recommends having a mentor/buddy system so that new hires can ask existing employees various questions concerning behaviour in meetings, use of office materials, or even daily breaks.

7.5 What can organizations do to help employees achieve high performance throughout their careers? Organizations should develop performance standards for employees and then evaluate employees on a regular basis. Through performance appraisal, employees learn whether they are performing effectively or whether they need help to improve, including additional training.

Performance management ensures that employees are rewarded for excellence. It also helps establish career goals and adapt ongoing professional development plans.

7.6 How do total rewards motivate employees? Total rewards contains five components: strategic compensation, benefits, work–life balance, performance management, and career development. These elements combine into one reward strategy that is integrated and results in happy, committed, and productive employees.

7.7 What can organizations do to maximize employee relations? Once an organization has attracted and motivated employees, retention becomes the next crucial component. Employee relations is the final part of the HRM process identified earlier in the chapter and completes the toolkit that is an effective and integrated model for the successful management of an organization's human resources.

SNAPSHOT SUMMARY

7.1 The Human Resource Management Process
Environmental Factors Affecting HRM

7.2 Human Resource Requirements
Job Analysis and Design
Human Resource Planning
Meeting Future Needs

7.3 Staffing the Organization
Recruitment
Selection

7.4 Orientation and Training
Orientation
Training

7.5 Performance Management
Performance Management System
What Happens When Performance Falls Short

7.6 Total Rewards: Five Key Components

7.7 Employee Relations
Occupational Health and Safety
Employee Engagement

MyManagementLab   Study, practise, and explore real management situations with these helpful resources:

- **Interactive Lesson Presentations:** Work through interactive presentations and assessments to test your knowledge of management concepts.
- **PIA (Personal Inventory Assessments):** Enhance your ability to connect with key concepts through these engaging self-reflection assessments.
- **Study Plan:** Check your understanding of chapter concepts with self-study quizzes.
- **Simulations:** Practise decision making in simulated management environments.

Discussion Questions

1. Describe the environmental factors that most directly influence the human resource management process.
2. What are the two types of interview questions that employers should use?
3. How are orientation and employee training alike? How are they different?
4. Describe three performance appraisal methods as well as the advantages and disadvantages of each.
5. How do recruitment, selection, orientation, and training directly affect workforce diversity?
6. Do you think there are moral limits on how far a prospective employer should delve into an applicant's life by means of interviews, tests, and background investigations? Explain your position.
7. Should managers offer flextime and other work–life balance initiatives? What special human resource management issues do these initiatives raise?
8. What are total rewards? How do the various components of total rewards lead to effective human resource management?

Developing Management Skills

Dilemma

Your instructor has asked class members to form teams to work on a major class project. You have worked on teams before and have not always been pleased with the results. This time you are determined to have a good team experience. You

have reason to believe that effective performance management might make a difference.

You also know that evaluating performance and giving feedback are important. You have heard that organizations are using competencies as the basis for managing performance. A competency is a combination of knowledge, skills, and abilities

(KSAs) used to improve performance. For example, negotiation or effective communications are competencies that are desirable in a group context.

With all of this in mind, write up a list of competencies that you would expect to find in strong team members.

Becoming a Manager

- Using the Internet, research different companies that interest you and check out what required competencies they list in their job descriptions.
- If you are working, note what types of competencies you see in your managers. What do they do that seems to be effective? Ineffective? What can you learn from this?

Developing Your Diagnostic and Analytical Skills: Dealing with a Difficult Person

Document your answers to the following questions about someone with whom you are not getting along. Implement your written action plan for how you will adapt your behaviour to influence this negative relationship.

1. Your typical approach has not been successful. Describe your approach.
2. What, in your opinion, is this person's personality and behavioural style?
3. How does this person react to your style?
4. What way(s) could you modify your behaviour to improve your relationship with this person?
5. Outline a specific action plan for your next meeting with this person.

Developing Your Interpersonal Skills: Volunteering

ABOUT THE SKILL
Volunteering is a good way to build up the experience that employers are seeking when recruiting college and university graduates. Participating in a volunteer internship can help job seekers build soft skills, technical skills, and communication skills.

TIPS TO BE A SUCCESSFUL VOLUNTEER OR INTERN
You can be an effective intern if you do the following:

- Set goals and follow through on them. Get advice from professionals in the workplace.
- Ask a lot of questions and keep a journal with daily notes of your activities and achievements.
- Avoid office politics by being professional, tactful, and diplomatic.
- Demonstrate an eagerness to learn.

- Join a professional association or organization associated with your studies. Attend networking events.

PRACTISING THE SKILL
An internship can help you develop your soft skills, such as flexibility, team building, leadership, and collaboration. Many recent graduates and newcomers to Canada lack relevant Canadian work experience. Internships help both the volunteer and the employer in evaluating the fit or compatibility, and companies often dip into their own intern pool when hiring.

Your Essential Management Reading List

Learning from key management experts can help us understand today's management theory and practice. What follows is a list of some of the top books about HR:

- *Games People Play*—Eric Berne
- *First, Break All the Rules: What the World's Greatest Managers Do Differently*—Marcus Buckingham and Curt Coffman
- *Who Moved My Cheese? An Amazing Way to Deal with Change in Your Work and in Your Life*—Spencer Johnson

Diversity Matters

Royal Bank received a lot of criticism when it was discovered that it had outsourced IT jobs to a foreign company, and then brought in temporary foreign workers to help move the jobs offshore. It turns out RBC is not the only one using the federal Temporary Foreign Worker Program, which admitted 213 516 temporary foreign workers in 2012. That number was three times higher than a decade earlier.[80]

The federal government views the temporary work program as a key weapon in its fight against the growing skills gap in Canada. Canada's immigration policy has been focused on bringing in people with specific occupational skills, such as petroleum engineers for the Alberta oil patch. They are looking at an "expression of interest" model that would allow employers and governments to pick from an online pool of applicants based on local labour-market needs.

Critics contend that Canada's relatively high unemployment rate indicates we have a problem with workers who do not want to work in available jobs, due to everything from pay to health and safety. Canadian employers are slow to recognize foreign credentials, so immigrants who are twice as likely to be university grads are almost three times more likely to be working in low-skilled jobs.[81] Other complaints centre on the budget cuts that have gutted programs that were set up to support immigrants settling into Canadian life. One of the keys to surviving the skills gap is to make sure immigrants thrive in higher skilled jobs. Employers need to emphasize the benefits of diversity in orientation and training programs and ensure that immigrants are accepted in the workplace.

Hey, You're the Boss Now!

The interview is used almost universally as part of the employee selection process. Not many of us have ever been hired without having gone through one or more interviews. Interviews can be valid and reliable selection tools, but they need to be structured and well organized.

You can be an effective interviewer by using the following eight suggestions for interviewing job candidates:[82]

1. **Review the job description and job specifications.** Be sure that prior to the interview you have reviewed pertinent information about the job. Why? Because this will provide you with valuable information with which to assess the job candidate. Furthermore, knowing the relevant job requirements will help eliminate interview bias.

2. **Prepare a structured set of situational and behavioural questions that you want to ask all job applicants.** By having a set of prepared questions, you are able to better compare all candidates' answers against a common base. Use a standardized evaluation form.

3. **Before meeting a candidate, review his or her application form and résumé.** By doing this preparation, you will be able to create a complete picture of the candidate in terms of what is represented on the résumé or application and what the job requires. You can also begin to identify areas to explore during the interview: Areas that are not clearly defined on the résumé or application but are essential to the job can become a focal point in your discussion with the candidate.

4. **Open the interview by putting the applicant at ease and providing a brief preview of the topics to be discussed.** Interviews are stressful for job candidates. If you indicate upfront that you want a successful outcome for both of you and engage in a bit of small talk at the beginning, you can give the candidate time to adjust to the interview setting. By providing a preview of topics to come, you are giving the candidate an agenda, which helps the candidate begin to frame what he or she will say in response to your questions.

5. **Ask your questions and listen carefully to the candidate's answers.** Select follow-up questions that flow naturally from the answers given. Focus on the candidate's responses as they relate to information you need to ensure that the person meets your job requirements. If you are still uncertain, use a follow-up question to probe further for information.

6. **Give the candidate a chance to ask questions.** Typically, at the start of the interview, you would let candidates know there will be an opportunity to ask questions at the end, or, if you prefer, throughout the interview.

7. **Close the interview by telling the applicant what is going to happen next.** Applicants are anxious about the status of your hiring decision. Be upfront with candidates regarding others who will be interviewed and the remaining steps in the hiring process. Let the person know your time frame for making a decision. In addition, tell the applicant how you will notify him or her about your decision.

8. **Write your evaluation of the applicant while the interview is still fresh in your mind.** Do not wait until the end of the day, after interviewing several people, to write your analysis of each candidate. Memory can (and often will) fail you! The sooner after an interview you write down your impressions, the better chance you have of accurately noting what occurred in the interview and your perceptions of the candidate.

3BL: The Triple Bottom Line

Human resource management is part of the solution when it comes to the triple bottom line. Consider the following benefits that accrue in the three main areas of 3BL:

PEOPLE
Immigrants provide innovation, creativity, and high levels of skills and education.

PROFIT
Inclusive workplaces feature higher job satisfaction and lower recruiting and turnover costs.

PLANET
A broader labour supply pool provides long-term sustainability and avoids the necessity of meeting labour shortages with higher compensation and benefit packages.

THINKING STRATEGICALLY ABOUT 3BL
The New Brunswick government has invested more than $5 million in its Aboriginal population. In January 2010, it invested $1 million for Aboriginal students to complete postsecondary education.[83] This investment was followed in October 2011 by $4 million for an employment training program in information and communications technology.[84] These strategic initiatives are meant to address a labour shortage and increase Aboriginal participation in the workforce. What other strategies could the government use to enhance employment opportunities for Aboriginal peoples?

Team Exercises

Networking: The 30-Second Commercial

Networking is a skill that can be very valuable for students to use for job hunting and making contacts. Think of it as building relationships with a variety of people whom you may be able to help or receive help from in the future. Before attending a networking event, you should learn to develop your "30-second commercial."[85] This tool is like an elevator pitch, which is a quick summary of you, an organization, or even a product or service. The name suggests that it should be possible to deliver the summary in the time span of an elevator ride. Venture capitalists on shows like CBC's *Dragon's Den*[86] often judge the quality of an idea by the quality of its elevator pitch and will ask entrepreneurs for their elevator pitches in order to quickly weed out bad ideas and weak teams. Your 30-second commercial can be used in many situations, such as job interviewing and even dating!

When you meet a potential contact, you should state your purpose early in the conversation. Your initial discussion should be brief and to the point. You are meeting this person because they are in the field or industry you want to explore, so your goal is not to get a job but to obtain information from them about the industry.

Here are two templates that you can use to build a 30-second commercial. You have five minutes to create your commercial. Divide into pairs, greet each other with a firm, professional handshake, and take turns saying your commercial. Circulate among other students and practise your commercial. Obtain written feedback from one classmate.

OPTION A

- Your name
- Your current status *(student, program, school)*
- What were your major accomplishments? *(academic or work, list three and results)*
- What do you want to do next? *(seek information on this industry, learn more about role X, learn more about the organization, etc.)*

OPTION B

- I'm *(name)*. I'm a *(_ year student)* with *(university, college, school)*. Most recently, I worked at *(company)* as a *(job title)*, where I *(list a few duties)*. Whether at school or in the workplace, I bring three key strengths to the table: (___, ___, ___). At this time, I am seeking *(information, background, details, etc.)* in this field as I am considering a career in this industry.

Continue to polish and develop your personal 30-second commercial—you never know when it may come in handy.

For more information, see Julia McKinnell, "The Introvert's Guide to Networking," *Maclean's*, August 26, 2010, and Derek Sankey, "Don't Overlook 'Face Time' in Job Search," *Ottawa Citizen*, November 16, 2011.

Be the Consultant

You have been hired by a company to give some guidance on its job interview questions. A lawyer told managers of the company that several of their questions do not meet Canadian legislation requirements and provided them with sample revised questions. Turn the remainder of the bad questions into good interview questions.

No	Instead
What is your age?	Are you of legal working age?
Do you have kids?	Are there any restrictions on your ability to travel as necessary?
Are you a Canadian citizen?	Are you legally entitled to work in Canada?
What are your strengths and weaknesses?	
Tell me about yourself.	
Why should I hire you for this job?	
What interests you about our company?	
Do you ever abuse alcohol or drugs?	
If you were a *Lost* character, who would you be?	
Do you get along well with people?	

Earlier in the chapter the Tips for Managers looked at behavioural and situational questions. Turn these closed-ended questions that can be answered with a simple yes into more suitable behavioural and situational questions.

Questions	
Are you good at handling stress?	
Do you work well in teams?	
Are you an ethical person?	

Business Cases

Wellington West

Bay Street is the centre of Canada's financial district, but a Winnipeg-based brokerage firm proved that having its headquarters in Toronto was not a requirement for success. Wellington West started as a small investment boutique, formed a financial services division and an energy and mining investment division, and grew to become one of Canada's sparkling success stories. Few companies have been named to both the 50 Best Managed Companies in Canada and the 50 Best Employers in Canada, but Wellington West did it numerous times.[87]

Wellington West derived its competitive advantage from three areas: a client-centric approach, its unique organizational culture, and employee ownership.[88] The company's culture allowed it to draw employees seeking an alternative to large Canadian banks, opting instead for a large firm that operates like a boutique.[89] Wellington West became a firm that was built both for and by financial advisers. Another major core principle was employee ownership. More than 90 percent of the 650 employees became shareholders.[90] Founder and CEO Charlie Spiring summed it up as follows: "Ownership is a powerful thing. No one washes a rental car."

The growth that Wellington West achieved was astounding. In 1994, the company had one office, had revenue of $2.5 million, and managed $250 million worth of assets. By 2008, Wellington West had 51 offices and $133 million in revenue, and was managing over $10 billion worth of client assets.[91] The success started from the top, and CEO Spiring was named to Canada's Top 40 Under 40 and won an Entrepreneur of the Year award from Ernst & Young.

Ultimately, Wellington West's success led to it being a popular target for acquisition. In 2011, the energy and investment mining arm of Wellington West was acquired by National Bank. National Bank Financial co-CEO Ricardo Pascoe said the $333 million acquisition would allow the company to pursue a leadership position in investment banking for mid-cap energy and mining companies in Canada. "What we're really going after," he said, "is Wellington West's client relationship and their research coverage."[92]

In late August 2012, Wellington West Financial Services was acquired by Manulife Financial. "This transaction allows us to build on our position as one of Canada's premier investment firms and reflects our commitment to independent financial advice in Canada," said Rick Annaert, chief executive of Manulife Securities. "There is a natural cultural fit between our two firms."[93]

What can National Bank and Manulife do to maintain Wellington West's strong corporate culture that has traditionally been somewhat "anti-bank"?

Love Among the Cubicles

You can probably recall an infamous workplace romance disaster such as Bill Clinton and his intern or David Letterman and his assistants, which might be the reason so many employers are cautious about intra-office love. Some companies in the United States require couples to sign waivers dubbed "love contracts" vowing that they will not sue their employers if the relationship does not work out. In Canada, companies tend to manage it on an ad hoc basis. "I don't want to know," says Laurie Sproule, a senior manager with a large Ontario manufacturer. "As long as it doesn't spill out and interfere with others, I really don't care."[94]

Nina Cole, an organizational behaviour expert from Ryerson University, conducted a study investigating coworker perceptions about office romance. "The latest generation to enter the workforce is quite matter of fact about this sort of thing," she indicates. "They don't think it's a big deal at all."[95] Studies have shown some perks associated with office romances: more engaged and happier employees, as well as a corporate culture that attracts and retains staff. Other benefits include higher job satisfaction and fewer sick days. Happy couples working together are more likely to stay later, be more creative, and have less personality conflicts with other members of the team.[96] Powerful results. In Sweden, a review of 37 000 employees in 1500 workplaces showed the rate of divorce of couples who worked together was lower by half than the overall average.[97]

Companies like Southwest Airlines and AT&T have publicly come out in support of office dating. Southwest has 1200 married couples among their staff of 35 000. Company spokesperson Michelle Agnew attests that it is one of the reasons people enjoy coming to work, as long as people are being appropriate about it. The only policy they have in this area is that a couple cannot be in a supervisor-subordinate relationship, so they tend to reassign one member of the couple.[98] Companies should also be aware of two employees dating in small departments, but otherwise businesses should embrace office romance.

Two famous couples who met at the office are Bill and Melinda Gates and Olivia Chow and late NDP leader Jack Layton. Melinda was a marketing manager and Bill was the chairman when they met at a Microsoft event. Olivia and Jack met in 1985 when they were both campaigning for the school board. Eventually both became Members of Parliament.

CHAPTER

8 Leadership

EPA/Landov

The top business bestseller of 2013 was *Lean In: Women, Work, and the Will to Lead* by Sheryl Sandberg. She advocated that women should be more ambitious, or "lean in" to their careers. Major companies like Cisco and PriceWaterhouseCoopers established Lean In Circles in their offices.[1] Sandberg was Facebook's chief operating officer and, along with Yahoo's CEO Marissa Mayer, was evidence of the rise of female executives in technology firms. But an important distinction is that Sandberg and Mayer are not just powerful female executives: They are major players in their industry.

One of the interesting aspects of the tech industry supportive to female leadership is its median age under 30, with a generation espousing values such as egalitarianism, openness, and community engagement. The reality is that every company's workforce will be overrun with millennials, and companies will have to change and become more gender-neutral. A report by American Express noted that since 1997, women-owned companies have outpaced the number of new businesses by 59 percent to 41 percent, and they are outperforming most businesses in terms of employment and revenue growth.[2]

In Canada, RBC became the first of the big banks to appoint a female chair of its board of directors, Kathleen Taylor. The Ontario Securities Commission announced in late 2013 that it wants companies on the TSX to publicly disclose the actions they are taking to increase the number of senior female executives.[3]

Why is leadership so important? Because leaders in organizations are the ones who make things happen. If leadership is so important, it is only natural to ask: What differentiates leaders from nonleaders? What is the most appropriate style of leadership? What can you do if you want to be seen as a leader? In this chapter, we try to answer these and other questions about what it means to be a leader.

Think About It

What does it mean to be a female leader for today's organizations? Put yourself in Sheryl Sandberg's shoes: What kinds of challenges would you face as a female leader in the technology sector?

8.1 **Tell** How do leaders and managers differ?

PERSONAL INVENTORY ASSESSMENT

And the Survey Says...

The following are critical leadership capabilities required in Canadian health care organizations:

82% championing change

59% strategic alignment

59% develop others

49% build teams

35% self-development

35% encourage innovation[7]

MANAGERS VERSUS LEADERS

Let us begin by clarifying the distinction between managers and leaders. *Leadership* and *management* are two terms that are often confused and typically viewed as separate. What is the difference between them?

Managers and leaders act in different but complementary ways. Leaders cope with change to transform organizations, while managers cope with the complexity of keeping organizations running effectively and efficiently. As organizations deal with much more rapid change, management and leadership are seen as integrated roles rather than separate functions.[4] Exhibit 8-1 illustrates the basic distinction between managers and leaders. **Leaders** provide vision and strategy to the organization; managers implement that vision and strategy, coordinate and staff the organization, and handle day-to-day problems. **Leadership** is the process of influencing individuals or groups toward the achievement of goals.

Can managers be leaders? Should leaders be managers? Because no one yet has shown that leadership ability is a handicap to a manager, we believe that all managers should ideally be leaders. One of the major functions of management is to lead. However, not all leaders have the capabilities or skills of effective managers, and thus not all leaders should be managers. An individual who can set vision and strategy is not necessarily able to plan, organize, and control. Mark Henderson, president and CEO of Ericsson Canada, believes that "managers and leaders don't have all the answers, but strong leadership seems to utilize the knowledge of the employees and the collective power of their motivation and experience."[5]

Researchers have begun organizing traits around the Big Five personality framework.[6] They have found that most of the dozens of traits that emerged in various leadership reviews fall under one of the Big Five personality traits (extroversion, agreeableness, conscientiousness, emotional stability, and openness to experience). This approach has resulted in consistent and strong support for traits as predictors of leadership.

Researchers have agreed that traits alone are not sufficient to explain effective leadership, because explanations based solely on traits ignore the interactions of leaders and their group members as well as situational factors. Possessing the appropriate traits only makes it more likely that an individual would be an effective leader. Therefore, leadership research from the late 1940s to the mid-1960s concentrated on the preferred behavioural styles that leaders demonstrated. Researchers wondered whether there was something unique in what effective leaders *did*—in other words, in their *behaviour*.

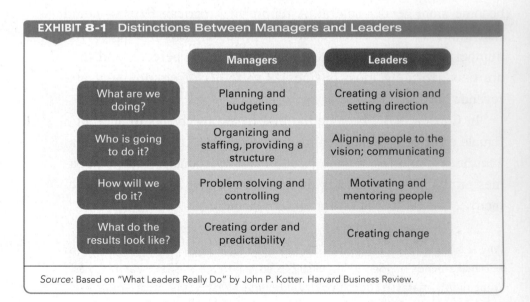

EXHIBIT 8-1 Distinctions Between Managers and Leaders

	Managers	Leaders
What are we doing?	Planning and budgeting	Creating a vision and setting direction
Who is going to do it?	Organizing and staffing, providing a structure	Aligning people to the vision; communicating
How will we do it?	Problem solving and controlling	Motivating and mentoring people
What do the results look like?	Creating order and predictability	Creating change

Source: Based on "What Leaders Really Do" by John P. Kotter. Harvard Business Review.

---

leader
Someone who can influence others and provide vision and strategy to the organization.

leadership
The process of influencing individuals or groups toward the achievement of goals.

What Do Early Leadership Theories Tell Us About Leadership?

Leaders. Groups. **Long History!**

- Early leadership theories focused on:
  - The **person** (*leader trait theories*)
  - The **behaviours**—how the leader interacted with his or her group members—(*behavioural theories*)
- Are there specific traits or behaviours leaders of tech companies, like Sheryl Sandberg, should have?

1 THE LEADER What Traits Do Leaders Have?

- **WHAT DO YOU KNOW ABOUT LEADERSHIP?** When asked that question, most people cite a list of qualities they admire in leaders—intelligence, charisma, decisiveness, enthusiasm, strength, bravery, integrity, self-confidence, and so on.

- That's the **trait theories of leadership** in a nutshell—the search for traits or characteristics that differentiate leaders from nonleaders.

- If this concept was valid, *all leaders would have to possess those unique and consistent characteristics,* making it easy to find leaders in organizations.

- Not going to happen. Despite the best efforts of researchers, finding a set of traits that would always differentiate a leader (the person) from a nonleader has not happened.

Sergiu Ungureanu/Shutterstock

- Attempts to identify traits consistently with *leadership* (the process, not the person) have been more successful. See Exhibit 8-2 for those eight traits.[8]

trait theories of leadership
Theories that isolate characteristics (traits) that differentiate leaders from nonleaders.

EXHIBIT 8-2 Eight Traits Associated with Leadership

1 Drive.
Leaders exhibit a high effort level. They have a relatively high desire for achievement; they are ambitious; they have a lot of energy; they are tirelessly persistent in their activities; and they show initiative.

2 Desire to lead.
Leaders have a strong desire to influence and lead others. They demonstrate the willingness to take responsibility.

3 Honesty and integrity.
Leaders build trusting relationships between themselves and followers by being truthful or non-deceitful and by showing high consistency between word and deed.

4 Self-confidence.
Followers look to leaders for an absence of self-doubt. Leaders, therefore, need to show self-confidence in order to convince followers of the rightness of their goals and decisions.

5 Cognitive intelligence.
Leaders need to be intelligent enough to gather, synthesize, and interpret large amounts of information, and they need to be able to create visions, solve problems, and make correct decisions.

6 Emotional intelligence.
Leaders need to be aware of their emotions and those of others, and they need to be able to use those emotions effectively when making decisions.

7 Job-relevant knowledge.
Effective leaders have a high degree of knowledge about the company, industry, and technical matters. In-depth knowledge allows leaders to make well-informed decisions and to understand the implications of those decisions.

8 Extroversion.
Leaders are energetic, lively people. They are sociable, assertive, and rarely silent or withdrawn.

Sources: Based on S. A. Kirkpatrick and E. A. Locke, "Leadership: Do Traits Really Matter?" *Academy of Management Executive.* May 1991, pp. 48–60; and T. A. Judge, J. E. Bono, R. Iiies, and M. Werner, "Personality and Leadership: A Qualitative and Quantitative Review," *Journal of Applied Psychology,* August 2002, pp. 765–780.

What Now?

- TRAITS alone were not sufficient for identifying leaders. Why? Explanations based solely on traits ignored the interactions of leaders and their group members as well as situational factors.

- Possession the appropriate traits only made it *more likely* that an individual would be an effective leader.

- Leadership research from the late 1940s to the mid-1960s turned to finding preferred behavioural styles that leaders demonstrated.

Was there something unique in what leaders did—in their words or behaviour?

Vege/Fotolia

THE BEHAVIOURS What Behaviours Do Leaders Exhibit?

- Would **behavioural theories of leadership** provide more definitive answers about the nature of leadership?

- If behavioural theories could identify critical behavioural determinants of leadership, people could be trained to be leaders—the premise behind management development programs.

UNIVERSITY OF IOWA[4]	OHIO STATE[5]	UNIVERSITY OF MICHIGAN[6]	MANAGERIAL GRID[7]
Behavioural Dimension	**Behavioural Dimension**	**Behavioural Dimension**	**Behavioural Dimension**
Democratic style: involving subordinates, delegating authority, and encouraging participation	**Consideration**: being considerate of followers' ideas and feelings	**Employee oriented**: emphasized interpersonal relationships and taking care of employees' needs	**Concern for people**: measured leader's concern for subordinates on a scale of 1 to 9 (low to high)
Autocratic style: dictating work methods, centralizing decision making, and limiting participation	**Initiating structure**: structuring work and work relationships to meet job goals	**Production oriented**: emphasized technical or task aspects of job	**Concern for production**: measured leader's concern for getting job done on a scale 1 to 9 (low to high)
Laissez-faire style: giving group freedom to make decisions and complete work	**CONCLUSION**	**CONCLUSION**	**CONCLUSION**
CONCLUSION	High–high leader (high in consideration and high in initiating structure) achieved high subordinate performance and satisfaction, but not in all situations	Employee-oriented leaders were associated with high group productivity and higher job satisfaction.	Leaders performed best with a 9,9 style (high concern for production and high concern for people).
Democratic style of leadership was most effective, although later studies showed mixed results.			

What Now?

- Dual nature of leader behaviours—that is, focusing on the work to be done and on employees—is an important characteristic in each of these studies.

- Leadership researchers were discovering that predicting leadership success involved something more complex than isolating a few leader traits or preferable behaviours.

- They began looking at situational influences. *Specifically, which leadership styles might be suitable in different situations, and what were these different situations?*

Fotolia

---

behavioural theories of leadership
Theories that isolate behaviours that differentiate effective leaders from ineffective leaders.

8.3 **Describe** How do contingency theories of leadership improve our understanding of leadership?

PERSONAL INVENTORY ASSESSMENT

CONTINGENCY THEORIES OF LEADERSHIP

Contingency theories of leadership developed after it became clear that identifying traits or key behaviours was not enough to understand what made good leaders. Contingency researchers considered whether different situations required different styles of leadership. To illustrate how situations might affect the ability to lead, consider the fate of an American who was recruited to run Canadian companies. Successful Texas oilman J. P. Bryan was given two chances to restore profitability at Canadian companies—Gulf Canada Resources (now ConocoPhillips) and Canadian 88 Energy (which later became Esprit Exploration)—and failed in both attempts.[9] This example suggests that one's leadership style may need to be adjusted for different companies and employees, and perhaps even for different countries, an observation consistent with research findings that not all leaders can lead in any situation.[10]

In this section, we examine two contingency theories of leadership—Hersey and Blanchard's Situational Leadership and path-goal theory. Both of these theories focus on the relationship of the leader to followers, and there is broad support for the idea that this relationship is important.[11] Each theory attempts to answer *if-then* contingencies (that is, *if* this is the situation, *then* this is the best leadership style to use).

Hersey and Blanchard's Situational Leadership

Paul Hersey and Ken Blanchard developed a leadership theory that has gained a strong following among management development specialists.[12] This contingency theory of leadership, called **Situational Leadership® (SL)**, focuses on followers' readiness. Hersey and Blanchard argue that successful leadership is achieved by selecting the right leadership style, which is contingent on the level of the followers' readiness. Before we proceed, we need to clarify two points: why a leadership theory focuses on the followers and what is meant by the term *readiness*.

The emphasis on the followers in leadership effectiveness reflects the reality that the followers are the ones who accept or reject the leader. Regardless of what the leader does, effectiveness depends on the actions of his or her followers. This fact is an important dimension that has been overlooked or underemphasized in most leadership theories. **Readiness**, as defined by Hersey and Blanchard, refers to the extent to which people have the ability and willingness to accomplish a specific task.

SL uses the same two leadership dimensions that Fred Fiedler, a psychologist at the University of Washington who pioneered the study of leadership behaviours, identified in his contingency model of leadership: task and relationship behaviours. However, Hersey and Blanchard go a step further by considering each as either high or low and then combining them into four specific leadership styles (see Exhibit 8-3), described as follows:

- *Telling* (high task–low relationship): The leader defines roles and tells people what, how, when, and where to do various tasks.
- *Selling* (high task–high relationship): The leader provides both directive and supportive behaviour.
- *Participating* (low task–high relationship): The leader and follower share in decision making; the main role of the leader is facilitating and communicating.
- *Delegating* (low task–low relationship): The leader provides little direction or support.

The final component in SL theory is follower readiness, described in four stages:

- *R1:* People are both *unable* and *unwilling* to take responsibility for doing something. They are neither competent nor confident.
- *R2:* People are *unable* but *willing* to do the necessary job tasks. They are motivated but currently lack the appropriate skills.

Situational Leadership (SL)
A leadership theory that focuses on the readiness of followers.

readiness
The extent to which people have the ability and willingness to accomplish a specific task.

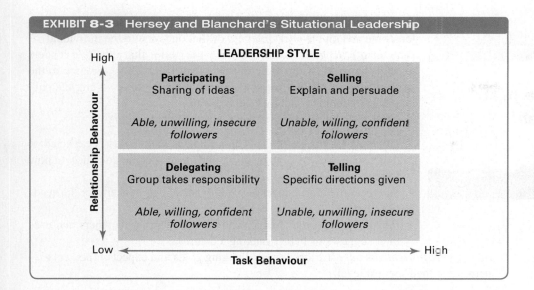

EXHIBIT 8-3 Hersey and Blanchard's Situational Leadership

LEADERSHIP STYLE

| **Participating**
Sharing of ideas

*Able, unwilling, insecure
followers* | **Selling**
Explain and persuade

*Unable, willing, confident
followers* |
| **Delegating**
Group takes responsibility

*Able, willing, confident
followers* | **Telling**
Specific directions given

*Unable, unwilling, insecure
followers* |

Relationship Behaviour (vertical axis, Low to High)

Task Behaviour (horizontal axis, Low to High)

- *R3:* People are *able* but *unwilling* to do what the leader wants.
- *R4:* People are both *able* and *willing* to do what is asked of them.

SL essentially views the leader–follower relationship as similar to that of a parent and child. Just as a parent needs to give up control as a child becomes more mature and responsible, so, too, should a leader. As followers reach high levels of readiness, the leader responds not only by continuing to decrease control over their activities, but also by continuing to decrease relationship behaviour. SL says if followers are *unable* and *unwilling* to do a task, the leader needs to give clear and specific directions; if followers are *unable* and *willing,* the leader needs to display high task orientation to compensate for the followers' lack of ability and high relationship orientation to get followers to "buy into" the leader's desires; if followers are *able* and *unwilling*, the leader needs to use a supportive and participative style; and if employees are both *able* and *willing*, the leader does not need to do much.

SL has intuitive appeal. It acknowledges the importance of followers and builds on the logic that leaders can compensate for ability and motivational limitations in their followers. Yet research efforts to test and support the theory generally have been disappointing.[13] Why? Possible explanations include internal inconsistencies in the model itself as well as problems with research methodology. So despite its appeal and wide popularity, any endorsement of the SL theory should be made with caution.

Path-Goal Theory

Currently, one of the most respected approaches to understanding leadership is **path-goal theory**, which states that a leader's job is to assist his or her followers in attaining their goals and to provide the necessary direction and support to ensure that their goals are compatible with the overall objectives of the group or organization. Developed by University of Toronto Professor Martin Evans in the late 1960s, the path-goal theory was subsequently expanded upon by Robert House (formerly at the University of Toronto and now at the Wharton School of Business). Path-goal theory is a contingency model of leadership that takes key elements from the expectancy theory of motivation (see Chapter 9, page 222) (a theory postulating that an individual tends to act in a certain

path-goal theory
A leadership theory that says the leader's job is to assist his or her followers in attaining their goals and to provide the necessary direction and support to ensure that their goals are compatible with the overall objectives of the group or organization.

A goal without a plan is just a wish!

French writer Antoine de Saint-Exupery (1900–1944)

way based on the expectation that the act will be followed by a given outcome and on the attractiveness of that outcome to the individual).[14] The term *path-goal* is derived from the belief that effective leaders clarify the path to help their followers get from where they are to the achievement of their work goals and make the journey along the path easier by reducing roadblocks and pitfalls.

Path-goal theory identifies four leadership behaviours:

- *Directive leader.* Leader lets subordinates know what is expected of them, schedules work to be done, and gives specific guidance on how to accomplish tasks.
- *Supportive leader.* Leader is friendly and shows concern for the needs of followers.
- *Participative leader.* Leader consults with group members and uses their suggestions before making a decision.
- *Achievement-oriented leader.* Leader sets challenging goals and expects followers to perform at their highest level.

In contrast to Fiedler's view that a leader could not change his or her behaviour, House assumed that leaders are flexible. In other words, path-goal theory assumes that the same leader can display any or all of these leadership styles, depending on the situation.

Path-goal theory proposes two situational or contingency variables that moderate the leadership behaviour–outcome relationship: *environmental* factors that are outside the control of the follower (including task structure, formal authority system, and the work group) and factors that are part of the personal characteristics of the *follower* (including locus of control, experience, and perceived ability). Environmental factors determine the type of leader behaviour required if subordinate outcomes are to be maximized; personal characteristics of the follower determine how the environment and leader behaviour are interpreted. The theory proposes that leader behaviour will not be effective if it is redundant with what the environmental structure is providing or is incongruent with follower characteristics. Exhibit 8-4 gives some illustrations of leadership behaviour tailored to the situation.

Research on the path-goal theory is generally encouraging. Although not every study has found support, the majority of the evidence supports the logic underlying the theory.[15] In summary, employee performance and satisfaction are likely to be positively influenced

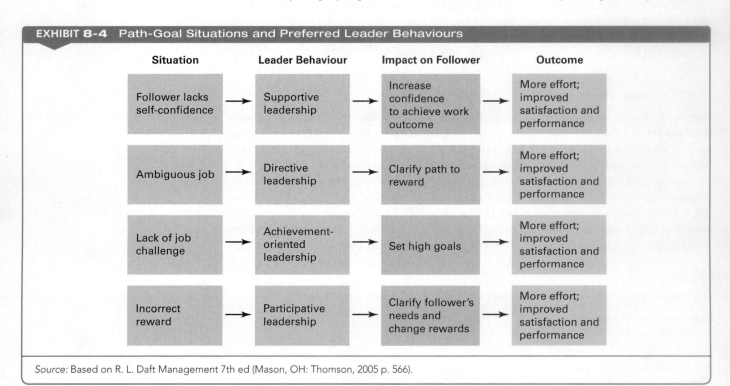

EXHIBIT 8-4 Path-Goal Situations and Preferred Leader Behaviours

Situation	Leader Behaviour	Impact on Follower	Outcome
Follower lacks self-confidence	Supportive leadership	Increase confidence to achieve work outcome	More effort; improved satisfaction and performance
Ambiguous job	Directive leadership	Clarify path to reward	More effort; improved satisfaction and performance
Lack of job challenge	Achievement-oriented leadership	Set high goals	More effort; improved satisfaction and performance
Incorrect reward	Participative leadership	Clarify follower's needs and change rewards	More effort; improved satisfaction and performance

Source: Based on R. L. Daft Management 7th ed (Mason, OH: Thomson, 2005 p. 566).

when the leader compensates for shortcomings in either the employee or the work setting. However, if the leader spends time explaining tasks when they are already clear or when the employee has the ability and experience to handle them without interference, the employee is likely to see such directive behaviour as redundant or even insulting.

LEADING CHANGE

Most of the leadership theories presented so far in this chapter have described **transactional leaders**—leaders who guide or motivate their followers in the direction of established goals by clarifying role and task requirements.[16] But another kind of leadership is needed for leading change in organizations. Two types of leadership have been identified in situations where leaders have inspired change: charismatic–visionary leadership and transformational leadership.

Charismatic–Visionary Leadership

Jeff Bezos (pictured), founder and CEO of Amazon. com, is a person who exudes energy, enthusiasm, and drive.[17] He is fun-loving (his legendary laugh has been described as a flock of Canada geese on nitrous oxide), but has pursued his vision for Amazon with serious intensity and has demonstrated an ability to inspire his employees through the ups and downs of a rapidly growing company. Bezos is what we call a **charismatic leader**—an enthusiastic, self-confident leader whose personality and actions influence people to behave in certain ways.

Reed Saxon/AP Images

Jeff Bezos showing off Amazon.com tablets.

8.4 **Explain** What do charismatic and transformational leaders do?

P I A
PERSONAL INVENTORY ASSESSMENT

CHARACTERISTICS OF CHARISMATIC LEADERS Several authors have attempted to identify the personal characteristics of charismatic leaders.[18] The most comprehensive analysis identified five such characteristics that differentiate charismatic leaders from non-charismatic ones: Charismatic leaders have a vision, are able to articulate that vision, are willing to take risks to achieve that vision, are sensitive to both environmental constraints and follower needs, and exhibit behaviours that are out of the ordinary.[19]

EFFECTS OF CHARISMATIC LEADERSHIP What can we say about the charismatic leader's effect on his or her followers? An increasing body of evidence shows impressive correlations between charismatic leadership and high performance and satisfaction among followers.[20] Research indicates that people who work for charismatic leaders are motivated to exert extra work effort and express greater satisfaction, because they like their leaders.[21] One of the most-cited studies of the effects of charismatic leadership was done at the University of British Columbia in the early 1980s by Jane Howell (now at the University of Western Ontario) and Peter Frost.[22] They found that those who worked under a charismatic leader generated more ideas, produced better results, reported higher job satisfaction, and showed stronger bonds of loyalty. Howell concludes, "Charismatic leaders know how to inspire people to think in new directions."[23]

transactional leaders
Leaders who guide or motivate their followers in the direction of established goals by clarifying role and task requirements.

charismatic leader
An enthusiastic, self-confident leader whose personality and actions influence people to behave in certain ways.

Charismatic leadership also affects overall company performance. Robert House and colleagues studied 63 American and 49 Canadian companies (including Nortel Networks, Molson, Gulf Canada, and Manulife Financial) and found that "between 15 and 25 percent of the variation in profitability among the companies was accounted for by the leadership qualities of their CEO."[24] Charismatic leaders led more profitable companies. However, a recent study of the impact of a charismatic CEO on subsequent organizational performance found no relationship.[25] Despite this finding, charisma is still believed to be a desirable leadership quality.

Charismatic leadership may have a downside, however, as we see from the recent accounting scandals and high-profile bankruptcies of North American companies. WorldCom's Bernard Ebbers and Enron's Kenneth Lay "seemed almost a breed apart, blessed with unique visionary powers" when their companies' stock prices were growing at phenomenal rates in the 1990s.[26] After the scandals, however, there was some agreement that CEOs with less vision and more ethical and corporate responsibility might be more desirable.

BECOMING CHARISMATIC   Can people learn to be charismatic leaders? Or are charismatic leaders born with their qualities? Although a small number of experts still think that charisma cannot be learned, most believe that individuals can be trained to exhibit charismatic behaviours.[27] For example, researchers have succeeded in teaching undergraduate students to "be" charismatic. How? The students were taught to articulate a sweeping goal, communicate high performance expectations, exhibit confidence in the ability of subordinates to meet those expectations, and empathize with the needs of their subordinates; they learned to project a powerful, confident, and dynamic presence; and they practised using a captivating and engaging voice tone. The researchers also trained the student leaders to use charismatic nonverbal behaviours including leaning toward the follower when communicating, maintaining direct eye contact, and having a relaxed posture and animated facial expressions. In groups with these "trained" charismatic leaders, members had higher task performance, higher task adjustment, and better adjustment to the leader and to the group than did group members who worked in groups led by noncharismatic leaders.

One last thing we need to say about charismatic leadership: It may not always be needed to achieve high levels of employee performance. Charismatic leadership may be most appropriate when the follower's task has an ideological purpose or when the environment involves a high degree of stress and uncertainty.[28] For this reason, charismatic leaders most often surface in the arenas of politics, religion, or war; or when a business firm is starting up or facing a survival crisis. For example, Martin Luther King Jr. used his charisma to bring about social equality through nonviolent means, and Steve Jobs achieved unwavering loyalty and commitment from Apple Computer's employees by articulating a vision of a company that would become a world leader.

VISIONARY LEADERSHIP   Although the term *vision* is often linked with charismatic leadership, **visionary leadership** goes beyond charisma—it is the ability to create and articulate a realistic, credible, and attractive vision of the future that improves on the present situation.[29] This vision, if properly selected and implemented, is so energizing that it "in effect jump-starts the future by calling forth the skills, talents, and resources to make it happen."[30]

A vision should offer clear and compelling imagery that taps into people's emotions and inspires enthusiasm to pursue the organization's goals. It should be able to generate possibilities that are inspirational and unique, and offer new ways of doing things that are clearly better for the organization and its members. Visions that are clearly articulated and have powerful imagery are easily grasped and accepted. For example, Michael Dell (founder of Dell) created a vision of a business that sells and delivers a finished personal

visionary leadership
The ability to create and articulate a realistic, credible, and attractive vision of the future that improves on the present situation.

computer directly to a customer in less than a week. The late Mary Kay Ash's vision of women as entrepreneurs selling products that improved their self-image guided her cosmetics company, Mary Kay Cosmetics.

What skills do visionary leaders have? Once the vision is identified, these leaders appear to have three skills that are related to effectiveness in their visionary roles.[31] First is the *ability to explain the vision to others* by making the vision clear in terms of required goals and actions through clear oral and written communication. The second skill is the *ability to express the vision not just verbally but through behaviour*, which requires behaving in ways that continuously convey and reinforce the vision. The third skill is the *ability to extend or apply the vision to different leadership contexts*. For example, the vision has to be as meaningful to the people in accounting as it is to those in production, and to employees in Halifax as it is to those in Toronto.

Transformational Leadership

Some leaders are able to inspire followers to transcend their own self-interests for the good of the organization and are capable of having a profound and extraordinary effect on their followers. These individuals are **transformational leaders**. Examples include Frank Stronach, chair of Aurora, Ontario–based Magna International; and Mogens Smed, CEO of Calgary-based DIRTT (Doing It Right This Time) and former CEO of SMED International. Prime Minister Stephen Harper was named *Time* magazine's 2006 Canadian Newsmaker of the Year, in part because of his transformational style. *Time* contributing editor Stephen Handelman explained the choice as follows: "[Harper] has set himself the messianic tasks of remaking Canadian federalism by curbing Ottawa's spending powers and overhauling Canada's health care and social welfare system." Handelman predicted that should Harper win a Conservative majority in the next election, "he may yet turn out to be the most transformational leader since Trudeau."[32]

Transformational leaders pay attention to the concerns and developmental needs of individual followers; they change followers' awareness of issues by helping those followers look at old problems in new ways; and they are able to excite, arouse, and inspire followers to put out extra effort to achieve group goals.[33]

Transformational leaders turn followers into believers on a vision, working toward what they believe is really important. "Part of a leader's role is to set the vision for the company and to communicate that vision to staff to get their buy-in," explains Dave Anderson of WorkSafeBC.[34] Transformational leadership is more than charisma, since the transformational leader attempts to empower followers to question not only established views but even those views held by the leader.[35]

The evidence supporting the superiority of transformational leadership over transactional leadership is overwhelmingly impressive. Studies that looked at managers in different settings, including the military and business, found that transformational leaders were evaluated as more effective, higher performers, and more promotable than their transactional counterparts.[36] In addition, evidence indicates that transformational leadership is strongly correlated with lower turnover rates, higher productivity, and higher employee satisfaction.[37] Finally, subordinates of transformational leaders may trust their leaders and their organizations more and feel that they are being fairly treated, which in turn may positively influence their work motivation (see Chapter 9).[38] However, transformational leadership should be used with some caution in non–North American contexts, because its effectiveness may be affected by cultural values concerning leadership.[39]

transformational leaders
Leaders who inspire followers to transcend their own self-interests for the good of the organization, and who have a profound and extraordinary effect on their followers.

| 8.5 | **Explain** What are some current issues in leadership? |

CURRENT ISSUES IN LEADERSHIP

Do men and women lead differently? A study by UBC's Sauder School of Business found that female corporate directors are less motivated then men in building empires and are less likely to destroy shareholder value through mergers and acquisitions. Another study indicated that women are less likely to publicly display the mistakes of a talented subordinate to keep them in check.[40]

In this section, we look at some of the issues that leaders face today, including managing power, developing trust, providing ethical leadership, providing virtual leadership, providing team leadership, and understanding gender differences in leadership.

Managing Power

Where do leaders get their power—that is, their capacity to influence work actions or decisions? Five sources of leader power have been identified: legitimate, coercive, reward, expert, and referent.[41]

Legitimate power and authority are the same. Legitimate power represents the power a leader has as a result of his or her position in the organization. People in positions of authority are also likely to have reward and coercive power, but legitimate power is broader than the power to coerce and reward.

Coercive power is the power that rests on the leader's ability to punish or control. Followers react to this power out of fear of the negative results that might occur if they do not comply. As a manager, you typically have some coercive power, such as being able to suspend or demote employees or to assign them work they find unpleasant or undesirable.

Reward power is the power to give positive benefits or rewards. These rewards can be anything that another person values. In an organizational context, that might include money, favourable performance appraisals, promotions, interesting work assignments, friendly colleagues, and preferred work shifts or sales territories.

Expert power is influence that is based on expertise, special skills, or knowledge. As jobs have become more specialized, managers have become increasingly dependent on staff "experts" to achieve the organization's goals. If an employee has skills, knowledge, or expertise that is critical to the operation of a work group, that person's expert power is enhanced.

Finally, **referent power** is the power that arises because of a person's desirable resources or personal traits. If I admire and identify with you, you can exercise power over me because I want to please you. Referent power develops out of admiration of another and a desire to be like that person. If you admire someone to the point of modelling your behaviour and attitudes after him or her, that person has referent power over you.

Most effective leaders rely on several different forms of power to affect the behaviour and performance of their followers. For example, Lieutenant Commander Geoffrey Wadley, commanding officer of one of Australia's state-of-the-art submarines, the HMAS *Sheean,* employs different types of power in managing his crew and equipment. He gives orders to the crew (legitimate), praises them (reward), and disciplines those who commit infractions (coercive). As an effective leader, he also strives to have expert power (based on his expertise and knowledge) and referent power (based on his being admired) to influence his crew.[42]

adam121/Fotolia

When you're the boss, you pull the strings

legitimate power
The power a leader has as a result of his or her position in the organization.

coercive power
The power a leader has through his or her ability to punish or control.

reward power
The power a leader has to give positive benefits or rewards.

expert power
The influence a leader has based on his or her expertise, special skills, or knowledge.

referent power
The power a leader has because of his or her desirable resources or personal traits.

Developing Trust

After union members reluctantly agreed to $850 million a year in concessions that they believed were necessary to keep their company from bankruptcy in 2004, Air Canada's employees were stunned at president and CEO Robert Milton's after-the-fact disclosure of lucrative compensation policies and pension protections designed to retain key executives. Milton and his chief restructuring officer, Calin Rovinescu, were to receive 1 percent of the airline's shares, potentially worth an estimated $21 million, if the proposed takeover by Victor Li was successful. Any trust that employees had in Milton's ability to lead the airline into the future was eroded. In the end, the deal with Li collapsed when union members could not agree to further concessions relating to their pension plans.[43]

Milton's behaviour illustrates how fragile leader trust can be. In today's uncertain environment, an important consideration for leaders is building trust and credibility. Before we can discuss ways leaders can build trust and credibility, we have to know what trust and credibility are and why they are so important.

The main component of credibility is honesty. Surveys show that honesty is consistently singled out as the number-one characteristic of admired leaders. According to James Kouzes and Barry Posner, eminent scholars and leadership coaches, "Honesty is absolutely essential to leadership. If people are going to follow someone willingly, whether it be into battle or into the boardroom, they first want to assure themselves that the person is worthy of their trust." In addition to being honest, credible leaders are competent and inspiring.[44] They are personally able to effectively communicate their confidence and enthusiasm. Thus, followers judge a leader's **credibility** in terms of his or her honesty, competence, and ability to inspire.

creative soul/Fotolia

Trust is closely entwined with the concept of credibility, and, in fact, the terms are often used interchangeably. **Trust** is defined as the belief in the integrity, character, and ability of a person. Followers who trust a leader are willing to be vulnerable to the leader's actions because they are confident that their rights and interests will not be abused.[45] Research has identified five dimensions that make up the concept of trust:[46]

- *Integrity:* Honesty and truthfulness
- *Competence:* Technical and interpersonal knowledge and skills
- *Consistency:* Reliability, predictability, and good judgment in handling situations
- *Loyalty:* Willingness to protect a person, physically and emotionally
- *Openness:* Willingness to share ideas and information freely

Of these five dimensions, integrity seems to be the most critical when someone assesses another's trustworthiness.[47] However, both integrity and competence were seen in our earlier discussion of leadership traits as consistently associated with leadership.

Workplace changes have reinforced why such leadership qualities are so important. For example, the trend toward empowerment and self-managed work teams has reduced or eliminated many of the traditional control mechanisms used to monitor employees. If a work team is free to schedule its own work, evaluate its own performance, and even make its own hiring decisions, trust becomes critical. Employees have to trust managers to treat them fairly, and managers have to trust employees to conscientiously fulfill their responsibilities.

Also, leaders have to increasingly lead others who may not be in their immediate work group—members of cross-functional teams, individuals who work for suppliers or customers, and perhaps even people who represent other organizations through strategic alliances. These situations do not allow leaders the luxury of falling back on their formal

credibility
The degree to which someone is perceived as honest, competent, and able to inspire.

trust
The belief in the integrity, character, and ability of a person.

positions for influence. Many of these relationships, in fact, are fluid and fleeting; the ability to develop trust quickly is crucial to the success of the relationship.

Why is it important that followers trust their leaders? Research has shown that trust in leadership is significantly related to positive job outcomes, including job performance, job satisfaction, and organizational commitment.[48] Given the importance of trust in effective leadership, how should leaders build trust?

Providing Ethical Leadership

PERSONAL INVENTORY ASSESSMENT

The topic of leadership and ethics has received surprisingly little attention. Only recently have ethics and leadership researchers begun to consider the ethical implications of leadership.[49] Visit your local bookstore and you will find quite a few books on ethics and leadership. Why now? One reason is a growing general interest in ethics throughout the field of management. Another, without a doubt, is the recent corporate and government financial scandals that have increased the public's and politicians' concerns about ethical standards.

Ethics is part of leadership in a number of ways. For example, transformational leaders have been described as fostering moral virtue when they try to change the attitudes and behaviours of followers.[50] We can also see an ethical component to charisma. Unethical leaders may use their charisma to enhance their power over followers and use that power for self-serving purposes. On the other hand, ethical leaders may use their charisma in more socially constructive ways to serve others.[51] We also see a lack of ethics when leaders abuse their power and give themselves large salaries and bonuses while, at the same time, they seek to cut costs by laying off employees. Of course, trust, which is important to ethical behaviour, explicitly deals with the leadership traits of honesty and integrity.

As we have seen recently, leadership is not value-free. Providing moral leadership involves addressing the *means* that a leader uses in trying to achieve goals, as well as the content of those goals. As a recent study concluded, ethical leadership is more than being ethical; it is reinforcing ethics through organizational mechanisms such as communication and the reward system.[52] Thus, before we judge any leader to be effective, we should consider both the moral content of his or her goals *and* the means used to achieve those goals.

Providing Virtual Leadership

How do you lead people who are physically separated from you and where interactions are essentially reduced to written online communications? Pat O'Day, manager of a five-person virtual team at KPMG International, understands the challenges of providing online leadership. To help his team be more effective, O'Day says, "We communicate through email and conference calls and meet in person four times a year."[53]

What little research has been done in online leadership has focused on managing virtual teams.[54] This research suggests there are three fundamental challenges in providing online leadership: communication, performance management, and trust.

COMMUNICATION In a virtual setting, leaders may need to learn new communication skills in order to be seen as effective. To effectively convey online leadership, managers must realize they have choices in the words, structure, tone, and style of their online communications and be alert to expressions of emotions. In face-to-face communications, harsh *words* can be softened by nonverbal action. A smile and comforting gestures, for example, can lessen the blow behind words such as *disappointed, unsatisfactory, inadequate,* or *below expectations*. In online interactions, that nonverbal aspect does not exist.

The *structure* of words in online communication has the power to motivate or demotivate the receiver. Is the message made up of full sentences or just phrases? The latter is likely to be seen as curt and more threatening. Similarly, a message in ALL CAPS is the equivalent of shouting.

Leaders also need to be sure the *tone* of their message correctly conveys the emotions they want to send. Is the message formal or informal? Does it convey the appropriate

TIPS (FOR) MANAGERS

Technology and the Manager's Job

How do you lead people who are physically separated from you and with whom your interactions are primarily written digital communictions?[55] That is the challenge of being a virtual leader. And unfortunately, leadership research has been directed mostly at face-to-face and verbal situations. But we cannot ignore the reality that today's managers and their employees are increasingly being linked by technology rather than by geographic proximity. So what guidance would be helpful to leaders who must inspire and motivate dispersed employees?

It is easy to soften harsh words in face-to-face communication with nonverbal action. A smile or a comforting gesture can go a long way in lessening the blow behind strong words like *disappointed, unsatisfactory, inadequate,* or *below expectations.* That nonverbal component does not exist in online interactions. The *structure* of words in a digital communication also has the power to motivate or demotivate the receiver. A manager who inadvertently sends a message in short phrases or in ALL CAPS may get a very different response than if the message had been sent in full sentences using appropriate punctuation.

To be an effective virtual leader, managers must recognize that they have choices in the words and structure of their digital communications. They also need to develop the skill of "reading between the lines" in the messages they receive. It is important to try and decipher the emotional content of a message as well as the written content. Also, virtual leaders need to think carefully about what actions they want their digital messages to initiate. Be clear about what is expected and follow up on messages.

For an increasing number of managers, good interpersonal skills may include the abilities to communicate support and leadership through digital communication and to read emotion in others' messages. In this "new world" of communication, writing skills are likely to become an extension of interpersonal skills.

What challenges does a "virtual" leader face? How can virtual leaders use technology to help them be more effective leaders?

---

level of importance or urgency? Is the leader's writing style consistent with his or her oral style? For example, if a leader's written communication is more formal than his or her oral style, it will likely create confusion for employees and hinder the effectiveness of the message.

Online leaders must also choose a *style.* Do they use emoticons, abbreviations, jargon, and the like? Do they adapt their style to their audience? Observation suggests that some managers have difficulty adjusting to computer-based communications. For instance, they use the same style with their bosses that they use with their staff. Or they selectively use online communication to "hide" when delivering bad news. Finally, online leaders need to develop the skills of "reading between the lines" in the messages they receive so they can decipher the emotional components.

PERFORMANCE MANAGEMENT Another challenge of online leadership is managing performance. How? By defining, facilitating, and encouraging it.[56] As leaders *define* performance, they must ensure that all members of a virtual team understand the team's goals, their responsibilities in achieving those goals, and how goal achievement is going to be assessed. There should be no surprises or uncertainties about performance expectations. Although these issues are important managerial responsibilities in all situations, they are particularly critical in virtual work environments because there are no face-to-face interactions to convey expectations or address performance problems.

Online leaders also have a responsibility to *facilitate* performance. Facilitating involves reducing or eliminating obstacles to successful performance and providing adequate resources to get the job done. This task can be particularly challenging, especially if the virtual team is global, since the physical distance separating the leader and the team means it is not easy to get team members the resources they may need.

Finally, online leaders are responsible for *encouraging* performance by providing sufficient rewards that virtual employees really value. As we will see in Chapter 9, motivating employees can be difficult, even in work settings where there is face-to-face interaction. In a virtual setting, the motivational challenge can be even greater because the leader is not there in person to encourage, support, and guide. What can online leaders do? They can ask virtual employees what rewards are most important to them—pay, benefits, technology upgrades, opportunities for professional development, and so forth. Then, they can make sure the rewards are provided in a timely manner after major work goals have been achieved. Finally, any rewards program must be perceived as fair. This expectation is not any different from that of leaders in nonvirtual settings—employees want and expect rewards to be distributed fairly.

TRUST The final challenge of providing online leadership is the trust issue. In a virtual setting, there are numerous opportunities to violate trust. One possible trust issue is whether the system is being used to monitor and evaluate employees. The technology is there to do so, but leaders must consider whether that is really the best way to influence employee behaviour. T. J. Rodgers, founder and CEO of Cypress Semiconductor, found out the hard way that it might not be.[57] He built an in-house system that tracked goals and deadlines. If a department missed its target, the software shut down its computers and cancelled the manager's next paycheque. After realizing the system encouraged dishonesty, Rodgers ditched it. The experience made him understand that it was more important to create a culture in which trust among all participants is expected and required. In fact, the five dimensions of trust we described earlier—integrity, competence, consistency, loyalty, and openness—would be vital to the development of such a culture.

Team Leadership

Since leadership is increasingly taking place within a team context and more organizations are using work teams, the role of the leader in guiding team members is gaining importance. The role of team leader *is* different from the traditional leadership role. Many leaders are not equipped to handle the change to employee teams. As one consultant noted, "Even the most capable managers have trouble making the transition because all the command-and-control type things they were encouraged to do before are no longer appropriate. There's no reason to have any skill or sense of this."[58] This same consultant estimated that "probably 15 percent of managers are natural team leaders; another 15 percent could never lead a team because it runs counter to their personality—that is, they're unable to sublimate their dominating style for the good of the team. Then there's that huge group in the middle: Team leadership doesn't come naturally to them, but they can learn it."[59]

The challenge for many managers is learning how to become an effective team leader. They have to learn skills such as having the patience to share information, being able to trust others and to give up authority, and understanding when to intervene. Effective team leaders have mastered the difficult balancing act of knowing when to leave their teams alone and when to get involved. New team leaders may try to retain too much control at a time when team members need more autonomy, or they may abandon their teams at times when team members need support and help.[60]

One study of organizations that had reorganized themselves around employee teams found certain common responsibilities of all leaders. These tasks included coaching, facilitating, handling disciplinary problems, reviewing team and individual performance, training, and communication.[61] However, a more meaningful way to describe the team leader's job is to focus on two priorities: (1) managing the team's external boundary and (2) facilitating the team process.[62] These priorities entail four specific leadership roles (see Exhibit 8-5).

Leadership can seem like juggling many things at once.

EXHIBIT 8-5 Specific Team Leadership Roles

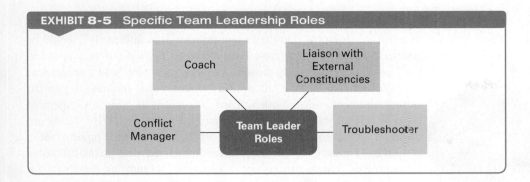

Team leaders are *liaisons with external constituencies*, which may include upper management, other organizational work teams, customers, or suppliers. The leader represents the team to other constituencies, secures needed resources, clarifies others' expectations of the team, gathers information from the outside, and shares that information with team members.

Team leaders are *troubleshooters*. When the team has problems and asks for assistance, team leaders sit in on meetings and try to help resolve the problems. Troubleshooting rarely involves technical or operational issues, because the team members typically know more about the tasks being done than does the leader. The leader is most likely to contribute by asking penetrating questions, helping the team talk through problems, and getting needed resources to tackle problems.

Team leaders are *conflict managers*. They help identify issues such as the source of the conflict, who is involved, the issues, the resolution options available, and the advantages and disadvantages of each. By getting team members to address questions such as these, the leader minimizes the disruptive aspects of intra-team conflicts.

Finally, team leaders are *coaches*. They clarify expectations and roles, teach, offer support, and do whatever else is necessary to help team members keep their work performance high.

Nathan Denette/Canadian Press Images

When Eva Aariak spoke to the Nunavut legislative assembly to explain why she should be elected the territory's premier, she emphasized that her leadership style included the ability to listen and encourage others to share their ideas. She considers herself a team player, which will work well with the territory's consensus style of government built from the principles of parliamentary democracy and Aboriginal values.

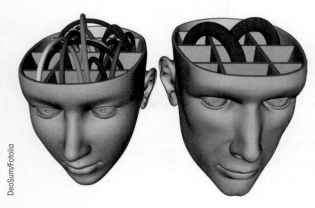

Men and women have many differences, including how their brains process communication.

DeoSum/Fotolia

Understanding Gender Differences and Leadership

There was a time when the question "Do males and females lead differently?" could be accurately characterized as a purely academic issue—interesting, but not very relevant. That time has certainly passed! Many women now hold management positions, and many more around the world will continue to join the management ranks. Women filled 20 percent of senior management roles globally in 2011 (down from 24 percent in 2009).[63] They are highly involved in smaller companies. Industry Canada reports that in 2012, 47 percent of all small to medium-sized enterprises had some degree of female ownership.[64] Moreover, a study by the Canadian Imperial Bank of Commerce estimates that since 1989 women-run businesses have increased 60 percent faster than those run by men.[65]

In other economically developed countries, the percentage of female managerial/administrative employees is as follows: Australia—37 percent; France—39 percent; Germany—38 percent; China—17 percent; Poland—36 percent; and Sweden—32 percent.[66] Misconceptions about the relationship between leadership and gender can adversely affect hiring, performance evaluation, promotion, and other human resource decisions for both men and women. For example, evidence indicates that a "good" manager is still perceived as predominantly masculine.[67] A warning before we proceed: This topic is controversial. If male and female styles differ, is one inferior? If there is a difference, is one gender more effective in leading than the other? These are important questions and we will address them shortly.

A number of studies focusing on gender and leadership style have been conducted.[68] Their general conclusion is that males and females *do* use different styles. Specifically, women tend to adopt a more democratic or participative style. Women are more likely to encourage participation, share power and information, and attempt to enhance followers' self-worth. They lead through inclusion and rely on their charisma, expertise, contacts, and interpersonal skills to influence others. Women tend to use transformational leadership, motivating others by transforming their self-interest into organizational goals. Men are more likely to use a directive, command-and-control style. They rely on formal position authority for their influence. Men use transactional leadership, handing out rewards for good work and punishment for bad.[69] However, the above findings have an interesting qualifier. The tendency of female leaders to be more democratic than males declines when women are in male-dominated jobs. In such jobs, apparently, group norms and male stereotypes influence women, and they are likely to act more autocratically.[70]

Another issue to consider is how male and female leaders are perceived in the workplace. A recent study sheds some light on this topic.[71] One major finding of this research was that men consider women to be less skilled at problem solving, which is one of the qualities often associated with effective leadership. Another finding was that both men and women believed women to be superior to men at "take care" behaviours and men superior to women at "take charge" behaviours. Such gender-based stereotyping creates challenges both for organizations and for leaders within those organizations. Organizations need effective leaders at all levels, but they need to ensure that stereotypical perceptions do not limit who those leaders might be.[72]

Although it is interesting to see how male and female leadership styles differ, a more important question is whether they differ in effectiveness. Some researchers have shown that males and females tend to be equally effective as leaders,[73] but an increasing number of studies have shown that women executives, when rated by their peers, employees, and bosses, score higher than their male counterparts on a wide variety of measures, including getting extra effort from subordinates and overall effectiveness in leading. Subordinates also reported more satisfaction with the leadership given by women.[74] Based on a summary of five studies, female managers performed better at motivating others, fostering communication, producing high-quality work, and listening to others.[75] Why these differences? One possible explanation is that in today's organizations, flexibility, teamwork and partnering, trust, and information sharing are rapidly replacing rigid structures, competitive individualism, control, and secrecy. In these types of workplaces, effective managers must use more social and interpersonal behaviours. They listen, motivate, and provide support to their people. They inspire and influence rather than control. Women seem to do those things better than men.[76] Elyse Allan, president and CEO GE Canada, believes that "Leadership is about conviction and a sense of responsibility that you don't give up halfway through"[77] and Ellen Moore, president and CEO Chubb Insurance Co. of Canada, is of the opinion that "You need to be able to set a clear course, something that is consistent so people understand where you're taking them."[78]

Although women seem to rate highly on those leadership skills needed to succeed in today's dynamic global environment, we do not want to fall into the same trap as the early leadership researchers who tried to find the "one best leadership style" for all situations. We know that there is no one *best* style for all situations. Instead, which leadership style is effective will depend on the situation. Even if men and women differ in their leadership styles, we should not assume that one is always preferable to the other.

Tips for Future Leaders gives some suggestions for being a better leader.

TIPS (FOR) FUTURE LEADERS

Tips for Future Leaders

* People work **with** you, not **for** you.

* **Spend time with people** at all levels and positions in the organization.

* Create a culture of **caring**—people do not care how much you know until they know how much you care.

* **Be persistent**. Re-evaluate and re-invent yourself.

* Support your organization's people. Look for the **good**, not the bad.

* Energize your team with a vision. Create a sense of **urgency**.

Summary of Learning Outcomes

8.1 **How do leaders and managers differ?** Managers are appointed to their positions. They have formal authority; this authority gives them their ability to influence employees. In contrast, leaders can be appointed or can emerge from within a work group. They provide vision and strategy and are able to influence others for reasons beyond formal authority. Though ideally all managers should be leaders, not all leaders can be managers, because they do not all have the ability to plan, organize, and control.

Sheryl Sandberg demonstrated the ability to both lead and manage at Facebook.

8.2 **What do early leadership theories tell us about leadership?** Researchers agree that traits alone are not sufficient for explaining effective leadership. Possessing the appropriate traits makes it only more likely that an individual would be an effective leader. In general, behavioural theories have identified useful behaviours that managers should have, but the research could not identify when these behaviours were most useful.

Sheryl Sandberg notes that one of her most useful leadership traits is being open and honest with her employees.

8.3 **How do contingency theories of leadership improve our understanding of leadership?** Contingency theories acknowledge that different situations require different leadership styles. The theories suggest that leaders may need to adjust their style to the needs of different organizations and employees, and perhaps different countries.

8.4 **What do charismatic and transformational leaders do?** While most leaders are transactional, guiding followers to achieve goals by clarifying role and task requirements, charismatic and transformational leaders inspire and influence their followers. Charismatic leaders are enthusiastic and self-confident leaders whose personality and actions motivate followers. They are known for having and articulating a vision, and for being willing to take risks to achieve that vision. Transformational leaders turn followers into believers on a mission and encourage followers to go beyond their own self-interests for the

greater good. Transformational leadership is more than charisma, since the transformational leader attempts to empower followers to question established views, even those views held by the leader.

8.5 **What are some current issues in leadership?** The major leadership issues today include managing power, developing trust, providing moral leadership, providing online leadership, and understanding gender differences and leadership.

Sheryl Sandberg's experience with tech companies illustrates the differences men and women can face in the workplace. She had to find a way to make her male counterparts and employees comfortable with her expertise, something a man in her position would probably not have had to do.

SNAPSHOT SUMMARY

8.1 **Managers Versus Leaders**

8.2 **What Do Early Leadership Theories Tell Us About Leadership?**

8.3 **Contingency Theories of Leadership**
Hersey and Blanchard's Situational Leadership
Path-Goal Theory

8.4 **Leading Change**
Charismatic–Visionary Leadership
Transformational Leadership

8.5 **Current Issues in Leadership**
Managing Power
Developing Trust
Providing Ethical Leadership
Providing Virtual Leadership
Technology and the Manager's Job
Team Leadership
Understanding Gender Differences and Leadership

MyManagementLab   Study, practise, and explore real management situations with these helpful resources:

- **Interactive Lesson Presentations:** Work through interactive presentations and assessments to test your knowledge of management concepts.
- **PIA (Personal Inventory Assessments):** Enhance your ability to connect with key concepts through these engaging self-reflection assessments.
- **Study Plan:** Check your understanding of chapter concepts with self-study quizzes.
- **Simulations:** Practise decision making in simulated management environments.

Discussion Questions

1. Discuss the strengths and weaknesses of the trait theory of leadership.
2. What similarities, if any, can you find between Hersey and Blanchard's Situational Leadership and path-goal theory?
3. What sources of power are available to leaders? Which ones are most effective?
4. "All managers should be leaders, but not all leaders should be managers." Do you agree or disagree with this statement? Support your position.
5. "Charismatic leadership is always appropriate in organizations." Do you agree or disagree? Support your position.
6. What kinds of campus activities could a full-time student do that might lead to the perception that he or she is a charismatic leader? In pursuing those activities, what might the student do to enhance this perception of being charismatic?

Developing Management Skills

Dilemma

You have worked hard at your organization and were rewarded with a promotion. What you may not have prepared for is the difficult situation of workplace friends now reporting to you. Fortunately experts indicate that you can both maintain those friendships and use them to be a better manager.[79]

Becoming a Manager

- Meet with each of your friends individually to discuss any concerns they may have.
- Do not create new boundaries—remind the team that you have not changed and that you are still there for support and advice.
- Do not assume that people will be resentful. Many will be very happy for you, and you can deal with the others on a one-on-one basis.
- Avoid venting about the new position with your friends.
- Offer your friends support and time and space to adapt to the changes.

Developing Your Diagnostic and Analytical Skills: Radical Leadership

Ricardo Semler, CEO of Semco Group of São Paulo, Brazil, is considered by many to be a radical. He has never been the type of leader that most people would expect to be in charge of a

multimillion-dollar business.[80] Why? Semler breaks all the traditional "rules" of leading and managing. He is the ultimate hands-off leader who does not even have an office at the company's headquarters. As the "leading proponent and most tireless evangelist" of participative management, Semler says his philosophy is simple: Treat people like adults and they will respond like adults.

Underlying the participative management approach is the belief that "organizations thrive best by entrusting employees to apply their creativity and ingenuity in service of the whole enterprise and to make important decisions close to the flow of work, conceivably including the selection and election of their bosses." According to Semler, his approach works well. But how does it work in reality?

At Semco, most of the trappings of organizations and management are absent. There are no organization charts, no long-term plans, no statements of corporate values, no dress codes, and no written rules or policy manuals. The company's 3000 employees decide their work hours and their pay levels. Subordinates decide who their bosses will be and also review their bosses' performance. The employees elect the corporate leadership and decide most of the company's new strategic initiatives. Each person has one vote—including Ricardo Semler.

At one of the company's plants outside São Paulo, there are no supervisors telling employees what to do. On any given day, an employee may decide to "run a grinder or drive a forklift, depending on what needs to be done." João Vendramin Neto, who is in charge of Semco's manufacturing, says that "the workers know the organization's objectives and they use common sense to decide for themselves what they should do to hit those goals."

Why did Semler decide that his form of radical leadership was necessary, and does it work? Semler did not pursue such radical self-governance out of some altruistic ulterior motive. Instead, he felt it was the only way to build an organization that was flexible and resilient enough to flourish in chaotic and turbulent times. He maintains that this approach has enabled Semco to survive the roller-coaster nature of Brazilian politics and the Brazilian economy. Although the country's political leadership and economy have gone from one extreme to another and countless Brazilian banks and companies have failed, Semco has survived. Not just survived—prospered. Semler says, "If you look at Semco's numbers, we've grown 27.5 percent a year for 14 years." Semler attributes this fact to flexibility—of his company and, most importantly, of his employees.

Questions

1. Describe Ricardo Semler's leadership style. What do you think the advantages and drawbacks of his style might be?

2. What challenges might a radically "hands-off" leader face? How could those challenges be addressed?

3. How could future leaders be identified in this organization? Would leadership training be important to this organization? Discuss.

4. What could other businesses learn from Semler's approach to leadership?

Your Essential Management Reading List

Learning from key management experts can help us understand today's management theory and practice. What follows is a list of some of the top books about leadership:

- *The Power of Habit*—Charles Duhigg
- *The End of Leadership*—Barbara Kellerman
- *The Lords of Strategy*—Walter Kiechel
- *Lean In: Women, Work, and the Will to Lead*—Sheryl Sandberg

Diversity Matters

Diversity is one of Royal Bank of Canada's (RBC) five core values. The company created a "Diversity Blueprint" to ensure visible senior leadership commitment, employee involvement, collaboration with partners, communication, and accountability. RBC would like to increase the representation of women, minorities, and newcomers to Canada in leadership positions, as well as maintain an inclusive and supportive work environment. It has set up mentoring programs, cultural competency awareness and training, business communications training, and networking events to help achieve its goals.[81] RBC recognizes that diversity provides incredible business and economic potential. Its belief is that harnessing diverse perspectives will drive innovation and growth for both RBC and the Canadian economy.

Hey, You're the Boss Now!

When you step into a leadership role for the first time, it can be very intimidating. Here are 10 tips to help you as a first-time manager:

- **Realize that you still have much to learn**—don't pretend you know all the answers.
- **Be an active listener and communicator**—encourage feedback.
- **Develop your time management skills**—this will help you with the extra workload.
- **Do not take all the credit**—share the spotlight with your team and recognize them regularly.
- **Create a learning environment**—learn from your new team and provide guidance.
- **Manage by walking around**—don't stay locked away in your office.
- **Embrace diversity**—respect your long-term employees and use them as mentors.
- **Delegation is your friend**—learn how to motivate, and don't expect employees to be perfect.
- **Look at the bigger picture**—take time to understand the business.
- **Network, network, network**—increase your team's visibility as well as your own.

Team Exercises

3BL: The Triple Bottom Line

The Center for Creative Leadership conducted a study of executives entitled "Leadership and the Triple Bottom Line."[82] The study found that the top five leadership competencies necessary for adopting 3BL approaches are as follows:

- long-term view (20 percent)
- communication (15 percent)
- influence (11 percent)
- scanning the external environment (9 percent)
- collaboration (8 percent)

The respondents further identified the importance of creating an organizational culture where 3BL approaches are accepted and aligned with strategy, values, rewards, and recognition. Beyond the cultural support, leaders must model

3BL behaviours in their professional and personal lives to successfully achieve organizational support. What other competencies do you think are important for leaders to be effective at maximizing the triple bottom line?

THINKING STRATEGICALLY ABOUT 3BL

A 3BL strategy is not enough. Organizations must develop the leadership capacity to manage 3BL opportunities and challenges. The leaders surveyed suggested that success with 3BL would come through an integrated approach, with key stakeholder involvement and a balanced perspective of long-term strategy and short-term results. Pick a small or medium-sized business in your community. Who are the key stakeholders you would recommend involving in order to support 3BL? Which of those stakeholders would be most opposed to 3BL?

The Pre–Post Leadership Assessment

OBJECTIVE

To compare characteristics intuitively related to leadership with leadership characteristics found in leadership theory.

PROCEDURE

Identify three people (e.g., friends, relatives, previous boss, public figures) whom you consider outstanding leaders. List why you feel each individual is a good leader. Compare your lists of the three people. Which traits, if any, are common to all three? Your instructor will lead the class in a discussion of leadership characteristics based on your lists. Students will call out what they identified, and your instructor will display the list on the screen or whiteboard. When all students have shared their lists, class discussion will focus on the following questions:

- What characteristics consistently appeared on students' lists?
- Were these characteristics more trait-oriented or behaviour-oriented?
- In what situations were these characteristics useful?
- What, if anything, does this exercise suggest about leadership attributes?

Be the Consultant: Hiring Ethical Leaders

Your consulting firm has been chosen to develop questions that might help organizations select more ethical leaders. You are familiar with behavioural interview questions that generally start with "Tell me about a time when you . . ." or "Give me an example of a situation in which you . . ."

You feel that four key areas where ethical leadership may come into difficulty are compromise, conflicting values, time pressure, and formal rules. In business situations, compromise is often necessary for things to happen. Sometimes that compromise might be a situation where your values were not in line with organizational values. Often leaders have to come to quick decisions or use a more informal style where they bend the rules to get something done.

Develop behavioural questions for the four areas mentioned above:

Compromise	
Conflicting values	
Time pressure	
Bending the rules	

What are other areas requiring ethical leadership?

Business Cases

Enbridge

Patrick Daniel took the helm as CEO of Calgary-based pipeline giant Enbridge Inc. in 2001 and faced crisis after crisis, such as a massive oil pipeline spill in Michigan and a heated controversy over the proposed Northern Gateway pipeline. He was awarded Canada's Outstanding CEO of the Year for 2011.[83] He retired and passed the baton to Al Monaco in 2012, confident in the number of bright young stars in the company and the strength of their long-range growth forecasts.[84]

Leadership at Enbridge is like that of many companies. Enbridge's strategy focuses on a combination of high growth, low risk, and steady income—a simple-sounding proposition that is very hard to maintain. As a result, Daniel indicates that Enbridge has been both aggressive in pursuing new business and cautious by being very disciplined in its analysis.

Canada's energy sector faces tumultuous change, such as lower energy prices, increased competition through deregulation, and public interest group criticism over pipeline projects. The NIMBY principle (Not In My Back Yard) is at odds with pipeline development. Daniel recounts earlier days where landowners felt it was their obligation to provide the right of way to serve Canadian development. That sentiment has changed dramatically. Enbridge's Energy4Everyone foundation features employees volunteering to install more efficient appliances and energy sources around the world, where the locals' attitude was "In my backyard, please." Daniel believes a key leadership competency in his position is patience—being able to calmly discuss all sides of the issue with various stakeholders. Daniel showed his strong leadership humility when he responded to a question about whether he should write a book on crisis management: "I don't think there is any rocket science. You take responsibility and then you go to work and fix things. It would be hard to stretch that into a book."

How should companies like Enbridge work with the Canadian public and various stakeholder groups to build support for the energy industry and reduce the NIMBY effect?

Leadership Legacy

A lot has been written about the late Steve Jobs.[85] How he took Apple, a niche business, and turned it into the most valuable company in the world as measured by market capitalization. How he was extremely charismatic and extremely compelling in getting people to join with him and believe in his vision. But how he was despotic, tyrannical, abrasive, uncompromising, and a perfectionist. So what *is* his leadership legacy?

Everything that Jobs did and how he did them was motivated by his desire to have Apple make innovative products—products that were "insanely great"—"insanely" being one of his favourite descriptors. That singular focus shaped his leadership style, which has been described as autocratic and yet persuasive. As one reporter said, Jobs "violated every rule of management. He was not a consensus builder but a dictator who listened mainly to his own intuition. He was a maniacal micromanager . . . He could be absolutely brutal in meetings." His verbal assaults on staff could be terrifying. The story is told that when Apple launched its first version of the iPhone that worked on 3G networks, it included MobileMe, an email system that was supposed to provide seamless synchronization features similar to that used by the fanatical corporate users of BlackBerrys. The problem? It didn't work well at all, and product reviews were quite critical. Since "Steve Jobs doesn't tolerate duds," it was not long after the launch that he gathered the MobileMe team in an auditorium on Apple's campus. According to a participant in that meeting, Jobs walked in—in his trademark black mock turtleneck and jeans—and "asked a simple question: 'Can you tell me what MobileMe is supposed to do?' Having received a satisfactory answer, he responded, 'So why the xxxx doesn't it do that?'" Then, for the next 30 minutes, Jobs blasted criticisms at the team. "You've tarnished Apple's reputation. You should hate each other for having let each other down." Ouch. And this was not the only example of his taking employees to task. He was tough on the people around him. When asked about his tendency to be rough on people, Jobs responded, "Look at the results. These are all smart people I work with, and any of them could get a top job at another place if they were truly feeling brutalized. But they don't."

On the other hand, Steve Jobs could be thoughtful, passionate, and "insanely" charismatic. He could "push people to do the impossible." And there is no argument with the fact that the results from the company he cofounded have been market-changing. From Macs to iPods to iPhones and iPads, Apple's products have revolutionized industries and created a fan base of consumers who are very loyal to the Apple brand and employees who are very loyal to the company.

Discussion Questions

1. Think about what you thought you knew about Steve Jobs prior to reading this business case. How would you have described his leadership style?
2. After reading this case, how would you describe his leadership style?
3. What were you most surprised about after reading this case?
4. Would Steve Jobs's leadership approach work for others? Discuss.

ROWE

Best Buy was one of the first companies to adopt a "results-only work environment" (ROWE), which is a program that goes beyond work–life balance and allows employees to decide when and where they want to work. By giving workers autonomy, they could be held accountable for achieving targets. Success would mean promotions; failure might mean termination. Best Buy scrapped the program in 2013, and CEO Hubert Joly called it "flawed from a leadership standpoint."[86]

Joly felt that the program had given employees too much independence and failed because it was based on the idea that delegation is always the right leadership style, instead of finding the right style of leadership for different employees. Best Buy employees complained of a divisive two-tiered system, with store-level employees sticking to strict schedules, unlike the corporate employees, who had complete freedom over their schedules.[87] Yahoo CEO Marissa Mayer came under fire when she cancelled Yahoo's work-from-home program so that employees could be more collaborative and innovative by working together.

Is ROWE dead? York University professor Souha Ezzedeen indicates that policies like ROWE are not an entitlement and may not be appropriate for a business, depending on its culture and lack of supportive management system.[88] A University of Toronto study on flextime found that it boosted profits for firms whose strategies were based on employee investment, but harmed firms that were focused on cutting costs. The Gap credited it with raising productivity by 22 percent among program participants. To have ROWE work successfully in your organization, it requires setting the right conditions:[89]

- Management support: Managers are there as "result coaches" to shape expectations, set consequences for unmet goals, and hold employees accountable.
- Maintaining camaraderie: The loss of the social aspect can be really challenging for ROWE, so managers need to make people still feel like part of a team.
- Employee education: All employees must buy in to the concept that it is none of their business where and when a colleague works, so that people do not feel like slackers when not at their desks.
- Workflow tools: Invest in good project management and scheduling software for planning communication and meetings.
- Patience: It takes time for managers to adapt, employees to buy in, and work processes to evolve.

Portraits in Leadership: Canada's Future Leaders Under 25

Raphaëlle Ferland was named one of Canada's future leaders under 25 by *Maclean's* in 2013. She graduated from the University of Ottawa with a civil law degree. Prior to her legal education, Raphaëlle graduated with honours from the Social Services Worker program at La Cité collégiale in Ottawa. She works two jobs: one with Gerami Law PC, and another with Public Works and Government Services Canada as a junior research analyst for the Special Investigations Directorate.[1]

Raphaëlle, 24, is an award-winning advocate for poverty and is currently establishing a charity for homelessness. Born in Montreal, Ferland's parents split up when she was still a baby. She and her brother lived with their dad, who remarried and switched jobs often, moving the family to Winnipeg, the Phillipines, Mississauga, and finally Gatineau, Quebec. She attended more than a dozen schools before she lost count. Ferland's home life was one of constant fighting and being asked to leave the house, the first time at age 12. By 16 she was homeless and lived on the streets for more than two years.[2] All the while she battled drugs, illness, violence, and prejudice. People would often tell her to "get a job" when she was on the street, but who would hire her without a phone number or an address to put on a résumé?

Ferland managed to stay in high school even while living on the streets. Her life changed when she found an apartment through the Youth Services Bureau of Ottawa. She began organizing conferences and speaking out about poverty. Most presenters at conferences have a PhD—very few have lived on the street. Ferland's time with the Youth Services Bureau was the turning point where she could deal with her health issues and drug use. Ferland plans a career in international human rights or social justice. Her advice to others is to believe that the light is at the end of the tunnel, and strive to get to it.[3]

***

Kendal Netmaker was also named one of Canada's future leaders under 25 by *Maclean's*. He opened Neechie Gear—"*neechie*" is slang for "my friend" in Cree—after winning $16 000 in two local business competitions, which allowed him to start his store in Saskatoon's Centre Mall. His vision was an athletic clothing company that would help kids get involved in sports, with profits from clothing sales supporting the 10 Aboriginal basketball, volleyball, and hockey teams in Saskatchewan, Alberta, and British Columbia.[4] His belief is that sports can solve many of the problems associated with life on the reserve, including helping to avoid the hardships that can come with alcohol.

Netmaker, 25, grew up on the Sweetgrass First Nations reserve. Raised alongside his three sisters by a single mother, he was one of the few Aboriginal children at his elementary school. Netmaker used sports to keep him out trouble. A Grade 5 friend's family paid his soccer fees and gave him rides to and from games when they discovered he could not afford to play. It was sports that provided Kendal with a scholarship to university. Netmaker came up with his business plan with the help of established community business mentors.

Neechie Gear represented Canada at the 2011 G20 Young Entrepreneur Summit in France, which Netmaker attended with Prime Minister Stephen Harper. Netmaker has also been nominated for three Saskatchewan Chamber of Commerce awards: Young Entrepreneur, Community Involvement, and Aboriginal Partnership.[5]

CHAPTER

9 Motivating Employees

Anatoly Maslennikov/Fotolia

Think About It

What motivates Gen Y employees to work at Yellow House? What has Grail Noble done to increase employee motivation?

How do you expand an independent consulting business without the money to hire staff?[1]

Grail Noble of Toronto-based Yellow House Events brought a Gen Y intern into her home office in 2006. That 23-year-old college graduate, who became her first employee later that year, convinced Noble to adopt a new corporate culture to harness the energy and quality work of Generation Y (those born between the late 1970s and the turn of the century). Six years later, Yellow House's revenue growth of 2395 percent had it ranking number 16 on *Profit* magazine's Top 200 fastest growing companies.[2]

Gen Ys, sometimes called millennials, are often stereotyped as self-absorbed, impatient, flighty, and so gratuitously confident they think they can run a company after a few days on the job. This tech-immersed age group has no doubt caused sleepless nights among many CEOs, because Gen Ys represent the future of the workforce. With an aging population and looming labour shortages, companies can ill afford to ignore these young people and their habits and desires.

But Gen Y is not as scary as it seems. As Noble's experiences demonstrate, tapping into their needs and motivations can unleash tremendous productivity. Since she started targeting young talent, Yellow House's revenue grew from less than $200 000 in 2005 to more than $10 million in 2013. Yellow House has landed new clients—including Virgin Mobile, Revlon, and Research In Motion—and differentiated its brand. When BlackBerry and its 65 percent of Yellow House's business did not renew in 2012, Noble was aggressive in prospecting and landed Google as a client. "It took careful planning, but by looking far into the future, we avoided the pitfalls," says Noble.[3] Part of Noble's success comes from her learning how best to manage millennials.

Having created an environment in which Gen Y workers could thrive, Noble hunted for opportunities to harness their youthful energy in ways that would put Yellow House ahead. She sought out as clients youth-oriented companies whose corporate cultures fit with hers. Many of these firms' marketing departments skew younger. and Noble recognizes the value of the social relationships her staff can forge with them. "I might have a great relationship with the CEO of a client, but ultimately most CEOs let the people who hold the budget decide which vendors they're going to hire," she explains. Moreover, event planning is a high-stakes game in which much can go wrong—and often does. Noble needs her team motivated and engaged to create truly memorable affairs. The best way to do that is to target brands they believe in. "Those are the clients we look for, because we believe in their product," says Noble. "We're in the experience business, and when you get face to face, authenticity is so important."[4]

Motivating and rewarding employees is one of the most important, and one of the most challenging, activities that managers perform. Successful managers, such as Grail Noble, understand that what motivates them personally may have little or no effect on others. Just because *you* are motivated by being part of a cohesive work team or by challenging work, do not assume everyone feels the same. Effective managers who want their employees to put forth maximum effort recognize that they need to know how and why employees are motivated and to tailor their motivational practices to satisfy the needs and wants of those employees.

Noble learned that Gen Y staffers have a blurry line between work and personal life. If they are engaged in their jobs, they are perfectly willing to log long hours in the office or take client calls at 11:00 p.m.—provided they can update their Facebook status and make personal calls at any hour of the workday. (Noble is usually the last person in the office each morning and sometimes has to kick staffers out at night.) "They don't see their work selves as different from their social selves," she explains. "What can be difficult is that they care more about where they work, what they're working on, and who they're working with than did past generations."[5]

Creating a fitting work environment has required Noble to make some adjustments. While she prefers working in silence, her young hires like to crank Top 40 tunes and create a veritable party atmosphere as they work. Noble found that it took time to allow herself to forget her workers' ages and relative lack of experience, and simply trust their ability to get a job done. Naturally, the Yellow House home office did not suffice for long. Gen Y staffers typically enjoy working in funky, open-concept spaces, so the company soon moved into an airy office in a nineteenth-century building in Toronto's Distillery Historic District.

....

In this chapter, we first look at some early motivation theories and then at contemporary theories. We finish by looking at several current motivation issues and present practical suggestions that managers can use to motivate employees.

....

9.1 **Tell** What is motivation?

PERSONAL INVENTORY ASSESSMENT

As we analyze the concept of motivation, keep in mind that the level of motivation varies both between individuals and within individuals at different times.

Sergey Nivens/Fotolia

I LOVE MY JOB

keepsmiling4u/Fotolia

A Canadian Policy Research Network[8] survey found that only 40 percent of Canadians are very satisfied with their jobs.[9]

WHAT IS MOTIVATION?

All managers need to be able to motivate their employees, and that requires an understanding of what motivation is. Many people incorrectly view motivation as a personal trait—a trait that some people have and others do not. Our knowledge of motivation tells us that we cannot label people that way. What we *do* know is that motivation is the result of the interaction between a person and a situation. Certainly, individuals differ in motivational drive but, overall, motivation varies from situation to situation. For example, your level of motivation probably differs among the various courses you take each term.

Motivation refers to an individual's willingness to exert high levels of effort to reach organizational goals, conditioned by the degree to which that effort satisfies some individual need. Although, in general, motivation refers to effort exerted toward any goal, here it refers to organizational goals because our focus is on work-related behaviour.

The three key elements in the definition of motivation are effort, organizational goals, and need. The *effort* element is a measure of intensity or drive.[6] A motivated person tries hard. But high levels of effort are unlikely to lead to favourable job performance unless the effort is channelled in a direction that benefits the organization.[7] Therefore we must consider the quality of the effort as well as its intensity. Effort that is directed toward, and is consistent with, *organizational goals* is the kind of effort that we should be seeking. Finally, we will treat motivation as a *need-satisfying* process.

A **need** is an internal state that makes certain outcomes appear attractive. An unsatisfied need creates tension, which an individual reduces by exerting effort. Because we are interested in work behaviour, this tension-reduction effort must be directed toward organizational goals. Therefore, inherent in our definition of motivation is the requirement that the individual's needs be compatible with the organization's goals. When the two do not match, individuals may expend high levels of effort that run counter to the interests of the organization. Incidentally, this situation is not all that unusual. Some employees regularly spend a lot of time talking with friends at work to satisfy their social need. They exert a great deal of effort, but little, if any, is being directed toward work.

Finding ways to motivate employees to achieve high levels of performance is an important organizational problem, and managers keep looking for a solution. The Towers Perrin 2014 Global Workforce Study found only 4 of 10 employees to be highly engaged, while almost 3 out of 10 were highly disengaged.[10] In light of these results, it is no wonder that both academic researchers and practising managers want to understand and explain employee motivation and engagement.

Grail Noble of Yellow House was interested in recognizing the unique characteristics of Gen Y employees.[11] She attended conferences and conducted research on the habits of today's younger workers. She learned that they wanted to be empowered on the job and also to work within an entrepreneurial culture. Noble adopted an open-book financial policy and treated her staff as owners of Yellow House. She further empowered her staff by dropping a lucrative customer that was making her staff miserable with their demands.

motivation
An individual's willingness to exert high levels of effort to reach organizational goals, conditioned by the degree to which that effort satisfies some individual need.

need
An internal state that makes certain outcomes appear attractive.

Early Theories of Motivation (1950s and 1960s)

9.2 **Define** How can needs help one be motivated?

Know these early theories because they (1) represent the foundation from which contemporary theories grew and (2) are still used by practising managers to explain employee motivation.

1 Maslow's Hierarchy of Needs Theory

Abraham Maslow—a psychologist—proposed that within every person is a hierarchy of five needs: self-actualization, esteem, social, safety, and physiological (see Exhibit 9-1).

EXHIBIT 9-1 Maslow's Hierarchy of Needs

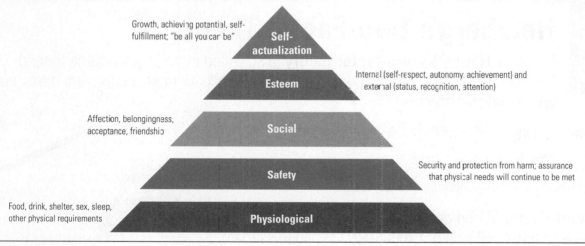

Growth, achieving potential, self-fulfillment; "be all you can be" — **Self-actualization**

Internal (self-respect, autonomy, achievement) and external (status, recognition, attention) — **Esteem**

Affection, belongingness, acceptance, friendship — **Social**

Security and protection from harm; assurance that physical needs will continue to be met — **Safety**

Food, drink, shelter, sex, sleep, other physical requirements — **Physiological**

Source: Maslow, Abraham H.; Frager, Robert D.; Fadiman, James, Motivation and Personality, 3rd Ed., ©1987. Reprinted and Electronically reproduced by permission of Pearson Education, Inc., New York, NY.

Each level must be substantially satisfied before the next need becomes dominant. An individual moves up the hierarchy from one level to the next. Lower-order needs are satisfied predominantly externally; higher-order needs are satisfied internally.

HOW is Maslow's hierarchy used to motivate employees?

Managers will do things to satisfy employees' needs. Remember: Once a need is substantially satisfied, it no longer motivates. This theory is widely popular among practising managers because it is easy to understand and intuitive.[12] However, there is no empirical support provided for the theory; other studies could not validate it.[13]

hierarchy of needs theory
Maslow's theory proposing a hierarchy of five human needs: physiological, safety, social, esteem, and self-actualization; as each need becomes satisfied, the next need becomes dominant.

2 McGregor's Theory X and Theory Y

Based on two assumptions about human nature:[14]

Marek/Fotolia

- **Theory X:** A negative view of people that assumes workers have little ambition, dislike work, want to avoid responsibility, and need to be closely controlled to work effectively.

- **Theory Y:** A positive view that assumes employees enjoy work, seek out and accept responsibility, and exercise self-direction.

To maximize employee motivation, use Theory Y practices—allow employees to participate in decisions, create responsible and challenging jobs, and encourage good group relations. However, there is no evidence to confirm either set of assumptions or that being a Theory Y manager is the only way to motivate employees.

3 Herzberg's Two-Factor Theory

Frederick Herzberg's **two-factor theory** (also called motivation-hygiene theory)—intrinsic factors are related to job satisfaction, while extrinsic factors are associated with job dissatisfaction.[15]

- popular theory from the 1960s to the early 1980s

- criticized for being too simplistic

- has influenced today's approach to job design

Research focus: When people felt exceptionally good (satisfied—see left-hand side of Exhibit 9-2) OR bad (dissatisfied—see right-hand side of exhibit) about their jobs. Replies showed these were *two different factors:*

andersphoto/Fotolia

- When people felt good about their work, they tended to cite intrinsic factors arising from the job content (the job itself), such as achievement, recognition, and responsibility.

- When they were dissatisfied, they tended to cite extrinsic factors arising from the job context, such as company policy and administration, supervision, interpersonal relationships, and working conditions.

Theory X
The assumption that employees have little ambition, dislike work, want to avoid responsibility, and must be closely controlled to perform effectively.

Theory Y
The assumption that employees can exercise self-direction, accept and seek out responsibility, and consider work a natural activity.

two-factor theory
Herzberg's theory that intrinsic factors are related to job satisfaction and motivation, whereas extrinsic factors are related to job dissatisfaction.

EXHIBIT 9-2 Herzberg's Two-Factor Theory

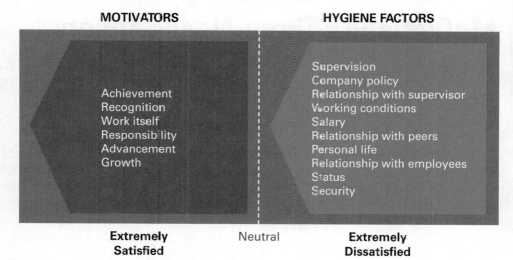

MOTIVATORS	HYGIENE FACTORS
Achievement Recognition Work itself Responsibility Advancement Growth	Supervision Company policy Relationship with supervisor Working conditions Salary Relationship with peers Personal life Relationship with employees Status Security

Extremely Satisfied   Neutral   **Extremely Dissatisfied**

Replies also provided a new view of satisfaction versus dissatisfaction (see Exhibit 9-3).

EXHIBIT 9-3 Contrasting Views of Satisfaction and Dissatisfaction

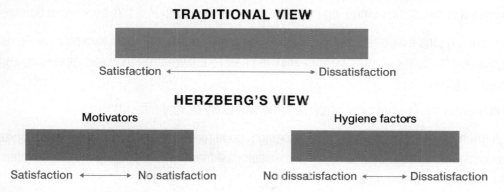

TRADITIONAL VIEW

Satisfaction ←——————————→ Dissatisfaction

HERZBERG'S VIEW

Motivators   Hygiene factors

Satisfaction ←——→ No satisfaction   No dissatisfaction ←——→ Dissatisfaction

Herzberg concluded that the traditional view—the opposite of satisfaction is dissatisfaction—was wrong. He believed that the factors that led to job satisfaction were separate and distinct from those that led to job satisfaction. Removing dissatisfying characteristics from a job did not necessarily make that job more satisfying (or motivating); it simply made people "less" dissatisfied. He proposed a dual continuum: The opposite of "satisfaction" is "no satisfaction," and the opposite of "dissatisfaction" is "no dissatisfaction."

Motivating Employees

1. When **hygiene factors** are adequate, people will not be dissatisfied, but they will not be motivated, either.

2. To motivate people, use the **motivators**.

olly/Fotolia

---

hygiene factors
Factors that eliminate job dissatisfaction, but do not motivate.

motivators
Factors that increase job satisfaction and motivation.

4 McClelland's Three-Needs Theory

David McClelland and his associates proposed the **three-needs theory**, which says three acquired (not innate) needs are the major motives in work, including:[16]

1 **need for achievement (nAch)**, which is the drive to succeed and excel in relation to a set of standards

2 **need for power (nPow)**, which is the need to make others behave in a way that they would not have behaved otherwise

3 **need for affiliation (nAff)**, which is the desire for friendly and close interpersonal relationships

nAch has been researched the most.

- People with a high nAch are striving for personal achievement rather than for the trappings and rewards for success.

- They have a desire to do something better or more efficiently than it has been done before.[17]

- They prefer (1) jobs that offer personal responsibility for finding solutions to problems, (2) receiving rapid and unambiguous feedback on their performance in order to tell whether they are improving, and (3) moderately challenging goals.

- High achievers avoid what they perceive to be very easy or very difficult tasks.

- A high nAch does not necessarily lead to being a good manager, especially in large organizations. Why? Because high achievers focus on their own accomplishments while good managers emphasize helping others accomplish their goals.[18]

- Employees can be trained to stimulate their nAch by being in situations where they have personal responsibility, feedback, and moderate risks.[19]

---

three-needs theory
McClelland's theory that the needs for achievement, power, and affiliation are major motives in work.

need for achievement (nAch)
The drive to excel, to achieve in relation to a set of standards, and to strive to succeed.

need for power (nPow)
The need to make others behave in a way that they would not have behaved otherwise.

need for affiliation (nAff)
The desire for friendly and close interpersonal relationships.

CONTEMPORARY THEORIES OF MOTIVATION

One of the challenges of motivating employees is linking productivity to rewards. Companies like Yellow House have to link productivity to rewards to ensure employees feel motivated.

The theories we discuss in this section represent contemporary explanations of employee motivation. Although they may not be as well known as some of the older theories we just discussed, they do have reasonable degrees of valid research support.[20] What are some contemporary theories of motivation? We look at goal-setting theory, four-drive theory, equity theory, and expectancy theory.

9.3 | **Describe** What are the contemporary theories of motivation?

Goal-Setting Theory

Before a big assignment or major class project presentation, has a teacher ever encouraged you to "just do your best"? What does that vague statement, "Do your best" mean? Would your performance on a class project have been higher had that teacher said you needed to score a 93 percent to keep your A in the class? Research on goal-setting theory addresses these issues, and the findings, as you'll see, are impressive in terms of the effect that goal specificity, challenge, and feedback have on performance.[21]

Substantial research support has been established for **goal-setting theory**, which says that specific goals increase performance and that difficult goals, when accepted, result in higher performance than do easy goals. *What does goal-setting theory tell us?*

1. Working toward a goal is a major source of job motivation. Studies on goal setting have demonstrated that specific and challenging goals are superior motivating forces.[22] Such goals produce a higher output than does the generalized goal of "do your best." The specificity of the goal itself acts as an internal stimulus.

2. Will employees try harder if they have the opportunity to participate in the setting of goals? Not always. In some cases, participatively set goals elicit superior performance; in other cases, individuals perform best when their manager assigns goals. However, participation is probably preferable to assigning goals when employees might resist accepting difficult challenges.[23]

3. We know that people will do better if they get feedback on how well they're progressing toward their goals because feedback helps identify discrepancies between what they have done and what they want to do. But all feedback is not equally effective. Self-generated feedback—where an employee monitors his or her own progress—has been shown to be a more powerful motivator than feedback coming from someone else.[24]

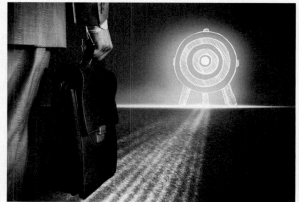

Three other contingencies besides feedback influence the goal-performance relationship: goal commitment, adequate self-efficacy, and national culture.

First, goal-setting theory assumes that an individual is committed to the goal. Commitment is most likely when goals are made public, when the individual has an internal locus of control, and when the goals are self-set rather than assigned.[25] Next, self-efficacy refers to an individual's belief that he or she is capable of performing a task.[26] The higher your self-efficacy, the more confidence you have in your ability to succeed in a task. So, in difficult situations, we find that people with low self-efficacy are likely to reduce their effort or give up altogether.

When a sales rep commits to making eight sales calls daily, this intention gives them a specific goal to try to attain.

goal-setting theory
The proposition that specific goals increase performance and that difficult goals, when accepted, result in higher performance than do easy goals.

whereas those with high self-efficacy will try harder to master the challenge.[27] In addition, individuals with high self-efficacy seem to respond to negative feedback with increased effort and motivation, whereas those with low self-efficacy are likely to reduce their effort when given negative feedback.[28] Finally, the value of goal-setting theory depends on the national culture. It is well adapted to Canada because its main ideas align reasonably well with the culture. It assumes that subordinates will be reasonably independent (not a high score on power distance), that people will seek challenging goals (low in uncertainty avoidance), and that performance is considered important by both managers and subordinates (high in assertiveness). Do not expect goal setting to lead to higher employee performance in countries where the cultural characteristics differ.

Exhibit 9-4 summarizes the relationships among goals, motivation, and performance. Our overall conclusion: *The intention to work toward hard and specific goals is a powerful motivating force.* Under the proper conditions, it can lead to higher performance. However, there is no evidence that such goals are associated with increased job satisfaction.[29]

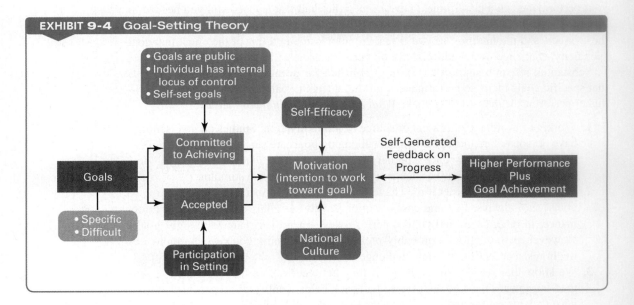

EXHIBIT 9-4 Goal-Setting Theory

Four-Drive Theory

Four-drive theory is a holistic theory developed by Harvard Business School professors Paul Lawrence and Nitin Nohria. It describes motivation in four categories: the drive to acquire, to bond, to learn, and to defend.[30] These drives interact with each other in varying degrees, depending on the individual and his or her external circumstances. The first three drives are considered "proactive" in the sense that we are always trying to fulfill them, independent of each other. The domination of one drive over the others can lead to a lack of balance in an employee's personal and work life. Exhibit 9-5 presents the four-drive theory.

The **drive to acquire** is the competitive drive for material goods, status, accomplishments, and power. This drive can lead to both greater performance and negative competition, so organizations can use the drive to bond to help minimize unhealthy competition.

The **drive to bond** is the social side of the equation, whereby we try to bond with others and engage in mutually beneficial relationships. These individual relationships can grow to include cooperation and collaboration with groups and teams in the workplace, especially when supported with team-based rewards and challenging goals.

---

four-drive theory
The theory that behaviour is influenced by our innate drives to acquire, bond, learn, and defend.

drive to acquire
The drive to seek, take control of, and retain objects and personal experiences.

drive to bond
The drive to form social relationships with others.

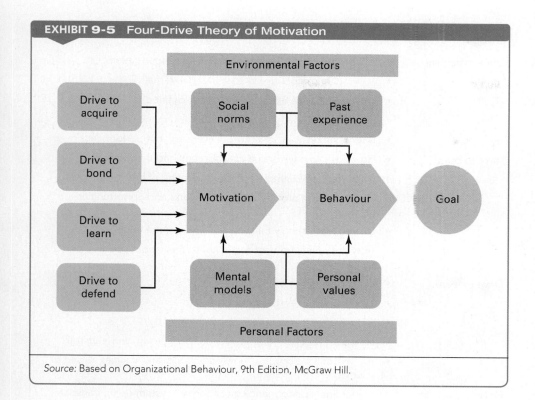

EXHIBIT 9-5 Four-Drive Theory of Motivation

Source: Based on Organizational Behaviour, 9th Edition, McGraw Hill.

The **drive to learn** is the drive to satiate curiosity and understand ourselves and the world around us. This drive is part of our need for growth and self-actualization discussed earlier. A work environment that allows for exploration can provide higher satisfaction, and learning new skills can be of greater importance than pay to some employees.

The **drive to defend** is all about self-protection. You may have faced the "fight-or-flight" response when defending yourself from danger, but perhaps also in relationships or dealing with your belief systems. This drive is the only reactive one and is typically triggered by threats. Communication can be used to correct employee misinformation that might cause unintentional threats in the workplace.

Most companies focus on the drive to acquire through pay and incentives, but often do not consider the impact of the other drives on employee engagement and motivation. Recognizing that employees want to bond, organizations could plan effective team-building activities that are more than just lip service and give the team a few hours of fun. We discussed the importance of efficiency and effectiveness in Chapter 1. However, organizations focused exclusively on efficiency through automation and standardization may be jeopardizing the drive to learn. They should instead spend more time on improving effectiveness and on how they structure their jobs and projects. A strong vision and corporate culture can provide employees with higher motivation that connects with their drive to defend. Exhibit 9-6 describes some of the organizational implications of four-drive theory.

The four-drive theory is based on substantive research on emotions and neural processes.[31] However, it does not sufficiently explain learned needs, and some critics argue that other drives could be included.

Each individual benefits the team, and the team benefits each individual.

drive to learn
The drive to satisfy our curiosity and understand ourselves and the world around us.

drive to defend
The drive to protect ourselves both physically and socially.

EXHIBIT 9-6	Organizational Implications of Four-Drive Theory
Drive to acquire	• Are rewards tied to performance in your organization?
	• Is your pay competitive internally and externally?
	• Are performance expectations clearly defined?
	• Do you know what constitutes high performance in your firm?
	• Is recognition appropriately provided for your performance?
Drive to bond	• How does your firm value collaboration and teamwork?
	• Does your firm's culture encourage sharing of best practices?
	• Does your firm provide support networks and opportunities for networking?
	• Do you feel strongly that you are a part of the team?
	• How does management show that it cares about you on a personal level?
Drive to learn	• Does your work interest you?
	• Can you learn new things at work?
	• Are your assignments varied and challenging?
	• How does your firm support your personal growth and learning?
	• Are you enhancing your knowledge, skills, and abilities as part of your work?
Drive to defend	• Is your firm's performance management system open, transparent, and fair?
	• Is your workplace free of hostility and intimidation?
	• Do your managers treat people with respect?
	• Do you support your company's vision and culture?
	• Is your workplace communication open—are you able to speak up?

Equity Theory

The term *equity* is related to the concept of fairness and equal treatment compared with others who behave in similar ways. Considerable evidence demonstrates that employees compare their job inputs and outcomes relative to others' and that inequities influence the degree of effort employees exert.[32]

Equity theory, developed by workplace and behavioural psychologist John Stacey Adams, proposes that employees perceive what they get from a job situation (outcomes) in relation to what they put into it (inputs) and then compare their input–outcome ratio with the input–outcome ratio of relevant others (see Exhibit 9-7). If employees perceive their ratio as equal to that of relevant others, a state of equity exists. In other words, they perceive that their situation is fair—that justice prevails. However, if the ratio is perceived as unequal, inequity exists, and they view themselves as under- or over-rewarded. Not all inequity (or equity) is real. It is the individual's *perception* that determines the equity of the situation.

What will employees do when they perceive an inequity? Equity theory proposes that employees might (1) distort either their own or others' inputs or outcomes, (2) behave in some way to induce others to change their inputs or outcomes, (3) behave in some way to change their own inputs or outcomes, (4) choose a different comparison person, or (5) quit their jobs. These types of employee reactions have generally proved to be accurate.[33] A review of the

equity theory
The theory that an employee compares his or her job's input–output ratio with that of relevant others and then responds to correct any inequity.

EXHIBIT 9-7 Equity Theory

Ratio of Output to Input	Employee 1's Perception
Employee 1 Employee 2	Inequity, under-rewarded
Employee 1 Employee 2	Equity
Employee 1 Employee 2	Inequity, over-rewarded

research consistently confirms the equity thesis: Whenever employees perceive inequity, they will act to correct the situation.[34] The result might be lower or higher productivity, improved or reduced quality of output, increased absenteeism, or voluntary resignation.

The **referent** against which individuals compare themselves is an important variable in equity theory.[35] Three referent categories have been defined: other, system, and self. The *other* category includes other individuals with similar jobs in the same organization but also includes friends, neighbours, or professional associates. On the basis of what they hear at work or read about in newspapers or trade journals, employees compare their pay with that of others. The *system* category includes organizational pay policies and procedures and the administration of the system. Whatever precedents have been established by the organization regarding pay allocation are major elements of this category. The *self* category refers to the input–outcome ratio that is unique to the individual. It reflects personal experiences and contacts and is influenced by criteria such as previous jobs or family commitments. The choice of a particular set of referents is related to the information available about the referents as well as to their perceived relevance. At Surrey, British Columbia–based Back in Motion Rehab, management decided that the highest-paid director's base salary should be less than two times the salary of the average staff member.[36] Because this policy uses the average staff member's pay as a referent, it sends the message that the output of the average staff member is truly valued.

Originally, equity theory focused on **distributive justice**, which is the perceived fairness of the amount and allocation of rewards among individuals. More recent research has focused on looking at issues of **procedural justice**, which is the perceived fairness of the process used to determine the distribution of rewards. This research shows that distributive justice has a greater influence on employee satisfaction than procedural justice, while procedural justice tends to affect an employee's organizational commitment, trust in his or her boss,

jovannig/Fotolia

When Toronto city councillors voted themselves an 8.9 percent pay raise in 2007, they were not thinking about possible budget shortfalls. Instead, they were responding to the idea that they were underpaid compared to other government decision makers who performed duties similar to their own. As councillors for the largest city in the country, with the largest budget, they were advised by a consulting firm that they should rank in the "top 25 percent of salaries for councillors across the country." Their salary before the raise was one of the lowest in the country.

referents
Those things individuals compare themselves against in order to assess equity.

distributive justice
Perceived fairness of the amount and allocation of rewards among individuals.

procedural justice
Perceived fairness of the process used to determine the distribution of rewards.

and intention to stay or quit.[37] What are the implications for managers? They should consider openly sharing information on how allocation decisions are made, follow consistent and unbiased procedures, and engage in similar practices to increase the perception of procedural justice. Employees who have an increased perception of procedural justice are likely to view their bosses and the organization as positive, even if they are dissatisfied with pay, promotions, and other personal outcomes.

Expectancy Theory

The most comprehensive and widely accepted explanation of employee motivation to date is the expectancy theory, developed by Victor Vroom, professor at the Yale School of Management.[38] Although the theory has its critics,[39] most research evidence supports it.[40]

Expectancy theory states that an individual tends to act in a certain way based on the expectation that the act will be followed by a given outcome and on the attractiveness of that outcome to the individual. It includes three variables or relationships (see Exhibit 9-8):

- *Expectancy, or effort–performance linkage.* The probability perceived by the individual that exerting a given amount of effort will lead to a certain level of performance.
- *Instrumentality, or performance–reward linkage.* The degree to which the individual believes that performing at a particular level is instrumental in attaining the desired outcome.
- *Valence, or attractiveness of reward.* The importance that the individual places on the potential outcome or reward that can be achieved on the job. Valence considers both the goals and needs of the individual.

This explanation of motivation might sound complex, but it really is not. It can be summed up in these questions: How hard do I have to work to achieve a certain level of performance, and can I actually achieve that level? What reward will I get for working at that level of performance? How attractive is the reward to me, and does it help me achieve my goals? Whether you are motivated to put forth effort (that is, to work) at any given time depends on your particular goals and your perception of whether a certain level of performance is necessary to attain those goals.

The key to expectancy theory is an understanding that an individual's goal and the links between effort and performance, between performance and rewards, and finally between rewards and individual goal satisfaction are related. Expectancy theory recognizes that there is no universal principle for explaining what motivates individuals and thus stresses that managers need to understand why employees view certain outcomes as attractive or unattractive. After all, we want to reward individuals with those things they value as

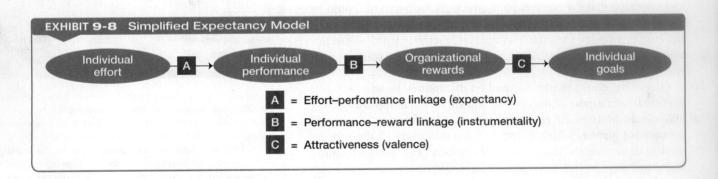

EXHIBIT 9-8 Simplified Expectancy Model

Individual effort → **A** → Individual performance → **B** → Organizational rewards → **C** → Individual goals

A = Effort–performance linkage (expectancy)
B = Performance–reward linkage (instrumentality)
C = Attractiveness (valence)

expectancy theory
The theory that an individual tends to act in a certain way based on the expectation that the act will be followed by a given outcome and on the attractiveness of that outcome to the individual.

positive. Expectancy theory also emphasizes expected behaviours. Do employees know what is expected of them and how they will be evaluated? Finally, the theory is concerned with perceptions; reality is irrelevant. An individual's own perceptions of performance, reward, and goal outcomes, not the outcomes themselves, will determine his or her motivation (level of effort). Exhibit 9-9 suggests how managers might increase employee motivation using expectancy theory.

EXHIBIT 9-9 Steps to Increasing Motivation Using Expectancy Theory

Improving Expectancy	Improving Instrumentality	Improving Valence
Improve the ability of the individual to perform	**Increase the individual's belief that performance will lead to reward**	**Make sure that the reward is meaningful to the individual**
• Make sure employees have the necessary skills for the task. • Provide training. • Assign reasonable tasks and goals.	• Observe and recognize performance. • Deliver rewards as promised. • Indicate to employees how previous good performance led to greater rewards.	• Ask employees what rewards they value. • Give rewards that are valued.

Integrating Contemporary Theories of Motivation

We have presented four contemporary motivation theories. You might be tempted to view them independently, but doing so would be a mistake. Many of the ideas underlying the theories are complementary, and you will better understand how to motivate people if you see how the theories fit together.[41]

Four-drive theory suggests that jobs and workplaces should provide an opportunity to fulfill the drives to acquire, bond, learn, and defend. The drives should be kept in balance so that employees are not overly influenced by any one drive.

Expectancy theory predicts that an employee will exert a high level of effort if he or she perceives that there is a strong relationship between effort and performance, performance and rewards, and rewards and satisfaction of personal goals. Each of these relationships is, in turn, influenced by certain factors. The level of individual performance is determined not only by the level of individual effort, but also by the individual's ability to perform and by whether the organization has a fair and objective performance evaluation system. The performance–reward relationship will be strong if the individual perceives that it is performance (rather than seniority, personal favourites, or some other criterion) that will be rewarded. The final link in expectancy theory is the rewards–goal relationship. Needs theories come into play at this point. Motivation is high to the degree that the rewards an individual receives for his or her high performance satisfy the dominant needs consistent with his or her individual goals.

Rewards also play a key part in equity theory. Individuals will compare the rewards (outcomes) they have received from the inputs or efforts they made with the input–outcome ratio of relevant others. Any inequities may influence the effort expended.

CURRENT ISSUES IN MOTIVATION

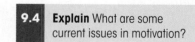
9.4 Explain What are some current issues in motivation?

One of the challenges managers face is how to motivate many different employee groups: students, new graduates, mothers returning to the workplace, and ethnic minorities, for example. Some companies find that older female employees want flexible hours and stimulating work, but are not looking to be promoted. Young college graduates working in head office, on the other hand, want a challenging, well-paid career and time to pursue personal interests and family life. Many employees want managers who help them.[42]

To keep her Yellow House staff engaged, Noble regularly solicits their opinions on almost everything, including new hires; she allows at least two employees to participate in interviews to ensure a candidate is a good cultural fit. She also offers pay increases before each employee's annual performance review; as a result, no one has asked for a raise, and Yellow House has lost only one employee to a competitor. The following diagram illustrates the link between employee engagement and key business outcomes such as absenteeism, turnover, productivity, and profitability.

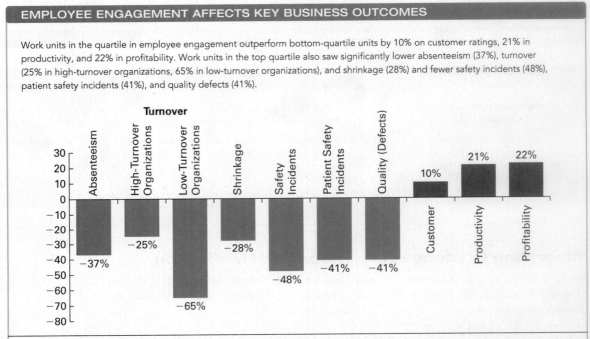

EMPLOYEE ENGAGEMENT AFFECTS KEY BUSINESS OUTCOMES

Work units in the quartile in employee engagement outperform bottom-quartile units by 10% on customer ratings, 21% in productivity, and 22% in profitability. Work units in the top quartile also saw significantly lower absenteeism (37%), turnover (25% in high-turnover organizations, 65% in low-turnover organizations), and shrinkage (28%) and fewer safety incidents (48%), patient safety incidents (41%), and quality defects (41%).

So far, we have covered a lot of the theoretical bases of employee motivation. Understanding and predicting employee motivation continues to be one of the most popular areas in management research. However, even current studies of employee motivation are influenced by several significant workplace issues—issues such as motivating unique groups of workers, designing effective rewards programs, and improving work–life balance. Let us take a closer look at each of these issues.

Motivating Unique Groups of Workers

MOTIVATING A DIVERSE WORKFORCE To maximize motivation in today's workforce, managers need to think in terms of *flexibility*. For example, studies tell us that men place more importance on having autonomy in their jobs than do women. In contrast, the opportunity to learn, convenient and flexible work hours, and good interpersonal relations are more important to women.[43] Baby Boomers may need more flextime as they manage the needs of their children and their aging parents. Gen-Xers want employers to add to their experience so they can develop portable skills. Meanwhile, millennials want more opportunities and the ability to work in teams.[44] Managers need to recognize that what motivates a single mother with two dependent children who is working full-time to support her family may be very different from what motivates a single part-time employee or an older employee who is working only to supplement his or her retirement income. A wide array of rewards is needed to motivate employees with such diverse needs.

There are also cross-cultural differences in motivation, which we discuss in *Diversity Matters* at the end of the chapter. Along with differences, there will be many cross-cultural consistencies in terms of what motivates employees. For example, the desire for interesting work seems important to almost all employees, regardless of their national culture. In a study of seven countries, employees in Belgium, Britain, Israel, and the United States ranked "interesting work" number one among 11 work goals, and this factor was ranked either second or third in Japan, the Netherlands, and Germany.[45] Similarly, in a study comparing job-preference outcomes among graduate students in Canada, the United States, Australia, and Singapore, growth, achievement, and responsibility were rated the top three and had identical rankings.[46] Both of these studies suggest some universality to the importance of intrinsic factors identified by Herzberg in his motivation-hygiene theory. Another recent study examining workplace motivation trends in Japan also seems to indicate that Herzberg's model is applicable to Japanese employees.[47]

MOTIVATING MINIMUM-WAGE EMPLOYEES Suppose that in your first managerial position after graduating you are responsible for managing a work group composed of minimum-wage employees. Offering more pay to these employees for high levels of performance is out of the question: Your company just cannot afford it.[48] In addition, many of these employees may have limited education and skills. What are your motivational options at this point? One of the toughest motivational challenges facing many managers today is how to achieve high performance levels from minimum-wage employees.

One trap we often fall into is thinking that people are motivated only by money. Although money is important as a motivator, it is not the only reward that people seek and that managers can use. What are some other types of rewards? Many companies use employee recognition programs such as employee of the month, quarterly employee performance award ceremonies, or other celebrations of employee accomplishment. For instance, at many fast-food restaurants such as Harvey's you will often see plaques hanging in prominent places that feature the "Crew Member of the Month." These types of programs highlight employees whose performance has been of the type and level the organization wants to encourage. Many managers also recognize the power of praise, but you need to be sure that these "pats on the back" are sincere and done for the right reasons; otherwise, employees can interpret such actions as manipulative.

We know from the motivation theories presented earlier that rewards are only part of the motivation equation. We need to look at other elements such as empowerment and career development assistance. We can look to expectancy theory for these insights. In service industries such as travel and hospitality, retail sales, child care, and maintenance, where pay for front-line employees generally does not get much higher than the minimum-wage level, successful companies are empowering these front-line employees with more authority to address customers' problems. By providing these opportunities to minimum-wage employees, you are preparing them for the future—one that ideally promises better pay. For many, this type of reward system is a strong motivator![49]

MOTIVATING PROFESSIONAL AND TECHNICAL EMPLOYEES In contrast to a generation ago, the typical employee today is more likely to be a highly trained professional with a postsecondary degree than a blue-collar factory worker. What special concerns should managers be aware of when trying to motivate a team of engineers at London, Ontario–based EllisDon, software designers at Vancouver-based Electronic Arts, or a group of consultants at Accenture?

Professionals are typically different from nonprofessionals.[50] They have a strong and long-term commitment to their field of expertise. Their loyalty is more often to their profession than to their employer. To keep current in their field, they need to regularly update their knowledge, and because of their commitment to their profession they rarely define their workweek as 8:00 a.m. to 5:00 p.m., five days a week.

What motivates professionals? Money and promotions typically are low on their priority list. Why? They tend to be well paid and enjoy what they do. In contrast, job challenge tends to be ranked high. They like to tackle problems and find solutions. Their chief reward in their jobs is the work itself. Professionals also value support. They want others to think that what they are working on is important.[51] That may be true for all employees, but professionals tend to be focused on their work as their central life interest, whereas nonprofessionals typically have other interests outside work that can compensate for needs not met on the job. The preceding points imply that managers should provide professional and technical employees

Marcio Jose Sanchez/AP Images

To attract, motivate, and retain employees, Google offers many different perks, including chef-prepared food, a gym, a masseuse, on-site car washes, haircuts, dry cleaning, free on-site doctor and dentist, and child care next door.

with new assignments and challenging projects. Give them autonomy to follow their interests and allow them to structure their work in ways they find productive. Reward them with educational opportunities—training, workshops, conferences—that allow them to keep current in their field and to network with their peers. Also reward them with recognition. Managers should ask questions and engage in other actions that demonstrate to their professional and technical employees that they are sincerely interested in what their employees are doing.

MOTIVATING CONTINGENT WORKERS   As many full-time jobs have been eliminated through downsizing and other organizational restructurings, the number of openings for part-time, contract, and other forms of temporary work have increased. Contingent workers do not have the security or stability that permanent employees have, and they do not identify with the organization or display the commitment that other employees do. Temporary workers also typically get little or no benefits such as health care or pensions.[52]

There is no simple solution for motivating contingent employees. For that small set of individuals who prefer the freedom of their temporary status—for example, some students, working mothers, and retirees—the lack of stability may not be an issue. Temporariness might also be preferred by highly compensated physicians, engineers, accountants, or financial planners who do not want the demands of a full-time job. But these are the exceptions. For the most part, temporary employees are not temporary by choice.

What will motivate involuntarily temporary employees? An obvious answer is the opportunity to become a permanent employee. In cases in which permanent employees are selected from a pool of temps, the temps will often work hard in hopes of becoming permanent. A less obvious answer is the opportunity for training. The ability of a temporary employee to find a new job is largely dependent on his or her skills. If the employee sees that the job he or she is doing can help develop marketable skills, then motivation is increased. From an equity standpoint, a manager should also consider the repercussions of mixing permanent and temporary workers when pay differentials are significant. When temps work alongside permanent employees who earn more and get benefits, too, for doing the same job, the performance of temps is likely to suffer. Separating such employees or perhaps minimizing interdependence between them might help managers decrease potential problems.[53]

Designing Effective Rewards Programs That Motivate Employees

Employee rewards programs play a powerful role in motivating for appropriate employee behaviour. In this section, we look at how managers can design effective rewards programs by using employee recognition programs and pay-for-performance programs. First, though, we should examine the issue of the extent to which money motivates.

duncanandison/Fotolia

People who value money score higher on attributes like sensation seeking, competitiveness, materialism, and control.

THE ROLE OF MONEY   The most commonly used reward in organizations is money. As one author notes, "Money is probably the most emotionally meaningful object in contemporary life: only food and sex are its close competitors as common carriers of such strong and diverse feelings, significance, and strivings."[54]

Little research attention has been given to individual differences in people's feelings about money, although some studies indicate that money is not employees' top priority.[55] A survey of 2000 Canadians discovered that trustworthy senior management and a good balance between work and personal or family life mattered more than pay or benefits when it came to employee satisfaction.[56]

A number of studies suggest that an individual's attitude toward money is correlated with personality traits and demographic factors.[57] People who desire money score higher on self-esteem, need for achievement, and Type A personality measures. Men seem to value money more than women. These studies suggest that individuals who value money will be more motivated by it than individuals who value other things.

What these findings suggest is that when organizations develop reward programs, they need to consider carefully what individuals value.

OPEN-BOOK MANAGEMENT   How can sharing information motivate employees? The 2012 list of Canada's 10 Most Admired Corporate Cultures included the Great Little Box Company, a one-stop manufacturer/distributor of boxes, displays, labels, and protective packaging. "Our culture is based on trust and respect," says James Palmer, Vice-President of Sales and Marketing. The company shares its financials and income with employees. As a result the Great Little Box Company is ranked among the top 100 employers in the country and has very high employee attraction and retention.[58] Many organizations of various sizes involve their employees in workplace decisions by opening up the financial statements (the "books"). They share that information so that employees will be motivated to make better decisions about their work and better able to understand the implications of what they do, how they do it, and the ultimate impact on the bottom line. This approach is called open-book management, and many organizations are using it.[59]

The goal of **open-book management** is to get employees to think like an owner by seeing the impact their decisions have on financial results. Because many employees do not have the knowledge or background to understand financials, they have to be taught how to read and understand the organization's statements. Once employees have this knowledge, however, managers need to regularly share the numbers with them. By sharing this information, employees begin to see the link between their efforts, level of performance, and operational results. Sharing information about a company's corporate social responsibility goals and objectives can also motivate employees to stay with the company.

EMPLOYEE RECOGNITION PROGRAMS   **Employee recognition programs** provide managers with opportunities to give employees personal attention and express interest, approval, and appreciation for a job well done.[61] These programs can take many forms. For instance, you can personally congratulate an employee in private for a good job. You can send a handwritten note or an email message acknowledging something positive that the employee has done. For employees with a strong need for social acceptance, you can publicly recognize accomplishments. To enhance group cohesiveness and motivation, you can celebrate team successes, perhaps by throwing a pizza party to celebrate a team's accomplishments.

One of the consistent themes that has emerged in the 13 years that Hewitt Associates has studied the 50 Best Companies to work for in Canada is the importance of recognition. A large number of the winning companies show appreciation for their employees frequently and visibly.[62]

PAY-FOR-PERFORMANCE PROGRAMS   What is in it for me? That is a question every person consciously or unconsciously asks before engaging in any form of behaviour. Our knowledge of motivation tells us that people act in order to satisfy some need. Before they do anything, they look for a payoff or reward. Although organizations may offer many different rewards, most of us are concerned with earning an amount of money that allows us to satisfy our needs and wants. In fact, a large body of research suggests that pay is far more motivational than some motivation theorists, such as Maslow and Herzberg, suggest.[63] Because pay is an important variable in motivation, we need to look at how we can use pay

And the Survey Says . . .[60]

The top five reasons small businesses invest in social responsibility:

92% A duty to give back to the community

77% The initiatives attract like-minded employees

75% Their customers expect social responsibility

73% The environment is part of their business decisions

62% There is a triple bottom line (3BL) impact in being socially responsible

open-book management
A motivational approach in which an organization's financial statements (the "books") are shared with all employees.

employee recognition programs
Reward programs that provide managers with opportunities to give employees personal attention and express interest, approval, and appreciation for a job well done.

to motivate high levels of employee performance. This concern explains the logic behind pay-for-performance programs.

Pay-for-performance programs are variable compensation plans that pay employees on the basis of a performance measure.[64] Piece-rate pay plans, wage-incentive plans, profit-sharing, and lump-sum bonuses are examples. What differentiates these forms of pay from more traditional compensation plans is that instead of paying a person for time on the job, pay is adjusted to reflect a performance measure. Performance measures might include such things as individual productivity, team or work-group productivity, departmental productivity, or the overall organization's profit performance.

Pay for performance is probably most compatible with expectancy theory. Specifically, if motivation is to be maximized, individuals should perceive a strong relationship between their performance and the rewards they receive. If rewards are allocated only on nonperformance factors—such as seniority, job title, or across-the-board pay raises—then employees are likely to reduce their efforts.

Pay-for-performance programs are popular; the number of employees affected by variable-pay plans has been rising in Canada. A 2007 survey of 314 firms by Hewitt Associates found that 80 percent of respondents had variable-pay programs in place, compared with 43 percent in 1994.[65] Pay-for-performance programs are more common for nonunionized employees than unionized ones, although more than 30 percent of unionized companies had such plans in 2002.[66] Prem Benimadhu, former vice-president of governance and human resource management with The Conference Board of Canada, noted, "Canadian unions have been very allergic to variable compensation."[67] In addition to wage uncertainty, employees may object to pay for performance if they feel that factors out of their control might affect the extent to which bonuses are possible.[68]

About 22 percent of Japanese companies have company-wide pay-for-performance plans.[69] However, one Japanese company, Fujitsu, dropped its performance-based program after eight years because it proved to be "flawed and a poor fit with Japanese culture."[70] Management found that some employees set goals as low as possible for fear of falling short. Others set extremely short-term goals. As a result, Fujitsu executives felt that ambitious projects that could produce hit products were being avoided.

Do pay-for-performance programs work? The evidence is mixed, at best.[71] One recent study that followed the careers of 1000 top economists found that they put in more effort early in their careers, at a time when productivity-related incentives had a larger impact.[72] A recent study of Finnish white-collar employees found that higher levels of payment and more frequent payments positively affected productivity, while lower levels of payment did not improve productivity.[73] A recent study in Canada looked at both unionized and nonunionized workplaces and found that variable-pay plans resulted in "increased productivity, a safer work environment, a better understanding of the business by employees, and little risk of employees losing base pay," according to Prem Benimadhu.[74] But there are also studies that question the effectiveness of pay-for-performance approaches, suggesting they can lead to less group cohesiveness in the workplace.[75]

If the organization uses work teams, managers should consider group-based performance incentives that will reinforce team effort and commitment. But whether these programs are individual based or team based, managers do need to ensure that they are specific about the relationship between an individual's pay and his or her expected level of appropriate performance. Employees must clearly understand exactly how performance—theirs and the organization's—translates into dollars on their pay-cheques.[76] Ottawa-based Lee Valley Tools uses quarterly newsletters to employees to let them know how much profit is forecast. The newsletter helps employees understand

pay-for-performance programs
Variable compensation plans that pay employees on the basis of some performance measure.

how hard work will pay off for them. Robin Lee, the company's president, says that "sharing information and profits promotes an atmosphere in which hard work, innovation, and efficiency pay off for everybody."[77]

The weak link between pay and performance is nowhere more evident than in the final type of rewards program we are going to look at—employee stock options.

STOCK OPTION PROGRAMS Executive bonus and stock option programs have come under fire because they seem to fly in the face of the belief that executive pay aligns with the organization's performance. What are stock option programs and what are they designed to do?

Stock options are a financial incentive that gives employees the right to purchase shares of company stock at some time in the future, at a set price. The original idea behind employee stock option plans was to turn employees into owners and give them strong motivation to work hard to make the company successful.[78] If the company was successful, the value of the stock went up, making the stock options valuable. In other words, there was a link between performance and reward. The popularity of stock options as a motivational and compensation tool skyrocketed during the dot-com boom in the late 1990s. Because many dot-coms could not afford to pay employees the going market-rate salaries, stock options were offered as performance incentives. As long as the market was rising, employees were willing to give up large salaries in exchange for stock options. However, when stock prices tanked in 2001, many individuals who joined and stayed with a dot-com for the opportunity to get rich through stock options found those stock options had become worthless. The declining stock market became a powerful demotivator.

Despite the risk of potential lost value and the widespread abuse of stock options, managers might want to consider them as part of their overall motivational program. An appropriately designed stock option program can be a powerful motivational tool for the entire workforce.[79]

Improving Work–Life Balance

While many employees continue to work an eight-hour day, five days a week, with fixed start and end times, organizations have started to implement programs to help employees manage their lives outside work. Many of the work–life balance programs that organizations have implemented are a response to the varied needs of a diverse workforce.

In addition to helping with errands and meals, contemporary companies are looking at a variety of scheduling options, including flextime, job sharing, and telework, to help employees balance work and personal life.

FLEXIBLE WORK SCHEDULES Many organizations have developed flexible work schedules that recognize different needs. For instance, a **compressed workweek** is a workweek in which employees work longer hours per day but fewer days per week. The most common form is four 10-hour days (a 4/40 program). However, organizations could design other types of schedules to fit employees' needs. Another alternative is **flexible work hours** (also popularly known as **flextime**), a scheduling option in which employees are required to work a specific number of hours per week but are free to vary those hours within certain limits. In a flextime schedule, all employees are required to be on the job for certain common core hours, but starting, ending, and lunch-hour times are flexible. Flextime is one of the most desired benefits among employees.[80] Employers have responded; a survey shows that 82 percent of Canadian employers expect to have flexible work arrangements by 2015 if not earlier.

stock options
A financial incentive that gives employees the right to purchase shares of company stock at some time in the future at a set price.

compressed workweek
A workweek in which employees work longer hours per day but fewer days per week.

flexible work hours (flextime)
A scheduling option in which employees are required to work a specific number of hours per week but are free to vary those hours within certain limits.

According to a 2010 Workopolis study, 53 percent of Canadian workers want a telework option to decrease commuting time and increase productivity.[81]

JOB SHARING Another scheduling option that can be effective in motivating a diverse workforce is **job sharing**—the practice of having two or more people split a full-time job. This type of job schedule might be attractive to individuals who want to work but do not want the demands and hassles of a full-time position.

TELEWORK Another alternative made possible by information technology is telecommuting or **telework**, in which employees work away from their office, usually at home, and are linked to the workplace by computer and other technology. Since many jobs are computer and Internet oriented, this job arrangement might be considered ideal for some people as there is no commuting, the hours are flexible, there is freedom to dress as you please, and there are few or no interruptions from colleagues. However, keep in mind that some employees miss the informal interactions at work that satisfy their social needs and provide a source of new ideas.

9.5 **Explain** What can managers learn from motivation theories?

FROM THEORY TO PRACTICE: SUGGESTIONS FOR MOTIVATING EMPLOYEES

We have covered a lot of information about motivation in this chapter. If you are a manager concerned with motivating your employees, what specific recommendations can you draw from the theories and issues discussed so far? Although there is no simple, all-encompassing set of guidelines, the following suggestions draw on what we know about motivating employees:

- *Recognize individual differences.* Almost every contemporary motivation theory recognizes that employees are not identical. They have different needs, attitudes, personalities, and other important individual variables. Managers may not be giving enough consideration to what employees really want in terms of pay and benefits from the workplace. A recent survey of 446 employers by Western Compensation and Benefits Consultants found that 94 percent listed competitive base salary as an important incentive. Only 52 percent of employers listed flexible scheduling as a good incentive.[82] Meanwhile, a Statistics Canada survey found that employees want "challenging work, continuous learning, flexible work arrangements, and better communication with their employers."[83] Eighty-seven percent of companies in the Western Compensation survey reported having difficulties attracting new employees in 2006. Companies may need to pay more attention to what their employees say that they want.
- *Match people to jobs.* A great deal of evidence demonstrates the motivational benefits of carefully matching people to jobs. For example, high achievers should have jobs that let them participate in setting moderately challenging goals and give them autonomy and feedback. Also, keep in mind that not everybody is motivated by jobs that are high in autonomy, variety, and responsibility.
- *Individualize rewards.* Because employees have different needs, what acts as a reinforcer for one may not for another. Managers should use their knowledge of employee differences to individualize the rewards they control, such as pay, promotions, recognition, desirable work assignments, autonomy, and participation.
- *Link rewards to performance.* Managers need to make rewards contingent on performance. Rewarding factors other than performance will reinforce only those other

job sharing
The practice of having two or more people split a full-time job.

telework
A job arrangement in which employees work at home and are linked to the workplace by computers and other technology.

factors. Important rewards such as pay increases and promotions should be given for the attainment of specific goals. Managers should also look for ways to increase the visibility of rewards, making them potentially more motivating.

- *Check the system for equity.* Employees should perceive that rewards or outcomes are equal to the inputs. On a simple level, experience, ability, effort, and other obvious inputs should explain differences in pay, responsibility, and other obvious outcomes. Remember that one person's equity is another's inequity, so an ideal reward system should weigh inputs differently in arriving at the proper rewards for each job.
- *Use recognition.* Use the power of recognition. In an economy where cost-cutting and layoffs are widespread (as we are experiencing in the current economy), recognition is a low-cost means to reward employees, and it is a reward that most employees consider valuable.
- *Do not ignore money.* It is easy to get so caught up in setting goals, creating interesting jobs, and providing opportunities for participation that you forget that money is a major reason why most people work. Some studies indicate that money is not the top priority of employees. Professor Graham Lowe at the University of Alberta and a colleague found that relationships in the workplace are more important than pay or benefits in determining job satisfaction.[84] Nevertheless, the allocation of performance-based wage increases, piecework bonuses, and other pay incentives is important in determining employee motivation. We are not saying that managers should focus solely on money as a motivational tool; rather, we are simply stating the obvious—if money is removed as an incentive, people are not going to show up for work. The same cannot be said for removing performance goals, enriched work, or participation.

Motivated employees lead to positive business outcomes.

9 Review and Apply

Summary of Learning Outcomes

9.1 **What is motivation?** Motivation refers to an individual's willingness to exert high levels of effort to reach organizational goals, conditioned by the degree to which that effort satisfies some individual need.

At Yellow House Events, one key way to motivate employees was to target brands that the employees believed in.

9.2 **How can needs help one be motivated?** According to needs theories, individuals have needs that, when fulfilled, will motivate them to perform well. While the theories do not account for all aspects of motivation, they do inform managers that individuals have different needs that should be considered when developing reward plans.

Yellow House Events discovered that as their Gen Y employees aged they developed different needs, and the company tried to address these needs to keep the employees motivated.

9.3 **What are the contemporary theories of motivation?** Equity theory proposes that employees compare their rewards and their productivity with others and then determine whether they have been treated fairly. Individuals who perceive that they are under-rewarded will try to adjust their behaviour to correct this imbalance. Expectancy theory explores the link between people's belief in whether they can do the work assigned, their belief in whether they will get the rewards promised, and the extent to which the reward is something they value. Most research evidence supports expectancy theory.

Noble offers her staff pay increases in advance of their annual performance review, ensuring that employees do not have to ask for raises or move to competitors for more salary.

9.4 **What are some current issues in motivation?** Current issues in motivation include motivating unique groups of workers, designing effective rewards programs, and improving work–life balance.

One of Yellow House's challenges was motivating employees who did not like working for certain lucrative clients. Noble

would occasionally "fire" clients to ensure that employees were motivated by the events that they were planning.

9.5 **What can managers learn from motivation theories?** Managers can motivate employees by recognizing individual differences, matching people to jobs, individualizing rewards, linking rewards to performance, checking the system for equity, using recognition, and not ignoring that money is a major reason why most people work.

Noble has worked hard to recognize the different needs of Gen Y employees and has allowed them to have flexible hours and blast music in the workplace. The company also has its employees participate in interviews for new hires to help keep current employees committed to the organization.

SNAPSHOT SUMMARY

9.1 **What Is Motivation?**

9.2 **Early Theories of Motivation (1950s and 1960s)**

9.3 **Contemporary Theories of Motivation**
Goal-Setting Theory
Four-Drive Theory
Equity Theory
Expectancy Theory
Integrating Contemporary Theories of Motivation

9.4 **Current Issues in Motivation**
Motivating Unique Groups of Workers
Designing Effective Rewards Programs that Motivate Employees
Improving Work–Life Balance

9.5 **From Theory to Practice: Suggestions for Motivating Employees**

MyManagementLab Study, practise, and explore real management situations with these helpful resources:

- **Interactive Lesson Presentations:** Work through interactive presentations and assessments to test your knowledge of management concepts.
- **PIA (Personal Inventory Assessments):** Enhance your ability to connect with key concepts through these engaging self-reflection assessments.
- **Study Plan:** Check your understanding of chapter concepts with self-study quizzes.
- **Simulations:** Practise decision making in simulated management environments.

Discussion Questions

1. How do needs affect motivation?
2. What are some possible consequences of employees' perceiving an inequity between their inputs and outcomes and those of others?
3. What can organizations do to create more motivating environments for their employees?
4. Most of us have to work for a living, and a job is a central part of our lives. Why then do managers have to worry about employee motivation issues?
5. Describe a task you have done recently for which you exerted a high level of effort. Explain your behaviour using the following motivation approaches: (1) the goal-setting theory, (2) four-drive theory, (3) equity theory, and (4) expectancy theory.
6. Describe several means that you might use to motivate (1) minimum-wage employees working for a small company that makes tortillas or (2) professional and technical employees working for a software design firm. Which of your suggestions do you think is best? Support your position.
7. Can an individual be too motivated? Discuss.

Developing Management Skills

Dilemma

You are in a team with six other management students and you have a major case analysis due in four weeks. The case project will count for 25 percent of the course mark. You are the team leader. Several team members are having difficulty motivating themselves to get started on the project. Identify ways you could motivate your team members using needs theories, expectancy theory, and equity theory. How will you motivate yourself?

Becoming a Manager

- Start paying attention to times when you are highly motivated and times when you are not as motivated. What accounts for the difference?
- When working on teams for class projects or on committees in student organizations, try different approaches to motivating others.
- If you are working, assess which of the four drives are strongest in motivating you at your job.
- As you visit various businesses, note what, if any, employee recognition programs these businesses use.
- Talk to practising managers about their approaches to employee motivation. What have they found works?

Developing Your Diagnostic and Analytical Skills: Twenty-First-Century Factory Town

ATCO Structures & Logistics is building a town in empty farmland about 100 km north of Regina.[85] BHP Billiton is opening the largest potash mine in the world in 2015, and the ATCO town will hold approximately 2500 employees, about 80 percent of whom are likely to be male. This $350 million complex will be open from 2015 to 2022, after which BHP will replace the topsoil and remove the roadways, restoring the land for future agricultural uses.

Work camps are common in mining, and traditionally they have featured shared rooms and group washrooms. ATCO is approaching its temporary town differently. Facilities will include 500 single bedrooms, each equipped with a bathroom, Wi-Fi, flat-screen TV, and mini-fridge. Lecture halls used for training during the day will provide broadcasts of hockey games and UFC fights, as well as card and video game tournaments. Worker priorities are changing, and ATCO is building a 20 000-square-foot fitness facility with a gym, two squash courts, a weight room, and an indoor running track with 360-degree window views. In a quintessentially Canadian move, ATCO is also putting in a full-sized outdoor hockey rink.

To keep employees occupied and stem the potential substance abuse problem featured in some camps, one out of every five residents at the facility will be there to look after the workers, including cooking, cleaning, maintenance, and security.

Questions

1. What is it like to work at one of BHP Billiton's mining camps? (Hint: Go to BHP Billiton's website and click on People and Careers.) What is your assessment of the company's philosophy toward employees?
2. What do you think is ATCO's biggest challenge in keeping employees occupied while living in a huge work camp?
3. If you were managing a team of potash miners and tradespeople, how would you keep them motivated?

Diversity Matters

In today's global business environment, managers cannot automatically assume that motivational programs that work in one location are going to work in others. Let us look at several theories to see if there is any cross-cultural transferability.

Maslow's hierarchy of needs proposes that people start at the physiological level and then move progressively up the hierarchy in order. This hierarchy, if it has any application at all, aligns with Canadian culture. In countries such as Japan, Greece, and Mexico, where uncertainty-avoidance characteristics are strong (that is, individuals prefer structured situations), security needs would be on the top of the needs hierarchy. Countries that score high on quality-of-life characteristics (that is, individuals value relationships and are concerned with the welfare of others)—Denmark, Sweden, Norway, the Netherlands, and Finland—would have social needs on top.[86] We would predict, for example, that group work will motivate employees more when a country's culture scores high on quality-of-life characteristics.

Equity theory has a relatively strong following in Canada. Given that Canadian-style reward systems are based on the assumption that employees are highly sensitive to equity in reward allocations, the theory's popularity is not surprising. In Canada, equity is meant to closely tie pay to performance. However, recent evidence suggests that in collectivist cultures (where individuals expect that others will look after and protect them), especially in the former socialist countries of Central and Eastern Europe, employees expect rewards to reflect their individual needs as well as their performance.[87] Moreover, consistent with a legacy of communism and centrally planned economies, employees exhibit a greater "entitlement" attitude—that is, they expect outcomes to be greater than their inputs.[88] These findings suggest that Canadian-style pay practices may need modification, especially in Russia and other former communist countries, in order to be perceived as fair by employees.

Hey, You're the Boss Now!

As a new manager, motivating employees can be one of the most challenging aspects of the job. There is no simple, all-encompassing set of motivational guidelines, but the following suggestions draw on the essence of what research says about motivating employees:[89]

1. **Recognize individual differences.** Almost every contemporary motivation theory recognizes that employees are not homogeneous. They have different needs. They also differ in terms of attitudes, personality, and other important individual variables.
2. **Match people to jobs.** A great deal of evidence demonstrates the motivational benefits of carefully matching people to jobs. People who lack the necessary skills to perform successfully will be disadvantaged. Redesign jobs to enhance motivation.
3. **Use goals.** You should ensure that employees have hard, specific goals and feedback on how well they are doing in pursuit of those goals. Employees will be more committed if goals are clear and set through participation.
4. **Ensure that goals are perceived as attainable.** Regardless of whether goals are actually attainable, employees who see goals as unattainable will reduce their effort. Be sure, therefore, that employees feel confident that increased effort can lead to achieving performance goals.
5. **Individualize rewards and ensure they are timely.** Because employees have different needs, what acts as a reinforcer for one may not do so for another. Use your knowledge of employee differences to individualize the rewards over which you have control. Some of the more obvious rewards that you can allocate include pay, promotions, autonomy, and the opportunity to participate in goal setting and decision making.
6. **Link rewards to performance.** You need to make rewards contingent on performance. Rewarding factors other than performance will reinforce only the importance of those other factors. Key rewards such as pay increases and promotions should be given for the attainment of employees' specific goals. Linking rewards to performance increases effort–performance and performance–reward expectancies.
7. **Check the system for equity.** Employees should perceive that rewards or outcomes are equal to the inputs given. On a simplistic level, experience, ability, effort, and other obvious inputs should explain differences in pay, responsibility, and other obvious outcomes.
8. **Link pay with performance.** It is easy to get so caught up in setting goals, creating interesting jobs, and providing opportunities for participation that you forget that money is a major reason why most people work. Thus, the allocation of performance-based wage increases, piecework bonuses, employee stock ownership plans, and other pay incentives are important in determining employee motivation.

Your Essential Management Reading List

Learning from key management experts can help you understand your own motivation better. Think about this quote from Richard Carlson: "Stress is nothing more than a socially acceptable form of mental illness." Here are some of the top books on motivation:

- *Don't Sweat the Small Stuff*—Richard Carlson
- *Outliers*—Malcolm Gladwell
- *The Power of Positive Thinking*—Norman Vincent Peale
- *Drive*—David Pink

Team Exercises

3BL: The Triple Bottom Line

Corporate sustainability practices can have a positive impact on recruitment, retention, and employee engagement. Towers Perrin's 2014 Global Workforce Study showed that a firm's reputation for social responsibility (including environmental work) is one of the top 10 drivers of employee engagement worldwide.[90] How do employers engage employees in their sustainability efforts? Some of the steps include public sustainability goals, senior executive support, and training, policies, and programs that integrate sustainability into employee roles.

THINKING STRATEGICALLY ABOUT 3BL

There are many ways to motivate employees to modify their behaviour and actions to become more sustainable:

- recognition
- management feedback
- salary and bonuses
- benefits
- competition/peer inducements
- modified job requirements
- opportunities for growth

All of these incentives need to be aligned with organizational goals or there will be incongruence and any behavioural changes will be short-lived. Different organizations could use combinations of the above incentives that fit their culture. For example, Intel ties corporate sustainability goals to its annual performance bonus.[91] Which of the above incentives would have the greatest impact on your behaviour?

What Rewards Motivate You?

Employees at Radialpoint in Montreal can get their laundry washed, dried, and folded for them at work. At trucking company Groupe Robert, based in Rougemont, Quebec, employees are entered into monthly draws for concerts and shows; each employee receives a Christmas food basket; and birthday cards are personally signed by the CEO. At Brantford, Ontario–based S. C. Johnson & Son, employees and their families can take holidays at the company's resort in Muskoka. The company also provides an on-site massage therapist. All of these companies believe that there is more to rewards than just cash.

All of the following traditional and offbeat benefits are currently offered at various Canadian firms. Rank them individually for yourself, putting those that are most likely to motivate you at the top of your list. Now compare your top five choices with the members of your group. What differences did you find? Why?

Flextime	Dental insurance	Pets at work	Company car
Telework	Vision insurance	Fitness memberships	Subsidized cafeteria
Paid vacation	Life insurance	On-site day care	Annual birthday gift
Management development plan	Retirement plan	Clothing allowance	Transportation voucher
Family picnics and parties	Profit sharing/stock purchase plan	Children's college/university tuition	Benefits for unmarried domestic partners
Paid sick days	Daily nap time	Tuition refund	Free snacks and candy
Child and elder care referral services	Flexible spending plan	Non-work-related courses	Ability to keep frequent flier miles
Bring your own device (BYOD)	Employee assistance program	Laundry/dry cleaning service	Company-sponsored teams

How Can You Motivate Others?

This exercise is designed to increase your awareness of how and why you motivate others and to help you focus on the needs of those you are attempting to motivate.

STEP 1

Break into groups of five to seven people. Each group member is to respond individually to the following situations:

Situation 1: You are the owner and president of a 50-employee organization that provides call-centre services to a number of local businesses. Your company has two major units. Customer Care answers questions from customers about malfunctioning technology (computers, cellphones, home networks). Sales and Marketing makes telemarketing calls to people's homes. Employees who work in Sales and Marketing phone people and try to sell them cellphone plans and/or Internet access at reduced prices. They also conduct market research via the phone, calling people to ask them to answer survey questions. Employees who work in Customer Care often receive calls from irate customers who are having technical difficulties. Employees who work in Sales and Marketing often encounter irate people when they phone to sell them something or conduct a survey, particularly at dinnertime. Your goal is to motivate all 50 employees to their highest level of effort.

Task 1: Look at the table listing 10 factors you could use to motivate your employees. Rank the factors from most important to least important (1 to 10), placing your rankings in the Task 1 column.

Situation 2: Consider now that you are one of the 50 employees who has been given insight into what motivates you.

Task 2: As an employee, look again at the factors listed in the table and think about what would motivate you most effectively. Again, rank the factors from most important to least important (1 to 10), and place your rankings in the Task 2 column.

STEP 2

Each member should share his or her prioritized lists (the lists from Tasks 1 and 2) with the other members of the group.

STEP 3

After each member has presented his or her lists, the group should respond to the following questions:

1. Are each individual's lists (Task 1 and Task 2) similar or dissimilar to the others? What do the differences or similarities suggest to you?
2. What have you learned about how and why to motivate others, and how can you apply this information?

Work Factor	Task 1 Rank	Task 2 Rank
Recognition for customer accomplishments		
A variety of tasks (sales and customer service)		
Seeing the results of my work		
Opportunity for advancement		
Being compensated for enhanced performance		
A comfortable physical working environment		
Job security		
Equity in access to benefits		
Interesting work		

Be the Consultant

Microfinance institutions (MFIs) provide financial services to poor and low-income individuals (microfinance), including microcredit, savings, money transfers, insurance, and payment services.[92] A local MFI has engaged your consulting firm to advise it on the benefits of incorporating sustainability practices internally and with clients.

Particularly, the MFI is interested in your firm answering the following questions:

1. How will sustainability practices increase the motivation of employees?
2. How can sustainability provide added value to clients?
3. How will sustainability practices of clients lead to decreased credit risk?
4. Which stakeholders might put pressure on MFIs to have better sustainability performance?

Business Cases

DevFacto Technologies

Micromanagement-free zone: DevFacto cofounders Chris Izquerdo and David Cronin aimed to create a company that values open communication and innovation. To do so meant embracing diversity, enticing creativity, and ensuring constant collaboration. Chris and David, software developers who had suffered through rigidly bureaucratic work environments in their own careers, felt a self-directed and engaged workforce would drive efficiency and productivity. "The two most important aspects of our business are our culture and our people," said Cronin.[93] "If you give them a purpose that's larger than themselves, you can lead them to results."[94] Thus their vision for DevFacto emerged as a team of doers without any micromanaging, needless policies, or even an HR department.

DevFacto is an ideas and solutions company in Canada based in Calgary. Started in 2007, it provides technology, services, and solutions for companies to allow them to focus on their core competences. Their services range from SharePoint business intelligence solutions to enterprise mobile solutions to application and software development.

The company has grown to 115 people on its payroll and has a satellite office in Regina, but it is more engaged than ever. It earned its third straight spot on the 50 Best Small and Medium Employers (BSME) in Canada, and its annual turnover rate is less than 2 percent. Not every employee is suited to be a self-starter, so the firm conducts a lengthy culture-fit interview with Cronin or a regional director at the satellite office. What Cronin looks for is intrinsic motivation that drives a potential employee to constantly improve. Since the company operates a flat structure, employees are regularly called for group interviews to assess candidates. Any employee can veto a hire who they do not feel will fit in.

Einar Westerlund, from the Queen's School of Business Centre for Business Venturing, works with BSME firms and believes that self-direction is a major driver of engagement. Giving employees influence over their workload and ongoing projects "allows them to map a lot of their own work direction," says Westerlund.[95] Rather than bosses holding employees accountable to budgets and deadlines, employees do it at DevFacto. It promotes collective decision making and helps people understand their roles more fully. CEO Izquierdo takes this a step further with open-book management. The company uses an internal social network for checking in, with "all hands on deck" staff meetings, and for sharing financial information.[96]

Its approach is not without challenges. Cronin is candid when he admits he spends a lot of time involved with issues that other companies handle via polices and procedures or micromanagement. However, these problems are rare and he prefers to let employees lead the way. "Our approach is: Let's find something that's a win–win. We talk about it."[97]

Discussion Questions

1. What types of rewards are suited to this type of work environment?
2. Which contemporary theory of motivation is most applicable to DevFacto?

Ubisoft Entertainment SA

Ubisoft is a worldwide network of studios that create, publish, and distribute entertainment and services with world-renowned brands like Just Dance and Tom Clancy's Splinter Cell video game series. The company's sales in 2014 were in excess of $1.5 billion, thanks to gaming experiences available on all popular platforms, including consoles, mobile phones, tablets, and PCs.[98] It took 10 teams in 6 countries over 13 international time zones to create *Assassin's Creed: Unity*—in which a fictional French assassin stalks his prey in 1789 Paris. This huge four-year undertaking presented major practical and logistical challenges along with difficult creative and technical hurdles. Ubisoft's innovative approach to international collaboration and employee engagement helped it overcome these challenges.[99]

The Montreal studio led the project, providing coordination for nine other units stationed in Toronto, France, Ukraine, Romania, China, and Singapore. In the creative environment of making video games, things like production, project management, and various other managerial tasks are usually at odds with the creative process. What Ubisoft did was free up creators to focus on the game's vision and reassigned all the other management functions. Its goal was to engage and empower employees to be innovative and creative at all levels of the company. Creative directors at Ubisoft do not have staff reporting to them so that they can focus 100 percent on the content. Managers typically have seven to ten people reporting to them, which gives teams more ownership and less dependency on other studios.[100] Staff in the same roles at different studios are encouraged to collaborate with each other. This allows ideas and best practices to be shared between studios without management intervention.[101]

The Toronto office is an example of employee engagement and work–life balance on steroids. Their open-concept office features a Ubigallery showcasing the works of Ontario art graduates, whiteboards in every room to stimulate the creative process, subsidized hot lunches, and a Friday evening scotch tasting club. It adds more than 100 people a year, but still focuses on fostering a strong team culture. To that end, every new employee gets a Nerf gun on his or her first day, and the staff have Nerf battles to break the ice.[102]

Discussion Questions

1. What are the risks of separating the creative side from the production side?
2. What are the challenges of running a decentralized organization in multiple countries?

Nevin Markwart

Nevin Markwart is President and CEO of Canoe Financial Corporation in Calgary. He is a prime example of what a motivated self-starter can achieve in his or her career with the right attitude, timing, and support. With Canoe, Nevin oversees a $3 billion portfolio. Prior to tracking stocks, he tracked stats.[103] In 1981 Nevin was playing hockey with the Western Hockey League's Regina Pats. He was a first-round pick of the Boston Bruins and played in the NHL for almost nine seasons. Hockey taught Nevin the concept of relying on a team, and he also learned through several rehab stints in the American Hockey League that you have to get better every day or you may be replaced.

Nevin began working with St. Laurent Associates as an investment representative while playing in the AHL and NHL. On behalf of the NHL Players' Association, he set up its first 401(k), a defined-contribution pension account. Nevin received his MBA from Northeastern in 1994 and had several roles in asset management companies. Nevin's experience in the NHL had taught him the rewards of teamwork, which he found was replicated more in private investment companies that were willing to allow employees to take risks and be rewarded for their success, as well as relying on a team structure.[104] He also discovered the importance of a mentor, finding someone who "basically spent 30 seconds with me every day for seven years," recalled Markwart.[105] He learned to focus on the details on a daily basis and to make minor corrections, which led to tremendous success.

Mark Greenberg/ZUMA Press/Newscom

CHAPTER

10 Understanding Groups and Teams

Think About It

What makes a team different from any group of people? Sir Richard Branson's philosophy has not changed from when he started his first venture, *Student* magazine. "Do something you enjoy and your enthusiasm will rub off on others, ensuring a committed and spirited team," said Branson. "I have felt that one of my most important jobs is to attract and motivate great people who genuinely feel their job is more important than just money."[5]

Forty years ago Sir Richard Branson launched Virgin Records. He launched Virgin Atlantic when he and 50 passengers were stranded in Puerto Rico because American Airlines cancelled a flight. He chartered a 50-person plane and charged every passenger $39. Today Virgin Galactic is offering suborbital flights for $200 000. "First we're taking people to suborbital travel, then orbital," says Branson. "One day, maybe even hotels in space—who's to know? Whatever happens, it's going to be ridiculously exciting. It's the start of a whole new era."[1]

The Virgin Group has expanded worldwide and includes Virgin Mobile Canada. To build an empire and become a billionaire, Branson has always demonstrated a strong entrepreneurial flare and an unwavering belief in the value of employees and teams.

Virgin has always been a bit anti-establishment. Branson encourages that with a program called "Refresh," a series of mandatory daylong training and team-building exercises for all employees, regardless of rank and position. At one February session, employees learned about body language from a police detective, learned how to imitate IndyCar pit crew tire changes, and used silent tag-team relays to prepare their lunches.[2]

Branson believes a leader needs to have good interpersonal skills to bring out the best in his or her team. "You need to be good at praising, and you need to be great at building a team and not trying to do everything yourself," says Branson. He suggests not taking all the credit and also "taking the knocks when things go wrong."[3]

All Virgin employees are empowered and open to new ideas. According to Branson, "You've got to have a yes mentality. You've got to be willing to take risks and allow people to fall flat on their face on occasion." Branson suggests that supporting employees who have taken risks and failed encourages them to take risks and succeed.[4] "Managers should never rule by fear," says Branson. He believes that enthusiasm, genuine openness, and camaraderie with your people works better.[6] Virgin adopts flexible working hours and other supportive policies, which encourages collaboration and team spirit.

Work teams are one of the realities—and challenges—of managing in today's dynamic global environment. Teams are widely used in Canada. Thousands of organizations have made the move to restructure work around teams rather than individuals. Why? What do these teams look like? What stages of development do teams go through? Like the challenges Sir Richard Branson faced, how can business owners create effective employee teams? These are a few of the types of questions we answer in this chapter. First, however, let us begin by developing our understanding of group/team behaviour.

UNDERSTANDING GROUPS AND TEAMS

10.1 **Tell** What are the stages of team development?

Because most organizational work is done by individuals who are part of a work team or group, managers need to understand team/group behaviour. The behaviour of a team is not simply the sum total of the behaviours of all the individuals in the team. Why? Because individuals act differently in teams than they do when they are alone. Therefore, if we want to understand organizational behaviour more fully, we need to study teams.

Though teams and groups can differ depending on their purpose, we use "groups" and "teams" interchangeably in our theoretical discussions below (conforming to how scholars have written their research) because we are discussing teams or groups in the workplace. Interchanging these terms simply underscores that the processes for groups and teams are similar, although formal work teams/groups involve more synergy.

What Is a Team?

Most of you are already familiar with teams, especially if you have watched organized sports events. Although a sports team has many of the same characteristics as a work team, work teams *are* different from informal groups and have their own unique traits. **Work teams** are two or more interacting and interdependent individuals whose members work intensely on a specific, common goal using their positive **synergy** (combined efforts that are greater than the sum of individual efforts), individual and mutual accountability, and complementary skills. In a work team, the combined individual efforts of team members result in a level of performance that is greater than the sum of those individual inputs by generating positive synergy through coordinated effort. Exhibit 10-1 provides some examples of different types of teams in today's organizations.

Informal Groups

Employees also belong to *informal groups*. Unlike work teams or groups, these informal groups have no need or opportunity to engage in collective work that requires joint effort. Informal groups are social and occur naturally in the workplace in response to the need for social contact. For example,

A team is a group whose individual efforts result in a performance that is greater than the sum of the individual inputs.

---

work team
Two or more interacting and interdependent individuals whose members work intensely on a specific, common goal using their positive synergy, individual and mutual accountability, and complementary skills.

synergy
Combined efforts that are greater than the sum of individual efforts.

EXHIBIT 10-1 Types of Teams in Organizations

Team Type	Description	Example
Cross-functional teams	Employees who are experts in various functions; task interdependence is limited as each member works with other employees in different departments.	Calgary-based Canadian Pacific Railway (CPR) uses cross-functional teams to figure out ways to cut costs. All the functional areas affected by the cost cutting are represented.
Problem-solving teams	Employees from the same department or functional area who are trying to improve work activities or solve specific problems.	The RCMP uses a drug task force separate from its main policing operations to address issues related to the manufacture, sale, and use of illegal drugs.
Self-managed teams	Employees with high autonomy who are responsible for an entire work process or segment. Unlike a problem-solving team, the team is also responsible for managing itself.	Muskoseepi Park in Grand Prairie, Alberta, is operated by a self-managed team whose members are accountable to each other and do not have direct daily supervision.
Advisory teams	Teams that provide feedback and recommendations to organizational decision makers.	Nova Scotia Business Inc. uses an advisory team to keep on top of community issues throughout the province.
Virtual teams	Teams that use information technologies to link physically dispersed members.	Microsoft's staff in Richmond, British Columbia, are part of a virtual team with members in Redmond, Washington, and other global centres.

Source: Based on S. A. Kirkpatrick and E. A. Locke, "Leadership: Do Traits Really Matter?" *Academy of Management Executive.* May 1991 pp. 48-60; and T. A. Judge, J. E. Bono, R. Iiies and M. Werner, "Personality and Leadership: A Qualitative and Quantitative Review," *Journal of Applied Psychology,* Aug 2002 pp. 765–780 6Ce Exh 8-2, p. 235; originally 10e p. 37. 2 CONTACT: Rozella Cribbs-Grant.

three employees from different departments who regularly eat lunch together are an informal group. Informal groups tend to form around friendships and common interests.

Stages of Team Development

PERSONAL INVENTORY ASSESSMENT

Team development is a dynamic process. Most teams and groups are in a continual state of change, although there is a general pattern that describes how most of them develop. Professor Bruce Tuckman of Ohio State University developed a five-stage model of small group development.[7] As shown in Exhibit 10-2, these five stages are *forming, storming, norming, performing,* and *adjourning.*

Stage I, **forming**, has two aspects. First, people join the team either because of a work assignment or for some other benefit desired (such as status, self-esteem, affiliation, power, or security).

Once the team's membership is in place, the second part of the forming stage begins: the task of defining the team's purpose, structure, and leadership. This phase is characterized by a great deal of uncertainty. Members are "testing the waters" to determine what types of behaviour are acceptable. This stage is complete when members begin to think of themselves as part of a team.

Stage II, **storming**, is one of intragroup conflict. Members accept the existence of the team but resist the control that the team imposes on individuality. Further, there is conflict over who will control the team. When this stage is complete, there will be a relatively clear hierarchy of leadership within the team and agreement on the team's direction. Conflict helps the team clarify roles and leads to some level of belonging for team members, although teams with major problems can sometimes get stuck in this stage.

Stage III is one in which close relationships develop and the team demonstrates cohesiveness. There is now a strong sense of team identity and camaraderie. This **norming** stage is complete when the team structure solidifies and the team has assimilated a

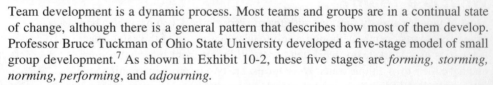

forming
The first stage of team development in which people join the group and then define the team's purpose, structure, and leadership.

storming
The second stage of team development, which is characterized by intragroup conflict.

norming
The third stage of team development, which is characterized by close relationships and cohesiveness.

EXHIBIT 10-2 Stages of Team Development

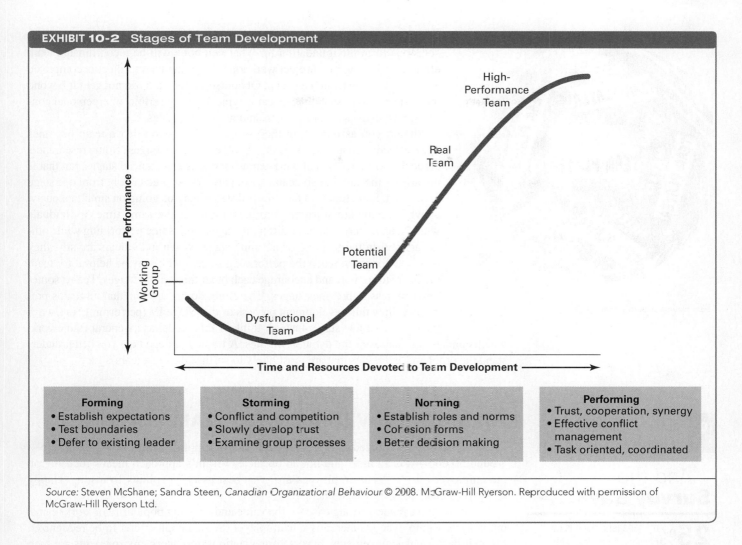

Source: Steven McShane; Sandra Steen, *Canadian Organizational Behaviour* © 2008. McGraw-Hill Ryerson. Reproduced with permission of McGraw-Hill Ryerson Ltd.

common set of expectations of what defines correct member behaviour. Members are involved and begin to support each other.

Stage IV is **performing**. The team structure at this point is fully functional and accepted by team members. Team energy has moved from getting to know and understand each other to performing the task at hand. Team purpose and roles are clear, and achievement leads to pride and high productivity.

Performing is the last stage in the development of permanent work teams. Temporary teams—such as project teams, task forces, and similar groups that have a limited task to perform—have a fifth stage, **adjourning**. In this stage, the team prepares to disband. High levels of task performance are no longer the team's top priority. Instead, attention is directed at wrapping up activities, perhaps with some sort of ceremony to help members seek closure. Responses of team members vary at this stage. Some are upbeat, basking in the team's accomplishments. Others may be saddened by the loss of camaraderie and friendships gained during the work team's life.

Many of you have probably experienced each of these stages in working on a class team project. Team members are selected and then meet for the first time. There is a "feeling out" period to assess what the team is going to do and how it is going to do it. This phase is usually rapidly followed by a battle for control: Who is going to be in charge? Once this issue is resolved and a "hierarchy" is agreed on, the team identifies specific aspects of the task, who is going to do them, and dates by which the assigned work needs to be completed.

performing
The fourth stage of team development, in which the team structure is fully functional and accepted by team members.

adjourning
The final stage of team development for temporary teams, in which members are concerned with wrapping up activities rather than task performance.

iQoncept/Fotolia

Team players stick together.

General expectations are established and agreed on by each member. These decisions form the foundation for what you hope will be a coordinated team effort culminating in a project well done. Once the team project is completed and turned in, the team breaks up. Of course, some teams do not get far beyond the first or second stage; these teams typically have serious interpersonal conflicts, turn in disappointing work, and get lower grades.

Should you assume from the preceding discussion that a team becomes more effective as it progresses through the first four stages? Some researchers argue that effectiveness of work teams increases at advanced stages, but that is not always the case.[8] Also, teams do not always proceed clearly from one stage to the next. Sometimes, in fact, several stages may be going on simultaneously, as when teams are storming and performing at the same time. Individuals within a team may also be at different stages, with some performing while others are still in the forming or norming stage. When individuals are shy, they may take longer to reach the performing stage, and it may be helpful for team members to support and encourage each other through the stages. Teams sometimes regress to previous stages. Therefore, do not assume that all teams precisely follow this development process or that Stage IV (performing) is always the most desirable stage. Instead, think of this model as a general framework, which emphasizes that teams are dynamic entities. A framework can help you better understand the problems and issues that are most likely to surface during a team's life.

TURNING INDIVIDUALS INTO TEAM PLAYERS

10.2 **Define** How do individuals become team players?

And the
Survey Says...[10]

25% of managers feel it is most challenging to deal with issues between team coworkers

22% of managers feel it is most challenging to motivate team members

70% of employees say that the biggest benefit of workplace friendships is that they create a more supportive workplace

85% of *Fortune 1000* companies used team- or group-based pay to some degree

83% of respondents identified teams as a key ingredient to organizational success

40% of senior executives said that meeting deadlines was the most important characteristic of a good team player

37% of workers feel more productive in a small group

69% of workers said their teams were not given enough resources

Richard Branson recognized that the large number of employees in the Virgin Group—around 50 000—was an asset and not an obstacle. Virgin's approach means focusing on the employees first. "Your employees are your best asset," explains Branson. "Happy employees make for happy customers."[9]

So far, we have made a strong case for the value and growing popularity of work teams, but not every employee is inherently a team player. Some people prefer to be recognized for their individual achievements. In some organizations, too, work environments are such that only the strong survive. Creating teams in such an environment may meet some resistance. Countries differ in terms of the degree to which individuals are encouraged by societal institutions to be integrated into groups. Teams fit well in countries that score high on collectivism, where working together is encouraged. But what if an organization wants to introduce teams into an individualistic society like that of Canada? The job becomes more difficult.

The Challenges of Creating Team Players

One substantial barrier to work teams is the individual resistance that may exist. Employees' success, when they are part of teams, is no longer defined in terms of individual performance. Instead, success is a function of how well the team as a whole performs. To perform well as team members, individuals must be able to communicate openly and honestly with one another, to confront differences and resolve conflicts, and to place lower priority on personal goals for the good of the team. For many employees, these demands are difficult and sometimes impossible assignments.

The challenge of creating team players will be greatest when the national culture is highly individualistic and the teams are being introduced into an established organization that has historically valued individual achievement.[11] These organizations prospered by hiring and rewarding corporate stars, and they bred a competitive work climate that encouraged individual achievement and recognition. In this context, employees can experience culture shock caused by a sudden shift in the focus to teamwork.[12]

Team players do not just appear. A lot of hard work is required to get team members to gel. That is why baseball teams, like the Toronto Blue Jays, go to spring training every year—to prepare themselves as a team for the upcoming season.

Three Key Aspects of Group Behaviour

1 Roles

Behaviour patterns expected of someone who occupies a given position in a social unit. We adjust our **roles** to the group we belong to at the time. Employees attempt to determine what behaviours are expected of them by reading their job descriptions, getting suggestions from their bosses, and watching what their cowokers do. Role conflict happens when an employee has conflicting role expectations.

Dr. Meredith Belbin suggests that understanding your role within a particular team helps you enhance your strengths and address your weaknesses as a team member. This creates a stronger team with better individual contributors. Exhibit 10-3 lists the nine roles that Dr. Belbin summarized. It is beneficial to ensure that the group is balanced in terms of these roles.

Kwest/shutterstock

EXHIBIT 10-3 Belbin's Team Roles

Action-Oriented Roles	Shaper	Drives the team to improve Dynamic, loves pressure
	Implementer	Adept at putting ideas into action Practical, reliable, organized
	Completer Finisher	Ensures timely completion Painstakingly thorough, efficient
People-Oriented Roles	Coordinator	Acts as a chairperson of the team Clarifies goals, delegates clearly
	Team Worker	Encourages cooperation Perceptive, diplomatic, great listener
	Resource Investigator	Explores opportunities Outgoing, enthusiastic, networker
Thought-Oriented Roles	Plant	Generates ideas and approaches Creative, adept at problem solving
	Monitor-Evaluator	Sees all the options Assesses accurately and strategically
	Specialist	Provides specialized skills Single-minded, self-starting

Source: Pearson Canada

role
Behaviour patterns expected of someone who occupies a given position in a social unit.

2 Norms

Acceptable standards shared by a group's members. Each group has its own unique set of **norms**. Most organizations have common norms that typically focus on:

- effort and performance
  - probably the most widespread norm
  - can be extremely powerful in affecting an individual employee's performance
- dress codes (what is acceptable to wear to work)

We often adjust our behaviour to align with a group's norms. We all want to be accepted by groups to which we belong, which makes us susceptible to conformity pressures.

mogen creative/Shutterstock

3 Group Size

The size of a group affects that group's behaviour, but the effect depends on what criteria you are looking at.

Small groups (five to seven members) **are better at:**

- completing tasks faster
- figuring out what to do
- getting a job done

lantapix/shutterstock

Large groups (12 or more members) **are better at:**

- problem solving
- finding facts
- gaining diverse input

lantapix/shutterstock

Drawbacks of large groups:

Individual productivity of each group member declines as the group expands, which is known as social loafing[13]—reducing effort because dispersion of responsibility encourages individuals to slack off. When a group's results cannot be attributed to any single person, individuals may be tempted to become "free riders" and coast on the group's efforts because they think their contributions cannot be measured.

norms
Standards or expectations that are accepted and shared by a group's members.

In contrast, the challenge for management is less demanding when teams are introduced in places in which employees have strong collectivist values—such as Japan or Mexico. The challenge of forming teams will also be less in new organizations that use teams as their initial means of structuring work. For instance, Saturn Corporation (an American organization owned by General Motors) was designed around teams from its start. Everyone at Saturn was hired on the understanding that they would be working in teams, and the ability to be a good team player was a hiring prerequisite. *Diversity Matters* at the end of the chapter considers how you can help team members from different cultures work together more effectively.

Shaping Team Behaviour

Several options are available for managers who are trying to turn individuals into team players. The three most popular ways include proper selection, employee training, and rewarding the appropriate team behaviours. Let us look at each of these.

SELECTION Some individuals already possess the interpersonal skills to be effective team players. When hiring team members, in addition to checking on the technical skills required to successfully perform the job, the organization should ensure that applicants can fulfill team roles.

As we have mentioned before, some applicants have been socialized around individual contributions and, consequently, lack team skills, as might some current employees whose jobs are being restructured into teams. When faced with such candidates, a manager can do several things. First, and most obvious, if a candidate's team skills are woefully lacking, do not hire that candidate. If successful performance requires interaction, rejecting such a candidate is appropriate. On the other hand, a good candidate with only some basic team skills can be hired on a probationary basis and required to undergo training to shape him or her into a team player. If the skills are not learned or practised, the individual may have to be let go for failing to master the skills necessary for performing successfully on the job.

TRAINING Performing well in a team involves a set of behaviours. As we discussed in Chapter 9, new behaviours can be learned. Even a large portion of people who were raised on the importance of individual accomplishment can be trained to become team players. Training specialists can conduct workshops that allow employees to experience the satisfaction that teamwork can provide. The workshops usually cover such topics as team problem solving, communication, negotiation, conflict resolution, and coaching skills. It is not unusual, too, for these employees to be exposed to the five stages of team development that we discussed earlier.[14] At Verizon Communications, for example, trainers focus on how a team goes through various stages before it gels. Employees are reminded of the importance of patience, because teams take longer to do some things—such as make decisions—than do employees acting alone.[15]

REWARDS The organization's reward system needs to encourage cooperative efforts rather than competitive ones. For example, Lockheed Martin Aeronautics Company has organized its 20 000-plus employees into teams. Rewards are structured to return a percentage increase in the bottom line to the team members on the basis of achievements of the team's performance goals.

Promotions, pay raises, and other forms of recognition should be given to employees who are effective collaborative team members. Recognition of teamwork does not mean that individual contribution is ignored, but rather that it is balanced with selfless contributions to the team. Examples of behaviours that should be rewarded include training new colleagues, sharing information with teammates, helping resolve team conflicts, and mastering new skills in which the team is deficient.[16] Finally, managers cannot forget the inherent rewards that employees can receive from teamwork. Work teams provide camaraderie. It is exciting and satisfying to be an integral part of a successful team. The opportunity to engage in personal development and to help teammates grow can be a very satisfying and rewarding experience for employees.[17]

TURNING GROUPS INTO EFFECTIVE TEAMS

The Virgin Group believes that building teamwork improves the bottom line and is key to attracting and retaining good employees. Employees working together effectively understand each other's jobs and make fewer mistakes.

Employees are encouraged to develop strong friendships. Many companies discourage employees from having fun at work, becoming friends, and even falling in love. Virgin has been able to create a fun, inclusive, energetic atmosphere, and the friendships and romances formed along the way have made it a stronger company. Branson summed it up best when he said, "Some say managers should avoid forging friendships with employees because it makes letting someone go even more difficult. To me that's the point—it should hurt."[18]

Teams are not automatic productivity enhancers; they can also be disappointments. The challenge is to create effective teams. Effective teams have a number of characteristics, which we review below. In addition, teams need to build group cohesiveness, manage group conflict, and prevent social loafing to perform well. For more insights into creating effective teams, see *Developing Your Interpersonal Skills—Creating Effective Teams* at the end of the chapter.

Characteristics of Effective Teams

Research on teams provides insights into the characteristics associated with effective teams.[19] Let us look more closely at these characteristics, which are shown in Exhibit 10-4.

CLEAR GOALS High-performance teams have a clear understanding of the goals to be achieved. Members are committed to the team's goals; they know what they are expected to accomplish and understand how they will work together to achieve these goals.

RELEVANT SKILLS Effective teams are composed of competent individuals who have the necessary technical and interpersonal skills to achieve the desired goals while working well together. This last point is important, since not everyone who is technically competent has the interpersonal skills to work well as a team member.

MUTUAL TRUST Effective teams are characterized by high levels of mutual trust among members. Members believe in each other's ability, character, and integrity. But as you probably know from personal relationships, trust is fragile. For team members to have mutual trust, they must believe that the team is capable of getting the task done and that "the team will not harm the individual or his or her interests."[20] Maintaining this trust requires careful attention by managers.

PERSONAL INVENTORY ASSESSMENT

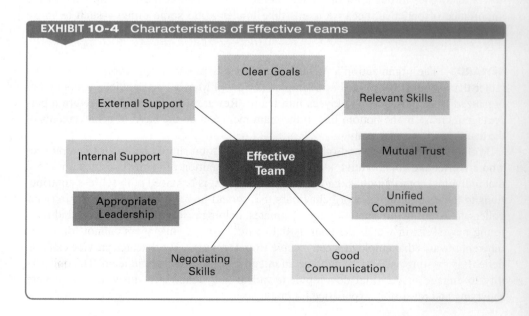

EXHIBIT 10-4 Characteristics of Effective Teams

UNIFIED COMMITMENT Unified commitment is characterized by dedication to the team's goals and a willingness to expend extraordinary amounts of energy to achieve them. Members of an effective team exhibit intense loyalty and dedication to the team and are willing to do whatever it takes to help their team succeed.

GOOD COMMUNICATION Not surprisingly, effective teams are characterized by good communication. Members convey messages, verbally and nonverbally, to each other in ways that are readily and clearly understood. Also, feedback helps to guide team members and to correct misunderstandings. Like a couple who have been together for many years, members on high-performing teams are able to quickly and efficiently share ideas and feelings.

NEGOTIATING SKILLS Effective teams are continually making adjustments as to who does what. This flexibility requires team members to possess negotiating skills. Since problems and relationships are regularly changing in teams, members need to be able to confront and reconcile differences.

APPROPRIATE LEADERSHIP Effective leaders can motivate a team to follow them through the most difficult situations. How? By clarifying goals, demonstrating that change is possible by overcoming inertia, increasing the self-confidence of team members, and helping members to more fully realize their potential. Increasingly, effective team leaders act as coaches and facilitators. They help guide and support the team but do not control it.

INTERNAL AND EXTERNAL SUPPORT The final condition necessary for an effective team is a supportive climate. Internally, the team should have a sound infrastructure, which means having proper training, a clear and reasonable measurement system that team members can use to evaluate their overall performance, an incentive program that recognizes and rewards team activities, and a supportive human resource system. The right infrastructure should support members and reinforce behaviours that lead to high levels of performance. Externally, managers should provide the team with the resources needed to get the job done.

BUILDING GROUP COHESIVENESS Intuitively, it makes sense that groups in which there is a lot of internal disagreement and lack of cooperation are less effective in completing their tasks than are groups in which members generally agree, cooperate, and like each other. Research in this area has focused on **group cohesiveness**, or the degree to which members are attracted to each other and share the group's goals. Cohesiveness is important because studies have shown it to be related to a group's productivity.[22]

Research has generally shown that highly cohesive groups are more effective than less cohesive ones.[23] However, this relationship between cohesiveness and effectiveness is more complex. A key moderating variable is the degree to which the group's attitude aligns with its goals or with the goals of the organization.[24] The more cohesive a group is, the more its members will follow its goals. If the goals are desirable (e.g., high output, quality work, cooperation with individuals outside

As Roger Fisher and William Ury explain in their book *Getting to Yes*, win–win negotiation has four rules: one, separate the people from the issue; two, focus on interests and information, not positions; three, generate numerous alternatives; and four, develop an objective standard on which to base results of the negotiation.

PERSONAL INVENTORY ASSESSMENT

Tangerine does a fantastic job of empowering employees. The bank's employees have no job titles and no offices. Anyone can talk to anyone, and leaders focus on removing obstacles instead of creating them. Its CEO welcomes feedback and input from the team, negative or positive, and employees are not policed on their collaborative environment.[21]

group cohesiveness
The degree to which group members are attracted to each other and share the group's goals.

Increasing Group Cohesiveness

Increasing socioemotional cohesiveness

❋ **Small** groups typically have better communication.

❋ Find opportunities to celebrate **achievements** and enhance **status**.

❋ **Time spent together** develops friendship and communication.

❋ Find **commonalities** between members.

❋ Build a strong and united team by focusing on **environmental threats**.

Increasing instrumental cohesiveness

❋ Make the group harder to join so members feel a sense of **initiation**.

❋ Communicate frequently about the group's **goal(s)**.

❋ Provide a higher degree of **positive dependence** between group members so they understand that they need each other.

❋ Ensure free exchange of ideas to focus each group member's special talents toward a **problem**.

❋ Recognize and equitably reinforce member **cooperation**.

PERSONAL INVENTORY ASSESSMENT

the group), a cohesive group is more productive than a less cohesive group. But if cohesiveness is high and attitudes are unfavourable, productivity decreases. If cohesiveness is low and goals are supported, productivity increases, but not as much as when both cohesiveness and support are high. When cohesiveness is low and goals are not supported, cohesiveness has no significant effect on productivity.

Most studies of cohesiveness focus on *socioemotional cohesiveness*: the "sense of togetherness that develops when individuals derive emotional satisfaction from group participation."[25] There is also *instrumental cohesiveness*: the "sense of togetherness that develops when group members are mutually dependent on one another because they believe they could not achieve the group's goal by acting separately." Teams need to achieve a balance between these two types of cohesiveness to function well. *Tips for Managers—Increasing Group Cohesiveness* indicates how to increase both socioemotional and instrumental cohesiveness.

Managing Group Conflict

Another important group process is how a group manages conflict. As a group performs its assigned tasks, disagreements inevitably arise. When we use the term **conflict**, we are referring to *perceived* differences that result in some form of interference or opposition. Whether the differences are real or not is irrelevant. If people in a group perceive that differences exist, then there is conflict. Our definition encompasses the full range of conflict—from subtle or indirect acts to overt acts such as strikes, riots, or wars.

Over the years, three different views have evolved regarding conflict.[26] One view argues that conflict must be avoided—that it indicates a problem within the group. We call this the **traditional view of conflict**. A second view, the **human relations view of conflict**, argues that conflict is a natural and inevitable outcome in any group and need not be negative but, rather, has the potential to be a positive force in contributing to a group's performance. The third and most recent perspective proposes that not only can conflict be a positive force in a group, but also that some conflict is *absolutely necessary* for a group to perform effectively. This third approach is called the **interactionist view of conflict**.

The interactionist view does not suggest that all conflicts are good. Some conflicts are seen as supporting the goals of the work group and improving its performance; these are **functional conflicts** of a constructive nature. Other conflicts are destructive and prevent a group from achieving its goals. These are **dysfunctional conflicts**. Exhibit 10-5 illustrates the challenge facing managers. They want to create an environment in which there is healthy conflict that will help the group reach a high level of performance.

What differentiates functional from dysfunctional conflict? The evidence indicates that you need to look at the *type* of conflict.[27] Three types have been identified: task, relationship, and process.

---

conflict
Perceived differences that result in some form of interference or opposition.

traditional view of conflict
The view that all conflict is bad and must be avoided.

human relations view of conflict
The view that conflict is a natural and inevitable outcome in any group and has the potential to be a positive force in contributing to a group's performance.

interactionist view of conflict
The view that some conflict is absolutely necessary for a group to perform effectively.

functional conflicts
Conflicts that support the goals of the work group and improve its performance.

dysfunctional conflicts
Conflicts that are destructive and prevent a group from achieving its goals.

EXHIBIT 10-5 Conflict and Group Performance

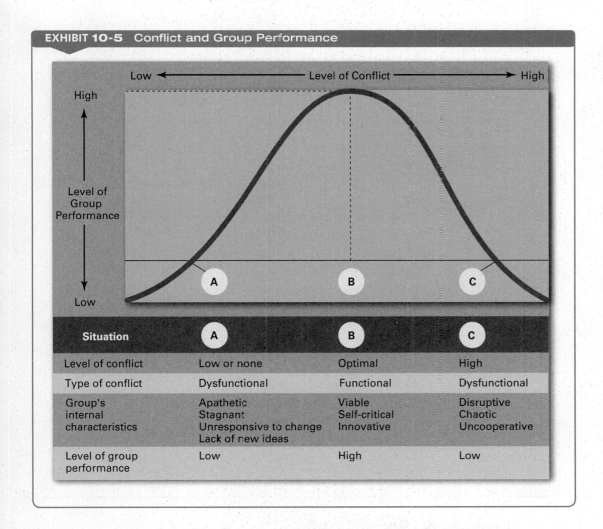

Situation	A	B	C
Level of conflict	Low or none	Optimal	High
Type of conflict	Dysfunctional	Functional	Dysfunctional
Group's internal characteristics	Apathetic Stagnant Unresponsive to change Lack of new ideas	Viable Self-critical Innovative	Disruptive Chaotic Uncooperative
Level of group performance	Low	High	Low

Task conflict relates to the content and goals of the work. **Relationship conflict** is based on interpersonal relationships. **Process conflict** relates to how the work gets done. Studies demonstrate that relationship conflicts are almost always dysfunctional. Why? It appears that the friction and interpersonal hostilities inherent in relationship conflicts increase personality clashes and decrease mutual understanding, thereby hindering the completion of organizational tasks. On the other hand, low levels of process conflict and low-to-moderate levels of task conflict are functional. For process conflict to be productive, it must be kept to a minimum. Intense arguments about who should do what become dysfunctional when they create uncertainty about task roles, increase the time taken to complete tasks, and lead to members working at cross-purposes. A low-to-moderate level of task conflict consistently demonstrates a positive effect on group performance because it stimulates discussions of ideas that help groups be more innovative.[28] Because we have yet to devise a sophisticated measuring instrument for assessing whether a given task, relationship, or process conflict level is optimal, too high, or too low, the manager must make intelligent judgments.

When group conflict becomes dysfunctional, what can managers do? Exhibit 10-6 describes five conflict resolution options: avoiding, accommodating, forcing, compromising, and collaborating.[29] Keep in mind that no one option is ideal for every situation. Which approach to use depends on the manager's desire to be more or less cooperative and more or less assertive.

task conflict	**relationship conflict**	**process conflict**
Conflict over content and goals of the work.	Conflict based on interpersonal relationships.	Conflict over how the work gets done.

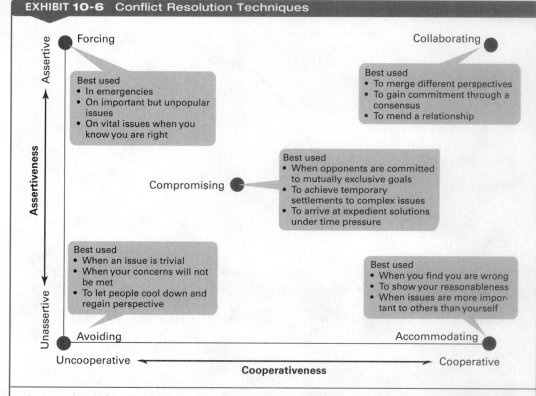

EXHIBIT 10-6 Conflict Resolution Techniques

Source: Adapted from K. W. Thomas, "Conflict and Negotiation Processes in Organizations." in Handbook of Industrial and Organizational Psychology, vol. 3, 2nd ed., ed. M D Dunnette and L. M. Hough (Palo Alto, CA: Consulting Psychologists Press, 1992), p. 668; and C. K. W De Dreu, A. Evers, B. Beersma, E. S. Kluwer, and A. Nauta, "A Theory-Based Measure of Conflict Management Strategies in the Workplace." Journal of Organizational Behaviour 22, no 6 (September 2001). pp. 645–668.

Preventing Social Loafing

One of the more important findings related to group size is **social loafing**, which is the tendency of individuals to expend less effort when working with others than when working individually.[30] Social loafing is much more likely to happen in larger groups. This finding directly challenges the logic that the group's productivity should at least equal the sum of the productivity of each group member. What causes social loafing? It may be caused by a belief that others in the group are not doing their fair share. If you see others as lazy or inept, you can re-establish equity by reducing your effort. Another explanation is the dispersion of responsibility. Because the results of the group cannot be attributed to any one person, the relationship between an individual's input and the group's output is clouded. In such situations, individuals may be tempted to become "free riders" and coast on the group's efforts. In other words, there will be a reduction in efficiency when individuals think that their contribution cannot be measured.

For managers, the implications of social loafing are significant. When managers use collective work situations to enhance morale and teamwork, they must also have a way to identify individual efforts. If this is not done, they must weigh the potential losses in productivity from using groups against any possible gains in employee satisfaction.[31]

10.4 Explain What are some of the current challenges in managing teams?

CURRENT CHALLENGES IN MANAGING TEAMS

Managers face some current challenges in managing global teams. They also have to determine when it is best to use a team.

social loafing
The tendency of individuals to expend less effort when working collectively than when working individually.

Managing Global Teams

Two characteristics of today's organizations are obvious: They are global and work is increasingly done by groups or teams. This reality means that any manager is likely, at some point in time, to have to manage a global team. What do we know about managing global teams? We know there are both drawbacks and benefits to using them.

GROUP MEMBER RESOURCES IN GLOBAL TEAMS In global organizations, understanding the relationship between group performance and group member resources is more challenging because of the unique cultural characteristics represented by members of a global team. In addition to recognizing team members' abilities, skills, knowledge, and personality, managers need to be familiar with and clearly understand the cultural characteristics of the groups and the group members they manage.[32] For example, is the global team from a culture in which uncertainty avoidance is high? If so, members will not be comfortable dealing with unpredictable and ambiguous tasks. Also, as managers work with global teams, they need to be aware of the potential for stereotyping, which has been shown to be a problem.[33]

GROUP STRUCTURE Some of the structural areas where we see differences in managing global teams include conformity, status, social loafing, and cohesiveness.

Research suggests that conformity to social norms tends to be higher in collectivist cultures than in individualistic cultures.[34] However, groupthink tends to be less of a problem in global teams because members are less likely to feel pressured to conform to the ideas, conclusions, and decisions of the group.[35]

Also, the importance of status varies among cultures. The French, for example, are extremely status conscious. Also, countries differ on the criteria that confer status. Status for Latin Americans and Asians tends to come from family position and formal roles held in organizations. In contrast, although status is important in countries such as Canada and Australia, it tends to be less "in your face" and is usually based on accomplishments rather than on titles and family history. Managers should be sure to understand who and what holds status when interacting with people from a culture different from their own. A Canadian manager who does not understand that office size is not a measure of a Japanese executive's position or who fails to grasp the importance the British place on family genealogy and social class is likely to unintentionally offend others and lessen his or her interpersonal effectiveness.

Social loafing has a Western bias and is most prevalent in individualistic cultures, such as Canada and the United States, which are dominated by self-interest. It is not consistent with collectivistic societies, in which individuals are motivated by in-group goals. In studies comparing employees from the United States with employees from the People's Republic of China and Israel (both collectivistic societies), the Chinese and Israelis did not tend to engage in social loafing. In fact, they actually performed better in a group than when working alone.[36]

Cohesiveness is another group structural element where managers may face special challenges. In a cohesive group, members are unified and "act as one." There is a great deal of camaraderie, and group identity is high. In global teams, however, cohesiveness is often more difficult to achieve because of higher levels of mistrust, miscommunication, and stress.[37]

GROUP PROCESSES The processes global teams use to do their work can be particularly challenging for managers. Communication problems often arise because not all team members may be fluent in the team's working language. This language barrier can lead to inaccuracies, misunderstandings, and inefficiencies.[38] However, research has also shown that a multicultural global team is better able to make use of the diversity of ideas represented if a wide range of information is used.[39]

Managing conflict in global teams, especially when those teams are virtual teams, is not easy. Conflict in multicultural teams can interfere with how information is used by the team. However, research shows that in collectivistic cultures, a collaborative conflict management style can be most effective.[40]

The Chinese have what is called social striving, where individual performance is improved by staying focused as a team.

Beware! Teams Are Not Always the Answer

Despite considerable success in the use of teams, they are not necessarily appropriate in all situations. Teamwork takes more time and often more resources than individual work; it has increased communication demands and an increased number of conflicts to be managed and meetings to be run. In the rush to enjoy the benefits of teams, some managers have introduced them into situations in which the work is better done by individuals. A study by Statistics Canada found that the introduction of teamwork lowered job turnover in the service industries, for both high- and low-skilled employees. However, manufacturing companies experienced higher job turnover if they introduced teamwork and formal teamwork training, compared with not doing so (15.8 percent versus 10.7 percent).[41] Exhibit 10-7 helps answer the question of whether the work of your group would be better done in teams or individually.

Researchers have outlined the conditions under which organizations would find teams more useful: "when work processes cut across functional lines; when speed is important (and complex relationships are involved); when the organization mirrors a complex, differentiated, and rapidly changing market environment; when innovation and learning have priority; when the tasks that have to be done require online integration of highly interdependent performers."[42]

EXHIBIT 10-7   Deciding When to Use Teams

Use teams if . . .
- employees buy-in on purpose
- job can't be completed unless people work together
- rewards can be provided for team performance
- ample resources and support are available
- teams have clear authority over how work gets done
- strong, unambiguous management support

Don't use teams if . . .
- individuals would prefer working alone
- the job tasks are independent or too interdependent
- rewards are more suited to individual effort and performance
- required resources are not available
- autocratic management
- rigid hierarchical organizational structure

Summary of Learning Outcomes

10.1 **What are the stages of team development?** The five stages are forming, storming, norming, performing, and adjourning. These stages describe how teams evolve over time, although teams do not necessarily go through these stages in a completely linear fashion. Some researchers argue that the effectiveness of work teams increases at advanced stages, but the reality is not that simple. The assumption may be generally true, but what makes a team effective is a complex issue. Instead, think of this model as a general framework of how teams develop.

Virgin Group uses formal recognition programs to recognize team success, helping teams bond by identifying star contributors, highlighting teams in company newsletters, and hosting parties for employees. It has created a team environment where employees from different Virgin companies collaborate to work on projects and share updates and tips.

10.2 **How do individuals become team players?** Many individuals resist being team players. To improve the odds that a team will function well, managers can select the right people to be on a team, train individuals in how to work on teams, and make sure that rewards encourage individuals to be cooperative team players.

Branson believes in leading by listening—Virgin conducts regular satisfaction surveys along with frequent informal employee meetings to ensure effective, two-way communication with employees. Employees are able to speak freely with a high level of trust. This practice has led to employees working together to provide both positive and constructive feedback.

10.3 **How can groups become effective teams?** The characteristics associated with effective teams include clear goals, relevant skills, mutual trust, unified commitment, good communication, negotiating skills, appropriate leadership, and internal and external support. To be effective, teams also need to build group cohesiveness, manage group conflict, and prevent social loafing.

Virgin also uses company awards to motivate employees to pull together. When the London office was going

through a big move, it was a hectic several months with long days and long nights preparing for the move. After the move, Branson threw a pirate-themed party to thank the group for all the hard work. They ended up on the front page of the newspaper and the event did wonders for reviving the team spirit.

10.4 **What are some of the current challenges in managing teams?** Managers face a variety of challenges in managing global teams. The cultural differences of the team members may lead to more conflict, at least initially. As well, there may be an increase in communication difficulties. Another challenge that managers face is to consider whether a team is really necessary to get the work done.

Virgin Group manages companies all over the world, with 50 000 employees. Virgin Mobile Canada employees need to communicate with employees in other countries and utilize virtual teams for marketing and pricing decisions.

SNAPSHOT SUMMARY

10.1 **Understanding Groups and Teams**
What Is a Team?
Informal Groups
Stages of Team Development

10.2 **Turning Individuals into Team Players**
The Challenges of Creating Team Players
Shaping Team Behaviour

10.3 **Turning Groups into Effective Teams**
Characteristics of Effective Teams
Managing Group Conflict
Preventing Social Loafing

10.4 **Current Challenges in Managing Teams**
Managing Global Teams
Beware! Teams Are Not Always the Answer

MyManagementLab Study, practise, and explore real management situations with these helpful resources:

- **Interactive Lesson Presentations:** Work through interactive presentations and assessments to test your knowledge of management concepts.
- **PIA (Personal Inventory Assessments):** Enhance your ability to connect with key concepts through these engaging self-reflection assessments.
- **Study Plan:** Check your understanding of chapter concepts with self-study quizzes.
- **Simulations:** Practise decision making in simulated management environments.

 PERSONAL INVENTORY ASSESSMENT

Discussion Questions

1. Contrast (1) self-managed and cross-functional teams; and (2) virtual and face-to-face teams.

2. What problems might surface in teams during each of the five stages of team development?

3. Do you believe mutual trust is important in developing high-performing work teams? Why?

4. Why might a manager want to stimulate conflict in a group or team? How could conflict be stimulated?

5. All work teams are work groups, but not all work groups are work teams. Do you agree or disagree with this statement? Discuss.

6. Would you prefer to work alone or as part of a team? Why? Support your response with data from your self-assessments.

7. Describe a situation in which individuals, acting independently, outperform teams in an organization.

Developing Management Skills

Dilemma

One of your instructors has just informed your class that you will be working on a new major assignment worth 30 percent of your course mark. The assignment is to be done in teams of seven. Realistically you will need to function as a virtual team, because each of you has a different work and class schedule so that there is almost no time when more than three people could meet face to face. As you know, virtual teams have benefits, but they can also face problems. How will you build group cohesiveness in this team? What norms might help the team function, and how should the norms be decided? What will you do to prevent social loafing?

How to manage a virtual team:

- What do we need to operate as an effective virtual team?
- What should our team start doing?
- What should our team stop doing?
- How should our team monitor our progress?
- What are our virtual team meeting protocols?
- What are our technology protocols?
- What are our roles, expectations, goals, and behaviour standards?
- How should our group manage conflict?

Developing Your Interpersonal Skills: Creating Effective Teams

ABOUT THE SKILL

A team is different from a group because its members are committed to a common purpose, have a set of specific performance

goals, and hold themselves mutually accountable for the team's results. Teams can produce outputs that are greater than the sum of the individual contributions of its members. The primary force that makes a work group an effective team—that is, a real high-performing team—is its emphasis on performance.

STEPS IN DEVELOPING THE SKILL

Managers and team leaders have a significant impact on a team's effectiveness. You can be more successful at creating an effective team if you use the following nine suggestions:[43]

1. **Establish a common purpose.** An effective team needs a common purpose to which all members aspire. This purpose is a vision and is broader than any specific goals. The common purpose provides direction, momentum, and commitment for team members.

2. **Assess team strengths and weaknesses.** Team members will have different strengths and weaknesses. Knowing these strengths and weaknesses can help the team leader build on the strengths and compensate for the weaknesses.

3. **Develop specific individual goals.** Specific individual goals help lead team members to achieve higher performance. In addition, specific goals facilitate clear communication and help maintain the focus on getting results.

4. **Get agreement on a common approach for achieving goals.** Goals are the ends a team strives to attain. Defining and agreeing on a common approach ensures the team's unity regarding the means for achieving those ends.

5. **Encourage acceptance of responsibility for both individual and team performance.** Successful teams make members individually and jointly accountable for the team's purpose, goals, and approach. Members understand

what they are individually responsible for and what they are jointly responsible for.

6. **Build mutual trust among members.** When there is trust, team members believe in the integrity, character, and ability of each other. When trust is lacking, members are unable to depend on each other. Teams that lack trust tend to be short-lived.

7. **Maintain an appropriate mix of team member skills and personalities.** Team members come to the team with different skills and personalities. To perform effectively, teams need three types of skills. First, teams need people with technical expertise. Next, they need people with problem-solving and decision-making skills to identify problems, generate alternatives, evaluate those alternatives, and make competent choices. Finally, teams need people with good interpersonal skills.

8. **Provide needed training and resources.** Team leaders need to make sure that their teams have both the training and the resources they need to accomplish their goals.

9. **Create opportunities for small achievements.** Building an effective team takes time. Team members have to learn to think and work as a team. New teams cannot be expected to hit home runs every time they come to bat, especially at the beginning. Instead, team members should be encouraged to try for small achievements first.

PRACTISING THE SKILL

You are the leader of a five-member project team that has been assigned the task of moving your engineering firm into the new booming area of high-speed rail construction. You and your team members have been researching the field, identifying specific business opportunities, negotiating alliances with equipment vendors, and evaluating high-speed rail experts and consultants from around the world.

Throughout the process, Tonya, a highly qualified and respected engineer, has challenged everything you say during team meetings and in the workplace. For example, at a meeting two weeks ago, you presented the team with a list of 10 possible high-speed rail projects that had been identified by the team and started evaluating your organization's ability to compete for them. Tonya contradicted virtually all your comments, questioned your statistics, and was quite pessimistic about the possibility of contracts. After this latest display of displeasure, two other group members, Liam and Ahmed, came to you and complained that Tonya's actions were damaging the team's effectiveness. You originally put Tonya on the team for her unique expertise and insight. What should you say to Tonya, and how can you help get the team on the right track to reach its full potential?

Diversity Matters

Understanding and managing teams composed of people who are similar can be difficult. Add in diverse members and managing teams can be even more of a challenge. However, the benefits to be gained from the diverse perspectives, skills, and abilities often more than offset the extra effort.[44] How can you meet the challenge of coordinating a diverse work team? It is

important to stress four critical interpersonal behaviours: understanding, empathy, tolerance, and communication.

You know that people are not the same, yet they need to be treated fairly and equitably. Differences (cultural, physical, or other) can cause people to behave in different ways. Team leaders need to understand and accept these differences. Each and every team member should be encouraged to do the same.

Empathy is closely related to understanding. As a team leader, you should try to understand others' perspectives.

Tolerance is another important interpersonal behaviour in managing diverse teams. Even though you understand that people are different and you empathize with them, accepting different perspectives or behaviours is not easy. But it is important to be tolerant in dealing with diverse ages, gender, and cultural backgrounds—to allow team members the freedom to be themselves. Part of being tolerant is being open-minded about different values, attitudes, and behaviours.

Finally, open communication is vital in managing a diverse team. Diversity problems may intensify if people are afraid or unwilling to openly discuss issues that concern them. Communication within a diverse team needs to be two-way. If a person wants to know whether a certain behaviour is offensive to someone else, it is best to ask. Likewise, a person who is offended by someone else's behaviour should explain his or her concerns and ask that person to stop. As long as these communication exchanges are handled in a nonthreatening, low-key, and friendly manner, they generally will have positive outcomes. Finally, it helps to have an atmosphere within the team that supports and celebrates diversity.

Put yourself in the place of an Asian woman who has joined a team of Caucasian and Hispanic men. How can you be made to feel more welcome and comfortable with the team? As the Asian woman, what could you do to help the team get along well together and also help your transition to the team?

Hey, You're the Boss Now!

As a new manager in an organization, it is quite likely you will be part of a team or even managing a team. One of the key challenges that prevent successful team collaboration and performance is social loafing, which causes members of a team working together to exert less effort than they would if they worked alone.

To avoid this tendency, here are some team considerations that must be addressed prior to embarking on a collaborative project:

- **Is a team needed?** That should always be the first question. Perhaps it's time to break up an existing work team.
- **Identifiability.** Individuals can hide in a crowd. Make individual contributions identifiable to the team frequently. Divide the tasks so that each person has his or her own individual deliverables that are easy to measure and evaluate.
- **Diversity.** Do not always pick the "star players" or "big thinkers," as they may battle for leadership. You need varying skills and abilities in a team. Studies have shown that people tend to work harder if they expect some of their colleagues to perform poorly.

- **Shared goals.** Team loyalty is higher if the team truly desires the goal. The members of the team will care more about the team's success rather than their own individual success.
- **Group size.** Keep group size to a minimum so that it is easier to account for everyone's work. The larger the group, the more each individual can hide behind its size. Amazon is known for having "two-pizza teams," which means that if two pizzas are not enough to feed the team, then the team is too large.
- **Group cohesiveness.** The members of your group should like each other and want to work together to pursue the same goals. That doesn't mean they are friends, as sometimes friends on a team can be a problem. They need to have a feeling of unity so that they do not want to slack off and let down the rest of the group.

Your Essential Management Reading List

Learning from key management experts can help you understand today's management theory and practice, how teams work, and how you can work more effectively on them. What follows is a list of some of the top books on teams:

- *How to Win Friends and Influence People*—Dale Carnegie
- *The Mentor Leader: Secrets to Building People and Teams That Win Consistently*—Tony Dungy
- *The Five Dysfunctions of a Team*—Patrick Lencioni
- *The 17 Essential Qualities of a Team Player: Becoming the Kind of Person Every Team Wants*—John Maxwell

Team Exercises

3BL: The Triple Bottom Line

Richard Branson, founder of the Virgin Group of companies, decided that an entrepreneurial approach to sustainability would be most effective if based on a team model. Branson established a charitable foundation and sought involvement from everyone working with the Virgin Group. Rather than simply write cheques to charities, Virgin employees wanted to be a true partner to charitable organizations and leverage internal operations for sustainability.

Virgin Unite was launched as an integral part of the Virgin Group rather than a charitable arm. Employees wanted it to be a way of connecting people and entrepreneurial ideas to make sustainability happen. Virgin Unite provides the means for the groups to connect with each other. Virgin employees join with leaders and workers at existing businesses who are concerned with making profit while helping people and the planet.[45]

THINKING STRATEGICALLY ABOUT 3BL

The focus on entrepreneurial sustainability is a new way of doing business, where people are willing to say "screw business as usual" and look beyond financial profit as the only driving force for companies like Virgin. How would you apply entrepreneurial sustainability to a large Canadian company like Tim Hortons? What nonprofit associations could it partner with to become more sustainable?

Be the Consultant: Conducting Effective Meetings

A team meeting can be of vital importance to the success of your academic projects. Conducting effective meetings takes diligence and practice. Here are some tips.

1. Prepare for the meeting.	• Plan the meeting carefully: Who, what, when, where, why, and how many? • Distribute the agenda and any relevant materials before the meeting. • Begin the meeting with the agenda and get all participants to agree on the items/expectations. • Review action items from previous meetings.
2. Ensure the chair is prepared.	• Vary the chairs of meetings to involve members more effectively. • Discussions and behaviours become predictable with one chair—mix it up for creativity and participation.
3. Maintain the focus.	• Encourage problem solving and explore various alternatives. • Encourage conflict of ideas, not personalities. • Do not allow any member to manipulate the agenda.
4. Establish ground rules.	• Encourage participation by all—draw out the quiet ones and quiet the talkative ones. • Stay on track and maintain momentum. • Allow people to fill different roles (harmonizers, gatekeepers, compromisers).
5. Maximize the chair's role.	• Start on time, and set clear time limits. • Use a note-taker and timekeeper as required. • The leader stimulates and controls the discussion, keeps the meeting on task, and summarizes all the points discussed. • Get feedback *during* the meeting to optimize meeting processes and norms.

6. Ensure effective decision making.	• Groups typically vote or reach consensus; consensus is more difficult and time consuming but provides the best decision making. • Summarize agreements. • Even if individuals do not agree 100 percent with the decision, they are more likely to support it (or less likely to oppose it) when their opinions have been heard. • Identify additional data needed to make decisions.
7. Clarify deliverables and next steps.	• Evaluate the meeting. • End the meeting by clarifying what happens next. • What actions need to follow, who is responsible, and by when? • Schedule the next meeting before you leave. • Follow up on action items after the meeting.

Business Cases

Whole Foods Canada

Walk in any one of the 10 Canadian Whole Foods Markets and you will see eye-popping displays of fresh and healthy food. What you may not see is the continuous innovation happening thanks to effective leadership and empowered employees working in teams. Every store features about a dozen self-directed teams who make decisions about their work units with very little management control. Each team in all 10 stores meets continuously, with each store meeting monthly as a team as well.

Team meetings are an opportunity for team members to communicate openly, solve problems, and share information. They are the backbone of the stores' operation, leading to company innovations and improvements. This promotes team accountability and reinforces the company's values. Teams compete in many ways: against their own goals for sales, growth, and productivity; against other teams in their store and also their region.[46] Whole Foods has an open-book management philosophy, right down to a radical open-salary policy. All teams can view every team's performance, as well as submit peer reviews and benchmark each other. Even with competition the teams still manage to collaborate by sharing knowledge and best practices so that all teams get better.[47]

Whole Foods teams approve new hires for full-time jobs. New recruits generally go through a temporary employment of about 30 days, after which team members vote on whether they should stay. Employees take this seriously since they receive monthly bonuses based on team performance. If the teams find ways to lower costs, they share in the savings generated.[48]

Team self-responsibility leads to employee empowerment. Whole Foods employees do not need to be supervised in order to ensure job performance. That trust leads to higher performance than could be achieved otherwise. Whole Foods views control as a way of creating the conditions that allow for self-direction. With shared values, team members develop a greater sense of responsibility from each other.[49]

Whole Foods is passionate about helping people eat well and live longer. The company wants to teach customers that healthy eating makes a difference, as does sustainable supply and caring for the planet. That message would not get through without employees who believe in it and are ambassadors of the brand. Since the employees are passionate about their jobs and believe in the company's purpose and core values, they serve customers with the same passion.[50] Teams are responsible for developing new ideas by analyzing customer feedback. This way innovation happens as a democratic process within the team, through small working improvements seeking to provide more customer value. It is not about a single genius coming up with brilliant ideas. Whole Foods believes that if an individual comes up with an idea and shares it with other members of his or her team, the team collaborates and improves upon the idea.[51]

Discussion Questions

1. Is sharing information worth the risk of revealing important information to competitors?
2. What would each of these self-directed teams need to be successful?
3. How would the way store managers manage be different in this team-based organization as opposed to other supermarkets?

Toyota Canada

The Toyota Production System (TPS) has been copied by rivals and other organizations in various industries. Lean-manufacturing experts have extolled the virtues of TPS so often that it is referred to in textbooks around the world. But for Toyota it is successful because of the company's belief in employee collaboration and teamwork. Although many companies proudly proclaim their team culture, at Toyota the endorsement seems well deserved and sincere. Teamwork is one of Toyota's core values, along with trust, continuous improvement, long-term thinking, standardization, innovation, and problem solving. In addition, four management principles (the 4P model) guide employees: problem solving, people and partners, process, and philosophy.

The idea behind these principles is that "Good Thinking Means Good Product." Another interesting detail about Toyota is its belief that efficiency alone cannot guarantee success. The company recognizes that teams of employees are more than several pairs of hands but represent *chie*—the wisdom of experience. So . . . how does Toyota's culture reflect its emphasis on teamwork?

First, individualism—a prominent value in Western culture—is deemphasized. Instead, Toyota emphasizes systems in which people and processes and products are seen as intertwined value streams. As we noted earlier, employees are trained to be problem solvers with an important responsibility to make the production system leaner and better. Next, Toyota's hiring process "weeds out" those who are not oriented to teamwork. Job applicants must not only be competent and possess technical skills, but must exhibit strong teamwork capabilities, such as the ability to trust their team, comfort in solving problems collaboratively, and motivation to achieve collective outcomes.

Next—and this should not come as a surprise—Toyota structures its work around teams. Every Toyota employee knows the Thomas Merill adage, "All of us are smarter than any of us." Teams are used not only in production but at every level and in every function. "Toyota University" illustrates its view on continual education. Job rotation is commonly used to build individual competencies that benefit the whole team.

Finally, Toyota considers employee teams to be the power centre of the organization. The leader serves the team—not the other way around. When asked whether he would feature himself in an advertisement, the former CEO of Toyota said, "No. We want to show everybody in the company. The heroes. Not one single person." At Toyota Canada, employees have long resisted attempts to unionize because they are happy. In April 2014, Unifor, Canada's largest private-sector union, withdrew its application to represent Toyota workers because it did not have sufficient support from employees. That could change in the future, but as long as Toyota continues to focus on employees, it may not.

Discussion Questions

1. Do you think Toyota has succeeded because of its team-oriented culture, or do you think it could have succeeded without it?
2. How does Toyota emphasize teamwork throughout the organization?
3. How would the way managers manage be different in this team-based organization?
4. Would you be comfortable working in such an environment as this? Why or why not?

Ontario Realty Corporation

The Ontario Realty Corporation (ORC) manages real estate for the Ontario public service. Greg Dadd was CEO when the decision was made to build up his team's abilities in delivering top-notch customer service.

Dadd held a three-day retreat for his managers to "take a look at what they wanted to accomplish at ORC, involve people in sharing information, and develop solutions that we all owned." The retreat was used to facilitate discussions on continuous improvement and involved people across every region and all functional areas. Break-out groups were used to brainstorm, look at issues from fresh perspectives, and build networks with other colleagues.

ORC made the retreat even more tactical by inviting a key client to discuss what they were looking for in customer service. The client's perspective was used as a litmus test when solutions were proposed during the retreat. Dadd was able to build a stronger team as a result of the retreat. He put together all the customer service solutions in a work plan during the retreat so that momentum was not lost and the ORC team was committed to following through.[52]

Discussion Questions

1. ORC recently merged with Infrastructure Ontario as a cost savings measure. What will that mean to this team environment?
2. Have you been on a team-building retreat? Was it successful?

CHAPTER

11 Foundations of Control

Curling Canada/Michael Burns

Curling is an iconic national pastime played by more than 1 million Canadians. In Sochi, Canada won gold in both men's and women's curling, and the men's, women's and wheelchair teams are all ranked number one in the world. During the 2014 Olympic Games, the men's and women's curling finals were two of the top five most watched events on CTV.[1]

In the mid 2000s, the Canadian Curling Association (CCA) was facing a seven-figure deficit and hired Greg Stremlaw as its new CEO in 2007. The CCA adopted a new policy governance model and began a top-down restructuring program that focused on financial controls and the association's bottom line. Stremlaw created a new business plan with clear operational objectives. The new strategies have led to a large increase in sponsorship from companies such as Tim Hortons, Ford, and Great Western Brewery.[2]

The CCA established two major financial controls that have put the association back on firm footing and helped turn the major deficit into a $2 668 725 surplus in 2013–2014. Stremlaw established a long-term financial reserve fund to protect the CCA against future financial problems and also began a curling assistance program to support the grassroots network of curling centres and member associations.

In today's competitive global marketplace, managers want their organizations to achieve high levels of performance, and one way they can do that is by searching out the best practices successful organizations are using. By comparing themselves against the best, managers look for specific performance gaps and areas for improvement—areas where better controls over the work being done are needed.

As we will see in this chapter, Greg Stremlaw understands the importance of management controls. No matter how thorough the planning, a decision may still be poorly implemented without a satisfactory control system in place. This chapter describes controls for monitoring and measuring performance. It also looks at how to create a well-designed organizational control system.

Think About It

What is organizational control? Look at the decisions Greg Stremlaw made. How did he use control to turn around the financial fortunes of the Canadian Curling Association?

11.1 **Tell** What is control?

PERSONAL INVENTORY ASSESSMENT

Control helps an organization adapt to change, discover errors, reduce costs, add value, detect opportunities, deal with complexity, and aid teamwork.

alexmillos/Shutterstock

WHAT IS CONTROL?

Both the viewing public and NASA officials were devastated by the tragic *Columbia* shuttle disaster in February 2003. Investigations of the tragedy suggest that organizational safety controls may not have been as thorough as they should have been.[3] When problems were spotted, managers might have been too quick to dismiss them as non-life-threatening, and in this situation that choice may have led to disastrous consequences. Although most managers will not face such tragic consequences if they ignore signs that something may be wrong, this example does point out the importance of control.

What is **control**? It is the process of monitoring activities to ensure that they are being accomplished as planned, and correcting any significant deviations. All managers should be involved in the control function, even if their units are performing as planned. Managers cannot really know whether their units are performing properly until they have evaluated what activities have been done and compared the actual performance with the desired standard.[4] An effective control system ensures that activities are completed in ways that lead to the attainment of the organization's goals. The criterion that determines the effectiveness of a control system is how well it facilitates goal achievement. The more a control system helps managers achieve their organization's goals, the better the system.[5]

Performance Standards

To achieve control, performance standards must exist. These standards are the specific goals created during the planning process. **Performance** is the end result of an activity. Whether that activity is hours of intense practice before a concert or race, or carrying out job responsibilities as efficiently and effectively as possible, performance is what results from that activity.

Managers are concerned with **organizational performance**—the accumulated end results of all the organization's work activities. It is a complex but important concept. Managers need to understand the factors that contribute to a high level of organizational performance. After all, they do not want (or intend) to manage their way to mediocre performance. They *want* their organizations, work units, or work groups to achieve high levels of performance, no matter what mission, strategies, or goals are being pursued.

Measures of Organizational Performance

All managers must know what organizational performance measures will give them the information they need. The most frequently used organizational performance measures include organizational productivity, organizational effectiveness, and industry and company rankings.

ORGANIZATIONAL PRODUCTIVITY **Productivity** is the overall output of goods or services produced divided by the inputs needed to generate that output. Organizations strive to be productive. They want the most goods and services produced using the least amount of inputs. Output is measured by the sales revenue an organization receives when those goods and services are sold (selling price × number sold). Input is measured by the costs of acquiring and transforming the organizational resources into the outputs.

ORGANIZATIONAL EFFECTIVENESS In Chapter 1, we defined managerial effectiveness as goal attainment. Can the same interpretation apply to organizational effectiveness? Yes, it can. **Organizational effectiveness** is a measure of how appropriate organizational

---

control
The process of monitoring activities to ensure that they are being accomplished as planned, and correcting any significant deviations.

performance
The end result of an activity.

organizational performance
The accumulated end results of all the organization's work activities.

productivity
The overall output of goods or services produced divided by the inputs needed to generate that output.

organizational effectiveness
A measure of how appropriate organizational goals are and how well an organization is achieving those goals.

goals are and how well an organization is achieving those goals. It is a common performance measure used by managers in designing strategies, work processes, and work activities, and in coordinating the work of employees.

INDUSTRY AND COMPANY RANKINGS   There is no shortage of different types of industry and company rankings. The rankings for each list are determined by specific performance measures. The companies listed in the 50 Best Employers in Canada are ranked based on answers given by managers to a leadership team survey, an employee opinion survey, and a human resource survey designed by Hewitt Associates, a compensation and benefits consultant.[7] The companies listed in the *PROFIT* 200: Canada's Fastest Growing Companies are ranked based on their percentage sales growth over the past five years. Private and publicly traded companies that are over 50 percent Canadian-owned and are headquartered in Canada nominate themselves, and then *PROFIT* editors collect further information about eligible companies.[8]

The companies listed in *Report on Business Magazine's* Top 1000 are measured by assets. They are ranked according to after-tax profits in the most recent fiscal year, excluding extraordinary gains or losses.[6]

Why Is Control Important?

Planning can be done, an organizational structure can be created to efficiently facilitate the achievement of goals, and employees can be motivated through effective leadership. Still, there is no assurance that activities are going as planned and that the goals managers are seeking are, in fact, being attained. Control is important, therefore, because it is the final link in the four management functions. Control is the only way managers know whether organizational goals are being met and, if not, the reasons why. The value of the control function lies in its relation to planning, empowering employees, and protecting the organization and workplace.

In Chapter 3 we described goals as the foundation of planning. Goals give specific direction to managers. However, just stating goals or having employees accept your goals is no guarantee that the necessary actions to accomplish those goals have been taken. As the old saying goes, "The best-laid plans often go awry."

Managing is an ongoing process, and controlling activities provides the critical link back to planning (see Exhibit 11-1). If managers did not control, they would have no way of knowing whether their goals and plans were on target and what future actions to take.

The effective manager needs to follow up to ensure that what others are supposed to do is, in fact, being done and that their goals are, in fact, being achieved.

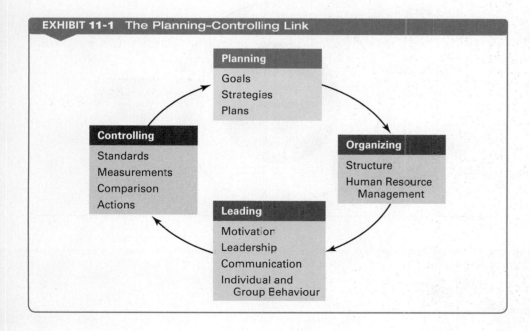

EXHIBIT 11-1   The Planning–Controlling Link

Planning
Goals
Strategies
Plans

Organizing
Structure
Human Resource Management

Leading
Motivation
Leadership
Communication
Individual and Group Behaviour

Controlling
Standards
Measurements
Comparison
Actions

Another reason control is important is employee empowerment. Many managers are reluctant to empower their employees because they fear employees will do something wrong for which the manager will be held responsible. Thus, many managers are tempted to do things themselves and avoid empowering. This reluctance, however, can be reduced if managers develop an effective control system that provides information and feedback on employee performance.

The final reason that managers control is to protect the organization and the physical workplace.[9] Given today's environment, with heightened security alerts and surprise financial scandals, managers must have plans in place to protect the organization's data, employees, and infrastructure.

<table>
<tr><td>**11.2**</td><td>**Define** What is the control process?</td></tr>
</table>

THE CONTROL PROCESS

The **control process** is a three-step process: measuring actual performance, comparing actual performance against a standard, and taking managerial action to correct deviations or inadequate standards (see Exhibit 11-2). The control process for managers is similar to what you might do as a student at the beginning of the term: set goals for yourself for studying and marks, and then evaluate your performance after midterms, determining whether you have studied enough or need to study more in order to meet whatever goals you set for your marks.

Measuring Performance

To determine what actual performance is, a manager must acquire information about it. The first step in control, then, is measuring. Let us consider how we measure and what we measure.

HOW WE MEASURE Four sources of information frequently used by managers to measure actual performance are personal observations, statistical reports, oral reports, and written reports. In the workplace, personal observation is sometimes known as management by walking around. It can provide hands-on and detailed coverage of activities, but is time consuming and distracting when it comes to employees. Reports provide a more complete data source but may suffer when it comes to interpretation and subjective factors. For most managers, using a combination of approaches increases both the number of input sources and the probability of getting reliable information.

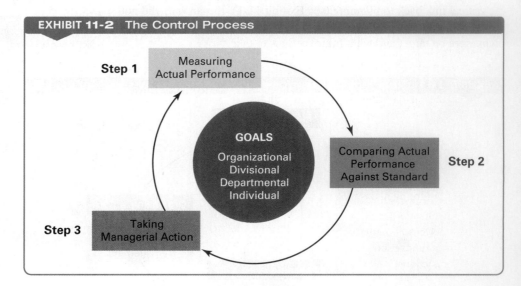

EXHIBIT 11-2 The Control Process

Step 1 — Measuring Actual Performance

GOALS — Organizational, Divisional, Departmental, Individual

Step 2 — Comparing Actual Performance Against Standard

Step 3 — Taking Managerial Action

control process
A three-step process that includes measuring actual performance, comparing actual performance against a standard, and taking managerial action to correct deviations or inadequate standards.

WHAT WE MEASURE *What* we measure is probably more critical to the control process than *how* we measure. Why? The selection of the wrong criteria can result in serious dysfunctional consequences. Besides, what we measure determines, to a great extent, what people in the organization will attempt to excel at.[10] For example, if employees are evaluated by the number of big-ticket items they sell, they may not help customers who are looking for less expensive items.

Some control criteria are applicable to any management situation. For example, because all managers, by definition, coordinate the work of others, criteria such as employee satisfaction or turnover and absenteeism rates can be measured. Most managers also have budgets set in dollar costs for their areas of responsibility. Keeping costs within budget is, therefore, a fairly common control measure. However, any control system needs to recognize the diversity of activities that managers do. A production manager at a paper tablet manufacturer might use measures such as quantity of paper tablets produced per day and per labour-hour, scrap rate, and/or percentage of rejects returned by customers. On the other hand, the manager of an administrative unit in a government agency might use the number of client requests processed per hour or the average time required to process paperwork. Marketing managers often use measures such as percentage of market held, average dollars per sale, number of customer visits per salesperson, or number of customer impressions per advertising medium.

Most jobs and activities can be expressed in tangible and measurable terms. However, when a performance indicator cannot be stated in quantifiable terms, managers should use subjective measures.

Although subjective measures have significant limitations, they are better than having no standards at all and ignoring the control function. If an activity is important, the excuse that it is difficult to measure is unacceptable.

Comparing Performance Against a Standard

The comparing step determines the degree of variation between actual performance and the standard. Although some variation in performance can be expected in all activities, it is critical to determine the acceptable **range of variation**. Deviations that exceed this range become significant and need the manager's attention. In the comparison stage, managers are particularly concerned with the size and direction of the variation. An example can help make this concept clearer.

Chris Tanner is sales manager for Beer Unlimited, a distributor of specialty beers in the Prairies. Tanner prepares a report during the first week of each month that describes sales for the previous month, classified by brand name. Exhibit 11-3 displays both the sales goal (standard) and the actual sales figures for the month of July.

Should Tanner be concerned about July's sales performance? Sales were a bit higher than originally targeted, but does that mean there were no significant deviations? Even though overall performance was generally quite favourable, he may need to examine several brands more closely. However, the number of brands that deserve attention depends on what he believes to be *significant*. How much variation should Tanner allow before corrective action is taken?

The deviation on three brands (Maple Brown Ale, Full Moon, Black Cat Lager) is very small and does not need special attention. On the other hand, are the shortages for Premium Lager and Blanche de Chambly brands significant? That is a judgment Tanner must make. Premium Lager sales were 15 percent below his goal. This deviation is significant and needs attention. He should look for a cause. In this instance, Tanner attributes the decrease to aggressive advertising and promotion programs by the big domestic producers,

Some variation may be acceptable.

range of variation
The acceptable degree of variation between actual performance and the standard.

EXHIBIT 11-3 Sales Performance Figures for July, Beer Unlimited

Brand	(number of cases)		
	Standard	Actual	Over (Under)
Premium Lager (Okanagan Spring, Vernon)	1075	913	(162)
India Pale Ale (Alexander Keith's, Halifax)	800	912	112
Maple Brown Ale (Upper Canada Brewery, Toronto)	620	622	2
Blanche de Chambly (Brasseries Unibroue, Quebec)	160	110	(50)
Full Moon (Alley Kat, Edmonton)	225	220	(5)
Black Cat Lager (Paddock Wood Brewing, Saskatoon)	80	65	(15)
Bison Blonde Lager (Agassiz, Winnipeg)	170	286	116
Total cases	**3130**	**3128**	**(2)**

Labatt and Molson Coors. Because Premium Lager is his company's number-one selling microbrew, it is most vulnerable to the promotion clout of the big domestic producers. If the decline in sales of Premium Lager is more than a temporary slump (that is, if it happens again next month), then Tanner will need to cut back on inventory stock.

An error in understating sales can be as troublesome as an overstatement. For example, is the surprising popularity of Bison Blonde Lager (up 68 percent) a one-month anomaly, or is this brand becoming more popular with customers? If the brand is increasing in popularity, Tanner will want to order more product to meet customer demand, so as not to run short and risk losing customers. Again, he will have to interpret the information and make a decision. Our Beer Unlimited example illustrates that both overvariance and undervariance in any comparison of measures may require managerial attention.

BENCHMARKING OF BEST PRACTICES We first introduced the concept of benchmarking in Chapter 3. Remember that **benchmarking** is the search for the best practices among competitors or noncompetitors that lead to their superior performance. The **benchmark** is the standard of excellence against which to measure and compare.[11] At its most fundamental level, benchmarking means learning from others.[12] As a tool for monitoring and measuring organizational performance, benchmarking can be used to help identify specific performance gaps and potential areas for improvement.[13] To ensure the company is on track, Montreal-based BouClair, a home-decorating store, benchmarks everything against past performance and also against what other leading retailers are doing. "If a particular department or category is up 40 percent in sales over last year but we said we expected it to grow at 60 percent, then we are going to investigate and find out why," Gerry Goldberg, president and CEO, says.[14] "Then we look at our own same-store sales increases and compare them to the best companies out there. That's how we measure our efficiency and our productivity."

Managers should not look just at external organizations for best practices. It is also important for them to look inside their own organization for best practices that can be shared. Research shows that best practices frequently already exist within an organization but usually go unidentified and unused.[15] In today's environment, organizations striving for high performance levels cannot afford to ignore such potentially valuable information. Some companies have already recognized the potential of internally benchmarking best practices as a tool for monitoring and

An organization can benchmark almost anything.

benchmarking
The search for the best practices among competitors or noncompetitors that lead to their superior performance.

benchmark
The standard of excellence against which to measure and compare.

> **EXHIBIT 11-4   Steps to Successfully Implement an Internal Benchmarking Best-Practices Program**
>
> 1. *Connect best practices to strategies and goals.* The organization's strategies and goals should dictate what types of best practices might be most valuable to others in the organization.
> 2. *Identify best practices throughout the organization.* Organizations must have a way to find out what practices have been successful in different work areas and units.
> 3. *Develop best-practices reward and recognition systems.* Individuals must be given an incentive to share their knowledge. The reward system should be built into the organization's culture.
> 4. *Communicate best practices throughout the organization.* Once best practices have been identified, that information needs to be shared with others in the organization.
> 5. *Create a best-practices knowledge-sharing system.* There needs to be a formal mechanism for organizational members to continue sharing their ideas and best practices.
> 6. *Nurture best practices on an ongoing basis.* Create an organizational culture that reinforces a "we can learn from everyone" attitude and emphasizes sharing information.
>
> *Source:* Based on T. Leahy, "Extracting Diamonds in the Rough," *Business Finance.* August 2000, pp. 33–37.

measuring performance. For example, to improve diversity within the company, Saskatoon, Saskatchewan–based Yanke Group, a trucking company, is committed to hiring First Nations and people with disabilities. Yanke reviews its employment equity benchmarks quarterly.[16] Toyota Motor Corporation developed a suggestion-screening system to prioritize best practices based on potential impact, benefits, and difficulty of implementation. General Motors sends employees—from upper management to line employees—to different plants, where they learn about internal and external best practices.[17] Exhibit 11-4 provides a summary of what managers must do to implement an internal benchmarking best-practices program.

Taking Managerial Action

The third and final step in the control process is taking managerial action. Managers can choose among three possible courses of action: They can do nothing; they can correct the actual performance; or they can revise the standard. Because "doing nothing" is fairly self-explanatory, let us look more closely at the other two options.

CORRECT ACTUAL PERFORMANCE   If the source of the performance variation is unsatisfactory work, the manager will want to take corrective action. Examples of such corrective action might include changing strategy, structure, compensation practices, or training programs; redesigning jobs; or firing employees.

A manager who decides to correct actual performance has to make another decision: Should immediate or basic corrective action be taken? **Immediate corrective action** corrects problems at once to get performance back on track. **Basic corrective action** looks at how and why performance has deviated and then proceeds to correct the source of deviation. It is not unusual for managers to rationalize that they do not have the time to take basic corrective action and therefore must be content to perpetually "put out fires" with immediate corrective action. Effective managers, however, analyze deviations and, when the benefits justify it, take the time to pinpoint and correct the causes of variance.

Cultura Creative/Alamy

Toronto-based Celestica redesigned its manufacturing process to cut waste. It did so by watching how factory workers carried out their duties, and then designing more efficient processes. Workers at its Monterrey, Mexico, plant "reduced equipment setup time by 85 percent, shortened time between receiving an order and shipping it by 71 percent, reduced floor space used by 34 percent, reduced consumables by 25 percent, reduced scrap by 66 percent and reduced the investment in surface-mount technology (SMT) lines by 49 percent."[18]

---

immediate corrective action
Corrective action that corrects problems at once to get performance back on track.

basic corrective action
Corrective action that looks at how and why performance deviated and then proceeds to correct the source of deviation.

To return to our Beer Unlimited example, taking immediate corrective action on the negative variance for Premium Lager, Chris Tanner might contact the company's retailers and have them immediately drop the price on Premium Lager by 5 percent. However, taking basic corrective action would involve more in-depth analysis by Tanner. After assessing how and why sales deviated, he might choose to increase in-store promotional efforts, increase the advertising budget for this brand, or reduce future purchases from the brewery. The action Tanner takes will depend on the assessment of the brand's potential profitability.

REVISE THE STANDARD   Possibly the variance was a result of an unrealistic standard—the goal may have been too high or too low. In such instances, the standard needs corrective attention, not the performance. For example, if individuals are exceeding the standard or have no difficulty meeting the standard, perhaps the standard should be raised. In our example, Chris Tanner might need to raise the sales goal (standard) for Bison Blonde Lager to reflect its growing popularity, at 116 cases higher than anticipated.

The more troublesome problem is revising a performance standard downward. If an employee, work team, or work unit falls significantly short of reaching its goal, their natural response is to shift the blame for the variance to the goal. For example, students who make a low grade on a test often attack the grade cut-off standards as too high. Rather than acknowledge that their performance was inadequate, students argue that the standards are unreasonable. Similarly, salespeople who fail to meet their monthly quotas may attribute the failures to unrealistic quotas. It may be true that when a standard is too high it can result in a significant variation and may even contribute to demotivating those employees being measured. But keep in mind that if employees or managers do not meet the standard, the first thing they are likely to attack is the standard. If you believe that the standard is realistic, fair, and achievable, hold your ground. Explain your position; reaffirm to the employee, team, or unit that you expect future performance to improve; and then take the necessary corrective action to turn that expectation into reality.

Summary of Managerial Decisions

Exhibit 11-5 summarizes the manager's decisions in the control process. Standards evolve out of goals that are developed during the planning process. These goals provide the basis for the control process, which is essentially a continuous flow between measuring,

EXHIBIT 11-5   Managerial Decisions in the Control Process

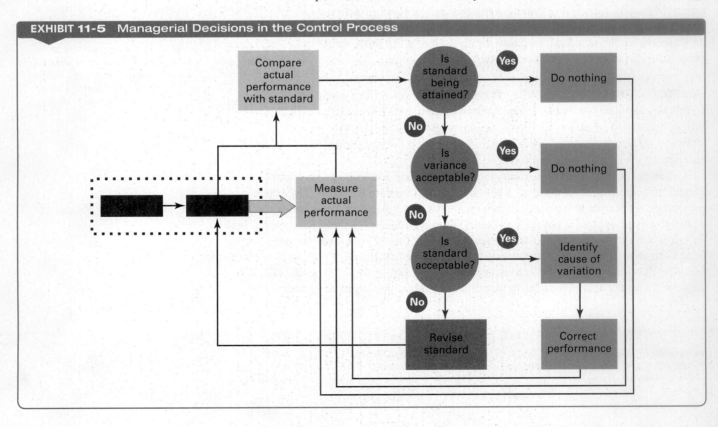

comparing, and taking managerial action. Depending on the results of comparing, a manager's decision about what course of action to take might be to do nothing, revise the standard, or correct the performance.

WHEN TO INTRODUCE CONTROL

11.3 Describe When should controls be introduced?

Managers can implement controls *before* an activity begins, *during* the time the activity is going on, or *after* the activity has been completed. The first type is called *feedforward control*, the second is *concurrent control*, and the last is *feedback control* (see Exhibit 11-6).

Feedforward Control

The most desirable type of control—**feedforward control**—prevents anticipated problems since it takes place before the actual activity.[19] Let us look at some examples of feedforward control.

When McDonald's Canada opened its first restaurant in Moscow, it sent company quality control experts to help Russian farmers learn techniques for growing high-quality potatoes and to help bakers learn processes for baking high-quality breads. Why? Because McDonald's strongly emphasizes product quality no matter what the geographical location. It wants a cheeseburger in Moscow to taste like one in Winnipeg. Still another example of feedforward control is the scheduled preventive maintenance programs on aircraft done by airlines. These programs are designed to detect and prevent structural damage that might lead to an accident.

The key to feedforward controls is taking managerial action *before* a problem occurs. Feedforward controls are desirable because they allow managers to prevent problems rather than having to correct them later after the damage (such as poor-quality products, lost customers, lost revenue, and so forth) has already been done. Unfortunately, these controls require timely and accurate information that often is difficult to obtain. As a result, managers frequently end up using the other two types of control.

Concurrent Control

Concurrent control, as its name implies, takes place while an activity is in progress. When control is enacted while the work is being performed, management can correct problems before they become too costly.

The best-known form of concurrent control is direct supervision. When managers use **management by walking around**, a term used to describe a manager who is out in the work area and interacting directly with employees, they are using concurrent control. When a

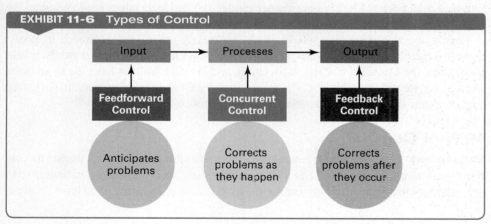

EXHIBIT 11-6 Types of Control

Input	Processes	Output
Feedforward Control	Concurrent Control	Feedback Control
Anticipates problems	Corrects problems as they happen	Corrects problems after they occur

---

feedforward control
A type of control that focuses on preventing anticipated problems, since it takes place before the actual activity.

concurrent control
A type of control that takes place while an activity is in progress.

management by walking around
A term used to describe a manager who is out in the work area and interacting directly with employees.

manager directly oversees the actions of employees, he or she can monitor their actions and correct problems as they occur. Although, obviously, some delay occurs between the activity and the manager's corrective response, the delay is minimal. Problems usually can be addressed before much resource waste or damage has been done. Also, technical equipment (computers, computerized machine controls, and so forth) can be programmed for concurrent controls. You may have experienced concurrent control when using a computer program such as word-processing software that alerts you to misspelled words or incorrect grammatical usage as you type. In addition, many organizational quality programs rely on concurrent controls to inform employees if their work output is of sufficient quality to meet standards.

Feedback Control

The most popular type of control relies on feedback. In **feedback control**, the control takes place *after* the activity is done. For example, when McDonald's executives learned that a suspected criminal ring had allegedly stolen millions of dollars in top prizes in their customer games, the theft was discovered through feedback control.[20] Even though the company took corrective action once the problem was discovered, the damage had already occurred.

As the McDonald's example shows, the major drawback of this type of control is that by the time the manager has the information, the problems have already occurred—leading to waste or damage. But for many activities, feedback is the only viable type of control available. Financial statements are an example of feedback controls. If, for example, the income statement shows that sales revenues are declining, the decline has already occurred. At this point, the manager's only option is to try to determine why sales have decreased and to correct the situation.

Feedback controls have two advantages.[21] First, feedback provides managers with meaningful information on how effective their planning efforts were. Feedback that indicates little variance between standard and actual performance is evidence that the planning was generally on target. If the deviation is significant, a manager can use that information when formulating new plans to make them more effective. Second, feedback control can enhance employee motivation. People want information on how well they have performed, and feedback control provides that information. However, managers should be aware of recent research that suggests individuals raise their goals when they receive positive feedback but lower their goals when they receive negative feedback.[22] (To learn how to give feedback effectively, see *Developing Management Skills* at the end of the chapter.)

11.4 Explain What methods of control do managers use?

METHODS OF CONTROL

The Canadian Curling Association implemented a new corporate governance structure. It followed John Carver's Policy Governance model of board leadership, which required the CCA to be governed in an organized, planned, and highly disciplined manner.[23]

Ideally, every organization would like to efficiently and effectively reach its goals. Does this mean the control systems organizations use are identical? In other words, would Matsushita, the Canadian Curling Association, and WestJet Airlines have the same types of control systems? Probably not. There are generally three main approaches to designing control systems: market, bureaucratic, and clan controls (see Exhibit 11-7).[24]

Market Control

Market control is an approach to control that emphasizes the use of external market mechanisms, such as price competition and relative market share, to establish the standards used in the control system. Organizations that use the market control approach often have divisions

---

feedback control
A type of control that takes place after a work activity is done.

market control
An approach to control that emphasizes the use of external market mechanisms, such as price competition and relative market share, to establish the standards used in the control system.

EXHIBIT 11-7 Characteristics of Three Approaches to Designing Control Systems	
Type of Control	Characteristics
Market	Uses external market mechanisms, such as price competition and relative market share, to establish standards used in the system. Typically used by organizations whose products or services are clearly specified and distinct and that face considerable marketplace competition.
Bureaucratic	Emphasizes organizational authority. Relies on administrative and hierarchical mechanisms, such as rules, regulations, procedures, policies, standardization of activities, well-defined job descriptions, and budgets to ensure that employees exhibit appropriate behaviours and meet performance standards.
Clan	Regulates employee behaviour by the shared values, norms, traditions, rituals, beliefs, and other aspects of the organization's culture. Often used by organizations in which teams are common and technology is changing rapidly.

set up as profit centres and evaluated by the percentage of total corporate profits contributed. For instance, at Japan's Matsushita, which supplies a wide range of products throughout the world, the various divisions (audiovisual and communication networks, components and devices, home appliances, and industrial equipment) are evaluated according to the profit each generates.

Bureaucratic Control

Another approach to control is **bureaucratic control**, which emphasizes organizational authority and relies on administrative rules, regulations, procedures, and policies. The CCA provides a good example of bureaucratic control. The achievement of financial profit is part of the culture at the nonprofit association. The mandate is slightly different than for a corporation, however, because all the money CCA generates is fed back into the sport of curling. Greg Stremlaw is given freedom to run the association as he sees fit, but the board governance model expects him to adhere closely to budgets and to stay within corporate guidelines.

Clan Control

Clan control is an approach to control in which employee behaviour is regulated by the shared values, norms, traditions, rituals, beliefs, and other aspects of the organization's culture. While market control relies on external standards and bureaucratic control is based on strict hierarchical mechanisms, clan control is dependent on the individuals and the groups in the organization (the clan) to identify appropriate and expected behaviours and performance measures. At Calgary-based WestJet Airlines, individuals are well aware of the expectations regarding appropriate work behaviour and performance standards, and employees are encouraged to keep costs low.[25]

Most organizations do not rely totally on just one of these approaches to design an appropriate control system. Instead, they choose to emphasize either bureaucratic or clan control, and then add some market control measures. The key is to design an appropriate control system that helps the organization efficiently and effectively reach its goals. We consider clan culture in more detail than the other types of control systems because it provides control that is both more flexible and more enduring than either market or bureaucratic control. As we mentioned earlier, clan control is regulated by organizational culture. When employees are guided by a strong set of organizational values and norms, they can be empowered to make decisions that will benefit the organization in the long run.

bureaucratic control
An approach to control that emphasizes organizational authority and relies on administrative rules, regulations, procedures, and policies.

clan control
An approach to control in which employee behaviour is regulated by the shared values, norms, traditions, rituals, beliefs, and other aspects of the organization's culture.

KEEPING TRACK: What Gets Controlled?

Countless activities are taking place in different organizational locations and functional areas.

11.5 **Explain** How do financial and information controls help managers monitor performance?

1 Keeping Track of an Organization's Finances

Want to earn a profit?
You need financial controls.
Traditional financial controls include:

- **Ratio analysis** (see Exhibit 11-8). Ratios are calculated using selected information from the organization's balance sheet and income statement.

Ekaterina Tarasenkov/Fotolia

EXHIBIT 11-8 Popular Financial Ratios

Objective	Ratio	Calculation	Meaning
Liquidity ratios: measure an organization's ability to meet its current debt obligations	Current ratio	$\dfrac{\text{Current Assets}}{\text{Current liabilities}}$	Tests the organization's ability to meet short-term obligations
	Acid test	$\dfrac{\text{Current assets} - \text{Inventories}}{\text{Current liabilities}}$	Tests liquidity more accurately when inventories turn over slowly or are difficult to sell
Leverage ratios: examine the organization's use of debt to finance its assets and whether it's able to meet the interest payments on the debt	Debt to assets	$\dfrac{\text{Total debt}}{\text{Total assets}}$	The higher the ratio, the more leveraged the organization
	Times interest earned	$\dfrac{\text{Profits before interest and taxes}}{\text{Total interest changes}}$	Measures how many times the organization is able to cover its interest expenses
Activity ratios: assess how efficiently a company is using its assets	Inventory turnover	$\dfrac{\text{Sales}}{\text{Inventory}}$	The higher the ratio, the more efficiently inventory assets are being used
	Total asset turnover	$\dfrac{\text{Sales}}{\text{Total assets}}$	The fewer assets used to achieve a given level of sales, the more efficiently management is using the organization's total assets
Profitability ratios: measure how efficiently and effectively the company is using its assets to generate profits	Profit margin on sales	$\dfrac{\text{Net profit after taxes}}{\text{Total sales}}$	Identifies the profits that are being generated
	Return on investment	$\dfrac{\text{Net profit after taxes}}{\text{Total assets}}$	Measures the efficiency of assets to generate profits

- **Budget analysis.** Budgets are used for both planning and controlling.
  - **Planning tool:** Indicates which work activities are important and what and how much resources should be allocated to those activities.
  - **Controlling tool:** Provides managers with quantitative standards against which to measure and compare resource consumption. Significant deviations require action, and the manager examines what has happened and why and then takes necessary action.

Economic value added (EVA) is a tool that measures corporate and divisional performance.

EVA = after-tax operating profit minus the total annual cost of capital.[26]

- As a performance control tool, EVA focuses managers' attention on earning a rate of return over and above the cost of capital.

- About 30 percent of Canadian companies use EVA, including Montreal-based Rio Tinto Alcan; Montreal-based Domtar; Markham, Ontario—based Robin Hood Multifoods; and Montreal-based cable company Cogeco.[27]

- When EVA is used as a performance measure, employees soon learn that they can improve their organization's or business unit's EVA either by using less capital (figuring out how to spend less) or by investing capital in high-return projects (projects that will bring in more money, with fewer expenses).

Market value added (MVA) adds a market dimension. It is a tool that measures the stock market's estimate of the value of a firm's past and expected capital investment projects.

- If the company's market value (value of all outstanding stock plus the company's debt) is greater than all the capital invested in it (from shareholders, bondholders, and retained earnings), it has a positive MVA.

- If the company's market value is less than all the capital invested in it, the MVA will be negative, indicating that managers have destroyed wealth.

- Studies have shown that EVA is a predictor of MVA and that consecutive years of positive EVA generally lead to a high MVA.[28]

economic value added (EVA)
A financial tool that measures corporate and divisional performance; calculated by taking after-tax operating profit minus the total annual cost of capital.

market value added (MVA)
A financial tool that measures the stock market's estimate of the value of a firm's past and expected capital investment projects.

2 Keeping Track of an Organization's Information

A **Information**—*a critical tool for controlling other organizational activities.*

WHY Managers need the **RIGHT INFORMATION** at the **RIGHT TIME** and in the **RIGHT AMOUNT** to help them monitor and measure organizational activities:

- about what is happening within their area of responsibility

- about the standards to be able to compare actual performance with the standard

- to help them determine if deviations are acceptable

- to help them develop appropriate courses of action

Morenina/Shutterstock

Information is important.

HOW? A **MANAGEMENT INFORMATION SYSTEM** (MIS):

- can be manual or computer based, although most organizational MIS are computer-supported applications

- implies order, arrangement, and purpose

- focuses specifically on providing managers with information (processed and analyzed data), not merely data (raw, unanalyzed facts)

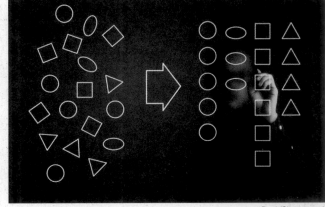

Dusit/Shutterstock

management information system (MIS)
A system used to provide management with needed information on a regular basis.

3 Keeping Track of **Employee Performance**

- Are employees doing their jobs as planned and meeting goals that have been set?

- If not, employee counselling or employee discipline may be needed.

Mike Charles/Shutterstock

4 Keeping Track Using a **Balanced Scorecard Approach**

A balanced scorecard approach looks at more than the financial perspective by typically looking at four areas that contribute to a company's performance:

1. financial
2. customer
3. internal processes
4. people/innovation/growth assets

Sharifulin Valery Itar-Tass Photos/Newscom

luna2631/Fotolia

11.6 Explain What are some current issues in control?

FINANCIAL AND INFORMATION CONTROLS

The Canadian Curling Association had a deficit of more than $1 million in the mid 2000s. Thanks to the introduction of financial and information controls as part of a governance overhaul, the CCA had a $2 668 725 surplus in 2013–2014.

One of the primary purposes of every business is to earn a profit. To achieve this goal, managers need financial controls and accurate information. Managers might, for example, carefully analyze quarterly income statements for excessive expenses. They might also perform several financial ratio tests to ensure that sufficient cash is available to pay ongoing expenses, debt levels have not risen too high, and assets are being used productively. Or they might look at newer financial control tools such as EVA (economic value added) to see if the company is creating economic value. Managers can control information and use it to control other organizational activities.

CURRENT ISSUES IN CONTROL

The Canadian Curling Association, like virtually all nonprofit organizations, has a board of directors that looks after the interests of members. In recent years, corporate governance has come under scrutiny because of corporate scandals. Many boards were not overseeing management as well as they might have.

The CCA used Carver's Policy Governance model to strengthen its board policies in recent years. The primary duty of the CCA board is to "approve, monitor and provide guidance on the strategic planning process." While the president and CEO and senior management team create the strategic plan, the board has to review and approve it. The board's role also includes identifying the principal risks of the CCA's business and managing and monitoring these risks, as well as approving the CCA's strategic plans, annual budget, and financial plans.

Control is an important managerial function. What types of control issues do today's managers face? We look at five: balanced scorecard, corporate governance, cross-cultural differences, and workplace concerns.

The employees of Tempe, Arizona–based Integrated Information Systems thought there was nothing wrong with exchanging copyrighted digital music over a dedicated office server they had set up. Like office betting on college basketball games, it was technically illegal, but harmless—or so they thought. But after the company had to pay a $1.5 million settlement to the Recording Industry Association of America, managers wished they had controlled the situation better.³⁰

VRD/Fotolia

Balanced Scorecard

The balanced scorecard approach to performance measurement was introduced as a way to evaluate organizational performance from more than just the financial perspective.³¹ The **balanced scorecard** is a performance measurement tool that examines four areas that contribute to an organization's performance: financial, customer, internal business process, and learning and growth assets. Exhibit 11-9 illustrates how the balanced scorecard is measured. The financial area looks at activities that improve the short- and long-term performance of the organization. The customer area looks at the customer's view of the organization, whether customers return, and whether they are satisfied. The internal business process looks at how production and operations, such as order fulfillment, are carried out. The learning and growth area looks at how well the company's employees are being managed for the company's future.

According to this approach, managers should develop goals in each of the four areas and then measure to determine if these goals are being met. For example, a company might include cash flow, quarterly sales growth, and return on investment (ROI) as measures for success in the

balanced scorecard
A performance measurement tool that looks at four areas that contribute to an organization's performance: financial, customer, internal business process, and learning and growth assets.

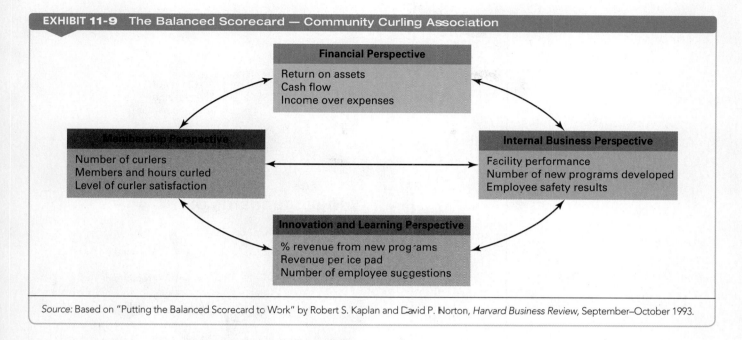

EXHIBIT 11-9 The Balanced Scorecard — Community Curling Association

Financial Perspective
Return on assets
Cash flow
Income over expenses

Membership Perspective
Number of curlers
Members and hours curled
Level of curler satisfaction

Internal Business Perspective
Facility performance
Number of new programs developed
Employee safety results

Innovation and Learning Perspective
% revenue from new programs
Revenue per ice pad
Number of employee suggestions

Source: Based on "Putting the Balanced Scorecard to Work" by Robert S. Kaplan and David P. Norton, *Harvard Business Review*, September–October 1993.

financial area. It might include percentage of sales coming from new products as a measure of customer goals. It might include dollars spent toward training, or number of courses taken by employees, as a measure of learning and growth. The intent of the balanced scorecard is to emphasize that all of these areas are important to an organization's success and that there should be a balance among them.

Although a balanced scorecard makes sense, managers still tend to focus on areas that drive their organization's success.[32] Their scorecards reflect their strategies. If those strategies centre on the customer, for example, then the customer area is likely to get more attention than the other three areas. Yet you really cannot focus on measuring only one performance area because, ultimately, other performance areas will be affected.

Many companies are starting to use the balanced scorecard as a control mechanism, including Bell Canada, British Airways, and Hilton Hotels. The Ontario Hospital Association uses a scorecard for 89 hospitals that is designed to evaluate four main areas: clinical use and outcomes, financial performance and financial condition of the hospital, patient satisfaction and how the hospital is investing for the future. The scorecard is purposefully designed to recognize the synergies among each of these measures. After hospitals are evaluated on the scorecard measures, the results of the scorecard evaluations are made available to patients, giving them an objective basis for choosing a hospital. The association provides the reports on its website.[33]

Corporate Governance

Although Andrew Fastow, Enron's former chief financial officer, had an engaging and persuasive personality, that still does not explain why Enron's board of directors failed to raise even minimal concerns about management's questionable accounting practices. The board even allowed Fastow to set up off-balance-sheet partnerships for his own profit at the expense of Enron's shareholders.

Corporate governance, the system used to govern a corporation so that the interests of corporate owners are protected, failed abysmally at Enron, as it did at many of the other companies caught in recent financial scandals. In the aftermath of these scandals, there have been increased calls for better corporate governance. Two areas in which corporate governance is being reformed are the role of boards of directors and financial reporting. The concern over corporate governance exists in Canada and globally.[34] For example, 75 percent of

corporate governance
The system used to govern a corporation so that the interests of corporate owners are protected.

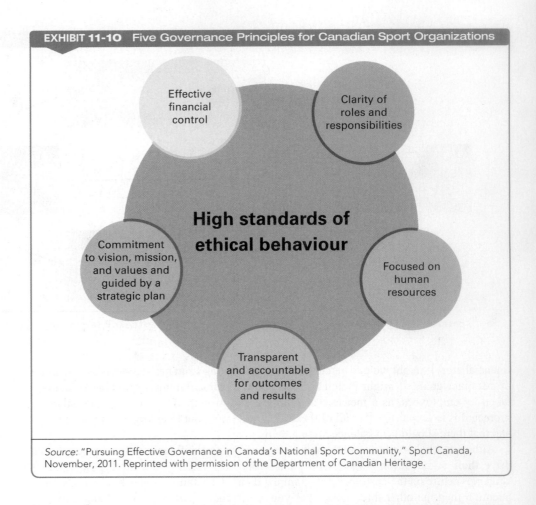

EXHIBIT 11-10 Five Governance Principles for Canadian Sport Organizations

High standards of ethical behaviour

Effective financial control

Clarity of roles and responsibilities

Commitment to vision, mission, and values and guided by a strategic plan

Focused on human resources

Transparent and accountable for outcomes and results

Source: "Pursuing Effective Governance in Canada's National Sport Community," Sport Canada, November, 2011. Reprinted with permission of the Department of Canadian Heritage.

senior executives at U.S. and Western European corporations expect their boards of directors to take a more active role in improving corporate governance.[35]

THE ROLE OF BOARDS OF DIRECTORS The original purpose of a board of directors was to have a group, independent from management, looking out for the interests of shareholders who, because of the corporate structure, were not involved in the day-to-day management of the organization. However, it has not always worked that way in practice. Board members often enjoy a cozy relationship with managers in which board members "take care" of the CEO and the CEO "takes care" of the board members.

This quid pro quo arrangement is changing. In the United States, since the passage of the *Sarbanes-Oxley Act* in 2002, demands on board members of publicly traded companies in the United States have increased considerably.[36] The Canadian Securities Administrators rules, which came into effect in March 2004, strive to tighten board responsibility somewhat, though these rules are not as stringent as those developed in the United States. To help sport organizations govern their affairs more effectively, Sport Canada developed five governance principles for Canadian sport organizations (see Exhibit 11-10 for a list of five governance principles).[37]

FINANCIAL REPORTING In addition to expanding the role of boards of directors, the Canadian Securities Administrators rules require more financial disclosure by organizations but, unlike the *Sarbanes-Oxley Act* of the United States, do not require senior managers to provide a qualitative assessment of an organization's internal compliance control. Still, these types of changes should lead to somewhat better information—information that is more accurate and reflective of the firm's financial condition.

These types of changes should lead to somewhat better information—information that is more accurate and reflective of the firm's financial condition.

Comugnero Silvana/Fotolia

Cross-Cultural Differences

The concepts of control that we have discussed so far are appropriate for an organization whose units are not geographically separated or culturally distinct. But what about global organizations? Will control systems be different, and what should managers know about adjusting controls for cross-cultural differences?

Methods of controlling people and work can be quite different in different countries. The differences we see in organizational control systems of global organizations are primarily in the measurement and corrective action steps of the control process. In a global corporation, managers of foreign operations tend to be less directly controlled by the home office, if for no other reason than that distance keeps managers from being able to observe work directly. Because distance creates a tendency to formalize controls, the home office of a global company often relies on extensive formal reports for control. The global company may also use the power of information technology to control work activities. For instance, the Japanese-based retailer Seven & i Holdings, which owns the 7-Eleven convenience store chain, uses automated cash registers not only to record sales and monitor inventory, but also to schedule tasks for store managers and to track managers' use of the built-in analytical graphs and forecasts. If managers do not use them enough, they are told to increase their activities.[38]

Technology's impact on control is most evident in comparisons of technologically advanced nations with those that are less technologically advanced. In Canada, global-minded managers use indirect control devices—especially computer-generated reports and analyses—in addition to standardized rules and direct supervision to ensure that work activities are going as planned. In less technologically advanced countries, managers tend to rely more on direct supervision and highly centralized decision making as means of control.

Also, constraints on what corrective actions managers can take may affect managers in foreign countries, because laws in some countries do not allow managers the option of closing facilities, laying off employees, taking money out of the country, or bringing in a new management team from outside the country.

Finally, another challenge for global companies in collecting data for measurement and comparison is comparability. For instance, a company's manufacturing facility in Mexico might produce the same products as a facility in Scotland. However, the Mexican facility might be much more labour intensive than its Scottish counterpart (to take strategic advantage of lower labour costs in Mexico). If the top-level executives were to control costs by, for example, calculating labour costs per unit or output per employee, the figures would not be comparable. Global managers must address these types of control challenges.

Workplace Concerns

Today's workplace presents considerable control challenges for managers. From monitoring employees' computer use at work to protecting the workplace from disgruntled employees, managers must control the workplace to ensure that the organization's work can be carried out efficiently and effectively as planned. In this section, we look at two major workplace concerns: workplace privacy and employee theft.

WORKPLACE PRIVACY If you work, do you think you have a right to privacy at your workplace? What can your employer find out about you and your work? You might be surprised by the answers!

Employers can (and do), among other things, read your email (even those marked "personal" or "confidential"), tap your smartphone, monitor your computer screen, store and review computer files, and monitor you in an employee washroom or dressing room. These actions are not all that uncommon. Nearly 57 percent of Canadian companies have Internet-use policies restricting employees' personal use of the Internet.[39] Employees of the City of Vancouver are warned that their computer use is monitored, and a desktop agent icon of a spinning head reminds them that they are being watched.

PERSONAL INVENTORY ASSESSMENT

Why do managers feel they must monitor what employees are doing? A big reason is that employees are hired to work, not accessing social media, placing bets at online casinos, or shopping for presents for family or friends. An Ipsos-Reid poll found Canadians spend 1.6 billion hours a year online at work for personal reasons, an average of 4.5 hours a week per employee.[40] That lost time represents a significant cost to businesses. Conservative estimates suggest that personal use of the Internet at work costs Canadian businesses more than $16 billion annually in lost productivity.[41]

Another reason that managers monitor employee email and computer use is that they do not want to risk being sued for creating a hostile workplace environment because of offensive messages or an inappropriate image displayed on a coworker's computer screen. Concern about racial or sexual harassment is one of the reasons why companies might want to monitor or keep backup copies of all email. This electronic record can help establish what actually happened and can help managers react quickly.[42]

Finally, managers want to ensure that company secrets are not being leaked.[43] Although protecting intellectual property is important for all businesses, it is especially important in high-tech industries. Managers need to be certain that employees are not, even inadvertently, passing information on to others who could use that information to harm the company.

Even with the workplace monitoring that managers can do, Canadian employees do have some protection through the Criminal Code, which prohibits unauthorized interception of electronic communication. The *Personal Information Protection and Electronic Documents Act*, which went into effect in early 2004, gives employees some privacy protection, but it does not make workplace electronic monitoring illegal. Under existing laws, if an individual is aware of a corporate policy of surveillance and does not formally object, or remains at the job, the monitoring is acceptable.[44] Unionized employees may have a bit more privacy with respect to their computers. The Canada Labour Code requires employers operating under a collective agreement to disclose information about plans for technological change. This information might provide unions with an opportunity to bargain over electronic surveillance.

Because of the potentially serious costs, and given the fact that many jobs now entail work that involves using a computer, many companies are developing and enforcing workplace monitoring policies. The responsibility for workplace monitoring falls on managers, who must develop some type of viable workplace monitoring policy. What can managers do to maintain control in a way that is not demeaning to employees? They should develop a clear and unambiguous computer-use policy and make sure that every employee knows about it. For example, managers should tell employees upfront that their computer use may be monitored at any time and provide clear and specific guidelines as to what constitutes acceptable use of company email systems and the Web. The Bank of Montreal blocks access to "some of the dubious sites that are high risk," such as Playboy.com and other pornographic sites. The bank has developed policies about appropriate and inappropriate use of the Internet, which are emailed to all employees several times a year.[45]

EMPLOYEE THEFT   Would you be surprised to find out that up to 75 percent of Canadian organizations have reported experiencing employee theft and fraud?[46] It is a costly problem. Air Canada, which has run a campaign against employee theft, noted that the airline "is right in line with industry standards for employee theft, and that means as much as 9 percent of stock such as office supplies and on-board products is taken each year."[47] A 2012 Retail Council of Canada study found that 33 percent of theft was due to employees, and that the overall cost of theft was more than $4 billion.[48]

Employee theft is defined as any unauthorized taking of company property by employees for their personal use.[49] It can range from embezzlement to fraudulent filing of expense

employee theft
Any unauthorized taking of company property by employees for their personal use.

reports to removing equipment, parts, software, and office supplies from company premises. While retail businesses have long faced serious potential losses from employee theft, loose financial controls at startups and small companies and the ready availability of information technology have made employee stealing an escalating problem in all kinds and sizes of organizations. Employee theft is a control issue. Managers need to educate themselves about this problem and be prepared to deal with it.[50]

Why do employees steal? The answer depends on whom you ask.[51] Experts in various fields—industrial security, criminology, clinical psychology—all have different perspectives. Industrial security people propose that people steal because the opportunity presents itself through lax controls and favourable circumstances. Criminologists say it is because people have financial pressures (such as personal financial problems) or vice-based pressures (such as gambling debts). Clinical psychologists suggest that people steal because they can rationalize whatever they are doing as correct and appropriate behaviour ("everyone does it," "they had it coming," "this company makes enough money and they will never miss anything this small," "I deserve this for all that I put up with," and so forth).[52] Although each of these approaches provides compelling insights into employee theft and has been instrumental in program designs to deter it, unfortunately employees continue to steal.

What can managers do to deter or reduce employee theft or fraud? We can use the concepts of feedforward, concurrent, and feedback controls to identify actions managers can take.[53] Exhibit 11-11 summarizes several possible control measures.

EXHIBIT 11-11 Control Measures for Deterring or Reducing Employee Theft or Fraud

Feedforward	Concurrent	Feedback
Use careful prehiring screening.	Treat employees with respect and dignity.	Make sure employees know when theft or fraud has occurred—not naming names but letting people know this is not acceptable.
Establish specific policies defining theft and fraud and discipline procedures.	Openly communicate the costs of stealing.	Use the services of professional investigators.
Involve employees in writing policies.	Let employees know on a regular basis about their successes in preventing theft and fraud.	Redesign control measures.
Educate and train employees about the policies.	Use video surveillance equipment if conditions warrant.	Evaluate your organization's culture and the relationships of managers and employees.
Have professionals review your internal security controls.	Install "lock-out" options on computers, telephones, and email.	
	Use corporate hotlines for reporting incidents.	
	Set a good example.	

Summary of Learning Outcomes

11.1 **What is control?** Control is the process of monitoring activities to ensure that they are being accomplished as planned and correcting any significant deviations. Managers can measure a variety of performances, but the most frequently used ones are organizational productivity, organizational effectiveness, and industry rankings.

When Greg Stremlaw joined the Canadian Curling Association, he and the board immediately changed the culture to run the nonprofit association like a business, while introducing financial controls to help turn the association's fortunes around.

11.2 **What is the control process?** The control process is a three-step process: measuring actual performance, comparing actual performance against a standard, and taking managerial action to correct deviations or inadequate standards.

The CCA regularly reviews all aspects of Canadian curling teams to ensure that their performance is up to world standards and to correct any deviations. With the men's, women's, and wheelchair teams all ranked number one in the world, there are not many deviations being corrected.

11.3 **When should controls be introduced?** Managers can implement controls before an activity begins (feedforward control), during the time the activity is going on (concurrent control), and after the activity has been completed (feedback control).

The CCA mainly uses concurrent control and feedback control because of the nature of the sport of curling.

11.4 **What methods of control do managers use?** There are three different approaches to designing control systems: market, bureaucratic, and clan control. Market control emphasizes the use of external market mechanisms, such as price competition and relative market share, to establish the standards used in the control system. Bureaucratic control emphasizes organizational authority and relies on administrative rules, regulations, procedures, and policies. Under clan control, employee behaviours are regulated by the shared values, norms, traditions, rituals, beliefs, and other aspects of the organization's culture.

Control is often needed to improve organizational performance, as Greg Stremlaw found when he took over the CCA and had to shrink the association's large deficit.

11.5 **How do financial and information controls help managers monitor performance?** Financial ratio analysis allows managers to monitor how efficiently and profitably the organization uses its assets, debt, inventories, and the like. Budget analysis provides managers with quantitative standards against which to measure and compare resource consumption. Economic value added (EVA) is a tool that measures corporate and divisional performance, while market value added (MVA) measures the stock market's estimate of the value of a firm's past and expected capital investment projects. Information may be used both as a tool to help managers control other organizational activities and as an organizational area that managers need to control.

At the CCA, Greg Stremlaw uses traditional financial controls and other measures of performance, including the brand impressions and value produced by the CCA through sponsorship and the www.curling.ca platform.

11.6 **What are some current issues in control?** Important current issues in control include the balanced scorecard (looking at financial, customer, internal business process, and learning and growth assets), corporate governance, cross-cultural differences, and workplace concerns.

The CCA has a board of directors that looks after the interests of members. The primary duty of the CCA board is to "approve, monitor and provide guidance on the strategic planning process." The board also approves the CCA's strategic plans, annual budget, and financial plans.

SNAPSHOT SUMMARY

11.1 What Is Control?
Performance Standards
Measures of Organizational Performance
Why Is Control Important?

11.2 The Control Process
Measuring Performance
Comparing Performance Against a Standard
Taking Managerial Action
Summary of Managerial Decisions

11.3 When to Introduce Control
Feedforward Control
Concurrent Control
Feedback Control

11.4 Methods of Control
Market Control
Bureaucratic Control
Clan Control

11.5 Keeping Tract: What Gets Controlled?

11.6 Current Issues in Control
Balanced Scorecard
Corporate Governance
Cross-Cultural Differences
Workplace Concerns

MyManagementLab Study, practise, and explore real management situations with these helpful resources:

- **Interactive Lesson Presentations:** Work through interactive presentations and assessments to test your knowledge of management concepts.
- **PIA (Personal Inventory Assessments):** Enhance your ability to connect with key concepts through these engaging self-reflection assessments.
- **Study Plan:** Check your understanding of chapter concepts with self-study quizzes.
- **Simulations:** Practise decision making in simulated management environments.

Discussion Questions

1. What is the role of control in management?
2. What are the advantages and disadvantages of feedforward control?
3. Describe the financial control measures managers can use.
4. What can management do to implement a benchmarking best practices program?
5. How are planning and control linked? Is the control function linked to the organizing and leading functions of management? Explain.
6. Why is feedback control the most popular type of control? Justify your response.

Developing Management Skills

Dilemma

Your parents have let you know they are expecting a big party for their twenty-fifth wedding anniversary and have put you in charge of planning it. Develop a timeline for carrying out the project and then identify ways to monitor progress toward getting the party planned. How will you know that your plans have been successful? At what critical points do you need to examine your plans to make sure that everything is on track?

PRACTISING THE SKILL

Think of a skill you would like to acquire or improve, or a habit you would like to break. Perhaps you would like to learn a foreign language, start exercising, quit smoking, ski better, or spend less. For the purpose of this exercise, assume you have three months to make a start on your project and all the necessary funds. Draft a plan of action that outlines what you need to do, when you need to do it, and how you will know that you have successfully completed each step of your plan. Be realistic, but do not set your sights too low either. Review your plan. What outside help or resources will you require? How will you get them? Add these to your plan. Ask someone to follow the steps in your plan. What modifications did the person suggest you make, if any?

Applying Feedforward, Concurrent, and Feedback Controls

You will be assigned one or more of the following tasks:

1. You are a consultant to a manager of a small retail clothing store. Over the past six months, the manager has noticed that a significant amount of inventory has gone missing. The manager is not sure whether it is employees or customers who are taking things from the store. The manager has a somewhat limited budget but wants to know what possibilities there are for controlling inventory. You have agreed to present a set of recommendations, identifying feedforward, concurrent, and feedback mechanisms that the manager might use.
2. You are a student in a business program at a local college or university. Several of your professors have expressed an interest in developing some specific controls to minimize opportunities for students to cheat on homework assignments and exams. Because you find cheating offensive, you and some other students have volunteered to write a report outlining some suggestions that might be used to control possible cheating (1) before it happens, (2) while in-class exams or assignments are being completed, and (3) after it has happened.
3. Devise control measures for each of the tasks involved in delivering a beverage to a Starbucks customer. Determine whether the measure is a feedforward, concurrent, or a feedback control.

Be prepared to present your suggestions before the rest of the class.

Diversity Matters

Most Canadian organizations feature a wide range of people with cultural differences. This cultural diversity is strengthened by having effective feedback, team-building activities, and interpersonal communication. When individuals interact they learn to appreciate each other's culture; consequently, the organizational culture becomes inclusive. Employees need to be sensitive to cross-cultural differences in communication and feedback.

Studies have found that European-Canadians are more likely to seek positive versus negative individual feedback, while East Asians are more likely to seek negative feedback due to less ego concern with the positive evaluations of others. European-Canadians are also less likely than East Asians to seek public feedback. Also, European-Canadians prefer feedback from a supervisor instead of a peer, while East Asians are less likely to seek feedback when it comes from a supervisor.[54]

By better understanding the type of feedback sought and the associated motivations of diverse employees, managers can create an environment where feedback provides the necessary performance evaluation without interpersonal conflict.[55]

Hey, You're the Boss Now!

One of the more critical feedback sessions will occur when you, as a manager, are using feedback control to address performance issues. You can be more effective at providing feedback if you use the following 10 suggestions:[56]

1. **Schedule the feedback session in advance, and be prepared.** One of the biggest mistakes you can make is to treat feedback control lightly. Simply calling in an employee and giving feedback that is not well organized serves little purpose for you or your employee. For feedback to be effective, you must plan ahead. Identify the issues you wish to address and cite specific examples to reinforce what you are saying. Set aside the time for the meeting with the employee. Make sure that what you do is done in private and can be completed without interruptions. That may mean closing your office door (if you have one), holding phone calls, and the like.
2. **Put the employee at ease.** Regardless of how you feel about the feedback, you must create a supportive climate for the employee. Recognize that giving and receiving feedback can be an emotional event, even when the feedback is positive. By putting your employee at ease, you begin to establish a supportive environment in which understanding can take place.
3. **Make sure the employee knows the purpose of the feedback session.** What is the purpose of the meeting? That is something any employee will wonder. Clarifying what you are going to do sets the appropriate stage for what is to come.
4. **Focus on specific rather than general work behaviours.** Feedback should be specific rather than general. General statements are vague and provide little useful information—especially if you are attempting to correct a problem.
5. **Keep comments impersonal and job-related.** Feedback should be descriptive rather than judgmental or evaluative, especially when you are giving negative feedback. No matter how upset you are, keep the feedback job-related and never criticize someone personally because of an inappropriate action. You are censuring job-related behaviour, not the person.
6. **Support feedback with hard data.** Tell your employee how you came to your conclusion about his or her performance. Hard data help your employees identify with specific behaviours. Identify the "things" that were done correctly and provide a detailed critique. If you do need to criticize, state the basis of your conclusion that a good job was not completed.

7. **Direct the negative feedback toward work-related behaviours that the employee controls.** Negative feedback should be directed toward work-related behaviours that the employee can do something about. Suggest what he or she can do to improve the situation. This practice helps take the sting out of the criticism and offers guidance to an individual who understands the problem but does not know how to resolve it.

8. **Let the employee speak.** Get the employee's perceptions about what you are saying, especially if you are addressing a problem. Of course, you are not looking for excuses, but you need to be empathetic to the employee and hear his or her side. Letting the employee speak involves your employee and just might provide information you were unaware of.

9. **Ensure that the employee has a clear and full understanding of the feedback.** Feedback must be concise and complete enough that your employee clearly and fully understands what you have said. Consistent with active listening techniques, have your employee rephrase the content of your feedback to check whether it fully captures your meaning.

10. **Detail a future plan of action.** Performing does not stop simply because feedback occurred. Good performance must be reinforced and new performance goals set. However, when performance deficiencies have been identified, time must be devoted to helping your employee develop a detailed, step-by-step plan to correct the situation. This plan includes what has to be done, when, and how you will monitor the activities. Offer whatever assistance you can to help the employee, but make it clear that it is the employee, not you, who has to make the corrections.

Your Essential Management Reading List

Learning from key management experts can help you understand today's management theory and practice and how controls can be effectively used in your personal and work lives. Here are some of the top books on control:

- *The Wealthy Barber*—Lance Chilton
- *Enterprise Risk Management: From Incentives to Controls*—James Lam
- *Nine Minutes on Monday*—James Robbins
- *The Dragon's Den Guide to Investor-Ready Business Plans*—John Vyge

Team Exercises

3BL: The Triple Bottom Line

Germany's Siemens has been doing business in Canada for 100 years and recently made a radical change to move away from nuclear energy to focus on green power, sustainable cities, and health care.[57] The move started when the German government announced it would stop its nuclear power plants, all built by Siemens. The German action was a response to the 2011 nuclear disaster in Fukushima, Japan, which focused attention on the high risk posed by nuclear power. In Canada, Siemens made a $20 million investment in a wind turbine blade manufacturing facility in Tillsonburg, Ontario.[58] Recently Siemens signed an agreement with the Ontario government to develop projects such as smart-grid electric vehicles, wind and solar power, water treatment, and energy conservation.[59] Siemens has developed a model for Canadian cities to enhance their environmental performance. The city finances the necessary energy-saving measures, with the savings in energy and operational costs guaranteed by Siemens. To date, more than 6500 buildings have been modernized with savings of $2 billion and a carbon reduction of 9 million tonnes.[60]

Siemens is an example of an industry giant working collaboratively with Canadian municipal governmental partners to achieve sustainability in green energy. Vancouver recently adopted an "EcoDensity Charter," which focuses on limiting sprawl, reducing the carbon footprint, and expanding housing options.[61]

THINKING STRATEGICALLY ABOUT 3BL

Companies like Siemens that are looking at green power instead of nuclear energy might put in place several measures of energy performance, such as pollution prevention, process safety, employee health and safety, and customer perception targets. These measures provide them with a way of evaluating their move away from nuclear energy. What kind of measures could you put in place to gauge community perceptions concerning Siemens's switch to green power? How could the Canadian nuclear industry convince Siemens to continue using nuclear energy?

Be the Consultant: Financing a New Business Venture

Your friend is starting a video game company and has asked for your help in putting together a business plan. She is especially concerned with sources of financing and whether she should use debt or equity financing. She has asked for your recommendations.

Which of the following sources should she consider?

What costs of operating a business are there apart from rent and raw materials?

Source	When and how to use	Comments
Bootstrapping	The company is started with personal finances, borrowed or donated equipment, and using only the finances generated through revenue	• Maintains full ownership and control • Difficult to source certain items • Lack of financing can cripple the business
Family and friends	Might be the most viable source if the business model is untested or the venture is brand new or unique	• May be willing to accept low (or zero) interest rates • Terms must be clearly spelled out to avoid conflict and disappointment
Banks	Can provide operating lines of credit to help with cash flow Term loans can help with fixed assets and equipment	• Lack of credit history can be a major impediment • Leasing equipment might be a better way
Venture capitalists	Provide seed money in exchange for equity in the company	• Are less risk averse • Can expect large returns in short periods
Angel investors	Providing personal funds for the business to be repaid or for equity in the business	• Often more interested in medium-sized ventures; harder to get for small businesses • May provide mentorship
Other	Government grants; financial cooperatives	• Time consuming • Small amounts available typically

Business Cases

Facebook

The "Hacker Way" is Facebook's organizational culture, and it originates with CEO Mark Zuckerberg. The culture is equal parts egalitarian, risk-taking, collaborative, innovative, driven, and irreverent.[62] In 2008, Facebook started a process called Bootcamp to encapsulate its culture for new employees. Facebook grows so rapidly—more than 6000 employees have been hired since January 2009—that Bootcamp provides a hands-on glimpse into the company's values and culture.

Bootcamp is a six-week journey for every engineering hire, no matter how senior, and includes one-on-one sessions with mentors and in-depth talks from senior engineers. New hires unlearn old habits as they work on real software bugs right from day one. The program helps show them the ropes and initiates them into Facebook's urgent, do-it-now culture.[63] Joel Seligstein, Facebook's Bootcamp "Yoda," describes the program as learning "to think about how to attack challenges and how to meet people."[64] The result of Bootcamp is a culture that teaches employees how to act and react, how to tackle problems independently, and how to take risks to keep Facebook growing rapidly and successfully. Bootcamp is also adept at using feedforward controls as part of orientation and training. As employees learn organizational culture, managers can also assess employee behaviours that might lead to problems in the future.

One new recruit was working on a software bug and crashed part of Facebook, but the company culture is very tolerant of failure, as evidenced by its "Move Fast and Break Things" motto. Slogans like "We Hack Therefore We Are" are plastered everywhere around the office. Bootcamp helps keep Facebook nimble, and the culture of constant change helps provide its competitive advantage over rivals. It is not uncommon for employees to walk right up to Mark Zuckerberg to talk about an engineering fix or a company problem. This form of concurrent control is actually bottom-up instead of top-down and has proven very effective at correcting problems before they end up costing Facebook money or customers. To ensure these controls succeed, the organizational structure is kept purposefully flat so that Zuckerberg remains hands-on with Facebook. Periodically, Facebook has all-night "Hackathons," where engineers try out new software ideas that often become company products.[65]

As Facebook acquires more companies, such as Instagram, WhatsApp, and Oculus, Zuckerberg is fashioning the company into a social media holding company.[66] Part of the goal is to obtain feedback about new products and services separate from Facebook users. Previous applications were forced on Facebook users, but now Zuckerberg can obtain feedback about these applications anonymously without risk of negative publicity for Facebook.

Discussion Questions

1. What information is needed for feedforward controls to be effective?
2. How effective would concurrent control be at Facebook if it were top-down only?
3. Is there a better way for Zuckerberg to collect feedback on new business ventures?

Balanced Scorecard—Your Local Credit Union

More than one-third of Canadians use a credit union. They have been innovators in the Canadian financial services industry, including some exciting firsts. Credit unions were the first to offer full-service ABMs, open mortgages, registered education plans, daily interest savings, and the first Canadian institutions to lend to women in their own names.

Credit unions compete with the strong Canadian big banking sector, and to do so effectively requires sustainable revenue growth, effective capital management, and

leadership. Credit unions can use metrics to help set strategy, evaluate results, and solicit feedback on future strategic actions.

The use of a balanced scorecard can be for the credit union as a whole as well as for individual departments. Metrics from the scorecard are used to evaluate activities and projects, but a scorecard can also provide insight into how the credit union derives value to the employees taking part instead of the value added to the organization. The scorecard is a powerful evaluative tool but also has great potential for driving HR activities. An example of a scorecard that could be used by a credit union is presented in the below figure.

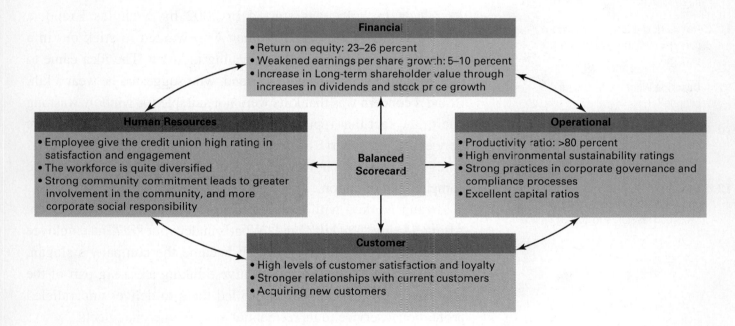

Financial
- Return on equity: 23–26 percent
- Weakened earnings per share growth: 5–10 percent
- Increase in Long-term shareholder value through increases in dividends and stock price growth

Human Resources
- Employee give the credit union high rating in satisfaction and engagement
- The workforce is quite diversified
- Strong community commitment leads to greater involvement in the community, and more corporate social responsibility

Balanced Scorecard

Operational
- Productivity ratio: >80 percent
- High environmental sustainability ratings
- Strong practices in corporate governance and compliance processes
- Excellent capital ratios

Customer
- High levels of customer satisfaction and loyalty
- Stronger relationships with current customers
- Acquiring new customers

Instead of developing metrics based on available data, a credit union could create the desired metrics and then formulate plans on how to collect the required data. For example, if diversity was one of the key overall organizational objectives, the balanced scorecard could track compensation, turnover, and cost per hire for women, visible minorities, Aboriginals, and persons with disabilities.

Discussion Questions

1. Why are metrics important, and how they can contribute to improved performance and profitability?
2. Analyze the metrics that are currently being used for the hypothetical credit union balanced scorecard. What recommendations would you make?

CHAPTER

12 Managing Innovation and Change

Men in Kilts

Think About It

Many change management programs consume massive resources but ultimately fail to solve the problems for which they were created.[1] The reason for this failure is the focus on "big splashes" instead of continuous improvement. Like a dieter who loses weight and then later puts it all back on, if change is not sustainable, it will not stick. What should Nicholas Brand do to understand the change that is required in his organization? How can Chris Carrier develop a long-term plan for change and work to keep the company on track?

Men In Kilts was started in 2002 by Nicholas Brand, a Vancouver-based Scotsman who wanted to stick out in a dime-a-dozen window-cleaning industry. The idea came to him through discussions with a friend, who suggested he wear a kilt. Brand's concern was that kilts were not suitable for window washing due to the fact that typical kilts are heavy, do not dry quickly, are very expensive (up to $1000 each), and can only be dry-cleaned. His wife is a seamstress, however, and she was able to make kilts for the company out of cotton.

Brand worked with his employees to come up with a slogan. After rejecting "Got kilt?" and "What's under your kilt?" an employee blurted out, "No peeking!" which became the company's slogan. Employee suggestions and innovative thinking are a big part of the company's success, and have also led them to deliver unparalleled professional service to its residential and commercial clients.

What does an innovative slogan and company name produce? Men In Kilts just opened its eleventh franchise. Men In Kilts has appeared on MSNBC, *Good Morning America*, and *Breakfast Television*. In January 2015, after 23 years running his own multimillion-dollar window-cleaning company, Chris Carrier became CEO of Men In Kilts. He bleeds tartan and is excited about the opportunity to assist in growing Men In Kilts across North America. Chris has a sharp focus on the support, service, and growth of existing franchise locations while providing a strong foundation for new partners to flourish.

Big companies and small businesses, universities and colleges, and governments at all levels are being forced to significantly change the way they do things. Although change has always been a part of the manager's job, it has become even more important in recent years. In this chapter, we describe the forces that lead to change and how managers can manage change. We conclude by looking at the critical concerns managers face when managing change today.

HOW IMPORTANT IS INNOVATION TO COMPANIES?

12.1 **Tell** How can managers encourage innovation in an organization?

"Innovation is the key to continued success."
—Ajay Banga, CEO of MasterCard

"We innovate today to secure the future."
—Sophie Vandebroek, Chief Technology Officer of Xerox Innovation Group

These two quotes reflect how important innovation is to organizations.[2] Success in business today demands innovation. In the dynamic, chaotic world of global competition, organizations must create new products and services and adopt state-of-the-art technology in order to compete successfully.[3]

What companies come to mind when you think of successful innovators? Apple, with its cool work and entertainment gadgets? Facebook, for its 1-billion-plus users? Nissan, for creating the Leaf, the first mass-market all-electric car? Or even maybe Foursquare, a startup that revved up the social-local-mobile trend by having users "check in" at locations, unlocking quirky badges and special offers from merchants.[4] What is the secret to the success of these innovator champions? What can other managers do to make their organizations more innovative? In the following pages, we will try to answer those questions as we discuss the factors behind innovation.

How Are Creativity and Innovation Related?

Creativity refers to the ability to combine ideas in a unique way or to make unusual associations between ideas.[5] A creative organization develops unique ways of working or novel solutions to problems. For instance, at Mattel, company officials introduced "Project Platypus," a special group that brings together people from all disciplines—engineering, marketing, design, and sales—and tries to get them to "think outside the box" in order to "understand the sociology and psychology behind children's play patterns." To help make this kind of thinking happen, team members embark on such activities as imagination exercises, group crying, and stuffed-bunny throwing. What does throwing stuffed bunnies have to do with creativity? It is part of a juggling lesson where team members learn to juggle two balls and a stuffed bunny. Most people can easily learn to juggle two balls but cannot let go of that third object. Creativity, like juggling, is learning to let go—that is, to "throw the bunny."[6] Creativity by itself isn't enough, though.

PERSONAL INVENTORY ASSESSMENT

The outcomes of the creative process need to be turned into useful products or work methods—in other words, **innovation**. Thus, the innovative organization is characterized by its ability to channel creativity into useful outcomes. When managers talk about changing an organization to make it more creative, they usually mean they want to stimulate and nurture innovation.

PERSONAL INVENTORY ASSESSMENT

What Is Involved in Innovation?

Some people believe that creativity is inborn; others believe that with training, anyone can be creative. The latter group views creativity as a fourfold process:[7]

1. *Perception* involves the way you see things. Being creative means seeing things from a unique perspective. One person may see solutions to a problem that others cannot or will not see at all. The movement from perception to reality, however, does not occur instantaneously.
2. Instead, ideas go though a process of *incubation*. Sometimes employees need to sit on their ideas, which does not mean sitting and doing nothing. Rather, during this

---

creativity
The ability to produce novel and useful ideas.

innovation
The process of taking a creative idea and turning it into a useful product, service, or method of operation.

McCarony/Fotolia

3M's "15 dream time" policy was responsible for the creation of the Post-it. Google allows employees to spend 20 percent of their time on side projects that are not part of their job description. How could your organization create a program to develop and pilot test innovative ideas?

incubation period, employees should collect massive amounts of data that are stored, retrieved, studied, reshaped, and finally moulded into something new. It is common for this period to last for years. Think for a moment about a time you struggled for an answer on a test. Although you tried hard to jog your memory, nothing worked. Then, suddenly, like a flash of light, the answer popped into your head. You found it!

3. *Inspiration* in the creative process is similar. Inspiration is the moment when all your efforts successfully come together. Although inspiration leads to euphoria, the creative work is not complete. It requires an innovative effort.

4. *Innovation* involves taking that inspiration and turning it into a useful product, service, or way of doing things. Thomas Edison is often credited with saying that "Creativity is 1 percent inspiration and 99 percent perspiration." That 99 percent, or the innovation, involves testing, evaluating, and retesting what the inspiration found. It is usually at this stage that an individual involves others more in what he or she has been working on. Such involvement is critical because even the greatest invention may be delayed or lost if an individual cannot effectively deal with others in communicating and achieving what the creative idea is supposed to do.

How Can a Manager Foster Innovation?

The systems model (inputs → transformation process → outputs) can help you understand how organizations become more innovative.[8] If an organization wants innovative products and work methods (*outputs*), it has to take its *inputs* and *transform* them into those *outputs*. Those *inputs* include creative people and groups within the organization. But having creative people is not enough. The *transformation process* requires having the right environment to turn those inputs into innovative products or work methods. This "right" environment—that is, an environment that stimulates innovation—includes three variables: the organization's structure, culture, and human resource practices (see Exhibit 12-1).

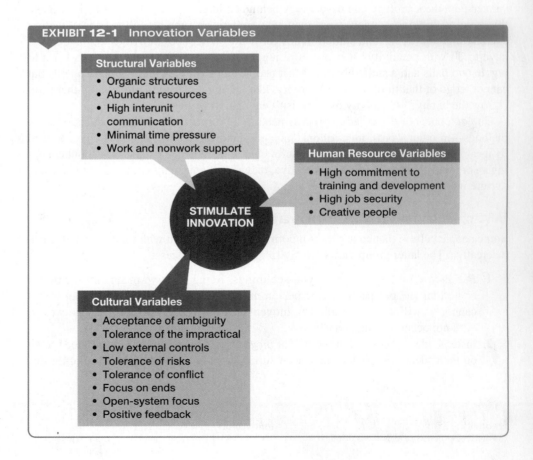

EXHIBIT 12-1 Innovation Variables

Structural Variables
- Organic structures
- Abundant resources
- High interunit communication
- Minimal time pressure
- Work and nonwork support

Human Resource Variables
- High commitment to training and development
- High job security
- Creative people

STIMULATE INNOVATION

Cultural Variables
- Acceptance of ambiguity
- Tolerance of the impractical
- Low external controls
- Tolerance of risks
- Tolerance of conflict
- Focus on ends
- Open-system focus
- Positive feedback

How Do Structural Variables Affect Innovation?

Research into the effect of structural variables on innovation shows five things:[9]

1. An organic-type structure positively influences innovation. Because this structure is low in formalization, centralization, and work specialization, it facilitates the flexibility and sharing of ideas that are critical to innovation.
2. The availability of plentiful resources provides a key building block for innovation. With an abundance of resources, managers can afford to purchase innovations, can afford the cost of instituting innovations, and can absorb failures.
3. Frequent communication between organizational units helps break down barriers to innovation.[10] Cross-functional teams, task forces, and other such organizational designs facilitate interaction across departmental lines and are widely used in innovative organizations.
4. Extreme time pressures on creative activities are minimized despite the demands of white-water-rapids-type environments. Although time pressures may spur people to work harder and may make them feel more creative, studies show that it actually causes them to be less creative.[11]
5. When an organization's structure explicitly supports creativity, employees' creative performance can be enhanced. Beneficial kinds of support include encouragement, open communication, readiness to listen, and useful feedback.[12]

Bulletproof vests are bulky and unstylish. Toronto tailor Garrison Bespoke created a custom three-piece bulletproof suit used by executives in the mining, oil, and finance industries. The suits cost $20 000 and use carbon nanotubes, which look and feel like cotton but behave like steel.

How Does an Organization's Culture Affect Innovation?

Innovative organizations tend to have similar cultures.[13] They encourage experimentation, reward successes, and celebrate mistakes. An innovative organization is likely to have the following characteristics:

- *Accepts ambiguity.* Too much emphasis on objectivity and specificity constrains creativity.
- *Tolerates the impractical.* Individuals who offer impractical, even foolish, answers to what-if questions are not stifled. What at first seems impractical might lead to innovative solutions.
- *Keeps external controls minimal.* Rules, regulations, policies, and similar organizational controls are kept to a minimum.
- *Tolerates risk.* Employees are encouraged to experiment without fear of consequences should they fail. Mistakes are treated as learning opportunities.
- *Tolerates conflict.* Diversity of opinions is encouraged. Harmony and agreement between individuals or units are *not* assumed to be evidence of high performance.
- *Focuses on ends rather than means.* Goals are made clear, and individuals are encouraged to consider alternative routes toward meeting the goals. Focusing on ends suggests that there might be several right answers to any given problem.
- *Uses an open-system focus.* Managers closely monitor the environment and respond to changes as they occur. For example, at Starbucks, product development depends on "inspiration field trips to view customers and trends." Visiting local Starbucks and other restaurants in other countries helps get a better sense of local cultures.

TIPS FOR MANAGERS

Creating a More Innovative Work Environment

* **Communicate openly** about the problems facing the organization.
* Use a blog or email **suggestion box** and reward the top suggestions.
* Provide **training** to supervisors to listen without judgment.
* Visibly **reward innovative behaviours**.
* Provide **protective mechanisms** for employees that make mistakes to reduce fear of punishment or embarrassment.

behaviours, and fashions, which leads to different ideas and different ways to think about things.

- *Provides positive feedback.* Managers provide positive feedback, encouragement, and support so employees feel that their creative ideas receive attention.

What Human Resource Variables Affect Innovation?

Innovative organizations (1) actively promote the training and development of their members so their knowledge remains current, (2) offer their employees high job security to reduce the fear of getting fired for making mistakes, and (3) encourage individuals to become **idea champions**, actively and enthusiastically supporting new ideas, building support, overcoming resistance, and ensuring that innovations are implemented. Research finds that idea champions have common personality characteristics: extremely high self-confidence, persistence, energy, and a tendency toward risk taking. They also display characteristics associated with dynamic leadership. They inspire and energize others with their vision of the potential of an innovation and through their strong personal conviction in their mission. They are also good at gaining the commitment of others to support their mission. In addition, idea champions have jobs that provide considerable decision-making discretion. This autonomy helps them introduce and implement innovations in organizations.[14]

How Does Design Thinking Influence Innovation?

We introduced you to the concept of design thinking in a previous chapter. Well, undoubtedly, there is a strong connection between design thinking and innovation. "Design thinking can do for innovation what TQM did for quality."[15] Just as total quality management provides a process for improving quality throughout an organization, design thinking can provide a process for coming up with things that do not exist. When a business approaches innovation with a design thinking mentality, the emphasis is on getting a deeper understanding of what customers need and want. It entails knowing customers as real people with real problems—not just as sales targets or demographic statistics. But it also entails being able to convert those customer insights into real and usable products. For instance, at Intuit, the company behind TurboTax software, founder Scott Cook felt "the company wasn't innovating fast enough."[16] So he decided to apply design thinking. He called the initiative "Design for Delight," and it involved customer field research to understand their "pain points"—that is, what most frustrated them as they worked in the office and at home. Then, Intuit staffers brainstormed (they nicknamed it "painstorm") a "variety of solutions to address the problems, and experiment with customers to find the best ones." For example, one pain point uncovered by the Intuit team was how customers could take pictures of tax forms to reduce typing errors. Some younger customers, used to taking photos with their smartphones, were frustrated that they could not just complete their taxes on their mobiles. To address this, Intuit developed a mobile app called SnapTax, which the company says has been downloaded more than a million times since it was introduced in 2010. That is how design thinking works in innovation. Clayton Christensen, a Harvard Business School professor, first coined the theory *disruptive innovation*, in which successful businesses become fixated on honing existing products, leaving them vulnerable to upstart companies with cheaper, technologically advanced products. Read more about this theory in Christensen's book, one of the titles in *Your Essential Management Reading List* at the end of the chapter.

idea champions
Individuals who actively and enthusiastically support new ideas, build support for them, overcome resistance to them, and ensure that innovations are implemented.

ORGANIZATIONAL CULTURE

Organizational culture is a system of shared meaning and beliefs held by organizational members that determines, in large degree, how they act. It represents a common perception held by an organization's members that influences how they behave. In every organization, there are values, symbols, rituals, myths, and practices that have evolved over time.[17] These shared values and experiences mainly determine what employees perceive and how they respond to their world.[18] When faced with problems or issues, the organizational culture—the way we do things around here—influences what employees can do and how they conceptualize, define, analyze, and resolve issues.

12.2 How does organizational culture affect innovation and change?

Our definition of organizational culture implies three things:

- Culture is a *perception*. Individuals perceive the organizational culture on the basis of what they see, hear, or experience within the organization.
- Culture is *shared*. Even though individuals may have different backgrounds or work at different organizational levels, they tend to describe the organization's culture in similar terms.
- Culture is a *descriptive* term. Culture is concerned with how members perceive the organization, not with whether they like it. It describes rather than evaluates.

Research suggests there are seven dimensions that capture the essence of an organization's culture.[19] These dimensions are described in Exhibit 12-2. Each dimension ranges from low (not very typical of the culture) to high (very typical of the culture). Appraising an organization on these seven dimensions gives a composite picture of the organization's

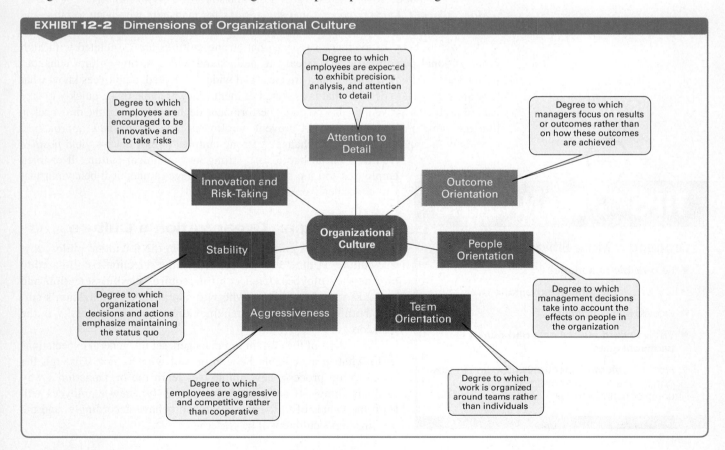

EXHIBIT 12-2 Dimensions of Organizational Culture

organizational culture
A system of shared values, norms, and beliefs held by organization members that determines, in large degree, how employees act.

culture. In many organizations, one of these cultural dimensions is often emphasized more than the others and essentially shapes the organization's personality and the way organization members work. For example, at Sony Corporation the focus is on product innovation. The company "lives and breathes" new-product development (outcome orientation), and employees' work decisions, behaviours, and actions support that goal. In contrast, WestJet Airlines has made its employees a central part of its culture (people orientation). However, its admission of engaging in corporate espionage against Air Canada may cause employees to question WestJet's corporate values.

Strong Versus Weak Cultures

Although all organizations have cultures, not all cultures have an equal impact on employees' behaviours and actions. **Strong cultures**—cultures in which the key values are deeply held and widely shared—have a greater influence on employees than do weak cultures. The more employees accept the organization's key values and the greater their commitment to those values, the stronger the culture is.

Whether an organization's culture is strong, weak, or somewhere in between depends on factors such as the size of the organization, how long it has been around, how much turnover there has been among employees, and the intensity with which the culture began.

Some organizations do not make clear what is important and what is not. This lack of clarity is a characteristic of weak cultures. In such organizations, culture is unlikely to greatly influence managers. Most organizations, however, have moderate to strong cultures. There is relatively high agreement on what is important, what defines "good" employee behaviour, what it takes to get ahead, and so forth. *Tips for Managers—Creating a More Ethical Culture* provides some suggestions for managers who want to build and maintain a more ethical culture in the workplace.

A growing body of evidence suggests that strong cultures are associated with high organizational performance.[20] It is easy to understand why a strong culture enhances performance. After all, when values are clear and widely accepted, employees know what they are supposed to do and what is expected of them. They are able to act quickly to take care of problems, preventing any potential performance decline. However, the drawback is that the same strong culture might prevent employees from trying new approaches, especially during periods of rapid change.[21] Strong cultures do not always yield *positive* results.[22] Enron had a very strong and unethical culture. It enabled employees and top management to engage in unethical behaviour that was concealed from public scrutiny.

Developing an Organization's Culture

An organization's culture is derived from the founders' philosophy. The culture, in turn, strongly influences the selection criteria used to hire new employees. Clan control requires careful selection and socialization of employees who will support the organization's culture, both of which include making sure to manage diversity in the workforce.

The actions of the current top managers set the general expectations as to what is acceptable behaviour and what is not. Through the socialization process, new employees learn the organization's way of doing things. If socialization is successful, new employees will learn the values of the organization and behave accordingly, and the organization's culture will be preserved.

TIPS (FOR) MANAGERS

Creating a More Ethical Culture

* Be a **visible role model**.
* Communicate **ethical expectations**.
* Provide **ethics training**.
* Visibly **reward ethical acts and punish unethical ones**.
* Provide **protective mechanisms** so employees can discuss ethical dilemmas and report unethical behaviour without fear.

strong cultures
Organizational cultures in which the key values are deeply held and widely shared.

How Employees Learn Culture

Culture is transmitted to employees in a number of ways. The most significant are stories, rituals, material symbols, and language.

STORIES An organization's "stories" typically are related to significant people or events, such as the organization's founders, rule-breaking, reactions to past mistakes, and so forth.[23] They help employees learn the culture by anchoring the present in the past, providing explanations and legitimacy for current practices, and showing what is important to the organization.[24]

RITUALS An organization's rituals are repetitive sequences of activities that express and reinforce the values of the organization, the goals that are most important, and the people who are most important.[25] One well-known ritual is Walmart's company chant that employees say at the beginning of each workday.

MATERIAL SYMBOLS An organization's material symbols convey to employees who is important, the degree of equality desired by top management, and the kinds of behaviour (e.g., risk-taking, conservative, authoritarian, participative, individualistic, and so on) that are expected and appropriate. The layout of an organization's facilities, how employees dress, the types of automobiles provided to top executives, and the availability of corporate aircraft are examples of material symbols.

LANGUAGE Many organizations and units within organizations use language as a way to identify members of a culture. By learning this language, members attest to their acceptance of the culture and their willingness to help preserve it. New employees are frequently overwhelmed with acronyms and jargon that, after a short period of time, become a natural part of their language. Once learned, the language acts as a common denominator to unite members of a given culture.

HOW CULTURE AFFECTS MANAGERS An organization's culture does more than influence employee behaviour; it also constrains a manager's decision-making options in all management functions. Exhibit 12-3 shows the major areas of a manager's job that are affected by the culture in which he or she operates.

EXHIBIT 12-3 Managerial Decisions Affected by Organizational Culture

Planning	Organizing
• The degree of risk that plans should contain	• How much autonomy should be designed into employees' jobs
• Whether plans should be developed by individuals or teams	• Whether tasks should be done by individuals or in teams
• The degree of environmental scanning in which management will engage	• The degree to which department managers interact with each other

Leading	Controlling
• The degree to which managers are concerned with increasing employee job satisfaction	• Whether to impose external controls or to allow employees to control their own actions
• The appropriate leadership style(s)	• What criteria should be emphasized in employee performance evaluations
• Whether all disagreements—even constructive ones—should be eliminated	• What repercussions will result from exceeding one's budget

Changing Organizational Culture

When W. James McNerney Jr. became CEO of 3M Company, he brought with him managerial approaches from his old employer, General Electric. He soon discovered that what was routine at General Electric was unheard of at 3M. For example, he was the only one who showed up at meetings without a tie. His blunt, matter-of-fact, and probing style of asking questions caught many 3M managers off guard. McNerney soon realized that he would need to address the cultural issues before tackling any needed organizational changes.[26]

A culture takes a long time to form; once established, it tends to become entrenched. Strong cultures are particularly resistant to change because employees have become deeply committed to them.

The explosion of the space shuttle *Columbia* in 2003 highlights how difficult changing an organization's culture can be. An investigation into the explosion found that the causes were remarkably similar to the reasons given for the *Challenger* disaster 17 years earlier.[27] Although foam striking the shuttle was the technical cause, NASA's organizational culture was the real problem. Joseph Grenny, a NASA engineer, noted that "The NASA culture does not accept being wrong." The culture does not accept that "there's no such thing as a stupid question." Instead, "the humiliation factor always runs high."[28] Consequently, people do not speak up. As this example shows, if, over time, a certain culture becomes inappropriate to an organization and a handicap to management, there may be little a manager can do to change it, especially in the short run. Even under favourable conditions, cultural changes have to be viewed in years, not weeks or even months.

Understanding the Situational Factors

What "favourable conditions" might facilitate cultural change? The evidence suggests that cultural change is most likely to take place when most or all of the following conditions exist:

- *A dramatic crisis occurs.* A crisis can be the shock that weakens the status quo and makes people start thinking about the relevance of the current culture. Examples are a surprising financial setback, the loss of a major customer, or a dramatic technological innovation by a competitor.
- *Leadership changes hands.* New top leadership, who can provide an alternative set of key values, may be perceived as more capable of responding to the crisis than the old leaders were. Top leadership includes the organization's chief executive but might include all senior managers.
- *The organization is young and small.* The younger the organization, the less entrenched its culture. Similarly, managers can communicate new values more easily in a small organization than in a large one.
- *The culture is weak.* The more widely held the values and the higher the agreement among members on those values, the more difficult it will be to change. Conversely, weak cultures are more receptive to change than are strong ones.[29]

These situational factors help explain why a company such as Microsoft faces challenges in reshaping its culture. For the most part, employees like the old ways of doing things and do not always see the company's problems as critical.

How Can Cultural Change Be Accomplished?

Now we ask the question: If conditions are right, how do managers go about changing culture? The challenge is to unfreeze the current culture, implement the new "ways of doing things," and reinforce those new values. No single action is likely to have the impact necessary to change something that is widely accepted and highly valued. Thus, there needs to be a comprehensive and coordinated strategy for managing cultural change, as shown in *Tips for Managers—Strategies for Managing Cultural Change.*

TIPS FOR MANAGERS

Strategies for Managing Cultural Change

✷ Set the tone through management behaviour. Managers, particularly top management, need to be **positive role models**.

✷ **Create new stories, symbols, and rituals** to replace those currently in vogue.

✷ Select, promote, and support employees who **adopt the new values** that are sought.

✷ **Redesign socialization processes** to align with the new values.

✷ Change the reward system to **encourage acceptance** of a new set of values.

✷ Replace unwritten norms with **formal rules and regulations** that are tightly enforced.

✷ **Shake up current subcultures** through transfers, job rotation, and/or terminations.

✷ Work to get peer-group consensus through **employee participation** and creation of a climate with a high level of trust.

As you can see, these suggestions focus on specific actions that managers can take to change the ineffective culture. Following these suggestions, however, is no guarantee that a manager's change efforts will succeed. Organizational members do not quickly let go of values they understand that have worked well for them in the past. Managers must, therefore, be patient. Change, if it comes, will be slow, and managers must stay constantly alert to protect against any return to old familiar practices and traditions.

FORCES FOR CHANGE

12.3 What are forces for change?

PERSONAL INVENTORY ASSESSMENT

If it were not for change, the manager's job would be relatively easy. Planning would be simple because tomorrow would be no different from today. The issue of effective organizational design would also be solved, because the environment would be free from uncertainty and there would be no need to adapt. Similarly decision making would be dramatically streamlined—the outcome of each alternative could be predicted with almost certain accuracy. The manager's job would, indeed, be simplified if, for example, competitors did not introduce new products or services, customers did not demand new and improved products, government regulations were never modified, or employees' needs never changed. But that is not the way it is. Change is an organizational reality.[30] Managing change is an integral part of every manager's job. In Chapter 2 you learned about the external and internal forces that constrain managers. These same forces also bring about the need for change. Let us look briefly at these forces.

External Forces

The external forces that create the need for change come from various sources. Chipotle's entry into the Canadian market will have a major impact on existing competitors, such as Tim Hortons and McDonald's, who must consider change as a way of adapting to new competition.

Government laws and regulations are a frequent impetus for change. For example, the Canadian Generally Accepted Accounting Principles (GAAP) have been replaced by the International Financial Reporting Standards (IFRS). This change requires Canadian publicly accountable companies to change the way they disclose financial information and enact corporate governance to allow for greater transparency in financial reporting.

Technology also creates the need for change. For example, technological improvements in diagnostic equipment have created significant economies of scale for hospitals. Assembly-line technology in other industries is changing dramatically as organizations replace human labour with robots. In the greeting card industry, email and the Internet have changed the way people exchange greeting cards. The move from locally installed to web-based software and computing will create a major shift for companies. The cloud will provide lower costs, higher efficiency, and greater innovation but may increase security concerns.[31]

The fluctuation in *labour markets* also forces managers to change. Organizations that need certain kinds of employees must change their human resource management activities to attract and retain skilled employees in the areas of greatest need. For example, health care organizations facing severe nursing shortages have had to change the way they schedule work hours.

Economic changes, of course, affect almost all organizations. For example, global recessionary pressures force organizations to become more cost-efficient. But even in a strong economy, uncertainties about interest rates, federal budget deficits, and currency exchange rates create conditions that may force organizations to change.

Internal Forces

In addition to the external forces just described, internal forces also create the need for change. These internal forces tend to originate primarily from the internal operations of the organization or from the impact of external changes.

A redefinition or modification of an organization's *strategy* often introduces a variety of changes. For instance, when TransCanada realized the Keystone pipeline project was at risk, diversification and risk management became a major focal point in its corporate strategy. Previously its strategy had a much smaller Asian component as it focused on the U.S. market, but with the need to diversify TransCanada moved quickly to Energy East. This $12-billion project aims to repurpose one of the two parallel pipes that make up the Canadian gas mainline.[32]

An organization's *workforce* is rarely static. Its composition changes in terms of age, education, ethnic background, sex, and so forth. Take, for example, an organization in which a large number of older executives, for financial reasons, decide to continue working instead of retiring. There might be a need to restructure jobs in order to retain and motivate younger managers. The compensation and benefits system might also need to be adapted to reflect the needs of this older workforce.

The introduction of new *equipment* represents another internal force for change. Employees may have their jobs redesigned, need to undergo training on how to operate the new equipment, or be required to establish new interaction patterns within their work groups.

Finally, *employee attitudes* such as job dissatisfaction may lead to increased absenteeism, more voluntary resignations, and even labour strikes. Such events often lead to changes in management policies and practices.

Two Views of the Change Process

We can use two very different metaphors to describe the change process.[33] One metaphor envisions the organization as a large ship crossing calm waters. The ship's captain and crew know exactly where they are going because they have made the trip many times before. Change comes in the form of an occasional storm, a brief distraction in an otherwise calm and predictable trip. In the other metaphor, the organization is seen as a small raft navigating a raging river with uninterrupted white-water rapids. Aboard the raft are half a dozen people who have never worked together before, who are totally unfamiliar with the river, who are unsure of their eventual destination, and who, as if things were not bad enough, are travelling at night. In the white-water rapids metaphor, change is an expected and natural state, and managing change is a continuous process. These two metaphors present very different approaches to understanding and responding to change. Let us take a closer look at each one.

THE CALM WATERS METAPHOR   Up until the late 1980s, the **calm waters metaphor** more or less described the situation that managers faced. This metaphor is best illustrated by the three-step description of the change process developed by Kurt Lewin, often recognized as the founder of social psychology (see Exhibit 12-4).[34]

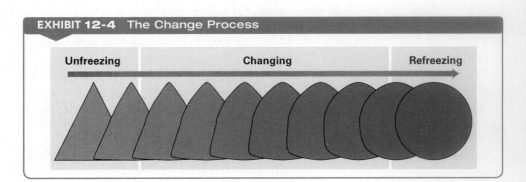

EXHIBIT 12-4   The Change Process

Unfreezing   Changing   Refreezing

calm waters metaphor
A description of organizational change that likens that change to a large ship making a predictable trip across a calm sea and experiencing an occasional storm.

According to Lewin, successful change can be planned and requires *unfreezing* the status quo, *changing* to a new state, and *refreezing* to make the change permanent. The status quo can be considered an equilibrium state. To move from this equilibrium, unfreezing is necessary. Unfreezing can be thought of as preparing for the needed change. It can be achieved by increasing the *driving forces*, which are forces that drive change and direct behaviour away from the status quo; decreasing the *restraining forces*, which are forces that resist change and push behaviour toward the status quo; or combining the two approaches. Driving forces include the environmental changes discussed earlier, but could also be the introduction of new competitors or technologies. Driving forces create the necessary urgency for change but are often not enough to overcome employee resistance to change without strategies to reduce the restraining forces. Employee involvement would be one example of a strategy geared toward enhancing organizational change efforts.[35]

Once unfreezing is done, the change itself can be implemented. However, merely introducing change does not ensure that the change will take hold. The new situation needs to be *refrozen* so that it can be sustained over time. Unless this last step is taken, there is a strong chance that the change will be short-lived as employees revert back to the old equilibrium state—that is, the old ways of doing things. The objective of refreezing, then, is to stabilize the new situation by reinforcing the new behaviours.

Note how Lewin's three-step process treats change simply as a break in the organization's equilibrium state. The status quo has been disturbed, and change is necessary to establish a new equilibrium state. However, a calm waters environment is not what most managers face today.[36]

THE WHITE-WATER RAPIDS METAPHOR   The **white-water rapids metaphor** is consistent with our discussion of uncertain and dynamic environments in Chapters 2 and 3. It is also consistent with a world that is increasingly dominated by information, ideas, and knowledge.[37] We can see how the metaphor applies to Microsoft, which is currently facing an uncertain and dynamic environment after dominating the software industry for many years.

To get a feeling of what managing change might be like when you have to continuously manoeuvre in uninterrupted and uncertain rapids, consider attending a college or university that has the following rules: Courses vary in length. Unfortunately, when you sign up, you do not know how long a course will run. It might go for 2 weeks or 30 weeks. Furthermore, the instructor can end a course any time he or she wants, with no prior warning. If that is not bad enough, the length of the class changes each time it meets: Sometimes the class lasts 20 minutes; other times it runs for 3 hours. The time of the next class meeting is set by the instructor during this class. There is one more thing. All exams are unannounced, so you have to be ready for a test at any time. To succeed in this type of environment, you would have to be incredibly flexible and able to respond quickly to changing conditions. Students who are overly structured, slow to respond, or uncomfortable with change would not survive.

Growing numbers of managers are coming to accept that their jobs are very much like what students would face in such a college or university. The stability and predictability of the calm waters metaphor do not exist. Disruptions in the status quo are not occasional and temporary, and they are not followed by a return to calm waters. Many managers never get out of the rapids. They face constant change, bordering on chaos.

Is the white-water rapids metaphor an exaggeration? No! Although you would expect this type of chaotic and dynamic environment in high-tech industries, even organizations in non-high-tech industries are faced with constant change.

Ian Anderson

Author Ian Anderson, pictured second from the left, experiences the metaphor first-hand in Costa Rica.

white-water rapids metaphor
A description of organizational change that likens that change to a small raft navigating a raging river.

PUTTING THE TWO VIEWS IN PERSPECTIVE Does *every* manager face a world of constant and chaotic change? No, but the number who do not is dwindling. Managers in such businesses as telecommunications, computer software, and women's clothing have long confronted a world of white-water rapids. These managers used to envy their counterparts in such industries as banking, utilities, oil exploration, publishing, and air transportation, where the environment was historically more stable and predictable. However, those days of stability and predictability are long gone!

Today, any organization that treats change as an occasional disturbance in an otherwise calm and stable world runs a great risk. Too much is changing too fast for an organization or its managers to be complacent. It is no longer business as usual. Managers must be ready to efficiently and effectively manage the changes facing their organizations or their work areas. Nevertheless, managers have to be certain that change is the right thing to do at any given time.

12.4 What is organizational change and what are some common approaches to change?

WHAT IS ORGANIZATIONAL CHANGE?

Most managers, at one point or another, will have to make changes in some aspects of their workplace. We classify these changes as **organizational change**—any alteration of people, structure, or technology (see Exhibit 12-5). Organizational changes often need someone to act as a catalyst and assume the responsibility for managing the change process—that is, a **change agent**. Who can be change agents?

We assume that changes are initiated and coordinated by a manager within the organization. However, the change agent could be a nonmanager—for example, a change specialist from the HR department or even an outside consultant with expertise in change implementation. For major system-wide changes, an organization often hires outside consultants to provide advice and assistance. Because they are from the outside, they offer an objective perspective that insiders may lack. However, outside consultants are usually at a disadvantage because they have a limited understanding of the organization's history, culture, operating procedures, and people. Outside consultants are also likely to initiate more drastic change than insiders would (which can be either a benefit or a disadvantage) because they do not have to live with the repercussions after the change is implemented. In contrast, internal managers who act as change agents may be more thoughtful, but possibly overcautious, because they must live with the consequences of their decisions.

As change agents, managers are motivated to initiate change because they are committed to improving their organization's performance. Initiating change involves identifying what types of

While other potash producers are suffering profit losses of up to 50 percent, Canada's Allana Potash opened a new mine in Ethiopia. It is using solution mining to be effective in the country's scorching temperatures, typically above 45 degrees Celsius. This innovative technique is cheaper than open pit or shaft mining.[38]

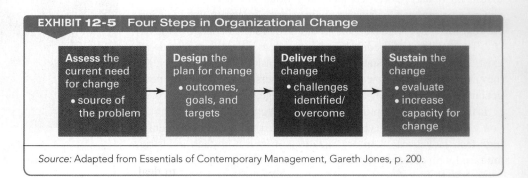

EXHIBIT 12-5 Four Steps in Organizational Change

Assess the current need for change	**Design** the plan for change	**Deliver** the change	**Sustain** the change
• source of the problem	• outcomes, goals, and targets	• challenges identified/ overcome	• evaluate • increase capacity for change

Source: Adapted from *Essentials of Contemporary Management,* Gareth Jones, p. 200.

organizational change
Any alteration of people, structure, or technology in an organization.

change agent
Someone who acts as a catalyst and assumes the responsibility for managing the change process.

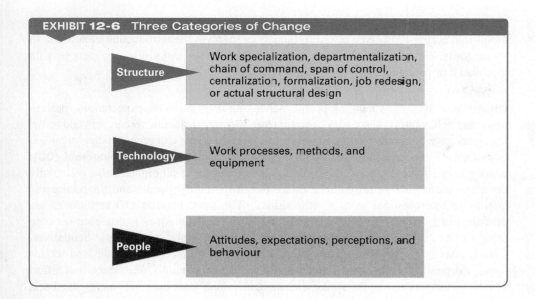

EXHIBIT 12-6   Three Categories of Change

Structure — Work specialization, departmentalization, chain of command, span of control, centralization, formalization, job redesign, or actual structural design

Technology — Work processes, methods, and equipment

People — Attitudes, expectations, perceptions, and behaviour

changes might be needed and putting the change process in motion. But managing organizational change has another key aspect. Managers must manage employee resistance to change. What types of organizational change might managers need to make, and how do managers deal with resistance to change?

Types of Change

What *can* a manager change? The manager's options fall into three categories: structure, technology, and people (see Exhibit 12-6). Changing *structure* includes any alteration in authority relations, coordination mechanisms, employee empowerment, job redesign, or similar structural variables. Changing *technology* encompasses modifications in the way work is performed or the methods and equipment that are used. Changing *people* refers to changes in employee attitudes, expectations, perceptions, and behaviour.

CHANGING STRUCTURE   We discussed organizational structure issues in Chapter 5. Managers' organizing responsibilities in the sphere of structure include such activities as choosing the organization's formal design, allocating authority, and determining the degree of formalization. Once those structural decisions have been made, however, they are not final. Changing conditions or changing strategies brings about the need to make structural changes.

What options does a manager have for changing structure? The manager has the same ones we introduced in our discussion of organizational structure and design. A few examples should make this clear. Recall from Chapter 5 that an organization's structure is defined in terms of work specialization, departmentalization, chain of command, span of control, centralization and decentralization, and formalization. Managers can alter one or more of these *structural elements*.

Another option would be to make major changes in the actual *structural design*. For example, the design change might involve a shift from a functional to a product structure or the creation of a project structure design. The Department of Fisheries and Oceans (DFO) has successfully used co-management in the Atlantic region, with management teams featuring representatives from industry, key stakeholders, and the broader community.[39] Some government agencies and private organizations are looking to new organizational ventures, forming public–private partnerships (P3s) to deal with change. British Columbia's Canada Line, a rail-based rapid transit line built between Vancouver International Airport and downtown Vancouver before the 2010 Olympic Winter Games, was the first BC P3 project to launch. These partnerships are adept at reducing risk and obtaining better long-term financing.

Change management is always a challenge.

CHANGING TECHNOLOGY Managers can also change the technology used to convert inputs into outputs. This type of change generally involves the introduction of new equipment, tools, or methods; automation (replacing certain tasks done by people with machines); or computerization.

CHANGING PEOPLE Changing people—changing their attitudes, expectations, perceptions, and behaviours—is not easy. Yet, for over 30 years, academic researchers and actual managers have been interested in finding ways for individuals and groups within organizations to work together more effectively. The term **organizational development (OD)**, although occasionally used to refer to all types of change in an organization, essentially describes techniques or programs that are meant to change people and the nature and quality of interpersonal work relationships.[40] The most popular OD techniques are described in Exhibit 12-7. The common thread in these techniques is that each seeks to bring about changes in the organization's people. For example, executives at Scotiabank, Canada's second-largest bank, knew that the success of a new customer sales and service strategy depended on changing employee attitudes and behaviours. Managers used different OD techniques during the strategic change, including team building, survey feedback, and intergroup development. One indicator of how well these techniques worked in getting people to change was that every branch in Canada implemented the new strategy on or ahead of schedule.[41]

Making Change Happen Successfully

When changes are needed, who makes them happen? Who manages them? Although you may think change is the responsibility of top managers, actually managers at *all* organizational levels are involved in the change process. Employees may not be aware of all the

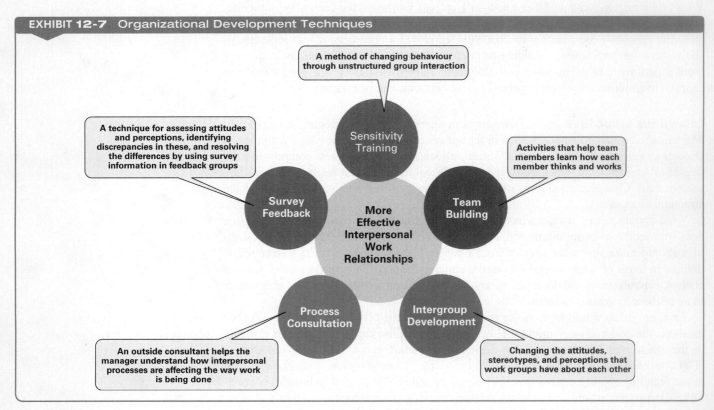

EXHIBIT 12-7 Organizational Development Techniques

A method of changing behaviour through unstructured group interaction

A technique for assessing attitudes and perceptions, identifying discrepancies in these, and resolving the differences by using survey information in feedback groups

Activities that help team members learn how each member thinks and works

Sensitivity Training

Survey Feedback

More Effective Interpersonal Work Relationships

Team Building

Process Consultation

Intergroup Development

An outside consultant helps the manager understand how interpersonal processes are affecting the way work is being done

Changing the attitudes, stereotypes, and perceptions that work groups have about each other

organizational development (OD)
Techniques or programs meant to change people and the nature and quality of interpersonal work relationships.

EXHIBIT 12-8 Mistakes Managers Make When Leading Change

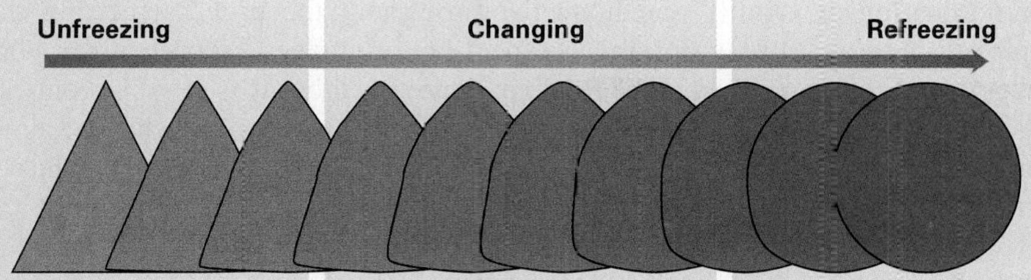

Unfreezing	Changing	Refreezing
• Being unaware of the gap between what employees know and what they actually do • Not creating awareness of the need to change • Not recognizing the hidden conflicts working against change	• Lacking a vision to create the desire for change • Under-communicating and not empowering employees to change • Unaware of the knowledge and ability required to change and training employees	• Stopping the change effort too quickly • Starting another change effort before the first is finished • Not adapting the culture to support the change • Lack of reinforcement through rewards and recognition

external driving forces for change, which means that managers must inform them about changes in competition, consumer preferences, government regulations, and other aspects of the external environment. Employees who are aware that the company is facing adversity are more likely to change their habits to help transform the situation.[42]

Even with the involvement of all levels of managers in change efforts, change processes do not always work the way they should. In fact, a global study of organizational change concludes that "Hundreds of managers from scores of US and European companies [are] satisfied with their operating prowess . . . [but] dissatisfied with their ability to implement change."[43] One of the reasons change fails is that managers do not really know how to introduce change in organizations. Professor John Kotter of Harvard Business School identifies a number of places where managers make mistakes when leading change. These mistakes are illustrated in Exhibit 12-8. We should also note that recent research emphasizes the need in change processes to manage the "hard stuff" as well as the "soft" or people issues in order to be successful.[44]

How can managers make change happen successfully? Managers can increase the likelihood of making change happen successfully in three ways. First, they should focus on making the organization ready for change. Exhibit 12-9 summarizes the characteristics of organizations that are ready for change.

EXHIBIT 12-9 Characteristics of Change-Capable Organizations

- *Link the present and the future.* Think of work as more than an extension of the past; think about future opportunities and issues and factor them into today's decisions.
- *Make learning a way of life.* Change-friendly organizations excel at knowledge sharing and management.
- *Actively support and encourage day-to-day improvements and changes.* Successful change can come from the small changes as well as the big ones.
- *Ensure diverse teams.* Diversity ensures that things won't be done the way they are always done.
- *Encourage mavericks.* Since their ideas and approaches are outside the mainstream, mavericks can help bring about radical change.
- *Shelter breakthroughs.* Change-friendly organizations have found ways to protect those breakthrough ideas.
- *Integrate technology.* Use technology to implement changes.
- *Build and deepen trust.* People are more likely to support changes when the organization's culture is trusting and managers have credibility and integrity.

Source: Based on P.A. McLagan. "The Change Capable Organization," Training & Development, January 2003 pp.50-58

Second, managers need to understand their own role in the change process. Managers facilitate change by creating a simple, compelling statement of the need for change; communicating constantly and honestly throughout the process; getting as much employee participation as possible; respecting employees' apprehension about the change but encouraging them to be flexible; removing those who resist but only after all possible attempts have been made to get their commitment to the change; aiming for short-term change successes since large-scale change can take a long time; and setting a positive example.[45]

Third, managers need to encourage employees to be change agents—to look for those day-to-day improvements and changes that individuals and teams can make. When employees are involved in the change process, they are more likely to support the changes required. Employees also have the front-line knowledge that is crucial to providing key ideas. For example, a recent study of organizational change found that 77 percent of changes at the work-group level were reactions to a specific, current problem or to a suggestion from someone outside the work group; and 68 percent of those changes occurred in the course of employees' day-to-day work.[46]

PERSONAL INVENTORY ASSESSMENT

Communicating Effectively When Undergoing Change

One study examined employee communications programs in 10 leading companies that had successfully undertaken major restructuring programs.[47] Eight factors were found to be related to the effectiveness of employee communications in these companies during times of change: (1) CEOs were committed to communication; (2) management matched their actions to their words; (3) two-way communication between managers and employees was encouraged; (4) the organization emphasized face-to-face communication; (5) managers shared responsibility for employee communication; (6) positive ways were found to deal with bad news; (7) messages were shaped for their intended audience; and (8) communication was treated as an ongoing process. Because the companies studied came from a variety of industries and organizational settings, the authors propose that these eight factors should apply to many types of organizations.

Perhaps the most important lesson from this research is that employees facing change need to be told what is happening and why, in very direct language, in order to reduce their fears. Good communication makes the process of change go more smoothly.

Global Organizational Development

Much of what we know about global organizational development (OD) practices has come from North American research. However, managers need to recognize that some OD techniques, although effective in North American organizations, may not be appropriate for organizations or organizational divisions based in other countries.[48] For example, a study of OD interventions showed that "multirater (survey) feedback as practised in the United States is not embraced in Taiwan" because the cultural value of "saving face is simply more powerful than the value of receiving feedback from subordinates."[49] What is the lesson for managers? Before using the same techniques to implement behavioural changes, especially across different countries, managers need to be sure that they have taken into account cultural characteristics and whether the techniques "make sense" for the local culture.

12.5 | **Explain** What are some common approaches to manage employee stress and resistance to change?

MANAGING EMPLOYEE STRESS

As a student, you have probably experienced stress when finishing class assignments and projects, taking exams, or finding ways to pay rising tuition costs, which may mean juggling a job and school. Then there is the stress associated with getting a decent job after graduation. Even after you have landed that job, your stress is not likely to stop. For many employees, organizational change creates stress. A dynamic and uncertain environment characterized by mergers, restructurings, forced retirements, and downsizing has created a large number of employees who are overworked and stressed out.[50]

According to the Vanier Institute of the Family, employees' stress-related disorders cost Canadian businesses an estimated $12 billion per year.[51] A 2012 Ipsos-Reid survey of Canadian businesses showed that three-quarters of Canadians were experiencing an uncomfortable level of stress.[52] A *Globe and Mail* survey in 2014 found that 36 percent of Canadians identify work as their biggest source of stress, ahead of money and family.[53] In this section, we review what stress is, what causes it, how to identify its symptoms, and what managers can do to reduce it.

Take a vacation from stress!

Sergey Nivens/Fotolia

Managing Resistance to Change

Change can be a threat to people in an organization. Organizations can build up inertia that motivates people to resist changing their status quo, even though change might be beneficial. Why do people resist change and what can be done to minimize their resistance?

WHY PEOPLE RESIST CHANGE   Resistance to change is well documented.[55] Why *do* people resist change? An individual is likely to resist change for the following reasons: uncertainty, habit, concern over personal loss, team dynamics, and the belief that the change is not in the organization's best interest.[56]

Change replaces the known with ambiguity and uncertainty. When you finish school, you will be leaving an environment where you know what is expected of you to join an organization where things are uncertain. Employees in organizations are faced with similar uncertainty and sometimes fear what they do not know. For example, when quality control methods based on sophisticated statistical models are introduced into manufacturing plants, many quality control inspectors have to learn new methods. Some inspectors may fear they will be unable to do so and might, therefore, develop a negative attitude toward the change or behave poorly if required to use those new methods.

Another cause of resistance is that we do things out of habit. Every day, when you go to school or work, you probably go the same way. If you are like most people, you find a single route and use it regularly. Human beings are creatures of habit. Life is complex enough—we do not want to have to consider the full range of options for the hundreds of decisions we make every day. To cope with this complexity, we rely on habits or programmed responses. When confronted with change, this tendency to respond in our accustomed ways becomes a source of resistance. Employees need to be forced out of their comfort zones when their habits are no longer organizationally appropriate.[57]

The third cause of resistance is the fear of losing something already possessed. Change threatens the investment you have already made in the status quo. The more people have invested in the current system, the more they resist change. Why? They fear the loss of status, money, authority, friendships, personal convenience, or other economic benefits that they value. This factor helps explain why older employees tend to resist change more than younger employees. Older employees have generally invested more in the current system and thus have more to lose by changing.

Team dynamics such as norms and values may also conflict with the organizational changes needed, and the behaviours of the members will serve to discourage individuals from embracing the change.[58]

A final cause of resistance is a person's belief that the change is incompatible with the goals and interests of the organization. An employee who believes that a proposed new job procedure will reduce product quality or productivity can be expected to resist the change.

And the
Survey Says... [54]

27% of businesses say the biggest hurdle to change is empowering others to act on the change.

46% of individuals say they would give up some of their salary for more personal time.

50% or more of employee resistance to change could have been avoided with effective change management.

77% of managers say they work 41 to 60 hours a week.

31% of managers believe that innovation happens by accident at their companies.

25% of employees say their companies encourage innovation as a mandate.

What Reaction Do Employees Have to Organizational Change?

1 What Is **Stress?**

- **Stress**—response to anxiety over intense demands, constraints, or opportunites.[59]

- Not always bad; can be positive, especially when there's potential gain. Functional stress allows a person to perform at his or her highest level at crucial times.

- Often associated with constraints (an obstacle that prevents you from doing what you desire), demands (the loss of something desired), and opportunities (the possibility of something new, something never done).
  Examples: Taking a test or having your annual work performance review.

- Although conditions may be right for stress to surface, it does not mean it will.

Too much stress can also have tragic consequences. In Japan, there is a stress phenomenon called **karoshi** (pronounced kah-roe-she), which is translated as death from overwork.

EXHIBIT 12-10 What Are the Symptoms of Stress?

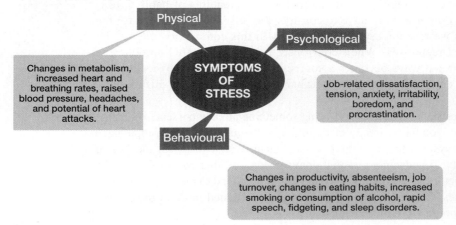

stress
Response to anxiety over intense demands, constraints, or opportunities.

karoshi
A Japanese term that refers to a sudden death caused by overworking.

2 What Causes Stress? Stressors

Job-related factors:

- Examples: Pressures to avoid errors or complete tasks in a limited time period; changes in the way reports are filed; a demanding supervisor; unpleasant coworkers

1. **Task demands:** Stress due to an employee's job—job design (autonomy, task variety, degree of automation); working conditions (temperature, noise, etc.); physical work layout (overcrowded or in visible location with constant interruptions; work quotas, especially when excessive;[60] high level of task interdependence with others. (FYI: Autonomy lessens stress.)

2. **Role demands:** Stress due to an employee's particular role.
   - **Role conflicts**—expectations that may be hard to reconcile or satisfy
   - **Role overload**—created when an employee is expected to do more than time permits
   - **Role ambiguity**—created when role expectations are not clearly understood. Employee is not sure what he or she is to do.

3. **Interpersonal demands**—Stress due to other employees; little or no support from colleagues; poor interpersonal relationships

4. **Organizational structure**—Stress due to excessive rules; no opportunity to participate in decisions that affect an employee

5. **Organizational leadership**—Stress due to managers' supervisory style in a culture of tension, fear, anxiety, unrealistic pressures to perform in the short run, excessively tight controls, and routine firing of employees who do not measure up.

---

stressors
Factors that cause stress.

role conflicts
Work expectations that are hard to satisfy.

role overload
Having more work to accomplish than time permits.

role ambiguity
When role expectations are not clearly understood.

Personal factors:
Life demands, constraints, opportunities of any kind

PIA
PERSONAL INVENTORY ASSESSMENT

1 Family issues, personal economic problems, and so forth

- Cannot just ignore. Managers need to be understanding of these personal factors.[61]

A Question of Ethics

One in five companies offers some form of stress management program.[62] Although such programs are available, many employees may choose not to participate. They may be reluctant to ask for help, especially if a major source of that stress is job insecurity. After all, there is still a stigma associated with stress. Employees do not want to be perceived as being unable to handle the demands of their job. Although they may need stress management now more than ever, few employees want to admit that they are stressed.

Discuss this:

- What can be done about this paradox?
- Do organizations even have an ethical responsibility to help employees deal with stress?

2 Employees' personalities— Type A or Type B

- **Type A personality**—chronic sense of time urgency, excessive competitive drive, difficulty accepting and enjoying leisure time; more likely to show symptoms of stress

- **Type B personality**—little to no sense of time urgency or impatience

- Stress comes from the hostility and anger associated with Type A behaviour. Surprisingly, Type Bs are just as susceptible.

Beyond Fotomedia GmbH/Alamy

Type A personality
People who have a chronic sense of urgency and an excessive competitive drive.

Type B personality
People who are relaxed and easygoing and accept change easily.

How Can Stress Be Reduced?

1 **General guidelines:**

- Not all stress is dysfunctional.
- Stress can never be totally eliminated!
- Reduce dysfunctional stress by controlling job-related factors and offering help for personal stress.

2 **Job-related factors:**

- **Employee selection**—provide realistic job previews and make sure an employee's abilities match the job requirements
- **On-the-job**—improve organizational communications to minimize ambiguity; use a performance planning program such as MBO to clarify job responsibilities, provide clear performance goals, and reduce ambiguity through feedback; redesign job, if possible, especially if stress can be traced to boredom (increase challenge) or to work overload (reduce the workload); allow employees to participate in decisions and to gain social support.[63]

1bestofphoto/Alamy

3 **Personal factors:**

- Not easy for a manager to control directly
- Ethical considerations

Does a manager have the **right to intrude**—even subtly—
in an employee's personal life?

- If the manager believes it is ethical and the employee is receptive, consider:
  - Employee assistance and wellness programs,[64] which are designed to assist employees in areas where they might be having difficulties (financial planning, legal matters, health, fitness, or stress)[65]
  - **Employee assistance programs (EAPs)**[66]—the rationale is to get a productive employee back on the job as quickly as possible
  - **Wellness programs**—the rationale is to keep employees healthy

Samantha Craddock/Alamy

---

employee assistance programs (EAPs)
Programs offered by organizations to help employees overcome personal and health-related problems.

wellness programs
Programs offered by organizations to help employees prevent health problems.

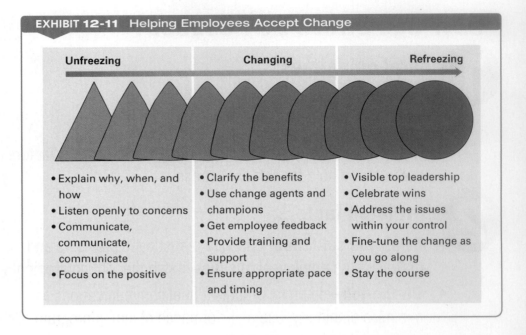

EXHIBIT 12-11 Helping Employees Accept Change

Unfreezing	Changing	Refreezing
• Explain why, when, and how • Listen openly to concerns • Communicate, communicate, communicate • Focus on the positive	• Clarify the benefits • Use change agents and champions • Get employee feedback • Provide training and support • Ensure appropriate pace and timing	• Visible top leadership • Celebrate wins • Address the issues within your control • Fine-tune the change as you go along • Stay the course

TECHNIQUES FOR REDUCING RESISTANCE When managers see resistance to change as dysfunctional, they can choose from a variety of actions to deal with it.[67] Exhibit 12-11 shows how to manage resistance at the unfreezing, changing, and refreezing stages. Actions include communicating the reasons for change, getting input from employees, choosing the timing of change carefully, and showing management support for the change process. Providing support to employees to deal with the stress of the change is also important.

The actions a manager chooses depend on the type and source of the resistance. In general, resistance is likely to be lower if managers involve people in the change, offer training where needed, and are open to revisions once the change has been implemented. For more suggestions on reducing resistance, see *Developing Your Interpersonal Skills—Managing Resistance to Change* at the end of the chapter.

Common Approaches to Organizational Change

Change occurs daily in organizations. There are many common approaches to organizational change, but action research and appreciative inquiry are two of the leading approaches.[68]

Managers need to do more than just tell their employees what to do.

ACTION RESEARCH Kurt Lewin's action research approach has a problem-solving view that change is based on changing employee attitudes and behaviours along with collecting data to diagnose the organizational problems in more detail. This approach relies on Lewin's earlier discussion about *unfreezing* the status quo, *changing* to a new state, and *refreezing* to make the change permanent.

Typically an outside consultant is the original change agent. Employees are highly involved in data collection and analysis, and the nature and timing of the change are determined. Once the change is introduced, organizational and team systems are then redesigned to support the refreezing process. Action research is highly participative and employees work with the consultant to understand the changes required and build commitment.[69] Exhibit 12-12 illustrates the action research approach.

Texelart/Fotolia

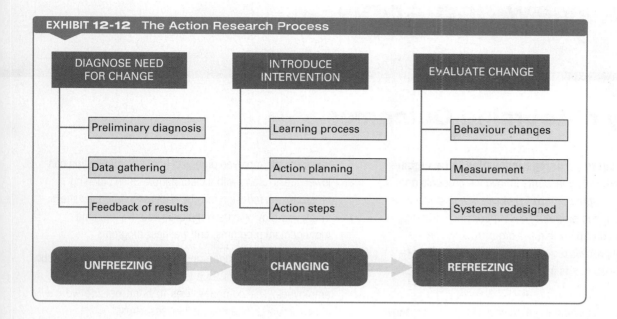

EXHIBIT 12-12   The Action Research Process

APPRECIATIVE INQUIRY   Appreciative inquiry (AI) is a more positive approach than action research. AI begins by investigating what the organization is doing well. Searching for the organization's strengths can help create a vision of what it could become. Like parents who focus on highlighting the positive aspects of a child's behaviour instead of the negative, AI uncovers successful events and teams within an organization and uses that knowledge as a guidepost for the change effort.[70] Canadian Tire successfully launched a major AI effort, which solicited feedback from employees across the country to come up with six key values that defined "The Canadian Tire Way." Employees used AI to visualize a positive future for Canadian Tire.[71] The four stages of AI are illustrated in Exhibit 12-13.

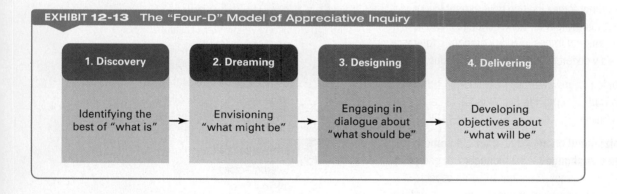

EXHIBIT 12-13   The "Four-D" Model of Appreciative Inquiry

12 Review and Apply

Summary of Learning Outcomes

12.1 How can managers encourage innovation in an organization? If an organization wants innovative products and work methods (*outputs*), it has to take its *inputs* and *transform* them into those outputs. Those *inputs* include creative people and groups within the organization. The *transformation process* requires having the right environment to turn those inputs into innovative products or work methods.

Men In Kilts took ideas from its employees about the company slogan and what type of kilts they should wear.

12.2 How does organizational culture affect innovation and change? Innovative organizations tend to have similar cultures, which encourage experimentation, reward both successes and failures; and celebrate mistakes. An innovative organization is likely to have the following characteristics: *accepts ambiguity, tolerates the impractical, keeps external controls minimal, tolerates risk and conflict, focuses on ends rather than means, uses an open-system focus, and provides positive feedback.*

12.3 What are forces for change? Forces for change are internal and external. External forces include government laws and regulations, technology, labour market changes, and economic changes. Internal forces include company strategy, an organization's workforce, and employee attitudes.

Men In Kilts wanted to grow the business through franchising and hired Chris Carrier to provide higher levels of service and support to franchisees.

12.4 What is organizational change and what are some common approaches to change? Most managers, at one point or another, will have to make changes in some aspects of their workplace—any alteration of people, structure, or technology. Action research looks at solving some organizational problem by researching and diagnosing the need for change, introducing the intervention, and then changing employee attitudes and behaviours to stabilize the change. Appreciative inquiry focuses more on the positive side to create future success through analysis of organizational strengths. The four steps are discovery, dreaming, designing, and delivering.

12.5 What are some common approaches to manage employee stress and resistance to change? Managers need to make sure that an employee's abilities match the job

requirement. Improved organizational communication can lower stress, along with a clear performance planning program. Job redesign may be necessary to reduce stress. Employers may also use employee counselling, time management programs, and wellness programs.

Men In Kilts has an open and collaborative culture. The success of the business is due to the quality service provided by employees. The company likes to bond outside work with social activities to reduce employees' stress.

SNAPSHOT SUMMARY

12.1 How Important Is Innovation to Companies?
How Are Creativity and Innovation Related?
What Is Involved in Innovation?
How Can a Manager Foster Innovation?
How Do Structural Variables Affect Innovation?
How Does an Organization's Culture Affect Innovation?
What Human Resource Variables Affect Innovation?
How Does Design Thinking Influence Innovation?

12.2 Organizational Culture
Strong Versus Weak Cultures
Developing an Organization's Culture
How Employees Learn Culture
Changing Organizational Culture
Understanding the Situational Factors
How Can Cultural Change Be Accomplished?

12.3 Forces for Change
External Forces
Internal Forces
Two Views of the Change Process

12.4 What Is Organizational Change?
Types of Change
Making Change Happen Successfully
Communicating Effectively When Undergoing Change
Global Organizational Development

12.5 Managing Employee Stress
Managing Resistance to Change
Common Approaches to Organizational Change

Discussion Questions

1. Discuss the external and internal forces for change.
2. Why is handling change an integral part of every manager's job?
3. Describe two approaches to managing organizational change.
4. Explain why people resist change and how resistance might be managed.
5. Who are change agents? Do you think that a low-level employee could act as a change agent? Explain.
6. How would an organization decide between action research and appreciative inquiry? Explain briefly how each brings about organizational change.

Developing Management Skills

Dilemma

Think of something you would like to change in your personal life. It could be your study habits, your fitness and nutrition, the way you interact with others, or anything else of interest to you. What values and assumptions have encouraged the behaviour that currently exists (the one you want to change)? What driving and restraining forces can you address in order to make the desired change? Here are some tips for making a change in your life:

- Accept the change instead of resisting it, and find the potential benefits and new opportunities the change may bring.
- Familiarize yourself with the new aspects as quickly as possible, but be patient and recognize that you cannot master everything at once.
- Be organized. Make a list of what needs to be done to make the change happen, and focus on one change at a time.
- Ask "How?" rather than "Why?" "How can I use the support of others to facilitate the transition?" Change can be intimidating, but asking the right questions can make you more comfortable with what is going on around you.
- Gain back control. Change can take control away from you, so stare down your challenges.

Developing Your Interpersonal Skills: Managing Resistance to Change

Kurt Lewin's force field analysis model was discussed earlier in the chapter. This exercise will help you apply the model to a real-life situation.[72] Lewin suggests that whenever driving forces are greater than restraining forces, the status quo will change.

ABOUT THE SKILL

Driving forces are both attitudes to change and the emotions surrounding those attitudes. Developing your emotional intelligence will help you understand the forces operating within you and others.

STEPS IN DEVELOPING THE SKILL

The following steps can be used as a guide to following Lewin's force field analysis:

1. **Clarify your vision of the change you want to see.** Write down the goal you have for a particular situation (school success, health and nutrition, career development, etc.). The vision of the desired future will help you clarify the goal.
2. **List the driving forces.** Record the forces that are favourable to the change you would like to achieve. List them in the first column of a four-column chart.
3. **List the restraining forces.** Record the forces that oppose your change or might limit your effectiveness. List these in the third column.
4. **Rate the driving and restraining forces.** In column two, rate each driving force from 1 (weak) to 5 (strong); in column four rate each restraining force from 1 (weak) to 5 (strong).
5. **Develop a strategy.** Decide which of the forces could be influenced most easily. Come up with a strategy to strengthen the driving forces or weaken the restraining

forces. Note that reducing the impact of restraining forces is often easier. If you look at your ratings, can you figure out a way to raise the scores of the driving forces or reduce the scores of the restraining forces?

6. **Develop your action plan.** What steps can you take that will have the greatest impact? Identify the resources you will need and come up with a basic implementation plan.

PRACTISING THE SKILL

You are the regional manager of two successful restaurants that employ bartenders and servers. One of the restaurants is downtown and the other is in a highly populated suburb. Each of the teams of bartenders and servers tends to work almost exclusively with others doing the same job. Servers in the downtown restaurant earn less pay and have no duties behind the bar. Servers in the suburban restaurant often fill in behind the bar.

In your professional reading, you have come across the concept of cross-training restaurant staff and giving them more varied responsibilities, which in turn has been shown to improve customer satisfaction while lowering costs. You call the two team leaders, Sue and Scott, into your office to explain that you want the bartending teams to move to this approach. To your surprise, both team leaders are opposed to the idea.

Sue says she and the other downtown bartenders feel they are needed in the main bar, where they fill the most vital role in the restaurant. They have developed special talents in mixology and pouring, and often work in difficult and stressful circumstances with a much younger clientele. The downtown bartenders think the suburban bartenders have relatively easy jobs for the pay they receive, since they also spend time serving customers in the restaurant.

Scott, the leader of the suburban bartenders, tells you his group believes the downtown bartenders lack the special training and extra experience required to work with the senior IT executives who frequent their restaurant, as well as the special skills needed to serve and tend bar. The bartenders claim they have heavier responsibilities and do more exacting work, because they have responsibilities as servers as well.

What should you do about your idea to introduce more cross-training for the restaurant teams?

Hey, You're the Boss Now!

Innovation requires a team approach, and what is needed to stimulate innovation is beyond possible for only one person to achieve. As a new supervisor, you need to find roles for your team members.

Idea champions	Innovation rarely happens without someone to initiate and advocate for the idea. Anyone in the organization can be an idea champion.
Constructive coworkers	They rally behind ideas but also constructively identify or refine the problem. They may also bring other unique problems to the group for input and reflection.
Coaches	Managers must encourage innovative behaviours, and they must allocate time and budget to ideas. They may also need to be a coach and facilitator.

For one of your thornier organizational problems, try this team brainstorming technique to stimulate innovation:

1. Whoever is having the problem states to the group his/her view of the problem.
2. The group brainstorms potential definitions or alternative statements of the problem, being careful to identify symptoms separately from the problem.
3. The problem owner selects a few of these new problem statements for further review.
4. One or more of those reviewed problem definitions are brought back to the group, who then brainstorm potential solutions.
5. The problem owner selects one or more of the solutions for further analysis or research.
6. The problem owner may decide to use the group again for further development of the solutions.

You may also need to break down certain common roadblocks in organizations that stifle creativity and innovation:[73]

- people afraid of making mistakes
- lack of resources for projects
- no time to be innovative
- lack of expertise or staff without the required skills
- lack of a shared vision of the benefits of innovation

Diversity Matters

Intuitively, most managers accept that organizations benefit from a diverse workforce, and new research has shown that diversity unlocks innovation and drives market growth.[74] The research examined two types of diversity: *inherent* and *acquired*. Inherent diversity involves traits you are born with, such as gender, ethnicity, and sexual orientation. Acquired diversity deals more with traits gained from experience, such as working in another company or with a diverse client base. When both types of diversity are present, it is referred to as 2-D diversity.

Companies with 2-D diversity out-innovate and out-perform others in terms of higher market share and capitalizing on new markets. The results discovered that 2-D diversity stimulates innovation by creating an "outside the box" idea-generating environment, as inherently diverse contributors understand the unmet needs in under-leveraged markets.[75] Companies whose employee populations match their client populations in inherent diversity develop much deeper understandings of those clients.

Inherent diversity is the first step, but leaders also need acquired diversity to shape a culture that is open to innovation and change. Here are six actions[76] that were found to unlock innovation in individuals and organizations:[77]

- ensuring that everyone is heard
- creating a safe environment for creativity and unique ideas

- giving team members decision-making authority
- sharing credit for success
- giving actionable feedback
- implementing ideas and suggestions from the team

Your Essential Management Reading List

Learning from key management experts can help you understand today's management theory and practice. Here is a list of some of the more influential management books on change

and innovation, as well as 1-800-GOT-JUNK's CEO Brian Scudamore's favourite on small business:

- *The E-Myth: Why Most Small Businesses Don't Work and What to Do About It*—Michael Gerber
- *The Innovator's Dilemma*—Clayton Christensen
- *Leading Change*—John Kotter
- *Switch: How to Change Things When Change Is Hard*—Chip Heath and Dan Heath

Team Exercises

3BL: The Triple Bottom Line

HOW CAN COMPANIES MAKE THE CHANGE TOWARD SUSTAINABILITY?

Moving toward the triple bottom line requires vision from the outset. Businesses move to sustainability in an attempt to improve economic performance, enhance corporate image, reduce the environmental impact of their actions, and attract and retain top employees. External forces for change certainly can have a strong influence on the move to sustainability, but companies need to be able to drive this process even when the external forces are not apparent.

An important first step is to decide how much of the organization should be involved in 3BL. Sustainability can be implemented in all facets of the organization, but often the best place to start is with its products and services.[78] Westport Innovations of Vancouver, for example, develops environmental technologies and services that enable vehicles to operate on clean-burning alternative fuels.[79] Companies need to look at their products to see if they can be made from non-toxic, renewable materials, or even if there is another use for their product. Nike Grind[80] uses recycled shoes to make sport surfaces like playgrounds. Other areas where companies can consider sustainability include processes, its business model, and the supplier value chain.[81]

Functional areas of a company can implement sustainability in its processes and practices. The facilities team of Ottawa's Algonquin College designed the largest Leadership in Environmental and Energy Design (LEED) platinum-certified building in Canada as part of the new Centre for Construction Excellence.[82] Human resource departments can build their 3BL presence through recruitment and training. Finance departments can provide more detailed reporting of sustainability initiatives.

The last piece of the puzzle is having the right change leadership in place. Earlier in the chapter change agents were discussed. Change agents responsible for 3BL would be charged with facilitating training and education, gathering 3BL resources, linking employees to experts, coordinating meetings, and problem-solving 3BL issues.

THINKING PRACTICALLY ABOUT 3BL

How can companies demonstrate leadership to the industry concerning the need for 3BL?

Walmart Canada held a Green Business Summit in Vancouver in 2010. The Summit demonstrated to the attendees that all businesses could work together to accelerate change toward triple bottom line goals. The outcome was ShareGreen.ca, an open website where companies and individuals can share case studies of green business practices with a positive impact on return on investment (ROI).[83]

Overcoming Resistance to Change

OBJECTIVES

- to explore resistance to change
- to investigate the planning necessary to overcome resistance

THE SITUATION

You have been promoted to HR Manager in a large IT organization with three divisions: a helpdesk staffing agency, a network consulting branch, and a software development unit. There are three VPs, and each administers one of the divisions. The VP of the software development unit has been struggling.

The president has just informed you that he will be emailing staff in the software division tomorrow to announce he is consolidating the software development and the network consulting under one division. Only one of the VPs will run the two divisions, and the other VP will become a manager and report to the VP. Two supervisors will report to the manager. All employees from the former separate divisions will report to the two supervisors.

The president is well respected in the industry for his technical ability, and you have established a strong working relationship with him over the past five years. He has grown the company from 25 employees to over 2000 in the past 10 years. He has developed a reputation for making quick decisions that have led to issues such as a lack of coordination, frustrated staff, and even high turnover. This decision is his alone, and he has not obtained feedback or involved anyone else in the decision. He has asked you to create a draft email to staff outlining all of the changes. You have some experience with managing change at a previous company and have decided that you will provide some recommendations to the president by tomorrow on how to manage his desired consolidation more effectively.

PROCEDURE

1. Divide into groups of five to seven—you are acting as the HR Manager in the scenario.
2. Each group should identify the forces causing resistance to the change in the scenario.
3. Each group should develop a set of recommendations for the president.
4. Reassemble the class and hear each group's recommendations and explanations.
5. After each group has presented, the other consulting groups should pose probing questions about the presenting group's recommendations.

Be the Consultant: The Celestial Aerospace Company

OBJECTIVES

- to illustrate how forces for change and stability must be managed in organizations
- to illustrate the effects of alternative change techniques on the relative strength of forces for change and forces for stability

THE SITUATION

The marketing division of the Celestial Aerospace Company (CAP) has gone through two major reorganizations in the past seven years. Initially, the structure changed from a functional

to a matrix form, which did not satisfy some functional managers; nor did it lead to organizational improvements. The managers complained that the structure confused the authority and responsibility relationships. In reaction to these complaints, senior management returned to the functional form, which maintained market and project teams managed by project managers with a few general staff personnel. No functional specialists were assigned to these groups. After the change, problems began to surface. Project managers complained they could not obtain the necessary assistance from functional staff. It not only took more time to obtain assistance but also created problems in establishing stable relationships with functional staff members. Because these problems affected customer service, project managers demanded a change in the organizational structure.

Faced with these complaints and demands from project managers, senior management is pondering yet another reorganization for the division. They have requested an outside consultant (you) to help them in their reorganization plan—one that will provide some stability to the structure, address their issues, and help the organization achieve its strategic goals.

PROCEDURE

1. Divide into groups of five to seven and take the role of consultants.
2. Each group should identify the forces necessitating the change and the resistance to that change in the company.
3. Each group should develop a set of strategies for dealing with the resistance to change and for implementing those strategies.
4. Reassemble the class and hear each group's recommendations and explanations.
5. After each group has presented, the other consulting groups should pose probing questions about the presenting group's recommendations.

Business Cases

1-800-GOT-JUNK?

Eighteen thousand expired cans of sardines.[84] Fifty garden gnomes. A mechanical bull. Trophies from a nudist colony. These objects are just some of the weird items that Vancouver-based 1-800-GOT-JUNK? customers have asked the uniformed people in the freshly scrubbed blue trucks to haul away. Company founder and CEO Brian Scudamore discovered a lucrative niche between "trash cans and those big green bins dropped off by" the giant waste haulers. But even in such an uncomplicated business as hauling people's junk, Scudamore must be concerned with managing change and innovation.

1-800-GOT-JUNK? is an award-winning company with a corporate staff of about 300 individuals. "With a vision of creating the 'FedEx' of junk removal," says Scudamore, "I dropped

out of university with just one year left to become a full-time JUNKMAN! Yes, my father, a liver transplant surgeon, was not impressed, to say the least." However, in 2011, the company had more than 200 franchises, and system-wide revenues were over $100 million.[85] Not surprisingly, Scudamore's father is a little more understanding these days about his son's business. Since 1997, the company has grown exponentially. The company made the list of *Entrepreneur* magazine's 100 fastest-growing franchises in 2005 and 2006. It was named one of the Best Employers in Canada by *Canadian Business*, and Scudamore won the International Franchise Association's Entrepreneur of the Year award. Scudamore also started two newer franchises: Wow 1 Day Painting and You Move Me.

Hauling junk would be, to most people's minds at least, a pretty simple business. However, the company Scudamore founded is a "curious hybrid." It has been described as a blend of "old economy and new economy." The company's service—hauling away trash—has been done for hundreds, if not thousands, of years. But 1-800-GOT-JUNK? also relies heavily on up-to-date information technology and has the kind of organizational culture that most people associate with high-tech startups. The company uses its 1-800-GOT-JUNK? call centre to do the booking and dispatching for all its franchise partners. The franchise partners also use the company's proprietary intranet and customer relationship management site—dubbed JunkNet—to access schedules, customer information, real-time reports, and so forth. According to Scudamore's philosophy, this approach allowed franchise partners to "work on the business" instead of "work in the business." On any given day, all a franchisee has to do is open up JunkNet to see the day's schedule. If a new job comes in during a workday, the program automatically sends an alert to the franchisee. Needless to say, the company's franchisees tend to be quite tech-savvy. In fact, some of them have installed GPS devices in their trucks to help find the most efficient routes on a job. Others use online navigation sites. With the price of gas continuing to increase, this type of capability is important.

1-800-GOT-JUNK? has a culture that would rival any high-tech startup. The head office is known as the Junktion. Grizzly, Scudamore's dog, comes to the office every day and helps employees relieve stress by playing catch anytime, anywhere. Each morning at exactly 10:55, all employees at the Junktion meet for a seven-minute huddle, where they share good news, announcements, metrics, and problems they are encountering. Visitors to the Junktion have to join the group huddle, too. One of the most conspicuous features of the Junktion is the "Vision Wall," which contains the varied outputs of Scudamore's brainstorms. Other members of the executive team have visions for the company's future as well. Periodically they will wander through the offices of Genome Sciences Centre, the tenant occupying the space above them, to visualize a future when GOT-JUNK? has expanded so sufficiently that it will take over that office space. Scudamore does not use a permanent desk, instead preferring to sit in different spaces to talk with people and get a sense of what is going on in the business.

Company franchisees are also encouraged to take initiative and be innovative. For example, the Toronto franchise, which has 12 trucks, sometimes gets a blue truck motorcade going down Yonge Street through the heart of the city as a way to be noticed and to publicize its services. Despite the company's success to date, Scudamore is wondering whether he is prepared to face whatever changes may happen in the environment in the years to come.

Discussion Questions

1. How would you advise Scudamore to make 1-800-GOT-JUNK? a "change-capable" organization?
2. 1-800-GOT-JUNK? uses a large bell in the office that employees ring every time they have a good idea. Is this an effective way to stimulate innovation?
3. Scudamore built a mini-library for employees, where they are encouraged to read in order to grow and learn. What other ways could Scudamore encourage change among employees?

Prairie General Hospital

When you think about the significant changes that have occurred in people's lives over the past five decades, clearly the advances in medical science would be at the top of such a list. Diseases have been eradicated, and medical procedures and devices have helped save thousands of lives. But do not be too quick to conclude that the health care industry is a model of innovation and efficiency.[86]

Hospitals, in general, have one of the most archaic and costly operating systems of any group of large organizations. Nearly 95 percent of all hospitals currently use procedures and record-keeping systems that were implemented more than 50 years ago. Many doctors and technicians prefer to function the way they have always done. Individuals in this industry have been highly reluctant to accept and use new technologies.

Doctors and hospital administrators at Prairie General Hospital, however, refuse to be part of "the old guard." Consider the following incident that happened in the emergency room at Prairie General. A middle-aged patient was brought in by his wife to the emergency room (ER). The patient, who was very overweight, was complaining of shortness of breath and dizziness. Although the patient claimed he was fine, his wife made him go to the hospital. Immediately the staff at Prairie General went to work. While nurses hooked the patient up to heart monitoring equipment and checked his vital signs, a resident wheeled over an emergency room cart, which contained a laptop computer. Logging in the patient's identification number, the ER doctor noticed that the patient had had an electrocardiogram (EKG) in the past year. By reviewing the past EKG records and comparing them with current heart monitoring results, the doctor determined the patient was in the middle of a heart attack. Within 10 minutes of seeing the patient, doctors had determined that he was suffering from a blocked artery. Clot-busting drugs were swiftly administered, and the patient was immediately taken to the cardiac lab, where an emergency angioplasty was performed to open up the clogged artery. Within a day, the patient was back on his feet and ready to go home. In most other hospitals, the patient might not have been so lucky!

Prairie General is unusual in the health care industry. This hospital is investing money in technology that enables it to provide better service at a lower cost. Through its system, called CareWeb, more than 1 million patient records are available. Each of these records contains all previous medical orders, such as lab test results and prescriptions, for every patient. When a patient comes to the hospital, that individual's health history is easily retrievable and can be used to assist in the current diagnosis.

What has been the effect of this technology change on Prairie General? The system is saving the hospital more than $1 million each year. It has reduced errors in patient care by more than 90 percent, and reduced prescription errors and potential adverse drug interactions by more than 50 percent. Patient charts are now available in moments rather than hours or days. Patients are discharged more than 30 minutes faster than they had been before CareWeb was implemented.

Cost savings, time savings, increased patient care, and saved lives—all these benefits make you wonder why every hospital is not making such changes!

Discussion Questions

1. Describe the types of changes that have occurred at Prairie General in terms of structure, technology, and people. Cite examples.
2. Why do you think the medical profession resists changing to systems such as CareWeb? Explain.
3. Assume you were going to make a presentation to a group of hospital staff (doctors and administrators) on why they should invest in technology such as CareWeb. How would you attempt to overcome their resistance to change and their attitude about continuing to do what they have always done? Discuss.

Endnotes

CHAPTER 1

1. J. Geddes, "The Power Issue: The 50 Most Important People in Canada," *Maclean's*, December 2, 2013, pp. 18–20.

2. "Naheed Nenshi's Biography," http://blog.calgarymayor.ca/p/biography.html.

3. K. A. Tucker and V. Allman, "Don't Be a Cat-and-Mouse Manager," *Gallup Business Journal*, http://businessjournal.gallup.com/content/12574/dont-be-a-cat-and-mouse-manager.aspx.

4. See the *Tenth Annual Survey of Canada's Most Respected Corporations*, conducted by Ipsos-Reid and sponsored by KPMG, which asks 250 of Canada's leading CEOs to indicate which corporations they most respect in eight categories, http://www.rbc.com/newsroom/pdf/CMRC2004En.pdf.

5. "WorkUSA 2004/2005: Effective Employees Drive Financial Results," Watson Wyatt Worldwide, Washington, DC.

6. D. J. Campbell, "The Proactive Employee: Managing Workplace Initiative," *Academy of Management Executive*, August 2000, pp. 52–66.

7. J. S. McClenahen, "Prairie Home Champion," *IndustryWeek*, October 2005, pp. 45–47.

8. J. Geddes, "The Power Issue: The 50 Most Important People in Canada," *Maclean's*, December 2, 2013, pp. 18–20.

9. P. Drucker, *Management: Tasks, Responsibilities, Practices* (New York: Harper & Row, 1974).

10. H. Fayol, *Industrial and General Administration* (Paris: Dunod, 1916).

11. For a comprehensive review of this question, see C. P. Hales, "What Do Managers Do? A Critical Review of the Evidence," *Journal of Management*, January 1986, pp. 88–115.

12. D. Burnett Vachon and C. Lavis, "Women in Leadership: Perceptions and Priorities for Change, Report," May 2013. The Conference Board of Canada.

13. S. J. Carroll and D. A. Gillen, "Are the Classical Management Functions Useful in Describing Managerial Work?" *Academy of Management Review*, January 1987, p. 48.

14. Ibid.

15. H. G. Barkema, J. A. C. Baum, and E. A. Mannix, "Management Challenges in a New Time," *Academy of Management Journal*, October 2002, pp. 916–930; M. A. Hitt, "Transformation of Management for the New Millennium," *Organizational Dynamics*, Winter 2000, pp. 7–17; T. Aeppel, "Power Generation," *Wall Street Journal*, April 7, 2000, p. A11; "Rethinking Work," *Fast Company*, April 2000, p. 253; "Workplace Trends Shifting over Time," *Springfield News Leader*, January 2, 2000, p. 7B1; "Expectations: The State of the New Economy," *Fast Company*, September 1999, pp. 251–264; T. J. Tetenbaum, "Shifting Paradigms: From Newton to Chaos," *Organizational Dynamics*, Spring 1998, pp. 21–33; T. A. Stewart, "Brain Power: Who Owns It, How They Profit from It," *Fortune*, March 17, 1997, p. A11; W. H. Miller, Leadership at a Crossroads," *IndustryWeek*, August 19, 1996, pp. 42–56; M. Scott,

"Interview with Dee Hock," *Business Ethics*, May–June 1996, pp. 37–41; J. O. C. Hamilton, S. Baker, and B. Vlasic, "The New Workplace," *BusinessWeek*, April 29, 1996, pp. 106–117.

16. Industry Canada, *Key Small Business Statistics, July 2012*. http://www.ic.gc.ca/eic/site/061.nsf/eng/h_02689.html.

17. Ibid.

18. Canada Post, *2010 Annual Report: Making Necessary Change*, http://www.canadapost.ca/cpo/mc/assets/pdf/aboutus/annualreport/ar_2010-e.pdf.

19. S A. Hewlett, M. Marshall, L. Sherbin, and T. Gonsalves, "Innovation, Diversity and Market Growth," *Center for Talent Innovation*, 2013. Retrieved from Conference Board of Canada, *Human Capital in Review Focus on Diversity & Inclusion*, vol. 4, no. 1, 2014.

20. Ibid.

21. U.S. Bureau of Labor Statistics, "Employment Projections 2010–2020 Summary," February 1, 2012 (http://www.bls.gov/news.release/ecopro.nr0.htm). Also http://www.newswire.ca/en/story/1311403/the-millennial-influence-say-hello-to-the-new-workplace.

22. Pew Research Center, "Millennials—A Portrait of Generation Next," 2010. Retrieved from Diane Piktialis and Kent A. Greenes, *Bridging the Gaps*, The Conference Board, 2008.

23. Jeanne C. Meister and Karie Willyerd, "Mentoring Millennials," *Harvard Business Review*, May 2010.

24. See Shopify, "Shopify Marks Fifth Anniversary," Press Release, September 13, 2011, http://www.shopify.com/press/articles/shopify-marks-fifth-anniversary.html.

25. S. Silcoff, "A Rare Startup Success Story: Shopify Hits $1-Billion Milestone," *Globe and Mail*, December 11, 2013. Retrieved from http://www.theglobeandmail.com/report-on-business/small-business/sb-money/business-funding/a-rare-startup-success-story-shopify-hits-1-billion-milestone/article15892998/.

26. Ibid.

27. Industry Canada, *Small Business Branch: Key Small Business Statistics, August 2013*. Retrieved from https://www.ic.gc.ca/eic/site/061.nsf/vwapj/KSBS-PSRPE_August-Aout2013_eng.pdf/$FILE/KSBS-PSRPE_August-Aout2013_eng.pdf.

28. See K. Chow, "Fastest-Growing Companies: Shopify," *Business Journal*, May 16, 2011, http://www.obj.ca/Other/Special-Reports/2011-05-16/article-2507771/FASTEST-GROWING-COMPANIES%3A-Shopify/1; Shopify, "Shopify Announces Build-A-Business Competition," Press Release, 2012, http://www.shopify.com/press/articles/shopify-announces-build-a-business-competition.html.

29. See FuEL Awards, "Meet the Judges," http://www.fuelawards.ca/judges.

30. See Shopify, "Shopify Announces $7 Million Series A Funding from Bessemer, FirstMark, and Felicis," Press Release, December 13, 2010, http://www.shopify.com/press/articles/7-million-series-a-funding.html.

CHAPTER 2

1. Adam Waterous, "The Keystone XL Delay Was a Gift to Canada," *Globe and Mail*, April 4, 2012, http://www.theglobeandmail.com/news/opinions/opinion/the-keystone-xl-delay-was-agift-to-canada/article2391122.

2. TransCanada. "Keystone XL Pipeline Project," TransCanada Corporation, http://www.transcanada.com/keystone.html.

3. AP, "Thwarted on US Oil Pipeline, Canada Looks to China," *Canadian Business*, January 29, 2012, http://www.canadianbusiness.com/article/68160—thwarted-on-us-oil-pipeline-canada-looks-to-china.

4. "Obama Changes Course, Fast-tracks Keystone Pipeline," *CTV News*, http://www.ctv.ca/CTVNews/TopStories/20120322/keystone-pipeline-announcement-120322/#ixzz2PQn5ISXc.

5. Adam Waterous, "The Keystone XL Delay Was a Gift to Canada," *Globe and Mail*, April 4, 2012, http://www.theglobeandmail.com/news/opinions/opinion/the-keystone-xl-delay-was-agift-to-canada/article2391122.

6. AP, "Thwarted on US Oil Pipeline, Canada Looks to China," *Canadian Business*, January 29, 2012, http://www.canadianbusiness.com/article/68160—thwarted-on-us-oil-pipeline-canada-looks-to-china.

7. "Bottled Water in Canada," Euromonitor International, March 2015, http://www.euromonitor.com/bottled-water-in-canada/report.

8. J. S. Harrison and C. H. St. John, "Managing and Partnering with External Stakeholders," *Academy of Management Executive*, May 1996, pp. 46–60.

9. A. J. Hillman and G. D. Keim, "Shareholder Value, Stakeholder Management, and Social Issues: What's the Bottom Line?" *Strategic Management Journal*, March 2001, pp. 125–139; and J. Kotter and J. Heskett, *Corporate Culture and Performance* (New York: Free Press, 1992).

10. G. Lamphier, "Alberta Oil Exports Threatened by Surging U.S. Output," *Ottawa Citizen*, April 19, 2012; G. Lamphier, "Cheap Natural Gas Can Work to Alberta's Advantage," *Edmonton Journal*, April 28, 2012, p. B1.

11. T. S. Mescon and G. S. Vozikis, "Federal Regulation—What Are the Costs?" *Business*, January–March 1982, pp. 33–39.

12. J. Thorpe, "Inter-Provincial Trade Barriers Still a Concern for Executives 'Handicapping Country Economically,'" *Financial Post* (*National Post*), September 13, 2004, p. FP2.

13. R. Annan, for Goodmans LLP, "Merger Remedies in Canada," Competition Bureau, November 4, 2005, http://www.competitionbureau.gc.ca/eic/site/cb-bc.nsf/vwapj/richard-annan.pdf/$file/richard-annan.pdf.

14. See "Frito Lay Eliminating Trans Fat from Some Snacks," Halifax Live.com, February 23, 2004, http://www.halifaxlive.com/snack_02232004_769.php.

15. G. Bonnell, "Food Industry Rushes to Drop Trans Fats," *Calgary Herald*, March 11, 2004, p. D1.

16. See "Banning Bad Fats," *CBC News*, November 6, 2006, http://www.cbc.ca/news/background/fats/banning_badfats.html.

17. Dave Collyer, President, Canadian Association of Petroleum Producers (CAPP), "Canadian Oil and Gas Industry Outlook—Opportunities & Challenges," (presentation to the Association of Professional Engineers and Geoscientists of Alberta [APEGA], Calgary, April 19, 2012); Global Clean Energy Congress and Exhibition, Calgary, November 1–3, 2011, http://www.capp.ca/getdoc.aspx?dt=PDF&docID=206748; Oil & Gas Sector Outlook 2012, Supplement to *Canadian Business*, April 30, 2012.

18. E. Huston, "Helping Millennials Help You—Managing Your Young Workforce," The Conference Board Executive Action Series, no. 402, May 2013.

19. Canadian Association of Petroleum Producers (CAPP), "2010 Responsible Canadian Energy Report," http://www.rce2010.ca.

20. Sustainable Development Technology Canada (SDTC), "Clean Technologies Help Green the Patch," SDTC Information Feature, *Globe and Mail*, February 27, 2012.

21. C. Gillis and A. Kingston, "The Great Pet Food Scandal," *Maclean's*, April 30, 2007, www.macleans.ca/business/companies/article.jsp?content=20070430_104326_104326; "Company Overview of Menu Foods Income Fund," *Bloomberg Businessweek*, http://investing.businessweek.com/research/stocks/snapshot/snapshot.asp?capId=3206215; D. George-Cosh, "Menu Foods Hammered as Customer Walks," *Globe and Mail*, June 13, 2007, p. B15.

22. "Is Corporate Canada Being 'Hollowed Out'?" *CBC News*, May 27, 2007, http://www.cbc.ca/news/background/mergers/hollowed-out.html.

23. "Global 500, Countries, Canada," *CNN Money*, http://money.cnn.com/magazines/fortune/global500/2011/countries/Canada.html.

24. Ibid.

25. A. Shama, "Management Under Fire: The Transformation of Management in the Soviet Union and Eastern Europe," *Academy of Management Executive*, vol. 7, no. 1 (1993), pp. 22–35.

26. World Trade Organization (WTO), WTO Policy Issues for Parliamentarians (Geneva: WTO, 2001), p. 1, www.wto.org/english/res_e/booksp_e/parliamentarians_e.pdf.

27. B. Mitchener, "A New EU, but No Operating Manual," *Wall Street Journal*, December 16, 2002, p. A10.

28. Statistics Canada, "Imports, Exports and Trade Balance of Goods on a Balance-of-Payment Basis, by Country or Country Grouping," CANSIM, Table 228-0003, May 10, 2005, http://www.statcan.gc.ca/tables-tableaux/sum-som/l01/cst01/gblec02aeng.htm.

29. See Standing Committee on Foreign Affairs, Mexico: Canada's Other NAFTA Partner, vol. 3, March 2004, http://www.parl.gc.ca/Content/SEN/Committee/373/fore/rep/rep03mar04-e.htm; Foreign Affairs and International Trade Canada, "The NAFTA's Impact," http://www.international.gc.ca/trade-agreementsaccords-commerciaux/agr-acc/nafta-alena/nafta5_section04.aspx?lang=en&view=d.

30. Association of Southeast Asian Nations (ASEAN), "Gross Domestic Product in ASEAN, at Current Prices (Nominal), in US Dollars," Table 5, *Macroeconomic Indicators*, February 15, 2011, www.aseansec.org/stat/Table5.pdf.

31. Council of Canadians, "Trans-Pacific Partnership," http://www.international.gc.ca/trade-agreements-accords-commerciaux/agr-acc/tpp-ptp/index.aspx?lang=eng.

32. BRICS, Fourth BRICS Summit, New Delhi, March 29, 2012, http://www.bricsindia.in.

33. This section is based on materials from the World Trade Organization website, www.wto.org.

34. J. Cowan, "The Next Free Trade Quagmire," *Canadian Business*, November 13, 2013, p. 26.

35. G. Abramovich, "Google's China Syndrome," *DM News*, June 20, 2006, http://www.dmnews.com/cms/dm-news/search-marketing/37089.html.

36. G. Hofstede, *Culture's Consequences: International Differences in Work-Related Values*, 2nd ed. (Thousand Oaks, CA: Sage, 2001), pp. 9–15; and G. Hofstede, "The Cultural Relativity of Organizational Practices and Theories," *Journal of International Business Studies*, Fall 1983, pp. 75–89.

37. Based on C. Gillis and A. Kingston, "The Great Pet Food Scandal," *Maclean's*, April 30, 2007, http://www.macleans.ca/business/companies/article.jsp?content=20070430_104326_104326; and D. Barboza and A. Barrionuevo, "Filler in Animal Feed Is Open Secret in China," *New York Times*, April 30, 2007.

38. D. Barboza and A. Barrionuevo, "Filler in Animal Feed Is Open Secret in China," *New York Times*, April 30, 2007.

39. C. A. Barlett and S. Ghoshal, *Managing Across Borders: The Transnational Solution*, 2nd ed. (Boston: Harvard Business School Press, 2002); and N. J. Adler, *International Dimensions of Organizational Behavior*, 4th ed. (Cincinnati, OH: South-Western College Publishing, 2002), pp. 9–11.

40. D. A. Aaker, Developing Business Strategies, 5th ed. (New York: John Wiley & Sons, 1998); and J. A. Byrne, "Borderless Management," *BusinessWeek*, May 23, 1994, pp. 24–26.

41. G. A. Knight and S. T. Cavusgil, "A Taxonomy of Born-Global Firms," *Management International Review*, vol. 45, no. 3 (2005), pp. 15–35; S. A. Zahra, "A Theory of International New Ventures: A Decade of Research," *Journal of International Business Studies*, January 2005, pp. 20–28; and B. M. Oviatt and P. P. McDougall, "Toward a Theory of International New Ventures," *Journal of International Business Studies*, January 2005, pp. 29–41.

42. Brendan B. Read, "More Bell(s) Tolling for Indian Outsourcing," TMCnet.com, http://call-center-software.tmcnet.com/topics/call-center-services/articles/50740-more-bells-tolling-indianoutsourcing.htm; Vikas Bajaj, "A New Capital of Call Centers," *New York Times*, November 25, 2011, http://www.nytimes.com/2011/11/26/business/philippines-overtakes-india-as-hub-ofcall-centers.html?pagewanted=all.

43. Mega Brands Inc., *Annual Report 2006*, http://www.megabrands.com/media/pdf/corpo/en/reports/2006_annual_report_en.pdf; Mega Brands Inc., "Mega Brands Reports Fourth Quarter and 2011 Results," Press Release, March 12, 2012, http://www.megabrands.com/media/pdf/corpo/en/PressReleaseQ4-20110314.pdf.

44. Industry Canada, International Trade, Canadian Economy (NAICS 11-91), http://www.ic.gc.ca/eic/site/cis-sic.nsf/eng/h_00029.html.

45. Ibid.

46. Industry Canada, International Trade, Canadian Economy (NAICS 11-91), https://www.ic.gc.ca/app/scr/sbms/sbb/cis/internationalTrade.html?code=11-91&lang=eng.

47. Derek Sankey, "U.S. Franchisors Eye Canada for Growth," *Financial Post*, November 17, 2009.

48. L. Frost, "Starbucks Lures French Café Society," Associated Press, January 16, 2004.

49. J. Lorinc, "Gunning for Growth," *Canadian Business*, October 20, 2014, pp. 17–18.

50. "How the Music Industry's Transformation Is Paving the Way for Monetization Opportunities," *Seeking Alpha*, November 26, 2010, http://seekingalpha.com/article/238741-how-the-musicindustry-s-transformation-is-paving-the-way-for-monetizationopportunities.

51. "How the Music Industry's Transformation Is Paving the Way for Monetization Opportunities," *Seeking Alpha*, November 26, 2010, http://seekingalpha.com/article/238741-how-the-musicindustry-s-transformation-is-paving-the-way-for-monetizationopportunities.

52. O. Ward, "Pop Goes Globalization," *Toronto Star*, March 13, 2004, p. A18.

53. A. Kreamer, "America's Yang Has a Yen for Asia's Yin," *Fast Company*, July 2003, p. 58; D. Yergin, "Globalization Opens Door to New Dangers," *USA Today*, May 28, 2003, p. 11 A; K. Lowrey Miller, "Is It Global Money?" *Newsweek*, December 16, 2002, pp. E4–E8; L. Gomes, "Globalization Is Now a Two-Way Street—Good News for the U.S.," *Wall Street Journal*, December 9, 2002, p. B1; J. Kurlantzick and J. T. Allen, "The Trouble with Globalism," *U.S. News & World Report*, February 11, 2002, pp. 38–41; J. Guyon, "The American Way," *Fortune*, November 26, 2001, pp. 114–120.

54. J. Guyon, "The American Way," *Fortune*, November 26, 2001, pp. 114–120.

55. Occupy Wall Street website, http://occupywallst.org; Occupy Movement page, *The Guardian*, http://www.guardian.co.uk/world/occupy-movement; Forum on "Understanding the Occupy Movement: Perspectives from the Social Sciences," *Berkeley Journal of Sociology*, http://bjsonline.org/2011/12/understandingthe-occupy-movement-perspectives-from-the-social-sciences;" Opinion Roundup: What Has the Occupy Movement Accomplished?" *CBC News*, November 23, 2011, http://www.cbc.ca/news/canada/story/2011/11/23/f-occupy-movement.html.

56. C. Harvey and M. J. Allard, *Understanding and Managing Diversity: Readings, Cases, and Exercises*, 2nd ed. (Upper Saddle River NJ: Prentice Hall, 2002); P. L. Hunsaker, *Training in Management Skills* (Upper Saddle River, NJ: Prentice Hall, 2001); and J. Greenberg, *Managing Behavior in Organizations: Science in Service to Practice*, 2nd ed. (Upper Saddle River, NJ: Prentice Hall, 1999).

57. Information from INDITEX company website, www.inditex; and M. Helft, "Fashion Fast-Forward," *Business* 2.0, May 2002, pp. 60–66.

58. Denise Deveau, "Cleaning Up in Pet Stores," *Financial Post*, April 2, 2012; Earth Rated Poop Bags website, ww.poopbags.ca.

59. Pet Food Association of Canada, "Pet Food Industry in Canada," http://www.pfac.com/about/industry/index.html.

60. T. Hanes, "Pet Owners Represent $6.5-billion a year business opportunity," *Globe and Mail*, April 8, 2013, http://www.theglobeandmail.com/report-on-business/small-business/starting-out/pet-owners-represent-65-billion-a-year-business-opportunity/article10430341.

61. "Joe Fresh Launches International Expansion In 23 Countries With Signing Of 3 Partnership Agreements," PR Newswire, February 20, 2014.

62. L. Nguyen, "Joe Fresh Global Expansion Will See 120 Stores In Europe, Mideast, South Korea," *The Canadian Press*, February 20, 2014.

63. "Joe Fresh Launches International Expansion In 23 Countries With Signing Of 3 Partnership Agreements," PR Newswire, February 20, 2014.

64. L. Nguyen, "Joe Fresh Global Expansion Will See 120 Stores In Europe, Mideast, South Korea," *The Canadian Press*, February 20, 2014.

65. C. O'Connor, "Extreme Pricing: At What Cost? Retailer Joe Fresh Sends Reps To Bangladesh As Death Toll Rises," Forbes.com, April 30, 2013.

66. Ibid.

67. Ibid.

68. A. Androich, "How well is Joe Fresh handling the Bangladesh factory disaster?" *Marketing Mag*, May 08, 2013, http://www.marketing-mag.ca/news/marketer-news/how-well-is-joe-fresh-handling-the-bangladesh-factory-disaster-78101#comments.

70. Ibid.

CHAPTER 3

1. R. Molz, "How Leaders Use Goals," *Long Range Planning*, October 1987, p. 91.

2. See, for example, J. A. Pearce II, K. K. Robbins, and R. B. Robinson Jr., "The Impact of Grand Strategy and Planning Formality on Financial Performance," *Strategic Management Journal*, March–April 1987, pp. 125–134; L. C. Rhyne, "Contrasting Planning Systems in High, Medium, and Low Performance Companies," *Journal of Management Studies*, July 1987, pp. 363–385; J. A. Pearce II, E. B. Freeman, and R. B. Robinson Jr., "The Tenuous Link Between Formal Strategic Planning and Financial Performance," *Academy of Management Review*, October 1987, pp. 658–675; D. K. Sinha, "The Contribution of Formal Planning to Decisions," *Strategic Management Journal*, October 1990, pp. 479–492; N. Capon, J. U. Farley, and J. M. Hulbert, "Strategic Planning and Financial Performance: More Evidence," *Journal of Management Studies*, January 1994, pp. 22–38; C. C. Miller and L. B. Cardinal, "Strategic Planning and Firm Performance: A Synthesis of More Than Two Decades of Research," *Academy of Management Journal*, March 1994, pp. 1649–1685; and P. J. Brews and M. R. Hunt, "Learning to Plan and Planning to Learn: Resolving the Planning School/Learning School Debate," *Strategic Management Journal*, December 1999, pp. 889–913.

3. H. Mintzberg, *The Rise and Fall of Strategic Planning* (New York: Free Press, 1994).

4. Ibid.

5. G. Hamel and C. K. Prahalad, *Competing for the Future* (Boston: Harvard Business School Press, 1994).

6. D. Miller, "The Architecture of Simplicity," *Academy of Management Review*, January 1993, pp. 116–138.

7. P. N. Romani, "MBO by Any Other Name Is Still MBO," *Supervision*, December 1997, pp. 6–8; and A. W. Schrader and G. T. Seward, "MBO Makes Dollar Sense," *Personnel Journal*, July 1989, pp. 32–37.

8. P. N. Romani, "MBO by Any Other Name Is Still MBO," *Supervision*, December 1997, pp. 6–8; and R. Rodgers and J. E. Hunter, "Impact of Management by Objectives on Organizational Productivity," *Journal of Applied Psychology*, April 1991, pp. 322–336.

9. For additional information on goals, see, for example, P. Drucker, *The Executive in Action* (New York: HarperCollins Books, 1996), pp. 207–214; and E. A. Locke and G. P. Latham, *A Theory of Goal Setting and Task Performance* (Upper Saddle River, NJ: Prentice Hall, 1990).

10. J. D. Hunger and T. L. Wheelen, *Strategic Management*, 7th ed. (Upper Saddle River, NJ: Prentice Hall, 2000).

11. J. R. Schermerhorn Jr. and B. Wright, *Management*, 2nd Canadian Edition (Mississauga, ON: Wiley, 2011).

12. Ibid.

13. Ibid.

14. P. J. Brews and M. R. Hunt, "Learning to Plan and Planning to Learn: Resolving the Planning School/Learning School Debate," *Strategic Management Journal*, December 1999, pp. 889–913.

15. Paul J. H. Schoemaker and Cornelius A. J. M. van der Heijden, "Integrating Scenarios into Strategic Planning at Royal Dutch/Shell," *Planning Review 20, no. 3* (1992), pp. 41–46.

16. F. Jossi, "Take a Peek Inside," *HR Magazine*, June 2002, pp. 46–52; and R. A. Martins, "Continuous Improvement Strategies and Production Competitive Criteria: Some Findings in Brazilian Industries," *Total Quality Management*, May 2001, pp. 281–291.

17. See http://www.mapleleaf.ca/en/corporate/company-info/over-view (accessed November 14, 2011).

18. J. W. Dean Jr. and M. P. Sharfman, "Does Decision Process Matter? A Study of Strategic Decision-Making Effectiveness," *Academy of Management Journal*, April 1996, pp. 368–396.

19. Based on A. A. Thompson, Jr., A. J. Strickland III, and J. E. Gamble, *Crafting and Executing Strategy*, 14th ed. (New York: McGraw-Hill Irwin, 2005).

20. J. Magretta, "Why Business Models Matter," *Harvard Business Review*, May 2002, pp. 86–92.

21. M. Carpenter, G. Sanders, K. Harling, *Strategic Management*, Canadian ed. (Toronto: Pearson, 2012).

22. C. K. Prahalad and G. Hamel, "The Core Competence of the Corporation," *Harvard Business Review*, May–June 1990, pp. 79–91.

23. See P&G, "Core Strengths," http://www.pg.com/en_US/company/core_strengths.shtml.

24. See Kevin O'Marah and Debra Hofman, "The AMR Supply Chain Top 25 for 2010," *Gartner*, June 2, 2010, http://www.gartner.com/DisplayDocument?id=1379613.

25. See, for example, H. J. Cho and V. Pucik, "Relationship between Innovativeness, Quality, Growth, Profitability, and Market Value," *Strategic Management Journal*, vol. 26, no. 6 (2005), pp. 555–575; W. F. Joyce, "Building the 4+2 Organization," *Organizational Dynamics*, May 2005, pp. 118–129; R. S. Kaplan and D. P. Norton, "Measuring the Strategic Readiness of Intangible Assets," *Harvard Business Review*, February 2004, pp. 52–63; C. M. Fiol, "Managing Culture as a Competitive Resource: An Identity-Based View of Sustainable Competitive Advantage," *Journal of Management*, March 1991, pp. 191–211; T. Kono, "Corporate Culture and Long-Range Planning," *Long Range Planning*, August 1990, pp. 9–19; S. Green, "Understanding Corporate Culture and Its Relation to Strategy," *International Studies of Management and Organization*, Summer 1988, pp. 6–28; C. Scholz, "Corporate Culture and Strategy—The Problem of Strategic Fit," *Long Range Planning*, August 1987, pp. 78–87; and J. B. Barney, "Organizational Culture: Can It Be a Source of Sustained Competitive Advantage?" *Academy of Management Review*, July 1986, pp. 656–665.

26. A. Carmeli and A. Tischler, "The Relationships between Intangible Organizational Elements and Organizational Performance," *Strategic Management Journal*, vol. 25, no. 13, December 2004, pp. 1257–1278; P. W. Roberts and G. R. Dowling, "Corporate Reputation and Sustained Financial Performance," *Strategic Management Journal*, December 2002, pp. 1077–1093; and C. J. Fombrun, "Corporate Reputations as Economic Assets," in *Handbook of Strategic Management*, ed. M. A. Hitt, R. E. Freeman, and J. S. Harrison (Malden, MA: Blackwell Publishers, 2001), pp. 289–312.

27. "Johnson & Johnson Ranks No. 1 in National Corporate Reputation Survey for Seventh Consecutive Year," Harris Interactive Press Release, www.harrisinteractive.com, December 7, 2005.

28. M. Carpenter, G. Sanders, K. Harling, *Strategic Management*, Canadian ed. (Toronto: Pearson, 2012), p. 75.

29. H. Mintzberg, "The Strategy Concept I: Five Ps for Strategy," *California Management Review*, Fall 1987, pp. 11–24.

30. Based on A. A. Thompson, Jr., A. J. Strickland III, and J. E. Gamble, *Crafting and Executing Strategy*, 14th ed. (New York: McGraw-Hill Irwin, 2005).

31. Ibid.

32. A. Brandenburger and B. Nalebuff, *Co-opetition* (New York, NY: Currency/Doubleday, 1996).

33. M. Carpenter, G. Sanders, K. Harling, *Strategic Management*, Canadian ed. (Toronto: Pearson, 2012).

34. Based on E. A. Locke and G. P. Latham, *Goal-Setting: A Motivational Technique That Works!* (Upper Saddle River, NJ: Prentice Hall, 1984); and E. A. Locke and G. P. Latham, "Building a Practically Useful Theory of Goal Setting and Task Motivation," *American Psychologist*, September 2002, pp. 705–717.

35. From The ROI of D&I. Municipal World - Canada's Municipal Magazine. July 2013. volume 123, number 7. Copyright © 2013 by Municipal World Inc. Reprinted by permission.

36. "Sustainability & Community," SilverBirch Hotels, http://www.silverbirchhotels.com/about/environment.html; "Vision, Mission and Values," SilverBirch Hotels, http://www.silverbirchhotels.com/about/vision.html; "Our Story, SilverBirch Hotels," http://www.silverbirchhotels.com/about/history.html; "News." SilverBirch Hotels, http://www.silverbirchhotels.com/press; "Green Key," Hotel Association of Canada, http://www.hotelassociation.ca/site/programs/green_key.htm.

37. K. Jordan, *The Canadian Wine Industry: A Summary View* (Special Report for BMO Capital Markets), July 6, 2011; Agriculture and Agri-Food Canada, "The Canadian Wine Industry (NAICS 31213)," http://www4.agr.gc.ca/AAFC-AAC/display-afficher.do?id=1172244915663&lang=eng; Canada's Wine Economy—Ripe Robust Remarkable, www.canadianvintners.com; "A Canadian Success Story: Icewine Exports to China," Foreign Affairs, Trade and Development Canada, http://www.international.gc.ca/media_commerce/release_photo_distribution/2013/04/16b.aspx?lang=eng.

SUPPLEMENT 3

1. "Social and Mobile Statistics on a Global Scale, 2014," *Canadian Digital*. Posted by M. McKinnon, http://canadiansinternet.com/canadian-digital-social-mobile-statistics-global-scale-2014.

2. CNW, "Less Than a Fifth of Canadian Companies Use Social Media Effectively," *Canadian Newswire*, August 30, 2011, http://www.newswire.ca/en/story/832943/less-than-a-fifth-of-canadian-companies-use-social-media-effectively.

3. T. Dixon, *Communication, Organization, and Performance* (Norwood, NJ: Ablex Publishing Corporation, 1996), p. 281; P. G. Clampitt, *Communicating for Managerial Effectiveness* (Newbury Park, CA: Sage Publications, 1991); and L. E. Penley, E. R. Alexander, I. E. Jernigan, and C. I. Henwood, "Communication Abilities of Managers: The Relationship to Performance," *Journal of Management*, March 1991, pp. 57–76.

4. C. Thomas, "Best-Kept Secrets of the World's Best Companies: The Three Minute Huddle," *Business 2.0*, April 2006, p. 94.

5. V. Galt, "Top-Down Feedback," *Vancouver Sun*, February 15, 2003, pp. E1, E2.

6. Tips for Managers based on R. Kreitner and A. Kinicki, *Organizational Behavior*, 6th ed. (New York: McGraw-Hill/Irwin, 2004), p. 335. Reprinted by permission of McGraw-Hill Education.

7. M. Vallis, "Nasty E-mail from the Boss May Mean More Sick Days." *National Post*, January 9, 2004, pp. A1, A9. Study was done by George Fieldman, a psychologist at Buckinghamshire Chilterns University College, and presented at the 2004 Annual Occupational Psychology Conference of the British Psychological Society.

8. Derived from P. Kuitenbrouwer, "Office E-Mail Runs Amok," *Financial Post*, October 18, 2001, p. FP11.

9. See, for example, Jabra, *GenM: Defining the Workforce of Tomorrow*, 2012, http://campaigns.jabra.com/eCards/UK/6339_4_Jabra_GenM_Study_Booklet_final.pdf; Contact Centre Live, "Research Identifies Growing Mobile Work Culture & Frustration with Solutions Provided by IT Depts," March 13, 2012, http://www.callcentreclinic.com/news/market-research/research-identifies-growing-mobile-work-culture—frustration-with-solutions-provided-by-it-depts—46575.htm.

10. Information on *Second Life* based on A. Athavaley, "A Job Interview You Don't Have to Show Up For," *Wall Street Journal*, June 20, 2007, p. D1.

11. K. Hafner, "For the Well Connected, All the World's an Office," *New York Times*, March 30, 2000, p. D11.

12. B. McCrea, "A New Kind of Hookup," *Black Enterprise*, July 2007, p. 52

13. K. Cukier and V. Mayer-Schönberger, "The Financial Bonanza of Big Data," *Wall Street Journal*, March 8, 2013, p. A15.

14. Debbie Dimoff, "Connecting with Social Media" Pricewaterhouse Coopers LLP, 2011, http://www.pwc.com/ca/en/private-company/lets-talk/social-media.jhtml.

15. Jennifer Vivian, "Molson Coors Canada Incorporates Social Media into Its Employee Engagement Approach to Drive Performance, Productivity and Bottom Line Results," *Social Media for Business Performance*, February 6, 2012, http://smbp.uwaterloo.ca/2012/02/molson-coors-canada-incorporates-social-media-into-its-employee-engagement-approach-to-drive-performance-productivity-and-bottom-line-results/.

16. Derek Sankey, "Employers, Unions Making More Use of Social Media," *Postmedia News*, May 8, 2012, http://www.canada.com/business/Employers—unions+making+more+social+media/6547875/story.html.

17. "Pros and Cons of Social Media," *Canadian Business Network*, http://www.canadabusiness.ca/eng/page/2655/.

18. Ibid.

19. Debbie Dimoff, "Connecting with Social Media" PricewaterhouseCoopers LLP, 2011, http://www.pwc.com/ca/en/private-company/lets-talk/social-media.jhtml.

20. J. Langdon, "Differences between Males and Females at Work," *USA Today*, February 5, 2001, www.usatoday.com; J. Manion, "He Said, She Said," *Materials Management in Health Care*, November 1998, pp. 52–62; G. Franzwa and C. Lockhart, "The Social Origins and Maintenance of Gender Communication Styles, Personality Types, and Grid-Group Theory," *Sociological Perspectives*, vol. 41, no. 1 (1998), pp. 185–208; and D. Tannen, *Talking from 9 to 5: Women and Men in the Workplace* (New York: Avon Books, 1995).

21. "Workplace Communication Protocol, 2011 edition," *Canadian Business*, November 21, 2011.

CHAPTER 4

1. Derek Sankey, "Women Embrace Franchising," *Financial Post*, March 26, 2012, http://www.canada.com/technology/Women+embrace+franchising/6378913/story.html.

2. Ibid.

3. See "Canadian Franchise Statistics and Information," *Franshiseek Canada*, http://www.franchiseek.com/Canada/Franchise_Canada_Statistics.htm.

4. See Nurse Next Door™, "What Makes Us Unique," http://www.nursenextdoorfranchise.com/what-makes-us-unique/.

5. I. Wylie, "Who Runs This Team Anyway?" *Fast Company*, April 2002, pp. 32–33.

6. D. A. Garvin and M. A. Roberto, "What You Don't Know about Making Decisions," *Harvard Business Review*, September 2001, pp. 108–116.

7. W. Pounds, "The Process of Problem Finding," *Industrial Management Review*, Fall 1969, pp. 1–19.

8. P. C. Nutt, *Why Decisions Fail: Avoiding the Blunders and Traps that Lead to Debacles* (San Francisco, CA: Berrett-Koehler Publishers, 2002).

9. T. A. Stewart, "Did You Ever Have to Make Up Your Mind?" *Harvard Business Review*, January 2006, p. 12; and E. Pooley, "Editor's Desk," *Fortune*, June 27, 2005, p. 16.

10. J. G. March, "Decision-Making Perspective: Decisions in Organizations and Theories of Choice," in A. H. Van de Ven and W. F. Joyce (eds.), *Perspectives on Organization Design and Behavior* (New York: Wiley-Interscience, 1981), pp. 232–233.

11. See T. Shavit and A. M. Adam, "A Preliminary Exploration of the Effects of Rational Factors and Behavioral Biases on the Managerial Choice to Invest in Corporate Responsibility," *Managerial and Decision Economics*, April 2011, pp. 205–213; A. Langley, "In Search of Rationality: The Purposes Behind the Use of Formal Analysis in Organizations," *Administrative Science Quarterly*, December 1989, pp. 598–631; and H. A. Simon, "Rationality in Psychology and Economics," *Journal of Business* (October 1986), pp. 209–224.

12. See D. R. A Skidd, "Revisiting Bounded Rationality," *Journal of Management Inquiry*, December 1992, pp. 343–347; B. E. Kaufman, "A New Theory of Satisficing," *Journal of Behavioral Economics*, Spring 1990, pp. 35–51; and N. McK. Agnew and J. L. Brown, "Bounded Rationality: Fallible Decisions in Unbounded Decision Space," *Behavioral Science*, July 1986, pp. 148–161.

13. See, for example, G. McNamara, H. Moon, and P. Bromiley, "Banking on Commitment: Intended and Unintended Consequences of an Organization's Attempt to Attentuate Escalation of Commitment," *Academy of Management Journal*, April 2002, pp. 443–452; V. S. Rao and A. Monk, "The Effects of Individual Differences and Anonymity on Commitment to Decisions," *Journal of Social Psychology*, August 1999, pp. 496–515; C. F. Camerer and R. A. Weber, "The Econometrics and Behavioral Economics of Escalation of Commitment: A Re-examination of Staw's Theory," *Journal of Economic Behavior and Organization*, May 1999, pp. 59–82; D. R. Bobocel and J. P. Meyer, "Escalating Commitment to a Failing Course of Action: Separating the Roles of Choice and Justification," *Journal of Applied Psychology* (June 1994), pp. 360–263; and B. M. Staw, "The Escalation of Commitment to a Course of Action," *Academy of Management Review*, October 1981, pp. 577–587.

14. L. Alderman, "A Shoemaker That Walks but Never Runs," *New York Times Online*, October 8, 2010.

15. S. Maich, "Promises, Promises but Tax Bill Grows," *Financial Post (National Post)*, June 1, 2004, p. FP1.

16. K. R. Brousseau, M. J. Driver, G. Hourihan, and R. Larsson, "The Seasoned Executive's Decision-Making Style," *Harvard Business Review*, February 2006, pp. 111–121.

17. A. J. Rowe, J. D. Boulgarides, and M. R. McGrath, *Managerial Decision Making, Modules in Management Series* (Chicago: SRA, 1984), pp. 18–22.

18. C. Shaffran, "Mind Your Meeting: How to Become the Catalyst for Culture Change," *Communication World*, February–March 2003, pp. 26–29.

19. I. L. Janis, *Victims of Groupthink* (Boston: Houghton Mifflin, 1972); R. J. Aldag and S. Riggs Fuller, "Beyond Fiasco: A Reappraisal of the Groupthink Phenomenon and a New Model of Group Decision Processes," *Psychological Bulletin*, May 1993, pp. 533–552; T. Kameda and S. Sugimori, "Psychological Entrapment in Group Decision Making: An Assigned Decision Rule and a Groupthink Phenomenon," *Journal of Personality and Social Psychology*, August 1993, pp. 282–292.

20. R. G. Vleeming, "Machiavellianism: A Preliminary Review," *Psychology Reports*, February 1979, pp. 295–310.

21. See Richard Branson, "What Steve Jobs Taught Me by Kicking My Butt," *Canadian Business*, September 22, 2011, http://www.canadianbusiness.com/article/46349—branson-what-steve-jobs-taught-me-by-kicking-my-butt.

22. Based on J. Brockner, *Self Esteem at Work* (Lexington, MA: Lexington Books, 1988), Chapters 1–4.

23. See, for example, L. K. Michaelson, W. E. Watson, and R. H. Black, "A Realistic Test of Individual vs. Group Consensus Decision Making," *Journal of Applied Psychology*, vol. 74, no. 5 (1989), pp. 834–839; R. A. Henry, "Group Judgment Accuracy: Reliability and Validity of Postdiscussion Confidence Judgments," *Organizational Behavior and Human Decision Processes*, October 1993, pp. 11–27; P. W. Paese, M. Bieser, and M. E. Tubbs, "Framing Effects and Choice Shifts in Group Decision Making," *Organizational Behavior and Human Decision Processes*, October 1993, pp. 149–165; N. J. Castellan Jr., ed., *Individual and Group Decision Making* (Hillsdale, NJ: Lawrence Erlbaum Associates, 1993); and S. G. Straus and J. E. McGrath, "Does the Medium Matter? The Interaction of Task Type and Technology on Group Performance and Member Reactions," *Journal of Applied Psychology*, February 1994, pp. 87–97.

24. E. J. Thomas and C. F. Fink, "Effects of Group Size," *Psychological Bulletin*, July 1963, pp. 371–384; F. A. Shull, A. L. Delbecq, and L. L. Cummings, *Organizational Decision Making* (New York: McGraw-Hill, 1970), p. 151; A. P. Hare, *Handbook of Small Group Research* (New York: Free Press, 1976); M. E. Shaw, *Group Dynamics: The Psychology of Small Group Behavior*, 3rd ed. (New York: McGraw-Hill, 1981); P. Yetton and P. Bottger, "The Relationships among Group Size, Member Ability, Social Decision Schemes, and Performance," *Organizational Behavior and Human Performance*, October 1983, pp. 145–159.

25. A. Kleingeld, H. Van Tuijl, and J. A. Algera, "Participation in the Design of Performance Management Systems: A Quasi-Experimental Field Study," *Journal of Organizational Behaviour*, vol. 25, no. 7 (2004), pp. 831–854.

26. S. McShane and S. Steen, *Canadian Organizational Behaviour*, 7th ed. (Toronto, ON: McGraw-Hill, 2009), pp. 165–166.

27. D. Kahneman and A. Tversky, "Judgment under Uncertainty: Heuristics and Biases," *Science*, vol. 185 (1974), pp. 1124–1131.

28. Information for this section is taken from S. P. Robbins, *Decide & Conquer* (Upper Saddle River, NJ: Financial Times/Prentice Hall, 2004).

29. See, for example, B. M. Staw, "The Escalation of Commitment to a Course of Action," *Academy of Management Review*, October 1981, pp. 577–587; D. R. Bobocel and J. P. Meyer, "Escalating Commitment to a Failing Course of Action: Separating the Roles of Choice and Justification," *Journal of Applied Psychology*, June 1994, pp. 360–363; C. F. Camerer and R. A. Weber, "The Econometrics and Behavioral Economics of Escalation of Commitment: A Re-examination of Staw's Theory," *Journal of Economic Behavior and Organization*, May 1999, pp. 59–82; V. S. Rao and A. Monk, "The Effects of Individual Differences and Anonymity on Commitment to Decisions," *Journal of Social Psychology*, August 1999, pp. 496–515; and G. McNamara, H. Moon, and P. Bromiley, "Banking on Commitment: Intended and Unintended Consequences of an Organization's Attempt to Attenuate Escalation of Commitment," *Academy of Management Journal*, April 2002, pp. 443–452.

30. And the Survey Says box based on D. Kahneman, D. Lovallo, and O. Siboney, "Before You Make That Big Decision," *Harvard Business Review*, June 2011, pp. 50–60; P. Wang, "To Make Better Choices, Choose Less," *Money*, June 2010, pp. 111–114; B. Dumaine, "The Trouble with Teams," *Fortune*, September 5, 1994, pp. 86–92; A. S. Wellner, "A Perfect Brainstorm," *Inc.*, October 2003, pp. 31–35; "The Poll," *BusinessWeek*, August 21–28, 2006, p. 44; "Hurry Up and Decide," *BusinessWeek*, May 14, 2001, p. 16; J. MacIntyre, "Bosses and Bureaucracy," *Springfield, Missouri Business Journal*, August 1–7, 2005, p. 29; J. Crick, and "On the Road to Invention," *Fast Company*, February 2005, p. 16.

31. "The Critical Role of Teams," The Ken Blanchard Companies, http://www.kenblanchard.com/img/pub/pdf_critical_role_teams.pdf.

32. K. Davis and W. C. Frederick, *Business and Society: Management, Public Policy, Ethics*, 5th ed. (New York: McGraw-Hill, 1984), pp. 28–41, 76.

33. G. F. Cavanagh, D. J. Moberg, and M. Valasquez, "The Ethics of Organizational Politics," *Academy of Management Journal*, June 1981, pp. 363–374. See also F. N. Brady, "Rules for Making Exceptions to Rules," *Academy of Management Review*, July 1987, pp. 436–444, for an argument that the theory of justice is redundant with the prior two theories. See also T. Donaldson and T. W. Dunfee, "Toward a Unified Conception of Business Ethics: Integrative Social Contracts Theory," *Academy of Management Review*, April 1994, pp. 252–284; M. Douglas, "Integrative Social Contracts Theory: Hype over Hypernorms," *Journal of Business Ethics*, July 2000, pp. 101–110; and E. Soule, "Managerial Moral Strategies—In Search of a Few Good Principles," *Academy of Management Review*, January 2002, pp. 114–124, for discussions of integrative social contracts theory.

34. E. Soule, "Managerial Moral Strategies—In Search of a Few Good Principles," *Academy of Management Review*, January 2002, p. 117.

35. F. D. Sturdivant, *Business and Society: A Managerial Approach*, 3rd ed. (Homewood, IL: Richard D. Irwin, 1985), p. 128.

36. L. Bogomolny, "Good Housekeeping," *Canadian Business*, March 1, 2004, pp. 87–88; and Royal Bank of Canada (RBC), "Community & Sustainability," http://www.rbc.com/community-sustainability/index.html.

37. See Industry Canada, "Corporate Social Responsibility," http://www.ic.gc.ca/eic/site/csr-rse.nsf/eng/rs00129.html.

38. W. Dabrowski, "Tighter Guidelines Issued on Disclosure: Canada's 'Sarbanes,'" *Financial Post (National Post)*, March 30, 2004, p. FP1.

39. L. Bogomolny, "Good Housekeeping," *Canadian Business*, March 1, 2004, pp. 87–88.

40. Terry Eyden, "Global Survey on Business Ethics," *Accounting Web*, June 21, 2012, http://www.accountingweb.com/article/global-survey-business-ethics/219380; and J. Alexander, "On the Right Side," *World Business*, January–February 1997, pp. 38–41.

41. P. Richter, "Big Business Puts Ethics in Spotlight," *Los Angeles Times*, June 19, 1986, p. 29.

42. F. R. David, "An Empirical Study of Codes of Business Ethics: A Strategic Perspective" (paper presented at the 48th Annual Academy of Management Conference, Anaheim, California, August 1988).

43. P. S. Ridge, "Ethics Programs Aren't Stemming Employee Misconduct," *Wall Street Journal*, May 11, 2000, p. A1.

44. L. Bogomolny, "Good Housekeeping," *Canadian Business*, March 1, 2004, pp. 87–88.

45. A. K. Reichert and M. S. Webb, "Corporate Support for Ethical and Environmental Policies: A Financial Management Perspective," *Journal of Business Ethics*, May 2000; G. R. Weaver, L. K. Trevino, and P. L. Cochran, "Corporate Ethics Programs as Control Systems: Influences of Executive Commitment and Environmental Factors," *Academy of Management Journal*, February 1999, pp. 41–57; G. R. Weaver, L. K. Trevino, and P. L. Cochran, "Integrated and Decoupled Corporate Social Performance: Management Commitments, External Pressures, and Corporate Ethics Practices," *Academy of Management Journal*, October 1999, pp. 539–552; and B. Z. Posner and W. H. Schmidt, "Values and the American Manager: An Update," *California Management Review*, Spring 1984, pp. 202–216.

46. L. Nash, "Ethics without the Sermon," *Harvard Business Review*, November–December 1981, p. 81.

47. See, for example, R. A. Buccholz, *Essentials of Public Policy for Management*, 2nd ed. (Upper Saddle River, NJ: Prentice Hall, 1990).

48. M. Friedman, *Capitalism and Freedom* (Chicago: University of Chicago Press, 1962); and M. Friedman, "The Social Responsibility of Business Is to Increase Profits," *New York Times Magazine*, September 13, 1970, p. 33.

49. J. Bakan, *The Corporation* (Toronto: Big Picture Media Corporation, 2003).

50. Information from the Avon's website on its Corporate Citizenship, http://www.avonfoundation.org/causes/breast-cancer-crusade.

51. E. P. Lima, "Seeding a World of Transformation," *IndustryWeek*, September 6, 1999, pp. 30–31.

52. E. White, "PR Firms Advise Corporations on Social Responsibility Issues," *Wall Street Journal*, November 13, 2002, p. B10.

53. The Triple Bottom Line was first introduced in J. Elkington, *Cannibals with Forks: The Triple Bottom Line of 21st Century Business* (Stony Creek, CT: New Society Publishers, 1998).

54. See, for example, A. B. Carroll, "The Pyramid of Corporate Social Responsibility: Toward the Moral Management of Organizational Stakeholders," *Business Horizons*, July–August 1991, pp. 39–48.

55. This section has been influenced by E. Gatewood and B. Carroll, "The Anatomy of Corporate Social Response," *Business Horizons*, September–October 1981, pp. 9–16.

56. See, for example, P. Cochran and R. A. Wood, "Corporate Social Responsibility and Financial Performance," *Academy of Management Journal*, March 1984, pp. 42–56; K. Aupperle, A. B. Carroll, and J. D. Hatfield, "An Empirical Examination of the Relationship between Corporate Social Responsibility and Profitability," *Academy of*

Management Journal, June 1985, pp. 446–463; J. B. McGuire, A. Sundgren, and T. Schneeweis, "Corporate Social Responsibility and Firm Financial Performance," *Academy of Management Journal*, December 1988, pp. 854–872; D. M. Georgoff and J. Ross, "Corporate Social Responsibility and Management Performance" (paper presented at the National Academy of Management Conference, Miami, Florida, August 1991); S. A. Zahra, B. M. Oviatt, and K. Minyard, "Effects of Corporate Ownership and Board Structure on Corporate Social Responsibility and Financial Performance" (paper presented at the National Academy of Management Conference, Atlanta, Georgia, August 1993); "Social Responsibility and the Bottom Line," *Business Ethics*, July–August 1994, p. 11; D. B. Turban and D. W. Greening, "Corporate Social Performance and Organizational Attractiveness to Prospective Employees," *Academy of Management Journal*, June 1996, pp. 658–672; S. A. Waddock and S. B. Graves, "The Corporate Social Performance–Financial Performance Link," *Strategic Management Journal*, April 1997, pp. 303–319; and S. L. Berman, A. C. Wicks, S. Kotha, and T. M. Jones, "Does Stakeholder Orientation Matter? The Relationship between Stakeholder Management Models and Firm Financial Performance," *Academy of Management Journal*, October 1999, pp. 488–506.

57. D. J. Wood and R. E. Jones, "Stakeholder Mismatching: A Theoretical Problem in Empirical Research on Corporate Social Performance," *International Journal of Organizational Analysis*, vol. 3, no. 3 (1995), pp. 229–267.

58. See A. A. Ullmann, "Data in Search of a Theory: A Critical Examination of the Relationships among Social Performance, Social Disclosure, and Economic Performance of U.S. Firms," *Academy of Management Review*, July 1985, pp. 540–557; R. E. Wokutch and B. A. Spencer, "Corporate Saints and Sinners: The Effects of Philanthropic and Illegal Activity on Organizational Performance," *California Management Review*, Winter 1987, pp. 62–77; R. Wolfe and K. Aupperle, "Introduction to Corporate Social Performance: Methods for Evaluating an Elusive Construct," ed. J. E. Post, *Research in Corporate Social Performance and Policy*, vol. 13 (1991), pp. 265–268; and D. J. Wood and R. E. Jones, "Stakeholder Mismatching: A Theoretical Problem in Empirical Research on Corporate Social Performance," *International Journal of Organizational Analysis*, vol. 3 (1995), pp. 229–267.

59. D. Macfarlane, "Why Now?" *Report on Business Magazine*, March 2004, pp. 45–46.

60. J. V. Anderson, "Mind Mapping: A Tool for Creative Thinking," *Business Horizons*, January–February 1993, pp. 42–46; M. Loeb, "Ten Commandments for Managing Creative People," *Fortune*, January 16, 1995, pp. 135–136; M. Henricks, "Good Thinking," *Entrepreneur*, May 1996, pp. 70–73; H.-S. Choi and L. Thompson, "Old Wine in a New Bottle: Impact of Membership Change on Group Creativity," *Organizational Behavior and Human Decision Processes*, vol. 98, no. 2 (2005), pp. 121–132; R. Florida and J. Goodnight, "Managing for Creativity," *Harvard Business Review*, vol. 83, no. 7 (2005), pp. 124+; L. L. Gilson, J. E. Mathieu, C. E. Shalley, and T. M. Ruddy, "Creativity and Standardization: Complementary or Conflicting Drivers of Team Effectiveness?" *Academy of Management Journal*, vol. 48, no. 3 (2005), pp. 521–531; and K. G. Smith, C. J. Collins, and K. D. Clark, "Existing Knowledge, Knowledge Creation Capability, and the Rate of New Product Introduction in High-Technology Firms," *Academy of Management Journal*, vol. 48, no. 2 (2005), pp. 346–357.

61. Information for this box comes from B. C. McDonald and D. Hutcheson, "Dealing with Diversity Is Key to Tapping Talent," *Atlanta Business Chronicle*, December 18, 1998, p. 45A1; P. M. Elsass and L. M. Graves, "Demographic Diversity in Decision-Making Groups:

The Experience of Women and People of Color," *Academy of Management Review*, October 1997, pp. 946–973; and N. J. Adler, ed., *International Dimensions of Organizational Behavior*, 4th ed. (Cincinnati, OH: South-Western College Publishing, 2001).

62. "Toronto Blue Jays: Built to Win Yesterday," Batting Leader, http://battingleadoff.com/2014/01/09/toronto-blue-jays-built-to-win-yesterday/

63. D. D. Stanford, "Coke Has a Secret Formula for Orange Juice, Too," *Bloomberg Businessweek*, February 4–February 10, 2013, pp. 19–20; P. Sellers, "The New Coke," *Fortune*, May 21, 2012, pp. 138–144; and Adi Ignatious, "Shaking Things Up at Coca-Cola," *Harvard Business Review*, October 2011, pp. 94–99.

CHAPTER 5

1. "Annual Report," Empire Canada (2013).

2. See, for example, R. L. Daft, *Organization Theory and Design*, 6th ed. (St. Paul, MN: West Publishing, 1998).

3. W. Hillier, "BC Forest Fires: A Time of Need," *Canadian Underwriter*, vol. 72, no. 1 (2004), pp. 22–23.

4. For a discussion of authority, see W. A. Kahn and K. E. Kram, "Authority at Work: Internal Models and Their Organizational Consequences," *Academy of Management Review*, January 1994, pp. 17–50.

5. R. C. Morais, "The Old Lady Is Burning Rubber," *Forbes*, November 26, 2007, pp. 146–150.

6. D. Drickhamer, "Lessons from the Leading Edge," *Industry Week*, February 21, 2000, pp. 23–26.

7. D. Van Fleet, "Span of Management Research and Issues," *Academy of Management Journal*, September 1983, pp. 546–552.

8. See, for example, Nestlé's website, www.nestle.com; Ben Worthen, "Nestlé's Enterprise Resource Planning (ERP) Odyssey," *CIO*, May 15, 2002, http://www.cio.com/article/31066/Nestl_eacute_s_Enterprise_Resource_Planning_ERP_Odyssey.

9. Based on L. Millan, "Who's Scoffing Now? The Lemaire Brothers Started Out Using Recycled Fibre in One Small Paper Mill in Rural Quebec," *Canadian Business*, March 27, 1998, pp. 74–77; Cascades Inc., "Profile," www.cascades.com/profile; and Cascades Inc., *Resolutely Cascades: 2008 Annual Report*, http://www.cascades.com//client_file/upload/pdf/rapports/2008_annuel_an.pdf.

10. E. W. Morrison, "Doing the Job Well: An Investigation of Pro-Social Rule Breaking," *Journal of Management*, February 2006, pp. 5–28.

11. Ibid.

12. T. Burns and G. M. Stalker, *The Management of Innovation* (London: Tavistock, 1961).

13. D. Dougherty, "Re-imagining the Differentiation and Integration of Work for Sustained Product Innovation," *Organization Science*, September–October 2001, pp. 612–631.

14. A. D. Chandler, Jr., *Strategy and Structure: Chapters in the History of the Industrial Enterprise* (Cambridge, MA: MIT Press, 1962).

15. See, for instance, L. L. Bryan and C. I. Joyce, "Better Strategy through Organizational Design," *McKinsey Quarterly*, no. 2 (2007), pp. 21–29; D. Jennings and S. Seaman, "High and Low Levels of Organizational Adaptation: An Empirical Analysis of Strategy, Structure, and Performance," *Strategic Management Journal*, July 1994, pp. 459–475; D. C. Galunic and K. M. Eisenhardt, "Renewing the Strategy-Structure-Performance Paradigm," in B. M. Staw and L. L. Cummings (eds.), *Research in Organizational Behavior*, vol. 16 (Greenwich, CT: JAI Press, 1994), pp. 215–255; R. Parthasarthy and S. P. Sethi, "Relating Strategy and Structure to Flexible Automation:

A Test of Fit and Performance Implications," *Strategic Management Journal*, vol. 14, no. 6 (1993), pp. 529–549; H. A. Simon, "Strategy and Organizational Evolution," *Strategic Management Journal*, January 1993, pp. 131–142; H. L. Boschken, "Strategy and Structure: Re-conceiving the Relationship," *Journal of Management*, March 1990, pp. 135–150; D. Miller, "The Structural and Environmental Correlates of Business Strategy," *Strategic Management Journal*, January–February 1987, pp. 55–76; and R. E. Miles and C. C. Snow, *Organizational Strategy, Structure, and Process* (New York: McGraw-Hill, 1978).

16. See, for instance, P. M. Blau and R. A. Schoenherr, *The Structure of Organizations* (New York: Basic Books, 1971); D. S. Pugh, "The Aston Program of Research: Retrospect and Prospect," in A. H. Van de Ven and W. F. Joyce (eds.), *Perspectives on Organization Design and Behavior* (New York: John Wiley, 1981), pp. 135–166; and R. Z. Gooding and J. A. Wager III, "A Meta-Analytic Review of the Relationship between Size and Performance: The Productivity and Efficiency of Organizations and Their Subunits," *Administrative Science Quarterly*, December 1985, pp. 462–481.

17. See, for example, H. M. O'Neill, "Restructuring, Reengineering and Rightsizing: Do the Metaphors Make Sense?" *Academy of Management Executive*, vol. 8, no. 4 (1994), pp. 9–30; R. K. Reger, J. V. Mullane, L. T. Gustafson, and S. M. Demarie, "Creating Earthquakes to Change Organizational Mindsets," *Academy of Management Executive*, vol. 8, no. 4 (1994), pp. 31–41; and J. Tan, "Impact of Ownership Type on Environment–Strategy Linkage and Performance: Evidence from a Transitional Company," *Journal of Management Studies*, May 2002, pp. 333–354.

18. H. Mintzberg, *Structure in Fives: Designing Effective Organizations* (Upper Saddle River, NJ: Prentice Hall, 1983), p. 157.

19. R. J. Williams, J. J. Hoffman, and B. T. Lamont, "The Influence of Top Management Team Characteristics on M-Form Implementation Time," *Journal of Managerial Issues*, Winter 1995, pp. 466–480.

20. See, for example, R. E. Hoskisson, C. W. L. Hill, and H. Kim, "The Multidivisional Structure: Organizational Fossil or Source of Value?" *Journal of Management*, vol. 19, no. 2 (1993), pp. 269–298; I. I. Mitroff, R. O. Mason, and C. M. Pearson, "Radical Surgery: What Will Tomorrow's Organizations Look Like?" *Academy of Management Executive*, February 1994, pp. 11–21; T. Clancy, "Radical Surgery: A View from the Operating Theater," *Academy of Management Executive*, February 1994, pp. 73–78; M. Hammer, "Processed Change: Michael Hammer Sees Process as 'the Clark Kent of Business Ideas'—A Concept That Has the Power to Change a Company's Organizational Design," *Journal of Business Strategy*, November–December 2001, pp. 11–15; D. F. Twomey, "Leadership, Organizational Design, and Competitiveness for the 21st Century," *Global Competitiveness*, Annual 2002, pp. S31–S40; and G. J. Castrogiovanni, "Organization Task Environments: Have They Changed Fundamentally over Time?" *Journal of Management*, vol. 28, no. 2 (2002), pp. 129–150.

21. T. Starner, "Room for Improvement," *IQ Magazine*, March–April 2003, pp. 36–37.

22. Q. Hardy, "Google Thinks Small," *Forbes*, November 14, 2005, pp. 198–202.

23. See, for example, H. Rothman, "The Power of Empowerment," *Nation's Business*, June 1993, pp. 49–52; B. Dumaine, "Payoff from the New Management," *Fortune*, December 13, 1993, pp. 103–110; J. A. Byrne, "The Horizontal Corporation," *Business Week*, December 20, 1993, pp. 76–81; J. R. Katzenbach and D. K. Smith, *The Wisdom of Teams* (Boston: Harvard Business School Press, 1993); L. Grant, "New Jewel in the Crown," *U.S. News & World Report*, February 28, 1994, pp. 55–57; D. Ray and H. Bronstein, *Teaming Up: Making the Transition to a Self-Directed Team-Based Organization* (New York: McGraw Hill, 1995); and D. R. Denison, S. L. Hart, and J. A. Kahn, "From Chimneys to Cross-Functional Teams: Developing and Validating a Diagnostic Model," *Academy of Management Journal*, December 1996, pp. 1005–1023.

24. C. Fishman, "Whole Foods Is All Teams," *Fast Company, Greatest Hits*, vol. 1, 1997, pp. 102–113.

25. W. Hillier, "BC Forest Fires: A Time of Need," *Canadian Underwriter*, January 2004, pp. 22–23.

26. P. LaBarre, "This Organization Is Dis-Organization," *Fast Company*, www.fastcompany.com/magazine/03/oticon.html.

27. See, for example, G. G. Dess et al., "The New Corporate Architecture," *Academy of Management Executive*, August 1995, pp. 7–20.

28. S. C. Certo and S. T. Certo, *Modern Management*, 10th ed. (Upper Saddle River, NJ: Prentice Hall, 2006), p. 316; P. M. J. Christie and R. R. Levary, "Virtual Corporations: Recipe for Success," *Industrial Management*, July/August 1998, pp. 7–11; and C. C. Snow, R. E. Miles, and H. J. Coleman Jr., "Managing 21st Century Network Organizations," *Organizational Dynamics*, Winter 1992, pp. 5–20.

29. See, for example, W. H. Davidow and M. S. Malone, *The Virtual Corporation* (New York: HarperCollins, 1992); H. Chesbrough and D. Teece, "When Is Virtual Virtuous? Organizing for Innovation," *Harvard Business Review*, January–February 1996, pp. 65–73; G. G. Dess, A. Rasheed, K. J. McLaughlin, and R. L. Priem, "The New Corporate Architecture," *Academy of Management Executive*, August 1995, pp. 7–20; M. Sawhney and D. Parikh, "Break Your Boundaries," *Business 2.0*, May 2000, pp. 198–207; D. Pescovitz, "The Company Where Everybody's a Temp," *New York Times Magazine*, June 11, 2000, pp. 94–96; W. F. Cascio, "Managing a Virtual Workplace," *Academy of Management Executive*, August 2000, pp. 81–90; D. Lyons, "Smart and Smarter," *Forbes*, March 18, 2002, pp. 40–41; and B. Hedberg, G. Dahlgren, J. Hansson, and N. Goran Olve, *Virtual Organizations and Beyond: Discovering Imaginary Systems* (New York: John Wiley, 2001).

30. Based on G. Shaw, "Vancouver Law Firm Opens Virtual Branch Office," *Vancouver Sun*, September 26, 2007, p. F4.

31. "Virtual Organizations—Avatars and the Business World," 899ALK, https://899alk.wordpress.com/category/traditional-vs-modern-design (June 28, 2011).

32. R. E. Miles and C. C. Snow, "Causes of Failures in Network Organizations," *California Management Review*, vol. 34, no. 4 (1992), pp. 53–72; R. E. Miles and C. C. Snow, "The New Network Firm: A Spherical Structure Built on Human Investment Philosophy," *Organizational Dynamics*, Spring 1995, pp. 5–18; C. Jones, W. Hesterly, and S. Borgatti, "A General Theory of Network Governance: Exchange Conditions and Social Mechanisms," *Academy of Management Review*, October 1997, pp. 911–945; and R. E. Miles, C. C. Snow, J. A. Mathews, G. Miles, and H. J. Coleman, "Organizing in the Knowledge Age: Anticipating the Cellular Form," *Academy of Management Executive*, November 1997, pp. 7–24.

33. SMTnet, "Mitel Outsources Manufacturing to New Company," News Release, September 7, 2001, http://www.smtnet.com/news/index.cfm?fuseaction=view_news&news_id=1884.

34. J. Barthelemy and D. Adsit, "The Seven Deadly Sins of Outsourcing," *Academy of Management Executive*, vol. 17, no. 2 (2003), pp. 87–100.

35. K. Restivo, "Most Canadian Tech Firms Prefer Not to Outsource, Study Shows," *Financial Post (National Post)*, June 11, 2004, p. FP5.

36. PricewaterhouseCoopers LLP, *Embracing the New: The Business Insights® Survey of Canadian Private Companies 2011*, http://www.pwc.com/ca/en/private-company/publications/business-insights-2011-10-en.pdf.

37. S. Brearton, "Circles and Squares," *Canadian Business*, November 2014, p. 57–63.

38. Ibid.

39. T. Schadler, "2013 Mobile Workforce Adoption Trends," Forrester Research, Inc., Cambridge, MA.

40. C. E. Connelly and D. G. Gallagher, "Emerging Trends in Contingent Work Research," *Journal of Management*, November 2004, pp. 959–983.

41. P. Olson, "Tesco's Landing," *Forbes*, June 4, 2007, pp. 116–118; and P. M. Senge, *The Fifth Discipline: The Art and Practice of Learning Organizations* (New York: Doubleday, 1990).

42. D. A. Garvin, A. C. Edmondson, and F. Gino, "Is Yours a Learning Organization?" *Harvard Business Review*, March 2008, pp. 109–116; A. N. K. Chen and T. M. Edgington, "Assessing Value in Organizational Knowledge Creation: Considerations for Knowledge Workers," *MIS Quarterly*, June 2005, pp. 279–309; K. G. Smith, C. J. Collins, and K. D. Clark, "Existing Knowledge, Knowledge Creation Capability, and the Rate of New Product Introduction in High-Technology Firms," *Academy of Management Journal*, April 2005, pp. 346–357; R. Cross, A. Parker, L. Prusak, and S. P. Borgati, "Supporting Knowledge Creation and Sharing in Social Networks," *Organizational Dynamics*, Fall 2001, pp. 100–120; M. Schulz, "The Uncertain Relevance of Newness: Organizational Learning and Knowledge Flows," *Academy of Management Journal*, August 2001, pp. 661–681; G. Szulanski, "Exploring Internal Stickiness: Impediments to the Transfer of Best Practice within the Firm," *Strategic Management Journal*, Winter Special Issue, 1996, pp. 27–43; and J. M. Liedtka, "Collaborating across Lines of Business for Competitive Advantage," *Academy of Management Executive*, April 1996, pp. 20–37.

43. N. M. Adler, *International Dimensions of Organizational Behavior*, 4th ed. (Cincinnati, OH: South-Western College Publishing), 2002, p. 66.

44. P. B. Smith and M. F. Peterson, "Demographic Effects on the Use of Vertical Sources of Guidance by Managers in Widely Differing Cultural Contexts," *International Journal of Cross Cultural Management*, April 2005, pp. 5–26.

45. Based on P. L. Hunsaker, *Training in Management Skills* (Upper Saddle River, NJ: Prentice Hall, 2001), pp. 135–136 and 430–432; R. T. Noel, "What You Say to Your Employees When You Delegate," *Supervisory Management*, December 1993, p. 13; and S. Caudron, "Delegate for Results," *IndustryWeek*, February 6, 1995, pp. 27–30.

46. See, for example, Deloitte, "Organizing for Corporate Responsibility and Sustainability: How a Company's Organizational Structure and Governance Models Can Support CS&R Success," Deloitte Development LLC, 2009, http://www.corpgov.deloitte.com/site/us/board-governance/corporate-responsibility-and-sustainability/; Canadian Business for Social Responsibility (CBSR) and the Network for Business Sustainability, *Embedding Sustainability in Organizational Culture—Framework and Best Practices* (report emerging from the workshop "Embedding Sustainability into Corporate Cultures," presented February 23, 2010, in Toronto, Ontario, by CBSR and Network for Business Sustainability), http://www.cbsr.ca/sites/default/files/file/CultureReport_Final.pdf; Kathee Rebernak, "Where Sustainability Lives: A Path to Integration and Innovation," *Environmental Leader*, July 12, 2009, http://www.environmentalleader.com/2009/07/12/where-sustainability-lives-a-path-to-integration-and-innovation/.

47. Deloitte, "Organizing for Corporate Responsibility and Sustainability: How a Company's Organizational Structure and Governance Models Can Support CS&R Success," Deloitte Development LLC, 2009, http://www.corpgov.deloitte.com/site/us/board-governance/corporate-responsibility-and-sustainability/.

48. See the Nova Scotia Association of Social Workers (NSASW) website, http://www.nsasw.org; NSASW, "Board of Examiners Annual Report," January 1–December 31, 2010, http://www.nsasw.org/files/File/Board%20of%20Examiners/BOARD%20OF%20EXAMINERS-2011.pdf; and Richard G. Ramsay Management Consultants Inc., *The Nova Scotia Association of Social Workers: Organization Structure Review, Final Report*, October, 2009, http://www.nsasw.org/inner.php?id=70.

49. FAST COMPANY by A. Cohen. Copyright 2008 by Mansueto Ventures LLC. Reproduced with permission of Mansueto Ventures LLC in the format Textbook via Copyright Clearance Center.

50. See, for example, Northern Light Technologies, "About Us," http://www.nltinc.com/about.html; Levitt-Safety, "About Us," http://www.levitt-safety.com/Company/AboutUs/tabid/61/Default.aspx; and "As I See It," Interview with Bruce Levitt of Levitt-Safety Limited in *Embracing the New: The Business Insights® Survey of Canadian Private Companies 2011*, PricewaterhouseCoopers LLP, p. 25, http://www.pwc.com/ca/en/private-company/publications/business-insights-2011-10-en.pdf.

CHAPTER 6

1. B. Horovitz, "Starbucks CEO Reinvents the Spiel," *USA Today*, April 25, 2013, p. 3B; S. Jakab, "Starbucks Story Could Have a Bitter Edge," *Wall Street Journal*, April 25, 2013, p. C1; "Starbucks' Quest for Healthy Growth: An Interview with Howard Schultz," *McKinsey Quarterly*, no. 2 (2001), pp. 34–43; "Return to Glory," *Retail Traffic*, May/June 2011, p. 38; J. Jannarone, "Grounds for Concern at Starbucks," *Wall Street Journal*, May 3, 2011, p. C10; M. Morrison, "Bang for Its Starbucks: Hits No. 3 Despite Limited Ad Spending," *Advertising Age*, May 2, 2011, pp. 1+; W. Kendall, "A Long, Hard Grind," *Management Today*, May 2011, p. 27; "Howard Schultz, On Getting a Second Shot," *Inc.*, April 2011, pp. 52–54; "Starbucks Corp. Plans Retail Push," *Nation's Restaurant News*, April 4, 2011, p. 6; "Starbucks Marks 40th Anniversary," *Beverage Industry*, April 2011, p. 8; R. Lowenstein, "When Latte Lost Its Luster," *Wall Street Journal*, March 29, 2011, p. A17; H. Schultz, "How Starbucks Got Its Mojo Back," *Newsweek*, March 21, 2011, pp. 50–55; G. Charles, "Change Brewing at Starbucks," *Marketing*, January 2011, pp. 14–15; "Starbucks Outlines Strategies for Growth," *Beverage Industry*, January 2011, p. 14; H. Edwards, "Howard Schultz's Tall Order," *Marketing*, January 2011, p. 19; S. Berfield, "Starbucks: Howard Schultz vs. Howard Schultz," *BusinessWeek Online*, August 6, 2009; and J. Jargon, "Latest Starbucks Buzzword: 'Lean' Japanese Techniques," *Wall Street Journal*, August 4, 2009, p. A1.

2. D. Eng, "Cheesecake Factory's Winning Formula," *Fortune*, May 2, 2011, pp. 19–20, and D. McGinn, "Faster Food," *Newsweek*, April 19, 2004.

3. World Factbook 2011, www.cia.gov/library/publications/the-world-factbook.

4. Ibid.

5. "Canada Economy," *Economy Watch*, http://www.economywatch.com/world_economy/canada/?page=full.

6. B. Render, "The Humble, High-Tech Shipping Container," March 3, 2014, retrieved from Jay and Barry's OM Blog.

7. D. Michaels and J. L. Lunsford, "Streamlined Plane Making," *Wall Street Journal*, April 1, 2005, pp. B1+.

8. B. Render, "Before the Drones, Amazon Lets Loose the Robots," December 12, 2013, retrieved from Jay and Barry's OM Blog.

9. B. Render, "Rise of the Robots," March 31, 2014, retrieved from Jay and Barry's OM Blog.

10. B. Render, "Heinz Goes on a Diet," February 13, 2014, retrieved from Jay and Barry's OM Blog.

11. B. Render, "Speeding up McDonald's Drive-Thru," November 30, 2013, retrieved from Jay and Barry's OM Blog.

12. "Double-double lanes—How Tim Hortons Aims to Tackle One of the Biggest Dilemmas in Fast Food: Lon Drive-through Lineups," *Macleans*, July 9, 2012, p. 59.

13. C. Fredman, "The Devil in the Details," *Executive Edge*, April–May 1999, pp. 36–39.

14. http://new.skoda-auto.com/Documents/AnnualReports/skoda_auto_annual_report_2007_%20EN_FINAL.pdf (July 8, 2008); and T. Mudd, "The Last Laugh," *IndustryWeek*, September 18, 2000, pp. 38–44.

15. Based on "Honorary Members Form Impressive Lineup of Quality Thinkers," *Quality Progress*, March 2011, p. 17; "W. Edwards Deming," *Quality Progress*, November 2010, p. 17; R. Aguayo, *Dr. Deming: The American Who Taught the Japanese about Quality* (New York: Fireside Press, 1991); M. Walton, *The Deming Management Method* (New York: Penguin Group, 1986); and W. E. Deming, "Improvement of Quality and Productivity through Action by Management," *National Productivity Review*, Winter 1981–1982, pp. 12–22.

16. B. Render, "Chipotle's Operations Strategy for Faster Service," February 9, 2014, retrieved from Jay and Barry's OM Blog.

17. Q. H. Soon and Z. M. Udin, "Supply Chain Management from the Perspective of Value Chain Flexibility: An Exploratory Study," *Journal of Manufacturing Technology Management*, May 2011, pp. 506–526; G. Soni and R. Kodali, "A Critical Analysis of Supply Chain Management Content in Empirical Research," *Business Process Management*, April 2011, pp. 238–256; and J. H. Sheridan, "Managing the Value Chain," *IndustryWeek*, September 6, 1999, pp. 1–4, available online in archives at www.industryweek.com.

18. "Supply Chain Management: A New Narrative," *Strategic Direction*, March 2011, pp. 18–21; and J. H. Sheridan, "Managing the Value Chain."

19. T. Laseter, K. Ramdas, and D. Swerdlow. "The Supply Side of Design and Development," *Strategy & Business*, Summer 2003, p. 23; J. Jusko, "Not All Dollars and Cents," *IndustryWeek*, April 2002, p. 58; and D. Drickhamer, "Medical Marvel," *IndustryWeek*, March 2002, pp. 47–49.

20. See, for example, J. Jusko, "Procurement—Not All Dollars and Cents, *IndustryWeek*, April 4, 2002, www.industryweek.com.

21. D. Bartholomew, "The Infrastructure," *IndustryWeek*, September 6, 1999, p. 1.

22. G. Tannecz, "Forging the Chain," *IndustryWeek*, May 15, 2000, pp. 40–46.

23. T. Vinas, "A Map of the World: IW Value-Chain Survey," *IndustryWeek*, September 2005, pp. 27–34.

24. F. Panchak, "Shaping the Future of Manufacturing," *IndustryWeek*, January 2005, pp. 38–44; M. Hammer, "Deep Change: How Operational Innovation Can Transform Your Company," *Harvard Business Review*, April 2004, pp. 84–94; S. Levy, "The Connected Company, *Newsweek*," April 28, 2003, pp. 40–48; and J. Teresko, "Plant Floor Strategy," *IndustryWeek*, July 2002, pp. 26–32.

25. B. Render, "Creating More Resilient Supply Chains," August 10, 2014 retrieved from Jay and Barry's OM Blog.

26. B. Render, "Reducing the Risk of Supply Chain Disruptions," April 19, 2014, retrieved from Jay and Barry's OM Blog.

27. See J. H. Sheridan, "Now It's a Job for the CEO," *IndustryWeek*, March 20, 2000, pp. 22–30.

28. R. Norman and R. Ramirez, "From Value Chain to Value Constellation," *Harvard Business Review on Managing the Value Chain* (Boston: Harvard Business School Press, 2000), pp. 185–219.

29. B. Render, "Factory Apprenticeship Is Latest Model from Germany," December 1, 2013, retrieved from Jay and Barry's OM Blog.

30. See, for example, C. Lunan, "Workers Doing More in Less Time," *Charlotte Observer*, June 1, 2002, p. D1.

31. S. Leibs, "Getting Ready: Your Customers," p. 3.

32. See, for instance, L. Harrington, "The Accelerated Value Chain: Supply Chain Management Just Got Smarter, Faster, and More Cost-Effective, Thanks to a Groundbreaking Alliance between Intel and Technologies," *IndustryWeek*, April 2002, pp. 45–51.

33. Ibid.

34. B. Render, "The Case of the Vanishing Drugs," February 24, 2014, retrieved from Jay and Barry's OM Blog.

35. And the Survey Says box based on "Innovation Nation," *IndustryWeek*, November 2010, p. 15; "First-Hand Accounts," *IndustryWeek*, July 2008, p. 28; "State of the Workforce Report," *IndustryWeek*, November 2008, p. 18; "Sustainable Supply Chains," *IndustryWeek*, December 2008, p. 57; "Taking Charge of Mobile Workforce Costs," *IndustryWeek*, August 2009, p. 47; and "The Future of Manufacturing," *IndustryWeek*, November 2008, pp. 51–57.

36. See, for instance, L. Harrington, "The Accelerated Value Chain: Supply Chain Management Just Got Smarter, Faster, and More Cost-Effective, Thanks to a Groundbreaking Alliance between Intel and Technologies," *IndustryWeek*, April 2002, pp. 45–51; and J. H. Sheridan, "Managing the Value Chain."

37. J. H. Sheriden, "Managing the Value Chain," p. 3.

38. B. Render, "Speeding Up the Airline Boarding Process," January 27, 2014, retrieved from Jay and Barry's OM Blog.

39. "Guide to Airline Boarding Procedures," Seat Guru by tripadvisor, http://www.seatguru.com/articles/boarding_procedures.php.

40. W. J. Stevenson, and M. Hojati, *Operations Management*, 2nd Canadian edition (Toronto: McGraw-Hill Ryerson, 2004), p. 279.

41. G. Taninecz, "Forging the Chain," *IndustryWeek*, May 15, 2000, pp. 40–46.

42. Ibid.

43. Ibid.

44. M. Gooderham, "At These Companies, the Training Never Stops," *Globe and Mail*, October 14, 2010, http://www.theglobeandmail.com/report-on-business/careers/top-employers/at-these-companies-the-training-never-stops/article1215132.

45. D. Drickhamer, "On Target," *IndustryWeek*, October 16, 2000, pp. 111–112.

46. "Top Security Threats and Management Issues Facing Corporate America: 2003 Survey of Fortune 1000 Companies," *ASIS International* and *Pinkerton*, www.asisonline.org.

47. J. H. Sheridan, "Managing the Value Chain," p. 4.

48. S. Rosenbloom, "Solution, or Mess? A Milk Jug for a Green Earth," *New York Times Online*, June 30, 2008.

49. K. T. Greenfeld, "Taco Bell and the Golden Age of Drive-Thru," *Bloomberg BusinessWeek Online*, May 5, 2011; and S. Anderson, Associated Press, "Restaurants Gear Up for Window Wars," *Springfield, Missouri, News-Leader*, January 27, 2006, p. 5B.

50. B. Render, "Wal-Mart Ramps Up Global E-Commerce," February 22, 2014, retrieved from Jay and Barry's OM Blog.

51. Technology and the Manager's Job box based on S. Minter, "What Is Advanced Manufacturing?" *IndustryWeek*, August 2009, p. 7; J. Bush, "Russia's Factories Shift Gears," *BusinessWeek*, May 18, 2009, pp. 50–51; D. Blanchard, "A Manufacturer for All Seasons," *IndustryWeek*, December 2008, p. 7; J. Teresko, "Planning the Factory of the Future," *IndustryWeek*, December 2008, pp. 22–24; and J. Teresko, "Winning with Digital Manufacturing," *Industry-Week*, July 2008, pp. 45–47.

52. B. Render, "The Downside of Increasing Productivity," July 16, 2014, retrieved from Jay and Barry's OM Blog.

53. B. Render, "Productivity and Technology Down on the Farm," February 27, 2014, retrieved from Jay and Barry's OM Blog.

54. D. Bartholomew, "Quality Takes a Beating," *IndustryWeek*, March 2006, pp. 46–54; J. Carey and M. Arndt, "Making Pills the Smart Way," *BusinessWeek*, May 3, 2004, pp. 102–103; and A. Barrett, "Schering's Dr. Feelbetter?" *BusinessWeek*, June 23, 2003, pp. 55–56.

55. T. Vinas, "Six Sigma Rescue," *IndustryWeek*, March 2004, p. 12.

56. J. S. McClenahen, "Prairie Home Companion," *IndustryWeek*, October 2005, pp. 45–46.

57. "Best Managed: Congratulations to Canada's 50 Best Managed Companies of 2011," *Financial Post*, February 21, 2012, http://business.financialpost.com/2012/02/21/congratulations-to-canadas-50-best-managed-companies-of-2011.

58. W. Royal, "Spotlight Shines on Maquiladora," *IndustryWeek*, October 16, 2000, pp. 91–92.

59. See B. Whitford and R. Andrew (eds.), *The Pursuit of Quality* (Perth: Beaumont Publishing, 1994).

60. D. Drickhamer, "Road to Excellence," *IndustryWeek*, October 16, 2000, pp. 117–118.

61. "ISO Survey," ISO, http://www.iso.org/iso/home/standards/certification/iso-survey.htm.

62. "Customer Feedback Commitment," Town of Ajax, http://www.ajax.ca/en/insidetownhall/qualitymanagement.asp.

63. G. Hasek, "Merger Marries Quality Efforts," *IndustryWeek*, August 21, 2000, pp. 89–92.

64. J. Jusko, "An Elite Crew," *IndustryWeek*, March 2011, pp. 17–18; and M. Arndt, "Quality Isn't Just for Widgets," *BusinessWeek*, July 22, 2002, pp.72–73.

65. "Lean Six Sigma Success Stories by Industry," GoLeanSigma.com, http://www.goleansixsigma.com/lean-six-sigma-industry-success-stories.

66. "Helping Staples Use Lean Six Sigma to Drive Process Improvements that Enable High Performance," Accenture, 2009, http://www.accenture.com/sitecollectiondocuments/pdf/accenture_retail_staples_lean_six_sigma.pdf.

67. For a thorough overview of project management, see S. Berkun, *The Art of Project Management* (Upper Saddle River, NJ: Prentice Hall, 2005); or J. K. Pinto, *Project Management: Achieving Competitive Advantage and MS Project* (Upper Saddle River, NJ: Prentice Hall, 2007).

68. H. Maylor, "Beyond the Gantt Chart: Project Management Moving On," *European Management Journal* (February 2001), pp. 92–101.

69. For additional information on CPM, see W. A. Haga and K. A. Marold, "A Simulation Approach to the PERT/CPM Time-Cost Trade-Off Problem," *Project Management Journal*, June 2004, pp. 31–37.

70. B. Render, "Keeping Some Slack in the Operating Room," March 27, 2014, retrieved from Jay and Barry's OM Blog.

71. B. Render, "Lean Also Works in the Mining Industry," August 4, 2014, retrieved from Jay and Barry's OM Blog.

72. B. Render, "Making the Decision to Reshore," August 26, 2014, retrieved from Jay and Barry's OM Blog.

73. B. Render, "Otis Finds Reshoring Manufacturing Is Not Easy," May 6, 2014, retrieved from Jay and Barry's OM Blog.

74. "Women Matter. Gender diversity, a corporate performance driver," McKinsey and Company, 2007.

75. Based on R. Fisher and W. Ury, *Getting to Yes: Negotiating Agreement without Giving In* (New York: Penguin Books, 1986); J. A. Wall, Jr. and M. W. Blum, "Negotiations," *Journal of Management*, June 1991, pp. 273–303; and M. E. Roloff, L. L. Putnam, and L. Anastasiou, "Negotiation Skills," in J. O. Greene and B. R. Burleson (eds.), *Handbook of Communication and Social Interaction Skills* (Mahwah, NJ: Lawrence Erlbaum, 2003), pp. 801–833.

76. V. Galt, "Canadian Tire Applies Its 'Lean' Ideals to Hiring Process" *Globe and Mail*, February 23, 2012, http://www.theglobeandmail.com/report-on-business/careers/management/canadian-tire-applies-its-lean-ideals-to-hiring-process/article548381.

77. Ibid.

78. C. Simpson, "An iPhone Tester Caught in Apple's Supply Chain," *Bloomberg Business Week*, https://twitter.com/intent/user?screen_name=CamSimpsonNews, November 07, 2013, http://www.businessweek.com/articles/2013-11-07/an-iphone-tester-caught-in-apples-supply-chain#p1.

79. Ibid.

80. Ibid.

81. Ibid.

82. Ibid.

83. B. Render, "Rethinking Corporate Social Compliance in the Supply Chain," July 21, 2014, retrieved from Jay and Barry's OM Blog.

84. J. Ostrower and H. Kachi, "Boeing's 787 Resumes Service," *Wall Street Journal*, April 29, 2013, p. B3; J. Ostrower and T. Stynes, "Boeing Steers Past 787 Woes," *Wall Street Journal*, April 25, 2013, p. B2; S. Jakab, "Dreamliner's Woes Fail to Ground Boeing," *Wall Street Journal*, April 24, 2013, p. C1; N. Clark, "Boeing Begins Modifying 787 Batteries," *New York Times Online*, April 22, 2013; A. Pasztor, "How Boeing Rescued the 787," *Wall Street Journal*, April 20/21, 2013, p. B1+; C. Drew and J. Mouawad, "Boeing Fix for Battery Is Approved by F.A.A.," *New York Times Online*, April 19, 2013; H. Tabuchi, "Boeing Presents Solution for Dreamliner Problems," *New York Times Online*, March 15, 2013; S. Mayerowitz, "Former Workers: Boeing Rushed Dreamliner Project," *Springfield, Missouri, News-Leader*, January 26, 2013, p. 7A; D. Michaels, "Innovation Is Messy Business," *Wall Street Journal*, January 24. 2013, pp. B1+; S. Dubois, "Boeing's Dreamliner Mess: Simply Inevitable?" management.fortune.com, January 22, 2013; P. Kavilanz, "Dreamliner: Where in the World Its Parts Come From," money. cnn.com, January 18, 2013; "Boeing's Dreamliner Takes to the Skies," *USA Today*, October 21, 2011, p. 3B; P. Jonsson, "787 Dreamliner Takes Off at Last. When Can You Jump Aboard?" www.csmonitor.com, September 27, 2011; and W. J. Hennigan, "Boeing Delivers First 787 Dreamliner," *LA Times*, September 26, 2011.

85. V. Gupta, and M. V. Kumar, "The Making of Boeing's 787 Dreamliner," *IBS Center for Management Research*, 2006. Retrieved from each case collection, doi: 606-016-1.

86. Ibid.

CHAPTER 7

1. See the Calgary Chamber of Voluntary Organizations (CCVO) website, www.calgarycvo.org.

2. A. Burrowes and J. Coe, *Beyond the Boomers: A Guidebook for Building an Immigrant Workforce in the Nonprofit Sector* (Calgary, AB: CCVO, 2011), http://www.calgarycvo.org/sites/default/files/resources/201107_CCVO_DiversityWorkbook.pdf.

3. R. Roach, *The Nonprofit and Voluntary Sector in Alberta: Regional Highlights of the National Survey of Nonprofit and Voluntary Organizations*, (Toronto ON: Imagine Canada, 2006).

4. See, for example, Y. Y. Kor and H. Leblebici, "How Do Interdependencies among Human-Capital Deployment, Development, and Diversification Strategies Affect Firms' Financial Performance?" *Strategic Management Journal*, October 2005, pp. 967–985; D. E. Bowen and C. Ostroff, "Understanding HRM–Firm Performance Linkages: The Role of the 'Strength' of the HRM System," *Academy of Management Review*, April 2004, pp. 203–221; R. Batt, "Managing Customer Services: Human Resource Practices, Quit Rates, and Sales Growth," *Academy of Management Journal*, June 2002, pp. 587–597; A. S. Tsui, J. L. Pearce, L. W. Porter, and A. M. Tripoli, "Alternative Approaches to the Employee–Organization Relationship: Does Investment in Employees Pay Off?" *Academy of Management Journal*, October 1997, pp. 1089–1121; M. A. Huselid, S. E. Jackson, and R. S. Schuler, "Technical and Strategic Human Resource Management Effectiveness as Determinants of Firm Performance," *Academy of Management Journal*, January 1997, pp. 171–188; J. T. Delaney and M. A. Huselid, "The Impact of Human Resource Management Practices on Perceptions of Organizational Performance," *Academy of Management Journal*, August 1996, pp. 949–969; B. Becker and B. Gerhart, "The Impact of Human Resource Management on Organizational Performance: Progress and Prospects," *Academy of Management Journal*, August 1996, pp. 779–801; M. J. Koch and R. G. McGrath, "Improving Labor Productivity: Human Resource Management Policies Do Matter," *Strategic Management Journal*, May 1996. pp. 335–354; and M. A. Huselid, "The Impact of Human Resource Management Practices on Turnover, Productivity, and Corporate Financial Performance," *Academy of Management Journal*, June 1995, pp. 635–672.

5. "Maximizing the Return on Your Human Capital Investment: The 2005 Watson Wyatt Human Capital Index® Report," "WorkAsia 2004/2005: A Study of Employee Attitudes in Asia," and "European Human Capital Index 2002," Watson Wyatt Worldwide (Washington, D.C.).

6. See WorldatWork®, *Total Rewards Model*, (WorldatWork®, 2011), http://www.worldatwork.org/waw/adimLink?id=28330&nonav=y.

7. Adapted from Gareth Morgan, *Images of Organization*, (Thousand Oaks, CA: Sage Publications, 2006).

8. A. Burrowes and J. Coe, *Beyond the Boomers: A Guidebook for Building an Immigrant Workforce in the Nonprofit Sector* (Calgary, AB: CCVO, 2011), http://www.calgarycvo.org/sites/default/files/resources/201107_CCVO_DiversityWorkbook.pdf.

9. Deloitte Canada, "Congratulations to Canada's 50 Best Managed Companies," *National Post*, February 21, 2011.

10. Statistics Canada, "Labour Force Survey, August 2012," *The Daily* (Statistics Canada), http://www.statcan.gc.ca/daily-quotidien/120907/dq120907a-eng.htm.

11. Canadian Labour Market—Budget Information, Department of Finance, http://www.budget.gc.ca/2014/docs/jobs-emplois/pdf/jobs-emplois-eng.pdf.

12. Peter O'Neill, "Chamber Seeks Changes to EI to Combat Skills Shortage Crisis; President Says Ottawa Believes Its Own 'Propaganda' About the State of the Economy; 'Competitiveness' Should Be Its Mandate," *Vancouver Sun*, February 8, 2012: C2; Canadian Chamber of Commerce, "Taking on the Top 10 Barriers to Canadian Competitiveness," *Connect!*, February 8, 2012, http://www.chamber.ca/index.php/en/news/C197/taking-on-the-top-10-barriers-to-canadian-competitiveness; and Canadian Chamber of Commerce, "Top 10 Barriers to Competitiveness," *Connect!*, http://chambertop10.ca.

13. Working in Canada, "Canada Targets Skilled Trades," http://www.workingin-canada.com/visa/skills-in-demand/canada-targets-skilled-trades.

14. Human Resources and Skills Development Canada, "Canadians in Context—Aging Population," http://www4.hrsdc.gc.ca/.3ndic.1t.4r@-eng.jsp?iid=33.

15. "Canada's Foreign-Born Population Soars to 6.8 Million," *CBC News*, 2014. http://www.cbc.ca/news/canada/canada-s-foreign-born-population-soars-to-6-8-million-1.1308179.

16. See, for example, The Ontario Federation of Labour's Workers Under 30 Committee, "Myths about Unions," http://youth.ofl.ca/index.php/myths/; Lawrence Mishel and Matthew Walters, *How*

Unions Help All Workers (Washington, DC: Economic Policy Institite, 2003); A. Jilani, "Report: Five Things Unions Have Done for All Americans," *Think Progress*, March 5, 2011, http://thinkprogress.org/politics/2011/03/05/148930/top-five-things-unions/?mobile=nc.

17. Statistics Canada, "Unionization: Unionized Rates in First Half of 2006 and 2007," http://www.statcan.gc.ca/pub/75-001-x/topics-sujets/unionization-syndicalisation/unionization-syndicalisation-2007-eng.htm.

18. G. Dessler and N. Cole, *Human Resources Management in Canada*, 10th ed. (Toronto, ON: Pearson Prentice-Hall).

19. S. Armour, "Lawsuits Pin Target on Managers," *USA Today*, October 1, 2002, www.usatoday.com.

20. See, for example, C. Sleezer, T. Wentling, and R. Cude, eds., *Human Resource Development and Information Technology: Making Global Connections* (Norwell, MA: Kluwer Academic Publishers, 2001), pp. 89–104; W. F. Cascio, "From Business Partner to Driving Business Success: The Next Step in the Evolution of HR Management," in *The Future of Human Resource Management: 64 Thought Leaders Explore the Critical HR Issues of Today and Tomorrow*, M. Losey, S. Meisinger, and D. Ulrich, eds. (Hoboken, NJ: John Wiley & Sons, 2005), pp. 103–109; B. Luck, *Innovation of Technology: Business for a New Century*, 2010, http://www.scribd.com/?doc/?27947709/?Innovation-of-Technology-in-Business-Slides; and A. Walker, "Best Practices in HR Technology," in A. Walker and T. Perrin, eds., *Web-based Human Resources: The Technologies and Trends That Are Transforming HR* (New York, NY: McGraw-Hill, 2001), pp. 3–14.

21. W. Brockbank, "If HR Were Really Strategically Proactive: Present and Future Directions in HR's Contribution to Competitive Advantage," *Human Resource Management*, Winter 1999.

22. D. Sankey, "Technologies Extend HR Reach," *Ottawa Citizen*, November 9, 2011, http://www2.canada.com/ottawacitizen/story.html?id=a6638454-3711-422e-9c0e-1a40d1ac52f2.

23. Ibid.

24. D. Vanheukelom, "HR Tech's Future (and Present) in the Cloud," *Canadian HR Reporter*, October 10, 2011, http://www.hrreporter.com/articleview/11414-hr-techs-future-and-present-in-the-cloud.

25. "HRIS in 2010 (or Sooner!): Experts Predict Use of Wrist Mounted Devices, Virtual HR Access, and HR Voice Recognition," *Managing HR Information Systems*, February 2002, pp. 1–4.

26. E. Beauchesne, "Skills Training Rebounds: But Labour Shortage May Still Be Looming," *Telegram*, November 21, 2003, p. D1.

27. E. Komarnicki, Labour and Skills Shortages in Canada: Addressing Current and Future Challenges, *Report of the Standing Committee on Human Resources, Skills and Social Development and the Status of Persons with Disabilities* (2012).

28. "The Sick Day Scam," *Maclean's*, July 8, 2013, pp.40–42.

29. G. Dessler and N. Cole, *Human Resources Management in Canada*, 10th ed. (Toronto, ON: Pearson Prentice-Hall).

30. J. Sullivan, "Workforce Planning: Why to Start Now," *Workforce*, September 2002, pp. 46–50.

31. Based on A. Tomlinson, "The Many Benefits of Online Job Boards," *Canadian HR Reporter*, July 15, 2002, pp. 17–18. The Career webpage can be found at http://www.scotiabank.com/ca/en/0,,178,00.html.

32. T. J. Bergmann and M. S. Taylor, "College Recruitment: What Attracts Students to Organizations?" *Personnel*, May–June 1984, pp.

34–46; and A. S. Bargerstock and G. Swanson, "Four Ways to Build Cooperative Recruitment Alliances," *HR Magazine*, March 1991, p. 49.

33. S. Burton and D. Warner, "The Future of Hiring—Top 5 Sources for Recruitment Today," *Workforce Vendor Directory*, 2002, p. 75.

34. C. Eustace, "VPD: Virtual Police Department," *Vancouver Sun*, May 29, 2007, pp. A1–A2.

35. G. Shaw, "An Offer That's Hard to Refuse," *Vancouver Sun*, November 12, 2003, p. D5.

36. See, for example, J. P. Kirnan, J. E. Farley, and K. F. Geisinger, "The Relationship between Recruiting Source, Applicant Quality, and Hire Performance: An Analysis by Sex, Ethnicity, and Age," *Personnel Psychology*, Summer 1989, pp. 293–308; and R. W. Griffeth, P. Hom, L. Fink, and D. Cohen, "Comparative Tests of Multivariate Models of Recruiting Sources Effects," *Journal of Management*, vol. 23, no. 1 (1997), pp. 19–36.

37. Hub Pages, "The Average Cost of Employee Turnover," July 26, 2008, http://lifeislikethat.hubpages.com/hub/The-Average-Cost-of-Employee-Turnover.

38. See, for example, T. Janz, L. Hellervik, D. Gilmore. *Behavior Description Interviewing* (Newton, MA: Allyn and Bacon Publishers, 1986); S. J. Motowidlo, G. W. Carter, M. D. Dunnette, et al., "Studies of the Structured Behavioral Interview," *Journal of Applied Psychology*, vol. 77, no. 5 (1992), pp. 571–587; M. A. McDaniel, D. Whetzel, F. L. Schmidt, S. D. Maurer, "The Validity of Employment Interviews: A Comprehensive Review and Meta-Analysis," *Journal of Applied Psychology*, vol. 79, no. 4, (1994), pp. 599–616; and T. Janz, "Initial Comparisons of Patterned Behavior-Based Interviews versus Unstructured Interviews," *Journal of Applied Psychology*, vol. 67, no. 5 (1982), pp. 577–580.

39. G. W. England, *Development and Use of Weighted Application Blanks*, rev. ed. (Minneapolis: Industrial Relations Center, University of Minnesota, 1971); J. J. Asher, "The Biographical Item: Can It Be Improved?" *Personnel Psychology*, Summer 1972, p. 266; G. Grimsley and H. F. Jarrett, "The Relation of Managerial Achievement to Test Measures Obtained in the Employment Situation: Methodology and Results," *Personnel Psychology*, Spring 1973, pp. 31–48; E. E. Ghiselli, "The Validity of Aptitude Tests in Personnel Selection," *Personnel Psychology*, Winter 1973, p. 475; I. T. Robertson and R. S. Kandola, "Work Sample Tests: Validity, Adverse Impact, and Applicant Reaction," *Journal of Occupational Psychology*, vol. 55, no. 3 (1982), pp. 171–183; A. K. Korman, "The Prediction of Managerial Performance: A Review," *Personnel Psychology*, Summer 1986, pp. 295–322; G. C. Thornton, *Assessment Centers in Human Resource Management* (Reading, MA: Addison-Wesley, 1992); C. Fernandez-Araoz, "Hiring without Firing," *Harvard Business Review*, July–August, 1999, pp. 108–120; and A. M. Ryan and R. E. Ployhart, "Applicants' Perceptions of Selection Procedures and Decisions: A Critical Review and Agenda for the Future," *Journal of Management*, vol. 26, no. 3 (2000), pp. 565–606.

40. A. Wahl, "People Power," *Canadian Business*, March 29–April 11, 2004, p. 58.

41. C. L. Cooper, "The Changing Psychological Contract at Work: Revisiting the Job Demands–Control Model," *Occupational and Environmental Medicine*, June 2002, p. 355; D. M. Rousseau and S. A. Tijoriwala, "Assessing Psychological Contracts: Issues, Alternatives and Measures," *Journal of Organizational Behavior*, vol. 19, no. S1

(1998), pp. 679–695; and S. L. Robinson, M. S. Kraatz, and D. M. Rousseau, "Changing Obligations and the Psychological Contract: A Longitudinal Study," *Academy of Management Journal*, February 1994, pp. 137–152.

42. "2011 Industry Report," *Training Magazine*, November 2011, www.trainingmag.com.

43. D. Sankey, "Canadian Companies Skimp on Training," *National Post*, June 27, 2007, p. WK3.

44. H. Dolezalek, "2005 Industry Report," *Training*, December 2005, pp. 14–28.

45. B. Hall, "The Top Training Priorities for 2003," *Training*, February 2003, p. 40.

46. S. Purba, "When Reviews Deserve a Failing Grade," *Globe and Mail*, June 11, 2004, p. C1.

47. K. Clark, "Judgment Day," *U.S. News & World Report*, January 13, 2003, pp. 31–32; E. E. Lawler III, "The Folly of Forced Ranking," *Strategy & Business*, Third Quarter 2002, pp. 28–32; K. Cross, "The Weakest Links," Business2.com, June 26, 2001, pp. 36–37; J. Greenwald, "Rank and Fire," *Time*, June 18, 2001, pp. 38–39; D. Jones, "More Firms Cut Workers Ranked at Bottom to Make Way for Talent," *USA Today*, May 30, 2001, p. B11; and M. Boyle, "Performance Reviews: Perilous Curves Ahead," *Fortune*, May 28, 2001, pp. 187–188.

48. J. McGregor, "The Struggle to Measure Performance," *Business-Week*, January 9, 2006, pp. 26–28.

49. D. Jones, "Study: Thinning Herd from Bottom Helps," *USA Today*, March 14, 2005, p. 1B.

50. S. E. Cullen, P. K. Bergey, and L. Aiman-Smith, "Forced Distribution Rating Systems and the Improvement of Workforce Potential: A Baseline Simulation," *Personnel Psychology*, Spring 2005, pp. 1–32.

51. J. McGregor, "The Struggle to Measure Performance," *Business-Week*, January 9, 2006, pp. 26–28.

52. R. D. Bretz Jr., G. T. Milkovich, and W. Read, "The Current State of Performance Appraisal Research and Practice: Concerns, Directions, and Implications," *Journal of Management*, June 1992, p. 331.

53. M. Debrayen and S. Brutus, "Learning from Others' 360-Degree Experiences," *Canadian HR Reporter*, February 10, 2003, pp. 18–19.

54. M. Johne, "It's Good PR to Keep Employees Loyal," *Globe and Mail*, September 20, 2002, p. C1.

55. M. A. Peiperl, "Getting 360° Feedback Right," *Harvard Business Review*, January 2001, pp. 142–147.

56. Based on WorldatWork®, *Total Rewards Model*, (WorldatWork®, 2011), http://www.worldatwork.org/waw/adimLink?id=28330& nonav=y.

57. This section based on R. I. Henderson, *Compensation Management in a Knowledge-Based World*, 9th ed. (Upper Saddle River, NJ: Prentice Hall, 2003).

58. L. R. Gomez-Mejia, "Structure and Process of Diversification, Compensation Strategy, and Firm Performance," *Strategic Management Journal*, vol. 13, no. 5 (1992), pp. 381–397; and E. Montemayor, "Congruence between Pay Policy and Competitive Strategy in High-Performing Firms," *Journal of Management*, vol. 22, no. 6 (1996), pp. 889–908.

59. E. E. Lawler III, G. E. Ledford Jr., and L. Chang, "Who Uses Skill-Based Pay and Why," *Compensation & Benefits Review*, March–April 1993, p. 22; G. E. Ledford, "Paying for the Skills, Knowledge and Competencies of Knowledge Workers," *Compensation & Benefits Review*, July–August 1995, pp. 55–62; C. Lee, K. S. Law, and P. Bobko, "The Importance of Justice Perceptions on Pay Effectiveness: A Two-Year Study of a Skill-Based Pay Plan," *Journal of Management*, vol. 26, no. 6 (1999), pp. 851–873.

60. J. D. Shaw, N. Gupta, A. Mitra, and G. E. Ledford Jr., "Success and Survival of Skill-Based Pay Plans," *Journal of Management*, February 2005, pp. 28–49.

61. Information from Hewitt Associates Studies, "Hewitt Study Shows Pay-for-Performance Plans Replacing Holiday Bonuses," December 6, 2005; "Salaries Continue to Rise in Asia Pacific," Hewitt Annual Study Reports, November 23, 2005; and CLA Personnel, "Hewitt Associates Study Reveals Salary Increases Remain Flat," Info CLA, http://www.clapersonnel.ca/en_employ_articles_ details.asp?id=2086.

62. Based on G. Dessler and N. Cole, *Human Resources Management in Canada*, 10th ed. (Toronto, ON: Pearson Prentice-Hall), Chapter 13.

63. C. Oglesby, "More Options for Moms Seeking Work–Family Balance," *CNN.com*, May 10, 2001.

64. J. Miller and M. Miller, "Get a Life!" *Fortune*, November 28, 2005, pp. 108–124.

65. M. Elias, "The Family-First Generation," *USA Today*, December 13, 2004, p. 5D.

66. F. Hansen, "Truths and Myths about Work/Life Balance," *Work-force*, December 2002, pp. 34–39.

67. M. M. Arthur, "Share Price Reactions to Work–Family Initiatives: An Institutional Perspective," *Academy of Management Journal*, August 2003, pp. 497–505.

68. N. P. Rothbard, T. L. Dumas, and K. W. Phillips, "The Long Arm of the Organization: Work–Family Policies and Employee Preferences for Segmentation," paper presented at the 61st Annual Academy of Management meeting, Washington, D.C., August 2001.

69. Based on WorldatWork®, *Total Rewards Model*, (WorldatWork®, 2011), http://www.worldatwork.org/waw/adimLink?id=28330 &nonav=y.

70. D. E. Super and D. T. Hall, "Career Development: Exploration and Planning," in *Annual Review of Psychology*, vol. 29, eds. M. R. Rosenzweig and L. W. Porter (Palo Alto, CA: Annual Reviews, 1978), p. 334.

71. D. E. Super, "A Life-Span Life Space Approach to Career Development," *Journal of Vocational Behavior*, Spring 1980, pp. 282–298. See also E. P. Cook, and M. Arthur, *Career Theory Handbook* (Upper Saddle River, NJ: Prentice Hall, 1991), pp. 99–131; and L. S. Richman, "The New Worker Elite," *Fortune*, August 22, 1994, pp. 56–66.

72. Based on G. Dessler and N. Cole, *Human Resources Management in Canada*, 10th ed. (Toronto, ON: Pearson Prentice-Hall), Chapter 14.

73. Ibid.

74. "Employers Underestimate Extent of Sexual Harassment, Report Says," *Vancouver Sun*, March 8, 2001, p. D6.

75. Ibid.

76. John Gibbons, *Employee Engagement A Review of Current Research and Its Implications* (Ottawa, ON: The Conference Board of Canada, November 2006).

77. J. K. Harter, F. L. Schmidt, T. L. Hayes, "Business-Unit-Level Relationship between Employee Satisfaction, Employee Engagement, and Business Outcomes: A Meta-Analysis," *Journal of Applied Psychology*, vol. 87, no. 2, (2002), pp. 268–279.

78. J. A. LePine, A. Erez, and D. E. Johnson, "The Nature and Dimensionality of Organizational Citizenship Behavior: A Critical Review and Meta-Analysis," *Journal of Applied Psychology*, vol. 87, no. 1 (2002), pp. 52–65.

79. See WorldatWork®, *Total Rewards Model*, (WorldatWork®, 2011), http://www.worldatwork.org/waw/adimLink? id=28330&nonav=y.

80. "Filling the Gaps," *Maclean's*, September 16, 2013, pp. 40–41.

81. Ibid.

82. Based on S. P. Robbins and D. A. DeCenzo, *Fundamentals of Management*, 4th ed. (Upper Saddle River, NJ: Prentice Hall, 2004), p. 194.

83. Communications New Brunswick, "New Initiatives to Help Aboriginal Students Pursue Post-Secondary Education," Government of New Brunswick News Release, January 6, 2010, http://www.gnb.ca/cnb/news/pet/2010e0007pe.htm.

84. "New Brunswick Invests in Training for Aboriginal Peoples," *Canadian HR Reporter*, October 7, 2911, http://www.hrreporter.com/articleprint.aspx?articleid=11403.

85. Laura A. DeCarlo, "The 30-Second Commercial: What's Unique about You?" The Global Career Services Network, http://www.careerdirectors.com/members/articles/I01.pdf.

86. *Dragon's Den*, Canadian Broadcasting Corporation, http://www.cbc.ca/dragonsden.

87. Wellington West, *Rock Steady, Annual Report 2008*, http://www.wellwest.ca/documents/reports/WW_AR_2008.pdf.

88. Ibid.

89. Ibid.

90. M. Cash, "Steady Growth Brings $333-M Payoff—National Bank Buys Wellington West," *Winnipeg Free Press*, May 27, 2011, http://www.winnipegfreepress.com/business/steady-growth-brings-333-m-payoff-122710338.html.

91. Wellington West, *Rock Steady, Annual Report 2008*, http://www.wellwest.ca/documents/reports/WW_AR_2008.pdf.

92. M. Cash, "Steady Growth Brings $333-M Payoff—National Bank Buys Wellington West," *Winnipeg Free Press*, May 27, 2011, http://www.winnipegfreepress.com/business/steady-growth-brings-333-m-payoff-122710338.html.

93. A. Hopkins, "Manulife Buys Financial Planning Firm Wellington West," Reuters, August 29, 2012, http://www.reuters.com/article/2012/08/29/us-manulife-wellingtonwest-idUSBRE87S11F20120829; "Manulife Acquires Wellington West Arm," *Winnipeg Free Press*, August 30, 2012, http://www.winnipegfreepress.com/business/manulife-acquires-wellington-west-arm-167960166.html.

94. "Love among the Cubicles," *Maclean's*, May 14, 2012, pp. 24–28.

95. Ibid.

96. Ibid.

97. Ibid.

98. Ibid.

CHAPTER 8

1. P. Preville, "Women in Business," *Canadian Business*, Winter 2013/2014, pp. 26–27.

2. Ibid.

3. Ibid.

4. See, for example, "Feature Interview with Peter Drucker," *Training & Development Magazine* (September 1998); J. Kotter, "What Leaders Really Do," *Harvard Business Review*, vol. 68 (1990), pp. 103–111; and H. Mintzberg, In Conversation, *CBC Ideas*, The Canadian Broadcasting Corporation, 1999.

5. "Portraits in Leadership 2011," *Canadian Business* and the Ted Rogers Leadership Centre, Ryerson University, www.canadianbusiness.com/portraits.

6. See T. A. Judge, J. E. Bono, R. Ilies, and M. Werner, "Personality and Leadership: A Review" (paper presented at the 15th Annual Conference of the Society for Industrial and Organizational Psychology, New Orleans, 2000); T. A. Judge, J. E. Bono, R. Ilies, and M. W. Gerhardt, "Personality and Leadership: A Qualitative and Quantitative Review," *Journal of Applied Psychology*, August 2002, pp. 765–780; and D. A. Hofmann and L. M. Jones, "Leadership, Collective Personality, and Performance," *Journal of Applied Psychology*, vol. 90, no. 3 (2005), pp. 509–522.

7. Advancing Canadian Health Leadership, CHLNet, http://chlnet.ca/CHLNet-Leadership-Benchmarking-Study-Final-Report.pdf

8. See D. S. Derue, J. D. Nahrgang, N. Wellman, and S. E. Humphrey, "Trait and Behavioral Theories of Leadership: An Integration and Meta-Analytic Test of Their Relative Validity," *Personnel Psychology*, Spring 2011, pp. 7–52; T. A. Judge, J. E. Bono, R. Ilies, and M. W. Gerhardt, "Personality and Leadership: A Qualitative and Quantitative Review," *Journal of Applied Psychology*, August 2002, pp. 765–780; and S. A. Kirkpatrick and E. A. Locke, "Leadership: Do Traits Matter?" *Academy of Management Executive*, May 1991, pp. 48–60.

9. R. McQueen, "The Long Shadow of Tom Stephens: He Branded MacBlo's Crew as Losers, Then Made Them into Winners," *Financial Post* (*National Post*), June 22, 1999, pp. C1, C5.

10. A. J. Mayo and N. Nohria, "Zeitgeist Leadership," *Harvard Business Review*, vol. 83, no. 10 (2005), pp. 45–60.

11. H. Wang, K. S. Law, R. D. Hackett, D. Wang, and Z. X. Chen, "Leader–Member Exchange as a Mediator of the Relationship between Transformational Leadership and Followers' Performance and Organizational Citizenship Behavior," *Academy of Management Journal*, vol. 48, no. 3 (June 2005), pp. 420–432.

12. P. Hersey and K. Blanchard, "So You Want to Know Your Leadership Style?" *Training & Development*, February 1974, pp. 1–15; and P. Hersey and K. Blanchard, *Management of Organizational Behavior: Leading Human Resources*, 8th ed. (Englewood Cliffs, NJ: Prentice Hall, 2001).

13. See, for example, C. F. Fernandez and R. P. Vecchio, "Situational Leadership Theory Revisited: A Test of an Across-Jobs Perspective," *Leadership Quarterly*, vol. 8, no. 1 (1997), pp. 67–84; and C. L. Graeff, "Evolution of Situational Leadership Theory: A Critical Review," *Leadership Quarterly*, vol. 8, no. 2 (1997), pp. 153–170.

14. R. J. House, "A Path-Goal Theory of Leader Effectiveness," *Administrative Science Quarterly*, September 1971, pp. 321–338; R. J. House and T. R. Mitchell, "Path-Goal Theory of Leadership," *Journal of Contemporary Business*, Autumn 1974, p. 86; and R. J. House, "Path-

Goal Theory of Leadership: Lessons, Legacy, and a Reformulated Theory," *Leadership Quarterly*, Fall 1996, pp. 323–352.

15. J. C. Wofford and L. Z. Liska, "Path-Goal Theories of Leadership: A Meta-Analysis," *Journal of Management*, Winter 1993, pp. 857–876; M. G. Evans, "R. J. House's 'A Path-Goal Theory of Leader Effectiveness,'" *Leadership Quarterly*, Fall 1996, pp. 305–309; C. A. Schriesheim and L. L. Neider, "Path-Goal Leadership Theory: The Long and Winding Road," *Leadership Quarterly*, Fall 1996, pp. 317–321; A. Somech, "The Effects of Leadership Style and Team Process on Performance and Innovation in Functionally Heterogeneous Teams," *Journal of Management*, vol. 32, no. 1 (2006), pp. 132–157; and S. Yun, S. Faraj, and H. P. Sims, "Contingent Leadership and Effectiveness of Trauma Resuscitation Teams," *Journal of Applied Psychology*, vol. 90, no. 6 (2005), pp. 1288–1296.

16. B. M. Bass and R. E. Riggio, *Transformational Leadership*, 2nd ed. (Mahwah, NJ: Lawrence Erlbaum Associates, Inc., 2006), p. 3.

17. F. Vogelstein, "Mighty Amazon," *Fortune*, May 26, 2003, pp. 60–74.

18. J. A. Conger and R. N. Kanungo, "Behavioral Dimensions of Charismatic Leadership," in *Charismatic Leadership*, eds. J. A. Conger and R. N. Kanungo (San Francisco: Jossey-Bass, 1988), pp. 78–97; G. Yukl and J. M. Howell, "Organizational and Contextual Influences on the Emergence and Effectiveness of Charismatic Leadership," *Leadership Quarterly*, Summer 1999, pp. 257–283; and J. M. Crant and T. S. Bateman, "Charismatic Leadership Viewed from Above: The Impact of Proactive Personality," *Journal of Organizational Behavior*, February 2000, pp. 63–75.

19. J. A. Conger and R. N. Kanungo, *Charismatic Leadership in Organizations* (Thousand Oaks, CA: Sage, 1998).

20. K. S. Groves, "Linking Leader Skills, Follower Attitudes, and Contextual Variables via an Integrated Model of Charismatic Leadership," *Journal of Management*, April 2005, pp. 255–277; J. J. Sosik, "The Role of Personal Values in the Charismatic Leadership of Corporate Managers: A Model and Preliminary Field Study," *Leadership Quarterly*, April 2005, pp. 221–244; A. H. B. deHoogh, D. N. den Hartog, P. L. Koopman, H. Thierry, P. T. van den Berg, J. G. van der Weide, and C. P. M. Wilderom, "Leader Motives, Charismatic Leadership, and Subordinates' Work Attitudes in the Profit and Voluntary Sector," *Leadership Quarterly*, February 2005, pp. 17–38; J. M. Howell and B. Shamir, "The Role of Followers in the Charismatic Leadership Process: Relationships and Their Consequences," *Academy of Management Review*, January 2005, pp. 96–112; J. Paul, D. L. Costley, J. P. Howell, P. W. Dorfman, and D. Trafimow, "The Effects of Charismatic Leadership on Followers' Self-Concept Accessibility," *Journal of Applied Social Psychology*, September 2001, pp. 1821–1844; J. A. Conger, R.N. Kanungo, and S. T. Menon, "Charismatic Leadership and Follower Effects," *Journal of Organizational Behavior*, vol. 21, 2000, pp. 747–767; R. W. Rowden, "The Relationship between Charismatic Leadership Behaviors and Organizational Commitment," *Leadership & Organization Development Journal*, January 2000, pp. 30–35; G. P. Shea and C. M. Howell, "Charismatic Leadership and Task Feedback: A Laboratory Study of Their Effects on Self-Efficacy," *Leadership Quarterly*, Fall 1999, pp. 375–396; S. A. Kirkpatrick and E. A. Locke, "Direct and Indirect Effects of Three Core Charismatic Leadership Components on Performance and Attitudes," *Journal of Applied Psychology*, February 1996, pp. 36–51; D. A. Waldman, B. M. Bass, and F. J. Yammarino, "Adding to Contingent-Reward Behavior: The Augmenting Effect of Charismatic Leadership," *Group & Organization Studies*, December 1990, pp. 381–394; and R. J. House,

J. Woycke, and E. M. Fodor, "Charismatic and Noncharismatic Leaders: Differences in Behavior and Effectiveness," in *Charismatic Leadership*, eds. J. A. Conger and R. N. Kanungo (San Francisco: Jossey-Bass, 1988), pp. 103–104.

21. T. Dvir, D. Eden, B. J. Avolio, and B. Shamir, "Impact of Transformational Leadership on Follower Development and Performance: A Field Experiment," *Academy of Management Journal*, vol. 45, no. 4 (2002), pp. 735–744; R. J. House, J. Woycke, and E. M. Fodor, "Charismatic and Noncharismatic Leaders: Differences in Behavior and Effectiveness," in *Charismatic Leadership in Organizations*, eds. J. A. Conger and R. N. Kanungo (Thousand Oaks, CA: Sage, 1998), pp. 103–104; D. A. Waldman, B. M. Bass, and F. J. Yammarino, "Adding to Contingent-Reward Behavior: The Augmenting Effect of Charismatic Leadership," *Group & Organization Studies*, December 1990, pp. 381–394; S. A. Kirkpatrick and E. A. Locke, "Direct and Indirect Effects of Three Core Charismatic Leadership Components on Performance and Attitudes," *Journal of Applied Psychology*, February 1996, pp. 36–51; and J. A. Conger, R. N. Kanungo, and S. T. Menon, "Charismatic Leadership and Follower Outcome Effects" (paper presented at the 58th Annual Academy of Management Meetings, San Diego, CA, August 1998).

22. J. M. Howell and P. J. Frost, "A Laboratory Study of Charismatic Leadership," *Organizational Behavior & Human Decision Processes*, vol. 43, no. 2 (April 1989), pp. 243–269.

23. "Building a Better Boss," *Maclean's*, September 30, 1996, p. 41.

24. Ibid.

25. B. R. Agle, N. J. Nagarajan, J. A. Sonnenfeld, and D. Srinivasan, "Does CEO Charisma Matter? An Empirical Analysis of the Relationships among Organizational Performance, Environmental Uncertainty, and Top Management Team Perceptions of CEO Charisma," *Academy of Management Journal*, February 2006, pp. 161–174.

26. A. Elsner, "The Era of CEO as Superhero Ends Amid Corporate Scandals," *Globe and Mail*, July 10, 2002, www.globeandmail.com.

27. J. A. Conger and R. N. Kanungo, "Training Charismatic Leadership: A Risky and Critical Task," in *Charismatic Leadership*, eds. J. A. Conger and R. N. Kanungo (San Francisco: Jossey-Bass, 1988), pp. 309–323; S. Caudron, "Growing Charisma," *IndustryWeek*, May 4, 1998, pp. 54–55; and R. Birchfield, "Creating Charismatic Leaders," *Management*, June 2000, pp. 30–31.

28. R. J. House, "A 1976 Theory of Charismatic Leadership" in *Leadership: The Cutting Edge*, eds. J. G. Hunt and L. L. Larson (Carbondale, IL: Southern Illinois University Press, 1977); R. J. House and R. N. Aditya, "The Social Scientific Study of Leadership: Quo Vadis?" *Journal of Management*, vol. 23, no. 3 (1997), pp. 316–323; and J. G. Hunt, K. B. Boal, and G. E. Dodge, "The Effects of Visionary and Crisis-Responsive Charisma on Followers: An Experimental Examination," *Leadership Quarterly*, Fall 1999, pp. 423–448.

29. This definition is based on M. Sashkin, "The Visionary Leader," in *Charismatic Leadership*, eds. J. A. Conger and R. N. Kanungo (San Francisco: Jossey-Bass, 1988), pp. 124–125; B. Nanus, *Visionary Leadership* (New York: Free Press, 1992), p. 8; N. H. Snyder and M. Graves, "Leadership and Vision," *Business Horizons*, January–February 1994, p. 1; and J. R. Lucas, "Anatomy of a Vision Statement," *Management Review*, February 1998, pp. 22–26.

30. B. Nanus, *Visionary Leadership* (New York: Free Press, 1992), p. 8.

31. Based on M. Sashkin, "The Visionary Leader," in *Charismatic Leadership*, eds. J. A. Conger and R. N. Kanungo (San Francisco: Jossey-Bass, 1988), pp. 128–130; and J. R. Baum, E. A. Locke, and S. A. Kirkpatrick, "A Longitudinal Study of the Relation of Vision and

Vision Communication to Venture Growth in Entrepreneurial Firms," *Journal of Applied Psychology*, February 1998, pp. 43–54.

32. See "Harper Named *Time*'s Top Canadian Newsmaker," *CBC News*, December 17, 2006, www.cbc.ca/canada/story/2006/12/17/time-harper.html.

33. J. M. Howell and B. Shamir, "The Role of Followers in the Charismatic Leadership Process: Relationships and Their Consequences," *Academy of Management Review*, vol. 30, no. 1 (2005), pp. 96–112.

34. L. Manfield, "Creating a Safety Culture from Top to Bottom," *Worksafe Magazine*, February 2005, pp. 8–9; "Canadian CEOs Give Themselves Top Marks for Leadership!" *Canada Newswire*, September 9, 1999.

35. B. J. Avolio and B. M. Bass, "Transformational Leadership, Charisma, and Beyond" (working paper, School of Management, State University of New York, Binghamton, 1985), p. 14.

36. R. S. Rubin, D. C. Munz, and W. H. Bommer, "Leading from Within: The Effects of Emotion Recognition and Personality on Transformational Leadership Behavior," *Academy of Management Journal*, October 2005, pp. 845–858; T. A. Judge and J. E. Bono, "Five-Factor Model of Personality and Transformational Leadership," *Journal of Applied Psychology*, October 2000, pp. 751–765; B. M. Bass and B. J. Avolio, "Developing Transformational Leadership: 1992 and Beyond," *Journal of European Industrial Training*, January 1990, p. 23; and J. J. Hater and B. M. Bass, "Supervisors' Evaluation and Subordinates' Perceptions of Transformational and Transactional Leadership," *Journal of Applied Psychology*, November 1988, pp. 695–702.

37. R. F. Piccolo and J. A. Colquitt, "Transformational Leadership and Job Behaviors: The Mediating Role of Core Job Characteristics," *Academy of Management Journal*, April 2006, pp. 327–340; O. Epitropaki and R. Martin, "From Ideal to Real: A Longitudinal Study of the Role of Implicit Leadership Theories on Leader-Member Exchanges and Employee Outcomes," *Journal of Applied Psychology*, July 2005, pp. 659–676; J. E. Bono and T. A. Judge, "Self-Concordance at Work: Toward Understanding the Motivational Effects of Transformational Leaders," *Academy of Management Journal*, October 2003, pp. 554–571; T. Dvir, D. Eden, B. J. Avolio, and B. Shamir, "Impact of Transformational Leadership on Follower Development and Performance: A Field Experiment," *Academy of Management Journal*, August 2002, pp. 735–744; N. Sivasubramaniam, W. D. Murry, B. J. Avolio, and D. I. Jung, "A Longitudinal Model of the Effects of Team Leadership and Group Potency on Group Performance," *Group & Organization Management*, March 2002, pp. 66–96; J. M. Howell and B. J. Avolio, "Transformational Leadership, Transactional Leadership, Locus of Control, and Support for Innovation: Key Predictors of Consolidated-Business-Unit Performance," *Journal of Applied Psychology*, December 1993, pp. 891–911; R. T. Keller, "Transformational Leadership and the Performance of Research and Development Project Groups," *Journal of Management*, September 1992, pp. 489–501; and B. M. Bass and B. J. Avolio, "Developing Transformational Leadership: 1992 and Beyond," *Journal of European Industrial Training*, January 1990, p. 23.

38. R. Pillai, C. A. Schriesheim, and E. S. Williams, "Fairness Perceptions and Trust as Mediators of Transformational and Transactional Leadership: A Two-Sample Study," *Journal of Management*, vol. 25, 1999, pp. 897–933.

39. G. M. Spreitzer, K. H. Perttula, and K. Xin, "Traditionality Matters: An Examination of the Effectiveness of Transformational Leadership in the United States and Taiwan," *Journal of Organizational Behavior*, vol. 26, no. 3 (2005), pp. 205–227.

40. P. Preville, Women in Business, *Canadian Business*, Winter 2013/2014, pp. 26–27.

41. See J. R. P. French Jr. and B. Raven, "The Bases of Social Power," in *Group Dynamics: Research and Theory*, eds. D. Cartwright and A. F. Zander (New York: Harper & Row, 1960), pp. 607–623; P. M. Podsakoff and C. A. Schriesheim, "Field Studies of French and Raven's Bases of Power: Critique, Reanalysis, and Suggestions for Future Research," *Psychological Bulletin*, May 1985, pp. 387–411; R. K. Shukla, "Influence of Power Bases in Organizational Decision Making: A Contingency Model," *Decision Sciences*, July 1982, pp. 450–470; D. E. Frost and A. J. Stahelski, "The Systematic Measurement of French and Raven's Bases of Social Power in Workgroups," *Journal of Applied Social Psychology*, April 1988, pp. 375–389; and T. R. Hinkin and C. A. Schriesheim, "Development and Application of New Scales to Measure the French and Raven (1959) Bases of Social Power," *Journal of Applied Psychology*, August 1989, pp. 561–567.

42. See the Royal Australian Navy website, www.navy.gov.au.

43. J. Partridge and J. Saunders, "Milton's Right-Hand Man Quits Air Canada," *Globe and Mail*, April 7, 2004, p. A1.

44. J. M. Kouzes and B. Z. Posner, *Credibility: How Leaders Gain and Lose It, and Why People Demand It* (San Francisco: Jossey-Bass, 1993), p. 14.

45. Based on L. T. Hosmer, "Trust: The Connecting Link between Organizational Theory and Philosophical Ethics," *Academy of Management Review*, April 1995, p. 393; R. C. Mayer, J. H. Davis, and F. D. Schoorman, "An Integrative Model of Organizational Trust," *Academy of Management Review*, July 1995, p. 712; and G. M. Spreitzer and A. K. Mishra, "Giving Up Control Without Losing Control," *Group & Organization Management*, June 1999, pp. 155–187.

46. P. L. Schindler and C. C. Thomas, "The Structure of Interpersonal Trust in the Workplace," *Psychological Reports*, October 1993, pp. 563–573.

47. H. H. Tan and C. S. F. Tan, "Toward the Differentiation of Trust in Supervisor and Trust in Organization," *Genetic, Social, and General Psychology Monographs*, May 2000, pp. 241–260.

48. K. T. Dirks and D. L. Ferrin, "Trust in Leadership: Meta-Analytic Findings and Implications for Research and Practice," *Journal of Applied Psychology*, August 2002, pp. 611–628.

49. This section is based on R. B. Morgan, "Self- and Co-Worker Perceptions of Ethics and Their Relationships to Leadership and Salary," *Academy of Management Journal*, February 1993, pp. 200–214; E. P. Hollander, "Ethical Challenges in the Leader–Follower Relationship," *Business Ethics Quarterly*, January 1995, pp. 55–65; J. C. Rost, "Leadership: A Discussion about Ethics," *Business Ethics Quarterly*, January 1995, pp. 129–142; R. N. Kanungo and M. Mendonca, *Ethical Dimensions of Leadership* (Thousand Oaks, CA: Sage Publications, 1996); J. B. Ciulla, ed., *Ethics: The Heart of Leadership* (New York: Praeger Publications, 1998); J. D. Costa, *The Ethical Imperative: Why Moral Leadership Is Good Business* (Cambridge, MA: Perseus Press, 1999); and N. M. Tichy and A. McGill, eds., *The Ethical Challenge: How to Build Honest Business Leaders* (New York: John Wiley & Sons, 2003).

50. J. M. Burns, *Leadership* (New York: Harper & Row, 1978).

51. J. M. Avolio, S. Kahai, and G. E. Dodge, "The Ethics of Charismatic Leadership: Submission or Liberation?" *Academy of Management Executive*, May 1992, pp. 43–55.

52. L. K. Trevino, M. Brown, and L. P. Hartman, "A Qualitative Investigation of Perceived Executive Ethical Leadership: Perceptions from Inside and Outside the Executive Suite," *Human Relations*, January 2003, pp. 5–37.

53. C. Kleiman, "Virtual Teams Make Loyalty More Realistic," *Chicago Tribune*, January 23, 2001, p. B1.

54. B. J. Alge, C. Wiethoff, and H. J. Klein, "When Does the Medium Matter? Knowledge-Building Experiences and Opportunities in Decision-Making Teams," *Organizational Behavior and Human Decision Processes*, vol. 91, no. 1 (2003), pp. 26–37; C. O. Grosse, "Managing Communication within Virtual Intercultural Teams," *Business Communication Quarterly*, December 2002, pp. 22–38; M. M. Montoya-Weiss, A. P. Massey, and M. Song, "Getting It Together: Temporal Coordination and Conflict Management in Global Virtual Teams," *Academy of Management Journal*, December 2001, pp. 1251–1262; M. L. Maznevski and K. M. Chudoba, "Bridging Space over Time: Global Virtual-Team Dynamics and Effectiveness," *Organization Science*, vol. 11 (2000), pp. 473–492; W. F. Cascio, "Managing a Virtual Workplace," *Academy of Management Executive*, August 2000, pp. 81–90; A. M. Townsend, S. M. DeMarie, and A. R. Hendrickson, "'Virtual Teams' Technology and the Workplace of the Future," *Academy of Management Executive*, August 1998, pp. 17–29.

55. I. Wanasika, J. P. Howell, R. Littrell, and P. Dorfman, "Managerial Leadership and Culture in Sub-Saharan Africa," *Journal of World Business* (April 2011), pp. 234–241.

56. W. F. Cascio, "Managing a Virtual Workplace," *Academy of Management Executive*, August 2000, pp. 88–89.

57. N. Desmond, "The CEO Dashboard," *Business 2.0*, August 2002, p. 34.

58. S. Caminiti, "What Team Leaders Need to Know," *Fortune*, February 20, 1995, p. 93.

59. Ibid., p. 100.

60. N. Steckler and N. Fondas, "Building Team Leader Effectiveness: A Diagnostic Tool," *Organizational Dynamics*, Winter 1995, p. 20.

61. R. S. Wellins, W. C. Byham, and G. R. Dixon, *Inside Teams* (San Francisco: Jossey-Bass, 1994), p. 318.

62. N. Steckler and N. Fondas, "Building Team Leader Effectiveness: A Diagnostic Tool," *Organizational Dynamics*, Winter 1995, p. 21.

63. Ray Williams, "Women Don't Have a Whole Lot to Celebrate on Equality Front," *Financial Post*, March 19, 2012, http://business.financialpost.com/2012/03/19/women-dont-have-a-whole-lot-to-celebrate-in-equality-picture.

64. Statistics Canada, *Survey on Financing of Small and Medium Enterprises*, 2009 (Ottawa: Statistics Canada, 2009); Industry Canada, *Key Small Business Statistics* (Ottawa: Industry Canada, 2009).

65. Canadian Imperial Bank of Commerce, "Women Entrepreneurs: Leading the Change," 2005, www.cibc.com/ca/small-business/article-tools/women-entrepreneurs.html.

66. United Nations, Statistics and Indicators on Women and Men, Table 5f: Women Legislators and Managers, http://mdgs.un.org/unsd/demographic/products/indwm/default.htm.

67. G. N. Powell, D. A. Butterfield, and J. D. Parent, "Gender and Managerial Stereotypes: Have the Times Changed?" *Journal of Management*, vol. 28, no. 2 (2002), pp. 177–193.

68. A. H. Eagly and B. T. Johnson, "Gender and Leadership Style: A Meta-Analysis," *Psychological Bulletin*, September 1990, pp. 233–256; A. H. Eagly and S. J. Karau, "Gender and the Emergence of Leaders: A Meta-Analysis," *Journal of Personality and Social Psychology*, May 1991, pp. 685–710; J. B. Rosener, "Ways Women Lead," *Harvard Business Review*, November–December 1990, pp. 119–125; A. H. Eagly, M. G. Makhijani, and B. G. Klonsky, "Gender and the Evaluation of Leaders: A Meta-Analysis," *Psychological Bulletin*, January 1992, pp. 3–22; A. H. Eagly, S. J. Karau, and B. T. Johnson, "Gender and Leadership Style among School Principals: A Meta-Analysis," *Educational Administration Quarterly*, February 1992, pp. 76–102; L. R. Offermann and C. Beil, "Achievement Styles of Women Leaders and Their Peers," *Psychology of Women Quarterly*, March 1992, pp. 37–56; R. L. Kent and S. E. Moss, "Effects of Size and Gender Role on Leader Emergence," *Academy of Management Journal*, October 1994, pp. 1335–1346; C. Lee, "The Feminization of Management," *Training*, November 1994, pp. 25–31; H. Collingwood, "Women as Managers: Not Just Different: Better," *Working Woman*, November 1995, p. 14; J. B. Rosener, *America's Competitive Secret: Women Managers* (New York: Oxford University Press, 1995); and J. Cliff, N. Langton, and H. Aldrich, "Walking the Talk? Gendered Rhetoric vs. Action in Small Firms," *Organizational Studies*, vol. 26, no. 1 (2005), pp. 63–91.

69. See F. J. Yammarino, A. J. Dubinsky, L. B. Comer, and M. A. Jolson, "Women and Transformational and Contingent Reward Leadership: A Multiple-Levels-of-Analysis Perspective," *Academy of Management Journal*, February 1997, pp. 205–222; M. Gardiner and M. Tiggemann, "Gender Differences in Leadership Style, Job Stress and Mental Health in Male- and Female-Dominated Industries," *Journal of Occupational and Organizational Psychology* September 1999, pp. 301–315; C. L. Ridgeway, "Gender, Status, and Leadership," *Journal of Social Issues*, Winter 2001, pp. 637–655; W. H. Decker and D. M. Rotondo, "Relationships among Gender, Type of Humor, and Perceived Leader Effectiveness," *Journal of Managerial Issues*, Winter 2001, pp. 450–465; J. M. Norvilitis and H. M. Reid, "Evidence for an Association between Gender-Role Identity and a Measure of Executive Function," *Psychological Reports*, February 2002, pp. 35–45; N. Z. Selter, "Gender Differences in Leadership: Current Social Issues and Future Organizational Implications," *Journal of Leadership Studies*, Spring 2002, pp. 88–99; J. Becker, R. A. Ayman, and K. Korabik, "Discrepancies in Self/Subordinates' Perceptions of Leadership Behavior: Leader's Gender, Organizational Context, and Leader's Self-Monitoring," *Group & Organization Management*, June 2002, pp. 226–244; A. H. Eagly and S. J. Karau, "Role Congruity Theory of Prejudice toward Female Leaders," *Psychological Review*, July 2002, pp. 573–598; and K. M. Bartol, D. C. Martin, and J. A. Kromkowski, "Leadership and the Glass Ceiling: Gender and Ethnic Influences on Leader Behaviors at Middle and Executive Managerial Levels," *Journal of Leadership & Organizational Studies*, Winter 2003, pp. 8–19.

70. M. Gardner and M. Tiggemann, "Gender Differences in Leadership Style, Job Stress and Mental Health in Male- and Female-Dominated Industries," *Journal of Occupational and Organizational Psychology*, September 1999, pp. 301–315.

71. "Women 'Take Care,' Men 'Take Charge:' Stereotyping of U.S. Business Leaders Exposed," *Catalyst* (New York, 2005).

72. C. Hymowitz, "Too Many Women Fall for Stereotypes of Selves, Study Says," *Wall Street Journal*, October 24, 2005, p. B1; B. Kantrowitz, "When Women Lead," *Newsweek*, October 24, 2005, pp. 46–61; and "Why Can't Women Be Leaders Too?" *Gallup Management Journal*, gmj.gallup.com, October 13, 2005.

73. J. M. Norvilitis and H. M. Reid, "Evidence for an Association between Gender-Role Identity and a Measure of Executive Function," *Psychological Reports*, February 2002, pp. 35–45; W. H. Decker and D. M. Rotondo, "Relationships among Gender, Type of Humor, and Perceived Leader Effectiveness," *Journal of Managerial Issues*, Winter 2001, pp. 450–465; H. Aguinis and S. K. R. Adams, "Social-Role versus Structural Models of Gender and Influence Use in Organizations: A Strong Inference Approach," *Group & Organization Management*, December 1998, pp. 414–446; A. H. Eagly, S. J. Karau, and M. G. Makhijani, "Gender and the Effectiveness of Leaders: A Meta-Analysis," *Psychological Bulletin*, vol. 117 (1995), pp. 125–145.

74. A. H. Eagly, M. C. Johannesen-Schmidt, and M. L. van Engen, "Transformational, Transactional, and Laissez-Faire Leadership Styles: A Meta-Analysis Comparing Women and Men," *Psychological Bulletin*, vol. 129, no. 4 (July 2003), pp. 569–591; K. M. Bartol, D. C. Martin, and J. A. Kromkowski, "Leadership and the Glass Ceiling: Gender and Ethnic Influences on Leader Behaviors at Middle and Executive Managerial Levels," *Journal of Leadership & Organizational Studies*, Winter 2003, pp. 8–19; and R. Sharpe, "As Leaders, Women Rule," *BusinessWeek*, November 20, 2000, pp. 74–84.

75. R. Sharpe, "As Leaders Women Rule," *Business Week*, November 20, 2000, p. 75.

76. K. M. Bartol, D. C. Martin, and J. A. Kromkowski, "Leadership and the Glass Ceiling: Gender and Ethnic Influences on Leader Behaviors at Middle and Executive Managerial Levels," *Journal of Leadership & Organizational Studies*, Winter 2003, pp. 8–19.

77. From Elyse Allan president and CEO of GE Canada. Copyright © by GE Canada. Reprinted by permission.

78. From Ellen Moore president and CEO of Chubb Insurance Co. of Canada. Copyright © by Chubb Insurance Co. of Canada. Reprinted by permission.

79. Jacqueline Nelson, "How to Be Your Best Friend's Boss," *Canadian Business*, March 5, 2012.

80. L. M. Fisher, "Ricardo Semler Won't Take Control," *Strategy+Business*, Winter 2005, pp. 78–88; R. Semler, *The Seven-Day Weekend: Changing the Way Work Works* (New York: Penguin Group, 2004); A. J. Vogl, "The Anti-CEO," *Across the Board*, May–June 2004, pp. 30–36; G. Colvin, "The Anti-Control Freak," *Fortune*, November 26, 2001, p. 22; and R. Semler, "Managing without Managers," *Harvard Business Review*, September–October 1989, pp. 76–84.

81. "RBC Diversity Blueprint 2012–2015," http://www.rbc.com/diversity/pdf/rbc-diversity-blueprint.pdf.

82. Laura Quinn and Jessica Baltes, "Leadership and the Triple Bottom Line" (white paper for the Centre for Creative Leadership, 2007), http://www.ccl.org/leadership/pdf/research/tripleBottomLine.pdf.

83. See C. Cattaneo, "The Oil Patch Crusader," *Financial Post Magazine*, November 1, 2011, http://business.financialpost.com/2011/11/01/the-oil-patch-crusader/; and investor information from Enbridge's website, http://www.enbridge.com/InvestorRelations.aspx.

84. G. Pitts, "Enbridge's retiring CEO wishes pipelines weren't such a hot topic," *Globe and Mail*, June 28, 2012.

85. D. Archer and A. Cameron, "Collaborative Leadership," www.trainingjournal.com, June 2012, pp. 35–38; J. Katzenbach, "The Steve Jobs Way," *Strategy+Business Online*, April 23, 2012; W. Isaacson, "The Real Leadership Lessons of Steve Jobs," *Harvard Business Review*, April 2012, pp. 93–102; R. Williams, "Why Steve Jobs Was Not a Leader," www.psychologytoday.com, April

7, 2012; R. Foroohar, "The Leadership Lessons of Steve Jobs," business.time.com, February 16, 2012; R. Foroohar, "What Would Steve Do?" www.time.com, February 27, 2012; F. E. Allen, "Steve Jobs Broke Every Leadership Rule. Don't Try It," www.forbes.com, August 27, 2011; J. Nocera, "What Makes Steve Jobs Great," *New York Times Online*, August 26, 2011; A. Sharma and D. Grant, "The Stagecraft of Steve Jobs," *Strategy+Business Online*, June 10, 2011; and A. Lashinsky, "How Apple Works: Inside the World's Biggest Startup," tech.fortune.com, May 9, 2011.

86. "Out of Office? Out of luck," *Maclean's*, November 18, 2013, pp. 54–57.

87. Ibid.

88. Ibid.

89. "Give Staff Freedom without Creating Chaos," *Canadian Business*, April 2014, p.16.

SUPPLEMENT 4

1. Gerami Law PC, https://www.geramilaw.com

2. "Canada's Future Leaders under 25," *Maclean's*, April 12, 2013, http://www.macleans.ca/news/canada/future-leaders-under-25/#ferland

3. Ibid.

4. Ibid.

5. Ibid.

CHAPTER 9

1. Chris Atchison, "The Gen Y Whisperer," *Profit*, June 1, 2011, http://www.profitguide.com/article/28252—the-gen-y-whisperer.

2. "Profit 200—2012 Rankings: #16, Yellow House Events Inc.," *Profit*, http://www.profitguide.com/microsite/profit200/2012/16-Yellow-House-Events.

3. "Grail Noble," PROFIT/*Chatelaine* W100, http://www.profitguide.com/microsite/profitw100/2014/ranking/14-yellowhouse-events-inc.

4. From Chris Atchison (2011) One of Canada's Fastest-Growing Companies chose to embrace the unique preferences of Millennial workers. Was it worth the risk?, Roger Media Inc. Copyright © 2011 by Chris Atchison. Reprinted by permission.

5. Ibid.

6. G. P. Latham and C. C. Pinder, "Work Motivation Theory and Research at the Dawn of the Twenty-First Century," *Annual Review of Psychology*, vol. 56, no. 1 (2005), pp. 485–516; and C. C. Pinder, *Work Motivation in Organizational Behavior* (Upper Saddle River, NJ: Prentice Hall, 1998), p. 11. See also E. A. Locke and G. P. Latham, "What Should We Do about Motivation Theory? Six Recommendations for the Twenty-First Century," *Academy of Management Review*, vol. 29, no. 3 (July 1, 2004), pp. 388–403.

7. See, for example, T. R. Mitchell, "Matching Motivational Strategies with Organizational Contexts," in *Research in Organizational Behavior*, vol. 19, eds. B. M. Staw and L. L. Cummings (Greenwich, CT: JAI Press, 1997), pp. 60–62; and R. Katerberg and G. J. Blau, "An Examination of Level and Direction of Effort and Job Performance," *Academy of Management Journal*, June 1983, pp. 249–257.

8. Graham Lowe, *21st Century Job Quality: Achieving What Canadians Want* (Ottawa, ON: Canadian Policy Research Networks, Research Report W|37, September 2007), http://www.cprn.org/doc.cfm?doc=1745&l=en.

9. See "Job Satisfaction Wanes, but SHRM Survey Shows Majority of U.S. Employees Satisfied," *PR Newswire-US Newswire*, October 3, 2012, http://www.prnewswire.com/news-releases/job-satisfaction-wanes-but-shrm-survey-shows-majority-of-us-employees-satisfied-172521231.html; and Society for Human Resource Management (SHRM), *2012 Job Satisfaction and Engagement Research Report* (SHRM, October 3, 2012), http://www.shrm.org/Research/Survey-Findings/Articles/Pages/2012EmployeeJobSatisfaction.aspx.

10. P. Towers, *The 2014 Global Workforce Study: Driving Engagement through a Consumer-Like Experience,* August 2014.

11. Chris Atchison, "The Gen Y Whisperer," *Profit*, June 1, 2011, http://www.profitguide.com/article/28252—the-gen-y-whisperer.

12. S. P. Robbins and T. A. Judge, *Essentials of Organizational Behavior*, 11th ed. (Upper Saddle River, NJ: Prentice Hall, 2010).

13. M. S. Christian, A. S. Garza, and J. E. Slaughter, "Work Engagement: A Quantitative Review and Test of Its Relations with Task and Contextual Performance," *Personnel Psychology*, Spring 2011, pp. 89–136; V. T. Ho, S-S Wong, and C. H. Lee, "A Tale of Passion: Linking Job Passion and Cognitive Engagement to Employee Work Performance," *Journal of Management Studies*, January 2011, pp. 26–47; D. R. May, R. L. Gilson, and L. M. Harter, "The Psychological Conditions of Meaningfulness, Safety and Availability and the Engagement of the Human Spirit at Work," *Journal of Occupational and Organizational Psychology*, March 2004, pp. 11–37; R. T. Keller, "Job Involvement and Organizational Commitment as Longitudinal Predictors of Job Performance: A Study of Scientists and Engineers," *Journal of Applied Psychology*, August 1997, pp. 539–545; W. Kahn, "Psychological Conditions of Personal Engagement and Disengagement at Work," *Academy of Management Journal* (December 1990), pp. 692–794; and P. P. Brooke, Jr., D. W. Russell, and J. L. Price, "Discriminant Validation of Measures of Job Satisfaction, Job Involvement, and Organizational Commitment," *Journal of Applied Psychology*, May 1988, pp. 139–145. Also, see, for example, J. Smythe, "Engaging Employees to Drive Performance," *Communication World*, May–June 2008, pp. 20–22; A. B. Bakker and W. B. Schaufeli, "Positive Organizational Behavior: Engaged Employees in Flourishing Organizations," *Journal of Organizational Behavior*, February 2008, pp. 147–154; U. Aggarwal, S. Datta, and S. Bhargava, "The Relationship between Human Resource Practices, Psychological Contract, and Employee Engagement—Implications for Managing Talent," *IIMB Management Review*, September 2007, pp. 313–325; M. C. Christian and J. E. Slaughter, "Work Engagement: A Meta-Analytic Review and Directions for Research in an Emerging Area," *AOM Proceedings*, August 2007, pp. 1–6; C. H. Thomas, "A New Measurement Scale for Employee Engagement: Scale Development, Pilot Test, and Replication," *AOM Proceedings*, August 2007, pp. 1–6; A. M. Saks, "Antecedents and Consequences of Employee Engagement," *Journal of Managerial Psychology*, vol. 21, no. 7 (2006), pp. 600–619; and A. Parsley, "Road Map for Employee Engagement," *Management Services*, Spring 2006, pp. 10–11.

14. Mercer, *IndustryWeek*, April 2008, p. 24.

15. J. M. George, "The Wider Context, Costs, and Benefits of Work Engagement," *European Journal of Work & Organizational Psychology*, February 2011, pp. 53–59; and "Employee Engagement Report 2011," BlessingWhite Research, http://www.blessingwhite.com/eee__report.asp (January 2011), pp. 7–8.

16. A. J. Elliott and P. G. Devine, "On the Motivational Nature of Cognitive Dissonance: Dissonance as Psychological Discomfort," *Journal of Personality and Social Psychology*, September 1994, pp. 382–394.

17. L. Festinger, *A Theory of Cognitive Dissonance* (Stanford, CA: Stanford University Press, 1957); C. Crossen, "Cognitive Dissonance Became a Milestone in 1950s Psychology," *Wall Street Journal*, December 4, 2006, p. B1; and Y. "Sally" Kim, "Application of the Cognitive Dissonance Theory to the Service Industry," *Services Marketing Quarterly*, April–June 2011, pp. 96–112.

18. H. C. Koh and E. H. Y. Boo, "The Link between Organizational Ethics and Job Satisfaction: A Study of Managers in Singapore," *Journal of Business Ethics*, February 15, 2001, p. 309.

19. See, for example, W. D. Crano and R. Prislin, "Attitudes and Persuasion," *Annual Review of Psychology*, 2006, pp. 345–374; and J. Jermias, "Cognitive Dissonance and Resistance to Change: The Influence of Commitment Confirmation and Feedback on Judgment Usefulness of Accounting Systems." *Accounting, Organizations, and Society*, March 2001, p. 141.

20. M. L. Ambrose and C. T. Kulik, "Old Friends, New Faces: Motivation Research in the 1990s," *Journal of Management* 25, no. 3 (1999), pp. 231–292.

21. D. A. Harrison, D. A. Newman, and P. L. Roth, "How Important Are Job Attitudes?: Meta-Analytic Comparisons of Integrative Behavioral Outcomes and Time Sequences," *Academy of Management Journal*, April 2006, pp. 305–325.

22. G. Chen, R. E. Ployhart, H. C. Thomas, N. Anderson, and P. D. Bliese, "The Power of Momentum: A New Model of Dynamic Relationships Between Job Satisfaction Change and Turnover Intentions," *Academy of Management Journal*, February 2011, pp. 159–181.

23. I. Arnsdorf, "No More New Kid on Campus," *Wall Street Journal*, August 5, 2010, pp. D1+.

24. CPP, Inc., Myers-Briggs Type Indicator® (MBTI®), http://www.cpp.com/products/mbti/index.asp (2011); and J. Llorens, "Taking Inventory of Myers-Briggs," *T&D*, April 2010, pp. 18–19.

25. Ibid.

26. See, for instance, J. Overbo, "Using Myers-Briggs Personality Type to Create a Culture Adapted to the New Century," *T&D*, February 2010, pp. 70–72; K. Garrety, R. Badham, V. Morrigan, W. Rifkin, and M. Zanko, "The Use of Personality Typing in Organizational Change: Discourse, Emotions, and the Reflective Subject," *Human Relations*, February 2003, pp. 211–235.

27. P. Moran, "Personality Characteristics and Growth-Orientation of the Small Business Owner Manager," *Journal of Managerial Psychology*, July 2000, p. 651; and M. Higgs, "Is There a Relationship between the Myers-Briggs Type Indicator and Emotional Intelligence?" *Journal of Managerial Psychology*, September–October 2001, pp. 488–513.

28. J. M. Digman, "Personality Structure: Emergence of the Five Factor Model," in M. R. Rosenweig and L. W. Porter, eds., *Annual Review of Psychology*, vol. 41 (Palo Alto, CA: Annual Reviews, 1990), pp. 417–440; O. P. John, "The Big Five Factor Taxonomy: Dimensions of Personality in the Natural Language and in Questionnaires," in L. A. Pervin, ed., *Handbook of Personality Theory and Research* (New York: Guilford Press, 1990), pp. 66–100; and M. K. Mount, M. R. Barrick, and J. P. Strauss, "Validity of Observer Ratings of the Big Five Personality Factors," *Journal of Applied Psychology*, April 1996, pp. 272–280.

29. Barrick and Mount, "Autonomy as a Moderator of the Relationship between the Big Five Personality Dimensions and Job Performance."

30. P. R. Lawrence and N. Nohria, *Driven: How Human Nature Shapes Our Choices* (San Francisco: Jossey-Bass, 2002).

31. S. McShane and S. Steen, *Canadian Organizational Behaviour*, 7th ed. (Toronto, ON: McGraw-Hill, 2009), p. 113.

32. J. S. Adams, "Inequity in Social Exchanges," in *Advances in Experimental Social Psychology*, vol. 2, ed. L. Berkowitz (New York: Academic Press, 1965), pp. 267–300; and M. L. Ambrose and C. T. Kulik, "Old Friends, New Faces: Motivation Research in the 1990s," *Journal of Management*, vol. 25, no. 3 (1999), pp. 231–292.

33. See, for example, P. S. Goodman and A. Friedman, "An Examination of Adams' Theory of Inequity," *Administrative Science Quarterly*, September 1971, pp. 271–288; E. Walster, G. W. Walster, and W. G. Scott, *Equity: Theory and Research* (Boston: Allyn & Bacon, 1978); and J. Greenberg, "Cognitive Reevaluation of Outcomes in Response to Underpayment Inequity," *Academy of Management Journal*, March 1989, pp. 174–184.

34. See, for example, M. R. Carrell, "A Longitudinal Field Assessment of Employee Perceptions of Equitable Treatment," *Organizational Behavior and Human Performance*, February 1978, pp. 108–118; R. G. Lord and J. A. Hohenfeld, "Longitudinal Field Assessment of Equity Effects on the Performance of Major League Baseball Players," *Journal of Applied Psychology*, February 1979, pp. 19–26; and J. E. Dittrich and M. R. Carrell, "Organizational Equity Perceptions, Employee Job Satisfaction, and Departmental Absence and Turnover Rates," *Organizational Behavior and Human Performance*, August 1979, pp. 29–40.

35. P. S. Goodman, "An Examination of Referents Used in the Evaluation of Pay," *Organizational Behavior and Human Performance*, October 1974, pp. 170–195; S. Ronen, "Equity Perception in Multiple Comparisons: A Field Study," *Human Relations*, April 1986, pp. 333–346; R. W. Scholl, E. A. Cooper, and J. F. McKenna, "Referent Selection in Determining Equity Perception: Differential Effects on Behavioral and Attitudinal Outcomes," *Personnel Psychology*, Spring 1987, pp. 113–127; and C. T. Kulik and M. L. Ambrose, "Personal and Situational Determinants of Referent Choice," *Academy of Management Review*, April 1992, pp. 212–237.

36. A. Wahl, J. Castaldo, Z. Olijnyk, E. Pooley, and A. Jezovit, "The Best Workplaces in Canada 2007," *Canadian Business*, April 23, 2007, pp. 39–61. http://resources.greatplacetowork.com/article/pdf/the_best_workplaces_in_canada_2007.pdf.

37. See, for example, R. C. Dailey and D. J. Kirk, "Distributive and Procedural Justice as Antecedents of Job Dissatisfaction and Intent to Turnover," *Human Relations*, March 1992, pp. 305–316; D. B. McFarlin and P. D. Sweeney, "Distributive and Procedural Justice as Predictors of Satisfaction with Personal and Organizational Outcomes," *Academy of Management Journal*, August 1992, pp. 626–637; M. A. Konovsky, "Understanding Procedural Justice and Its Impact on Business Organizations," *Journal of Management*, vol. 26, no. 3, 2000, pp. 489–511; J. A. Colquitt, "Does the Justice of One Interact with the Justice of Many? Reactions to Procedural Justice in Teams," *Journal of Applied Psychology*, August 2004, pp. 633–646; J. Brockner, "Why It's so Hard to Be Fair," *Harvard Business Review*, March 2006, pp. 122–129; and B. M. Wiesenfeld, W. B. Swann, Jr., J. Brockner, and C. A. Bartel, "Is More Fairness Always Preferred? Self-Esteem Moderates Reactions to Procedural Justice," *Academy of Management Journal*, October 2007, pp. 1235–1253.

38. V. H. Vroom, *Work and Motivation* (New York: John Wiley, 1964).

39. See, for example, H. G. Heneman III and D. P. Schwab, "Evaluation of Research on Expectancy Theory Prediction of Employee Performance,"

Psychological Bulletin, July 1972, pp. 1–9; and L. Reinharth and M. Wahba, "Expectancy Theory as a Predictor of Work Motivation, Effort Expenditure, and Job Performance," *Academy of Management Journal*, September 1975, pp. 502–537.

40. See, for example, V. H. Vroom, "Organizational Choice: A Study of Pre- and Post-decision Processes," *Organizational Behavior and Human Performance*, April 1966, pp. 212–225; L. W. Porter and E. E. Lawler III, *Managerial Attitudes and Performance* (Homewood, IL: Richard D. Irwin, 1968); W. Van Eerde and H. Thierry, "Vroom's Expectancy Models and Work-Related Criteria: A Meta-Analysis," *Journal of Applied Psychology*, October 1996, pp. 575–586; and M. L. Ambrose and C. T. Kulik, "Old Friends, New Faces: Motivation Research in the 1990s," *Journal of Management*, vol. 25, no. 3 (1999), pp. 231–292.

41. See, for example, M. Siegall, "The Simplistic Five: An Integrative Framework for Teaching Motivation," *Organizational Behavior Teaching Review*, vol. 12, no. 4 (1987–1988), pp. 141–143.

42. S. Butcher, "Relentless Rise in Pleasure Seekers," *Financial Times*, July 6, 2003; "Tesco Pilots Student Benefits," *Employee Benefits*, November 7, 2003, p. P12; and Tesco PLC, *Corporate Responsibility Report 2009*, pp. 40–45, http://www.investis.com/plc/storage/tesco_cr_09.pdf.

43. J. R. Billings and D. L. Sharpe, "Factors Influencing Flextime Usage among Employed Married Women," *Consumer Interests Annual*, vol. 45 (Ames, IA: American Council on Consumer Interests, 1999), pp. 89–94; and I. Harpaz, "The Importance of Work Goals: An International Perspective," *Journal of International Business Studies*, First Quarter 1990, pp. 75–93.

44. N. Ramachandran, "New Paths at Work," *US News & World Report*, March 20, 2006, p. 47; S. Armour, "Generation Y: They've Arrived at Work with a New Attitude," *USA Today*, November 6, 2005, pp. B1+; R. Kanfer and P. L. Ackerman, "Aging, Adult Development, and Work Motivation," *Academy of Management Review*, July 2004, pp. 440–458; and R. Bernard, D. Cosgrave, and J. Welsh, *Chips and Pop: Decoding the Nexus Generation* (Toronto: Malcolm Lester Books, 1998).

45. I. Harpaz, "The Importance of Work Goals: An International Perspective," *Journal of International Business Studies*, First Quarter 1990, pp. 75–93.

46. G. E. Popp, H. J. Davis, and T. T. Herbert, "An International Study of Intrinsic Motivation Composition," *Management International Review*, January 1986, pp. 28–35.

47. R. W. Brislin, B. MacNab, R. Worthley, F. Kabigting Jr., and B. Zukis, "Evolving Perceptions of Japanese Workplace Motivation: An Employee-Manager Comparison," *International Journal of Cross-Cultural Management*, April 2005, pp. 87–104.

48. P. Falcone, "Motivating Staff without Money," *HR Magazine*, August 2002, pp. 105–108.

49. Ibid.

50. See, for example, M. Alpert, "The Care and Feeding of Engineers," *Fortune*, September 21, 1992, pp. 86–95; G. Poole, "How to Manage Your Nerds," *Forbes ASAP*, December 1994, pp. 132–136; and T. J. Allen and R. Katz, "Managing Technical Professionals and Organizations: Improving and Sustaining the Performance of Organizations, Project Teams, and Individual Contributors," *Sloan Management Review*, Summer 2002, pp. S4–S5.

51. "One CEO's Perspective on the Power of Recognition," *Workforce Management*, February 27, 2004, www.workforce.com; and R. Fournier, "Teamwork Is the Key to Remote Development—

Inspiring Trust and Maintaining Motivation Are Critical for a Distributive Development Team," *InfoWorld*, March 5, 2001, p. 48.

52. R. J. Bohner Jr. and E. R. Salasko, "Beware the Legal Risks of Hiring Temps," *Workforce*, October 2002, pp. 50–57.

53. J. P. Broschak and A. Davis-Blake, "Mixing Standard Work and Nonstandard Deals: The Consequences of Heterogeneity in Employment Arrangements," *Academy of Management Journal*, April 2006, pp. 371–393; M. L. Kraimer, S. J. Wayne, R. C. Liden, and R. T. Sparrowe, "The Role of Job Security in Understanding the Relationship between Employees' Perceptions of Temporary Workers and Employees' Performance," *Journal of Applied Psychology*, March 2005, pp. 389–398; and C. E. Connelly and D. G. Gallagher, "Emerging Trends in Contingent Work Research," *Journal of Management*, November 2004, pp. 959–983.

54. D. W. Krueger, "Money, Success, and Success Phobia," in *The Last Taboo: Money as a Symbol and Reality in Psychotherapy and Psychoanalysis*, ed. D. W. Krueger (New York: Brunner/Mazel, 1986), pp. 3–16.

55. T. R. Mitchell and A. E. Mickel, "The Meaning of Money: An Individual-Difference Perspective," *Academy of Management*, July 1999, pp. 568–578.

56. This paragraph is based on Graham Lowe, *21st Century Job Quality: Achieving What Canadians Want*, Research Report W|37, Work and Learning (Ottawa, ON: Canadian Policy Research Networks, September 2007).

57. This paragraph is based on T. R. Mitchell and A. E. Mickel, "The Meaning of Money: An Individual-Difference Perspective," *Academy of Management*, July 1999, pp. 568–578. The reader may want to refer to the myriad references cited in the article.

58. "CN's Remarkable Story of Transformation in Canadian Business," *Financial Post*, February 4, 2013, http://business.financialpost.com/2013/02/04/cns-remarkable-story-of-transformation-in-canadian-business.

59. G. Miller and T. Lawson, "The Effect of an Informational Option on the Fundamental Attribution Error," *Personality and Social Psychology Bulletin*, June 1989, pp. 194–204. See also G. Charness and E. Haruvy, "Self-Serving Bias: Evidence from a Simulated Labour Relationship," *Journal of Managerial Psychology*, July 2000, p. 655; and T. J. Elkins, J. S. Phillips, and R. Konopaske, "Gender-Related Biases in Evaluations of Sex Discrimination Allegations: Is Perceived Threat a Key?" *Journal of Applied Psychology*, April 2002, pp. 280–293.

60. "Is Giving Back Worthwhile?" *Canadian Business*, May 2014, p. 22.

61. F. Luthans and A. D. Stajkovic, "Provide Recognition for Performance Improvement," in *Principles of Organizational Behavior*, ed. E. A. Locke (Oxford, UK: Blackwell, 2000), pp. 166–180.

62. "Secrets of Their Success (and Failure)," *Report on Business*, January 2006, pp. 54–55.

63. S. L. Rynes, B. Gerhart, and L. Parks, "Personnel Psychology: Performance Evaluation and Pay for Performance," *Annual Review of Psychology*, vol. 56, no. 1 (2005), p. 572; and A. M. Dickinson, "Are We Motivated by Money? Some Results from the Laboratory," *Performance Improvement*, vol. 44, no. 3 (March 2005), pp. 18–24.

64. R. K. Abbott, "Performance-Based Flex: A Tool for Managing Total Compensation Costs," *Compensation and Benefits Review*, March–April 1993, pp. 18–21; J. R. Schuster and P. K. Zingheim, "The New Variable Pay: Key Design Issues," *Compensation and Benefits Review*, March–April 1993, pp. 27–34; C. R. Williams and

L. P. Livingstone, "Another Look at the Relationship between Performance and Voluntary Turnover," *Academy of Management Journal*, April 1994, pp. 269–298; and A. M. Dickinson and K. L. Gillette, "A Comparison of the Effects of Two Individual Monetary Incentive Systems on Productivity: Piece Rate Pay Versus Base Pay Plus Incentives," *Journal of Organizational Behavior Management*, Spring 1994, pp. 3–82.

65. Canadian Newswire (CNW), "Calgary Salary Increases Reach New Heights, According to Hewitt," news release, www.newswire.ca/en/releases/archive/September2007/06/c5734.html; G. Teel, "City Leads Nation in Salary Increases," *Calgary Herald*, September 7, 2007; Hewitt Associates, "Hewitt Study Shows Pay-for-Performance Plans Replacing Holiday Bonuses," news release, December 6, 2005; and P. Brieger, "Variable Pay Packages Gain Favour: Signing Bonuses, Profit Sharing Taking Place of Salary Hikes," *Financial Post (National Post)*, September 13, 2002, p. FP5.

66. E. Beauchesne, "Pay Bonuses Improve Productivity, Study Shows," *Vancouver Sun*, September 13, 2002, p. D5; and The Conference Board of Canada, "Variable Pay Offers a Bonus for Unionized Workplaces," news release, September 12, 2002.

67. "Hope for Higher Pay: The Squeeze on Incomes Is Gradually Easing Up," *Maclean's*, November 25, 1996, pp. 100–101.

68. Hewitt Associates, LLC, "Hewitt Study Shows Base Pay Increases Flat for 2006 with Variable Pay Plans Picking Up the Slack," August 31, 2005.

69. E. Beauchesne, "Pay Bonuses Improve Productivity, Study Shows," *Vancouver Sun*, September 13, 2002, p. D5; and "More than 20 Percent of Japanese Firms Use Pay Systems Based on Performance," *Manpower Argus*, May 1998, p. 7.

70. M. Tanikawa, "Fujitsu Decides to Backtrack on Performance-Based Pay," *New York Times*, March 22, 2001, p. W1.

71. G. D. Jenkins Jr., N. Gupta, A. Mitra, and J. D. Shaw, "Are Financial Incentives Related to Performance? A Meta-Analytic Review of Empirical Research," *Journal of Applied Psychology*, October 1998, pp. 777–787.

72. T. Coupé, V. Smeets, and F. Warzynski, "Incentives, Sorting and Productivity Along the Career: Evidence from a Sample of Top Economists," *Journal of Law Economics & Organization*, vol. 22, no. 1 (April 2006), pp. 137–167.

73. A. Kauhanen and H. Piekkola, "What Makes Performance-Related Pay Schemes Work? Finnish Evidence," *Journal of Management and Governance*, vol. 10, no. 2 (2006), pp. 149–177.

74. E. Beauchesne, "Pay Bonuses Improve Productivity, Study Shows," *Vancouver Sun*, September 13, 2002, p. D5.

75. P. A. Siegel and D. C. Hambrick, "Pay Disparities within Top Management Groups: Evidence of Harmful Effects on Performance of High-Technology Firms," *Organization Science*, vol. 16, no. 3 (May–June 2005), pp. 259–276; S. Kerr, "Practical, Cost-Neutral Alternatives That You May Know, but Don't Practice," *Organizational Dynamics*, vol. 28, no. 1 (1999), pp. 61–70; and E. E. Lawler, *Strategic Pay* (San Francisco: Jossey Bass, 1990); and J. Pfeffer, *The Human Equation: Building Profits by Putting People First* (Boston: Harvard Business School Press, 1998).

76. T. Reason, "Why Bonus Plans Fail," *CFO*, January 2003, p. 53; and J. D. Day, P. Y. Mang, A. Richter, and J. Roberts, "Has Pay for Performance Had Its Day?" *McKinsey Quarterly*, no. 4 (November 2002).

77. V. Sanderson, "Sweetening Their Slice: More Hardware and Lumberyard Dealers Are Investing in Profit-Sharing Programs as a

Way to Promote Employee Loyalty," *Hardware Merchandising*, May–June 2003, p. 66.

78. W. J. Duncan, "Stock Ownership and Work Motivation," *Organizational Dynamics*, Summer 2001, pp. 1–11.

79. P. Brandes, R. Dharwadkar, and G. V. Lemesis, "Effective Employee Stock Option Design: Reconciling Stakeholder, Strategic, and Motivational Factors," *Academy of Management Executive*, February 2003, pp. 77–95; J. Blasi, D. Kruse, and A. Bernstein, *In the Company of Owners: The Truth About Stock Options* (New York: Basic Books, 2003).

80. "Health Club Membership, Flextime Are Most Desired Perks," *Business West*, September 1999, p. 75.

81. ACT Conferencing, "Utilize Collaboration Tools to Make Virtual Meetings More Productive," *ACT Conferencing's Corporate Communication Blog*, August 28, 2012, http://blog.actconferencing.com/default.aspx?Tag=unified%20communications%20and%20collaboration.

82. D. Penner, "Survey: Top Pay Trumps Work-Life Balance," *The Gazette* (Montreal), March 10, 2007, p. G2.

83. "What Employees Want," *CMA Management*, vol. 75, no. 7 (October 2001), p. 8.

84. Information in this paragraph is based on D. Grigg and J. Newman, "Labour Researchers Define Job Satisfaction," *Vancouver Sun*, February 16, 2002, p. E2.

85. Jacqueline Nelson, "A 21st-century Factory Town," *Canadian Business*, April 16, 2012.

86. G. Hofstede, "Motivation, Leadership and Organization: Do American Theories Apply Abroad?" *Organizational Dynamics*, Summer 1980, p. 55.

87. J. K. Giacobbe-Miller, D. J. Miller, and V. I. Victorov, "A Comparison of Russian and U.S. Pay Allocation Decisions, Distributive Justice Judgments and Productivity under Different Payment Conditions," *Personnel Psychology*, Spring 1998, pp. 137–163.

88. S. L. Mueller and L. D. Clarke, "Political–Economic Context and Sensitivity to Equity: Differences between the United States and the Transition Economies of Central and Eastern Europe," *Academy of Management Journal*, June 1998, pp. 319–329.

89. K. Clark, "Perking Up the Office," *U.S. News & World Report*, November 22, 1999, p. 73: L. Brenner, "Perks That Work," *Business-Week Frontier*, October 11, 1999, pp. F22–F40.

90. P. Towers, The 2014 Global Workforce Study: Driving Engagement through a Consumer-Like Experience, August 2014.

91. Jackie Pitera, "Aligned Incentives and Engaged Employees Improve Triple Bottom Line Performance," *Environmental Leader*, August 4, 2011, http://www.environmentalleader.com/2011/08/04/aligned-incentives-and-engaged-employees-improve-triple-bottom-line-performance.

92. Canadian International Development Agency (CIDA), "Microfinance: The Government of Canada Supports Microfinance in Developing Countries," CIDA website, http://www.acdi-cida.gc.ca/acdi-cida/ACDI-CIDA.nsf/eng/RAC-1110131744-PG5.

93. "The DevFacto Team," DevFacto, www.devfacto.com/company. Reprinted by permission from David Cronin.

94. "Agents of Agency," *Canadian Business*, Special Report—Canada's Best Employers, December 2014, pp. 69–70.

95. Ibid.

96. Ibid.

97. Ibid.

98. "Our News," Ubisoft, http://toronto.ubisoft.com/en/ubisoft-our-news.

99. S. Khan, "The Massive Creative Collaboration Behind Ubisoft," *Fast Company*, November 13, 2014.

100. Ibid.

101. Ibid.

102. "Office Space: Ubisoft," *Canadian Business*, August 2014, pp. 14–15.

103. "Management: Career Arc," *Canadian Business*, November 2014, p. 32.

104. Ibid.

105. Ibid.

CHAPTER 10

1. J. Ankeny, "Richard Branson on Building an Empire," *Entrepreneur*, June 19, 2012, http://www.entrepreneur.com/article/223639.

2. Ibid.

3. Ibid.

4. Ibid.

5. R. Branson, "Empowering Employees," *Entrepreneur*, January 17, 2011, http://www.entrepreneur.com/article/217880.

6. Ibid.

7. B. W. Tuckman and M. C. Jensen, "Stages of Small-Group Development Revisited," *Group and Organizational Studies*, December 1977, pp. 419–427; and M. F. Maples, "Group Development: Extending Tuckman's Theory," *Journal for Specialists in Group Work*, Fall 1988, pp. 17–23.

8. L. N. Jewell and H. J. Reitz, *Group Effectiveness in Organizations* (Glenview, IL: Scott, Foresman, 1981); and M. Kaeter, "Repotting Mature Work Teams," *Training*, April 1994, pp. 54–56.

9. R. Branson, "Five Rules for Good Business," *Entrepreneur*, July 30, 2012, http://www.entrepreneur.com/article/223979.

10. And the Survey Says box based on J. Yang and P. Trap, "As a Manager, It's Most Challenging to . . . ," *USA Today*, April 19, 2011, p. 1B; J. Yang and K. Gelles, "Workplace Friendships," *USA Today*, April 13, 2010, p. 1B; K. Merriman, "Low-Trust Teams Prefer Individualized Pay," *Harvard Business Review*, November 2008, p. 32; B. J. West, J. L. Patera, and M. K. Carsten, "Team Level Positivity: Investigating Positive Psychological Capacities and Team Level Outcomes," *Journal of Organizational Behavior*, February 2009, p. 249; J. Yang and K. Simmons, "Traits of Good Team Players," *USA Today*, November 21, 2007, p. 1B; J. Yang and M. E. Mullins, "Workers More Productive in Small Groups," *USA Today*, January 10, 2007, p. 1B; and M. Weinstein, "Coming Up Short? Join the Club," *Training*, April 2006, p. 14.

11. See, for example, J. E. Salk and M. Y. Brannien, "National Culture, Networks, and Individual Influence in a Multinational Management Team," *Academy of Management Journal*, April 2000, p. 191; B. L. Kirkman, C. B. Gibson, and D. L. Shapiro, "Enhancing the Implementation and Effectiveness of Work Teams in Global Affiliates," *Organizational Dynamics*, Summer 2001, pp.

12–30; and B. L. Kirkman and D. L. Shapiro, "The Impact of Cultural Values on Employee Resistance to Teams: Towards a Model of Globalized Self-Managing Work Team Effectiveness," *Academy of Management Review*, July 1997, pp. 730–757.

12. S. Stern, "Teams that Work," *Management Today*, June 2001, p. 48.

13. Asch, "Effects of Group Pressure upon the Modification and Distortion of Judgments."

14. R. M. Yandrick, "A Team Effort," *HR Magazine*, June 2001, pp. 136–141.

15. Ibid.

16. M. A. Marks, C. S. Burke, M. J. Sabella, and S. J. Zaccaro, "The Impact of Cross-Training on Team Effectiveness," *Journal of Applied Psychology*, February 2002, pp. 3–14; and M. A. Marks, S. J. Zaccaro, and J. E. Mathieu, "Performance Implications of Leader Briefings and Team Interaction for Team Adaptation to Novel Environments," *Journal of Applied Psychology*, December 2000, p. 971.

17. C. Garvey, "Steer Teams with the Right Pay: Team-Based Pay Is a Success When It Fits Corporate Goals and Culture, and Rewards the Right Behavior," *HR Magazine*, May 2002, pp. 71–77.

18. R. Branson, "Friends with (Health) Benefits," *Canadian Business,* July 2014, p.32.

19. G. R. Jones and G. M. George, "The Experience and Evolution of Trust: Implications for Cooperation and Teamwork," *Academy of Management Review*, July 1998, pp. 531–546; A. R. Jassawalla and H. C. Sashittal, "Building Collaborative Cross-Functional New Product Teams," *Academy of Management Executive*, August 1999, pp. 50–63; R. Forrester and A. B. Drexler, "A Model for Team-Based Organization Performance," *Academy of Management Executive*, August 1999, pp. 36–49; V. U. Druskat and S. B. Wolff, "The Link between Emotions and Team Effectiveness: How Teams Engage Members and Build Effective Task Processes," *Academy of Management Proceedings*, CD-ROM, 1999; M. Mattson, T. Mumford, and G. S. Sintay, "Taking Teams to Task: A Normative Model for Designing or Recalibrating Work Teams," *Academy of Management Proceedings*, CD-ROM, 1999; J. D. Shaw, M. K. Duffy, and E. M. Stark, "Interdependence and Preference for Group Work: Main and Congruence Effects on the Satisfaction and Performance of Group Members," *Journal of Management*, vol. 26, no. 2 (2000), pp. 259–279; G. L. Stewart and M. R. Barrick, "Team Structure and Performance: Assessing the Mediating Role of Intrateam Process and the Moderating Role of Task Type," *Academy of Management Journal*, April 2000, pp. 135–148; J. E. Mathieu, T. S. Heffner, G. F. Goodwin, E. Salas, and J. A. Cannon-Bowers, "The Influence of Shared Mental Models on Team Process and Performance," *Journal of Applied Psychology*, April 2000, pp. 273–283; J. M. Phillips and E. A. Douthitt, "The Role of Justice in Team Member Satisfaction with the Leader and Attachment to the Team," *Journal of Applied Psychology*, April 2001, pp. 316–325; J. A. Colquitt, R. A. Noe, and C. L. Jackson, "Justice in Teams: Antecedents and Consequences of Procedural Justice Climate," *Personnel Psychology*, vol. 55 (2002), pp. 83–100; M. A. Marks, M. J. Sabella, C. S. Burke, and S. J. Zaccaro, "The Impact of Cross-Training on Team Effectiveness," *Journal of Applied Psychology*, February 2002, pp. 3–13; and S. W. Lester, B. W. Meglino, and M. A. Korsgaard, "The Antecedents and Consequences of Group Potency: A Longitudinal Investigation of Newly Formed Work Groups," *Academy of Management Journal*, April 2002, pp. 352–368.

20. D. R. Ilgen, J. R. Hollenbeck, M. Johnson, and D. Jundt, "Teams in Organizations: From Input-Process-Output Models to IMOI Models," *Annual Review of Psychology*, vol. 56, no. 1 (2005), pp. 517–543.

21. J. Morgan, "The 12 Habits of Highly Collaborative Organization," *Forbes*, July 30, 2013, http://www.forbes.com/sites/jacobmorgan/2013/07/30/the-12-habits-of-highly-collaborative-organizations.

22. C. R. Evans and K. L. Dion, "Group Cohesion and Performance: A Meta-Analysis," *Small Group Research*, May 1991, pp. 175–186; B. Mullen and C. Copper, "The Relation between Group Cohesiveness and Performance: An Integration," *Psychological Bulletin*, March 1994, pp. 210–227; P. M. Podsakoff, S. B. MacKenzie, and M. Ahearne, "Moderating Effects of Goal Acceptance on the Relationship between Group Cohesiveness and Productivity," *Journal of Applied Psychology*, December 1997, pp. 974–983.

23. See, for example, L. Berkowitz, "Group Standards, Cohesiveness, and Productivity," *Human Relations*, November 1954, pp. 509–519; and B. Mullen and C. Copper, "The Relation between Group Cohesiveness and Performance: An Integration," *Psychological Bulletin*, March 1994, pp. 210–227.

24. S. E. Seashore, *Group Cohesiveness in the Industrial Work Group* (Ann Arbor: University of Michigan, Survey Research Center, 1954).

25. Paragraph based on R. Kreitner and A. Kinicki, *Organizational Behavior*, 6th ed. (New York: Irwin, 2004), pp. 459–461.

26. This section is adapted from S. P. Robbins, *Managing Organizational Conflict: A Nontraditional Approach* (Upper Saddle River, NJ: Prentice Hall, 1974), pp. 11–14. Also, see D. Wagner-Johnson, "Managing Work Team Conflict: Assessment and Preventative Strategies," Center for the Study of Work Teams, University of North Texas, 1999; and M. Kennedy, "Managing Conflict in Work Teams," Center for the Study of Work Teams, University of North Texas, 1998.

27. See K. A. Jehn, "A Multimethod Examination of the Benefits and Detriments of Intragroup Conflict," *Administrative Science Quarterly*, June 1995, pp. 256–282; K. A. Jehn, "A Qualitative Analysis of Conflict Type and Dimensions in Organizational Groups," *Administrative Science Quarterly*, September 1997, pp. 530–557; K. A. Jehn, "Affective and Cognitive Conflict in Work Groups: Increasing Performance through Value-Based Intragroup Conflict," in *Using Conflict in Organizations*, eds. C. K. W. DeDreu and E. Van deVliert (London: Sage, 1997), pp. 87–100; K. A. Jehn and E. A. Mannix, "The Dynamic Nature of Conflict: A Longitudinal Study of Intragroup Conflictand Group Performance," *Academy of Management Journal*, April 2001, pp. 238–251; and C. K. W. DeDreu and A. E. M. Van Vianen, "Managing Relationship Conflict and the Effectiveness of Organizational Teams," *Journal of Organizational Behavior*, May 2001, pp. 309–328.

28. C. K. W. DeDreu, "When Too Little or Too Much Hurts: Evidence for a Curvilinear Relationship between Task Conflict and Innovation in Teams," *Journal of Management*, February 2006, pp. 83–107.

29. K. W. Thomas, "Conflict and Negotiation Processes in Organizations," in *Handbook of Industrial and Organizational Psychology*, vol. 3, 2nd ed., eds. M. D. Dunnette and L. M. Hough, pp. 651–717 (Palo Alto, CA: Consulting Psychologists Press, 1992).

30. See D. R. Comer, "A Model of Social Loafing in Real Work Groups," *Human Relations*, June 1995.

31. S. G. Harkins and K. Szymanski, "Social Loafing and Group Evaluation," *Journal of Personality and Social Psychology*, December 1989, pp. 934–941.

32. B. L. Kirkman, C. B. Gibson, and D. L. Shapiro, "Exporting Teams: Enhancing the Implementation and Effectiveness of Work Teams in Global Affiliates," *Organizational Dynamics*, Summer 2001, pp. 12–29; J. W. Bing and C. M. Bing, "Helping Global Teams Compete," *Training & Development*, March 2001, pp. 70–71; P. Christopher Earley and E. Mosakowski, "Creating Hybrid Team Cultures: An Empirical Test of Trans-national Team Functioning," *Academy of Management Journal*, February 2000, pp. 26–49; J. Tata, "The Cultural Context of Teams: An Integrative Model of National Culture, Work Team Characteristics, and Team Effectiveness," *Academy of Management Proceedings*, CD-ROM, 1999; D. I. Jung, K. B. Baik, and J. J. Sosik, "A Longitudinal Investigation of Group Characteristics and Work Group Performance: A Cross-Cultural Comparison," *Academy of Management Proceedings*, CD-ROM, 1999; and C. B. Gibson, "They Do What They Believe They Can? Group-Efficacy Beliefs and Group Performance across Tasks and Cultures," *Academy of Management Proceedings*, CD-ROM, 1996.

33. R. Bond and P. B. Smith, "Culture and Conformity: A Meta-Analysis of Studies Using Asch's [1952, 1956] Line Judgment Task," *Psychological Bulletin*, January 1996, pp. 111–137.

34. I. L. Janis, *Groupthink*, 2nd ed. (New York: Houghton Mifflin Company, 1982), p. 175.

35. See P. C. Earley, "East Meets West Meets Mideast: Further Explorations of Collectivistic and Individualistic Work Groups," *Academy of Management Journal*, April 1993, pp. 319–348; and P. C. Earley, "Social Loafing and Collectivism: A Comparison of the United States and the People's Republic of China," *Administrative Science Quarterly*, December 1989, pp. 565–581.

36. See P. C. Earley, "Social Loafing and Collectivism: A Comparison of the United States and the People's Republic of China," *Administrative Science Quarterly*, December 1989, pp. 565–581; and P. C. Earley, "East Meets West Meets Mideast: Further Explorations of Collectivistic and Individualistic Work Groups," *Academy of Management Journal*, April 1993, pp. 319–348.

37. N. J. Adler, *International Dimensions of Organizational Behavior*, 4th ed. (Cincinnati, OH: South-Western College Publishing, 2002), p. 142.

38. K. B. Dahlin, L. R. Weingart, and P. J. Hinds, "Team Diversity and Information Use," *Academy of Management Journal*, December 2005, pp. 1107–1123.

39. N. J. Adler, *International Dimensions of Organizational Behavior*, 4th ed. (Cincinnati, OH: South-Western College Publishing, 2002), p. 142.

40. S. Paul, I. M. Samarah, P. Seetharaman, and P. P. Mykytyn, "An Empirical Investigation of Collaborative Conflict Management Style in Group Support System-Based Global Virtual Teams," *Journal of Management Information Systems*, Winter 2005, pp. 185–222.

41. D. Brown, "Innovative HR Ineffective in Manufacturing Firms," *Canadian HR Reporter*, April 7, 2003, pp. 1–2.

42. R. Forrester and A. B. Drexler, "A Model for Team-Based Organization Performance," *Academy of Management Executive*, August 1999, p. 47. See also S. A. Mohrman, with S. G. Cohen and A. M. Mohrman Jr., *Designing Team-Based Organizations* (San Francisco: Jossey-Bass, 1995); and J. H. Shonk, *Team-Based Organizations* (Homewood, IL: Business One Irwin, 1992).

43. Based on P. L. Hunsaker, *Training in Management Skills* (Upper Saddle River, NJ: Prentice Hall, 2001), Chapter 12.

44. Based on L. Copeland, "Making the Most of Cultural Differences at the Workplace," *Personnel*, June 1988, pp. 52–60; C. R. Bantz, "Cultural Diversity and Group Cross-Cultural Team Research," *Journal of Applied Communication Research*, February 1993, pp. 1–19; L. Strach and L. Wicander, "Fitting In: Issues of Tokenism and Conformity for Minority Women," *SAM Advanced Management Journal*, Summer 1993, pp. 22–25; M. L. Maznevski, "Understanding Our Differences: Performance in Decision-Making Groups with Diverse Members," *Human Relations*, May 1994, pp. 531–552; F. Rice, "How to Make Diversity Pay," *Fortune*, August 8, 1994, pp. 78–86; J. Jusko, "Diversity Enhances Decision Making," *IndustryWeek*, April 2, 2001, p. 9; and K. Lovelace, D. L. Shapiro, and L. R. Weingart, "Maximizing Cross-Functional New Product Teams' Innovativeness and Constraint Adherence: A Conflict Communications Perspective," *Academy of Management Journal*, August 2002, pp. 779–793.

45. R. Branson, "How Virgin Unite Connects Philanthropy with Entrepreneurialism," *Canadian Business*, February 20, 2012.

46. A. Cuenllas, "Whole Foods Case Study: A Benchmark Model of Management for Hospitality," Hospitality Net—Industry News, February 11, 2013, http://www.hospitalitynet.org/news/4059396.html.

47. Ibid.

48. Ibid.

49. Ibid.

50. Ibid.

51. Ibid.

52. *Ontario Realty Corporation (ORC) Annual Report 2005–2006* (Toronto, ON: ORC, 2006).

CHAPTER 11

1. "Curling as a Business Model: The Off-Ice Success of the Canadian Curling Association," *Canadian Business Journal*, March 12, 2012, http://www.cbj.ca/business_in_action/mar_12/canadian_curling_association.html.

2. See the Canadian Curling Association website, www.curling.ca; "Curling as a Business Model: The Off-Ice Success of the Canadian Curling Association," *Canadian Business Journal*, March 12, 2012, http://www.cbj.ca/business_in_action/mar_12/canadian_curling_association.html.

3. J. Kluger and B. Liston, "A Columbia Culprit?" *Time*, February 24, 2003, p. 13.

4. K. A. Merchant, "The Control Function of Management," *Sloan Management Review*, Summer 1982, pp. 43–55.

5. E. Flamholtz, "Organizational Control Systems as a Managerial Tool," *California Management Review*, Winter 1979, p. 55.

6. "Top 1000: Ranking Canada's Top 1000 Public Companies by Profit," *Globe and Mail: Report on Business Magazine*, June 28, 2012, http://www.theglobeandmail.com/report-on-business/rob-magazine/top-1000/2012-rankings-of-canadas-top-1000-public-companies-by-profit/article4371923.

7. Aon Hewitt, "Best Employers in Canada," https://ceplb03.hewitt.com/bestemployers/canada/pages/currentlist2011.htm.

8. J. McElgunn, "Profit 200 Overview: Who Are Canada's Fastest-Growing Companies?" *Profit*, June 1, 2012, http://www.profitguide.com/microsite/profit200/2012.

9. P. Magnusson, "Your Jitters Are Their Lifeblood," *BusinessWeek*, April 14, 2003, p. 41; S. Williams, "Company Crisis: CEO Under Fire," *Hispanic Business*, March 2003, pp. 54–56; T. Purdum, "Preparing for the Worst," *IndustryWeek*, January 2003, pp. 53–55; and S. Leibs, "Lesson from 9/11: It's Not about Data," *CFO*, September 2002, pp. 31–32.

10. S. Kerr, "On the Folly of Rewarding A, While Hoping for B," *Academy of Management Journal*, December 1975, pp. 769–783.

11. Y. F. Jarrar and M. Zairi, "Future Trends in Benchmarking for Competitive Advantage: A Global Survey," *Total Quality Management*, December 2001, pp. 906–912.

12. M. Simpson and D. Kondouli, "A Practical Approach to Benchmarking in Three Service Industries," *Total Quality Management*, July 2000, pp. S623–S630.

13. K. N. Dervitsiotis, "Benchmarking and Paradigm Shifts," *Total Quality Management*, July 2000, pp. S641–S646.

14. See "Entrepreneur: BouClair," Roynat Capital Business Profiles, *National Post*, www.canada.com/nationalpost/entrepreneur/bouclair.html.

15. T. Leahy, "Extracting Diamonds in the Rough," *Business Finance*, August 2000, pp. 33–37.

16. "Recognizing Commitment to Diversity," *Canadian HR Reporter*, November 3, 2003, p. 12.

17. B. Bruzina, B. Jessop, R. Plourde, B. Whitlock, and L. Rubin, "Ameren Embraces Benchmarking as a Core Business Strategy," *Power Engineering*, November 2002, pp. 121–124; and T. Leahy, "Extracting Diamonds in the Rough," *Business Finance*, August 2000, pp. 33–37.

18. Celestica.com; E. Alini, "The Future of Manufacturing in Canada," *Maclean's*, http://www.macleans.ca/economy/business/economy-up-off-the-factory-floor; and "Powering Prosperity Award Nominations 2015," Ontario Sustainable Energy Association, http://www.ontario-sea.org/Page.asp?PageID=924&ContentID=4726.

19. H. Koontz and R. W. Bradspies, "Managing through Feedforward Control," *Business Horizons*, June 1972, pp. 25–36.

20. "An Open Letter to McDonald's Customers," *Wall Street Journal*, August 22, 2001, p. A5.

21. W. H. Newman, *Constructive Control: Design and Use of Control Systems* (Upper Saddle River, NJ: Prentice Hall, 1975), p. 33.

22. R. Ilies and T. A. Judge, "Goal Regulation across Time: The Effects of Feedback and Affect," *Journal of Applied Psychology*, vol. 90, no. 3 (May 2005), pp. 453–467.

23. John Carver and Miriam Carver, "Carver's Policy Governance® Model in Nonprofit Organizations," PolicyGovernance.com, http://www.carvergovernance.com/pg-np.htm.

24. W. G. Ouchi, "A Conceptual Framework for the Design of Organizational Control Mechanisms," *Management Science*, August 1979, pp. 833–838; and W. G. Ouchi, "Markets, Bureaucracies, and Clans," *Administrative Science Quarterly*, March 1980, pp. 129–141.

25. Based on P. Fitzpatrick, "Wacky WestJet's Winning Ways: Passengers Respond to Stunts that Include Races to Determine Who Leaves the Airplane First," *National Post*, October 16, 2000, p. C1.

26. F. Hansen, "The Value-Based Management Commitment," *Business Finance*, September 2001, pp. 2–5.

27. M. Acharya and T. Yew, "A New Kind of Top 10," *Toronto Star*, June 30, 2002, p. C01.

28. K. Lehn and A. K. Makhija, "EVA and MVA as Performance Measures and Signals for Strategic Change," *Strategy & Leadership*, May–June 1996, pp. 34–38.

29. "Trailing Indicator—Canada's Average Debtor," *Canadian Business*, April 30, 2012, p. 74.

30. J. Yaukey and C. L. Romero, "Arizona Firm Pays Big for Workers' Digital Downloads," *Springfield News-Leader*, May 6, 2002, p. 6B.

31. R. S. Kaplan and D. P. Norton, "How to Implement a New Strategy without Disrupting Your Organization," *Harvard Business Review*, March 2006, pp. 100–109; L. Bassi and D. McMurrer, "Developing Measurement Systems for Managing in the Knowledge Era," *Organizational Dynamics*, May 2005, pp. 185–196; G. M. J. de Koning, "Making the Balanced Scorecard Work (Part 2), *Gallup Business Journal*, http://businessjournal.gallup.com/content/12571/making-balanced-scorecard-work-part.aspx; G. M. J. de Koning, "Making the Balanced Scorecard Work (Part 1), *Gallup Business Journal*, http://businessjournal.gallup.com/content/12208/making-balanced-scorecard-work-part.aspx; K. Graham, "Balanced Scorecard," *New Zealand Management*, March 2003, pp. 32–34; K. Ellis, "A Ticket to Ride: Balanced Scorecard," *Training*, April 2001, p. 50; T. Leahy, "Tailoring the Balanced Scorecard," *Business Finance*, August 2000, pp. 53–56; and R.S. Kaplan and D. P. Norton, "Using the Balanced Scorecard as a Strategic Management System," *Harvard Business Review*, vol. 74, no. 1 (January–February 1996), pp. 75–85.

32. T. Leahy, "Tailoring the Balanced Scorecard," *Business Finance*, August 2000, pp. 53–56.

33. "Hospital Reports," Ontario Hospital Association (OHA), http://www.oha.com/KnowledgeCentre/Library/HospitalReports/Pages/HospitalReports.aspx; and T. Leahy, "Tailoring the Balanced Scorecard," *Business Finance*, August 2000, pp. 53–56.

34. "A Revolution Where Everyone Wins: Worldwide Movement to Improve Corporate-Governance Standards," *BusinessWeek*, May 19, 2003, p. 72.

35. J. S. McClenahen, "Executives Expect More Board Input," *IndustryWeek*, October 2002, p. 12.

36. D. Salierno, "Boards Face Increased Responsibility," *Internal Auditor*, June 2003, pp. 14–15.

37. R. Corbett, "Sport Canada Introduces Governance Principles for Sport Organizations," Sport Law & Strategy Group, November 8, 2011, http://www.sportlaw.ca/2011/11/sport-canada-to-introduce-governance-principles-for-sport-organizations/.

38. N. Shirouzu and J. Bigness, "7-Eleven Operators Resist System to Monitor Managers," *Wall Street Journal*, June 16, 1997, p. B1.

39. E. O'Connor, "Pulling the Plug on Cyberslackers," *StarPhoenix*, May 24, 2003, p. F22.

40. Ibid.

41. Kathryn Leger, "'Stealing' Time at Work on Net," *Gazette* (Montreal), April 4, 2008, www2.canada.com/montrealgazette/news/business/story.html?id=32125d78-a479-497a-ae19-4f461ea18060.

42. D. Hawkins, "Lawsuits Spur Rise in Employee Monitoring," *U.S. News & World Report*, August 13, 2001, p. 53; L. Guernsey, "You've Got Inappropriate Mail," *New York Times*, April 5, 2000, p. C11; and

R. Karaim, "Setting E-Privacy Rules," *Cnnfn Online*, December 15, 1999.

43. E. Bott, "Are You Safe? Privacy Special Report," *PC Computing*, March 2000, pp. 87–88.

44. E. O'Connor, "Pulling the Plug on Cyberslackers," *StarPhoenix*, May 24, 2003, p. F22.

45. A. Tomlinson, "Heavy-Handed Net Policies Push Privacy Boundaries," *Canadian HR Reporter*, December 2, 2002, pp. 1–2.

46. C. Sorensen, "Canada Ranks High in Employee Theft: Global Survey Findings," *National Post*, May 28, 2004, p. FP9.

47. A. Perry, "Back-to-School Brings Pilfering: Some Employees Raid Office for Kids," *Toronto Star*, August 30, 2003, p. B01.

48. Joshua Bamfield, *Global Retail Theft Barometer 2007: Monitoring the Costs of Shrinkage and Crime on the Global Retail Industry* (Nottingham, UK: Centre for Retail Research, 2007), http://www.globalretailtheftbarometer.com/pdf/Global-Retail-Theft-Barometer-2007.pdf; "Detering Employee Theft," Watchdog Loss Prevention for Businesses, March 22, 2012, http://watchdogloss.com/blog/detering-employee-theft/; and C. Powell, "Pro Thieves: They're Shopping More Often," *Canadian Grocer*, May 2, 2011, http://www.canadiangrocer.com/top-stories/grocery-theft-gone-in-30-seconds-6162.

49. J. Greenberg, "The STEAL Motive: Managing the Social Determinants of Employee Theft," in *Antisocial Behavior in Organizations*, eds. R. Giacalone and J. Greenberg (Newbury Park, CA: Sage, 1997), pp. 85–108.

50. "Crime Spree," *BusinessWeek*, September 9, 2002, p. 8; B. P. Niehoff and R. J. Paul, "Causes of Employee Theft and Strategies That HR Managers Can Use for Prevention," *Human Resource Management*, Spring 2000, pp. 51–64; and G. Winter, "Taking at the Office Reaches New Heights: Employee Larceny Is Bigger and Bolder," *New York Times*, July 12, 2000, p. C11.

51. This section is based on J. Greenberg, *Behavior in Organizations: Understanding and Managing the Human Side of Work*, 8th ed. (Upper Saddle River, NJ: Prentice Hall, 2003), pp. 329–330.

52. A. H. Bell and D. M. Smith, "Why Some Employees Bite the Hand that Feeds Them," *Workforce*, May 16, 2000.

53. A. H. Bell and D. M. Smith, "Protecting the Company Against Theft and Fraud," *Workforce*, May 16, 2000; J. D. Hansen, "To Catch a Thief," *Journal of Accountancy*, March 2000, pp. 43–46; and J. Greenberg, "The Cognitive Geometry of Employee Theft," in *Dysfunctional Behavior in Organizations: Nonviolent and Deviant Behavior*, eds. S. B. Bacharach, A. O'Leary-Kelly, J. M. Collins, and R. W. Griffin (Stamford, CT: JAI Press, 1998), pp. 147–193.

54. H. A. MacDonald, D. J. Brown, and L. M. Sulsky, *A Cross-Cultural Examination of the Motivational Differences in Feedback Seeking*, August 2008, Academy of Management Annual Meeting Proceedings.

55. Ibid.

56. Based on P. L. Hunsaker, *Training in Management Skills* (Upper Saddle River, NJ: Prentice Hall, 2001), pp. 60–61.

57. See "100 Years Siemens in Canada," http://www.siemens.com/entry/ca/en/; and Jared Mitchell, "Green Giant: Interview with Peter Loescher, President and CEO of Siemens AG," *Canadian Business*, November 16, 2011, http://www.canadianbusiness.com/article/57428—green-giant.

58. "Siemens Wind Energy Facility to Create 300 Jobs in Tillsonburg, Ontario," *The Green Pages*, December 2, 2010, http://thegreenpages.ca/ca/2010/12/02/siemens_wind_energy_facility_t.

59. Siemens Canada, "Siemens Canada Limited Signs MOU with Ontario Government," Press Release, May 20, 2011, http://www.siemens.ca/web/portal/en/press/Pages/MOU-signed-with-Ontario-Government.aspx.

60. Jared Mitchell, "Green Giant: Interview with Peter Loescher, President and CEO of Siemens AG," *Canadian Business*, November 16, 2011, http://www.canadianbusiness.com/article/57428—green-giant.

61. City of Vancouver, *Greenest City 2020 Action Plan* (Vancouver, BC: City of Vancouver, 2012), http://vancouver.ca/files/cov/Greenest-city-action-plan.pdf.

62. M. Swift, "A Look Inside Facebook's 'Bootcamp' for New Employees," *Toronto Star*, April 18, 2012, http://www.thestar.com/business/article/1163373—a-look-inside-facebook-s-bootcamp-for-new-employees.

63. Jessica Guynn, "The Grunts Are Geeks at Facebook Bootcamp," *Los Angeles Times*, August 1, 2010, http://articles.latimes.com/2010/aug/01/business/la-fi-facebook-bootcamp-20100801.

64. M. Swift, "A Look Inside Facebook's 'Bootcamp' for New Employees," *Toronto Star*, April 18, 2012, http://www.thestar.com/business/article/1163373—a-look-inside-facebook-s-bootcamp-for-new-employees.

65. Facebook, "Hackathon," https://www.facebook.com/hackathon.

66. C. Sorensen, "Facebook Grows Apart," *Maclean's*, June 2, 2014, pp. 34–35.

CHAPTER 12

1. "BP's Fiona MacLeod: A Change Agent Sees Change Addiction," *Knowledge Wharton*, July 8, 2009, http://knowledge.wharton.upenn.edu/article.cfm?articleid=2280.

2. A. Saha-Bubna and M. Jarzemsky, "MasterCard President Is Named CEO," *Wall Street Journal*, April 13, 2010, p. C3; and S. Vandebook, "Quotable," *IndustryWeek*, April 2010, p. 18.

3. R. M. Kanter, "Think Outside the Building," *Harvard Business Review*, March 2010, p. 34; T. Brown, "Change by Design," *BusinessWeek*, October 5, 2009, pp. 54–56; J. E. Perry-Smith and C. E. Shalley, "The Social Side of Creativity: A Static and Dynamic Social Network Perspective," *Academy of Management Review*, January 2003, pp. 89–106; and P. K. Jagersma, "Innovate or Die: It's Not Easy, but It Is Possible to Enhance Your Organization's Ability to Innovate," *Journal of Business Strategy*, January–February 2003, pp. 25–28.

4. "The World's 50 Most Innovative Companies," *Fast Company*, March 2011, pp. 66+; and G. Colvin, "The World's Most Admired Companies," *Fortune*, March 21, 2011, pp. 109+.

5. These definitions are based on T. M. Amabile, *Creativity in Context* (Boulder, CO: Westview Press, 1996).

6. C. Salter, "Mattel Learns to 'Throw the Bunny,'" *Fast Company*, November 2002, p. 22; and L. Bannon, "Think Tank in Toyland," *Wall Street Journal*, June 6, 2002, pp. B1, B3.

7. C. Vogel and J. Cagan, *Creating Breakthrough Products: Innovation from Product Planning to Program Approval* (Upper Saddle River, NJ: Prentice Hall, 2002).

8. R. W. Woodman, J. E. Sawyer, and R. W. Griffin, "Toward a Theory of Organizational Creativity," *Academy of Management Review*, April 1993, pp. 293–321.

9. T. M. Egan, "Factors Influencing Individual Creativity in the Workplace: An Examination of Quantitative Empirical Research," *Advances in Developing Human Resources*, May 2005, pp. 160–181; N. Madjar, G. R. Oldham, and M. G. Pratt, "There's No Place Like Home? The Contributions of Work and Nonwork Creativity Support to Employees' Creative Performance," *Academy of Management Journal*, August 2002, pp. 757–767; T. M. Amabile, C. N. Hadley, and S. J. Kramer, "Creativity Under the Gun," *Harvard Business Review*, August 2002, pp. 52–61; J. B. Sorensen and T. E. Stuart, "Aging, Obsolescence, and Organizational Innovation," *Administrative Science Quarterly*, March 2000, pp. 81–112; G. R. Oldham and A. Cummings, "Employee Creativity: Personal and Contextual Factors at Work," *Academy of Management Journal*, June 1996, pp. 607–634; and F. Damanpour, "Organizational Innovation: A Meta-Analysis of Effects of Determinants and Moderators," *Academy of Management Journal*, September 1991, pp. 555–590.

10. P. R. Monge, M. D. Cozzens, and N. S. Contractor, "Communication and Motivational Predictors of the Dynamics of Organizational Innovations," *Organization Science*, May 1992, pp. 250–274.

11. T. M. Amabile, C. N. Hadley, and S. J. Kramer, "Creativity Under the Gun," *Harvard Business Review*, August 2002, pp. 52–61.

12. N. Madjar, G. R. Oldham, and M. G. Pratt, "There's No Place Like Home? The Contributions of Work and Nonwork Creativity Support to Employees' Creative Performance," *Academy of Management Journal*, August 2002, pp. 757–767

13. See, for instance, J. E. Perry-Smith, "Social Yet Creative: The Role of Social Relationships in Facilitating Individual Creativity," *Academy of Management Journal*, February 2006, pp. 85–101; C. E. Shalley, J. Zhou, and G. R. Oldham, "The Effects of Personal and Contextual Characteristics on Creativity: Where Should We Go from Here?" *Journal of Management*, vol. 30, no. 6 (2004), pp. 933–958; J. E. Perry-Smith and C. E. Shalley, "The Social Side of Creativity: A Static and Dynamic Social Network Perspective"; J. M. George and J. Zhou, "When Openness to Experience and Conscientiousness Are Related to Creative Behavior: An Interactional Approach," *Journal of Applied Psychology*, June 2001, pp. 513–524; J. Zhou, "Feedback Valence, Feedback Style, Task Autonomy, and Achievement Orientation: Interactive Effects on Creative Behavior," *Journal of Applied Psychology*, vol. 83 (1998), pp. 261–276; T. M. Amabile, R. Conti, H. Coon, J. Lazenby, and M. Herron, "Assessing the Work Environment for Creativity," *Academy of Management Journal*, October 1996, pp. 1154–1184; S. G. Scott and R. A. Bruce, "Determinants of Innovative People: A Path Model of Individual Innovation in the Workplace," *Academy of Management Journal*, June 1994, pp. 580–607; R. Moss Kanter, "When a Thousand Flowers Bloom: Structural, Collective, and Social Conditions for Innovation in Organization," in B. M. Staw and L. L. Cummings, eds., *Research in Organizational Behavior*, vol. 10 (Greenwich, CT: JAI Press, 1988), pp. 169–211; and T. M. Amabile, *Creativity in Context* (Boulder, CO: Westview Press, 1996).

14. J. Ramos, "Producing Change That Lasts," *Across the Board*, March 1994, pp. 29–33; T. Stjernberg and A. Philips, "Organizational Innovations in a Long-Term Perspective: Legitimacy and Souls-of-Fire as Critical Factors of Change and Viability," *Human Relations*, October 1993, pp. 1193–2023; and J. M. Howell and C. A. Higgins, "Champions of Change," *Business Quarterly*, Spring 1990, pp. 31–32.

15. J. Liedtka and T. Ogilvie, *Designing for Growth: A Design Thinking Tool Kit for Managers*, (New York: Columbia Business School Press, 2011).

16. R. E. Silverman, "Companies Change Their Way of Thinking," *Wall Street Journal*, June 7, 2012, p. B8; and R. L. Martin, "The Innovation Catalysts," *Harvard Business Review*, June 2011, pp. 82–87.

17. H. L. Sirkin, P. Keenan, and A. Jackson, "The Hard Side of Change Management," *Harvard Business Review*, vol. 83, no. 10 (October 1 2005), pp. 108–118.

18. W. Pietersen, "The Mark Twain Dilemma: The Theory and Practice for Change Leadership," *Journal of Business Strategy*, September–October 2002, pp. 32–37; C. Hymowitz, "To Maintain Success, Managers Must Learn How to Direct Change," *Wall Street Journal*, August 13, 2002, p. B1; and J. E. Dutton, S. J. Ashford, R. M. O'Neill, and K. A. Lawrence, "Moves That Matter: Issue Selling and Organizational Change," *Academy of Management Journal*, August 2001, pp. 716–736.

19. P. A. McLagan, "The Change-Capable Organization," *Training & Development*, January 2003, pp. 50–58.

20. M. Young and J. E. Post, "Managing to Communicate, Communicating to Manage: How Leading Companies Communicate with Employees," *Organizational Dynamics*, Summer 1993, pp. 31–43.

21. M. Javidan, P. W. Dorfman, M. S. deLuque, and R. J. House, "In the Eye of the Beholder: Cross-Cultural Lessons in Leadership from Project GLOBE," *Academy of Management Perspective*, February 2006, pp. 67–90; and E. Fagenson-Eland, E. A. Ensher, and W. W. Burke, "Organization Development and Change Interventions: A Seven-Nation Comparison," *Journal of Applied Behavioral Science*, December 2004, pp. 432–464.

22. E. Fagenson-Eland, E. A. Ensher, and W. W. Burke, "Organization Development and Change Interventions: A Seven-Nation Comparison," *Journal of Applied Behavioral Science*, December 2004, p. 461.

23. See, for example, B. M. Staw, "Counterforces to Change," in *Change in Organizations*, eds. P. S. Goodman and Associates (San Francisco: Jossey-Bass, 1982), pp. 87–121; A. A. Armenakis and A. G. Bedeian, "Organizational Change: A Review of Theory and Research in the 1990s," *Journal of Management*, vol. 25, no. 3 (1999), pp. 293–315; C. R. Wanberg and J. T. Banas, "Predictors and Outcomes of Openness to Changes in a Reorganizing Workplace," *Journal of Applied Psychology*, February 2000, pp. 132–142; S. K. Piderit, "Rethinking Resistance and Recognizing Ambivalence: A Multidimensional View of Attitudes toward an Organizational Change," *Academy of Management Review*, October 2000, pp. 783–794; R. Kegan and L. L. Lahey, "The Real Reason People Won't Change," *Harvard Business Review*, November 2001, pp. 85–92; M. A. Korsgaard, H. J. Sapienza, and D. M. Schweiger, "Beaten before Begun: The Role of Procedural Justice in Planning Change," *Journal of Management*, vol. 28, no. 4 (2002), pp. 497–516; and C. E. Cunningham, "Readiness for Organizational Change: A Longitudinal Study of Workplace, Psychological and Behavioral Correlates," *Journal of Occupational and Organizational Psychology*, December 2002, pp. 377–392.

24. J. P. Kotter and L. A. Schlesinger, "Choosing Strategies for Change," *Harvard Business Review*, March–April 1979, pp. 107–109; P. Strebel, "Why Do Employees Resist Change?" *Harvard Business Review*, May–June 1996, pp. 86–92; J. Mariotti, "Troubled by Resistance to Change," *IndustryWeek*, October 7, 1996, p. 30; and A.

Reichers, J. P. Wanous, and J. T. Austin, "Understanding and Managing Cynicism about Organizational Change," *Academy of Management Executive*, February 1997, pp. 48–57.

25. S. McShane and S. Steen, *Canadian Organizational Behaviour,* 7th ed. (Toronto, ON: McGraw-Hill, 2009), p. 357.

26. C. Hymowitz, "How Leader at 3M Got His Employees to Back Big Changes," *Wall Street Journal*, April 23, 2002, p. B1; and J. Useem, "Jim McNerney Thinks He Can Turn 3M from a Good Company into a Great One—With a Little Help from His Former Employer: General Electric," *Fortune*, August 12, 2002, pp. 127–132.

27. M. L. Wald and J. Schwartz, "Shuttle Inquiry Uncovers Flaws in Communication," *New York Times*, August 4, 2003, http://www.nytimes.com/2003/08/04/us/shuttle-inquiry-uncovers-flaws-in-communication.html.

28. Ibid.

29. See, for example, R. H. Kilmann, M. J. Saxton, and R. Serpa, eds., *Gaining Control of the Corporate Culture* (San Francisco: Jossey-Bass, 1985); and D. C. Hambrick and S. Finkelstein, "Managerial Discretion: A Bridge between Polar Views of Organizational Outcomes," in *Research in Organizational Behavior*, vol. 9, eds. B. M. Staw and L. L. Cummings (Greenwich, CT: JAI Press, 1987), p. 384.

30. C. R. Leana and B. Barry, "Stability and Change as Simultaneous Experiences in Organizational Life," *Academy of Management Review*, October 2000, pp. 753–759.

31. J. Gallaugher, *Information Systems: A Manager's Guide to Harnessing Technology*, v. 1.0 (Flat World Knowledge, 2010), http://catalog.flatworldknowledge.com/catalog/editions/p61083.

32. "Features, Stop Sweating Keystone (TransCanada Has)," *Canadian Business*, August 2014, p. 53–54.

33. The idea for these metaphors came from J. E. Dutton, S. J. Ashford, R. M. O'Neill, and K. A. Lawrence, "Moves That Matter: Issue Selling and Organizational Change," *Academy of Management Journal*, August 2001, pp. 716–736; B. H. Kemelgor, S. D. Johnson, and S. Srinivasan, "Forces Driving Organizational Change: A Business School Perspective," *Journal of Education for Business*, January–February 2000, pp. 133–137; G. Colvin, "When It Comes to Turbulence, CEOs Could Learn a Lot from Sailors," *Fortune*, March 29, 1999, pp. 194–196; and P. B. Vaill, *Managing as a Performing Art: New Ideas for a World of Chaotic Change* (San Francisco: Jossey-Bass, 1989).

34. K. Lewin, *Field Theory in Social Science* (New York: Harper & Row, 1951).

35. S. McShane and S. Steen, *Canadian Organizational Behaviour,* 7th ed. (Toronto, ON: McGraw-Hill, 2009), pp. 354–355.

36. For contrasting views on episodic and continuous change, see K. E. Weick and R. E. Quinn, "Organizational Change and Development," in *Annual Review of Psychology*, vol. 50, ed. J. T. Spence, J. M. Darley, and D. J. Foss (Palo Alto, CA: Annual Reviews, 1999), pp. 361–386.

37. G. Hamel, "Take It Higher," *Fortune*, February 5, 2001, pp. 169–170.

38. S. Findlay, "Ethiopian Potash Heats Up," *Canadian Business*, March 2014, p. 12.

39. D. E. Lane, R. L. Stephenson, "Fisheries Co-management: Organization, Process, and Decision Support, *Journal of Northwest Atlantic Fishery Science*, vol. 23 (1998), pp. 251–265, http://journal.nafo.int/J23/lane.pdf.

40. See, for example, T. C. Head and P. F. Sorensen, "Cultural Values and Organizational Development: A Seven-Country Study,"

Leadership & Organization Development Journal, March 1993, pp. 3–7; A. H. Church, W. W. Burke, and D. F. Van Eynde, "Values, Motives, and Interventions of Organization Development Practitioners," *Group & Organization Management*, March 1994, pp. 5–50; W. L. French and C. H. Bell Jr., *Organization Development: Behavioral Science Interventions for Organization Improvement*, 6th ed. (Upper Saddle River, NJ: Prentice Hall, 1998); N. A. Worren, K. Ruddle, and K. Moore, "From Organizational Development to Change Management," *Journal of Applied Behavioral Science*, September 1999, pp. 273–286; G. Farias, "Organizational Development and Change Management," *Journal of Applied Behavioral Science*, September 2000, pp. 376–379; W. Nicolay, "Response to Farias and Johnson's Commentary," *Journal of Applied Behavioral Science*, September 2000, pp. 380–381; and S. Hicks, "What Is Organization Development?" *Training & Development*, August 2000, p. 65.

41. T. White, "Supporting Change: How Communicators at Scotiabank Turned Ideas into Action," *Communication World*, April 2002, pp. 22–24.

42. S. McShane and S. Steen, *Canadian Organizational Behaviour,* 7th ed. (Toronto, ON: McGraw-Hill, 2009), p. 359.

43. P. A. McLagan, "Change Leadership Today," *Training & Development*, November 2002, p. 29.

44. H. L. Sirkin, P. Keenan, and A. Jackson, "The Hard Side of Change Management," *Harvard Business Review*, vol. 83, no. 10 (October 1, 2005), pp. 108–118.

45. W. Pietersen, "The Mark Twain Dilemma: The Theory and Practice for Change Leadership," *Journal of Business Strategy*, September–October 2002, pp. 32–37; C. Hymowitz, "To Maintain Success, Managers Must Learn How to Direct Change," *Wall Street Journal*, August 13, 2002, p. B1; and J. E. Dutton, S. J. Ashford, R. M. O'Neill, and K. A. Lawrence, "Moves That Matter: Issue Selling and Organizational Change," *Academy of Management Journal*, August 2001, pp. 716–736.

46. P. A. McLagan, "The Change-Capable Organization," *Training & Development*, January 2003, pp. 50–58.

47. M. Young and J. E. Post, "Managing to Communicate, Communicating to Manage: How Leading Companies Communicate with Employees," *Organizational Dynamics*, Summer 1993, pp. 31–43.

48. M. Javidan, P. W. Dorfman, M. S. deLuque, and R. J. House, "In the Eye of the Beholder: Cross-Cultural Lessons in Leadership from Project GLOBE," *Academy of Management Perspective*, February 2006, pp. 67–90; and E. Fagenson-Eland, E. A. Ensher, and W. W. Burke, "Organization Development and Change Interventions: A Seven-Nation Comparison," *Journal of Applied Behavioral Science*, December 2004, pp. 432–464.

49. E. Fagenson-Eland, E. A. Ensher, and W. W. Burke, "Organization Development and Change Interventions: A Seven-Nation Comparison," *Journal of Applied Behavioral Science*, December 2004, p. 461.

50. M. A. Cavanaugh, W. R. Boswell, M. V. Roehling, and J. W. Boudreau, "An Empirical Examination of Self-Reported Work Stress among U.S. Managers," *Journal of Applied Psychology*, February 2000, pp. 65–74; M. A. Verespej, "Stressed Out," *IndustryWeek*, February 21, 2000, pp. 30–34; J. Laabs, "Time-Starved Workers Rebel," *Workforce*, October 2000, pp. 26–28; and C. Daniels, "The Last Taboo," *Fortune*, October 28, 2002, pp. 137–144.

51. Elaine Lowe, *Social Innovations: Conversations on Work and Well-Being*, (Ottawa, ON: Vanier Institute of the Family, October 2005), p. 5, http://www.vanierinstitute.ca/modules/news/newsitem.php?ItemId=309.

52. "Three-Quarters (72%) of Canadians Are Experiencing an Uncomfortable Level of Stress; Number Jumps to Nine in Ten (90%) among 18–24 Year Olds," *Game Changers*, November 5, 2012, http://www.ipsos-na.com/news-polls/pressrelease.aspx?id=5870.

53. J. Adams, "Work Was The Biggest Stressor for Canadians in 2014: Survey," *The Huffington Post*, December 30, 2014, http://www.huffingtonpost.ca/2014/12/30/work-stress-canada-survey_n_6392340.html.

54. And the Survey Says box based on based on S. Schomer, "Under Pressure," *Fast Company*, April 2010, p. 112; "Organizational Change: Facebook Poll," *Harvard Business Review*, March 2010, p. 16; J. Yang and S. Ward, "I'd Rather Give Up," *USA Today*, March 4, 2010, p. 1B; M. Weinstein, "Missing Something," *Training*, January 2010, p. 6; J. MacIntyre, "Hard at Work," *Springfield Business Journal*, November 30–December 6, 2009, p. 16; J. MacIntyre, "Accidental Innovation," *Springfield Business Journal*, September 28–October 4, 2009, p. 22; and M. Healy and S. Ward, "Workplace Worries," *USA Today*, August 28, 2008, p. 1D.

55. See, for example, B. M. Staw, "Counterforces to Change," in *Change in Organizations*, eds. P. S. Goodman and Associates (San Francisco: Jossey-Bass, 1982), pp. 87–121; A. A. Armenakis and A. G. Bedeian, "Organizational Change: A Review of Theory and Research in the 1990s," *Journal of Management*, vol. 25, no. 3 (1999), pp. 293–315; C. R. Wanberg and J. T. Banas, "Predictors and Outcomes of Openness to Changes in a Reorganizing Workplace," *Journal of Applied Psychology*, February 2000, pp. 132–142; S. K. Piderit, "Rethinking Resistance and Recognizing Ambivalence: A Multidimensional View of Attitudes toward an Organizational Change," *Academy of Management Review*, October 2000, pp. 783–794; R. Kegan and L. L. Lahey, "The Real Reason People Won't Change," *Harvard Business Review*, November 2001, pp. 85–92; M. A. Korsgaard, H. J. Sapienza, and D. M. Schweiger, "Beaten before Begun: The Role of Procedural Justice in Planning Change," *Journal of Management*, vol. 28, no. 4 (2002), pp. 497–516; and C. E. Cunningham, "Readiness for Organizational Change: A Longitudinal Study of Workplace, Psychological and Behavioral Correlates," *Journal of Occupational and Organizational Psychology*, December 2002, pp. 377–392.

56. J. P. Kotter and L. A. Schlesinger, "Choosing Strategies for Change," *Harvard Business Review*, March–April 1979, pp. 107–109; P. Strebel, "Why Do Employees Resist Change?" *Harvard Business Review*, May–June 1996, pp. 86–92; J. Mariotti, "Troubled by Resistance to Change," *IndustryWeek*, October 7, 1996, p. 30; and A. Reichers, J. P. Wanous, and J. T. Austin, "Understanding and Managing Cynicism about Organizational Change," *Academy of Management Executive*, February 1997, pp. 48–57.

57. S. McShane and S. Steen, *Canadian Organizational Behaviour*, 7th ed. (Toronto, ON: McGraw-Hill, 2009), p. 357.

58. Ibid.

59. Adapted from the UK National Work-Stress Network, www.work-stress.net.

60. See, for example, "Stressed Out: Extreme Job Stress: Survivors' Tales," *Wall Street Journal*, January 17, 2001, p. B1.

61. See, for instance, S. Bates, "Expert: Don't Overlook Employee Burnout," *HR Magazine*, August 2003, p. 14.

62. Question of Ethics box based on D. Cole, "The Big Chill," *US News & World Report*, December 6, 2004, pp. EE2–EE5.

63. H. Benson, "Are You Working Too Hard?" *Harvard Business Review*, November 2005, pp. 53–58; B. Cryer, R. McCraty, and D. Childre, "Pull the Plug on Stress," *Harvard Business Review*, July 2003, pp. 102–107; C. Daniels, "The Last Taboo," *Fortune*, October 28, 2002, pp. 137–144; C. L. Cooper and S. Cartwright, "Healthy Mind, Healthy Organization—A Proactive Approach to Occupational Stress," *Human Relations*, April 1994, pp. 455–471; C. A. Heaney et al., "Industrial Relations, Worksite Stress Reduction and Employee Well-Being: A Participatory Action Research Investigation," *Journal of Organizational Behavior*, September 1993, pp. 495–510; C. D. Fisher, "Boredom at Work: A Neglected Concept," *Human Relations*, March 1993, pp. 395–417; and S. E. Jackson, "Participation in Decision Making as a Strategy for Reducing Job-Related Strain," *Journal of Applied Psychology*, February 1983, pp. 3–19.

64. T. Barton, "Brave Face," *Employee Benefits*, January 2011, p. 41; and "Employee Assistance Programs," *HR Magazine*, May 2003, p. 143.

65. S. Barrett, "Employee Assistance Programs," *Employee Benefits*, January 2011, pp. 49–52; "EAPs with the Most," *Managing Benefits Plans*, March 2003, p. 8; and K. Tyler, "Helping Employees Cope with Grief," *HR Magazine*, September 2003, pp. 55–58.

66. N. Faba, "The EAP Problem," *Benefits Canada*, March 2011, p. 7; D. A. Masi, "Redefining the EAP Field," *Journal of Workplace Behavioral Health* (January–March 2011), pp. 1–9; R. M. Weiss, "Brinksmanship Redux: Employee Assistance Programs' Precursors and Prospects," *Employee Responsibilities & Rights Journal* (December 2010), pp. 325–343; and F. Hansen, "Employee Assistance Programs (EAPs) Grow and Expand Their Reach," *Compensation and Benefits Review*, March–April 2000, p. 13.

67. J. P. Kotter and L. A. Schlesinger, "Choosing Strategies for Change," *Harvard Business Review*, March–April 1979, pp. 106–111; K. Matejka and R. Julian, "Resistance to Change Is Natural," *Supervisory Management*, October 1993, p. 10; C. O'Connor, "Resistance: The Repercussions of Change," *Leadership & Organization Development Journal*, October 1993, pp. 30–36; J. Landau, "Organizational Change and Barriers to Innovation: A Case Study in the Italian Public Sector," *Human Relations*, December 1993, pp. 1411–1429; A. Sagie and M. Koslowsky, "Organizational Attitudes and Behaviors as a Function of Participation in Strategic and Tactical Change Decisions: An Application of Path-Goal Theory," *Journal of Organizational Behavior*, January 1994, pp. 37–47; V. D. Miller, J. R. Johnson, and J. Grau, "Antecedents to Willingness to Participate in a Planned Organizational Change," *Journal of Applied Communication Research*, February 1994, pp. 59–80; P. Pritchett and R. Pound, *The Employee Handbook for Organizational Change* (Dallas: Pritchett Publishing, 1994); R. Maurer, *Beyond the Wall of Resistance: Unconventional Strategies That Build Support for Change* (Austin, TX: Bard Books, 1996); D. Harrison, "Assess and Remove Barriers to Change," *HRfocus*, July 1999, pp. 9–10; L. K. Lewis, "Disseminating Information and Soliciting Input during Planned Organizational Change," *Management Communication Quarterly*, August 1999, pp. 43–75; J. P. Wanous, A. E. Reichers, and J. T. Austin, "Cynicism about Organizational Change," *Group & Organization Management*, June 2000, pp. 132–153; K. W. Mossholder, R. P. Settoon, and A. A. Armenakis, "Emotion during Organizational Transformations," *Group & Organization Management*, September 2000, pp. 220–243; and S. K. Piderit, "Rethinking Resistance and Recognizing

Ambivalence: A Multidimensional View of Attitudes toward an Organizational Change," *Academy of Management Review*, October 2000, pp. 783–794.

68. T. M. Egan and C. M. Lancaster, "Comparing Appreciative Inquiry to Action Research: OD Practitioner Perspectives," *Organizational Development Journal*, vol. 23, no. 2 (Summer 2005): pp. 29–49.

69. S. McShane and S. Steen, *Canadian Organizational Behaviour,* 7th ed. (Toronto, ON: McGraw-Hill, 2009), pp. 364–365.

70. Ibid., pp. 365–367.

71. "Team Values the Canadian Tire Way," *Appreciative Inquiry Commons*, http://appreciativeinquiry.case.edu/practice/ppCT.cfm.

72. Based on K. Lewin, *Field Theory in Social Science* (New York: Harper & Row, 1951); and S. McShane and S. Steen, *Canadian Organizational Behaviour,* 7th ed. (Toronto, ON: McGraw-Hill, 2009).

73. B. Anderson, *Canadian Association Management*, 2nd ed., CSAE.

74. S. A. Hewlett, M. Marshall, and L. Sherbin, (2013) "How Diversity Can Drive Innovation," *Harvard Business Review*, December 2013.

75. Ibid.

76. Ibid.

77. Ibid.

78. L. Friedman, "Ladder of Sustainability: Moving Sustainable Business Practices," *Leadership Excellence*, http://www.enterprisedevelop.com/pdf/Ladder_Sustainability.pdf.

79. M. Shin, "Westport's Time to Shine," *Corporate Knights*, vol. 24 (2008), http://www.corporateknights.ca/article/westports-time-shine.

80. Information from Nike Grind website, http://www.nikereuseashoe.com/using-nike-grind.

81. L. Friedman, "Ladder of Sustainability: Moving Sustainable Business Practices," *Leadership Excellence*, http://www.enterprisedevelop.com/pdf/Ladder_Sustainability.pdf.

82. Algonquin College, "Sustainability: Explore the Sustainable Algonquin Centre for Construction Excellence," *Algonquin College website*, http://www2.algonquincollege.com/acce/home/sustainability.

83. Based on information from the ShareGreen website, http://www.sharegreen.ca/about.

84. Information from press kit on company's website, www.1800gotjunk.com; A. Wahl, "Canada's Best Workplaces: Overview," *Canadian Business*, April 26, 2007; "Fastest-Growing Franchises 2006 Rankings," *Entrepreneur*, April 29, 2006, http://www.entrepreneur.com/franchises/rankings/fastestgrowing-115162/2006,-4.html; J. Hainsworth, The Associated Press, "Canadian Company Finds Treasures in People's Trash," *Springfield News-Leader*, April 24, 2006, p. 5B; J. Martin, "Cash from Trash," *Fortune*, November 2003, pp. 52–56; and M. Carbonaro, "1-800-GOT-JUNK? Quickly Opens Second Area Site," *CNY Business Journal*, August 10, 2007.

85. Jeff Beer, "Q&A: Brian Scudamore, founder/CEO, 1-800-Got-Junk?" May 7, 2012, http://www.canadianbusiness.com/article/81127—q-a-brian-scudamore-founder-ceo-1-800-got-junk.

86. Based on M. Warner, "Under the Knife," *Business* 2.0, January 1, 2004, http://money.cnn.com/magazines/business2/business2_archive/2004/01/01/359617/index.htm.

Glossary

A

accountability. The need to report and justify work to a manager's superiors.

acquired diversity. A company's acquisition of a global mindset and social media skills to enable it to better understand and appreciate diversity.

activities. Actions that take place.

adjourning. The final stage of team development for temporary teams, in which members are concerned with wrapping up activities rather than task performance.

analytic style. A decision-making style characterized by a high tolerance for ambiguity and a rational way of thinking.

anonymous mentoring. Using a mentor outside an organization who can provide anonymity and perspective.

Association of Southeast Asian Nations (ASEAN). A trading alliance of 10 Southeast Asian countries.

authority. The rights inherent in a managerial position to tell people what to do and to expect them to do it.

B

balanced scorecard. A performance measurement tool that looks at four areas that contribute to an organization's performance: financial, customer, internal business process, and learning and growth assets.

basic corrective action. Corrective action that looks at how and why performance deviated and then proceeds to correct the source of deviation.

behavioural style. A decision-making style characterized by a low tolerance for ambiguity and an intuitive way of thinking.

behavioural theories of leadership. Theories that isolate behaviours that differentiate effective leaders from ineffective leaders.

behaviourally anchored rating scales (BARS). A performance appraisal method in which the evaluator rates an employee on examples of actual job behaviours.

benchmark. The standard of excellence against which to measure and compare.

benchmarking. The search for the best practices among competitors or noncompetitors that lead to their superior performance.

born globals. International companies that choose to go global from inception.

boundaryless organization. An organization that is not defined by a chain of command, places no limits on spans of control, and replaces departments with empowered teams.

bounded rationality. Limitations on a person's ability to interpret, process, and act on information.

Brazil, Russia, India, China, and South Africa (BRICS). An association of leading emerging economies aiming to create mechanisms for consultation and cooperation.

bureaucratic control. An approach to control that emphasizes organizational authority and relies on administrative rules, regulations, procedures, and policies.

business model. A strategic design for how a company intends to profit from its broad array of strategies, processes, and activities.

business model. A strategic design for how a company intends to profit from its strategies, work processes, and work activities.

C

calm waters metaphor. A description of organizational change that likens that change to a large ship making a predictable trip across a calm sea and experiencing an occasional storm.

capabilities. An organization's skills and abilities that enable it to do the work activities needed in its business.

career. The sequence of positions held by a person during his or her lifetime.

Caricom Single Market and Economy (CSME). An association of Caribbean countries aiming to create one large market.

centralization. The degree to which decision making is concentrated at a single point in the organization.

certainty. A condition in which a decision maker can make accurate decisions because the outcome of every alternative is known.

chain of command. The continuous line of authority that extends from the top of the organization to the lowest level and clarifies who reports to whom.

change agent. Someone who acts as a catalyst and assumes the responsibility for managing the change process.

charismatic leader. An enthusiastic, self-confident leader whose personality and actions influence people to behave in certain ways.

civil servants. People who work in a local, provincial, or federal government department.

clan control. An approach to control in which employee behaviour is regulated by the shared values, norms, traditions, rituals, beliefs, and other aspects of the organization's culture.

classical view. The view that management's only social responsibility is to maximize profits.

code of ethics. A formal statement of an organization's primary values and the ethical rules it expects its employees to follow.

coercive power. The power a leader has through his or her ability to punish or control.

compressed workweek. A workweek in which employees work longer hours per day but fewer days per week.

conceptual style. A decision-making style characterized by a high tolerance for ambiguity and an intuitive way of thinking.

concurrent control. A type of control that takes place while an activity is in progress.

conflict. Perceived differences that result in some form of interference or opposition.

control process. A three-step process that includes measuring actual performance, comparing actual performance against a standard, and taking managerial action to correct deviations or inadequate standards.

control. The process of monitoring activities to ensure that they are being accomplished as planned, and correcting any significant deviations.

controlling. A management function that involves monitoring actual performance, comparing actual performance to a standard, and taking corrective action when necessary.

core competencies. An organization's major value-creating skills, capabilities, and resources that determine its competitive weapons.

corporate governance. The system used to govern a corporation so that the interests of corporate owners are protected.

corporate social responsibility. A business's obligation, beyond that required by law and economics, to do the right things and act in ways that are good for society.

creativity. The ability to produce novel and useful ideas.

credibility. The degree to which someone is perceived as honest, competent, and able to inspire.

critical incidents. A performance appraisal method in which the evaluator focuses on the critical or key behaviours that separate effective from ineffective job performance.

critical path. The longest or most time-consuming sequence of events and activities required to complete a project in the shortest amount of time.

cross-functional teams. Work teams made up of individuals who are experts in various functional specialties.

Crown corporations. Commercial companies owned by the government but independently managed.

customer departmentalization. Grouping jobs on the basis of customers who have common needs or problems.

D

decentralization. The degree to which lower-level employees provide input or actually make decisions.

decision criteria. Criteria that define what is relevant in making a decision.

decision. A choice from two or more alternatives.

decision-making process. A set of eight steps that includes identifying a problem, selecting an alternative, and evaluating the decision's effectiveness.

delegation. The assignment of authority to another person to carry out specific duties, allowing the employee to make some of the decisions.

departmentalization. The basis on which jobs are grouped together.

diagonal communication. Communication that cuts across both work areas and organizational levels.

directional plans. Plans that are flexible and that set out general guidelines.

directive style. A decision-making style characterized by a low tolerance for ambiguity and a rational way of thinking.

discipline. Actions taken by a manager to enforce an organization's standards and regulations.

distributive justice. Perceived fairness of the amount and allocation of rewards among individuals.

divisional structure. An organizational structure that consists of separate business units or divisions.

downward communication. Communication that flows downward from managers to employees.

drive to acquire. The drive to seek, take control of, and retain objects and personal experiences.

drive to bond. The drive to form social relationships with others.

drive to defend. The drive to protect ourselves both physically and socially.

drive to learn. The drive to satisfy our curiosity and understand ourselves and the world around us.

dysfunctional conflicts. Conflicts that are destructive and prevent a group from achieving its goals.

E

economic value added (EVA). A financial tool that measures corporate and divisional performance; calculated by taking after-tax operating profit minus the total annual cost of capital.

effectiveness. Completing activities so that organizational goals are achieved.

efficiency. Getting the most output from the least amount of inputs.

employee assistance programs (EAPs). Programs offered by organizations to help employees overcome personal and health-related problems.

employee counselling. A process designed to help employees overcome performance-related problems.

employee empowerment. Giving more authority to employees to make decisions.

employee recognition programs. Reward programs that provide managers with opportunities to give employees personal attention and express interest, approval, and appreciation for a job well done.

employee theft. Any unauthorized taking of company property by employees for their personal use.

environmental complexity. The number of components in an organization's environment and the extent of the organization's knowledge about those components.

environmental uncertainty. The degree of change and the degree of complexity in an organization's environment.

equity theory. The theory that an employee compares his or her job's input–output ratio with that of relevant others and then responds to correct any inequity.

escalation of commitment. An increased commitment to a previous decision despite evidence that the decision might have been wrong.

ethics. Rules and principles that define right and wrong behaviour.

European Union (EU). A union of 27 European countries that forms an economic and political entity.

events. End points that represent the completion of major activities.

expectancy theory. The theory that an individual tends to act in a certain way based on the expectation that the act will be followed by a given outcome and on the attractiveness of that outcome to the individual.

expert power. The influence a leader has based on his or her expertise, special skills, or knowledge.

exporting. An approach to going global that involves making products at home and selling them abroad.

external environment. Outside forces and institutions that can potentially affect the organization's performance.

F

family-friendly benefits. Benefits that accommodate employees' needs for work–life balance.

feedback control. A type of control that takes place after a work activity is done.

feedforward control. A type of control that focuses on preventing anticipated problems, since it takes place before the actual activity.

flexible work hours (flextime). A scheduling option in which employees are required to work a specific number of hours per week but are free to vary those hours within certain limits.

foreign subsidiary. An approach to going global that involves a direct investment in a foreign country by setting up a separate and independent production facility or office.

formal communication. Communication that follows the official chain of command or is part of the communication required to do one's job.

formalization. The degree to which jobs within the organization are standardized and the extent to which employee behaviour is guided by rules and procedures.

forming. The first stage of team development in which people join the group and then define the team's purpose, structure, and leadership.

four-drive theory. The theory that behaviour is influenced by our innate drives to acquire, bond, learn, and defend.

franchising. An approach to going global in which a service organization gives a person or group the right to sell a product, using specific business methods and practices that are standardized.

functional conflicts. Conflicts that support the goals of the work group and improve its performance.

functional departmentalization. Grouping jobs by functions performed.

functional structure. An organizational structure that groups similar or related occupational specialties together.

G

Gantt chart. A planning tool that shows in bar graph form when tasks are supposed to be done and compares that with the actual progress on each.

general environment. Broad external conditions that may affect the organization.

geographical departmentalization. Grouping jobs on the basis of territory or geography.

global company. An international company that centralizes management and other decisions in the home country.

global sourcing. Purchasing materials or labour from around the world, wherever they are cheapest.

goals (objectives). Desired outcomes for individuals, groups, or entire organizations.

goal-setting theory. The proposition that specific goals increase performance and that difficult goals, when accepted, result in higher performance than do easy goals.

graphic rating scales. A performance appraisal method in which the evaluator rates an employee on a set of performance factors.

group cohesiveness. The degree to which group members are attracted to each other and share the group's goals.

group mentoring. Millennials sharing ideas in groups in a peer-to-peer format.

groupthink. The withholding by group members of different views in order to appear to be in agreement.

H

heuristics. Rules of thumb that managers use to simplify decision making.

hierarchy of needs theory. Maslow's theory proposing a hierarchy of five human needs: physiological, safety, social, esteem, and self-actualization; as each need becomes satisfied, the next need becomes dominant.

human relations view of conflict. The view that conflict is a natural and inevitable outcome in any group and has the potential to be a positive force in contributing to a group's performance.

human resource management process. Activities necessary for staffing the organization and sustaining high employee performance.

human resource planning. The process by which managers ensure that they have the right number and kinds of people in the right places at the right times, who are capable of effectively and efficiently performing assigned tasks.

hygiene factors. Factors that eliminate job dissatisfaction, but do not motivate.

I

idea champions. Individuals who actively and enthusiastically support new ideas, build support for them, overcome resistance to them, and ensure that innovations are implemented.

immediate corrective action. Corrective action that corrects problems at once to get performance back on track.

importing. An approach to going global that involves acquiring products made abroad and selling them at home.

informal communication. Communication that is not defined by the organization's structural hierarchy.

inherent diversity. The gender, racial, and socioeconomic diversity of an organization.

innovation. The process of taking a creative idea and turning it into a useful product, service, or method of operation.

insourcing. Developing products and services in-house.

integrative social contracts theory. A view of ethics proposing that ethical decisions be based on existing ethical norms in industries and communities in order to determine what constitutes right and wrong.

interactionist view of conflict. The view that some conflict is absolutely necessary for a group to perform effectively.

intuitive decision making. Making decisions on the basis of experience, feelings, and accumulated judgment.

ISO 9000. A series of international quality standards that set uniform guidelines for processes to ensure that products conform to customer requirements.

J

job analysis. An assessment that defines jobs and the behaviours necessary to perform them.

job description. A written statement of what a jobholder does, how the job is done, and why the job is done.

job design. The process of looking at a job to determine what set of tasks is required, how they are done, and in what order.

job sharing. The practice of having two or more people split a full-time job.

job specification. A statement of the minimum qualifications that a person must possess to perform a given job successfully.

joint venture. An approach to going global in which the partners agree to form a separate, independent organization for some business purpose; it is a type of strategic alliance.

K

karoshi. A Japanese term that refers to a sudden death caused by overworking.

L

labour union. An organization that represents employees and seeks to protect their interests through collective bargaining.

lateral communication. Communication that takes place among employees on the same organizational level.

leader. Someone who can influence others and provide vision and strategy to the organization.

leadership. The process of influencing individuals or groups toward the achievement of goals.

leading. A management function that involves motivating subordinates, directing the work of individuals or teams, selecting the most effective communication channels, and resolving employee behaviour issues.

legitimate power. The power a leader has as a result of his or her position in the organization.

licensing. An approach to going global in which a manufacturer gives another organization the right to use its brand name, technology, or product specifications.

line managers. Managers responsible for the essential activities of the organization, including production and sales.

long-term plans. Plans with a time frame beyond one year.

lower-level managers. Managers at the lowest level of the organization who manage the work of nonmanagerial employees directly or indirectly involved with the production or creation of the organization's products.

M

management by objectives (MBO). An approach to goal setting in which specific measurable goals are jointly set by employees and their managers, progress toward accomplishing those goals is periodically reviewed, and rewards are allocated on the basis of this progress.

management by walking around. A term used to describe a manager who is out in the work area and interacting directly with employees.

management functions. Planning, organizing, leading, and controlling.

management information system (MIS). A system used to provide management with needed information on a regular basis.

management roles. Specific categories of managerial behaviour.

management. Coordinating work activities so that they are completed efficiently and effectively with and through other people.

manager. Someone who works with and through other people by coordinating their work activities in order to accomplish organizational goals.

manufacturing organizations. Organizations that produce physical goods.

market control. An approach to control that emphasizes the use of external market mechanisms, such as price competition and relative market share, to establish the standards used in the control system.

market economy. An economic system in which resources are primarily owned and controlled by the private sector.

market value added (MVA). A financial tool that measures the stock market's estimate of the value of a firm's past and expected capital investment projects.

matrix structure. An organizational structure that assigns specialists from different functional departments to work on one or more projects.

mechanistic organization. An organization that is rigid and tightly controlled.

middle-level managers. Managers between the first-line level and the top level of the organization who manage the work of first-line managers.

motivation. An individual's willingness to exert high levels of effort to reach organizational goals, conditioned by the degree to which that effort satisfies some individual need.

motivators. Factors that increase job satisfaction and motivation.

multidomestic corporation. An international company that decentralizes management and other decisions to the local country.

multinational corporation (MNC). A broad term referring to any and all types of international companies that maintain operations in multiple countries.

multiperson comparisons. A performance appraisal method in which one individual's performance is compared with that of others.

N

national culture. The values and attitudes shared by individuals from a specific country that shape their behaviour and beliefs about what is important.

nearshoring. Relocating to a nearby country, perhaps one sharing the same border and a market with many geographic, economic, and political similarities.

need for achievement (nAch). The drive to excel, to achieve in relation to a set of standards, and to strive to succeed.

need for affiliation (nAff). The desire for friendly and close interpersonal relationships.

need for power (nPow). The need to make others behave in a way that they would not have behaved otherwise.

need. An internal state that makes certain outcomes appear attractive.

network organization. A small core organization that outsources major business functions.

nongovernmental organization (NGO). A nongovernmental organization that emphasizes humanitarian issues, development, and sustainability.

nonprofit sector. The part of the economy run by organizations that operate for purposes other than making a profit (that is, providing charity or services).

nonprogrammed decisions. Decisions that are unique and nonrecurring, and require custom-made solutions.

norming. The third stage of team development, which is characterized by close relationships and cohesiveness.

norms. Standards or expectations that are accepted and shared by a group's members.

North American Free Trade Agreement (NAFTA). An agreement among the Canadian, American, and Mexican governments in which barriers to free trade are reduced.

O

offshoring. Relocation of an operational process to a country not connected by land.

onshoring. Relocating to lower-cost cities within the same country.

open-book management. A motivational approach in which an organization's financial statements (the "books") are shared with all employees.

operational plans. Plans that specify the details of how the overall goals are to be achieved.

operations management. The study and application of the transformation process.

opportunities. Positive trends in external environmental factors.

organic organization. An organization that is highly adaptive and flexible.

organization. A deliberate arrangement of people who act together to accomplish some specific purpose.

organizational change. Any alteration of people, structure, or technology in an organization.

organizational culture. A system of shared values, norms, and beliefs held by organization members that determines, in large degree, how employees act.

organizational culture. A system of shared values, norms, and beliefs held by organizational members that determines, in large degree, how employees act.

organizational design. The process of developing or changing an organization's structure.

organizational development (OD). Techniques or programs meant to change people and the nature and quality of interpersonal work relationships.

organizational effectiveness. A measure of how appropriate organizational goals are and how well an organization is achieving those goals.

organizational performance. The accumulated end results of all the organization's work activities.

organizational processes. The way organizational work is done.

organizational structure. How job tasks are formally divided, grouped, and coordinated within an organization.

organizing. A management function that involves determining what tasks are to be done, who is to do them, how the tasks are to be grouped, who reports to whom, and where decisions are to be made.

orientation. The introduction of a new employee to his or her job and to the organization.

outsourcing. Relocation of an operational process such as manufacturing to another country.

P

path-goal theory. A leadership theory that says the leader's job is to assist his or her followers in attaining their goals and to provide the necessary direction and support to ensure that their goals are compatible with the overall objectives of the group or organization.

pay-for-performance programs. Variable compensation plans that pay employees on the basis of some performance measure.

performance management system. A process of establishing performance standards and evaluating performance in order to arrive at objective human resource decisions and to provide documentation in support of those decisions.

performance. The end result of an activity.

performing. The fourth stage of team development, in which the team structure is fully functional and accepted by team members.

PESTEL analysis. A way for a company to align its strategy with the external environment by analyzing six contextual factors that shape the external environment: political, economic, sociocultural, technological, environmental, and legal.

planned economy. An economic system in which all economic decisions are planned by a central government.

planning. A management function that involves defining goals, establishing a strategy for achieving those goals, and developing plans to integrate and coordinate activities.

plans. Documents that outline how goals are going to be met and describe resource allocations, schedules, and other necessary actions to accomplish the goals.

policy. A guideline for making a decision.

private sector. The part of the economy run by organizations that are free from direct government control; enterprises in this sector operate to make a profit.

privately held organizations. Companies whose shares are not available on the stock exchange but are privately held.

problem. A discrepancy between an existing and a desired state of affairs.

procedural justice. Perceived fairness of the process used to determine the distribution of rewards.

procedure. A series of interrelated sequential steps that a decision maker can use to respond to a structured problem.

process conflict. Conflict over how the work gets done.

process departmentalization. Grouping jobs on the basis of product or customer flow.

product departmentalization. Grouping jobs by product line.

productivity. The overall output of goods or services produced divided by the inputs needed to generate that output.

programmed decision. A repetitive decision that can be handled by a routine approach.

project management. The task of getting project activities done on time, within budget, and according to specifications.

project structure. An organizational structure in which employees continuously work on projects.

project. A one-time-only set of activities with a definite beginning and ending point.

public sector. The part of the economy directly controlled by government.

publicly held organization. A company whose shares are available on the stock exchange for public trading by brokers/dealers.

Q

quality management. A philosophy of management driven by continual improvement and responding to customer needs and expectations.

R

range of variation. The acceptable degree of variation between actual performance and the standard.

rational decision making. Making decisions that are consistent and value-maximizing within specified constraints.

readiness. The extent to which people have the ability and willingness to accomplish a specific task.

realistic job preview (RJP). A preview of a job that includes both positive and negative information about the job and the company.

recruitment. The process of locating, identifying, and attracting capable applicants.

referent power. The power a leader has because of his or her desirable resources or personal traits.

referents. Those things individuals compare themselves against in order to assess equity.

relationship conflict. Conflict based on interpersonal relationships.

reliability. The ability of a selection device to measure the same thing consistently.

reshoring. Companies that bring back production of goods to the home country.

resources An organization's assets—financial, physical, human, intangible—that are used to develop, manufacture, and deliver products or services to customers.

responsibility. The obligation or expectation to perform any assigned duties.

reverse mentoring. A junior employee providing insight and expertise on a certain topic to a senior executive.

reward power. The power a leader has to give positive benefits or rewards.

rights view of ethics. A view of ethics concerned with respecting and protecting individual liberties and privileges.

risk. A condition in which a decision maker is able to estimate the likelihood of certain outcomes.

role ambiguity. When role expectations are not clearly understood.

role conflicts. Work expectations that are hard to satisfy.

role overload. Having more work to accomplish than time permits.

role. Behaviour patterns expected of someone who occupies a given position in a social unit.

rule. An explicit statement that tells a decision maker what he or she can or cannot do.

S

satisfice. To accept solutions that are "good enough."

selection process. The process of screening job applicants to ensure that the most appropriate candidates are hired.

service organizations. Organizations that produce nonphysical products in the form of services.

shareholders. Individuals or companies that own stocks in a business.

short-term plans. Plans with a time frame of one year or less.

simple structure. An organizational structure with low departmentalization, wide spans of control, authority centralized in a single person, and little formalization.

single-use plans. A one-time plan specifically designed to meet the needs of a unique situation.

Situational Leadership (SL). A leadership theory that focuses on the readiness of followers.

Six Sigma. A quality standard that establishes a goal of no more than 3.4 defects per million units or procedures.

skill-based pay. A pay system that rewards employees for the job skills and competencies they can demonstrate.

slack time. The time difference between the critical path and all other paths.

social loafing. The tendency of individuals to expend less effort when working collectively than when working individually.

socioeconomic view. The view that management's social responsibility goes beyond making profits to include protecting and improving society's welfare.

span of control. The number of employees a manager can efficiently and effectively manage.

specific environment. The part of the external environment that is directly relevant to the achievement of an organization's goals.

specific plans. Plans that are clearly defined and leave no room for interpretation.

staff managers. Managers who work in the supporting activities of the organizations (such as human resources or accounting).

stakeholders. Any constituencies in the organization's external environment that are affected by the organization's decisions and actions.

standing plans. Ongoing plans that provide guidance for activities performed repeatedly.

stock options. A financial incentive that gives employees the right to purchase shares of company stock at some time in the future at a set price.

storming. The second stage of team development, which is characterized by intragroup conflict.

strategic alliance. An approach to going global that involves a partnership between a domestic and a foreign company in which both share resources and knowledge in developing new products or building production facilities.

strategic management process. A six-step process that encompasses strategic planning, implementation, and evaluation.

strategic management. What managers do to develop the organization's strategies.

strategic plans. Plans that apply to the entire organization, establish the organization's overall goals, and seek to position the organization in terms of its environment.

strategies. The decisions and actions that determine the long-run performance of an organization.

strengths. Any activities the organization does well or any unique resources it has.

stress. Response to anxiety over intense demands, constraints, or opportunities.

stressors. Factors that cause stress.

strong cultures. Organizational cultures in which the key values are deeply held and widely shared.

structured problems. Problems that are straightforward, familiar, and easily defined.

SWOT analysis. An analysis of the organization's strengths, weaknesses, opportunities, and threats.

synergy. Combined efforts that are greater than the sum of individual efforts.

T

task conflict. Conflict over content and goals of the work.

team structure. An organizational structure in which the entire organization is made up of work groups or teams.

telework. A job arrangement in which employees work at home and are linked to the workplace by computers and other technology.

theory of justice view of ethics. A view of ethics in which managers impose and enforce rules fairly and impartially, and do so by following all legal rules and regulations.

Theory X. The assumption that employees have little ambition, dislike work, want to avoid responsibility, and must be closely controlled to perform effectively.

Theory Y. The assumption that employees can exercise self-direction, accept and seek out responsibility, and consider work a natural activity.

threats. Negative trends in external environmental factors.

three-needs theory. McClelland's theory that the needs for achievement, power, and affiliation are major motives in work.

top-level managers. Managers at or near the top level of the organization who are responsible for making organization-wide decisions and establishing the plans and goals that affect the entire organization.

traditional goal setting. An approach to setting goals in which goals are set at the top of the organization and then broken into subgoals for each organizational level.

traditional view of conflict. The view that all conflict is bad and must be avoided.

trait theories of leadership. Theories that isolate characteristics (traits) that differentiate leaders from nonleaders.

transactional leaders. Leaders who guide or motivate their followers in the direction of established goals by clarifying role and task requirements.

transformation process. The process that converts resources into finished goods and services.

transformational leaders. Leaders who inspire followers to transcend their own self-interests for the good of the organization, and who have a profound and extraordinary effect on their followers.

transnational corporation (TNC) or borderless organization. A type of international company in which artificial geographical barriers are eliminated.

Trans-Pacific Partnership (TPP). A group of nine countries that is intending to revolutionize Asian trade relations.

trust. The belief in the integrity, character, and ability of a person.

two-factor theory. Herzberg's theory that intrinsic factors are related to job satisfaction and motivation, whereas extrinsic factors are related to job dissatisfaction.

Type A personality. People who have a chronic sense of urgency and an excessive competitive drive.

Type B personality. People who are relaxed and easygoing and accept change easily.

U

uncertainty. A condition in which a decision maker is not certain about the outcomes and cannot even make reasonable probability estimates.

unity of command. The management principle that states every employee should receive orders from only one superior.

universality of management. The reality that management is needed in all types and sizes of organizations, at all organizational levels, in all organizational work areas, and in organizations in all countries around the globe.

unstructured problems. Problems that are new or unusual and for which information is ambiguous or incomplete.

upward communication. Communication that flows upward from employees to managers.

utilitarian view of ethics. A view of ethics maintaining that ethical decisions are made solely on the basis of their outcomes or consequences.

V

validity. The proven relationship that exists between the selection device and some relevant job criterion.

value chain management (VCM). The process of managing the sequence of activities and information along the entire value chain.

value chain. The entire series of work activities that add value at each step from raw materials to finished product.

value. The performance characteristics, features, attributes, and other aspects of goods and services, for which customers are willing to give up resources.

variable pay. A pay system in which an individual's compensation is contingent on performance.

virtual organization. An organization that has elements of a traditional organization, but also relies on recent developments in information technology to get work done.

vision and mission. The purpose of the organization.

visionary leadership. The ability to create and articulate a realistic, credible, and attractive vision of the future that improves on the present situation.

W

weaknesses. Activities the organization does not do well or resources it needs but does not possess.

wellness programs. Programs offered by organizations to help employees prevent health problems.

white-water rapids metaphor. A description of organizational change that likens that change to a small raft navigating a raging river.

work specialization. The degree to which tasks in an organization are subdivided into separate jobs; also known as division of labour.

work team. Two or more interacting and interdependent individuals whose members work intensely on a specific, common goal using their positive synergy, individual and mutual accountability, and complementary skills.

World Trade Organization (WTO). A global organization of 153 member countries that deals with the rules of trade among nations.

NUMBERS/SYMBOLS

360-degree feedback. A performance appraisal method that uses feedback from supervisors, employees, coworkers, and customers in conjunction with another appraisal method.

Name/Organization Index

Subject Index

personal factors, 306, 307
  reducing stress, 307
stressors, 305
strong cultures, 292
structured problems, 84–85
stuck in the middle, 57
subsidiaries, 10, 32
sunk-costs error, 91
supplier power, 58, 59
suppliers, 20
supply chain management, 52, 136–137
supportive leader, 192
SWOT analysis, 53, 54
synergy, 239
system referent category, 221

T

tariff-free trade, 26
task conflict, 249
task demands, 305
team, 239
team development stages, 240–242
team leadership, 200–201, 247
teams
  see also groups
  advisory teams, 240
  conflict management, 248–249
  cross-functional teams, 107, 240
  current challenges in team management,
    250–251
  diversity in, 255
  effective teams, characteristics of, 246–248
  global teams, 251
  problem-solving teams, 240
  rewards, 245
  selection, 245
  self-managed teams, 240
  stages of team development, 240–242
  team behaviour, shaping, 245
  team players, creating, 242–245
  training, 245
  types of teams, 240
  understanding teams, 239–242
  virtual teams, 240
  when to use teams, 252
  work teams, 239
team structure, 117–118
technical employees, 225–226
technological conditions, 22–23, 55
technology
  change in, 295, 300
  dematerialization of the product, 143
  and human resource management process, 160–161
  investment in, and value chain management, 138
  and the manager's job, 143, 199
  and operations management, 142
  and structure, 115
  technology-based training methods, 169
teleconferencing, 169
telephone, 75
telework, 230
telling, 190

temporary foreign workers, 181
texting, 75
theory of justice view of ethics, 93
Theory X, 214
Theory Y, 214
thought-oriented roles, 243
threat of new entrants, 58
threat of substitutes, 58
threats, 53, 54
360-degree feedback, 170, 171
three-needs theory, 216
time frame, 48
times interest earned, 270
tolerance for ambiguity, 87
top-level managers, 4
total asset turnover, 270
total quality management, 290
total rewards, 172–175
  benefits, 173
  career development, 175
  performance and recognition, 175
  strategic compensation, 172–173
  work-life balance, 174
traditional goal setting, 46
traditional organizational designs, 116–117
traditional training methods, 169
traditional view of conflict, 248
training
  employee training, 140, 169
  teams, 245
trait theories of leadership, 187–188
transactional leaders, 193
transfers, 165
transformational leaders, 195
transformation process, 129, 288
transnational corporation (TNC), 30
Trans-Pacific Partnership (TPP), 25
triple constraint, 146
troubleshooting, 201
trust, 197–198, 200, 246
turnaround strategy, 57
two-factor theory, 214–215
Type A personality, 306
Type B personality, 306

U

uncertainty, 86
  environmental uncertainty, 33–34
  environmental uncertainty matrix, 33
  planning and uncertainty, 44
uncertainty avoidance, 27
unconscious reasoning, 83
unionization, 159–160
unit production, 115
unity of command, 109
universality of management, 2–3
University of Iowa, 189
University of Michigan, 189
unstructured problems, 85
upward communication, 69
utilitarian view of ethics, 92

List of Canadian Companies, by Province

QUEBEC

SASKATCHEWAN

List of International Companies, by Country